The Emergence of a National Market in Spain, 1650–1800

To Prof. Geoffrey Walker, in remembrance of his friendship and mastery,

Guillermo Pérez

Zaragoza, 29-IV-2019

The problem faced by most thinkers of the eighteenth century was not that of returning to an ancient world of public virtue, but of counting and remedying the costs of having departed from it, and using its image to ask whether it was possible to rediscover virtue in some form unknown to the ancients but accessible to the moderns.

John G. A. Pocock, Tanner Lectures on Human Values, 1989,
in Pocock (2002), p. 9.

The Emergence of a National Market in Spain, 1650–1800

Trade Networks, Foreign Powers and the State

Guillermo Pérez Sarrión

Translated by Daniel Duffield

Bloomsbury Academic
An imprint of Bloomsbury Publishing Plc

B L O O M S B U R Y
LONDON • OXFORD • NEW YORK • NEW DELHI • SYDNEY

Bloomsbury Academic
An imprint of Bloomsbury Publishing Plc

50 Bedford Square
London
WC1B 3DP
UK

1385 Broadway
New York
NY 10018
USA

www.bloomsbury.com

BLOOMSBURY and the Diana logo are trademarks of Bloomsbury Publishing Plc

First published as *La península comercial. Mercado, redes sociales y Estado en España en el siglo XVIII* by Marcial Pons, 2012

Paperback edition first published 2017

British Library Cataloguing-in-Publication Data
A catalogue record for this book is available from the British Library.

ISBN: HB: 978-1-4725-8645-2
PB: 978-1-3500-5617-6
ePDF: 978-1-4725-8646-9
ePub: 978-1-4725-8647-6

Library of Congress Cataloging-in-Publication Data
Names: Pâerez Sarriâon, Guillermo, author.
Title: The emergence of a national market in Spain, 1650-1800 : trade networks, foreign powers and the state / Guillermo Perez Sarrion ; translated by Daniel Duffield.
Other titles: Penâinsula comercial. English
Description: New York : Bloomsbury Academic, 2016. | Includes bibliographical references and index.
Identifiers: LCCN 2015043357 (print) | LCCN 2016023421 (ebook) | ISBN 9781472586452 (hardback) | ISBN 9781472586469 (PDF) | ISBN 9781472586476 (ePub) | ISBN 9781472586469 (ePDF)
Subjects: LCSH: Spain–Commerce–History–17th century. | Spain–Commerce–History–18th century. | Spain–Economic conditions–17th century. | Spain–Economic conditions–18th century. | BISAC: HISTORY / Europe / Western.
Classification: LCC HF3685 .P4713 2016 (print) | LCC HF3685 (ebook) | DDC 382.0946–dc23 LC record available at https://lccn.loc.gov/2015043357

Cover design: Sharon Mah
Cover image: *Plan en vista de las obras del Jalón, con la adventencia de haberse executado ya la mudada de el río, concluido enteramente los dos arcos de el puente y aumentado de muchos pies el alto de las murallas*, by Gregorio Sevilla, Luis Chimioni and Fernando Martínez, Zaragoza, manuscript, circa 1781.

Typeset by RefineCatch Limited, Bungay, Suffolk

This book was written as part of research project HAR 2011-29036-C02-01 Política económica, circulación internacional de ideas económicas y esfera pública en España, 1680–1840 *(2012–2015) funded by the Spanish Ministerio de Economía y Competitividad.*

Contents

Foreword

It would be well nigh impossible to précis the wealth of theoretical and empirical material contained within the pages of this book, so let us rather consider the author's intentions as stated in the preface. He proposes to address the construction of Spain's internal market in the eighteenth century in terms of the action of the commercial networks formed by merchants and traders from different regions of the country (in particular Catalonia) and even from abroad (especially France). The work thus links the national market and the development of networks, two of the key issues in recent historiography worldwide. Nevertheless, his standpoint is far from treating Spain as a uniform whole above and beyond marginal regional differences (a matter which has gained increasing currency since it was first raised by Antonio Domínguez Ortiz, as Roberto Fernández notes in his edition of *El mosaico español*, one of the master's key works), yet he rejects the more absurd constructions entertained by certain nationalists, who view their regions as if they were islands cut off and remote from the realities existing beyond their borders. Finally, economic life is presented in the author's dialectic as an activity stemming from the labours of the agents directly involved (producers and distributors), but which is also necessarily shaped by prevailing legal and political conditions (in this case the Enlightened Monarchy of the Bourbons), a reality all too often ignored by those who believe in the quasi-miraculous power of government and by those who view political institutions as an enemy of economic freedom, so that regulation becomes a purely negative factor which can only hinder the innate wisdom and free flow of impersonal market forces. These are of course problems which go far beyond the limits of the early modern period and remain absolutely current today, both in Spain and internationally.

The author's analysis reveals a chequered history of trade diasporas (held together not only by common origin but also by intangibles like personal honesty and reputation, the foundations of that trust claimed by the famous sixteenth-century merchant Simón Ruiz as essential to business, and which Xavier Lamíkiz has recently placed at the centre of his work on trade in the eighteenth century), political pressure and war, leveraged by the victors to further their trade interests (in the treaties of 1659 with France and 1667 with England before the mutation of the Peace of Utrecht and the arrangements between France and Spain known as the *Pactos de Familia*), and the action of the Spanish state, which belatedly adopted a mercantilist policy in an effort to narrow the ever widening economic gap opened up by the depression of the Habsburg dynasty's last years. The results were in fact reasonably positive, and were only compromised in the last years of the eighteenth century, which ended with the largely unexpected crisis that would eventually see the birth of modern Spain.

In painting this complex fresco of interregional and international interactions, the dialectics between local agents and state policy, and the expansion of markets around core growth centres, the author has been able to draw not only on his profound knowledge of the economic realities of Spain in the early modern period, but also on his experience as a visiting fellow at foreign universities and other research facilities, offering the fruits profusely yet with intelligence in this work. He also returned from his stays abroad with a trove of documents obtained from French and British archives, which he has skilfully blended with the muniments existing in Spain to weave a narrative that is rich in previously unpublished material, throwing new light on his subject. Besides his use of these tools and his solid academic credentials, one cannot but remark on his courage in delving unselfconsciously into a series of topics from which historians working outside the field of economic history usually retreat, to wit financial fluctuations, customs policy, monetary policy and debt restructuring, a matter which fills the front pages of the media even as I write this brief foreword after re-reading the suggestive pages of a book so full of food for thought.

This baggage without doubt allows him authoritatively to address a series of convergent issues concerned in the formation of the Spanish national market in a process which lasted throughout the eighteenth century. The chapters concerned with English and French influence in Spain from the end of the seventeenth century to the end of the eighteenth offer an unceasing stream of new detail obtained from the author's archival research, though without changing the general outlines of the story as it is already known. The English based their activity on trade colonies established at various Spanish ports, although the intermediaries who sold their goods in the interior were not their compatriots. Rather, they operated through networks formed in particular by Castilians, the Irish, the Maltese and Catalans. The French found it easier to enter Spain because they were both neighbours and Catholic, and by the end of the seventeenth century there were already some sixty thousand of them.

The War of Succession brought about far-reaching change. England was the main beneficiary of the Treaty of Utrecht both in metropolitan Spain (seizing the opportunity to acquire Gibraltar and Menorca) and overseas, although Spain strove to reverse this situation for the next fifty years, finally succeeding in the Americas in the mid-eighteenth century. France, meanwhile, had benefitted from its condition as Spain's ally in the war but now sought to gain ground in three ways, which the author clearly identifies. First, the French succeeded in reducing the cost of their export goods. Second, they established an uncontested predominance in fashion (a world that received hardly a mention in the historiography until very recently, either in Spain or elsewhere). Third, they enlisted the support of the Spanish government. Finally, the author notes by way of conclusion that this situation, which was always fluid, depended on the development of the reformist policies tenaciously applied by the new Bourbon dynasty (despite what some scholars may have claimed).

The government's action is dealt with in some of the book's most illuminating pages. The discussion includes summaries of known material (e.g. the rationalization of government) and uses new data to enrich our understanding (e.g. the suppression of the dry ports and the reform of the customs administration), but in other cases the author decides clearly between different options (for example, where he comes down in favour of the *catastro*, the single tax imposed in the realms of the former Crown of Aragon, which he defends against attack by certain radically nationalist historiographers).

He also advances his own arguments with conviction on issues like the monarchy's (eventually successful) endeavour to recover 'fiscal sovereignty', which began even while the War of Succession was still in progress and ended with the measures adopted in the 1720s (which still followed the pattern established in the time of the Catholic Monarchs while implementing a model that would not be changed either in Spain or in America until the eventual demise of the *Ancien Régime*), and the restructuring of public debt, which reduced the principal owed by the state by around one third and interest by almost 90 per cent (following the ground-breaking work of Rafael Torres). In the other sections, he considers agricultural, industrial and trade policy (highlighting the creation of the *Junta General de Comercio y Moneda* or Board of Trade and Currency, which was finally completed in 1730), as well as the naturality policy applied to all subjects of the monarchy's realms in the Iberian Peninsula, following a policy direction which, we might add, was already clearly marked during the reign of Philip II, and indeed before he even ascended the throne, in favour of the '*naturales de los reinos de España*', whatever the myths propagated from nationalist quarters about the exclusion of the kingdoms belonging to the Crown of Aragon from trade with America in the *carrera de Indias*.

To conclude, we may perhaps note a matter that the author himself does not find it necessary to remark upon, which is that the governments of Philip V were responsible for the immense majority of the reforms adopted. This only reinforces the argument that his reign was the heyday of Enlightenment reformism, in contrast to the conventional view, which attributes the leading role to Charles III, or even the more recent claim that Ferdinand VI was a key player, which, despite the valiant efforts at rehabilitation made by Diego Téllez and Josep Maria Delgado, he may have been at best while the Marquis of Ensenada still held the reins of power, implementing his agenda in the early years of Ferdinand's reign.

The final chapters of the book are devoted to a detailed examination of the trade networks referred to throughout the work. To begin with, the author identifies the different networks formed by French immigrants, which he groups in different categories depending on their impact. These comprised the networks of merchants from Labourd, Basse-Navarre and Béarn who settled in Spanish Navarre (described in a section that could stand alone as a monograph on that realm's tax and customs arrangements), the merchants and financiers established in Madrid, the merchant colonies specializing in trade with the Americas, the networks of temporary migrants scattered throughout the interior of Spain, and the core of settled migrants beneath the layers of more recent arrivals. Other interesting revelations include the absence of French migrants in Catalonia (in contrast to the earlier period considered in the classic study by Jordi Nadal and Emili Giralt) and their scant presence in the Basque provinces. Meanwhile, Navarre and Aragon served as entry points for a host of 'poor French' immigrants on their way to Valencia, Castile and Andalusia, who nevertheless sent home remittances worth some two million silver *reales* each year according to the author aside from the profits of the great merchant houses.

The commercial expansion of Catalonia in the eighteenth century was driven by economic growth in the region itself, and encouraged by the Bourbon reforms and by the fact that Catalan traders were at the same time Spanish (and not foreigners like the French and British). This trade diaspora is one of the best known thanks to the pioneering work of Pierre Vilar, subsequently expanded by data on the colony in Cadiz trading with the Americas, and by the work of Assumpta Muset on Catalan expansion into the interior of Spain through the establishment of stores and shops following three main trade routes radiating out from Barcelona, the first running down the Mediterranean coast to Andalusia, and the other two leading to Zaragoza, where they forked westwards towards Valladolid and southwest towards central Spain and Madrid. Within this framework, the *Compañía de Aragón* is singled out for special attention. The importance of this firm was first recognized by Luis Navarro over three decades ago, and it has since been the subject of no small number of papers by different scholars, among them the author himself, who had already written scores of pages on its history before the present work. He now presents it as a key case study for the business of managing agrarian rents and the grain trade conducted by Catalan peasants, who had grown rich from the emphyteutic systems applied to landholdings (*establiments*) and viticulture (*rabassa morta*) in the principality and had shifted their interests from farming to the lease of ecclesiastical and seigneurial rents, trading in wheat and other commodities, and making loans of grain for use as seed stock. In the long run, however, firms of this kind mostly fell victim to the crisis brought on by the War of Independence, withdrawing to Catalonia where they would reinvent themselves after the end of Napoleonic rule in Spain. In contrast, the author is deliberately much less concerned with the Barcelona-based companies involved in the colonial trade, given the geographical constraints imposed by a work which focuses on the formation of the interior market rather than an analysis of overseas trade flows, which are in any case better understood today because of researchers' persistent focus on traffic with the Americas.

He also leaves for later any broader analysis of Madrid's spectacular rise as a commercial and financial hub, a development which is outlined in David Ringrose's splendid, pioneering work. It would be especially interesting to see a reassessment of the role played by the company of the *Cinco Gremios Mayores* in the construction of the Canal Imperial de Aragón (the author being something of an expert on this monumental undertaking), and as assiduous buyers of public debt and close allies of the powerful Cadiz-based firm of Uztáriz, which has recently been readdressed by María Dolores Herrero in an able and timely study.

In any event, the building erected with such effort over the course of the eighteenth century was shaken to its foundations by the events that marked the end of the *Ancien Régime* in Spain – the outbreak of hostilities with England, the bankruptcy of the Royal Treasury, the disruption of colonial trade, a political crisis that undermined the very legitimacy of the monarchy, submission to the interests of Napoleon and military occupation by the French, the impact of independence movements in America, and profound social divisions (absolutists against liberals, *afrancesados* against patriots). To use the author's own words it was 'the end of the old reformist and nationalist dreams of the Spanish Enlightenment'.

However, significant progress had been made towards the creation of a national market thanks to the active endeavour of social networks throughout the eighteenth century, the cooperation of a government that was open to the reforms needed to revive the kingdom's economy, and the expansionary conditions that allowed the development of the transactional fabric in the trade peninsula which Guillermo Pérez Sarrión, today one of the leading scholars in the field of Spain's economic history in the early modern period, has reconstructed for us, painstakingly accumulating the documentary evidence, rigorously analysing contemporary testimony, authoritatively applying the apposite economic theory and skilfully weaving the data into the narrative to form a coherent and comprehensive whole.

Carlos Martínez Shaw
Baeza, 26 July 2011

Preface

One could start a book like this in many ways. I believe the best is encapsulated in the following statement: this work forms part of the literature which seeks to explain the events of the past as they actually happened. Under normal circumstances, this might seem obvious, but it is not so today, because history has now become something of a consumer good, though its study developed two and a half centuries ago as a tool to explain where society had come from, why it was like it was, and where it was going.

Truth is no longer demanded of history *qua* commodity, but rather entertainment and anecdote. We live in a world in which the citizen can buy a CD of Roman music online,[1] learn the *truth* about British imperialism or Nazi Germany from video games,[2] or spend a family day out for a small fee at a medieval theme park where the organizers stage a witch hunt in spring, jousting in summer and a Christmas nativity scene in the autumn and visitors can relax in the style of the Middle Ages at a 'real' market offering 'genuine' tenth-century belts and refreshment in the form of 'authentic' thirteenth-century beer.[3] Let us turn now to the predominance of anecdote in popular historical literature, the 'never before told' stories of people and events which occupy the shelves of airport bookshops, and the historical novels in which persuasive fictions mingle with fact without a word of warning for the reader. I do not pass judgement; this is simply the world we live in.

Beyond this, the facts remain, waiting to be discovered, described and interpreted. One might say 'reconstructed'. This is not, however, a task for the leisure industry but for history conceived as science, a task for historians. It is the purpose of the present study.

The Spanish title of this book, *La península comercial*, conjures an image which refers to its contents through two channels of signification. The first alludes to the interior market of the Iberian Peninsula and the traffic in goods running through it, viewed from the standpoint of trade networks, the key players in its development. The second refers to the north-eastern part of Spain, an area which runs from the Basque provinces through to Catalonia and Valencia, and stretches southwards as far as Madrid. I found this expression used by a senior functionary, perhaps an intendant, in a text written in the second half of the eighteenth century, though I am afraid I can no longer remember where. This functionary coined the phrase *península comercial* to describe the position of the former kingdom of Aragon in the Spanish monarchy of the eighteenth century after the War of Succession. In terms of commerce, he saw the kingdom as being like a peninsula surrounded on three sides by other realms which were in some way special from a fiscal and economic standpoint – Navarre to the west was a distinct and separate fiscal space, France to the north was a foreign land, and Catalonia to the east was fast becoming a uniquely different region within the economic and social panorama of Spain (see Chapter 7 for details). As the reader will see in the pages that follow, the metaphor is compelling. The central part of Spain's north-eastern region was a sparsely populated, almost empty space criss-crossed by travellers of all kinds bringing goods, information, cash and bills of exchange from the neighbouring realms. This means that the apparently overarching supra-regional uniformity in which the market developed in fact emerged in a geographical context of regional differences, which contemporaries would have observed on a daily basis. The current historiography prefers to ignore these differences, however. National history usually discusses a uniform territorial whole, sidestepping any interregional comparisons, while nationalist historians are interested only in events within their own regions as a unique and unrepeatable story isolated from any outside influence.

The main argument of this book is that the economic growth which occurred in Spain at the end of the *Ancien Régime* between the late seventeenth century and the early nineteenth century, and which provided the context for the emergence of the country's interior market had differential regional effects and was marked by the action of two key players who have so far gone almost unnoticed. These were the social groups organized in trade networks which activated and structured Spain's interior market, and the state.

While this study refers to the Spanish monarchy, the details often do not refer to the whole of the territory it controlled, focusing rather on the north-eastern regions. Again, this work does not describe all of the trade and social networks existing in eighteenth-century Spain. Rather, I have selected only some based on various factors: the little I actually know, what I wished to explain, the available sources, the territories where such networks operated, the publisher's entirely sensible demand for a book of reasonable length, and the capacity of the protagonists selected to prove or disprove my central thesis. Hence, I refer little to the networks of English merchants and their partners, but at considerable length to French social networks throughout Spain, to those of the Catalans nationally but especially in Aragon, and to the Basque and Navarrese networks nationally but above all in Madrid, the capital and the seat of the court, where other networks converged, although they are barely mentioned, or not at all. For example, the existence of migratory networks formed by Galicians and other people from the north of Spain is known, but they are hardly considered in this work. This does not mean that they were not important in themselves, but rather that I have not drawn on them to develop my argument. There were also networks of Valencians operating in New Castile, Aragonese in Valencia and numerous others about which little or nothing is actually known, although research may one day unearth some surprising results.

I believe an explanation is required for the absence of any more extensive discussion of Castilian networks. It should not be thought that they were unimportant. Quite the reverse in fact. The reason is that they pose three difficulties for the present study. In the first place, what is today known about such networks falls outside the chronological and spatial scope of this study. We know that influential networks of Castilians from Burgos existed in Europe, and especially in Flanders and France, in the fifteenth and sixteenth centuries,[4] and that their organization was based on permanent partners and *national* (i.e. Castilian) factors. This system was, however, undermined by the rise of the often non-national commission partner and the appearance of religious dissensions, leading to its decline in the late sixteenth century and early seventeenth.[5] However, the

Castilian networks were rebuilt in the eighteenth century, and they appear constantly, though in a more or less secondary role, in studies of the spread of intra-peninsular trade like the work of Ringrose, Yun and Bernardos.[6]

Visibility is another problem. Castilian networks are far from easy to identify as such in the sources I have consulted, which were chosen for other purposes. A third difficulty is that the networks in which I was originally interested were those formed by communities associated with some sort of territorial identity. However, the different naturalities belonging to the realms of the Spanish monarchy were merged into a Spanish naturality in the eighteenth century, as we shall see, and because of this it seems to me that the Castilians did not behave like an ordinary *national* community. There were too many of them, and it was obvious that they were a majority rather than a minority, forming the monarchy's political core. What the Castilians actually did, when they did anything, was to form cliques, which were not held together by Castilian origin or *nationality* like the groups formed by people who spoke a different language or professed a different religion, but rather by bonds of patronage and loyalty to a particular politician (e.g. the Marquis of Ensenada), or origin in a given district (e.g. La Mancha or Toledo) or even bishopric (e.g. Burgos).

As for the state, I shall refer not only to the Spanish government, but also to two others, England and France, which were both keenly interested in controlling the peninsular market (and also Spain's colonial markets, though that is another matter) and exerted an enormous influence over its development.

The present work is not concerned with regional history, but consists rather of a broad comparative study, addressing issues which fall within the general scope of Spanish history, including the international dimension, although such details as can be given tend to refer to the north-east of Spain, and to the historical territories belonging to this region.

Various issues implicit in my principal argument deserve to be made plain from the outset. To begin with, the combination of expansionary economic conditions following the crisis of the seventeenth century and the political changes wrought by the War of Succession had differential effects on growth in the various historical regions.

Another key point is that the emergence of economic regions in the eighteenth century was also a differential process. Even at this time, the economic regions did not exactly match their historical counterparts, and their development gave rise to economic contrasts which continued throughout the final integration of the national market in the nineteenth century following the bourgeois revolution and the appearance of a new liberal state.

The third point is concerned with the political conditions prevailing in Spain in the mid-seventeenth century. The Thirty Years' War, Spain's political crisis and the urgency of maintaining the colonial empire coincided with the rise of the mercantilist states of England and France, which kept up a fierce political and economic rivalry while expanding their colonial empires, propelling their own migratory networks abroad and seeking to expand their internal markets, which at the time were more developed than Spain's. In these circumstances, both countries separately concluded that gaining control of the Spanish market to treat it as an appendage of their own was a project that would be well worth the long-term effort required.

In the fourth and final place, the migratory and trade networks organized by the English, French, Basques, Navarrese, Catalans and others played a key role in structuring what would eventually become the internal market of Spain. Meanwhile, the development of such groups was driven in large part by obvious demographic factors and by the conditions established by the Spanish monarchy for the movement of both people and goods.

The Spanish state had been seriously weakened in the seventeenth century and it was able to afford only limited protection and support for the development of the interior market. After the War of Succession, however, the state underwent a process of far-reaching reforms, which took decades to complete but eventually allowed the implementation of an actively mercantilist economic policy. The state thus ceased to be a mere spectator, and began to intervene actively in economic affairs, shaping and moulding the development of the internal market in a process that was never wholly autonomous. The active role of the Bourbon state was, however, ended by the French Revolution of 1789 and the political circumstances linking it to its sister monarchy.

Based on the above, I have structured the text in seven chapters. The first, introductory chapter discusses the basic historiographical concepts of economic region, social networks, urban systems and the state which I have applied to marshal the facts.

The next three are concerned with English and French influence over the Spanish economy. The second chapter examines the reasons for the economic rivalry between England and France viewed from the perspective of their interest in the Spanish interior market, while the third and fourth chapters address the Franco–British struggle over the interior market and their efforts to wrest control of it from each other in the second half of the seventeenth century and in the eighteenth century and discuss the results of their actions from the standpoint of their mutual relations.

The fifth chapter delves into another of the central themes of the study, namely the restructuring of the Spanish state in the first half of the eighteenth century seen in relation to its ability to foster economic activity and develop a mercantilist (i.e. nationalist) policy capable of putting a check on British and French commercial dominance.

Finally, the last two chapters examine the actions of certain social networks in the Spanish interior from different perspectives. The sixth and seventh chapters are thus given over respectively to the long-standing French trade networks and to the new Catalan networks operating in the Spanish interior.

I believe it is only fair to point out here that the research strategy I followed to develop the argument presented in these pages initially included an analysis of Madrid, a privileged social environment in which the action of the social networks described here and others is clearly visible. For editorial reasons, however, I was persuaded to leave this topic aside for the present. Nevertheless, the reader should bear in mind that both the principal and secondary arguments contained in this book were formed in view of the wealth of evidence obtained in relation to what was even then a grand social crucible and the Spanish monarchy's main market.

A historian is never untouched by his own times, and I am no exception. The arrival of democracy in Spain (1975), the constitution of 1978 and the country's enthusiastic accession to the European project (1986) have generated spectacular progress for our society, but also hitherto unheard of problems. This is the case of nationalist movements like those of Catalonia and the Basque Country, who today question a constitution that was approved by the vast majority of Spaniards, raising challenges with uncertain outcomes.

History has always been and still remains a source of powerful arguments in political debate, because what could and should be questioned is all too often taken as hard fact. In order to place the more parochial nationalist historiography in its proper place alongside the hackneyed myths of the imperial history self-interestedly propagated by the Franco regime, I believe it is important to return once again to the enduring history of Spain's political community and to look at the sources with new eyes in order to ask what the country's different peoples and territories shared and what they did not. This, of course, means drawing comparisons and making evaluations.

It is what I have done, and the results seem to me to be positive for two reasons. In the first place, if the methodology applied in the analysis makes use not only of the territorial concept of the historical region per se viewed in isolation but also considers nation states, economic regions and social networks, the resulting picture of the political community is not a crude mosaic of discrete units or a uniform canvas, but a political and social space animated by myriad freely moving social agents, who were also aware of and influenced by events outside their home regions. Furthermore, this methodological strategy has another major advantage, insofar as it reflects what was really happening in Spanish society at a time when the national market, one of its key features, was still developing.

This work is the fruit of a research project which began tentatively towards the end of the 1990s and has since been thoroughly revised, over the course of several versions. It includes findings described in published papers and adds new data obtained in two research visits at the University of Cambridge, one of them for a fairly extended period, and numerous visits to Spanish and European archives, as well as references to hitherto little used printed sources and a considerable bibliography. All of this was made possible with the support of the Spanish Ministry of Education and Science, which funded the related research projects. Finally, I found the time, freedom and intellectual stimulus I needed to give final shape to the text, which more than once seemed to me unending given the diversity of the elements to be assembled, in another stay at the Newark campus of Rutgers University, New Jersey, which was funded by the University of Zaragoza.

I am extremely grateful to all of the people who have helped me complete this work. At moments of difficulty Carlos Martínez Shaw, and then Roberto Fernández Díaz, Asela Rodríguez de Laguna, Elpidio Laguna, Jesús Astigarraga Goenaga, Javier Usoz Otal, Carmen Corona Marzol, José Luis Gómez Urdáñez and José Antonio Biescas Ferrer were all kind enough to read parts of the text, and their assistance and comments were invaluable in improving the final version. They deserve full credit for this, but no blame for any errors I may have made in such an extensive work, which are entirely my own responsibility.

I owe an even greater debt to others. Almudena Domínguez held up a mirror which at all times brought me back to the image of a reality which it was all too easy to forget, and at the same time she provided constant encouragement while proving my most patient and critical reader. The necessarily anonymous students to whom I expounded these ideas over the years at the Universities of Zaragoza, Puerto Rico in San Juan-Río Piedras, Rutgers in Newark, Valencia and Jaume I in Castellón gave me the opportunity to ripen my thoughts and spurred me to put them onto paper, offering their attention, interest and questions. Many of these ideas have been discussed and some of the authors mentioned here have also taken part in the Modern History Seminar, which I have organized at the University of Zaragoza for over a decade now. Thanks are due for their attendance and ongoing attention.

I have endeavoured to present old problems in a new light, approaching the issues from different angles, which substantially change our view of them. I have also sought to absorb concepts from economic history, contemporary history, demographic and family history and even economic anthropology into my argument, however remote these disciplines may sometimes seem from modern history as such. I trust that works like the present one will help improve our understanding of the formation of Spain's interior market, revealing its international implications, the important social dimension of the process, the ways in which it drove the emergence of supra-regional differences, and the key role played by the Enlightenment state, which was much more important than has hitherto been recognized. It is not for me to judge whether I have achieved what I set out to do.

Rouvray, Bourgogne, August 2010

Transcription Criteria and Bibliographical References

The French and English texts cited respect the original wording and use of capital letters, but I have modernized spelling, punctuation and the use of diacritic marks to facilitate comprehension, as well as the separation of words that are nowadays written as compounds. Place names are given in English where variants exist. Abbreviations are indicated by a full stop where they are not expanded. Question marks are used where the reading of a letter or word is doubtful.

I have respected the wording and spelling of texts written in Spanish, though I have modernized the use of silent 'h' and 'b-v', the use of capitals and the use of diacritic marks. I have used acute accents where the original text contains a diacritic grave. I have not transcribed the diacritic tilde (~) where it is used over 'a' or 'o', but I have kept other symbols where possible.

I have tried in general to give the full titles of bibliographical references, and I have modernized the authors' spelling of titles following the criteria applied in library catalogues to facilitate location. I have endeavoured to include the original dates in citing bibliography and printed sources. The edition used is cited in the bibliography.

Abbreviations

ACN	*Actas de las cortes de Navarra* (1530–1829).
AESC	*Annales. Economies. Societés. Civilisations*, Paris.
AGG	Archivo General de Guipúzcoa, Tolosa, Guipúzcoa.
AGN	Archivo General de Navarra, Pamplona.
AGS	Archivo General de Simancas, Simancas, Valladolid.
AGS, DGR	AGS, Dirección General de Rentas Generales.
AGS, SSH	AGS, Secretaría y Superintendencia de Hacienda.
AHMB	Arxiu del Institut Municipal d'Història, Barcelona.
AHMB, FC	AHMB, Fons Comercial section.
AHN	Archivo Histórico Nacional, Madrid.
AHPZ	Archivo Histórico Provincial de Zaragoza, Zaragoza.
AHT	Arxiu Històric de Tarragona, Tarragona.
AHT, FC	AHT, Fons Comercial section.
AJPCB	Archivo de la Real Junta Particular de Comercio de Barcelona, Barcelona.
AMAE	Archivo del Ministerio de Asuntos Exteriores, Madrid.
AMAEP	Archive du Ministère des Affaires Étrangeres, La Courneuve, Paris.
AMAEP, CP	AMAEP, Correspondance Politique section.
AMAEP, MD	AMAEP, Memoires et Documents section.
AMAEP, MD, Esp.	AMAEP, MD, Espagne sub-section.
AMH	Archivo del Ministerio de Economía y Hacienda, Madrid.
ANF	Archives Nationales, Paris.
ANF, Aff. étr.	Archives Nationales, Affaires étrangeres section, Paris.
APL	Arxiu de la Pahería, Lérida.
APNP	Archivo Histórico de Protocolos Notariales, Pamplona.

BCAZ	Biblioteca de las Cortes de Aragón, Zaragoza.
BCB	Biblioteca de Catalunya, Barcelona.
BCB, Bonsoms	BCB, Fullets Bonsoms section.
BMH	Biblioteca del Ministerio de Hacienda, Madrid.
BNE	Biblioteca Nacional de España, Madrid.
CLDPE	*Colección legislativa de la deuda pública de España.*
COGR	*Colección de órdenes generales de Rentas.*
LL	*El libro de las leyes del siglo XVIII . . .*
NR	*Novísima recopilación de las leyes de España . . .*
NRN	*Novissima recopilacion de las leyes de el reino de Navarra . . .*
TNA	The National Archives, Kew, Richmond, Surrey [formerly Public Record Office].
TNA, BT	The National Archives, Board of Trade section.
TNA, CO	The National Archives, Colonial Office section.
TNA, SP	The National Archives, State Papers Foreign section.
RORG	Garriga, Juan Bautista, *Recopilación de órdenes de Rentas Generales. Por D. . . ., administrador general de las de Galicia.*

1

The Concepts

Market, Regions, Networks and State

National market and economic regions

Geographically aware historians of course know that events occur in time and space. However, it was only fairly recently that it occurred to economic historians, whose discipline tends to be national in scope, that the historical evolution of a country, and more specifically the key phenomenon of its economic development, could take place in more reduced spatial contexts. Indeed, a country's geographical structure strongly conditions its very existence. Let us, then, presuppose that the creation of a national market is crucial to the historical formation of a country and its economy, in order to investigate the importance of lower level analytic units in Spain, and how far these units match the politically devolved regions called *comunidades autónomas* today. The discussion will thus begin with the concept of the national market and then move on to that of regional economy, finally addressing the question of how far historical and economic regions actually existed in the past, and to what extent they overlapped.

For this approach to be possible, contemporary historiography is indebted to disciplines like economic analysis and modern history itself. The question as it arises today in Spain first emerged during the decade-long process (1975–1986) embracing the political transition at the end of the Franco dictatorship, when the *autonomic* (i.e. devolved or regionalized) state was created and Spain finally joined the European Union. In this period, political changes encouraged a disaggregated analysis of the national economy designed to reveal local disparities in economic development and meet regionalist demands. From a historical perspective, however, this is the point of arrival and not the starting point. The present work does not address the issue of the Autonomous Communities but rather a historical problem, and it therefore does not consider how today's national market might be disaggregated, but rather investigates the ways in which this aggregate market was formed.

Until now it has been generally accepted that the national market was formed in Spain in the nineteenth century, and that it did not come out of nothing. The recent concept of *national market* was first used by Emilio Sereni in the 1960s to describe the process leading up to the creation of the first Italian state, and at the same time it entered Spanish historiography via an important article published by Josep Fontana, who developed the new historiographical approach taken by Vicens Vives shortly beforehand, by relating the nascent consciousness of the bourgeoisie with the formation of a national market in nineteenth-century Spain and with the Catalan industrial revolution.[1] At that time, it was taken for granted that the formation of a domestic market was a necessary condition for an industrial revolution to take place, and this was not the case in eighteenth-century Spain, when only an aggregation of isolated rural cells existed with insignificant trade between them. Fontana defines the national market in the following terms:

> Despite its ambiguity, there is really no substitute for the term 'national market'. It serves on the one hand to draw a distinction with the foreign or international market, which lies beyond the bounds of a given political entity, and outside the scope of its laws, customs duties and so on. Yet it also reflects a qualitative difference with primitive forms of domestic trade, confined to minor exchanges in a local market. In this case, national does not mean fixed within a given geographical scope which is supposed to embrace all of the economic activities of a country at any given moment, but it is rather the expression of a limit towards which activities tend, and which they seek to reach as they progress and develop.[2]

In this approach there was still no mention of regions, whether economic or historic (which is perfectly understandable in the political circumstances of the Franco dictatorship).

Not long afterwards, the early work of Nicolás Sánchez Albornoz brought the question into the more limited field of economic analysis, for the first time establishing the existence of a national market and different economic regions through a factorial analysis of prices.[3]

These early studies reveal the appearance of the national market in conceptual terms, but they have little or nothing to say about its origins. When and how did the national market appear as a historical fact? The answer, which I have taken as a basic premise for the present work, is that it was formed after the emergence of various economic regions, and both of these processes together, rather than one alone, drove both the specialization of production and interregional inequalities from the outset.[4] It was likewise believed that the emergence of the national market was a purely economic development and that it occurred in the nineteenth century. Recently, however, it has been recognized that the process began in the eighteenth century and that it also had a social and political dimension, although neither of these arguments has been fully settled in the historiography to date.

Nevertheless, we now know more than in the 1960s. We know, for example, that Catalonia was the main industrial region of Spain at the end of the nineteenth century and had been for more than a century, and we know that the Basque provinces had begun to industrialize. However, it has also been found that other regions had embarked on early rural industrialization processes and had in fact deindustrialized again by this time. Meanwhile, the capital, Madrid, was still a 'colony of servants' according to the Catalan Balmes, and it had virtually no manufacturing industry. Indeed, it was only in the latter decades of the twentieth century that the city emerged as a major industrial region in its own right, with significant European connections.

This was the context for the birth of Catalan and Basque nationalism, ideologies which have since grown but have yet to find their place alongside the long tradition of Spanish centralism and a new constitutional and democratic nationalism. In view of its political consequences, the situation at the end of the nineteenth century has recently been so precisely defined by Álvarez Junco that it will be sufficient merely to cite his remarks:

> The specifically Spanish problem was not so much the country's backwardness as its unequal development, which naturally produced an equally unbalanced process of cultural modernization [. . .]. The differences in economic development existing in the early nineteenth century widened spectacularly in its last 25 years. Two industrial areas had developed around the two major cities of Barcelona and Bilbao, the only ones able to compete with the capital [. . .]. Galicia, meanwhile, lacked not only the industrial development that might have raised the region's importance and lent weight to its demands, but also the unquestionable primacy of any single city, where the intellectual elites could meet and organize their conflicts with Madrid. Furthermore, the discontent among the elite had an escape valve ready to hand in the form of emigration. As a consequence, Galician nationalism, which was always a minority ideology in any case, grew up in Madrid and in Buenos Aires [. . .] it was not sparse or imperfect industrial development that was crucial, but rather the fact that the developed regions were naught but islands, and none even of these harboured the seat of political power. Madrid was not an industrial powerhouse, and it had none of the European connections that might have made it an arbiter of cultural life. The same was true of the geographical regions, above all Andalusia and Castile, where the political elites were recruited. Neither Spain's capital city, where its politicians conducted the affairs of state, nor the places from where those politicians hailed were the country's most economically and culturally advanced.[5]

In this light, one can only wonder whether the process which created this situation did not actually begin during the *Ancien Régime*. To answer this question, it will first be necessary to clarify the regional realities of the developing national market.

The terms *polarized economic region*, *specialized economic region*,[6] or simply *economic region* have been used in the recent economic historiography in the context of developments in spatial economic analysis, without exception referring to the economic developments of the nineteenth century. According to Luis Germán, the term was already used by scholars like Von Thünen, Alfred Weber and Walter Christaller at the end of the nineteenth century to explain processes of industrial localization, and in 1920 Alfred Marshall explained the advantages obtained by industrialized areas, stating explicitly that the increasing returns[7] they were able to generate were driven by three concurring factors, namely significant economies of scale as a result of industrial concentration, larger labour markets, and greater availability of intermediate factors thanks to the spread of technological know-how. This model was later developed in detail by scholars like Emilio Sereni, Alfred Hirschmann and Gunnar Myrdal,[8] who added effects like the tendency for growth to spread to the nearby periphery from the core and the tendency of industrialized areas to accumulate competitive advantages, causing delayed reactions in outlying areas. Economic regions also drive labour migrations and transfers of capital from the centre (which are not particularly significant at the centre but may be very important at the periphery); and deregulation and expansion of the domestic market, causing deindustrialization and unfavourable terms of interregional trade, as well as the appearance of certain unfavourable economic policy measures in fields like customs and excise, tax policy and public investments.

In short, Luis Germán defines a polarized economic region as a set of hierarchically structured spaces, which develops from a series of locational advantages like the availability of natural resources and raw materials, the existence of an adequate labour force and access to the market. Meanwhile, such a region will have a core, which is normally its main city, and a periphery, and each of these parts will predominantly occupy itself with certain specialized productive functions.[9]

The concept of economic region has been applied especially to the nineteenth and twentieth centuries,[10] but hardly at all to the pre-industrial era and still less to Spain.[11] It will be worth a short digression to discuss in more detail the most ambitious attempt so far to apply it, contained in the recent compilation of papers published under the title *Historia económica regional de España, siglos XIX y XX*.[12]

Let us begin by noting that certain methodological problems arise as soon as we seek to apply a contemporary regional economic analysis to the *Ancien Régime*. When, as in the aforementioned publication, an analysis applies a spatial approach to today's Autonomous Communities, now recognized as NUTS statistical units by the European Union, it perforce ignores the existence of supra-regional or even infra-regional economic constituencies which do not conform with current regional boundaries. Another matter is that the mention of the *Ancien Régime* may be merely a polite dismissal. However, the history of the *Ancien Régime* should not be used solely to seek the antecedents of what the (almost entirely statistical) sources reveal about the beginnings of the bourgeois, liberal revolution in the early nineteenth century. The eighteenth century is not always the prelude to what was about to happen, in the same way that the economic history of the *Ancien Régime* is not always a story of failure, of something inevitably condemned to collapse and to disappear (as so often appears in works penned from the standpoint of contemporary history). In short, the history of any period must be interpreted from the standpoint of its own internal logic, not the logic of later developments.

This point is clearly revealed in the studies of the Spanish regions area considered in this work during the *Ancien Régime*, or at least in the eighteenth century. For example, the important migratory networks emanating from Cantabria are almost entirely overlooked, as are the region's coastal articulation with the Basque provinces and the rest of northern Spain and the fiscal privileges of the Cuatro Villas, the four coastal towns of San Vicente, Santander, Laredo and Castro Urdiales. In the Basque provinces and Navarre, an adequate analysis based on geographical factors and regional product specialization will ignore significant work like Azcona's studies of Navarrese trade. Some important facts are also overlooked: for example, both regions constituted differentiated fiscal spaces; there were significant commercial networks already in existence; and Navarre had economic connections with France which were not exactly those of foreign trade and differed from its connections with the Basque provinces. The nature of Aragon as an economic region integrated with Catalonia is alluded to, but this does not appear to be taken into account in the analysis of the principality, and various factors which drove regional industrialization in the nineteenth century are passed over, like the previous development of a regional market, its early economic integration with Aragon, and easy access to the rest of the Spanish domestic market. All of these factors were already in operation in the eighteenth century. In the analysis of Valencia, almost no mention is made of domestic and foreign markets, or of the development of rural industries. In fact, it is only in the analysis of La Rioja (then a part of Old Castile) that regional economic developments in the eighteenth century are taken into account as a contributing factor to understand the situation in the nineteenth century.[13]

The brief study of pre-industrial Madrid by García Delgado and Carrera deserves a separate discussion. It contains a detailed commentary on Ringrose's celebrated thesis about Madrid's role in the decline of Castile, which the authors question (and rightly, for Madrid was not the sole cause). However, they fail to consider his key work, *Spain, Europe and the 'Spanish Miracle' 1700–1900*, published in 1996, which formulates a rather more complex explanatory model based on a variant of the concept of economic region, as I shall explain below.

In my opinion, García Delgado and Carrera, following the thesis of Concepción de Castro, fail properly to account for the dynamic role of the capital in the Castilian cereals market (in itself debatable, and in any event not inconsistent with the absence of manufacturing in the surrounding region). Their discussion of the role of the royal factories created by the state in the eighteenth century is also unconvincing. This is because they make an overly hurried assessment of Madrid during the enlightenment, focusing basically on the nineteenth century and ignoring the origins of the modern capital. The role of the capital as a service city certainly increased in the twentieth century, but it did not begin then, as García Delgado and Carrera assert. We now know that Madrid had already become Spain's main capital market in the eighteenth century, and the development of rural manufacturing in the surrounding areas was stifled by large scale imports of French cloth, a situation which continued in the nineteenth century when the city switched to bringing in Catalan manufactures (this is mentioned), again from outside the region.[14] Nineteenth-century Madrid did not come out of nothing, then. It was already the rentier and financial capital of Spain, it was important in the markets for wool and bills of exchange, and it was the great emporium of the Spanish interior.

To end these remarks on the book, I shall consider E. Llopis' overarching analysis of the *Ancien Régime* origins of nineteenth-century economic disparities.[15] This scholar raises certain reservations which have nothing at all to do with omissions or weaknesses of approach, but rather with the possibilities offered by the statistical sources analysed.

The article attempts to measure regional GDP based on figures for the workforce employed in different sectors of the economy in 1787 and 1797. However, the resulting figures reveal nothing new, in my opinion, but only confirm what was already known, because the error margins of the census data are very high due to differences in the criteria applied to classify the occupations of the population.

An analysis is also made of population figures and densities per km^2, as well as a calculation of the percentage of city dwellers among the population as a whole. Both indices are unquestionably valuable, the former more than the latter.

The calculation of population density per km^2 in each province in 1787 is revealing: in the Basque provinces the population was significantly greater in relative terms (42.3 people/km^2) than in Cantabria (28.2), Navarre (21.6) or La Rioja (24.0); density in Catalonia (27.69) was higher than in Aragon (13.1); and in Valencia it was higher (34.9) than in the region known today as Castile-La Mancha (11.7), excluding Madrid and its current metropolitan area. These differences in population density were decisive. To begin with, they show where extensive agriculture could thrive in the nineteenth century, when major colonization schemes were launched. And though the author does not say so, they also reveal where and why there had been emigration in the preceding centuries, as in the case of the Basque provinces and also Galicia, where the population density in 1787 was no less than 45.8 people/km^2.

Meanwhile, estimations of the percentage of city dwellers would be more effective if the author had included corrective factors, because the criterion of counting any town with a population equal to or greater than 5,000 inhabitants as a city does not take into account the fact that numerous large towns existed in southern Spain, where settlement was highly concentrated, which could not be called cities, while a number of true cities with fewer than 5,000 people existed in the north, where settlement was more dispersed. The cities provided services and played a role in structuring the territory, a matter which is beyond the scope of a population figure, a reasonable but still relative benchmark.

A number of other points could be raised. To begin with, tithes are ignored as a source. However, the author is right to note the existence of different ownership structures for farmland, though he fails to explain how this affected the industrialization process. The same could be said of the description of industrial assets held by the regions which industrialized in the nineteenth and twentieth centuries (Catalonia, the Basque Country and Madrid), as no account is given of how these initial advantages influenced subsequent events. Furthermore, the author does not tell us why the existence of economic regions in the *Ancien Régime* was a factor in the emergence of specialized economic regions in the nineteenth century. The author also makes an assertion that is at once true and somewhat paradoxical, namely that the trajectories of the Spanish regions had in fact begun to diverge as early as the second half of the eighteenth century. This statement is important, and in my belief it is absolutely correct. Surprisingly, however, the author prefers to cite Angel García Sanz[16] in support of his position, rather than drawing on his own arguments.

To sum up, *Historia económica regional de España, siglos XIX y XX* is an important and competent series of articles on the principal subject of regional economic inequalities in the nineteenth and twentieth centuries, but it still fails properly to address the fact that the nineteenth-century economic regions had their origins in the *Ancien Régime*, when signs of regional and supra-regional economic integration were already apparent. Economic historians have now begun the task of describing these developments from the standpoint of their own historiographical criteria, as may be seen in another manual of the economic history of Spain, once again edited by Llopis.[17]

To say this is no more than to show the route taken by the historiography in recent years, and I shall give some examples.

In a more recent publication addressing the case of the regional price of wheat in Castile and León in the eighteenth century from an almost exclusively statistical standpoint, the authors, Llopis and Jerez, posit four conditions that must be met by any process of market integration and by the basic statistical techniques applied to determine its existence:

1. Progressive price convergence (static correlation).
2. Synchrony of movements in the prices of the same good in different markets (dynamic correlation).
3. Progressive asynchrony between the prices of different cereals in the same market (time series analysis); and
4. general reduction in inter-annual price volatility[18] (volatility measures).

Analysis of the sale prices reflected in 15 sets of private accounts kept between 1691 and 1788 shows that the sigma convergence or standard deviation of prices fluctuated between 0.1 and 0.3, which means that considerable convergence did occur, or to put it another way that price volatility was low, even though the mean distance between the markets analysed in this large region was 178 km. The conclusion is that trade had progressed in the agrarian economy and commercial structures had developed in Castile and León beyond what was previously believed.[19] Analysis of the prices of wheat and barley corroborates this finding,[20] confirming that the correlation did not yet exist between 1500 and 1650.[21]

The impression of convergence is borne out almost simultaneously for the whole of Spain. David Reher analysed seven series of grain prices (Pamplona, Barcelona, Valencia, Old Castile (Sandoval, Segovia), New Castile and Andalusia (Seville)) for the period 1500–1800, finding indices of between 0.16 and 0.22 for the standard deviation of markets with easy maritime supply routes like Barcelona and Valencia, and (surprisingly) Pamplona, the lowest for all Spain, while the indices for the interior were around twice as high.[22] The main point, however, is that the author provides definitive statistical proof to confirm the thesis I have argued, namely that the variability or volatility of markets decreased markedly over the course of the eighteenth century (although it rose between 1780 and 1820, only to fall again thereafter), suggesting that the integration of markets in Spain should therefore not be viewed as a nineteenth-century development, but as a process lasting some two hundred years, which began in the eighteenth century and ended towards the close of the nineteenth. In my opinion, the process in fact began in the late seventeenth century. Reher's other key idea is that a series of essentially political institutions including the municipal grain deposits and markets, the state, the army and charitable institutions played an important role in mitigating fluctuations in grain prices.[23] This is a factor which has been largely ignored to date.

The eighteenth century saw general economic progress in Spain, and both domestic and foreign trade grew while the domestic market expanded in a context in which prices were rising faster than wages.[24] An analysis of the integration of markets in north-eastern Spain before the nineteenth century would probably now be possible using the series published by Arizcun for Pamplona,[25] Feliu for Catalonia,[26] and Hamilton and Palop for Valencia,[27] though it would be necessary to seek new sources for the crucial market of Zaragoza with its close links to Barcelona, because the existing studies contain serious gaps and do not adequately cover the eighteenth century.[28] In fact, even wage series are now becoming available, allowing measurement of living standards.[29]

As a final reference, a recent work by Domínguez Martín,[30] somewhere between an academic essay and a short book, goes back as far as 1700 and tentatively recognizes the importance of the political events arising from the War of the Spanish Succession, although it has the same objectives as the collective work discussed above.[31] National and regional wealth are measured based on sound, reliable indicators drawn from the census of 1787, like the number of inhabitants, population density per km^2 and an urbanization index. This work also recognizes the existence of regional differences in the eighteenth century, identifying different paths in the development of the richest regions (Madrid, Catalonia, Valencia and the Balearic Islands), those which were less rich (the Basque provinces and Navarre) and the poor regions.[32]

In short, the concept of economic region as applied in the historiography of the nineteenth and twentieth centuries to the analysis of spatial disparities in economic growth can be successfully transferred to the eighteenth century, and this has in fact already been done in some notable cases.

Let us now turn our attention to another aspect of the subject which has so far received little attention from the standpoint of the long process of market integration and the creation of interregional inequalities. I refer, of course, to the actual protagonists of this process viewed in terms of the historical formation of networks.

Social networks and trade networks

The concepts of social class and the resulting relations of domination have been, are and are likely to remain essential to any analysis of the human role in economic growth for many years to come. However, in a network-centred work like the present one, the progress made in other fields of research may provide new tools capable of throwing light on the issues at hand. The functioning of social networks in economic contexts is best explained by the new economic sociology which emerged in the United States in the 1970s as a reformulation of the earlier analysis of interpersonal relationships proposed by Karl Polanyi, who first recognized that economic relations between individuals and companies are not played out in the abstract realm of some ideal market but are in fact always embedded in social networks.[33] Meanwhile, other social scientists have made some surprising discoveries about the laws which govern the operation of social networks in the modern world.[34] Adapted to the needs of historical research, these ideas have enormously influenced our understanding of social networks, and they have recently been applied by scholars like Imízcoz Beunza to study Basque and Navarrese networks in the eighteenth century.[35]

According to Mark D. Granovetter, every individual is a member of social networks, acting in spheres formed by three kinds of relations, namely *strong ties* (family, kinship and marriage ties, which are long-lasting and frequent), *weak ties* (professional acquaintanceships, occasional political acquaintanceships, occasional travel or business acquaintanceships, which generate give and take exchanges) and *absent ties* (with casual acquaintances like shopkeepers, neighbours, fellow travellers on the bus, which do not generate any exchanges). Meanwhile, the intensity of ties within sphere is mediated by four factors: the duration of personal relations over time, emotional intensity, mutual trust and exchanges of services and favours.[36] Economic relationships too exist and take place within social networks (*embeddedness*),[37] and these must also be considered, therefore, if we are to understand economic activity. In terms of individual economic behaviour, then, the success of each agent in acquiring new information and expanding his radius of economic action will be based above all on his ability to manage and expand relationships based on weak ties, as people whose relationships are based on strong ties tend always to move in the same tight-knit social circles.[38]

Historically, the development of Spain's economic regions and of its domestic market was driven by people organized in social networks, or more specifically in commercial or trade networks. The point here is not to digress into a discussion of units of social analysis, or to contrast the term 'network' with other categories like social class, family or domain. Rather, it is to understand that capitalist markets actually developed from the action of a network of factors,[39] one of which was the progressive coalescence of disparate groups of merchants, pedlars, mule drivers, sailors and others into organized trade networks, which sometimes resulted in the formation of companies.

These stratified concepts are not, however, the only ones applicable to the social networks of the past, which were highly complex and, indeed, of many different kinds. Ringrose, to whom I shall return below, identifies at least five types of network existing on two levels in eighteenth- and nineteenth-century Spain. On an initial or basic level, there were rural networks (formed by individuals, families and political confederates) structured around the web of mutual dependences created by the market; and there were migratory networks, which allowed people and information to flow between the countryside and the cities. Above these two basic kinds of networks, there were political networks (formed by provincial notables, the *colegiales mayores* and groups of nobles) driven by the interaction between the interests of the state and those of the respective families, the commercial networks and financial networks.[40]

Family and patron–client ties also formed networks in colonial society[41] and at court, where political networks developed out of the more or less organized pressure groups seeking to influence the decisions of an absolute monarchy, in a hierarchy that stretched from the party of the Marques de la Ensenada or Aragonese party[42] in Madrid to networks of local notables, whose objective was to control the decisions of municipal councils.

For some years now, the organization and functioning of social networks has also attracted increasing interest in the fields of economic anthropology, history of the family and social history. Let us now turn to consider the available references on the existence and functioning of commercial networks, beginning with Philip Curtin's work on *trade diasporas*, consisting of merchant colonies or minorities living as aliens in the host country or community. Referring at the world level to trade between the major civilizations rather than the internal trade of each such bloc, Curtin combines the concepts of history, economics and anthropology to identify and describe some common features of the communities responsible for this long-distance, *cross-cultural trade*:

1. They were foreigners or aliens, their behaviour was to some extent unpredictable, and communication was in principle difficult.
2. They tended to form urban and interurban networks based on a range of common identifying factors, including country, language, religion and kinship, and they were organized, sometimes only informally (sharing only a common culture), and sometimes politically, as in the case of the *chartered companies* which came to the fore in the states of seventeenth-century Europe.
3. Their social position may have been low if the host society despised trade or held it to be sinful or wicked, as in the case of Jews in Christian medieval Europe.
4. The merchant networks of independent cities sometimes coalesced in more or less formal alliances, as in the case of the Hanseatic League of northern Germany in the period between the thirteenth and fifteenth centuries, even driving the formation of networks of functional dependence between cities in the terms of *central-place theory* (Walter Christaller, August Lösch) and organizing dependency systems (André Gunder Frank, Arghiri Emmmanuel, Immanuel Wallerstein).
5. Trade diasporas and commercial networks sometimes developed strong internal social control systems in order to preserve their original cultural identity, and they sometimes used marriage as a way of ensuring the integration of the group.[43]

Philip Curtin's depiction of trade diasporas is of interest here because it is fully applicable not only to intra-European but also to intra-Spanish networks, especially in the period before industrialization.

However, these references do not throw light on some key aspects of trade networks. How, for example, do they develop? How are they formed? And what other factors serve to maintain the cohesion of the group? In this regard, it seems that religious or merely ethical values like honesty and reputation within the network played an important role in many merchant communities and were applied by them to their trading activities. Meanwhile, marriage alliances helped cement and maintain trading alliances between a principal merchant and his partners or agents in other ports or markets.

From the standpoint of economic anthropology, a recent study of Jewish merchants in the ports of the Maghreb in the late medieval period is illuminating because it refers to a more primitive stage in the development of the market,[44] allowing observation of the factors binding trade networks together at a time when travel was hazardous, commercial information was difficult to obtain, the rule of law was uncertain and putting up capital to trade in far-off lands was an enormously risky business.

At least by the late medieval period, international trade had become free and competitive, and it was in private hands, run by merchants through extensive commercial alliances and coalitions in different ports formed on the one hand by partners, which is to say other independent merchants who did not share their capital with the principal, and on the other principally by agents. These were merchants in another port who, unlike partners, did pool their capital with their principal.

These merchants and their agents formed commercial leagues or *coalitions*,[45] which in turn functioned as a de facto economic institution capable of private regulation outside the market at a time when there were still no official institutions to provide a secure legal framework for commercial relations (trade consulates were a later innovation) and the courts, such as they were, were unable to decide quickly and fairly in matters of payments and claims, the lifeblood of trade.

Analysis of surviving commercial letters from these later medieval, North African networks reveals how they worked. Each mercantile coalition was based on the moral concept of *reputation*, which underpinned and ensured *honesty*, so that an honest agent would obtain not only a salary and a share in the profits from transactions, but also a premium or additional earnings derived from his reputation. There were two (not incompatible) ways in which the agent of a merchant could demonstrate his honesty. The first was to show himself a god-fearing man (which meant he had internalized the moral value of honesty), and the second was to make representations of his honesty to the coalition in advance. The latter was the more usual course. Game theory predicts in such cases that the agent will choose the best alternative between two poles: he can either stay honest and reap the benefits in the long term within the trade coalition, or he can cheat in order to make immediate gains though at the cost of expulsion. Profits provided an incentive to stay honest, and the system depended on ensuring that each agent would believe that the risk of being shunned would outweigh the temptation of any dishonest earnings he could make in the short term, so that it would be better to earn less as an honest man within the network. If an agent did cheat his principal, the merchant would be highly unlikely to recover the debt, but the agent would automatically be expelled from the league.

Meanwhile, each merchant would form alliances with various agents and could at the same time act as an agent on behalf of other merchants; and his agents would likewise be merchants themselves, operating through other agents in their employ. Overall, the individual identities and reputations of all of a network's members formed a system of internal relations based on an implicit contract: each associate merchant employed only agents who were also members of the network and paid them the highest premium possible (in the form of salaries and lump-sum remuneration), but he would never employ an agent who had at any time defrauded a member of the coalition. Furthermore, a member of a coalition who cheated or took advantage of an agent who had previously swindled any other member of the coalition was not held to be dishonest himself.

Hence, a good reputation itself enhanced the implicit contract made by an agent within the network. A merchant who formed an association with an agent who was already a member of the network (and was therefore known to be honest) could safely pay less for his honesty than if his reputation had yet to be established. Moreover, investigation of a new agent's reputation involved additional costs, either in cash terms or in terms of the risk of losses caused by fraud. This, of course, encouraged merchants to contract agents who were already used by their peers in the network. The agent of a networked merchant could expect to continue doing business with his principal over the long run, precisely because he was employed within the network, a situation which maintained and enhanced his standing within the group, assuring his relations with other members.

In a network cemented by such moral values, family ties could be used to strengthen the group. From a social standpoint, the members of a network formed a peer group, and they tended to bring their children and family members into the coalition, and to hold an individual's kin morally responsible for any dishonesty on his part. The North African Jews of the eleventh century did not tend to maintain the family business (although this was not uncommon in other such networks). Rather, sons would begin by working with their father, but would gain their independence while he was still alive. Upon the father's death, his assets would be shared out and the business would disappear. There were good reasons for this tendency to integrate family members, for sons assured the honesty of fathers in old age. While an old agent might have money and be in a position to retire, he would still be unlikely to cheat, because he would not be alone in the punishment meted out but would also be ruined by his sons and kin.

One last, perhaps better-known benefit of belonging to such a league was that it provided information about prices, supply and demand for goods, distribution channels and so forth in times when such intelligence was hard (and costly) to come by. The members of a league undertook to exchange information which was crucial to their decisions to buy and sell, cutting transaction costs by allowing them to bring the right goods to the right market at the right time, and to obtain competitive advantages both personally and for the network as a whole. Expulsion from the group of course deprived the victim of access to information flows.

Such cohesive systems have applied successfully to the reality of trade networks at other times in history, in particular cementing the economic regions and national market in Spain. The market of the seventeenth and eighteenth centuries had progressed much since its forerunner of the eleventh century. The commercial world had grown incomparably wider, and it was by this time simply impossible for a merchant to know all of his partners and customers personally in any trade of a certain size. Ventures were undertaken pursuant to the terms of written contracts; the mercantile consulates of Europe had been functioning for centuries; and the state and its courts provided legal assurance of contractual performance, the payment of debts and reliable accounting. The development of trade relations was in fact much closer to the neoclassical economists' ideal of a mass of faceless buyers and sellers making decisions about utility and profit based on standard goods sold at equilibrium prices.

Two more factors are needed, however, to make this network model fully applicable to the latter centuries of feudalism and to inland markets with a relatively small radius like those considered here: namely, the crucial role of family, kinship and clan ties, and the increasing importance of state policy in countries like England, France and Spain (as well as French and English policy in the latter case), a matter we may leave for further discussion below. As for the family, the social historiography has increasingly underscored its role not only as a unit of social action at least until the nineteenth century, but also as the lever which made possible the expansion of client networks[46] and extended family groups,[47] explaining the true functioning of certain political institutions better than any other factor.[48] These networks were in all cases formed by family units bound by blood, and by other economic, cultural and educational ties.[49]

Recent discoveries about the importance of credit in pre-industrial society are intimately linked with the family. Investigating the social networks of rural pedlars and hawkers of one sort or another in early modern Europe, Fontaine shows that it was family ties to places of origin which allowed them to raise the necessary credit for their activities, based on personal trust backed by ties of neighbourhood and family.[50] Many of these pedlars originated from mountainous regions of Europe, and they played a key role in strengthening wider social ties throughout the market by selling popular books and ballads, and exchanging information, often orally in artisans' workshops, in marketplaces and at country fairs. Credit was one of the drivers of economic growth. Indeed, the emergence of a credit culture based on reputation and trust was a fundamental feature of England's economic progress between 1550 and 1720, as has recently been documented.[51]

Economic anthropology can help us determine the true nature of the market resulting from the interaction of such trade networks, applying the term to two kinds of economic exchanges, namely those between organizations, or the *firm-type economy*, which is what we know today, and the *bazaar-type economy*,[52] which takes its names from the souks and bazaars of the Middle East and the Orient and in its variant forms was the predominant kind of economy in the centuries before the Industrial Revolution. Indeed, it remains prevalent in many non-industrialized parts of the world to this day.

It may be worth explaining how the bazaar economy worked, because its mechanisms were applied in most local markets and fairs of the late medieval and early modern periods. The system consisted of flows of goods and services in which small consumer articles changed hands repeatedly along a chain of numerous individual vendors, intermediaries and pedlars between the producer and the end consumer. This kind of market is of course only tenuously linked with manufacturing activities.

The system rested on three pillars: a sliding price system involving bargaining, extensive internal credit networks, and constant diversification of risk and activities.

The bargaining-based sliding price system was used because the bazaar type economy lacks exact accounting mechanisms, and merely estimative calculations of value cannot precisely establish either production costs or the profit obtainable in transactions. Competition existed not between traders but between the buyer and the seller. Reselling was common and caution was the basic commercial rule, because cheating was always possible. Thus, the seller's primary goal was not to secure buyers or customers, or even to expand his business, but to be on the spot when a sale was in the offing and to maximize his profit. The bazaar system is not based on an objective theory of the value of goods, which depends on production costs, but on a subjective theory of value which depends on demand and works within an economic horizon that is always uncertain. In such an environment, there is but little room for long-run business planning, and still less is it possible for the kind of entrepreneurial culture to evolve in which regular income streams are preferred over immediate profits, a hallmark of the modern company.

In the case of internal credit networks, the second pillar of the system, there was a hierarchy between rich merchants who supplied credit (in the form of goods or cash) and smaller traders. This kind of credit may be more expensive than bank loans, but it has the advantage of cementing the position of traders in the market, because it strengthens mutual ties. Traders thus spent much of their time dunning debtors and avoiding creditors with the aim of maximizing the volume and flow of goods, while holding as much hard cash as possible.

The third element was the diversification of activities, goods, risks and profits. Trade took place basically in small, face-to-face transactions, and purchases above a certain volume were unusual because they required business specialization, capital and the assumption of increasing risks.

It was out of this substrate of simple, rule-of-thumb retail trade, lacking any kind of developed accounting systems or planning and based fundamentally on bargaining that the European guilds and mercantile companies of the modern age grew, and it was also in this milieu that the first interurban, interregional and international trading networks emerged.

Having established what the cohesive factors holding together trade diasporas and networks were, or may have been, we may now ask what determined their appearance, growth and decline in Europe and in Spain in the early modern period. One clear, though very general, case is that of emigrations from highland areas. It is well known that relative overpopulation in poor areas acts as a push factor in migrations, and the districts concerned usually, though not always, lacked abundant or fertile farmland so that demographic growth led inevitably either to occupational specialization or emigration. In England, the city of London exerted a powerful magnetic pull unmatched anywhere else in Western Europe, drawing in people both from the north of the kingdom and from as far afield as Scotland and Wales. In Western Europe, the great mountain range of the Alps was the main focus of emigration, along with the Massif Central in France and both sides of the Pyrenees from Catalonia right across to the Basque Country and then on to Galicia.

The logic of these migrations began with the mere export of surplus labour, but it drove the next wave to seek support from their forerunners both in choosing and establishing themselves at their destinations. Meanwhile, those who had left would often return, repatriating their earnings from abroad. As a result, wherever long-run labour migrations occurred in Europe, networks, associations and alliances began to emerge with the mere passage of time based on a range of identifying features, though in almost all such cases the original exodus was from highland areas. These people were seasonal labourers, mule drivers, pedlars and itinerant artisans who traded in products from their home regions or obtained in other places along their migration circuit. Meanwhile, in their destinations they formed stable groups of foreigners specializing in certain trades, and in some cases even groups of well-established merchants who enjoyed a relatively privileged social position.

Certain push factors proper to the laws of highland societies, which tended to favour inheritance through a single heir, also drove emigration, in turn generating trade networks and encouraging them to expand.[53] Meanwhile, family ties were further strengthened by the creation of partnerships. The most developed of these to have come to my attention was the Compañía de Chinchón, but this was just one of the companies formed by the trade networks of emigrants from the Haute Auvergne in Spain, discussed in more detail below. The company was formed by adult French emigrants from an earlier migratory cycle, who would take in new arrivals of at least 16 years of age sent by their families from the homeland. Upon emigrating, these young Frenchmen were beginning a cycle involving between two and six stages in Spain. In the first, lasting from their first to their third years in the country, they would learn Spanish and the shop trade, and in the second (fourth to seventh year), they would work in exchange for a quarter of a share in the host company, gradually beginning to share in its annual profits. When between seven and nine years had passed since their initial emigration, they would return to France, where they would spend around two years and would generally marry. After that, they would make up to five further stays in Spain, each of around two years, returning to France to rest (and to distribute profits) for equal periods of two years, making a total of 20 years. In each sojourn in Spain, they would receive a further one-eighth of a share in the company and its profits. Eventually, after 25–27 years' work and rest, each emigrant would own one full share in the company, which had 102 partners and capital totalling some 1,500,000 *livres tournois* at the time of its liquidation in 1808. A full partner could thus expect to retire at the age of around 44 with an annual income of up to 2,000 *livres*.[54] This system was based on family ties reinforced by the ties of partnership, and it worked well provided the company made profits, of course.

However, there is an evident contrast between the migratory networks formed as a result of the spatial and/or social division of labour, and those which emerged for reasons of poverty or overpopulation. The networks created, for example, in England and Catalonia in the eighteenth century belong to the former category, while the latter were found historically in many of the highland districts of modern Europe. The reasons for the success or failure of such alliances differed depending on the kind of network concerned.

One such factor was the expansion, contraction and eventual disappearance of family ties and inheritance in emigrants' places of origin. In the context of land ownership in the highlands, which was usually freehold or quasi freehold, emigrants would normally cooperate to maintain and enrich the family home. Where links were maintained, an emigrant would have an incentive to remain part of the migratory network, but if they faded, then he would not.

Differences in the nature of intermediate trading are also apparent depending on whether the network was a product of poverty or of the division of labour. Emigration from regions where social and spatial division of labour already existed tended quickly to generate trade in specialized products from the home districts. In contrast, the good traded initially by emigrants from highland areas was their labour itself, and their networks only later began to trade in other products. This contrast is found in Spain, for example, between the networks of Catalan and French migrants.

These factors may explain the succession of occupations in which migrants engaged, for example graduating in time from day labourer to *colporteur* or pedlar, small shopkeeper and eventually merchant. Occasionally, a man might succeed in making such a transition in his own lifetime, although the process would more usually last one or more generations.

In any event, factors like family origins and ties played a key role in the functioning of migratory and trade networks, and this role was internal rather than external. In the long run, the success or failure of such networks is a key explanatory factor for the creation of agrarian wealth and proto-industrialization phenomena in many rural and highland areas between the sixteenth and the nineteenth centuries. The networks active in Spain included those of migrants from the Auvergne, the Pyrenees, the Cameros district of La Rioja, the hinterland of Catalonia, the highland districts of Teruel and other areas.

Economic networks and urban systems

Recent historiography has utilized the concepts of national market and economic region, on one hand, and of economic and social networks on the other, as cited above. While doing so, however, scholars have also employed similar, interrelated concepts in order to multiply the explanatory power of the model. I refer, of course, to *urban systems* and *economic networks*, and specifically to the analysis of spatial urban systems and the economic networks which moved between them made by Ringrose in 1996 in a book about eighteenth- and nineteenth-century Spain which is as interesting as it is little cited.[55] The concept of the *urban system* is drawn from the field of human geography, and its function is very similar to that of the economic region. In this context, Ringrose analyses the formation and development of economic and social networks, which are defined in practically identical terms to those described above, in order to identify and explain who the protagonists in the development of the market were and how they operated. Finally, the author draws support from two other analytical instruments that are also used in geographical analysis, namely the concept of the nodal region and the theory of regional systems, which has for years been applied to the case of Madrid and its economic region and is here extended to Spain as a whole.

Ringrose's work is useful here because it provides an overview of how economic regions and social networks may have developed side by side in eighteenth-century Spain. As I interpret his reasoning,[56] the argument begins with the fact that economic networks, defined as organized groups of people carrying on a productive activity, basically moved goods, people and information at the local level. The most difficult networks to understand are those which moved people and information, as they operated in a context, like the Spanish economy of the time, which was subject to a marked dualism between a majority productive sector focused on self-sufficiency of consumption, and a minority market-based productive sector. In the case of self-consumption, outputs were produced mainly by family units with little specialization, which sought self-sufficiency as a means of ensuring their reproduction and as a defence against future risks. The networks operating at the local level sought above all to ensure mutual supply through cooperative mechanisms such as family rather than wage labour, and similar systems. The small part of output which peasants sent abroad rarely required more than one day's travel to local markets and fairs, and it included all kinds of goods produced by the family unit, including farm produce and proto-industrial manufactures, the spatial location of which was governed by a range of different factors. These short-range exchanges tended to enhance the commercial function of the existing social networks in the locality, which thus became economic networks.

In the context of local markets in the eighteenth century, the expansion of the state and the market obliged family units to seek cash with which to pay state and local taxes, and the rents due to local lords and the Church (who at this time also increasingly needed money). This in turn encouraged the peasantry to seek supplementary work as mule drivers, day labourers on other farms, in artisans' workshops, proto-industrial manufacturing, charcoal burning, woodcutting and in digging lime for building. Meanwhile, the monetization of rural life drove a spatial and social division of labour, and this in turn provided an incentive for the trade networks which had for centuries grown up from among the existing social networks rooted in the rural community, lineage, family and occupation.

At a wider level beyond the confines of the district or the region, economic activity was meanwhile acquiring a quite different tone. The spatial division of labour generated exchanges of commodities and, above all, of manufactures and luxury goods over greater distances and by various means. The ports handled transportation of bulk products (e.g. grain, wine and other commodities) from further afield, because at that time maritime transport was the cheapest option, while mule trains allowed transportation of higher value added goods such as manufactures, luxury products, people and information.

During the century of the Enlightenment, most economic regions were structured around one or two large cities with a market and sometimes a port, together with an urban network linked to them which in turn articulated the rural milieu, attracting goods that were regularly exchanged for money depending on transport costs, market value and profit. These exchanges needed specific trade networks, and as they grew they also drove the expansion of the original small networks existing at the local level.

In an urban system forming the backbone of an economic region, a principal city will centralize commercial services (e.g. insurance, credit, warehousing facilities and wholesalers), and other smaller cities will act as centres for the redistribution of urban services and goods, exporting local produce or re-exporting the output of a specialist district. What economists call 'institutional' and historians simply 'political' factors also play a role in such systems, which may sometimes be decisive. Matters such as a city's status as the capital, the presence of the royal court, and the agrarian rents received by rich, landholding nobles and the Church could only enhance the position of a city in such a system. The most obvious case in eighteenth-century Spain is of course Madrid, which was a major focus of consumption as the seat of the Court, although Seville and Zaragoza could also be mentioned, as home to some of the great noble families and important ecclesiastics.[57]

Let us now consider briefly how many such urban systems there might have been in pre-industrial Spain. Ringrose maintains that there were four distinct networks:

> The largest network was based on Barcelona and ran from the French border to Malaga and inland to Zaragoza. A second extended along the northern coast from Vigo to San Sebastian, with its coordinating centre in Bilbao. The third system loosely covered the Mesetas of Old and New Castile and was oriented to Madrid.

> Yet another network was based in Seville and encompassed the Guadalquivir valley, the coast from Algeciras to Portugal, and extended into Extremadura. It will be clear from the start that these networks overlap and that the inclusion or exclusion of some towns is a matter of debate. It is also apparent that Cadiz, as the eighteenth-century focal point for access to the political and commercial resources of the Indies, participated in distinctive ways in each regional system.[58]

The idea of analysing the development of the Spanish market from the standpoint of urban systems, or economic regions, which need not necessarily coincide with political regions is interesting and useful for two reasons. First, it allows the question of the market to be addressed without being shackled to the notion of the historical regions, which have gained a disproportionate presence in the historiography today as the forerunners of the Autonomous Communities into which the contemporary Spanish state is divided. This may be one reason why Ringrose's thesis has met with such little enthusiasm in certain nationalist circles, particularly in Catalonia. Second, it raises the possibility of undertaking a historical analysis which is not only, or even necessarily, confined to the regional sphere. Spanish regional history is too often merely a matter of documentary ease, as many of the sources of information are held in regional archives.

Having said this, Ringose's interpretation raises a number of worthwhile questions. I agree with him that the urban systems described do to some extent overlap, and that Cadiz was to some extent a part of all of them, as the centre from which American silver, and therefore payments, were distributed. However, the key issue is to align the general outline of his argument with the scope of this work, and to include certain features of the historical evidence. For the reasons I have already explained, I have concentrated in my argument on north-eastern Spain, the geographical area initially defined as including Aragon, Catalonia, Valencia, Navarre and Castile, and which therefore included parts of the systems organized around Bilbao (the northern coastal strip of the Bay of Biscay), Barcelona and Madrid.

To begin with, it is doubtful that an urban system must necessarily end at a political frontier. Not only do such systems hop easily over regional barriers, they need not even be national in scope. In the eighteenth century, Bayonne in France was probably the head of something like an urban system which included at least Pamplona and probably cities like Logroño and Zaragoza, where it overlapped with Barcelona. For myself, I have never been convinced that the economic space of Navarre was commercially dependent on Bilbao, and indeed the former kingdom was at least as important politically, and probably more so, than the three Basque provinces in the Spanish monarchy of the eighteenth century, unlikely though this may seem today.

While Ringrose's outline adequately combines the concept of long distance networks, it is less than certain that the urban system (I use Ringrose's term) organized around Barcelona would not have included something very like independent sub-systems. Indeed, the available historical evidence suggests that Valencia may have been much more independent of Barcelona as an urban system than has been claimed, and that it may have developed, or been in the process of developing its own urban system, reaching back into the Castilian and Aragonese hinterland to Requena, Cuenca and Teruel. In the area of maritime trade, then, Valencia may have fallen within the area of influence of Barcelona, but in terms of the goods traded by local networks, including essential commodities and certain relatively high value added manufactures, the city may already have formed, or at least been in the process of forming, its own urban system in the eighteenth century. An economic region centred on Valencia has indeed been recognized in the nineteenth century, and one may well ask whether it did not already exist a century earlier.

This leads to a third issue, which is the question of time. Whether our focus is on urban systems or economic regions, the areas concerned varied over time. The War of the Spanish Succession almost did away with internal customs posts in Spain, and economic conditions in the rest of the eighteenth century took care of the rest. As a consequence, Madrid's area of influence expanded into Castile in the period, at the same time spreading north-eastwards into Navarre and Aragon. Meanwhile, the influence of Barcelona penetrated westwards up the Ebro valley as far as Zaragoza, and it would seem to have reached Navarre by the end of the century. Finally, trade relations between Bayonne and Pamplona grew ever stronger.

One last matter is Madrid's unique role as the financial capital. The four urban systems or economic regions were far from uniform, and nor indeed were the historic regions, but the whole was conditioned by the fact that Madrid, which by the eighteenth century was already the largest centre of consumption, the capital and the seat of the Court, had also become principal recipient of rents. At the same time, the state would grow ever stronger in the eighteenth century. The conjunction of these two factors, as we shall see in detail below, was what determined the city's development as a financial centre.

Madrid became the principal credit market in Spain and the centre for the management of international debt and loans, so that the trade networks which organized tasks in cities like Bilbao, Seville and Barcelona were sooner or later obliged to establish contact with the capital in order to negotiate their bills of exchange and to manage their loans and, on occasions, certain major investments by the state. This explains, for example, the strategic importance of roads like the highway linking Madrid and Barcelona, that progressed gradually from being mainly an instrument for military communications to become a conduit for the communication of people, goods, financial information and bills of exchange.

The presence of the state

The last issue we shall address in this introductory chapter is the presence of the state and its influence on economic realities. More specifically, we may ask whether or not it played an active role in the creation of the economic regions and the incipient national market, and in the development of social networks, and if so how.

Thanks to works like that of Douglass C. North, economic historians in general have long acknowledged the state's importance in the development of the market. However, this matter has attracted notice in the Spanish historiography only recently. Referring to the tardy modernization of the Spanish economy in the nineteenth century, the so-called institutionalist school has given much weight to political issues, underscoring the weakness of property rights during the period of transition to the liberal revolution,[59] the failure of the state to reorganize its finances to meet the needs of society and, in the matter of trade, the failure significantly to reduce transaction and information costs. Various measures were in fact adopted in Spain to make the market more responsive, even during the reign of Ferdinand VII, including the Patents Act of 1826, the first Commercial Code of 1829, the creation of the Banco de San Fernando (the forerunner of the Bank of Spain) in 1829, and the founding of the Madrid Stock Exchange in 1831. However, all of these initiatives were hampered by problems like the belated creation of the railway network,[60] the lack of resources for the administration of justice and failure to modernize the tax system.[61]

This general view of the question is interesting, but I believe that the issues are best illuminated by the kind of approach which weighs the role and crisis of the absolutist state, the bourgeois liberal revolution and the emergence of the new liberal state as factors in the process that resulted in the disappearance of the old pre-industrial economy, and the rise of industrialization and the integrated national market.

This is precisely the approach taken by Josep Fontana in his seminal book *La quiebra de la monarquía absoluta, 1814–1820*, first published in 1971 and an obligatory reference in the field. Fontana's argument is presented in various versions in the different editions of the work, the last of which stresses the close relationship existing between the fiscal possibilities of the principal European states (England, the United Provinces, France and Spain), the development of their colonial empires, industrialization processes and social outcomes.[62] This approach appears to provide a more precise point of departure.

For a number of years now, Fontana has stressed the central role played by the capacity to raise revenues for military spending in the development of the absolutist European states (including Spain),[63] and he has recently underscored the importance of politics in the development of treasury departments and their part in economic growth. To put it briefly, his thesis is that the political revolutions which occurred in states like the United Provinces and England successfully enhanced their financial possibilities between the sixteenth and the eighteenth centuries. Revolution handed control of the monarchy to representative parliaments, strengthening the state and enhancing the certainty of transactions (through clear property rights and the freedom to contract), so that it had become much easier to borrow by the eighteenth century, because investors in the Amsterdam debt market were confident that interest on the debt would actually be paid. Hence, they were prepared to lend at lower interest rates, because they knew that debts would be assumed by the borrower's successors thanks to parliamentary controls. This in turn created a climate of political confidence allowing long-term investment, from which the countries concerned themselves benefitted.

> those states in which government was controlled by representative parliaments inspired confidence in investors, because it could be safely assumed that the members [of the government] would themselves take a keen interest in ensuring regular payments of a debt that was closely linked to their own business interests in many ways. Small investors thus chose to deposit their savings in securities

which they knew to be safe, allowing governments to obtain the funds they needed at very low rates of interest.[64]

In short, political change allowed England and the Netherlands access to abundant, cheap credit.

Other states had no such access. On the contrary, Fontana sees the political absolutism of France and Spain as an obstacle to economic modernization, or at least as a factor which did nothing to encourage it. According to his argument, the lack of political revolution meant that coercive feudal rents (tithes and seignieurial rights) were neither transferred to the state nor done away with, while the ever stronger absolutist states of the seventeenth and eighteenth centuries found themselves obliged to increase taxes, so that tax pressure including feudal rents in fact grew faster. Increasing fiscal needs were met by more taxes, but also by recourse to public debt, which expanded exponentially in the eighteenth century. In those states where the monarchy was subject to parliamentary control, however, it could not spend such monies just as it liked. In contrast, absolute monarchs felt themselves under no obligation to assume the debts of their predecessors, and were liable to suspend payments without seeking any prior arrangements with creditors, which of course undermined confidence. Lenders, who were not blind to the greater risks involved, made loans at higher rates of interest, demanding additional security and guarantees, while the debt markets heavily discounted the paper of the absolute monarchies. As a result, the state found itself obliged to borrow domestically in a process that was highly speculative and resulted in swingeing rates of interest on loans.

In this context, the processes of bourgeois revolution had decisive differential effects. The French Revolution reawakened confidence in the political system and in the national debt, and as payment came to be seen as certain debt prices rose in the stock exchanges, allowing the state to renegotiate loans at lower rates of interest. The crisis of the *Ancien Régime* in Spain only worsened the problem of debt, which increased exponentially between 1774 and 1808,[65] ruining numerous small investors who had purchased debt certificates in the eighteenth century. In the nineteenth century, sovereign debt traded at low prices in the stock exchange and continued to be negotiated at high rates of interest, which made it more profitable to purchase debt for its yield than to invest in business ventures, contributing to the lag in industrialization.[66]

The interpretative model is clear, and it would be difficult to devise another that would provide a better explanation of the divergent development of some nations, like England and the United Provinces, compared with others, like France and Spain, four countries which will appear again and again in the following chapters. In my opinion, the most novel feature of the argument is the way in which Fontana relates the emergence of progressively democratic regimes with long-run economic growth.

The consequences arising from this interpretative model are well known. I refer to Nadal's thesis about the failure of the industrial revolution, and Fontana's own arguments concerning the impossible progress of enlightened absolutism in the Bourbon Spain of the eighteenth century and the wholesomeness of bourgeois revolution, not to mention the widely accepted idea that the national market was not formed until the nineteenth century. In the end, then, the blame lies with absolute monarchy, which was unwilling or unable to mould itself to a parliamentary system.

This is not the place to assess these views, which are supported by a considerable weight of documentary evidence and detailed arguments. Given their importance, however, we would do well to consider certain matters which have so far been largely ignored but which will become important planks in the argument we shall construct in the following chapters. Indeed, it may perhaps begin to shift the generally negative view of the role played by the absolutist state in Spain's economic development.

It is frequently assumed as fact that there is a right route to progress and economic growth, which is the English and Dutch course, and there is a wrong route, which is that taken by the absolute monarchies of France and Spain. However, it might be well to begin by considering that these four nations were far from equal back in 1650, when the English revolution (1642–1688) first brought the differences in their political regimes into the open. Indeed, developments in any one significantly influenced the others.

The arguments supporting this statement will be presented in detail in the following chapters. England had an expanding trade empire and was undergoing far-reaching economic change, while France had the most powerful army in Europe. At the same time, both had tethered once powerful Spain in a situation of economic dependence through diplomatic instruments like the Treaty of the Pyrenees and the Anglo-Spanish treaty of 1667. This subordination explains much in my opinion. In the mercantilist struggle that took place over the hundred years before the French Revolution, Spanish politicians, whether or not of the enlightened faction, were faced not only with the hangover from the political, economic and social crises of the seventeenth century (economic decline, secession in Catalonia and Portugal, privatization and oligarchic control of the machinery of the state) and with the obsessive idea that the Spanish monarchy must be the champion of the Counter-Reformation (dominance of Scholasticism, intellectual censorship, the overwhelming share of the economy in the hands of the Church, the Inquisition, and the expulsion of the *Moriscos*), but also with a host of other problems derived from the country's political and economic dependence. Thus, the rulers of eighteenth-century Spain were faced with the political objective of rescuing the country from its backwardness and modernizing (output, domestic consumption, organization of the state and exploitation of the American market) from a situation of political subordination which did not affect other states. Seen from this angle, Spain's backwardness in the early eighteenth century cannot be explained only by internal factors.

We might also be wise to weigh more carefully the extent to which the state, as a composite monarchy until 1707 and an administrative monarchy thereafter, and almost always as an absolutist, though sometimes as an enlightened regime, was actually able to act and make any significant progress in overcoming Spain's difficulties and expanding the domestic market. Some of the actions taken are discussed below from a general point of view. Be this as it may, the crisis of the *Ancien Régime* put a final end to any such activity, which certainly existed though it may have been mediated and limited by a range of circumstances.

Let us here make certain other points related with the scale of this approach. So far, it is only the macro-analytic scenario which has been considered, in the form of changing economic conditions, the situation of the state, the decisions of monarchs and international relations. By switching to a micro-analytic focus, however, in order to examine how people actually operated either individually or as members of groups and networks, we may discover other protagonists and important new faces. Trade networks are a case in point. They operated throughout Spain, but also in England and France, and their functioning cannot have been identical in each country. As I shall argue in detail below, the development of trade networks in Spain was conditioned by certain highly specific factors.

The demographic decline which began in the second half of the sixteenth century only to worsen in the seventeenth attracted increasing numbers of French migrants, many fleeing the wars of religion. This was at first mainly a labour migration, and it was only in its later stages that commercial activity increased. However, the resulting trade networks were key to the penetration of French goods in the markets of the Spanish interior, especially after the upsurge of manufacturing in the second half of the seventeenth century. This early Gallic presence in the markets not only of the Spanish interior but also of the colonies, and the arrival of the English (though in a different way) are facts that cannot be ignored. In general, the early players in Spain's emerging domestic market, at the time when the economic regions were in the process of formation, were organized in extensive trade networks formed both by Spanish *naturals* (natives) and by foreigners, and the ways in which these networks functioned had important consequences for the development of the market itself.

Another important factor which tends to be overlooked is the peculiar development of the capital, Madrid. Beginning in the late sixteenth century, migrants from the northern provinces of Galicia, Asturias, Santander, the Basque Country and Navarre converged steadfastly on the new capital, a city which was not built around any earlier settlement, port, market or structured rural hinterland, but rather on its position as the seat of the monarchy, and it was for this reason that it concentrated political power and attracted a large rentier population. As a consequence, the migrant labour force was organized around the provision of services to the king, the nobility and the religious orders. The city did not develop any manufacturing for consumption by the rural populace or for export from a convenient port, as had occurred with the ventures of Welsh and Scottish migrants in London, and the Auvergnese in Paris. Rather the reverse: industrial activity was confined to supplying a small urban settlement where consumption was dominated by the sumptuous spending of the Court, the aristocracy and the major religious institutions, and at no time did it break the confines imposed by the guilds. The engine of economic development in the capital of Spain was thus completely different from other capitals like Paris, London and Amsterdam.

Another significant factor was the growth of clientelism as a form of political action and a social elevator, weakening individual responsibility for economic success and shifting it onto commercial, social or political networks. The sale of offices and the development of extensive client networks in modern Spain is a well-known phenomenon, but it has never to my knowledge been analysed from this perspective. In this regard, we may note the position of Hilton Root, who has argued that the increasing divergence between the state's role in economic policy in England and

France between 1642 and 1789 was caused by the differing incidence of corruption, venality, clientelism and patronage.[67]

The English Civil War and the Restoration both sought above all to limit the cronyism of the Stuart dynasty. From that time onwards, the ways in which government favours were used changed substantially, as the Whig oligarchy took to dispensing such benefits to buy political support in Parliament, but not to create monopolies, or to provide financial backing or fiscal benefits.[68] The venality of officials and enrichment of ministers (that is, cronyism) in France were far greater than in England, as demonstrated by the cases of Richelieu, Mazarino, Colbert and his nephew Nicolas Desmarets (Desmaretz). Meanwhile, the country's rulers were more easily able to govern by decree through the Conseil du Roi than their English counterparts, and numerous *arrêts* regulated the economy to an extraordinary degree. In England, meanwhile, ministers were liable to run into parliamentary opposition if they sought to promulgate similar orders in response to *private bills*, and they would frequently confine themselves to proposing laws or making recommendations so as to avoid any clash with the electorate. Though English ministers were not of course entirely innocent of cronyism, their writ ran above all in the civil service, the army, the navy, and foreign and colonial affairs, but they had much less direct influence over the domestic economy.[69]

According to Root, then, corruption and venality were rife in England, but clientelism was less widespread than in France, where corruption was less but cronyism was the norm. The impact of these vices on the development of domestic markets was very different:

> Corruption and cronyism thus constitute two politically mandated types of market imperfection: informal contracts in political markets that shape how economic market forces evolved over time. Corruption is open to market forces and indirectly allows for the allocation of resources according to a criterion of efficiency that cronyism lacks.

This is because:

> Cronyism restricts entry and exit from the market while corruption does not. In this sense cronyism is like credit rationing that limits funds to preferred clients and prevents some enterprises from getting funds at any price. Corruption, on the other hand, creates equal difficulties for all parties.[70]

As French clientelism was also based on secrecy, political favours could not be priced, because nobody outside the government or ministry concerned knew what they were really worth.

The ministries of the British Crown used corruption, nepotism, the payment of electoral expenses and bribery to ensure the loyalty of members of Parliament. Thus, they sold their favours to the highest bidder. As this corruption was not based on cronyism but on social groups which gravitated around political parties, it did not limit access to the market by *lobbies*, interest groups and companies, which might pay more or less for favours but were in any case well apprised of their worth. Thus, the issues raised in Parliament became the subject of wider debate, allowing room for the influence of public opinion. In France, the King's ministers in the eighteenth century largely enjoyed a reputation for incorruptibility, and their tight control of subordinates limited the scope for venality. However, cronyism led to discrimination between cliques, affecting access to the market and causing less efficient use of resources with scant regard for the maximization of utility and profits.[71]

I believe this whole argument can and should also be applied to the Spanish state, which was structured along French lines with an absolute monarch but no effective Parliament. However, this is not quite as straightforward as it might seem. In the first place, it is disingenuous to pretend that corruption and cronyism are merely market dysfunctions; that the allocation of economic resources is efficient under conditions of corruption and inefficient under cronyism; that corruption and cronyism are mutually exclusive; that the pecuniary value of royal appointments was not known; or that appointments to office were not made on the basis of competition between individuals as well as patronage. However, other aspects of the argument are perfectly applicable. It is well known that certain patronage networks were very important in some areas of the economy (e.g. procurement of food and supplies for the army), so that their members were indeed able to benefit from privileged information. As for corruption, which was limited in England because parliamentary information eventually became public, it is very likely that abuses were greater in Spain, because the forums which produced an incipient public opinion in that country did not develop in Spain until the latter decades of the eighteenth century. The dealings of Cabarrus in the 1780s and the political fall and trials of Condom, Cabarrus and Floridablanca, who were accused of embezzling public funds between 1789 and 1792, could only have occurred in the context of the change in mentality with regard to the political value of public and private interests which took place in France at the end of the eighteenth century, and which must also have affected Spain.

* * *

I cannot, of course, say with any precision how far the exploration of these factors might alter our perceptions of eighteenth-century Spanish society, or what the resulting image of that society might be. Our task here is to investigate the genesis of the national market in an absolute monarchy. However, any exploration of the origins of a phenomenon will inescapably be imbued with a certain conceptual ambiguity. An origin may be a cause, or it may be merely a beginning; it may mark the culmination of a process resulting in a steady state, or it may mark the starting point of a chain of consequences. According to Marc Bloch, the popular meaning of 'origin' refers to a start which explains something or, even more hazily, a complete explanation of that thing.[72]

Hence, it may be that all our endeavours here will not explain how or why a national market began to take shape in Spain, but it will at least help ensure that the history of the drawn-out end of the *Ancien Régime* in Spain will not consist solely (and I must stress solely) of a litany of inevitable backwardness, degenerate monarchs, corrupt politicians and Scholasticism. Spain was not merely a backward society which was rescued from the dark by the bright light of the bourgeois liberal revolution, but also a political community which was already behind its supposed competitors when the race for economic growth began.

This history may also reveal a more complex past, which is closer to the actual reality. This past should not only provide us with a genealogy of the present, important though this may be, but also with the keys to understand (if not to justify) the workings of the social machine and the policies of rulers whose social universe was very different to ours, and whose mental world relegated the ideas of progress and economic growth to a position far below their position in today's scale of values, important though they may have been to a few. *Ideas in context* is the title of a celebrated series of publications, but the phrase is also perfectly applicable here, for the ideas and facts presented must be read not only from the perspective of the present but also within the context in which they occurred if they are to be properly understood. This will be the task of the next chapters, which will lead us to examine the Spanish monarchy's difficult commercial relations with England and France.

2

England, France and the Spanish Market

In my opinion, any discussion of Spain's domestic market before the nineteenth century must begin with an explanation of the state of Spain after it emerged from the crisis of the seventeenth century and the Thirty Years' War. This leads naturally to a consideration of the economic changes occurring in England and France in the seventeenth and eighteenth centuries, which ultimately conditioned both countries' position with respect to the Spanish monarchy and market.

Let us start by exploring the economic transformations set in motion in the early modern period first in England and then in the whole of Great Britain,[1] though we may recall that similar developments also occurred in other European countries, if not with the same intensity. These changes gradually put an end to the feudal societies which had emerged in the medieval period in a process that gathered pace in the seventeenth century, by which time the market had become a true forum for economic activity. Internationally, the rulers of a few ever stronger states strove to establish a dominant position, which would provide wealth and power for themselves and their followers. This was the age of mercantilism, a period that was hard for all, but especially for the losers.

In this context, it is generally taken as read that the earliest and most far-reaching transformations occurred in England, where the alignment of the monarchy and the people behind the Protestant Reformation, the early dissolution of the monasteries, the subjection of the Church to the king and the weakening of the seignieurial system[2] combined to allow the early development of the country, which progressively raised its agricultural productivity and proto-industrial output in the sixteenth century, expanding the domestic market and organizing production structures around the great city of London, which was at once the country's political heart and its economic engine.[3]

England embarked on a radical shift in its trade patterns between 1550 and 1640 (the years of what Barry Supple called the 'trade revolution') before any other European country. In 1600 trade was still oriented basically towards Germany and the Low Countries, but by 1641, the year in which the English revolution began, it had changed almost beyond recognition driven by burgeoning trade flows under the control of new commercial networks operating in the Levant, the Indies, Southern Europe, the Mediterranean, the Near East and the Far East. This occurred not because of any particular growth in demand for woollen cloth, England's main manufactured export at the time, but because the new English traders brought with them a fresh outlook that was less in hock to religious and feudal preconceptions, allowing them quickly to see that exports of woollens and the so-called *new draperies* not only generated income in themselves but allowed the import of exotic goods, which could then be re-exported to other countries bringing in even larger profits.[4]

The powerful merchant elite of early seventeenth-century London was, then, able to accumulate profits not so much from imports and exports, but from the re-export of foreign goods from their home ports, which made English shipping essential to pan-European trade. Meanwhile, Portugal and Spain both jealously controlled access to their colonial empires and to those metropolitan areas where inflows of cash and precious metals from the colonies created pockets of wealth and high prices. It was precisely in such places where English goods could be most profitably sold. Only the Flemish and Dutch could compete with the English. Flanders was, of course, the jewel in the Spanish Crown both for its wealth and for the strength of its proto-industrial manufacturing, which inspired Franklin Mendels' reformulation of the theory of proto-industrialization.[5] Partly because of this, the basic objective of English policy in the seventeenth century was to achieve the subjection of the United Provinces while making war on Spain.[6]

Unlike other European countries, economic transformation in England was not the result of deliberate action by the state. Rather the reverse: it was change on the ground which drove shifts in the government's economic policy. In fact, the English revolution (1642–1689) realigned the structure of the state with the new economic interests of the landed gentry and the moneyed classes. Leaving aside the decisive impact of the revolution, there can be no question that this occurred partly because the power of English kings to impose land taxes had always been very limited, in contrast to other European monarchs. As a consequence, the growth of trade made the monarchy ever more dependent on customs duties. This was the result of a happy coincidence of interests, so that the financial security of the English state was made possible by the simultaneous expansion of trade.

Economic changes brought about profound social transformations[7] in England so that a political community gradually developed in which many livelihoods had become fully aligned with the market by the end of the seventeenth century,[8] while consumption had risen well above the levels found elsewhere in Europe[9] and an individual's social standing was defined by his household's credit, the *currency of reputation*.[10] All of this was founded on a profoundly mercantile, and mercantilist, economic culture, the best expression of which is to be found in works like *The Fable of the Bees* by Bernard Mandeville (1714),[11] one of the most widely read books in Europe in the eighteenth century,[12] or Daniel Defoe's less well known treatise on the morals of trade.[13] At this time, the English state was the strongest in Europe financially, because its revenues and credit allowed it to borrow massively, issuing debt without problems in the Amsterdam money market to pay for its wars.[14] Its success was such that it did not become necessary to establish a wealth or income tax in Great Britain until the end of the eighteenth century, although such taxes had already been instituted decades before in countries like Spain in the form of the *real contribución, equivalente, talla, catastro* and the *única contribución*.[15]

All of this contrasts starkly with the historical trajectory of France, an equally wealthy, larger and more heavily populated continental country, where the conflict between the Protestant Reformation and the Catholic Counter-Reformation plunged the land into a series of civil and religious wars that lasted from the mid-sixteenth century until the mid-seventeenth century, consolidating a peculiar form of feudalism while weakening mercantile capital and enormously strengthening the state. In contrast to England, the economic and political progress of France was led by the state, in particular in the second half of the seventeenth century.

In the early modern centuries, the rivalry between England and France was one of the key explanatory forces driving European history. While competition was initially political and religious, economic interests soon began to play a part, and this was the reason for both countries' ceaseless efforts to control what for the sake of simplicity we may call the Spanish market, which comprised both the colonies and the domestic market in the Iberian Peninsula. To understand the underlying factors in play, we need to examine this struggle from its beginning.

The rivalry between Great Britain and France

The commercial and political rivalry between Great Britain and France in the eighteenth century goes back at least to the middle of the seventeenth century, spanning what some have called the 'second' Hundred Years' War (a total of eight wars between 1689 and 1815). According to Crouzet,[16] there were two reasons for this conflict.

The first of these factors was the mercantilist notion that trade is merely a physical exchange which tends to equilibrium, so that the balance of trade is a zero sum game in which one country's expansion is only possible at the expense of another's. England already saw France as a potential rival before the Restoration. It was widely believed at that time that England was running a trade deficit and that this gave an advantage to Louis XIV, as well as providing cash for him to finance his army. Because of this, many merchants lobbied the crown to ban the import of French goods. In 1713, the English Parliament refused to make a trade treaty with France, and French goods like claret imported from Bordeaux, were either banned or burdened with heavy duties. At around the same time, the French had become convinced that England's ambition was to take over world trade.

The second factor was religious. To the English, it was clear that France had taken over Spain's former role as the great Catholic power, and anti-papist hatreds were soon turned towards the country, worsening markedly after the revocation of the Edict of Nantes and the persecution of the Huguenots by Louis XIV. Nevertheless, this religious tyranny was paradoxically beneficial for England, because it brought numerous French emigrants to the country, many of whom settled in London, contributing to the development of finance and assisting in the creation of the Bank of England. At the same time, many Jacobites and Irish malcontents left for France, where they mostly served in the army and navy although a few turned to trade and some became leading merchants.[17]

These may have been the original reasons for the confrontation, but they were certainly not the only ones. The conflict spread to the field of politics, culture and national self-awareness in the period before the French Revolution. Linda Colley has clearly documented how it was war against the *significant other* that was France which defined the birth of an early British identity and nationalism, and not the dialogue between the nations of England, Wales, Ireland and Scotland.[18]

It could be said, then, that it was a powerful imagined reality which forged a national identity in Great Britain based on ethnicity and a series of political and religious arguments referring to an exceptional country inhabited by a unique people, the jewel of Protestantism shining like a beacon for the countries of continental Europe in thrall to the spiritual tyranny and superstition of the Church of Rome. To British thinkers, insularity was a boon granted by divine Providence: it had protected the country from the conquests of the Catholic Counter-Reformation, and it had freed it from the need to maintain the kind of large standing army that had perpetuated the sway of despotism in Europe. In this context, France loomed large in the British imagination because it shared much of its primitive Germanic inheritance with the Anglo-Saxon tradition of the British Isles. The Saxons, or the Franks in France, were fierce defenders of their freedom, and in the late Roman Empire they had elected their princes, whose powers were limited. This was the basis for the British conviction of superiority over the French in the eighteenth century: they had won back their freedoms by revolution, while the French remained in the hands not only of the Catholic Church but also of a despotic monarchy represented by Louis XIV.[19]

On this view, all peoples of Germanic origin shared the same freedom-loving tradition and the same political institutions throughout Western Europe, including France and Spain. In the words of the influential English mercantilist Charles Davenant, writing around 1700:

> these several branches springing from the same stem, it must follow, that the fruit they bore would be near of a taste; by which we mean, that in their manners, laws, and principally in their politic government, they must of consequence, as indeed they did, very much resemble one another. And whoever looks into the ancient constitutions of England, France, Spain, Denmark, and Sweden will find, that all these nations had one and the same form of government; and though they might vary in some circumstances, yet they all agreed in certain fundamentals, which were, that the people should have their rights and privileges; that the nobles, or men of chief rank, should have some participation of power, and, that the regal authority should be limited by laws.[20]

It was this tradition which the English proudly claimed to uphold, though it was broken in Europe and had been abandoned by the French.

Then as now, this was not the only way of seeing things. With the ambivalence proper to an increasingly complex and plural society, the English held France and French lifestyles in high regard in the eighteenth century, and it could likewise be argued that the French were also very open to ideas from the other side of the English Channel. French diplomacy treated Great Britain as a special country, but not exactly as an enemy, despite the litany of wars between the two countries. There was an important colony of pro-French Britons in Paris, and in other parts of France. Meanwhile, France was a major influence on English thought and literature, and it was common for the upper classes of one country to travel to the other even when they were at war. These relations sank to a low point during the Napoleonic Wars (1793–1802 and 1803–1814), but not beforehand.[21]

What, then, were the forces that drove the rivalry between Great Britain and France? Was it war, or economic interest, feelings of ethnic superiority, or political and cultural pre-eminence? All of these factors were involved, to a greater or lesser extent. The rivalry was probably originally borne out of the economic transformations of the time, becoming stronger as continuous wars bolstered national identity and finally acquiring ideological form through the interpretations placed by seventeenth- and above all eighteenth-century thinkers on the history of their own and other countries. By 1641 the interests of London's mercantile elite were already one of the primary concerns of England's foreign policy, which took its final shape after the Glorious Revolution of 1688–1689. This in turn raises the question of the influence of French commercial interests on the foreign policy of the French monarchy in the second half of the seventeenth century.

The facts described here will, I believe, show that these interests were also very important, if not in the same way. The strong presence of French networks in Spain described in the following chapters should change our initial view of English dominance. As an island nation, England's foreign trade networks developed via maritime trade, which required large companies, considerable capital, shipyards and insurance. The organization of the state took this into account. There was no standing army, but the country had a large navy and customs duties were an essential source of revenue to finance it. In France, maritime trade was organized along similar lines to that of England, but the country also engaged in intense overland trade based on a very different business model. Emigrants not only traded in goods but also in labour. Many did not use letters of exchange or other international payment instruments, functioning with scant fixed capital but penetrating deeper into the host territory. These French migrants also left few archival records, but this does not mean their overall activity was unimportant in economic terms. Competing fiercely with Great Britain at sea, the French state eventually became aware of this difference, in particular with regard to Spain.

It is something of a habit among historians to ask questions about the past which cannot be readily answered. This is one such case. It is here taken as fact that France and England, as political entities, were in competition for the Spanish market in the seventeenth century. However, we may ask whether what we have called competition was not, or did not become, merely a mental construct of princes, diplomats and intellectuals, which in reality had little to do with actual events and circumstances. Did the agents of trade, the British and French merchants and migrants themselves, actually see themselves as being in competition for anything? Perhaps this is just another of those unanswerable questions for which we vainly seek a clear and convincing answer.

The image of the other: a game of mirrors between Great Britain, France and Spain

If we are to answer the question posed above, we will need to venture out beyond the narrow field of economic and social history, to consider how the princes and subjects of each monarchy saw each other, and how the Spanish viewed the English and the French. In short, we must consider the game of mirrors between the players in the wider struggle of mercantilist competition and political transformation in the seventeenth century. Our aim here is only to show that this double image did indeed exist, affecting not only politics but also, significantly, mercantile competition, an area in which both the states concerned and the elites which controlled them had much to say.

In France, a certain feeling of inferiority existed with regard to Great Britain,[22] and of superiority over Spain. For example, the officers of the French army were filled with admiring trepidation by the growing prosperity of the English. The reasons for England's superiority from the standpoint of French thinkers consisted, first and foremost, of the strength of its foreign trade, in which it sought to establish monopolies to shut out other countries; the enormous technological progress made in agriculture and manufacturing, which allowed the English to cut the cost of production in spite of the country's supposedly high wages; and a range of other institutional factors. However, they entertained a rather primitive idea of the reasons for the success of English textiles manufacturing, which most analysts attributed to the quality of the wool (good sheep and pastures) and the existence of special clays which facilitated the cleaning process. On the institutional plane, the key was believed to lie in the political system. After the English revolution, the country enjoyed legal protection for its freedoms and for property; the French, in contrast, were subject to taxation of property in the form of the land tax, but neither manufacturers nor merchants paid excise or customs duties. Meanwhile, it was correctly recognized that the English government enjoyed enormous political credit, which allowed it to borrow without problems, while the British aristocracy enthusiastically supported manufactures and trade.[23] Seeking to modernize the economic system in the early eighteenth century by creating paper money and the *Banque Générale*, a private, royal bank, in order to reduce the state's dependence on revenue farmers and financiers, John Law copied the British model. His idea was precisely that the power of absolute monarchy would facilitate matters. According to Tot:

> Il avoit médité long temps sur les causes qui avoient tant augmenté les revenus des Hollandois et des Anglois, en comparaison du revenu des autres nations. Il avoit reconnu que la manière d'administrer les finances, déterminoit la puissance ou la faiblesse d'un Etat, le bonheur ou le malheur des peuples. Que l'augmentation prodigieuse du revenu des Hollandais et des Anglais venôit de celle de leur commerce, et que les principaux moyens de cette augmentation étoient l'établissement de leurs banques et de leurs compagnies de commerce. Il avoit étudié attentivement les réglements et la méchanique de ces établissements, il comprit que l'on pouvoit les établir en France en moins de temps qu'ailleurs, et dans une plus grande perfection, parce que toute l'autorité y est réunie en la personne du Roy, au lieu que dans les républiques, les bonnes choses, quelques avantageuses qu'elles soient, sont très long-temps à s'y etabli, parque qu'il y a autant d'obstacles à surmonter, que de persones à persuader, non seulement contre leurs ancients préjugés, mais quelques fois encore contre leurs intérèts particuliers.[24]

Law was wrong. We know today that absolutism began to be questioned on the Continent almost as soon as parliamentarianism took hold in Great Britain. It was the high esteem in which the English political system was held, already widespread by the eighteenth century, that led many thinkers in France to adopt positions that were more or less openly critical of the *Ancien Régime*.[25] This reveals twin facts which I believe have not been properly recognized: the English were aware that their representative political system was economically more efficient, but on the Continent the French and Spanish likewise realized that it would be impossible for them to match these gains without far-reaching change in the political situation of their own countries. In the short term, cultural awareness of this fact had little practical effect, but in the long run it became a determining factor of the French Revolution and of its disastrous domino effects in Spain.

The fierce competition over trade between France and Great Britain in the eighteenth century was reflected in many fields, including the abundant French literature on the subject of political economy, and it is not hard to find chapter after chapter of debate comparing the wealth and resources of the two nations.[26] For example, Turgot lays great stress in his numerous works on the growth and renewal of manufacturing and the division of labour as a means of increasing foreign trade, aside from the general physiocratic view of agriculture as the foundation stone of the economy.[27] Trade was in fact the mirror in which many French thinkers looked, especially in relation to their competition with England, in the hope that the reflection they would see would be increasingly that of their own country.

Like the French with the English, the Spanish saw the arrival of the new Bourbon dynasty as holding out the hope of salvation from decadence and political and economic renewal,[28] although the view from Aragon and Catalonia was initially darkened by the experiences of French immigration and the occupation of Catalonia in the second half of the seventeenth century, and by the War of Succession. In the eighteenth century, France and the French were seen by enlightened Spanish travellers like the painter José Luzán,[29] the historian Antonio Ponz[30] and the politician Count de Aranda as an admirable country and culture, well worthy of emulation. This view began to change after 1760 as enlightened Spanish policy grew more nationalistic, and it was radically altered in 1789, when the French Revolution aroused fiercely anti-French sentiment which was soon accompanied by an anti-revolutionary political stance, as Aymes has recently shown.[31]

The French image of Spain was very different, being constructed on the basis of a strong feeling of superiority. The Spanish Crown had maintained fierce political competition with France in the sixteenth and seventeenth centuries, and the Black Legend of Spain, as it has been called, had already had time to work its poison throughout Europe. As a result, the image of Spain in eighteenth-century France was generally negative and gloomy. For example, the Jesuit *Journal de Trévoux*, which for years provided an unequalled panorama of the French and European Enlightenment, only rarely directed its attention to Spain, and normally only with reference to the country's decadence or to America.[32] A highly unflattering critique of the economic and social condition of Spain is found in the journal's commentary on an anonymous pamphlet titled *Considérations sur les finances d'Espagne* published in Dresden in 1753, which emphasizes the country's bad government, the unequal distribution of taxes, rampant fraud, runaway public debt and, above all, the dereliction of agriculture and manufacturing, and the excessive fiscal privileges and enormous landholdings of the church, at the same time highlighting the injustice of taxes like the *rentas provinciales* of Castile compared with the beneficent effects of the new cadastre in Catalonia.[33]

The importance attached to trade in France and the important role attributed to the state, at least for the purposes of foreign trade, may be observed in the *Encyclopédie*, in which the entry for 'Commerce' occupies nine pages.[34] In contrast, the importance of Spanish trade was minimal: the term *Espagne* occupies just one page containing a brief history of the country, whereafter the writer explains that Spain reached its zenith in the sixteenth century but had declined since the time of Philip IV for certain very specific reasons:

> En fin l'Inquisition, les moïnes, la fierté oisive [=haughty idleness] des habitants ont fait passer en d'autres mains les richesses du Nouveau-Monde. Ainsi ce beau royaume, qui imprima jadis tant de terreur à l'Europe, est par gradation tombé dans une décadence dont il aura de la peine à se relever.
>
> Peu puissant au-dehors, pauvre et faible au-dedans, nulle industrie ne seconde encore dans ces climats heureux, les présents de la nature. Les soies de Valence, les belles laines de l'Andalousie et de la Castille, les piastres et les marchandises du Nouveau-Monde, sont moins pour l'Espagne que pour les nations commerçantes [France, Great Britain and the Low Countries]; elles confient leur fortune aux Espagnols, et ne s'en son jamais repenties: cette fidélité singulière qu'ils avoient autrefois à garder les dépôts et dont Justin fait l'éloge, ils sont encore aujourd'hui; mais cette admirable qualité jointe à leur paresse [=indolence], forme un mélange, dont il résulte des effets qui leur sont nuisibles. Les autres peuples font sous leurs yeux le commerce de leur monarchie; et c'est vraissemblablement un bonheur pour l'Europe que le Mexique, le Pérou, et le Chily, soient possédés par une nation paresseuse.
>
> Ce seroit sans doute un événement bien singulier, si l'Amérique venoit à secoüer le joug de l'Espagne, et si pour lors un habile vice-roi des Indes, embrassant le parti del Ameriquains, les soûtenoit de la puissance et de son génie. Leur terres produiroient bien-tôt nos fruits; leurs habitants n'ayant plus besoin de nos marchandises, ni de nos denrées, nous tomberions à-peu près dans le même état de l'indigence, où nous étions il y a quatre siècles. L'Espagne, je l'avoue, paroit à l'abri de cette révolution, mais l'empire de la fortune est bien étendu, et la prudence peut-elle se flatter de prévoir et de vaincre tous les caprices?[35]

This text, tinged as it is with a certain disdain, is an example of the political Darwinism typical of the mercantilist mindset, according to which Spain had no industry and was of interest only as the guardian of its own empire. This was, of course, an entirely self-interested opinion, as the internal market of Spain was by this time to a great extent in the hands of French traders, as we shall see below. Moreover, when the enlightened French authors of the *Encyclopédie* wrote this in the mid-eighteenth century, the reality of Spain was already very different. As in the case of the English but in reverse, the French used Spain as a mirror which reflected an image of themselves as superior.

France had attained great political power in Spain, and the French trade diaspora occupied an important position both in the country's domestic market and in trade with America.

The examples given above clearly reveal how different were the images which the English and French entertained both of each other and of the Spanish. If we are to understand Anglo-French economic competition in Spain, then, it will be necessary to leave ideas to one side and to concentrate on economic events per se.

The importance of technology

The overseas trade of Great Britain and France grew rapidly but separately in the eighty years between 1713 and 1793, especially in their respective American colonies. French trade expanded faster, multiplying by six times between 1715 and 1740, and the key port of Bordeaux experienced prodigious growth, specializing in exports to America and the re-export of imported goods to northern Europe. The French also had access to Spanish colonial trade via the port of Cadiz, where they were dominant, exporting Breton linens to America and bringing back silver. This was the zenith of French trade. Great Britain, meanwhile, saw two moments of somewhat slower growth, and even recession, but its trade eventually took off after 1781.[36] The English were dominant in trade with the Far East, but they also developed strong links with Brazil via Portugal, which allowed them to obtain large amounts of gold.[37]

Nonetheless, mutual trade between Great Britain and France was very limited in the eighteenth century, despite smuggling between Kent and Dunkirk. The English imported brandy, lace and silk in this way. Indeed, some merchants informed the Board of Trade while negotiations were under way for a trade treaty with France in 1786 that a diplomatic instrument of this kind was unnecessary, as many British products were already smuggled across the Channel[38] in what was already a thriving trade in the seventeenth and early eighteenth centuries. Mutual trade in fact only attained a certain intensity between 1786 and 1793. Thereafter, interaction remained intense, but not the exchange of goods: the course of the French Revolution was enormously influenced by war with Great Britain, and the Continental blockade against Napoleon was a key driver of the industrial revolution in the British Isles. After the Napoleonic War, reciprocal trade grew rapidly in the nineteenth century, after tariff barriers were progressively lifted in the 1850s. A liberal, if not free trade, treaty was signed between the two nations in 1860. It was only around 1890, however, that Great Britain and France became major mutual customers.

The differences between the rates of economic growth in France and England in the early modern period are a matter which is rarely considered. The end of the process is common knowledge: both the radicalism of the French Revolution and the older, sustained reformism of the English gave rise to an industrial revolution which had spectacular effects in Great Britain in just a few decades but in France generated lasting long-run growth, so that the two countries reached the end of the nineteenth century in a similar condition. The end result may have been similar, but what about the beginning of the process and its subsequent development?

It is many years now since F. Crouzet (1966) first compared the economic growth of Great Britain and France in a seminal paper presenting very similar estimates for the growth in per capita income. The population of England and Wales increased from 5.1 to 10 million people (39 per cent) between 1700 and 1790, and gross domestic product grew by 90 per cent (according to figures published by P. Deane and G.D.H. Cole), while the French population rose from 21.5 to 26 million (28 per cent) at the same time as GDP grew some 260 per cent in relative terms. As population growth was higher in one case but GDP growth was lower, and vice versa, the conclusion is that the increase in per capita income was very similar in both countries. France lagged only slightly behind Great Britain in the early eighteenth century despite the stagnation of the seventeenth century, a period when England achieved slow but continuous growth in industrial output and trade. However, the method of estimating per capita income for the two countries was qualitatively different. England was more industrialized and employed more labour in manufacturing, which accounted for a larger share of GDP. It was also more urbanized than France and its foreign trade was larger.

However, the key factor in economic terms was the technology gap which the English succeeded in opening up with France at this time.[39] Meanwhile, the political changes that resulted in the dissolution of the monasteries, the early transformation of the feudal system, parliamentary control of the Exchequer and the establishment of a free press had also worked in favour of Great Britain. Even so, technology is the key explanatory factor underlying the relative advantage achieved by the English.

As Crouzet argued, it is now believed that differences between the economies of Great Britain and France in the eighteenth century were much smaller than had been thought, since many scholars fell into the heuristic trap of considering only the information offered by British visitors to France like Arthur Young and others, whose writings are often tendentious and Anglo-centric. In contrast, numerous writers stress England's clear and decisive technological advantage.[40] What made this possible, in my opinion, was the development of a culture that was less hidebound by dogma and the continuous stream of immigrants coming to England at a time when freedom of thought and action were suppressed or restricted in most other European countries. The immigrants' social networks were decisive in this regard.

This was not always so, however. In the sixteenth and seventeenth centuries, the English lagged behind France and Flanders in terms of technology, and let us not forget that the latter country was at that time under the suzerainty of the Spanish Crown. Flemish technology was the most advanced in Europe in many areas, better than that of the English and even of the Italians, as Ciriacono has shown in the field of hydraulic engineering.[41] France and the Walloon region of the Low Countries had already made considerable progress with the development of air-injection furnaces, charcoal furnaces and various processes involved in the manufacture of plate glass in the sixteenth and seventeenth centuries.

However, the field in which French influence was initially greatest was in the manufacture of the *new draperies*, consisting of lighter, cheaper textiles combining different woollen fabrics and types of wool, and wool woven together with other fabrics like linen and cotton. The Reformation and the wars of religion changed everything. After 1560, many Flemish and Walloon (French) weavers fled war, tumult and religious persecution in their homelands for England, where they were made welcome among their Protestant coreligionists. Furthermore, there was good will, living standards were higher, and life was cheaper. The refugees settled, and it was not long before the processes used in the manufacture of Continental goods were no longer secret. The immigrants did not keep their special manufacturing within their own communities for more than a generation, even in towns like Norwich and Canterbury where they were particularly numerous.

The outcome was that the English began to develop new models in the first half of the seventeenth century, and by 1650 exports of English cloth definable as belonging to the *new draperies* made up as much as 50 per cent of the total value of the country's exports. By the end of the seventeenth century, English fabrics were being imitated in the Low Countries and the same happed in France after 1700.[42] Hence, the religious tolerance of Anglican (Protestant) England was a determining factor in attracting the artisans who made English technology dominant in the long run, which brings us by a different route back to Weber's argument that capitalism arose out of the Protestant mentality.[43] Indeed so. However, its development was not only a matter of the cultural values inherent in anti-papist Protestantism but also owed much to the technology transfer caused by the emigration of religious dissidents.

As its presence in the economic life of the country increased, the French state responded to this challenge by seeking to reverse the situation by means of industrial espionage, and it was to a great extent successful. This strategy played a key role in the development of French manufacturing in the eighteenth century, and it was guided by the state through the efforts of figures like Trudaine and Tolozan, focusing particularly on Great Britain. This fact is as important as it is little known, so we shall consider it in more detail here. France was the nation which most assiduously planned and undertook the mission of industrial espionage. Its main target by some way was England, though the country in fact attracted spies from all over Europe. This shows that Great Britain, which had for a long time been a technological laggard was now a leader. The British were, of course, aware of this, and they made strenuous efforts to prevent the transfer of technologies abroad, forbidding emigration by skilled artisans and the export of certain types of machinery, which the French nonetheless acquired by clandestine methods.

The first important legislation in this regard was an Act of Parliament of 18 April 1717, which prohibited the employment of foreigners as craft artisans in Great Britain and forbade them from leaving the country without an official permit for a period of seven years after completing their apprenticeship. France was the reason for this draconian law: by this time the *Contrôleur General* had succeeded in organizing a regular flow of British artisan migrants over the Channel.[44]

In the first half of the eighteenth century, and indeed later, a number of French manufacturing inspectors, including Ticquet in 1738, Marc Morel in the same year, and Jubié in 1747, travelled discretely to Great Britain, returning with detailed reports on iron foundries, coal mining and other industries. English Jacobites like John Holker, who eventually joined the French army in 1745, also played a part. At the behest of Marc Morel, inspector of textiles manufactures in Rouen (himself the son of a merchant and an expert), Holker visited Lancashire in 1749 to investigate the manufacture of *cotton velvet*,[45] and the use of the new machines called calenders[46] to smooth and finish fabrics, having persuaded the recently appointed *Directeur de Commerce*, Daniel-Charles Trudaine, that he could be most useful by returning to Great Britain a spy. He also recruited Jacobite artisans and in the mid-eighteenth century he set up a factory making cotton fabrics in Sens and others in Bourges to manufacture woollens, cottons and silks. His son, also named John Holker, continued his work after 1767.[47]

French industrial espionage in Britain did not only target textiles. Shipyards, iron foundries, glass making, Newcomen's and Watt's steam engines, and state-of-the art textiles machinery in the late eighteenth century like the *water frame* and the *spinning mule* were all investigated.[48] Overall, technology transfers from Great Britain to France as a result of espionage were far greater than transfers in the other direction, and the English were seldom able to benefit from French inventions.[49] France was not, however, the only country to spy on Great Britain; Sweden, and to a lesser extent Denmark and Austria, also conducted their own industrial espionage.[50] Spain did so too, as far as it could.

In short, English technology reached France quickly, and despite a certain technology gap with Great Britain, the French were not far behind in the race between the two countries for economic progress and the conquest of markets in the eighteenth century. Their great advantage was that their domestic market was much larger, and it included the Spanish market, as we shall see below. This meant that 7 million people were competing against 35 million, without counting the colonies.

People were, of course, always more important than machines in this rivalry. The problem inherent in the spread of technology was not so much to learn about new kinds of machines as they were invented, which was relatively straightforward, but to learn how to use them. Hence, it was important not so much to obtain drawings or blueprints of new inventions, but to discover the manufacturing systems involved and the processes in which the machinery was used and could help boost productivity. Such know-how was in the hands of emigrant artisans, who banded together in organized groups when they moved. Getting hold of plans was thus a secondary matter for Enlightenment-era agents, and their goal was rather to bring back artisans who could operate the new inventions, almost all of which were based less on scientific theory than on the practical application of engineering skills and basic chemistry. This was in many respects similar to the ways in which emigrants structured the market in Spain, as we shall see below. Thus, the development of the market was due to a lesser extent to overall economic conditions or the effects of macroeconomic variables, though such factors played a role, than to the actions of people working together in migratory networks and productive communities.

The emigration of artisans can only be approximately quantified. Perhaps 400 *techniciens* migrated from Great Britain to France between 1717 and 1800, together with some 1,000 *ouvriers*, and some of these migrants returned home after a time. In any case they were a minority, although their importance belied their apparently small numbers. The government played an active role in technological development through the Academie des Sciences, a body which was far more dependent on the King, whose sole patronage provided the financial backing for its activity, than the British Royal Society. The French Academie des Sciences, which was dissolved in 1793, was charged with the specific missions of examining and testing all new technological instruments and systems as they appeared. Furthermore, the Bureau de Commerce also played an active role in fostering the manufacturing industry after 1740.[51]

I have made this short digression to compare the economic development of France and Great Britain in the first place because mutual competition was a key stimulus for French progress, and second, because the majority of enlightened Spaniards at this time were keen to follow in their neighbour's footsteps. The Spanish were well aware of the relationship between the technological innovation which drove Britain's economic growth and the parliamentary system as revealed in the following remarks penned by Juan Bautista Virio in 1792:

> No puedo pasar en silencio la observación que hará sin duda cualquiera persona reflexiva al inquirir en las causas esenciales de la prosperidad de la Nación Inglesa.
>
> Prescindiendo de la superioridad decidida de esta Nación en tiempos pasados, y bien aprovechada sobre las demás de Europa, tiene en su centro los resortes más oportunos para promover su felicidad.
>
> Habiendo concebido cualquiera persona algún nuevo arbitrio, alguna mejora o cosa semejante en beneficio peculiar o general, tiene acceso libre al Senado de la Nación. En él se reconoce por los trámites regulares e inalterables la utilidad de la propuesta, nueva ley o providencia; y aunque se diga mucho de partidos y oposiciones, nadie puede dudar que entre quinientos y más individuos de todas las ciudades, pueblos y provincias de que se compone la Cámara de los Comunes, el mayor número de ellos es de hombres habilísimos, distinguidos por sus raros talentos y luces superiores. Uniformándose, pues, éstos en su dictamen sobre ser algún objeto conducente a cualquier género de fomento de sus conciudadanos, nunca se frustra la ocasión o el momento oportuno; conceden su sanción, se examina de nuevo por iguales trámites en la Cámara de los Pares, la que convenciéndose de la oportunidad del intento concurre con la otra al propio fin;[52] y últimamente el Soberano con su aprobación constituye la propuesta o proyecto nuevo en ley, que no puede revocarse sin volverse a reconocer las causas para ello con igual pulso y consideración. Obtenida la sanción en la forma ya expresada, si es en beneficio de un particular, bien puede exercer libremente y llevar a toda su extensión las empresas que premeditaba, invirtiendo en ello sin zozobra sus caudales, en la segura confianza de que ningún proceder ni valimiento sobre la tierra puede interrumpir o molestarle en las operaciones de que pende su felicidad; pues, mediante los antecedentes referidos, toda la Nación está empeñada en sostenerle en los derechos tan legítimamente adquiridos.
>
> Si la nueva ley es benéfica a algún ramo de fomento especial de alguna provincia o distrito, igual confianza produce a los efectos más apreciables que se reconocen en una actividad general capaz de mudar la faz al distrito, a donde se extiende en brevísimo espacio de tiempo.
>
> No obstante que son innumerables los ramos y artículos de industria y de comercio, como cada Parlamentario es un celador cuidadoso que, según lo requiere el tiempo y las circunstancias en cuanto respectivamente entiende, propone al Senado las enmiendas, alteraciones, amplificaciones y nuevos auxilios que sus constituyentes[53] hubiesen estimado necesario, sucede que apenas se discurre por

> tales constituyentes o las Sociedades Patrióticas, fabriles, mercantiles, &c. alguna mejora de que cada ramo es susceptible; apenas se ha observado necesidad de corregir algún defecto que se ha descubierto o contrarrestar por algún medio indirecto a alguna providencia económica de país extranjero por la cual se podría deteriorar o atrasar algún ramo de fomento propio, no dexa de hacerse presente en la sesión inmediata del Parlamento por algún Miembro de él, que ha palpado por sí mismo los inconvenientes o la necesidad de una alteración.
>
> Esta facilidad y certeza en la consecución de los intentos se extiende a todas las partes de los Dominios Británicos, y por lo tanto no debe causar extrañeza que sean florecientes.[54]

In these circumstances, the Spanish, who like the French lacked a parliamentary system, acted in the same way, relying on industrial espionage and seeking to contract artisans who had the desired technological know-how. The Count de Aranda and others imported artisans, plans and machinery from Great Britain and elsewhere. At the same time, the *Junta de Comercio* or Board of Trade acquired considerable powers to set policy and encourage manufacturing, and the *reales sociedades económicas* (royal economic societies) were entrusted with testing new machines.

Additional problems existed in Spain, however, resulting from widespread intolerance of new ideas, the backwardness of the universities and the scant bent for innovation and technology among the educated elites. In these circumstances, the enlightened faction in Spain sought to turn around a historical process which was heading in the opposite direction to that of France and Great Britain, which were similar at least in that regard. For centuries Spain, as the defender of Catholicism and champion of the Counter-Reformation, had only expelled the minorities who were now proving crucial to the economic development of other countries. The Jews were expelled in 1492 and were never allowed to return. Protestants were never admitted. The Anglican British were not allowed to enter Spain, and the Protestant artisans of the Catholic Low Countries, who might have played the same decisive role in Castile as they did in England, were allowed to leave for Great Britain and the United Provinces. The Moriscos were expelled in the early seventeenth century, causing demographic decline and technological decay in the irrigation systems crucial to farming in the arid climate of Aragon and Valencia. An attempt was made to exterminate the Spanish gypsies in 1749.[55] Numerous Catholic French immigrants had been allowed to settle over a period of centuries and, as we shall see, these people played an important role in the economic growth of the eighteenth century, but they too were eventually expelled in successive phases between 1793 and 1812.[56]

The French state had begun to take on an increasing role in industrial espionage and economic development in the second half of the seventeenth century, just when the Habsburg dynasty in Spain was in its last throes. This was well known at the time, and logically the enlightened faction in Spain, influenced as they were by dynastic considerations, sought to solve the problem of the country's backwardness and piggyback on French progress by imitating the policies adopted in the neighbouring kingdom over half a century earlier. In this regard, they enjoyed the advantage of knowing in advance the results that could be achieved by establishing institutions that had been tried and tested in France, like the intendancies and the academies, and by standardizing some weights and measures and adopting a more active industrial strategy, among other policies. In short, they applied mercantilist policies in line with practices which had been developed over time as a result of the mutual competition between France and England.

Manufacturing policy in England and France

Since at least the 1930s, mercantilism has been defined and analysed from two opposing yet complementary standpoints. The first of these treats mercantilism as an economic system, which is to say as a set of theories that are more or less applicable to economic analysis, and the second as a policy applicable to the economic affairs of the state. For the present purposes, mercantilism will be treated as policy and practice, since this facet not only provided the basis for subsequent theorizing but also throws light on the realities underlying the actions of the French and English states.

The disintegration and restructuring of the medieval system of customs, and the success attained in the regulation of manufacturing and national trade were the pillars of the nascent economic practice of the new absolute monarchies. These policies developed in different circumstances and countries over the course of the sixteenth and seventeenth centuries, fundamentally in response to the interest of the state in directing economic activity for its own purposes, especially war, creating industries to manufacture textiles, arms and ships, and to generate cash. Mercantilism was based on a physical conception of wealth associated with the accumulation of gold and silver bullion.[57] It both fostered manufacturing, which strengthened the internal market and boosted consumption so as to provide an important source of tax revenues, and maintained protectionist customs barriers in pursuit of a favourable balance of trade. If the balance of trade was positive, the state could obtain revenues without touching the incomes of its subjects, while avoiding the need to address the thorny question of wealth inequalities.

In the seventeenth and eighteenth centuries, England and France each maintained a position of export dominance in Spain, and the question of their customs policies, which were evidently based on freedom of trade, is therefore less interesting than the efforts of the Spanish monarchy to maintain some form of protectionist barriers. We shall address this question later on. First, however, let us consider English and French manufacturing policy, which directly affected the exports of both countries. Once again, it is necessary to underline the difference between England, which had made a political revolution in order to bring the interests of the people, represented by Parliament, within the pale of political decision-making, and France, which remained an absolute monarchy.

Textiles manufacturing was increasingly regulated in both Great Britain and France until the English revolution, but thereafter policy diverged. In the sixteenth century, the Tudors sought to maintain and strengthen the medieval statutes governing textiles manufacturing, but they failed to develop the necessary institutions to ensure compliance. For example, pieces of cloth could be manufactured to any length or breadth at the beginning of the seventeenth century, but tacking was forbidden. The state also regulated the cereals market. In 1630, King Charles I still maintained the policy of banning imports of grain from one part of the country to another,[58] as was usual on the Continent. These corn laws were similar to the Spanish *tasa de granos*, which was not finally abolished until 1765.

However, changing times ushered in new ideas. The Puritan revolution ensured the increasing predominance of the *common law* over *statute law* made by the king and his Privy Council. Meanwhile, custom buttressed the medieval idea of natural freedom, which precluded intervention by the monarchy. Monopolies and guild ordinances based on royal privileges were frequently rejected by the judiciary in legal disputes, and the Statute of Monopolies approved by Parliament in 1623–1624 only consolidated the anti-privilege trend. After the Bill of Rights of 1689, the royal prerogative to grant privileges was sharply curtailed. The Statute of Artificers approved in 1603 under Elizabeth I set minimum wages for weavers, but it was no longer applied by the end of the seventeenth century, while the Act of Settlement and Removal approved by Parliament in 1662, which obliged the poor to stay in their home parishes and allowed them to be forcibly returned if they were found elsewhere, was never strictly enforced in the cities and had little effect on unmarried men.[59]

This allowed social mobility, resulting in strong migratory flows to London and other cities, and provided fresh hands in the growing manufacturing towns where demand for industrial labour was strong. In this context, the monarchy's interest in industrial interventionism declined after 1660 and especially after 1688, focusing rather on foreign trade and the creation of *joint stock companies* and *regulated companies*. The guilds did not finally disappear until the nineteenth century, but they retained only a certain power to enforce technical standards in textiles production under the Statute of Artificers of 1603. As a consequence, the regulation of manufacturing in England was hollowed out from within. Few laws were actually repealed in the eighteenth century, but still fewer were actually enforced. Meanwhile, neither central nor local government was able to regulate manufacturing output, and little by little the old medieval system just faded away.[60]

This was what made England different from the rest of Europe, and what explains its burgeoning agriculture, the flourishing proto-industries that drove colonial power, and the emergence of an area of relatively high consumption and wages, which were paid for by technology-based productivity gains.

Both the starting point and the destination were similar in France, but actual developments were very different. The regulation of manufactures, and above all textiles, began to be significant in the mid-fourteenth century after the Black Death, and the decrees of 1581, 1597 and 1673 eventually brought about a unification of the law. Under the decree of 1581, all artisans had to be registered and officially certified by the district magistrate. Meanwhile, the decree of 1597 allowed the master craftsmen of Paris and Lyon to practice their trades in any city in France, subject to due registration, while the craftsmen of other towns and cities, whether or not they had their own *parlement* could only practice in their respective districts. Finally, the decree promulgated in 1673 required guild approval for the qualification of any artisan. The state also developed considerable administrative machinery to control manufacturing.

The *intendents* who supervised the enforcement of manufacturing regulations were appointed by the king, but this office was never put up for sale. They reported hierarchically to a *contrôleur general*, and in the eighteenth century to a Conseil de Commerce. In 1669, the office of *inspecteur* or *commis des manufactures* was created to oversee the guilds as their immediate superiors with executive and legal powers.[61] Beginning in 1666, Colbert organized manufacturing via numerous ordinances or *reglèments*. In the most important sector of the textile industry, four ordinances were issued to regulate pure woollen fabrics, fabrics made out of a mixture of wool and other fibres, dyeing and the manufacture of hose. The manufacturing ordinances issued between 1666 and 1730 occupy seven tomes containing thousands of pages, and the ordinances of 1737 regulating the silks of Lyon, a city known as *la grande fabrique*, consisted of some 208 articles.[62]

This policy had different effects. It was in practice difficult to enforce such a torrent of regulations, and even more so outside of the cities. Excessive regulation sometimes discouraged innovation, as happened with the printers of imported cotton calico. When their trade was prohibited in 1670 they emigrated to the United Provinces and England, handing the advantage in this industry to France's competitors. Another important effect was to create a fiscal interest for the monarchy to maintain a hyper-regulated guild system, because the state charged a levy on the qualification of every master craftsman, and it directly appointed a given number of masters (*maîtres royales*) to each guild even if they did not meet the conditions established in the guilds' statutes.[63] This was one reason not to prune back the thicket of manufacturing regulations.

More importantly, however, the legislation referred to urban craft manufacturing organized by the guilds, but it failed to address the development of cottage industries, whether or not combined with agriculture. This activity was often intended merely for self-consumption, but in some cases of proto-industrial manufacturing the goods produced were destined for more distant markets. The *arrêt* of 1581 and later Colbert's ordinances in principle extended the system of guild control to all goods produced on the assumption that the guilds were omnipresent, absurd as this may seem today. For example, the wool ordinances of 1666 required that all production should be overseen by a master craftsman (article 34), local quality inspectors (article 39) and supervisory deputies (article 16). In practice, this overly hierarchical and hyper-regulated system frequently did not work in the rural world. In fact, the royal administration often looked the other way in the late seventeenth and early eighteenth centuries, especially in the case of the cheap coarse cloth known as *cadis* produced in the villages. This was in fact recognized, to the extent that the ordinances of 1677 governing the production of woollens in Montauban and other provinces of Languedoc explicitly stated that such low-priced cloth sold well outside the region, and in a concession made separately to the town of Gévaudan and the mountainous district of the Cevènnes, another major focus of rural manufacturing, local weavers were permitted to produce cloth without inspection or the requirement for makers' marks. Furthermore, the royal officials often turned a blind eye because the spread of the putting-out system meant that city merchants and manufacturers had an increasing interest in low-cost cottage industries like spinning. Cultural factors also played a part. In the seventeenth century, both government and the courts of law began to treat manufacturing as superior to farming, and the idea that it was necessary to combat idleness (*l'oisiveté* or *la fainéantise*) among the peasants took hold. Rural industry presented an ideal solution, as it employed every member of the family right down to children as young as four.[64]

Finally, the state created a whole new manufacturing sector, which was theoretically overseen by the guilds but was never wholly under their control. These were the so-called 'privileged manufactures' which arose from the trades linked to three centres of special interest to the Crown, namely the *métiers suivant la cour*, whose numbers increased rapidly from the late sixteenth century onwards, the *artistes du Louvre*, once again from the end of the sixteenth century, and the professions related with the Academie des Arts et de Sculpture after 1648.[65] The policy of creating privileged manufactures, which had already begun in the sixteenth century, was intended to provide luxury goods for consumption by the royal court, and in principle it had nothing to do with the production of goods for the domestic market. However, what was initially merely a royal caprice gradually became part of the mercantilist effort to avoid dependence on other countries for luxury articles like porcelain, glass, enamels and tapestries consumed by the court and the aristocracy.

The early modern view of mercantilism as an economic theory

To sum up, the starting point of French policy in the areas of manufacturing and trade was similar to that of the English, but developments in the two countries were very different. Paradoxically, however, the final destination of deregulated rural manufacturing was once again very similar. The hyper-regulated French guild system helped to maintain quality and protect domestic manufacturing, but it still left considerable room for low-wage cottage industries, while contributing to the development of a merchant class which initially emerged to serve the domestic and colonial markets but with the aid of the state eventually became highly competitive in foreign trade. Though France suffered a permanent technology gap, the problem was solved by industrial espionage and by quickly copying the industrial innovations produced by the English.[66] A further two vectors for the spread of French manufactures were fashion or *la mode*, which was effective until the mid-eighteenth century, and the networks of French emigrants.

Thus, the differences between English and French mercantilism lay especially in the role played by the state in each case, and in the interests which guided its actions. In a way, it could be said that mercantilism as economic practice and policy was constructed by the state in France, while in England it was developed ahead of, if not against, the state, which followed the expansion of trade, or at least accompanied it, but never took the lead.

In the world of ideas, however, events greatly favoured the English. The development of the new draperies as exportable mass consumption fabrics occurred in a revolutionary period (which had its key moments in 1641 and 1689) that definitively set bounds on royal power and imposed a doctrine of individual rights which did not exist in the absolute monarchies of France and Spain. This in turn generated a current of speculative thought which led to the birth of political economy as a system of specifically economic ideas, which the state no longer controlled because of the freedoms of expression and the press. In this situation, the representatives of the new society were able to address new problems unhindered. What in fact was trade? Was free trade a better way to achieve a favourable balance of trade? Would the creation of paper money increase wealth? What taxes should be collected and how should domestic and maritime wealth be conserved? When and how should the state borrow?[67] The new political economy considered the question of workhouses and whether the labour of the poor could or could not contribute to, or be used in, the development of proto-industrial manufacturing, generating trade, employment and wealth. All of these ideas were raised and applied through Parliament and a government appointed by the monarchy in the context of an increasingly representative system which attracted attention throughout Europe.

These new ideas took shape in a context which was not one of pure economic analysis, however. Contemporary thinkers were not seeking to create what is today the science we call economics, but to organize the chaotic market that existed in their own times. Finkelstein has recently shown that the early mercantilists constructed their ideas on the circulation of goods using organic similes, which they compared, for example, to the circulation of the blood in the human body, and referred to the structure of the political community in terms drawn from the nascent science of anatomy as the *body politic*. Likewise, early ideas about the national accounts drew on analogies with commercial accounting, natural philosophy and the science of mechanics (e.g. the theory of gravity) and mathematics, of which Sir Isaac Newton was the principal proponent. The same happened with early ideas about the balance of trade, which were based on psychological and political analogies like the self-regulating balance of individual interests and the balance of political forces in a representative parliamentary system.[68]

This current of thought developed almost simultaneously in France. The links between the intellectual elites of London, Paris and Amsterdam were too close for this to have been otherwise. In political terms, however, the new ideas were differently applied. In France, where Paris had already grown into a major city by the sixteenth century, the king rose to an almost unimaginable height of power and wealth in the seventeenth century, and the monarchy protected and regulated guild-based manufacturing to an extraordinary degree. Meanwhile, the active presence of government made mercantilist thought look more like the economic practice and policy of the state than a theory or philosophy. Mercantilism was not something that could be debated in a Parliament but what passed through the minds of royal officials considering the interests of the state. Even so, this policy was constructed on the basis of almost identical similes and analogies to those of the English, as may be observed in the extreme example of Colbert, who was of course a politician and not a writer or an academic. His fundamental idea was to maintain a favourable balance of trade in order to obtain silver bullion and cash and, according to the novel notions of the body spread by the sciences of anatomy and physiology (the circulation of the blood was discovered by William Harvey in 1628[69]), to ensure that the *body* of France with the king at its *head* was bathed in the *blood* of domestic wealth so that it could compete with and outdo the rival *bodies* of England, the United Provinces and Spain in the struggle for trade and riches.

One further point deserves attention. The taste for classical culture, the ancient world and the Roman past prevalent among the French nobility, who still played an important part in the government of the kingdom, and who had quasi-sovereign powers over their own estates, brought with it a revival of Catonism and antique ideas about economic activity. According to these doctrines, the creation of wealth was of no value or interest. The only merit lay in appropriating the wealth created or possessed by others. The ideal of the perfect man was a leisured landowner, while merchants, artisans and moneylenders were placed firmly at the bottom of the social ladder,[70] the very opposite of the ideal espoused by the triumphant new mercantilists. Just as the intellectual weight of the aristocracy differed in England and in France, so did the economic issues addressed and sometimes the approaches taken. In France, for example, there was an extensive literature, begun by Jean Bodin, on the question of taxes and their unification in a single tax that would be payable in proportion to wealth or income. This was far from being a priority matter in England, where customs revenues assured the state of its income. Some treatises and manifestos also advocated the freedom of individuals and groups of merchants to trade, although this was a minority debate which never fully developed because freedom of expression was more restricted than in England. It was further conditioned by a widening gap in political culture, for the French monarchy viewed any subject of the king travelling or trading abroad as providing a *patriotic* service, which is to say a personal service to the sovereign himself, as we shall see below.

In contrast, all the key features of English mercantilism as described by Finkelstein could also be applied to France, except one – the opposition between individual wealth and the state. The idea of economic growth in England was based on an analytic identity between the wealth of the state and its power, but the power of the state and the wealth of individuals frequently came into conflict, because individuals did not necessary pursue the common good:

> There was no similar identity between individual wealth and national power, because the drive for gain assumed to motivate merchants was understood to be capable of being (if not necessarily) in conflict with the common good.[71]

Hence, it was commonly supposed that individual interests were divorced from those of the state, in contrast to the French view.

The creation of the privileged manufactures in France

By analysing the role of the French state in promoting economic growth, we may obtain key references not only for the problems found in Spain, but also for many of the solutions adopted, and it will therefore be of interest to consider returning to the creation of privileged manufactures, a part of the state policy outlined above. I do not mean here the great, centralized factories set up in the service of the Court, but rather the policy of granting privileges to manufactures of all kind, which was also profusely applied in Spain.

It is a mistake to treat Colbert as the originator of state intervention in French manufacturing, as the policy had in fact already begun before his time. Richelieu's maxim was already to 'make the state opulent', and this idea subsisted throughout the eighteenth century, even in its latter decades when the physiocrats and liberals were preaching a discourse on political economy which had more words than substance. Analysis of the legislative statistics on privileges and ordinances in manufacturing and trade reveals that some 1,000 regulations were issued in the 70 years between 1683 and 1753, and a further 500 were decreed in the 36 years between 1753 and 1789, showing that legislative activity did not decline in the least in the time of the physiocrats and the beginnings of liberalism. Likewise, the number of letters of patent granting the title of *royal factory* (i.e. privileged factory) actually increased in the first half of the eighteenth century. Forty such titles were granted during the reign of Henri IV and 20 in the time of Louis XIII and his minister Cardinal Mazarin, compared with 113 in the reign of Louis XIV while Colbert was in office (until 1683) and no fewer than 243 in the period between 1683 and 1750. This reflects rapid growth, in particular affecting textiles manufacturing and iron working.[72]

Contrary to what has sometimes been thought, privileges were not granted out of any fear of competition but rather as a temporary means of incentivizing the emergence of new enterprises and circumventing the limits imposed by the guilds and other corporate organizations, which were in principle opposed to innovation of any kind.

There were different levels or degrees of state intervention in an industry. In the first place, a company might receive a merely honorific title to distinguish it socially from the guilds. In a step up, the state might purchase all or part of a factory's output, for example in the case of goods manufactured to the standards of quality required for consumption at Court or in the case of military procurements. Finally, it might award subsidies, loans or tax privileges.

In general, intervention was highly selective, and from the beginning of the seventeenth century the state was concerned in particular to support industries providing technological innovations, but only when these were genuine. Technological innovation was the key to obtaining aid from the state. Meanwhile, the monopolies granted on the manufacture and sale of goods were not perpetual but were limited to a fixed term of years. Such grants were certainly influenced by the situation of the entrepreneur in the bureaucratic maze at court, and in particular by his standing with the Bureau de Commerce, but they depended even more on the state's concern to support certain emerging industries which could compete with the British (whose technologies were immediately copied) or were otherwise of interest. Thus, the manufacture of silk and cotton thread received support but not silk fabrics or tapestries. Incentives were provided for paper mills, tanneries, porcelain, earthenware and stoneware factories, clockmakers, iron, copper and lead mines and foundries, which were important for the production of armaments. This was the case of the Le Creusot and Schneider factories.[73]

As a mercantilist doctrine, Colbertism took a quantitative approach, maintaining that international economic competition was a 'war of money' and that the state could only prosper at the expense of others. This was the reason for Colbert's obsession with breaking the dependence of French trade on the Dutch. At the same time, however, Colbert's mercantilism included a kind of commercial humanism, in which the interests of the individual and the state converged. Thus, the preamble to the privilege granted to the Compagnie Commercial du Nord in 1669 declared:

> Trade is the most fruitful means to reconcile the nations and to involve opposing spirits in a beneficial reciprocal dialogue. It creates and propagates richness in the most innocent way, and it brings happiness to the people and prosperity to the State.[74]

It is largely false, although the idea is common enough today, that a shift towards liberalism occurred in French economic culture and attitudes about 1750, producing a radical change in the political economy of the country which led to the abolition of the system of privileges and monopolies. In the mid-eighteenth century, Daniel Charles Trudaine, who became Directeur de Commerce in 1749, assisted by his own nominees as superintendents of trade, Vincent de Gournay and Isaac de Bacalan, ushered in what appeared to be a new policy of trade liberalization. Free trade in corn was decreed in 1754. In 1759, the manufacture of printed calicoes was permitted. In 1762, the free movement of labour throughout the country was allowed, as well as free trade at the ports. A decree of 1764 removed controls on grain exports, and Turgot adopted similar measures in the following years. By the time of the Revolution, the Constituent Assembly proclaimed the freedom of enterprise, and on 2 August 1791, the Allarde Act abolished the guilds of master craftsmen and the privileges of the royal factories. However, these liberalizing measures were not in fact in contradiction with the protection of French manufacturing. The physiocrats and other enlightened liberals had no difficulty in accepting the grant of privileges to innovative entrepreneurs, and to those who were able to offer technological secrets and new inventions, or who could show the possibility of developing a new trade. The liberalizing physiocratic discourse was, then, at all times accompanied by a strong dose of political pragmatism.[75]

Roland de la Platière's treatise *Manufactures, arts et métiers* defines the official doctrine of the French Enlightenment, recognizing that:

> exclusive privileges are fair and necessary in some cases, and they constitute a kind of reward for the work of developing the invention [i. e. innovation] of manufactures, processes and machinery, which are of utility to the public or to the great commercial companies.[76]

A declaration of 24 December 1762 established a limit of 15 years for the term of royal privileges, although it added: 'but the holders will be allowed the right to obtain an extension of the privilege where such is deemed appropriate', and the famous letter patent of 5 May 1779 ending the grant of royal factory concessions in fact continued to allow exceptions 'in favour of inventors or of new manufactures imported from abroad'.[77] Thus, the state continued to protect certain industries where it was found expedient to do so. This active industrial policy also had its equivalent in trade policy.

The importance of trade, and the significant role reserved for the state in its development, are clearly revealed under the heading 'Commerce' in the *Encyclopédie*.[78]

* * *

In the second half of the seventeenth century, the British and French were hard at work penetrating the peninsula market belonging the Spanish Crown, and not just America, through the agency of their different trade and social networks, seeking to grab as large a slice of this trade as possible. Both employed significant diplomatic and military resources in pursuit of their goals. Were these foreigners able to trade in Spain under the same conditions as the subjects of Phillip IV or Charles II? Perhaps more importantly, given that Spanish trade networks had been weakened by depression and fiscal and monetary crisis, did the British and French merchants in Spain enjoy the same status, or were there differences which might have lent either group a clear competitive advantage?

In order to answer this question, if only in outline, it is necessary to consider the civil and mercantile situation of both groups in Spain in light of the international treaties made by Great Britain and France with Spain in the seventeenth century, considering especially those aspects which might have an impact on the business conducted by their subjects. This will be the subject of the following chapters.

3

England, France and the Struggle for Spain, 1650–1715

The rivalry between Great Britain and France over the Spanish market was a drawn-out affair, played out over decades as the English and French states grew stronger, and Spain's power waned. Like other seventeenth-century rivalries, it was rooted in religious and political differences, compounded by the accretion of commercial interests. In its origin, it sprang from the religious conflict caused by the Protestant Reformation. At the end of the sixteenth century, the English had definitively broken with Rome; his 'Catholic Majesty' the king of Spain was the champion of the Counter-Reformation; and his 'Most Christian Majesty' the king of France, whose lands were hemmed in on all sides by Spanish domains, had already endured long years of religious strife and now disputed the leadership of the Catholic world with Spain, though as yet without success.

The emerging modern states were to a great extent shaped by the Thirty Years' War, which devastated Germany and Central Europe in the first half of the seventeenth century. The interests of princes, dressed up as reasons of state, also played an important role in structuring a world in which the old medieval monarchies now asserted their divine right to rule, although their power soon became self-justifying. On the pretext of protecting the faith of their subjects, kings sought to rise above the supposed limitations imposed by the ancient institutions of courts and Parliaments, and to create instruments of government to channel the absolute will of the monarch. The logic of direct government by the monarch, which had become the *raison d'etat*, resulted in a complex international diplomacy based on dynastic marriages and wars fought on religious and political grounds, which eventually reshaped the absolutist states after the Peace of Westphalia (1648) and the Treaty of the Pyrenees (1659).

This will, then, be the starting point for our analysis of English and French commercial and political interests in Spain and their subsequent development, not only because the peace treaties of 1648 and 1659 would change the political map of Europe for the next 150 years, but also because neither England nor France had yet attained the economic, political and intellectual ascendancy which they would soon achieve. Nonetheless, they were already adversaries, and rivals of Spain, and had been so since the sixteenth century. France came to the fore after its victory over Spain at Rocroi in 1643, while England waxed ever stronger in the years following the outbreak of Civil War in 1641 and its naval victories over the United Provinces during the Interregnum.

The long discussion which follows, taking up both Chapters 3 and 4, is based above all on legal texts and diplomatic sources. Both have their limitations. Legal sources frequently ignore the reality on the ground, as we shall see more than once in the following chapters, which among other matters describe numerous occasions on which Spanish lawmakers succeeded only in revealing their own ignorance of the state of affairs in their own cities and markets in their top-down efforts to organize and encourage growth in the country's internal trade. For better or for worse, however, the legal texts in question here were trade treaties, and they provided the measure for diplomatic action. In this light, they are more than deserving of analysis.

Diplomatic sources, meanwhile, are also prone to error, because they depend on the understanding of the diplomats who wrote them, and it would hardly be reasonable that a mere reading of their reports could shed light on behind-the-scenes negotiations and even shadier backstairs dealings (although they occasionally do, to our good fortune). Nevertheless, they too are essential for two reasons.

In the first place, a broad view of a country's diplomatic sources (and we are here considering a period of more than 150 years) will reveal the issues and problems with which its government was actually concerned. For example, it is striking how often both English and French diplomats report on the activities of their rival in Spain.

Second, and more importantly, governments act in light of the intelligence they can obtain, and this information remains in their archives. It was the French and English ambassadors and *envoyés extraordinaires* who supplied this information, assisted by other diplomatic agents including merchants, who frequently formed part of intelligence networks. From this standpoint, diplomatic sources are essential to understand the actions of the states concerned, which is precisely our goal. Their agents did not report realities but rather their perception of those realities, and by consulting the information so accumulated over a period of decades, we may elicit an understanding of French and English policy, which is the main focus of the present discussion.

The forward march of absolutism in France, Spain, England and elsewhere faced social resistance all over Europe, but only in England did the king eventually fail to impose his will on Parliament, which was able to set bounds on royal power. This parliamentary revolution occurred at a time of exponential growth in English manufacturing and the relentless expansion of its trade, which radically transformed the country's diplomacy, shifting it away from the principles that still drove the actions of states like France and Spain.

England and France leveraged the economic changes taking place at home to expand abroad, and their foreign policies gradually changed to support their gains. Both countries were intensely concerned with the physical conditions and financial terms of their foreign trade, and especially to strengthen their position against competitors, but they also sought increasingly to improve the legal and political protection enjoyed by their respective migratory and mercantile diasporas. Whether it was a matter of the monarch's military and political might or a consequence of the economic influence wielded by emigrants and merchants abroad, or a combination of both factors, the legal status of one nation's subjects in the territory of another became increasingly important in diplomatic relations, providing a decisive comparative advantage for those whose diplomats, armies and navies could wrest more favourable trading conditions from foreign powers. This was the goal of both Great Britain and France in Spain.

The immediate result was mutual economic warfare, in Spain's case against France, England and the United Provinces, its principal enemies. It has recently been shown that successive Spanish monarchs played an active part in blockades and trade embargoes, despite profound economic and political crisis at home.[1] Philip II, and especially Philip IV and Charles II clamped down on reciprocal trade whenever open military conflict arose, though this generally hurt the Spanish themselves more than their enemies, who enjoyed a favourable trade position in peacetime.

Alloza argues that the seventeenth-century conflict with England broke out when Cromwell, who was a defender of the freedom to trade in the Americas (to the benefit of the English), came to power in 1653. In reality, trouble was already in the wind. In 1604 and 1642 the English had made treaties with Portugal, which at the time belonged to the Spanish Crown, allowing them to trade on favourable terms in Portuguese colonies. Not long afterwards they supported the Portuguese revolt against Philip IV, and after the restoration of an independent monarchy in the country a new treaty was made in 1654 permitting the English to establish factories in Portugal, and leading in the long run to the strategic alliance sealed by the two countries in the Methuen Treaty of 1703.[2] In July 1654, meanwhile, England and Holland had reached an accommodation in the Treaty of Westminster, which ended the first Anglo-Dutch War, and the English had begun to impose the restrictions on Dutch shipping enshrined in the Navigation Acts, thereby laying the foundations for the future dominance of their merchant marine.

In this context, the Spanish authorities issued a *pragmática* or decree ordering the expulsion of the English from Spain and the seizure of their assets after the loss of Jamaica and the blockade of Cadiz begun by Cromwell's forces in 1654. The conflict eventually ended in 1667 with a treaty between Spain and England which re-established trade under terms that were highly favourable to the English, as we shall see below.[3] It is possible, as Alloza argues (with reference to maritime trade), that the decree initially hurt the English in Spain, and especially their merchants in Madrid, but I do not believe that trade with the Spanish hinterland was significantly affected. The English merchants established in the ports continued to bring in goods, whence they were taken into the interior by networks of Portuguese intermediaries, and Portuguese and Spanish smugglers.

Trade with France was regulated in detail in the Treaty of the Pyrenees made in 1659,[4] although the Spanish king ordered embargoes against the French after the War of Devolution broke out in 1667 and again in 1674. However, these measures were mitigated by the freedom with which the *Junta de Represalias* (or Reprisals Board) allowed naturalizations and by smuggling, which never ceased in the second half of the seventeenth century.[5]

Moreover, there were already numerous poor French immigrants living in Spain, who were attracted by the country's high wages and arrived by land, bringing with them such goods as they could peddle along the way. So French exports to Spain continued. All of these matters will be discussed in more detail below, but first it will be necessary to consider the trade treaties made by Spain with France and England, which had an enormous influence in the long run.

Trade with Spain in the treaties of 1659 and 1667

The international treaties made by the Spanish monarchy defined the terms of trade in the second half of the seventeenth century, as well as the legal position of French and English subjects in Spain. These consisted basically of the Treaty of the Pyrenees, made on 7 November 1659 (together with an annex signed on 27 November 1659), which established the terms of peace and trade between Spain and France, and the treaty made between Spain and England on 23 May 1659 and ratified some months afterwards.[6] Let us examine their contents, which were constantly referred to by contemporaries in the following decades. The substance of the two treaties was very different, as indeed were the commercial activities of the English and French in Spain.

The Treaty of the Pyrenees (1659)[7] put an end to the long war fought between the kings of Spain and France as part of the wider conflict known as the Thirty Years' War. Drawn up in both French and Spanish, the treaty is more concerned with political matters than with trade, which is dealt with only in the first 30 of its 124 articles. The rest of the text refers principally to the marriage of María Teresa of Austria, daughter of Philip IV, to Louis XIV (article 22);[8] the concomitant territorial arrangements, which were both numerous and complex; and the legal status, property and rights of the populations living in the county of Rousillon and the principality of Catalonia (articles 55–59),[9] which were finally split.

Let us begin by looking at the first thirty articles of the Treaty. Free trade was permitted in accordance with the 'laws and customs of the country' (article 5),[10] along with freedom of residence and navigation throughout all dominions, and the export of any products except contraband (especially arms). Trade in corn and other foodstuffs was expressly authorized, and the treaty also regulated the procedures applicable to the inspection of shipping and the control of maritime smuggling.[11]

The most interesting clauses are those governing the legal status of the French in Spain, and of the Spanish in France. The French were assured equal treatment with the English and Dutch in terms of the legal guarantees accorded to their goods and property in Spain (article 6).[12] Under the important article 9, meanwhile, the subjects of the French and Spanish sovereigns were subject to 'embargos y arrestos de justicia por las vias ordinarias, por causa de deuda, obligaciones y contratos válidos'.[13] Subjection to the ordinary courts of each country had a much greater effect on the French given the large number of migrants in Spain. However, this was more than offset by the right to appoint their own consuls by mutual consent (article 26),[14] which allowed the French state to place its officials in Spanish trade *entrepôts*. The consuls were vested with extraterritorial official and judicial powers, and their role was to resolve conflicts among French nationals living locally applying their own commercial and labour laws.[15] Furthermore, merchants were free to use attorneys and agents of their own choosing, and they were authorized to keep their books of account in French, Spanish, Flemish or whatever other language they pleased (article 25),[16] which not only saved them costs but also hindered inspection and prevented indiscretions. It was always an advantage for trade networks to use their own language.

Finally, the treaty established processes for the restitution of offices, property and financial claims existing before the peace was made, and for compensation for the seizure of enemy goods, and it also normalized the situation of benefices, curacies and other ecclesiastical offices granted by the kings of each country in occupied territories (articles 27–32).[17]

Given the fiscal, political and economic crisis afflicting Spain in 1659, the treaty assured the king of France a strong legal position for his subjects in the country. Meanwhile, the minute regulation of the seaborne trade in contraband goods contrasts with the minimal attention paid to overland smuggling, showing that the treaty was drawn up basically to resolve questions of maritime trade. The treaty makers were much occupied with the interests of merchants but hardly at all with the conditions of migrant labourers, artisans, pedlars, carriers and other small traders, and still less with the kind of cottage manufacturers who hawked such goods as they could carry from place to place on a mule or even on their own backs. Nevertheless, the treaty was also applied to such people. The legal status of the French remained unchanged throughout the second half of the seventeenth century. Spain and France made a further four treaties between 1659 and 1700 – at Aix-La-Chapelle (2 May 1668),[18] Nijmegen (10 August 1678),[19] Regensburg (15 August 1684)[20] and Rijswijk (20 September 1697)[21] – but none did more than tweak borders except the treaty of Rijswijk, which restored the situation existing before the Nine Years' War.[22] However, persistent conflict led to frequent trade bans between Spain and France in this period, although they did not generally last for long. Such bans were instituted at least in 1667,[23] 1673–1675,[24] 1684[25] and 1689.[26] Other legislation prohibited overland and maritime smuggling.[27] These interruptions were always considered temporary and did not prevent interegional trade. For example, the Spanish province of Guipúzcoa and the French province of Labort (today's Labourd) made an accord to continue reciprocal trade on 22 July 1653, despite the state of war existing between Spain and France.[28]

The other diplomatic instrument we shall examine is the Treaty of Peace, Alliance and Commerce made between Spain and England on 23 May 1667.[29] Written in Latin and Spanish rather than English and Spanish, it is very different from the treaty made with France, reflecting England's role in the Thirty Years' War and its expectations with regard to Spain now that it had become a commercial and maritime power. It contains only 40 articles, all of which are given over to trade. The treaty was first made on 17 December 1665[30] as a novation of the existing treaty of 1630, to which a further 19 articles were added, but it was subsequently amended and signed again on 23 May 1667, the date usually cited. The whole of the treaty concerns maritime commerce, as the only way in which trade could be conducted directly between Spain and Great Britain. However, the Treaty of Westminster made on 10 July 1654 between England and Portugal[31] already afforded the English a highly advantageous position for the penetration of their manufactures not only into the Portuguese Indies but also into the Spanish hinterland. Thus, the English could in fact trade overland with Spain via Portugal. The conditions established for English commercial dealings in Spain were more extensive, more detailed and more favourable than those obtained by the French. The treaty's commercial clauses established free trade between the two countries and with third nations, clearly benefitting the English given the structural gap in the balance of bilateral trade, while articles 12, 13 and others like them greatly facilitated smuggling through the ports.[32] Meanwhile, the legal status of British residents in Spain allowed them significant independence and immunity from Spanish laws. The kings of England and Spain undertook to respect maritime law (article 28), to notify each other or their representatives in advance of any arrests, recruitment of men or challenges to the entry of contentious goods, and to permit all of their subjects to bear arms and use them in self-defence (article 18). The key clause of the treaty, however, extends to the whole of the Spanish Crown the privileges and immunities already enjoyed for over two decades by English merchants in Andalusia under the royal *cédulas* and orders of 19 March, 26 June and 9 November 1645.[33] This legislation provided for the appointment of a *judge conservator* with special jurisdiction over each merchant colony, as well as other minor privileges (article 9). In addition to these benefits, the English were also granted any privileges enjoyed in Spain by subjects of France, citizens of the United Provinces of the Netherlands or the Hanseatic cities, or any other nations (article 38). Disputes between ships' captains and their crews were to be resolved solely[34] by the consul[35] of the nation concerned in port, or by the courts of the country in which the litigants were resident but not those of the country where they actually found themselves (article 19). This provision had important consequences, chief among them being that conflicts between the English in port were not resolved by the Spanish authorities but according to English law. Furthermore, it meant that the British consuls in Spain would be appointed by the King of Spain and would enjoy the same powers and competences as the consuls of other nations, and vice versa (article 27). Certain articles concerning commercial shipping are also of special interest and importance. For instance, each ship was required to carry a safe-conduct and a passport providing details of the vessel and its crew, and a declaration of cargo (article 14), yet the treaty itself provided mechanisms which allowed this information to be altered and facilitated contraband. Thus, article 7 authorized mutual free trade in goods produced either at home or in the colonies without requiring any declaration of either the consignee or the price, or requiring any explanation of possible 'errors' [*yerros*] made in recording the ship's cargo: 'y sin [recibir] vexación o molestia alguna por los yerros que suelen cometer los maestres de navíos en orden al registro de mercaderías o bienes de esta naturaleza'.[36]

This legalized deliberate mistakes in ships' manifests de facto, opening the legal floodgates to smuggling. The treaty also provided that all goods seized from legitimate prizes should be treated as the property of the privateer, and that duties should be paid on them once only, even if the vessel put in at more than one port. This effectively legalized such goods, and the practical outcome was to allow free circulation of English goods at Spanish ports. Furthermore, the penalties for maritime smuggling were very light, allowing confiscation only of contraband goods but not the rest of the cargo (unless the vessel was also carrying gold or silverware made in the country of origin) or the vessel itself. No measures were to be taken against the crew (articles 15 and 22).

Under article 10, English vessels were made exempt from inspection by officers of the law, the militia or magistrates, and the officers and crews of British ships could not be detained on land. Finally, if a ship was found to be carrying more goods than stated in the manifest, it would be allowed eight days to declare them, but if the officers decided for any reason not to do so, then only the goods in question would be confiscated but nothing more.

Overall, it could be said these arrangements left English smuggling practically unpunished, because no penalties applied to contraband cargos but only to goods unlawfully passed through customs. Meanwhile, only contraband goods could be confiscated, the captain could not be detained, and the ship and the rest of its cargo could not be seized. The same conditions also applied at sea. Taken together, articles 7 and 10 effectively legalized unlawful trade throughout Spain for several decades, until a royal *cédula* of 23 December 1716 sought once again to remedy the problem.[37] Article 8 further expanded the opportunity by authorizing trade in English colonial produce, specifying that all goods declared as such would be treated accordingly. This granted to the English the same treatment as had been accorded to the Dutch in 1648, which was in turn the same as that sought by the French in the treaty of 1659 with respect to the English.[38] The main point, however, was that a mere declaration made in London was to be taken as proof that the goods consigned in a ship's manifest were English, allowing merchants to pass off any goods they might wish to trade as English even if they were in fact French, Dutch, German or from anywhere else. This re-export trade was vital to the development of English commerce.

Finally, some articles of the treaty (principally articles 29 and 31) guaranteed the freedom of English companies to trade, adding to their already broad legal autonomy. Furthermore, merchants could engage any lawyers or legal agents they wished, and could not be obliged to disclose their records or accounts, which they could keep in any language, except voluntarily to avoid or resolve litigation. In the words of article 31:

> y no se les obligará a manifestar a ningunas personas sus registros o libros de quentas ni a darles [a los jueces] copias de ellos, si no es que puedan servir para evitar o terminar algún pleyto; y también será lícito [...] poner los libros de cuentas y correspondencia, que tuviesen en lengua española, inglesa, flamenca u otra cualquiera que les pareciese conveniente.[39]

Hence, language assured the secrecy of English (and French) merchants' books, but this was not all: their contents were also reserved and their possessors were practically immune from the action of the courts unless the merchants themselves decided to present accounts as evidence in their own favour.

According to article 29, meanwhile, counterparties could not be compelled to make payments in gold or copper coin or to accept payment in kind unless previously agreed. This prevented forced in-kind payments and ensured that all transactions had to be effected in silver or bills of exchange, the preferred means of payment for English traders, sparing them payments in billon coins, which were much disliked for the cost of conversion into silver and the effects of devaluation. At the same time, the regulation facilitated the circulation of assets and the transfer of profits abroad. In addition, the treaty established the right to repatriate inherited assets and cash (articles 33 *et seq.*), and the right to the return of distrained property recognized as belonging to subjects of the other country. Where this was impossible, goods would be paid for at fair value (article 32).

Examination of the Hispano-British trade treaty of 1667 reveals not only England's absolute domination of commerce between the two countries, but also the extent to which its predominantly maritime trading system differed from the French model. The British obtained guarantees allowing them to develop a whole network of extra-territorial courts in which only their own law prevailed. Only they defined who was included in the manifest as British, and their ships could put in freely at Spanish ports until they decided to stay in one, pay the requisite customs duties and enter Spanish territory. Their trade diasporas also enjoyed their own commercial, and in some respects also civil and criminal, jurisdiction thanks to the actions of the judges conservator, who though Spanish were in the service of the British, and the British consuls, a situation which clashed with the principles on which continental absolute states were based, limiting the sovereignty of the Spanish king – on this point more theoretical than real – in his own territory.

Above all, however, the treaty paved the way for smuggling. It removed on-board inspections; allowed English merchants to decide what goods to carry and in what amounts; excused errors in ships' manifests; and imposed only the lightest sanctions on contraband cargos. The treaty of 23 May 1667 remained in force for many years, and most of its articles were still in effect in the eighteenth century, including almost all of those discussed above.[40]

The commercial activities of the British and French in Spain in the seventeenth century were defined by the legal and political framework described, only adding to the monarchy's political weakness during the reign of Charles II. However, the War of Succession transformed the situation in the early eighteenth century. To understand these developments, we will need to consider the context in which the British and the French actually conducted their trade in Spain in the late seventeenth century. Let us, then, sketch out British and French trade interests around 1680, allowing us to gauge the impact of the ensuing changes, which would considerably strengthen the interests of the French. In this exercise, it is the general panorama that is important rather than the situation of any specific trade or area of activity, and we shall attend above all to the eyewitness accounts of contemporary merchants and diplomats.

English commercial interests in Spain in the 1680s

The activities of the English merchants in Spain and the role of the peninsular market in England's remarkable commercial expansion can best be understood through the words of their diplomatic representatives, who document the trades in which they engaged, who was involved, the prospects and the problems arising. While these sources offer little specific detail, they provide a precise overview of British trade policy in Spain.

The correspondence of English representatives in Madrid is voluminous, and there would be little point in considering it all here. British interests were as diverse as their trade, requiring wide-ranging diplomatic efforts to protect it and ensure further growth. The issues and accounts selected date from the 1680s, a fascinating moment both because it reveals the situation existing just before the weak succession to the last Habsburg king of Spain, Charles II, became a serious problem, and because the actions of certain local institutions and other circumstances of domestic politics during this decade affected foreign trade interests in peninsular Spain and the American dominions. Both the English and the French sought to benefit from events, manoeuvring to gain the advantage for their own dynastic interests and market position in a complex game involving both the Americas and Spain itself.

This is revealed in the correspondence of the English *envoy extraordinary*[41] to the court of Madrid, Lord Lansdowne, which is doubly interesting because it sheds light not only on relations between the British and the Spanish, but also on the activities of the French as he saw them.

Lord Lansdowne's early reports show that the English had received authorization to establish factories and envoys in Gibraltar between January and April 1686,[42] while the French were being shut out of the Spanish trade, with the result that goods sold by French merchants in Mexico in 1683, worth some 500,000 pesos, had still not been paid for and they were burdened with taxes in the peninsular markets.[43] We may recall here that a truce with France would be signed not long after (15 August 1686) under the Peace of Nijmegen. Some months earlier, the French had sent warships to Cadiz, threatening to attack if the debt was not paid promptly. In the end, Charles II decided to pay them half the worth of the galleons due to arrive in Seville.[44]

In general, the English correspondence reveals their concern for trade issues relating to the Canary Islands, the Americas, Puerto Rico and the English Antilles, and a relatively scant interest in mainland Spain.

Not long afterwards, Lansdowne reports that Charles II had devalued the gold and silver coinage in a *pragmática* issued on 14 October 1686, seriously hurting trade, including English interests:

> I have receaved letters from most of the Consuls and factors of our Nation, within this dominion, who unanimously complaine that this is so destructive to the com[m]erce that they are utterly undone unless there be some remedy, but as this buissness [sic] does not regarde our Nation particularly any more than all others, that traffick in these countrys, I shall take no measures herein but jointly with the Ministers of such other Princes as are most concerned[45]

This was because the Spanish authorities had ordered

> that the bills of exchange which were accepted before the publishing of it [i.e. the *pragmática*] shall be pay'd according to the old rate. Our merchants have inform'd me from several places that they will oblige them to sell their goods at the prices as formerly, without advancing in proportion to the value put upon the money, which will utterly ruine our commerce, and is contrary to the privileges granted formerly to our nation[46]

Lansdowne was referring to the privileges enjoyed by the English since the treaty of 1667 between England and Spain. Instantly sparking inflation, the devaluation had pushed up prices, spoiling short-term expectations and any cash transactions currently in progress. Moreover, it affected bills of exchange by automatically depreciating short-term debts (due at 20, 60 or 90 days) and causing uncertainty in claims for non-payment. All of this was especially damaging to the trade carried on by English merchants and others like them, who relied on this means of payment.[47]

Two days later, the envoy extraordinary outlined the position of the English with regard to the devaluation in a letter to the King of Spain, complaining of its effects on prices and credit, and noting that it could not have been His Majesty's intention to benefit the buyers of goods at the cost of the seller in the following terms:

> el grave perjuicio que resulta a los comerciantes, precissándoles a rezivir con la nueva extensión de la moneda de plata y oro el precio de las mercaderías que antes de la publicazión de la pragmática vendieron fiadas, habiendo contratado el precio y su paga por la justa estimación de la moneda según el valor que tenía al tiempo del concierto; y con la misma inspección los hombres de negocios que remitieron sus géneros a sus corresponsales en España regularon el precio conforme al valor de la moneda de oro y plata en estos Reynos, y en esta fe y confianza emplearon sus caudales y se vendieron sus mercaderías. Y aunque en las obligaciones y papeles que de su valor se hicieron no se especificaron las circunstanzias de haberse de satisfacer con el mismo valor, pesso y ley de la moneda (por no ser imaginable tal novedad) fue esa la verdadera inteligencia de los contrayentes, incluida virtualmente en sus convenziones [=contracts]; y es regla natural e infalible en todos los contratos y obligaciones que las pagas se deven hacer con el mismo valor y bondad intrínseca que tenía la moneda al t[iem]po de la oblig[aci]ón. Y nunca pudo ser conforme a la justificada intenzión de V. M[ajesta]d que el inglés que dio su mercadería en cien pessos, además de estar expuesto a la contingencia de no cobrar, o padeciendo el daño de la demora, aya de recibir la satisfacción con ochenta, quedando utilizado [=beneficiado] el comprador en veinte pessos y el vendedor da[m]nificado en ellos[48]

This letter illustrates the inner workings of English commerce, as well as noting a third adverse effect of devaluation in addition to inflation and the impact of the measure on the mechanisms used to clear bills of exchange, as explained above. The English merchants established in the British Isles conducted their business in Spain through factors, and both the parent house and its correspondents settled payments using bills of exchange at fixed prices. Devaluation, however, altered the value of the coinage, and in doing so it also affected outstanding balances, causing disputes over prices which not only affected relations between English merchants and their Spanish customers, but also between the metropolitan trading houses in Great Britain and their agents in Spain.

The text shows the havoc caused by the Habsburg dynasty's frequent manipulations of the currency in the seventeenth century. The English commercial system was similar to that employed by the French wholesalers trading either at the ports or overland, but very different to the methods employed by the networks of French migrants abounding in the Spanish hinterland, many of whom were engaged in retail trade and worked through channels in which personal relations (patronage, *nationality* and family) were crucial, but the use of bills of exchange was rare.

Not long afterwards, the English envoy extraordinary, Lansdowne, wrote to the Spanish king requesting that the terms of a second Royal Order issued on 18 November

1686, which provided for payment of bills of exchange at pre-devaluation prices, should be extended to all commercial contracts made by the English in Spain. He wrote to him

> que sin embargo de lo resuelto por la Pragmática [de 12–X–1686], las letras de cambio que se hubieran dado antes de su promulgazión se paguen con el mismo valor de la moneda que se recibió [. . .] debe esperar el [=este] inviado [extraordinario] que V. M[ajesta]d se servirá ordenar que lo mismo se entiende con todos los contractos y obligaciones y papeles hechos de deudas contraydas hasta la publicación de la pragmática por razón de las ventas que los comerciantes ingleses hicieron de sus mercaderías en cualq[uie]r comercio que uvieren tenido en los dominios de V. M[ajesta]d, mandando se paguen en la misma moneda, pesso, valor y ley que tenía antes de la pragmática.[49]

Lansdowne also protested that articles 2 and 9 of the treaty of 1667 established the right of the subjects of both nations to receive payment in the currency freely agreed in advance, but the devaluation resulting from the *pragmática* of 12 October 1686 had changed the value of the coinage and, therefore, it changed the terms of the treaty.[50]

The Marquis de Mancera replied to Lansdowne on behalf of the *Cámara de Castilla*, a standing committee of the Castilian Privy Council, denying his accusations and asserting Spain's strict compliance with the peace treaty.[51] Nevertheless, the protest was shortly taken up by a group of London merchants, whose arguments demonstrate that the adverse effects for their commercial practices, based as they were on bills of exchange, were far greater than for the Spanish. The commercial systems or 'circumstances' of the native Spanish and the English merchants were quite different:

> the Circumstances twixt the Natives and the english Mer[chan]ts [in Spain] are extreamly different, for it cannot Reasonably bee supposed that wee nor any other alliens keep any summes of money in cash, our estates there consisting chiefly in goods to sell, debts for goods sould, and some bills of exchange, soo that wee could not possibly equally sharre with Spainiards in the benefit of the extention [i. e. extension] of the value of the gold and silver;[52] but doe suffer extreamly by their detayneing of our debts, which hitherto wee forbeare to recover according to the value sett by the Pragmatica, because wee would not bee at soe greate a losse as will thereby fall on us.[53]

This testimony shows how the devaluation proportionally impaired the value of English commercial assets in Spain, which basically comprised goods and trade debts. In particular, the devaluation affected accounts receivable and bills of exchange. The English merchants largely conducted their trade in Spain through factories at ports like Tenerife, Orotava, Bilbao, La Corunna and Cadiz-Seville (leaving aside ports in the Americas), and they were the principal losers in every devaluation, which caused inflation in the Spanish interior but hardly affected those who had no use for bills of exchange or need to exchange currencies. Devaluation was, then, not only a ploy used by the monarchy to raise cash or reduce the public debt, but it could also be described as a defensive trade mechanism, insofar as it hurt foreign trade in goods in which the English merchants were the creditors and the king's Spanish subjects were the debtors.

We must also consider political circumstances if we are to understand matters from the merchants' standpoint. The servants of the King of Spain were not generally well disposed towards the English if we are to believe the complaints voiced by Lord Lansdowne.[54]

Further testimony is provided by a group of English merchants in Santa Cruz de Tenerife (Canary Islands), who wrote to their king in 1687 explaining that trade between Great Britain and the Spanish port was intense and profitable ('it exported as much of our manufactures as was imported in wines'). England imported some 12,000 pipes of Canary sack annually and exports were worth more than 100,000 pounds sterling. More than 100 English vessels put in at the Islands each year. Canary wines were highly profitable for the English Crown because customs were payable on imports, but consumption was in decline, partly because tastes had shifted in favour of French wines ('The general dislike many have to Canary wines; French wine being the modish now in request') but also because of problems of adulteration and high duties, which drove up prices. Hence, the merchants sought a cut in customs duties to help them increase both their imports and exports of English cloth to the Canary Islands, which spanned practically the whole range offered by the English textiles industry:

> Bays, says, cottons, plaines, Notherne & Westerne kersies, coarse cloaths, perpetuanas & serges, all sorts of hats & haberdas, hery wares (on several occasions), greate quantity of all sorts or grames and every yeare vast quantity of all sort of provisions both from England and Ireland as pilchards, herrings, beefe, butter, cheese, etc.[55]

Given their strategic position on the sea lanes to America, the Canary Islands were probably the Spanish territory where English trade was most developed.

However, the merchants' interests were not confined to factories at Spain's ports. They also had, or were beginning to have, a market for manufactured goods in the important consumer market that was Madrid. This is implied by the testimony of the new extraordinary envoy to Madrid, Lord Stanhope, referring to a *pragmática* issued in early December 1691:

> I expect y[ou]r Lo[rdshi]pps orders as to what I writ in my last concerning a buriall place four our nation here, which will now be granted if insested [=insisted]; on three or fourer [=four] days ago came out a pragmatica for reforming excesses in apparell, coaches, mournings, and w[hi]ch makes great wise at present, but they say is likely to be forgot in a month as all others [*pragmáticas*] have been before. It there seems to me to be a kind of implied prohibition in it of all silks, cloaths and stuffs of our [=ours] or any other forreign manufactory, because it allowes them only with the condition of being the same measure, weight, mark and make in all particulars w[hi]ch those of the like kind fabricated here in Spain, so that because it may concern our trade. I send your Lo[rdshi]pps herewith a copie of the pragmática.[56]

Madrid and its court were an attractive market for English woollens and silks, and it is interesting to note that the Spanish monarchy was already attempting to impose protectionist measures against them at this time. As we shall see below, this mirrors the efforts of the Aragonese Parliament, which still retained sovereignty over such matters, to establish protectionist measures against the French manufactures that dominated the regional market.

Even so, the minds of the English ambassadors were occupied not only with problems of trade but also, indeed even more so, with maintaining intact the significant legal and commercial privileges enjoyed by their compatriots. These were based on three royal *cédulas* issued on 19 March, 26 June and 9 November 1645, which granted the English merchants established in Andalusia the privilege of having their own magistrates or 'judges conservator'. Although these magistrates were Spanish, they were appointed by the English, over whom they had exclusive civil and criminal jurisdiction. Article 9 of the 1667 treaty extended the privileges of the English merchants in Andalusia to all dealings and contracts made by the English in Spanish dominions, and at the same time it assured the respective subjects and trade of each of the signatory monarchs equal privileges and exemptions in the territory of the other to those granted to the subjects of his Most Christian Highness the King of France, to the citizens of the United Provinces or to the merchants of the Hanseatic cities.[57] This placed the legal position of the English in Spain on the same level as that of the French, Dutch and Germans.

Not long afterwards, we find Stanhope concerned with the problem of upholding the legal and commercial privileges won by the English. In a memorandum of 1693, he requested that Francisco Reynoso y Mendoza, a Spaniard, be ratified as the judge conservator chosen by the English colony in the important winegrowing district of Puerto de Santa María in the province of Cádiz, in line with the practice followed for the last 48 years, and that he should not be relieved of jurisdiction in cases affecting royal revenues, as the monarchy wished.[58]

The jurisdictional prerogative should, then, prevail even against the king. Charles II's mercantilist aim, meanwhile, was to control any civil or criminal litigation involving English merchants that might affect the revenues due to the Spanish monarchy. This constituted a threat, because it would allow the Spanish magistrates and authorities to restrict the scope of English mercantile autonomy, enabling them to investigate their property and, still worse in Stanhope's opinion, to scrutinize their accounts.

> I acquainted your Lo[rdshi]pp with a new restriction they would put upon our judges conservators, excluding them w[hi]ch is an innovation that will be most prejudiciall to our merchants and expose their houses, warehouses and bookes to be visited at pleasure, w[hi]ch is expressely contrary to our Articles.[59]

English mercantile interests, meanwhile, were focused on opening the Spanish market to colonial goods. Under the trade treaties, the ambassador pressed for permission to import cocoa and tobacco from England's colonial plantations, two products which the Spanish monarchy was particularly keen to control because of the succulent excise duties they brought in.[60]

To end this brief summary of the trade issues that occupied the minds of English envoys at this time, let us consider one last matter. At some time between 1688 and 1693 (probably in the latter year), the Spanish monarchy imposed a double system for the examination of cargos loaded on board British vessels bound for Spain, which meant that each vessel had to register with the Spanish consul in London, the only one in England at that time, before setting out. The first protests appeared in 1693, and on 15 August 1695 Alexander Stanhope, England's envoy extraordinary, petitioned the King of Spain to allow English vessels free admission to Spanish ports provided they had proper papers issued by officials in their home ports:

> las mercaderías y géneros que los negociantes ingleses traen en sus navíos a los puertos de estos reynos, en particular a el de Bilbao, fuesen libremente admitidos al comercio trayendo sus cartas de mar y demás despachos necesarios de los magistrados de las partes de donde saliesen d[ic]os navíos[61]

No further requirements should be added, because it was impossible for all the ships of England, Scotland and Ireland to sail via London, and the Spanish consul could not appoint a delegate in every port even if he had the necessary authority, which he did not. Furthermore, Stanhope argued, the merchants were opposed to double examination of their cargos because of the damage caused to their bales in the process. Moreover, the Spanish consul in London acted under the authority of the King of Spain with the permission of the King of England, and his proper functions were confined to assisting and protecting Spanish nationals:

> se limita a agenciar las dependencias de sus nacionales, proteger[los] y asistirlos para su mejor avío y despacho cobrando de ellos los derechos de su consulado sin que en ningún tiempo se haya practicado otra cosa.

Consequently, Stanhope concluded, the King of England could not authorize the Spanish consul to examine British vessels in their home ports.[62]

The King of Spain had no option but to yield to this pressure with the face-saving excuse of the strict ban on trade between England and France ('[...] por complacer al Rey Británico y por el rigor con que está informado se prohibe en Inglaterra todo el comercio con Francia [...]'), as English and Dutch troops had laid siege to the town of Palamós (in the Spanish province of Gerona), at the time in the hands of the French.[63]

To sum up, contemporary accounts from the 1680s show that English trade with Spain had succeeded in establishing important positions in the Spanish interior. This was a factory trade based in the Spanish (and probably also Portuguese) ports, from where goods could be distributed to the hinterland via different routes and networks, and the whole system was moved by bills of exchange. By the turn of the century, Spain was surrounded by English commercial seas, and British traders continued to push their way into the country's internal market. The merchant communities in the ports, England's ally Portugal, Gibraltar and Menorca provided the entrepôts, but goods were carried into the interior not by networks of English traders but rather by Castilian, Irish, Maltese and Catalan intermediaries. The English in fact did not generally stray far from the coast, although their goods moved all round Spain.

French commercial interests in Spain in the 1680s

The French opposed English interests in the Spanish market with equally powerful forces, astutely employing the key advantage of geographical proximity on land and the presence of a numerous community of French migrants, who with time had built up extensive trade networks, constantly crossing the frontier between the two countries to export their manufactures and bring home the prized Spanish silver.

The legal situation of French trade in Spain at the end of the seventeenth century was defined by articles 5 to 27 of the 1659 Treaty of the Pyrenees, the clarificatory declaration of 6 March 1669 signed by Mariana of Austria, mother of Charles II and regent of Spain, and a further clarificatory ordinance of 2 December 1670, which granted French traders the same privileges as accorded to the merchants of England, the Hanseatic League and other nations. The Peace of Nijmegen made on 17 September 1679 after the war between Spain and France brought about no changes in trade matters.

The sources used by the highly developed French diplomatic service of the seventeenth century provide precise information about trade between Spain and France in the 1680s, and about the extensive networks of French migrants working and trading in the Iberian Peninsula.

At the end of the 1680s:

> [...] on estimoit qu'il y avoit alors en Espagne plus de soixante mille françois, répandus dans les différentes Provinces de cette monarchie, les uns faisoient le commerce en détail, d'autres étoient colporteurs,[64] portefais[65] ou domestiques dans les maisons, plusieurs d'entre eux ne portant en Espagne que leur industrie et leur travail [tous ceux-ci] faisoient tous les ans passer en France des sommes considérables [d'argent]. Les habitants des frontières du Royaume du côté des Pirinées vendoient en Aragon et dans la Navarre leurs bestiaux, leurs grains et d'autres denrées, ils en retiroient des laines et des huiles, et ce commerce faisait de plus passer dans les Provinces de nos frontières un grand nombre de piastres. Les Rochellais et ceux de Nantes envoyent de mesme à St. Sébastien et à Bilbao des morües[66] de Terre-Neuve, des sels et des fruits de France, qui leur donnoient des retours considérables d'argent [...][67]

This text perfectly illustrates the lifestyles and social status of the more than 60,000 people of French extraction living in the Iberian dominions of the Spanish monarchy in the seventeenth century. In principle, these French immigrants had laboured in low-status occupations or had entered domestic service, but over time they formed extensive networks of small traders, initially as pedlars and hawkers (*colporteurs*) although some eventually settled, carrying on a highly varied retail trade. These networks exported labour and manufactured goods from France, bringing home wool, oil and large sums in cash. The migrants conducted an intense overland trade. Two distinct trade flows may be discerned along the Basque, Navarrese and Aragonese frontier. On the one hand, coastal vessels plied between the Atlantic ports of France (La Rochelle and Nantes) and the Basque ports of Bilbao and San Sebastián, carrying agricultural produce, salt cod and sea salt, and on the other, long-distance overland traders from France exported high value-added products as well as mules and grain, tending to stay close to the frontier in the regions of Navarre and Aragon. On their return, these traders basically brought back Spanish silver.

By comparison, this was a very different system of trade from that carried on by the English, who were few in number, were located in the ports and used intermediaries to send their goods into the Spanish interior, transacting their business by means of accounts[68] and bills of exchange. In contrast, French merchants trading through the ports like the English, who also existed, joined forces with the extensive networks developed by their compatriots throughout Spain, trading their labour as well as goods. We may safely assume, meanwhile, that most small French businesses did not use double entry bookkeeping or keep account of their profits and losses, techniques proper to large merchants and companies engaged in international maritime trade. The scene described in the text cited above is incomplete, however, as it contains no allusion to the important French merchants and financiers in Madrid and Cadiz, although their presence in Madrid was still small at the end of the seventeenth century.

In short, the overland trade accounted for a large part of French commerce in Spain and it was based on very different organizational patterns from the factory system preferred by the English, for it was not only a way to earn profits but also involved an important social dimension. Because of this, trading conditions in the Spanish interior had more direct repercussions in France than in England. Furthermore, the British probably already had a broader, more diversified range of trading activities by this time. For the English, the type of commerce that was functionally most similar to the activities of the French in Spain was carried on with Ireland, Scotland, the United Provinces and Spanish Flanders, but this trade had little impact on England's internal markets except in the case of dealings with Flanders, a region which is beyond the scope of this work.

Returning to our text, which dates from 1716 although it refers to the latter years of the 1680s, we may observe one further matter: what had been a clear commercial expansion in Spain had met major, unforeseen obstacles, not only from the politically weak Spanish monarchy, but also from certain quarters in those regions like Navarre and Aragon which were governed according to their own local laws. There are frequent complaints about the obligation imposed by the monarchy upon settled Hispano-French immigrants, the so-called *franceses españoles*, to pay the same taxes as the Spanish:

> On continua d'obliger les françois établis en Espagne à payer les mêmes taxes, et à faire les mêmes corvées que les espagnols ...

Furthermore, the text reveals that the provinces of Guipúzcoa and Vizcaya raised objections to the appointment of consuls under the terms of the Treaty of the Pyrenees where local privileges were affected:

Les provinces de Guipuzcoa et de Biscaya refusent de recevoir le Sr. Noël que le Roy avait nommé pour aller à Saint Sebastien et à Bilbao exercer l'employ de consul en conséquence du 26e article du traité des Pirénées, elles avoient admis les consuls anglois et hollandois (…) les habitants des Provinces de Biscaya et de Guipuscoa prétendent n'être soumis aux stipulations des traités que lors qu'ils y ont expressément consenty en dérogeant à leurs franchises.[69]

Moreover, those French migrants who were not settled in Spain but moved back and forth over the border also met with intense resistance to the penetration of their manufactures in Navarre and, above all, in Aragon:

On continua de faire payer un droit par teste sur chaque françois entrant en Navarre et sortant de ce royaume, et ce droit étoit souvent exigé au double suivant le caprice des gouverneurs particuliers; […] Les difficultés que les françois éprouvoient en Aragon étoient encore plus considérables. Les états de cette Province y faisaient était plus avantageux à la France qu'à l'Espagne, et ils publiérent le 22 janvier 1686 une Ordonnance portant défense aux françois non mariés avec des espag[n]oles de trafiquer dans le royaume d'Aragon d'autres choses que de bestiaux, et aux françois mariés avec des espagnoles d'avoir des garçons de boutique françois; enjoignant aux autres de sortir du royaume [d'Aragon] dans trois mois.[70]

The informant also mentions local import duties established in Vizcaya and Guipúzcoa, certain taxes imposed by the regional Parliament or *Cortes* of Navarre and, in particular, to the Aragonese *Cortes* held in Calatayud and Zaragoza in 1677–1678 and in Zaragoza in 1684, which banned all imports of manufactured goods, doubled import and export duties, and greatly restricted the activities of French pedlars and traders in the Kingdom of Aragon (1686).[71]

The importance of the Aragonese position to the French can hardly be overstated. French migrants who were not married to Spanish women (i.e. those who were not naturalized) were not permitted to trade except in mules,[72] while those who had taken local wives, the *franceses españoles*, were not allowed French apprentices. French trade in Aragon was conducted by dense networks based on family, origin and patronage, formed by both settled, naturalized immigrants and temporary migrants, and in this context apprenticeships served to maintain and strengthen bonds with communities in the home country. There are no references to customs policy: the problem with Aragon was not a matter of the duties applied to goods but of the goods themselves, and of the endogamous system by which the migrants' networks reproduced themselves, which ensured that trade would always remain in French hands.

The Aragonese restrictions became law, and not even the King of Spain could prevent it. The French reaction was vigorous:

Le marquis de Senquières demanda par ordre du Roy [français] que cette ordonnance fût annulée, comme étant contraire aux traités de paix et tendant à ruiner le commerce des françois en Aragon; [et] le Roy d'Espagne écrivit au Vice Roy d'Aragon de faire surseoire l'exécution de cette ordonnance jusqu'à la

> prochaine séance des États,[73] et fit témoigner qu'il ne pouvoit en faire d'avantage le privilège des aragonais,[74] ne luy permettant pas de casser les ordonnances des états de cette province.[75] Cette surséance dura peu de tem[p]s, les consuls et échevins de Saragosse[76] firent exécuter l'ordonnance des États et interdirent tout commerce aux marchands françois. Le marquis de Senquières ne put obtenir du Roy d'Espagne un ordre contraire. Le Conseil d'État appréhendra de commettre l'autorité royale avec des sujets qui ne faisoient que ce qu'il leur plaisait, et que le Marquis de los Vélez fît entendre que si l'on vouloit agir d'autorité contre les aragonais, ils ne manqueroient pas de se roidir [=raidir], et que le seul moyen de les réduire était de leur faire appréhender d'être privés des marchandises qu'ils tiraient de France, et de n'avoir plus dans ce Royaume [que] le débit de celles qui leur étaient superflües.[77]

The unknown author of this text reveals the importance which the French attached to this legislation, at the same time highlighting the limits on the powers of the Spanish monarchy. The absolutist state of Spain had signed the Treaty of the Pyrenees, and the French therefore understood that it was universally applicable, although the Spanish king, who was the ruler of a *composite* rather than an absolute monarchy,[78] could not enforce compliance without taking regional institutions into account. Charles II's response to the Marquis de Senquières, conveyed via the Marquis de Vélez, is more than a little naïve. The punishment which the author of the text suggests for the stubbornly capricious Aragonese ('ces sujets qui ne faisoient que ce qu'il leur plaisit') was just what the regional *Cortes* sought. Textiles were the main French export to Aragon, and the Aragonese believed that this foreign competition was harming the kingdom's domestic manufactures. Hence, their aim was to encourage local production by the usual mercantilist method of a trade ban on French cloth. This was what both the English and French had done in their own domains, and it was what the King of Spain had done in the monarchy as a whole. Mercantilism was everywhere the dominant ideology.

The text goes on:

> Le Roy [français] n'approuva cet expédient et ordonna aux marquis de Senquières de continuer ses instances pour obtenir du Roy Catholique d'employer son autorité pour obliger les aragonais à révoquer une ordonnance aussi contraire à bon voisinage, aux lois du commerce et au traité des Pirénées.
>
> Les répresèntations qu'il fit en conséquence des ordres de sa Majesté furent inutiles, et l'on répondit au sieur le Vasseur, chargé des affaires du Roy à Madrid, depuis la mort du marquis de Senquières, que tous les sujets de la Monarchie d'Espagne entraient avec le Roy Catholique dans les traités, mais que ces traités devoient s'entendre en sorte qu'ils ne dérogeassent pas à leurs privilèges, a moins que la clause derogatoire ne fust expressement stipulée et que les états des Royaumes d'Espagne y eussent consentes.[79]

The question therefore depended on the political interpretation of the applicable clauses in the agreements between France and Spain. On one hand, they could be construed literally on the assumption that the king had absolute power and could apply the treaties without limit, or they could be interpreted taking into account that the king was the ruler of a composite monarchy formed by different realms each with their own laws, constitutions and political institutions, which could only be changed by means of regional pacts. The case is interesting because it reveals how the decision of the Parliament in a region like Aragon, taken in defence of the local market, clashed not only with the interests of the Spanish Crown but also with those of the French monarchy, which actively supported the position of its emigrant pedlars, carriers, traders and merchants. As this was an overland trade, it was doubly affected by the Aragonese decision, because the kingdom lay directly athwart the frontier, so that the French stood to lose not only their business in the region's own extensive territory but also the transportation and communication routes used by migrants in other parts of Spain, who would be left stranded because neither goods nor people could travel freely through Aragon.

The Aragonese legislation appears to have been seriously detrimental to French commercial interests, because it reduced the volume of trade flows to approximately one tenth of what they were before the ban:

> Les aragonais ont trouvé le secret d'exclure les françois de la frontière de tout ce qui pouvoit les faire subsister et [ils] sont dans cet état à présent que nos frontières portent plus de 200 m[il] écus tous les ans en Aragon pour des huiles et ne retirent pas la dixième partie de ce qu'ils retiroient autre fois, et qui à partager entre tous les peuples voisins de l'Aragon montoit à sept ou huit cent mil écus de revenant-bon.[80] C'est un pais, Monsieur, qui ne tiroit pas un denier de la France, et qui y devait y faire couler d'Espagne une source continuelle d'argent, mais là voilà absolument ravie si l'on n'y apporte les remèdes que les négociants interessés jugent nécessaires.[81]

France's traditionally positive trade balance with Aragon had changed drastically. The kingdom continued to export its oil, but French exports to Aragon had fallen and the flow of silver back across the border had been seriously reduced, if not entirely choked off. The French traders lobbied their king to take action against Spain.

However, Louis XIV, who had fought four wars against Spain (1665–1668, 1672–1678 and 1683–1684) since the accession of Charles II to the Spanish throne in 1665, had now launched what came to be known as the Nine Years' War or the War of the League of Augsburg (1688–1698) by attacking Spanish possessions in Flanders, Italy and Catalonia, where the French even took Barcelona in 1697. In these circumstances, there could be little room for negotiation. The maritime powers of England and the United Provinces allied themselves with the Holy Roman Emperor and Spain, taking decisive action to halt French expansionism. In any event, the political estrangement between Spain and France after 1688 was decisive for this issue, because it ended French pressure on Charles II to prevent the decision of the Aragonese *Cortes* from taking effect.[82]

Meanwhile, French bloody-handedness in Catalonia at the eastern end of the frontier provoked intense antipathy, in the long run costing them any significant presence in the principality in the eighteenth century. However, little changed at the western end. French influence in Navarre remained strong, and the region became the main route for the entry of migrants heading into the Spanish hinterland, and for diplomatic communication and overland trade between the Basque provinces of Spain, France and England. Apart from the regional bans on French traders imposed in Aragon in 1678 and 1686, which ended in 1707 when the kingdom's local laws were abolished, relations between the Navarrese, the Aragonese and the French never reached the pitch of hostility existing in Catalonia, and the bonds of proximity and very often family remained strong. However, it is not possible to provide further detail in this respect or make even approximate regional comparisons. The decision of the Aragonese Parliament to ban foreign trade may have helped local artisans and manufactures, though it was perhaps less beneficial to other segments of the population, and in any event it did not entail a complete break in relations with France. The English, at the time allies of Spain, were alert to all matters involving France and were well aware of the problem. Their version of events coincides only partly with that of the French, at least in the sources used by this author. The Aragonese are presented as a stubborn people and jealous defenders of their local laws, but they also refused to close the frontier completely or to cut off all relations with France, like the Navarrese and the inhabitants of Guipúzcoa. Referring to the Spanish Council of State, William Aglionby reported in 1692 that

> it was as difficult on their side to shutt up ye frontier towards France on all parts; that theire owne people were verry difficultly brought to breake of commerce with France in ye provinces of Navarra and Guipuscoa, but that those of Arragon had absolutely refus'd either to bannish the French from among them or to forbeare corresponding and having [trade] with them, pretending *fueros*[83] [sic] and privileges, through w[hi]ch it was not convenient at this time for the Govvernement to breake they being an obstinate sort of people.[84]

By this time, commerce between Bayonne and Navarre had been broken off.[85]

The War of Succession broke out shortly afterwards, and the victorious King Phillip V, who was supported by the French, abolished the local laws and privileges of Aragon in 1707. To understand this move, we may recall that the mercantilist policy of the Aragonese *Cortes* had been a thorn in the side of French trade twenty years before, and in this light, it may be that the end of Aragon's status as an autonomous region was not only a matter of reprisal or political rationalism after the kingdom's military defeat, but also a consequence of lobbying by the French allies of the new Bourbon monarch to stop the realms of Spain from using local laws and institutions to hinder cross-border trade. The end of political autonomy would permit the penetration of French manufactures into the Spanish interior, and at the same time it would allow the French to triumph over the English in their struggle for control of Spain's domestic market and the exclusion of competitors. The war did not affect all of Spain's autonomous territories equally, and the consequences for Aragon and Catalonia were not the same as for Guipúzcoa and Navarre, but this is not a matter that need be discussed here.

By the end of the seventeenth century, French pedlars were established in Madrid, freely selling their wares in competition with Spanish and Portuguese traders (who probably dealt in English cloth):

De tout temps les porteurs de malle ou colporteurs françois ont eu la liberté pendant la paix de vendre leurs marchandises dans les rües de Madrid, de même que les Portugais et les espagnols. Le marquis de Villars obtint en 1680 après la paix de Nimègue que cette liberté leur fut rendüe.[86]

Most of these French pedlars, who ranged all over the Spanish interior, entered the country at the western end of the frontier through the provinces of Vizcaya, Guipúzcoa and Navarre, where they circulated freely until they reached one of the four main customs posts of Castile. The easternmost of these was Ágreda in the province of Soria. The goods traded in the Spanish interior consisted of

nos brocards d'or, d'argent et de soye, et celuy de nos étoffes légères et toutes sortes d'ouvrages de mode venant de Paris et de Lyon.[87]

Linens and other fine stuffs were the main goods marketed by the French, who manifestly dominated the import trade in the interior of Spain, even if their wares were not always of the best quality and their trade was to a great extent dependent on fashion. This is clearly revealed by the response of the *Real Junta General de Comercio* or Royal Board of Trade to the French ambassador's complaints over a protectionist Castilian decree issued on 6 June 1683, justifying the legislation as necessary to redress the harm caused by the high prices of foreign, and especially French manufactures:

[...] [hay que] reparar el daño que había padecido [Castilla] con la introducción de las manufacturas estrangeras de Francia, y otras partes faltas de ley, peso y medida, adulteradas y falsificadas, y comerciadas por precios tan escesivos que es inexplicable y de gran dolor que se huviesen vendido a los que es notorio, siendo el que daba la ley al precio la codicia del estrangero, y no la justificación de su verdadero valor; y esto con incomparable exceso en los franceses, protegidos de su embaxador, y con el indulto o amparo de vivir en sus quarteles, que les rendían considerables conveniencias. Pero nada de esto podía causar admiración a un buen político; pues era preciso se resistiesen los extrangeros no con razón, sino por la sensibilidad de las conveniencias que podían perder, quando las estaban logrando sin medida ni ley en la paga de derechos, en la libertad de no poder ser sus casas registradas, y en dar precio a su antojo a los géneros, admitiéndoles los vasallos de esta monarquía por la novedad y veleidad de vestirse de sus manufacturas, apreciando más la apariencia exterior que la bondad intrínsica de los géneros nobles de Castilla [...][88]

In view of this passionate expression of grievances by the institution entrusted with guiding the mercantile policy of the last of the Spanish Habsburgs, as a final testimony to the state of Spain's foreign trade before the War of Succession, we may wonder how far Charles II's physical and political weakness may have agitated the perpetual trade tussles between the English and the French.

Both trade and diplomacy needed a postal service, and the main overland routes connecting Madrid to the Spanish Netherlands, France and England ran either through the Basque provinces, or from Pamplona to Bayonne and Bordeaux. Some time before the events described here, although exactly when is unclear, a regular, fortnightly overland service had been created connecting Spain with its possessions in Flanders and with Paris and London. Correspondence was essential to communicate political and commercial information, and to carry the all-important bills of exchange. Hence, when war broke out with France after 1690 the English petitioned their king to persuade the King of Spain to close the overland route through the Basque provinces and Pamplona on the (alleged) ground of insecurity, and at the same time they eagerly sought to establish a maritime postal service between La Corunna and Falmouth to carry all diplomatic and commercial correspondence. It was no accident that the ports chosen for this service were as far as possible from the coast of France and the English Channel. The response of the Count de Oñate, postmaster general to Charles II, which is cited at length in the box, perfectly describes the futility of closing the northern frontier to post and trade, the multifaceted strategy of commercial intermediation deployed by the English, the threat of espionage in maritime postal services, and the effects of Spain's political inferiority and commercial dependence on England.

The postal service through France and English trade in 1691

[Count of Oñate, Correo Mayor del Rey (postmaster general), in response to petitions made by the English extraordinary envoy, William Aglionby]

1°) Responde que no basta el que S. M. mande a sus súbditos y a los que no lo son [que] no escriban a Francia ni tengan con ella ni por ella comercio alguno con otros reynos, ni tan poco [=tampoco] que el correo mayor ordene a los correos mayores de sus dominios que confinan con la Francia ympidan y corten el paso de los correos ordinarios y ex[traordina]rios. Lo primero por q[u]e el escribir o el dejar de escribir los comerciantes a la parte donde quisieren es arbitrio libre de su voluntad, y que aunque no [se] les recivan cartas en los officios de correo mayor de la frontera son tantas las veredas y partes por donde yndependientes de los officios [de correo mayor] pueden encaminarles, que sería preciso poner un cordón cerrado en toda la Corona de Aragón, en la de Navarra y [en el] principado de Catahaluña, que aun desta suerte no se podría attajar; [a]demás de que las cartas sólo pueden incluyr noticias de las salidas de géneros y balores dellos, syendo evidente que en ellas no caben fardos, paquetes ny géneros, que es con lo que se trafica.

Añádese a esto que [los ingleses] tienen tantas puertas abiertas para el comercio que no sólo tienen los medios de Portugal, de Dinamarca, Génova y venecianos, que por ellos trafican y introducen quanto quieren, y en prueba desto se hace pres[en]te que de sólo de la República de Génova navegan hoy [a España] de treinta a treinta y tres baxeles, quando antes de esta última rottura de guerra sólo navegaban a estos reynos dos o tres o a lo sumo quatro. Pruébase esta verdad con saberse positivamente que desde el arribo de galeones acá han passado de Cádiz a Génova passados de ocho millones de plata, de donde se hace la distribuz[i]ón de lo que pertenece a los franceses, sin dudar que más de la mitad de ello es suyo [de los ingleses] y procede de sus effectos [comerciales, =letras de cambio].

2°) Presupone el agente inglés que los intereses de Corona a Corona no deben reparar en el daño o conveniencia de los súbditos. Esta proposiz[i]ón no es tan ynsubsistente que nadie la puede dudar [=poner en duda], porque a los reyes y a sus reynos los haze ricos o pobres el comercio y el que no le aya; porque dicho se está que el vasallo pobre no podrá conttribuir con nada al Prin[cip]e ni satisfacer a los impuestos con que esta gravado para servirle. Y si no pregúntese al dominio de Inglaterra y a las Provincias Unidas de Holanda en qué consiste su riqueza o poder sino en el comercio; y es tan preponderado esto en ambas naciones que hoy en día no dejan de comerciar (aunq[u]e [di]simuladamente) por medio de genoveses, dinamarqueses y venecianos, con la Francia.

3°) Supónese que la Francia saca grandes ventajas del passo de las cartas [por su territorio], séase descubriendo los designios de sus enemigos y descubriendo los secretos [comerciales y diplomáticos]. Respóndese que en lo que mira a utilizarse [=obtener beneficios] con lo que se le contribuye por el paso de los [correos] ordinarios, es cierto, pero también lo es el que la experiencia ha mostrado que es la forma más barata [de correo] para los súbditos de los dominios de S. M. y de las naziones que residen en ellos, porque la onça de carta, que ahora paga con seis r[eales] de plata, antes que se estableciesen los [correos] ordinarios en la forma que hoy están les costaba por las vías secretas que tenían a más de 24 y 26 [reales] de p[la]ta por onça, [a]demás del retrasso que experimentaban en sus correspondencias. Y en quanto a lo que mira al punto de que por el medio del curso que tienen los [correos] ordinarios [los franceses] adquieren noticias de todo lo que pasa, se responde que siendo tantos los portillos y pasos abiertos que hay para adquirirlas diariam[en]te no necesitábase esperar al paso de los [correos] ordinarios, que parten cada quince días.

En quanto al [=a la] presunción de que en Francia se interce[p]tan los desp[ach]os, [es] cierto que siempre se ha hablado en esta presunción, pero también lo es que nunca se ha verificado ni parece dable que [se haga] en la corta mansión que [los correos] hazen en el tránsito, pues precisamente se habría de interponer alguna dilación que calificase la sospecha. Y aunque desde que se introdujeron los paquebotes [de Falmouth a La Coruña] se dio orden a los oficios [del Correo Mayor] de Cádiz, Sevilla, Málaga y esta Corte diesen a entender convendría que usassen desta vía y no de la de tierra, y en esto se puso especial cuydado, a [los] tres o quatro ordinarios reconocieron el gran retraso que [se] les seguía en el recibo de sus cartas, [a]demás de los accidentes de la mar que no se sujetaron a preceptos humanos; no siendo dudable que aun quando [las cartas] llegasen con puntualidad a la Coruña y se transfiriesen a esta corte como caxa principal, en el tiempo que esto incluye reciben los comerciantes de Bilbao, Sevilla, Cádiz y Málaga, que son los centros principales del comercio, más de 15 días de retrasso en la forma en que hoy se practica.

Y desde que se quiso establecer la vía de la Coruña, se declararon [los] holandeses en que no querían que su correspondencia se sujetase a la llave precisa de que fuessen a parar a Inglaterra, y dieron a entender buscarían como dueños de sí mismos otras vías por donde establecer sus correspondencias, por ser punto muy celoso entre comerciantes que los unos tengan las noticias con preferencia a los otros.

4°) Presupone que establecida la correspondencia por la Coruña en derechura a Inglaterra, con el tiempo será de gran beneficio al comercio, frutos y manufacturas de España, que comprarán y consumirán ingleses. Respóndese que este es un supuesto muy hermoso a la vista, pero muy solapsado y perjudizial a todos los súbditos de S[u] M[ajesta] y especialmente a los del pays baxo [=Países Bajos españoles], pues no se deja de dudar que la máxima de [los] ingleses es hacerse [los dueños] absolutos de todo el comercio de España, y hazer precisos dependientes mendigos a las demás naciones, y especialmente al pays baxo [=Países Bajos españoles] dándoles los mendrugos que les sobran a los precios que quisieren después de haber desfrutado toda la nata de los útiles [=beneficios]; manifestando el mismo hecho esta infallible maniobra.

5°) Quiere esforçar que extinguida la correspondencia por tierra se les disminuyrá a los franceses los útiles [=beneficios] de sus comercios. Este punto queda satisfecho en el primero capítulo con decir que en las cartas no se pueden incluyr paquetes ni fardos, que es el alma del comercio, y esta providencia, si es que la puede haber que conviniera, no es del instituto del officio de Correo Mayor, sino de lo universal del gobierno, para embarasar que por los puertos ni aduanas no se introduzgan géneros prohibidos congines [=¿con fines?] de fábricas supuestas de naciones amigas como actualmente se está practicando en la Corte [de Madrid].

6°) Quiérese assentar que [los] ingleses hayan quitado y cortado enteramente la comunicación con la Francia y que toda su correspondencia pase por sólo los payses de sus confederados. Respóndese que no se duda que el ánimo del rey britt[áni]co haya sido el que supone, pero al mismo paso se ve están comerciando sus súbditos cautelosamente por medio de embarcaciones portuguesa, ginovesas, dinamarquesas y hamburguesas, como más diffusamente está respondido en uno de los cap[ítul]os precedentes.

[The remaining three points likewise insist that the overland post through France was cheaper, more secure and more punctual.]

Source: *Respuesta a las proposiciones hechas por el agente del rey británico para la interru[p]ción y paso de las cartas por Francia y razones en que la funda*, Count de Oñate, Correo Mayor del Rey, to Aglionby, 4–VI–1691, TNA, SP 94/75.

The Count de Oñate insists repeatedly that the English seek to shut down diplomatic and commercial correspondence between France and Spain, but at the same time they are busy selling their goods in both countries through Genoese, Venetian, Danish and Hanseatic intermediaries, even using Genoese ships to export silver arriving at Cadiz directly, although these monies were meant to be shared with the French companies established in the Andalusian port. Furthermore, the English would take more than half of the bullion eventually distributed (in Genoa), in an eloquent statement of their predominant trading position with the Americas via Cádiz.

The Marquis goes on to argue that switching the northern postal service to a maritime route via Falmouth instead of the overland route through France would not be without consequences, placing the correspondence of Dutch and Flemish merchants, the latter still subjects of the King of Spain, in English hands, which would allow ample room for commercial espionage. The proof of this is that the Dutch were resolutely determined that their own letters and bills of exchange should not travel in English ships, as contemporary sources show. The merchants of Spanish Flanders, England's other great trade competitors would likewise have seen their trade ruined.

The English envoy to Spain, William Aglionby, answered the Count de Oñate at length in punctilious French, very much in the diplomatic style of the times. However, the English diplomat is silent in the face of his Spanish counterpart's bitter accusations of England's backstairs trade with France, which in this author's opinion confirms the truth of the charge. Moreover, he cynically asserts that:

> la conduite de la nation angloise ajourdhuy ne fait rien voir de semblable, car elle soutient pour l'amour de ses alliés en bonne partie la plus généreuse du monde une guerre fort préjudiciable aux intérêts de son commerce, c'est pourquoy l'on se poyrroit bien passer de la censurer sy' injustement.[89]

To my mind, these scraps of information convey the idea that English trade in Spain, whether lawful or unlawful, became quite overbearing after the treaty of 1667, and that English goods passed without let or hindrance through the Spanish ports. England's trade and dynastic interests meant that it was directly interested in controlling the thorny issue of the succession to Charles II, and if possible imposing outcomes that would be to its own benefit.

Succession, war and shifting trade positions

The succession and war changed everything. The diplomatic game played out in Europe in these years in anticipation of the succession to the Spanish throne after the long-awaited death of the infirm Charles II is well known. According to the British Ambassador, Stanhope, the king was already very sick in 1695, and in June 1698 he feared he was dying after further bouts of illness.[90]

After two days of conversations with the Count of Oropesa and the Cardinal of Toledo, Charles II declared his nephew the Elector of Bavaria as his heir in writing at a secret meeting of the Council of State on 14 November 1698. Twelve days later, on 26 November, Stanhope believed this was only probable based on the information provided by his spies ('my intelligencer was not caertin [=certain] w[h]ether he named the Prince of Bavaria'), but two weeks later, on 10 December, he has certain ('all my intelligencers agree').[91] This wholly unexpected manoeuvre was attributed to a private pact between Charles II and the Elector of Bavaria, and its expected consequence was war with France, for which Spain was woefully unprepared in the opinion of the English ambassador:

> that has incouraged this court to make so bold a stepp and so likely to engage them speedly in a war with France in a time they are so wholly unprovided...

Stanhope expected England to support the German candidate against France by sending an army of 20,000 English, Dutch and Bavarian soldiers to Portugal, where they would be joined by 1,000 local men and would proclaim the Elector of Bavaria the heir to the throne in Madrid under the protection of the English fleet, imposing his claim on the French and his other opponents.[92]

The English narrative bears witness to the attention with which they followed the events of the succession. However, to provide further detail would only be to embark on a tedious litany of doubts, intrigues, cavils, secret agreements and diplomatic conspiracies. The final outcome was that Charles II named the Archduke Charles of Austria as his successor, but then on his deathbed suddenly chose Louis XIV's candidate, Phillip Duke of Anjou, the future Phillip V as his heir under the guidance of his counsellors. The ensuing War of the Spanish Succession (1700–1715) eventually settled a raft of new questions arising from the changes that had taken place in European politics since the end of the Thirty Years' War.

The conflict was partly an international and partly a civil war. Its political and military course are well known, and there is no need to go into detail here. However, there is one matter that needs explaining. In an international context of feudal monarchies, in which the marriages of kings and princes were a diplomatic instrument used to establish positions from which to make gains when realms and estates were bestowed on a monarch's heirs, wars of succession were to some extent natural, and war and diplomacy were intimately linked. However, time had changed this once immutable reality. In the seventeenth century, major states like the United Provinces of the Netherlands had emerged, which were not ruled by a king, and some monarchs, notably the King of England, did not wield absolute power. Above all, in some nations the economic interests of the elites had gained as much weight in foreign policy as the dynastic interests of their princes. While wars of succession continued until the mid-eighteenth century, at least until the War of the Austrian Succession, other purely mercantile and colonial conflicts like the Seven Years' War also occurred, as well as intermediate campaigns fought ostensibly over questions of succession in which economic affairs played at least as important a role as diplomatic interests.

The War of the Spanish Succession was one of these. Sandwiched between international dynastic interests and fratricidal local quarrels, was an intermediate level in which the belligerents sought to settle a decisive economic question: would it be the British or the French who would finally achieve a position of dominance in Spain's domestic market? The British already had a firm foothold in Portugal, whence they could export their goods throughout the Iberian Pensinsula, and they now sought to further their ambitions in Spain by supporting the Archduke Charles of Austria in the hope that his victory would not only bolster their already sound commercial position in the Spanish interior, but would also allow them to influence and subordinate the incipient Catalan manufacturing interest to their export strategy. On the other side, France supported the future Phillip V de Bourbon, hoping to improve its own commercial position and to leverage the dense social networks which its subjects had formed in regions like Aragon, Castile and Andalusia, establishing a solid presence in wide swathes of rural Spain, many of the country's cities and in the Court of Madrid.

The commercial interests of France and Great Britain thus played a key role in the war from the very outset. Shortly after the death of Charles II in 1701, the new extraordinary envoy from England, Francis Schonenberg, informed London that it had been proposed to ban the import of English baize 'pour favoriser le débit des étoffes de France. . .', and more importantly that the Duke de Harcourt, the new secretary to King Phillip V of Spain, was secretly planning with the French and Spanish Catholics to create a *Real Compañía de Comercio* in Spain in order to exclude the Protestant English and Dutch:

> Il est vrai que plusieurs commercants françois appuyés de quelques marchands anglais et flammands qui s'étant rendus catholiq[ue]s romains et se trouvant naturalisés en ces royaumes, en ont épousé l'animosité contre les puissances protestantes; ont formé l'idée d'une Société de Commerce à l'exclusion principalement des autres anglois et hollandais dont elle avrait de ruïner entièrement le commerce [anglais]. Le projet en a mesme été présenté au duc de Harcourt mais ce ministre n'ayant pas allors jugé à propos d'allarmer dans un point si sensible et l'Angleterre et l'Estat des Provinces Unies en mesme temps, trouva plus convenable d'en suspendre encore l'exécution, et de ne travailler que furtivement par des détours obliques à la ruine du l[eu]r commerce, à fin d'y réussir plus seurement. Il ne peut point que les sujets commercants des ces deux puissances se flattent; la France conjure fortement contre leurs négoces, et la perte en est inévitable si elles ne la détournent par des moÿens vigoureux et efficaces, ainsi que je l'ai écrit et répété.[93]

This testimony manifests the continued use of religion by the English to explain commercial competition between French, Flemish and English (probably Irish) Catholics on one hand and English and Dutch Protestants on the other, and it also reflects the envoy's real or pretended concern that the former were preparing for a trade war. Not long afterwards, Schonenberg complained of:

> les influences prédominantes de la France, qui tendent de plus en plus à l'entière ruine du peu de commerce que l'Angleterre se conserve encore en Espagne, jointes à l'aveugle dépendance de cette Cour-ci, qui paroit determinée si coûte à sacrifier au bon plaisir de celle de France tout ce qu'il i a de plus sacré dans la foi publique des traités les plus solemnels et inviolables[94]

The envoy exaggerated. English trade in Spain was far from small, but he evidently wished to convey the feeling that his country's interests were beset by the new pro-French rulers of Spain, arguing that their actions were in breach of the international treaties of 1659 and 1667. One thing is not in doubt, however, and that is England's interest in the Spanish domestic market.

War broke out in Spain in 1707 after a series of preparatory actions elsewhere, resulting in victory for Phillip V and his French allies, which brought about considerable changes in the position of both rivals in the Spanish interior market and in the Americas. The war finally ended some years later, producing a new situation, which was enshrined in a series of treaties, comprising the truce and armistice made in Madrid between Great Britain, France and Spain on 1 August and 1 November 1712, which ended hostilities,[95] and the two treaties of Utrecht of 1713–1716 between Great Britain and Spain. The agreements of 1712 are of little interest here because they lack commercial content, but the treaties of 1713–1716 are crucial.

The first Treaty of Peace and Friendship between Great Britain and Spain was signed in Utrecht on 13 July 1713. Its 27 articles were given over exclusively to territorial adjustments, and political and dynastic agreements. Although it did not contain any trade provisions as such, which were left for a subsequent treaty (article 8), it had important repercussions in this area due to the cession of Menorca and Gibraltar and Spanish permission for an English slave factory and monopoly in the Americas.[96]

The second Treaty of Trade and Friendship between Spain and England was made at Utrecht on 9 December and ratified in Madrid on 21 January 1714. It is the more important of the two because it sets out in detail the terms of British trade in Spain and in the Americas, including certain improvements in conditions.[97]

The treaty began by confirming and fully ratifying its predecessor of 23 May 1667, which was copied verbatim into the new document, as well as the royal *cédulas* and orders of 19 March, 26 June and 9 November 1645 and other documents containing petitions and royal concessions granted up to 1695, which together confirmed the continued jurisdiction of the judges conservator for English subjects in Spain (article 1). These documents, from which the English had profited since the mid-seventeenth century, did not form part of the 1667 treaty, but they were subsumed under that of 1713 which afforded them the status of diplomatic instruments, with the consequent benefits.[98]

Article 2 of the treaty granted complete freedom to trade, contract and seek the protection of the courts under the same terms as the most favoured nation (as provided in article 38 of the treaty of 23 May 1667), and the import and export duties applicable to British subjects were set at the lowest rates payable by any other nation. Article 3, meanwhile, established that commissioners appointed by each of the parties would establish a tariff within a period of three months which would unify the duties payable on goods entering or leaving Castile, Aragon, Valencia and Catalonia in the time of Charles II at the lowest rate prevailing:

> contendrá por menor los derechos que en adelante se hubieren de pagar por las mercaderías que se introduzcan o saquen de Castilla, Aragón, Valencia y Cataluña: arreglándolo de modo que se reduzcan a un solo derecho y un solo pago todas las

> diferentes imposiciones que en tiempo del último rey Carlos Segundo se pagaban baxo de varios nombres y en diferentes oficinas o caxas, comprehendidos también en ellos los reynos de Aragón y Valencia y el principado de Cataluña; exceptuando sólo a Guipúzcoa y Vizcaya, de que se hablará después.[99]

The treaty also stipulated that the duties payable in the ports of Puerto de Santa María and Cadiz should not be higher than in the times of Charles II before the war, and likewise in other ports. Also, duties at the ports of Guipúzcoa and Vizcaya and in other places not subject to Castilian laws, which were lower than in Cadiz, were not to be increased but would remain at the same levels existing in the time of Charles II:

> En cuanto a los puertos de Guipúzcoa y Vizcaya, u otros no sujetos a las leyes de Castilla, en los quales en tiempo de Carlos Segundo se pagaban menores derechos que los que se cobraban en Cádiz, o en el Puerto de Santa María, promete su Real Magestad Católica no aumentar por el nuevo arancel los tales derechos en los dichos lugares, pero [=y] que entretanto quedarán como en tiempo de Carlos Segundo. Pero las mercaderías que, después de introducidas en los puertos de Vizcaya y de Guipúzcoa, se llevaren por tierra a los reynos de Castilla o Aragon, satisfarán en el puerto de su primera entrada en dichos reynos los derechos que en tiempo de Carlos Segundo se pagaban allí, o los que se establecieran en el nuevo arancel.[100]

In short, the freedom of trade provided for in the treaty included the important proviso that Spain should simplify its customs duties to create a single tariff, which would not be higher than that existing immediately before the war. Meanwhile, the import and export duties charged at the ports of Guipúzcoa and Vizcaya, which were lower than Castilian duties before 1700, would remain unchanged. The importance of the English demand that the Spanish monarchy should unify customs duties can hardly be overstated. After all, such a measure would have been simply impossible before the War of Succession, because Spain comprised several different territories each with its own local laws and institutions, which the king could control only with difficulty or not at all. The abolition of local laws and the loss of such important territories in trade terms as Flanders had made it possible to address the creation of a Spanish *Zollverein*.

As agreed, the commissioners of both countries met not long afterwards to set tariffs, as reflected in the ratification signed by Phillip V on 21 January 1714,[101] in accordance with which the King:

> [...] ha convenido en suprimir así los diferentes derechos de entrada y salida contenidos en los antiguos aranceles mencionados, como los que pueden haberse impuesto después acá baxo de qualquier nombre y pretexto, y contentarse con uno solo y único derecho, que se cobrará igualmente a la entrada como a la salida del reyno a razón del diez por ciento del valor de todo género de mercaderías, ahora sea que la valuación de ella se haga por peso, por medida, por pieza, o sea por cálculo o estima [...][102]

The same tariffs would be charged in Aragon, Valencia and Catalonia, and goods would be marked with a lead seal,[103] a quittance would be issued, and customs duties and a list of goods showing reference prices would be displayed in public places within a period of three months. In the case of imports made via Vizcaya and Guipúzcoa, duties would be payable only when the goods crossed the frontier with Castile or Aragon.[104]

These agreements were of great importance for trade. Though it may have lost the war, Great Britain thus forced the reorganization of the Spanish customs system, imposing a 10 per cent tariff on goods and the design of a new tariff in collaboration with the local authorities. As we shall see, unified customs duties were not actually created until 1782, but the 10 per cent tariff was applied to imports and exports throughout the eighteenth century.

It may be of interest at this point to follow the tax chain applied to British goods after they had entered Spain. In accordance with article 5 of the Treaty of Trade and Friendship, after paying customs duties merchants could pay the sales taxes known as *alcabalas* and *cientos* either directly at the port of entry or at the point of sale on initial wholesale transactions, and they were not obliged to pay any further taxes of this kind if they could show the pertinent receipts and supporting documents. However, municipal and sales taxes were still payable on retail sales:

> Pero si algún comerciante vendiere por menor sus géneros estará obligado a pagar, baxo de las penas impuestas por las leyes, todas las cargas locales y municipales que por dicha venta se deben y acostumbran pagar, juntamente con los derechos de alcabalas y cientos y otros qualesquiera que hubiese.[105]

This important article was confirmed in the ratification of the treaty, and a period of two months was stipulated for payment of the *alcabalas* and *cientos*. These taxes would again become payable in the event of a second sale of the goods concerned.[106] Accordingly, the Spanish Crown ensured the collection of *alcabalas* and *cientos*, which were payable successively on each transaction. However, the English practised factory trade operating mainly in the wholesale line, so they could probably be sure that they would not be liable for *alcabalas* on second and subsequent transactions, which would be paid by the networks of third parties who carried their wares into the Spanish interior.

Other articles of the treaty notably improved the legal status of the English and the conditions under which they conducted their business. Ships' captains were required to carry two declarations of goods, one for the magistrate responsible for the repression of smuggling and the other for the local customs officer, and an inspection procedure was established under which bales and sacks could be opened once only in the presence of the owner or his factor and the customs officer. Where fraud was suspected, the anti-smuggling magistrates or officers could also be present (article 11). In the case of exports, cargo could be loaded in Cadiz, or other ports, after payment of export duties (article 17). Merchants could reside and freely lease warehouses in Vizcaya, Guipúzcoa and Santander (articles 4 and 14).

Any goods not included in tariffs could not be taxed at a rate higher than if they were (article 9), and most importantly:

> [. . .] si resultare pleyto entre los arrendadores o administradores de las aduanas y el comerciante sobre el valor de algunos géneros quedará al arbitrio de éste dexarlos al arrendador por el precio en que éstos los hubiesen estimado, el cual habrá de pagar luego en dinero de contado, rebaxándose solamente los derechos. Podrá también el comerciante dexar al arrendador o administrador en pago de los derechos parte de dichas mercaderías [. . .].[107]

Accordingly, if any dispute arose over the application of tariffs, or if they were held to be excessive, the English could choose between paying the duty or handing over the goods at the appraised price, which they could collect in cash although they could choose to pay duties in kind. This was a potentially abusive clause. In the early eighteenth century new stuffs were constantly arriving in Spain due both to technological progress and to the development of fashion in textiles. This was the reason for the interminable tariff lists showing unit values and the duty payable, to which new items were frequently added. Furthermore, the prices of these manufactures varied, a factor that was taken into account in various ways. As a result, conflicts were far from uncommon, and in these cases the English could choose the interpretation which best suited their own interests.

Article 15, which improved the legal status of the British, was no less important:

> En cuanto al juez conservador y a los otros [a los] que él hubiera de substituir, concedida esta libertad a otra qualquier nación extrangera, deben gozar igualmente de ella los súbditos ingleses, y en el interín y hasta que se haya dispuesto cosa fixa en esta materia, su Real Magestad Católica dará orden expresa a todos y qualesquier jueces de su reyno [. . .] que en todas las causas de los súbditos ingleses administren justicia y la hagan executar sin delación y sin inclinación, favor o afición a las partes. Consiente el Rey Católico que las apelaciones de las sentencias dadas en causas pertenecientes a los súbditos ingleses, se lleven al tribunal del consejo de Guerra de Madrid, y no a otra parte.[108]

This clause is important not only because it reasserts the exclusive jurisdiction of the judges conservator created in 1645 and confirmed in their powers by the treaties of 1667 and 1713, which extended the system to the Canary Islands,[109] but also because it required any appeals to be heard by the *Consejo de Guerra*. The English merchants were thus accorded military status, and in the eighteenth century this was an advantage, because military justice was more flexible and faster than the ordinary courts. Hence, if an English merchant became embroiled in any civil or commercial suit, he would enjoy certain advantages over his Spanish peers (for example, Catalan merchants could only appeal through the civil courts).

In short, the British obtained facilities of all kinds for their trade, not to mention for quasi legal smuggling, in the trade treaty between Great Britain and Spain signed, together with riders and annexes, in Utrecht on 9 December 1713 and ratified on 21 January 1714. In addition they gained Menorca and Gibraltar, which were ceded in the political treaty of 13 July 1713. Permission to establish a slave factory with monopoly rights was granted in the same year (26 March 1713). The trade treaty then raised their already privileged commercial status and, more importantly in the long run, it forced the new Bourbon dynasty to reform the customs system inherited from the seventeenth century and to establish a new tariff policy.

In the case of France, the treaty of 1659 remained in force. In this case, the explicit and evident dynastic connection made it unnecessary to make any further treaties after the peace of 1712. It was only in 1721, in fact, that France and Spain agreed to commence a policy of alliances in the shape of the *Pactos de Familia* after Phillip V had consolidated his grip on the throne and European policy had been reorganized.

This was the heritage received by Phillip V. Comparing the positions achieved by Great Britain and France in Spain, we may conclude that they were different but equal. The British had established a maritime network of entrepôts for their merchants and bases for their navy, with which the French were able to compete because their relative disadvantage in the creation of triangular trade networks with America and the Orient was offset by their physical proximity to Spain and, above all, by the densely woven trade and social networks built up over time as a result of population pressure in the homeland, their Catholic faith and political circumstances, an asset which the British could not hope to emulate.

4

The Struggle for Spain in the Eighteenth Century

The foregoing analysis of the terms of English and French trade in Spain fixed in the treaty of 1659 with France and the treaties of 1667 and 1713 with England shows the two adversaries equally well-positioned in the early eighteenth century. In this light, we may wonder how the contest developed over the course of what was a very eventful century. Once we understand how the rivals exploited their advantages to develop trade with the Spanish interior and the degree of their successes and failures, we will be in a position to consider how the new Bourbon monarchy may have influenced the course of events by renewing and strengthening the action of the state during the century of the Enlightenment, and how the British and French unexpectedly met with increasingly fierce competition from certain Spanish trade diasporas.

The effects of war on British trade: the dual legal status of the British

The Bourbon party and France won the War of the Spanish Succession (1700–1715), and the party of the Archduke Charles of Austria and England lost. Though this may seem obvious, it should not obscure the fact that events could have gone either way, and we therefore need to remember that a hypothetical victory for the British would have fitted neatly into their plan to control the Spanish market. Hardly had hostilities begun, when England made a brief – and secret – treaty with Archduke Charles of Austria in Barcelona on 10 July 1707, which ratified the treaties made by Philip IV and the treaty of 1667 (article 2) and conferred important privileges on the English in America and in the interior markets of the Iberian Peninsula, allowing them to wait up to six months before paying customs duties (article 4) and export products of all kinds to Spain (article 5), while providing for the two countries to design a new customs tariff, which would entail a maximum charge of 7 per cent of declared value on any goods that were not specifically listed (article 5). This percentage was even lower than the figure finally agreed with Philip V in 1715. Meanwhile, a secret pact between the parties provided for the creation of a mixed Hispano-English Company of the Indies to trade with the Americas; if this company could not be formed, ten English ships per year would be authorized to participate in the trade. The French were to be shut out altogether.[1] All of these privileges – the freedom to import products of all kinds, control of the new tariff, and the low fixed duty on the value of goods declared by the merchant – placed the

Spanish market in the hands of the English, while granting them almost free entry to the Americas and excluding the French. Obviously, the Archduke Charles signed the treaty to obtain English support in the war, revealing that the conflict was more than just a dynastic matter but also concerned control of Spain's metropolitan and American markets.

However, events did not go entirely as planned, and although the English eventually secured a strong position, it was less than they had hoped. After the war, Spain was exhausted and its internal trade needed time to recover. Both English and French diplomatic reports throw light on the situation of commerce, the position of each with respect to the control of trade in the Iberian Peninsula, and the post-war outlook.

Let us begin with the British, who were in principle the losers. In 1715, the envoy extraordinary, Paul Methuen, submitted a long report on the general state of Spain which included a wealth of detail reflecting the disorganization of the country's economy, beginning with the disparities in the taxes charged at each port to finance campaigning. According to Methuen, the priorities were to achieve a unification of tariffs, obtain reparations for all of the robberies and attacks on English merchants (provided for in the treaty of 9 December 1713), and ensure the continuation of the same legal status as had existed in the time of Charles II. In tones of superiority, the ambassador notes that the fiscal chaos at the ports also affects the French and Dutch, and that the French indeed appear to fare worse than the English themselves, even though he surmises an underlying French plan:

> the new impositions on trade are not particular to us alone, the French and Dutch merchants having had at least an equal share of them the first of which are used rather worse than ours or the Dutch. And I see no other reason why the French king should suffer his subjects to be treated as they are in Spain, unless it be that he hereby hopes to render the commerce of other nations in this country impracticable, and consequently to destroy the ancient channel of trade from Spain to the West Indies, in order to ingross it wholly to himself and carry it on directly from France to America.[2]

The idea that the French had instigated the nationalist reaction of the Spanish and were seeking to cripple international trade with the Americas via Cadiz in order to take over via France only displays the English government's anti-French obsession. Nevertheless, there was a grain of truth in Methuen's suspicions. The position of the King of Spain's ministers was not without reason: they had been humiliated on all sides, but especially by the French. When war broke out, the Spanish fleet was almost non-existent, and for almost 10 years it was French warships which shepherded the trade fleets to and from the Americas and patrolled the Spanish coastline, defending it against the English. Spain paid a high price for this service in both political and economic terms. French corsairs had massively penetrated the Americas, and their unlawful trade grew so fast up to 1709 that even the French merchants in Cadiz complained that they could hardly sell anything at American fairs, because when they arrived the markets were already full of goods, especially textiles, brought directly from the metropolis. Moreover, French ships were authorized to patrol and seize cargos from foreign vessels not only along the coast but also in port, allowing smuggling with impunity. Finally, the Treaty of the Pyrenees made in 1659 placed the French under the privileged jurisdiction of their own consuls, and any conflict between them was therefore beyond the authority of the Spanish courts.

All of this was the result of the strategy followed by Louis XIV, who was able practically to impose the decrees signed by the youthful King Philip V through Miguel Juan (or Michel-Jean) Amelot, who was not only the French ambassador but also a minister of Spain (as a member of the *Junta de Gabinete*), thereby subjecting policy to French interests. This hurt not only the interests of Spanish merchants, but also those of the English and Dutch, albeit to a lesser extent.[3]

Amelot himself confirms the truth of the matter, writing in 1708:

> Los continuos informes que me han llegado del Perú y Nueva España de [=sobre] la casi total ruina del comercio y de los derechos del Rey Católico, por medio de la abundancia de mercancías europeas que los comerciantes franceses han llevado a las Indias por la vía del mar del Sur, y también del norte, han más que inquietado a los españoles. Todos los que regresan de allí, incluso los franceses, hablan abiertamente del terrible desorden en el que ha caído todo. Entre los sufridos deberes de que estoy encargado, puede [=puedo] asegurar a Su Majestad que este es el que más dolores me causa, conociendo la justicia de las quejas contra nosotros, y viendo que lo que podría asegurar la grandeza del rey de España y traer una estrecha unión entre las dos naciones se vuelve completamente inútil para Su Católica Majestad . . . [la culpa es de] la licencia de nuestros mercaderes franceses, quienes por su insaciable codicia han hallado el medio de traer la ruina al comercio más rico del mundo.[4]

Amelot's testimony is correct, but it is more than a little doubtful that all of the blame for the ruin of the American trade lay with the French merchants, whether individually or acting in companies, for the ministers of Louis XIV had in fact expressly upheld this policy of commercial penetration. The question, then, is to what extent the King of France may have acted following only the personal whims and proposals of his noble counsellors. It is hardly likely that he would have followed such a policy without any say on the part of France's merchants, whose pressure groups also had a voice at the court of Versailles. Amelot was himself fully aware of their opinions and interests, having served as president of the *Conseil du Commerce*.[5] This casts some doubt on the conventional idea that commercial interests took pride of place in England's foreign policy after the Glorious Revolution, but that French policy was driven primarily by dynastic and feudal concerns and that trade was very much a secondary concern. To put it bluntly, this is an overstatement. The massive arrival of French merchants in the Americas suggests a very different scenario.

The situation changed after 1709, when Louis XIV withdrew the support of French troops and counsellors, a move which prompted the airing of grievances and a flurry of decrees designed to curtail Gallic impunity. These were the very measures that the English ambassador exaggeratedly described as humiliations of the French and other foreigners in his report of 1715 cited above.

However, war and the protection of French commerce certainly hurt both British and especially Spanish trade. The British ambassador's version points up the impoverishment caused by the conflict in the Spanish interior, the heavy burden of taxes and the collapse of English and Dutch trade, supplanted by the French.

> The kingdom is certainly in a much worse condition then [=than] can be well expressed, exhausted of every thing that is necessary towards its wellfare or defence, and particularly of men and money. The first of those wants has been gradually increasing for these two hundred years since the discovery of America, but the want of money which is occasioned by the loss of their trade with Great Britain and Holland during the late war, and the French having ingrossed that of the West Indies to themselves for these ten years past, was never more plainly seen or sensibly felt than now.
>
> The common people are in the outmost misery, of which I was an eye witness in my journey from Cadiz hither. Tho[ugh] I came only through that part of Spain which is the richest and most fertile of any. They have been oppressed with very heavy taxes and much more to since the peace, for it seems the Court did not think it their interest to lay such heavy burdens on them during the war; and the *donativos* which have been demanded have been so great and raised by soldiers with so much rigour, that many, after having sold all they had in ye world to pay them, are forced to enter into the army for bread, and live [=leave] their wives and families to starve at home.
>
> Most of the Grandes and those who were of the noblest blood and greatest fortunes in Spain are reduced to a more miserable condition in proportion than that of the common people. They had formerly the privilege to being exempted from all manner of taxes and a great part of their estates consisted in *juros* or [=of] a perpetual interest which they received out of some of the revenues of the Crown that were appropriated for that purpose. These *juros* since this King's coming to the Crown have been reduced to one fourth part of what they received before, and they do not know how long even will be paid [to] them. As to their estates in land, they are now equally taxed with those of their men, and not only so, but when the money the Court proposes to raise out of any Province falls short by the inability of the poorer sort to pay it or any other accidents, the summ [=sum] must be made good out of the estates of the nobility on those parts.[6]

The financial ruin of the nobility mentioned by the British envoy extraordinary was an important issue, resulting from the action taken by Philip V on acceding to the throne to reduce the interest paid on *juros*, an early form of (perpetual) public debt issued by the monarchy since the sixteenth century, which was slashed to just a quarter of the interest paid before the War of Succession. This had dire effects for the Castilian nobility, many of whom held debt of this kind. Interest on the *juros* was payable in cash and their incomes therefore fell proportionately, which would certainly have caused a sharp contracting in luxury spending, especially in Madrid. As we shall see, the interest on *censos* (a kind of perpetual loan secured against property) was also cut from 5 per cent to 3 per cent, among other reasons so that town councils could continue borrowing to pay war contributions. The resulting contraction in the incomes of the nobility in turn obliged their creditors to negotiate reductions in the principal on their *censos.*

> respecto de que la calamidad de los tiempos ha minorado el valor de las haciendas redituables, no habiendo alguna que produzca el rédito o frutos que antes (...) y que muchos acreedores censualistas (...) han minorado los réditos de los censos asegurando su paga con la moderación[7]

The war had, then, caused a sharp deterioration in consumption and trade in the Spanish interior. Furthermore, those among the nobility who had not fought on the side of the Bourbons had lost their civil and military offices at court. Among the impoverished noble houses that had been politically side-lined in this way, Methuen mentions the Duke of Medina Sidonia and the Marquis de Leganés,[8] although they were not alone.

The recurrent reports[9] explaining the difficult situation of English trade in Spain and the predominance of the French are undoubtedly true, but the situation did not last long. In 1713, the British made the highly favourable Treaties of Utrecht, which granted them the right to establish a new slave factory in the Americas, and in 1715 they obtained the first licences for two ships to trade directly with the Spanish domains across the Atlantic without passing through Cadiz. Trade once again became the predominant theme of British correspondence that same year, hardly had peace been made. The numerous instructions and papers which the envoy extraordinary, Paul Methuen, received from Secretary of State Stanhope, not to mention the voluminous papers he left to his successor Geoffrey Bubb on 31 August 1715, show that England was once again receiving full information on its trade in the Iberian Peninsula. Its informants were made up of the network of consuls and the numerous British merchants acting in concert with the diplomatic service.[10] The merchants and embassy together formed a powerful lobby in Madrid, sending continual memoranda and petitions to the King of Spain. The only notable absence was that of the British merchants in Barcelona, at the time still a city at war. In 1715 the British community there consisted of four merchants and the consul, although there were a number of other temporary residents.[11]

The English suffered setbacks in some ports. In Bilbao the new tax on tobacco ended a substantial part of their trade,[12] and much the same also happened in Cadiz and other parties. The British in Bilbao lost their dominant trading position to local Basque merchants or 'townes men' according to a contemporary source.[13]

Shortly afterwards, Methuen sent a memorandum in French to Cardinal del Giudice demanding fulfilment of the favourable terms agreed in the peace and trade treaties of 1713–1715, including ratification of the privileges and concessions granted to British merchants under the treaty of 1667, the limitation of taxes to the levels existing during the reign of Charles II, and the continuation of the system of judges conservator with the same privileges as had formerly existed:

> [...] que la nation française, qui a un commerce considérable avec ce royaume, a toujours fait et continue encore de le faire entièrement sur le même pied, n'ayant point d'autres traités de commerce qui subsistent entre la Couronne d'Espagne et

> de France que ceux qui ont été faits ou devant le tem[p]s du Roy Charles Second, ou durant le Règne de ce Prince [...][14]

Once again, we find here a comparison with the French. Furthermore, the treatment received by the British should be equal to that accorded to the Dutch under article 17 of the Treaty of Peace and Trade made on 26 June 1714 between Spain and the States General of the United Provinces.[15] Meanwhile, the reinstatement of the judges conservator, whose jurisdiction had been interrupted by the war, had become a key objective, because litigation against English merchants was heard directly by the *Consejo de Guerra* at this time.

Discussing the matter of changes in the land border with France, the diplomat Geoffrey Bubb reveals that the Basque provinces were now seen as being all one with Castile, because the interior customs posts between the two territories had been removed[16] and only port customs remained. He claims that the situation was similar to that of lands belonging to the Crown of Aragon, where internal customs posts were also being removed:

> [...] as the country has entirely chang'd its constitution, we cannot expect that the king will give the people that he has conquer'd the same privileges again, out of a compliment to our merchants; so that I suppose, as Aragon, Valencia and Catalonia, make at present a part of the Crown of Castille, so their commerce must be reduc'd to the standard of Cadiz; and as the quality of the effects traded for in all those provinces cannot be the same with that of Cadiz, I suppose that tariff would be defective in the other ports, and new must be made; for those now in being cannot serve because now all the duties must be paid at once, where as before one part was paid at landing in the Provinces & the rest at the entrance into Castille, which custom houses are now taken away.[17]

This testimony clearly shows that the war and the ensuing reorganization of customs had allowed the British to begin the negotiation of new tariffs, which were to include a single port tax for all products, by 1713. Until then, the duties on merchandise imported into Castile from the ports of Vizcaya, Guipuzcoa, Catalonia and Valencia, and over the highland passes into Aragon, had differed because they passed more than one customs post, first at the port (or pass) itself and then further inland on their way into the interior.

Methuen's and Bubb's accounts reveal their interest in the matter, although not how it was negotiated. As we have already mentioned in connection with the trade treaty of 1713, the British demanded a simplification of tariffs and sought to unify Spanish customs duties, reflecting the political weakness of Philip V's new monarchy at the end of the War of Succession. All of this has a bearing on the events unfolding when the Enlightenment government of Spain sought to develop a truly independent trade policy.

Geoffrey Bubb's report was despatched to London together with spies' copies of letters penned by two Spaniards (probably royal functionaries), describing a veritable invasion of French ships and manufactured goods in America as a result of the war and anticipating official measures to moderate their presence[18] (which had in fact been even greater six years earlier). Sooner or later, the British expected to make themselves indispensable as a counterweight:

> I have some reasons to beleive that this court is resolv'd to treat the French very indifferently everywhere, which considering the present situation of Spain is very odd policy, but must of necessity, sooner o later, throw them more into our hands, and I fancy they are capable here of taking a resolution of driving the French out of the Indes, upon encouragement from his Majesty, if they cannot get rid of them by other means [. . .].[19]

This would open up new opportunities for British trade in Spain.

All of this shows, in my opinion, that the British indeed planned to penetrate the Spanish interior market further; that British diplomacy was moved to a great extent by what the French were doing; and that in this situation, the Spanish monarchy had little chance of halting the spread of British and French trade networks. Meanwhile, there is absolutely no evidence that the British had any intention of changing their factory system in order to enhance their activity in the interior. This strategy was ideally suited to the American colonies, where large profits could be made quickly, as the English themselves recognized, but it was less effective in Spain itself, where the French were able to dominate the market among other reasons because they had their own commercial networks.

The British may have sought to establish their own social networks in Spain, but this possibility, if it existed, did not prosper for reasons of religion. As Protestants they were viewed with aversion by the Spanish monarchy, which had been a standard-bearer in the defence of Catholicism and remained an apologist of religious intolerance. The Jews had been expelled in 1492, and in 1558 they were specifically banned from entering Spain on pain of death[20] (a penalty that stayed for centuries). Since at least 1623 only Catholics had been allowed to immigrate.[21] This prohibition was made more specific in the early years of the eighteenth century: Philip V banned all non-Catholic English and Dutch nationals from residing in Spain by a royal decree of 16 April 1701 and a *bando* or edict of 16 June 1703.[22] British merchants were nevertheless able to operate in Spain as non-residents protected by the specific rights granted under the treaties. However, they enjoyed none of the rights or entitlements of subjects of the King of Spain.

This matter requires some further explanation. The English were not the only British nationals in Spain in 1715. There were also numerous Irish, who had fled to Spain to escape the English colonization of Ireland and religious strife. As Catholics and enemies of the British monarchy, their activities were a source of concern and were closely watched by the embassy in Madrid:

> Amongst the many forreigners that are employed in this King's service, which are chiefly Italians, French, Flemmings and Irish, the last have not the smallest share in employments and favour of court. There are five batallions of foot and two regiments of dragoons entirely of that nation, besides a great number of other

> officers and soldiers who are dispersed amongst the Spanish troops. You cannot well conceive the great inveteracy these gentlemen shaw on all occasions against their own country, his present Majesty and all the Royal Family. They are so little concerned to hide it that almost every day produces some new monstruous lie or story of their inventings against His Majesties Sacred Persons or the present establishment of the Crown, which [being] sho [=so] ridiculous in themselves do a great deal of mischief here amongst these ignorant and credulous people. For they had so possessed the court that Gr[eat] Brittain would inmediately declare war against Spain as as soon as they heard of Her late Maj[es]ties death, that they expected it every day, and were very surprized when they received His Maj[es]ties letters notifying His accession to the crown, to the King of Spain.[23]

Relatively little was known about the Irish presence in Spain until recently, though much has been learned in the last few years.[24] Catholic Ireland was one of the parts of Europe which began to produce a population surplus in the sixteenth century along with southern Italy, Scotland, the mountains of Switzerland and the Atlantic north of Spain, and in the context of the Counter-Reformation the Spanish monarchy found in the Irish a natural ally against England, especially after the Battle of Kinsale in 1602 (according to the Gregorian calendar, or 1601 in the Julian calendar, which was still in use in Great Britain at this time). Like other European monarchies, both Catholic and Protestant, the Spanish employed mercenaries, in this case to swell the ranks of their army in Flanders. Some 6,500 Irishmen served between 1586 and 1622, forming *national* companies and *tercios*. The mercenaries were recruited mainly from among the Irish poor, but there were also some nobles, who were greatly prized by the Spanish for their loyalty, which was rewarded in 1688 when they were admitted to all political and military offices belonging to the monarchy. These nobles also brought with them followings of peasants from their own lands, who tended to maintain the client–patron relations existing in the home country in the Spanish army. By emigrating in this way, nobles and vassals alike were exiled and could never return home, so that many had nowhere to go when their service ended and eventually drifted to Madrid.[25] The presence of Irish veterans at the Court provided the motive for the foundation of the *Hospital de San Patricio de los Irlandeses* in 1635,[26] while the repatriation of garrisons after the War of Succession led to the presence of five battalions of Irish foot and two regiments of dragoons in the capital. Some of these Irish émigrés became important politicians, and the chief among them, Ricardo Wall, was the mentor of leading Enlightenment figures like José Grimaldi, Rodríguez Campomanes, the Count de Aranda and Manuel de Roda.[27]

Hence it is possible that some Irish émigrés may have engaged in Anglo-Spanish trade, although they would in any event have been few in number.[28] They were enemies of the English, professing a different religion, and mutual distrust would have made any significant commercial activity unlikely. It is even more improbable that the Irish would have maintained mass connections with the English, who tended to operate through retail networks formed principally by Spanish and Portuguese traders.

The differing legal statutes applicable to resident and non-resident British nationals in Spain raises another question that cannot be ignored. The royal decree of 16 April

1701 mentioned above granted rights of residence to English and Dutch Catholics who had lived in the country for at least 10 years or who were married to Spanish women:

> [. . .] con la expresión de que los de una y otra nacion que fuesen católicos no deben gozar de otros algunos privilegios expresados en los capítulos de paces con aquellas naciones, reputándose en todo como mis vasallos.[29]

Furthermore, the *bando* of 16 June 1703 required English and Dutch Catholics who had been resident for 16 years or less and had no 'correspondence' with their home country to submit a certificate issued by their parish priest to the local magistrates.[30] This means that any such residents were by definition prohibited from conducting any wholesale commercial business abroad.

This enshrined the existence of two separate legal statutes. On the one hand, non-residents and residents of less than 10 years benefitted from the trade privileges granted under the treaties of 1667 and later 1713, while those who had been resident for more than 10 years could become naturalized Spaniards, but only if they could show that they were Catholics and swore that they had no 'correspondence or communication with the nations or vassals of crowns that are the enemies of Spain' (see note 30). Hence, they could not attain the status of residents if they traded with their compatriots.

In this light, it might be wondered what incentives could have existed for the English to extend their commercial networks from the ports into the interior. If the treaties of 1667 and 1713 granted English merchants such broad privileges, why should they have wished to change? The edicts issued at the start of the war would have discouraged any English merchant permanently resident in a Spanish port, or who was merely married to a Spanish woman, from converting to Catholicism whether out of conviction or convenience in order to become naturalized, which would have allowed him to hold public office and even become a functionary of the king, but would also have obliged him to give up his business. This measure, then, effectively strangled any possibility that British nationals like the Irish and English Catholics might have formed communities of any kind in Spain. It explains why it remained so difficult in the eighteenth century (in reality, why it became even more difficult) for communities of British residents to form and spread the factory trade of the ports throughout the interior of the Iberian Peninsula. Any British nationals in the interior were Catholics, and if they maintained any contact with the merchants at the ports, who were Anglicans, they risked serious penalties. As merchants, they could have no relations with Great Britain. The French, however, continued to enjoy the opportunity for contact with their homeland, and it will therefore be of interest next to examine how they achieved a position of ascendancy over the British in trade with the Spanish interior.

The legal status of the French

The years between 1686 and 1709 were a favourable time for the expansion of French trade, and we have already mentioned the circumstances which allowed them to penetrate Spain's American colonies en masse during the war. Meanwhile, the abolition of the local laws or *fueros* of Aragon and Catalonia had resulted in the disappearance of institutions with the legislative capacity to impose protectionist measures, and as we shall see below, the Spanish monarchy had gained full control over those territories' Pyrenean frontiers with France. When French trade in Spain was at its peak in 1709, the *envoyé extraordinaire* of the King of France, Jean Louis Dusson, Marquis de Bonnac, described the two main avenues for commercial penetration of the interior as the Cadiz route, running through Andalusia and southern Castile, and the Bayonne–Navarre route to Castile and Aragon. Exports of wool, mainly from Castile and Aragon, were made mainly through Navarre.

> La principale entrée de ce commerce [français] se fait par Cadix pendant la paix, ou nous portons par le moyen de nos vaisseaux beaucoup de manufactures de France qui se distribuent en suite dans les villes de l'intérieur. Ce même commerce a une autre entrée de terre par la Navarre d'où nous introduisons nos marchandises en Aragon et en Castille; par cette même entrée, nous retirons les laines de Castille et d'Aragon qui tombent à Bayonne pour être ensuite voiturées en France par mer ou par terre et fournies aux manufactureurs que fabriquent les drapeaux.[31]

When Bonnac wrote his report in 1709, the Castilian customs posts, where the main duties on products imported overland were paid, were on the borders of the Basque provinces and Navarre.

The *envoyé extraordinaire* further reveals that customs revenues had been assigned to a new tax farmer on 1 January 1705, who had requested the Spanish exchequer or *Consejo de Hacienda* to create a new duty. This was done by friends of the tax farmer assigned the revenues, who was without doubt Navarrese. To do so 'ont commis le juge des traites et le Directeur du Boureau de Vitoire, gens devoués au fermier et assez gages'.[32] The effect had been that the tariffs charged on French manufactures had doubled and even tripled. However, the French merchants in Madrid had protested, and the tariffs had been reduced again in early 1706. A new tariff was created on 16 September 1709,[33] reflecting the power of French interests.

The French merchants' room for manoeuvre began to shrink towards the end of 1709 after Louis XIV withdrew his declared political support for Philip V. However, this decline was a matter of degree which cannot be easily spelled out, although my impression is that their influence shifted from overwhelming to merely enormous. The Spanish customs authorities were quick to exploit the change, however. Complaints against the French merchants and their consuls multiplied, and a royal decree was issued on 30 October 1709 prohibiting foreigners from using bills of exchange,[34] which would obviously have greatly hampered wholesale trade in Madrid. The response of the French merchants in Madrid was to form a Corps des Commerçants before their judge conservator, Pascual Villacampa Pueyo,[35] and 'in their own name and in that of all *Corps des Commerce* of the [French] nation' they submitted a memorandum to the *envoyé extraordinaire*, the Marquis de Blecour, listing the privileges to be defended against 'the procedures and innovations essayed on the orders of the governor of the Royal Council of Castile'.[36]

Other anti-French measures were taken at the regional level. For instance, an order of 11 January 1710 raised customs duties on French goods entering Aragon by 5 per cent;[37] export duties on Aragonese wool were increased from 2 to 4 *reales* per *arroba* (approximately 25 lb.); and an order of 5 April 1710 repealed an earlier decree which had exempted French nationals who had settled in Aragon from the payment of extraordinary war taxes.[38] Until then, the settled and naturalized *franceses españoles* had benefitted from tax privileges in the Kingdom of Aragon, a region that had been sorely affected by the war. There can be only one explanation for this: France had imposed this exceptional treatment in September 1708, shortly after the abolition of the Aragonese *fueros* (June 1707), because it was in its interest at that moment to treat the Hispano-French population as its own nationals. Temporary French migrants and those who had settled in cities like Zaragoza maintained close ties with each other. Many were carriers, pedlars, tinkers, artisans and chapmen who sought the support of other French residents in the Spanish interior.

All of this eventually led the Spanish authorities to question who should actually be considered French and who should not. The question of naturalization will be discussed below, but for the present we may note that the requirements to acquire the condition of resident had already begun to change. In 1712, the legal status of the French was brought into line with new criteria determining residence:

> [. . .] todos los franceses casados con españolas teniendo bienes raíces y haviendo vivido diez años de continua habitación en España, o eserciendo en estos reynos oficios reservados por las leyes a los naturales de ellos, deben contribuir[39] respecto a goçar muchas prerrogativas de españoles, como también deben ser considerados como naturales (aunque no tengan bienes raíces) los franceses de oficios mecánicos que se huvieren casado con españoles y vivido diez años continuos en estos reynos.[40]

These lines reiterate the requirement for 10 years' residence demanded of the English, but there is not a word of religion. It was assumed that the French were Catholic.

The residence criteria applied to French nationals who had settled in Spain were more important to both governments than in the case of the English, because the French were numerous and also because they paid taxes. Some of the *franceses españoles* were involved in commerce, but there were also many, as we shall see, who practiced manual trades or worked as day labourers, forming more or less integrated communities. Their statute allowed them to engage in occupations that were closed to other foreigners, and not a few of them continued to speak French (at least in certain activities) and were in contact with their families and compatriots beyond the frontier. However, they were not permitted to occupy municipal office, and they owed no loyalty to the King of Spain. Those of them who became officially resident fell under the jurisdiction of the Spanish courts and they were required to pay taxes like anybody else. These were both important matters in times of war, but they would become even more so in the ensuing peace.

Between 1711 and 1716, the rulers of Spain undertook a legal reform (which was also related with the Hispano-British and Hispano-Dutch Treaties of Utrecht) that eventually determined the legal status of the French in Spain, affecting not only the merchants and financiers of Cadiz and Madrid, but also the French emigrants resident in the interior, who were far more numerous. In 1711, the new principal minister of the *Junta de Gabinete*, Baron de Bergeyck, tried without success to have any French national who had lived in Spain for a period of just one year considered settled or *resident*, while a decree of 1712 exempted French nationals from extraordinary (war) taxes provided they were not resident. In March 1714, the Spanish government formed a special commission including French merchants and consuls to consider the matter,[41] and a decree of 8 March 1716 issued in consultation with the *Junta de Extranjeros* established the conditions defining residents and mere transients. In view of its importance, we may cite this decree in full:

> Circunstancias que deben concurrir en los extrangeros para considerarse por vecinos de estos reynos.
>
> Debe considerarse por vecino, en primer lugar qualquier extrangero que obtiene privilegio de naturaleza; el que nace en estos Reynos; el que en ellos se convierte a nuestra santa fe católica; el que viviendo sobre sí, establece su domicilio; el que pide y obtiene vecindad en algun pueblo; el que se casa con muger natural de estos reynos, y habita domiciliado en ellos; y si es la muger extrangera, que casare con hombre natural, por el mismo hecho se hace del fuero y domicilio de su marido; el que se arrayga comprando y adquiriendo bienes raíces y posesiones; el que siendo oficial viene a morar y exercer su oficio; y del mismo modo el que mora y exerce oficios mecánicos, o tiene tienda en que venda por menor; el que tiene oficios de concejo públicos, honoríficos, o cargos de qualquier género que sólo pueden usar los naturales; el que goza de los pastos y comodidades que son propios de los vecinos; el que mora diez años con casa poblada en estos reynos; y lo mismo en todos los demás casos en que conforme a derecho común, reales órdenes y leyes adquiere naturaleza ó vecindad el extrangero, y que según ellas está obligado á las mismas cargas que los naturales, por la legal y fundamental razón de comunicar de sus utilidades; siendo todos estos legítimamente naturales, y estando obligados a contribuir como ellos; distinguiéndose los transeúntes en la exoneración de oficios concejiles, depositarías, receptorías, tutelas, curadurías, custodia de panes, viñas, montes, huéspedes, leva, milicias, y otras de igual calidad: y finalmente, que de la contribución de alcabalas y cientos nadie esté libre; y que sólo los transeúntes lo estén de las demás cargas, pechos o servicios personales, con que se distinguen unos de otros; debiendo declararse por comprehendidos todos aquellos en quienes concurran qualquiera de las circunstancias que quedan expresadas.[42]

This edict regularized a situation of residence that had little to do with the legal status of the English, who were untouched by the measure, since they had not formed any communities in the interior of Spain and the legal statute recognized in the peace and trade treaties of 1659, 1667 and 1713–1714 applied to the merchants in the ports. The legislation was concerned rather with the situation of more or less settled foreigners living in the interior, who were mostly French and numbered upwards of 60,000. In the seventeenth century, the legislation applied to these people had consisted of temporary edicts, local ordinances and above all laws emanating from peace and trade treaties that were in no wise designed for them.

Under a decree of 8 March 1716, all those who were Catholics, had been born in Spain and were legally resident (or who held office as town councillors, or whose communal rights had otherwise been recognized) became *vecinos* or townsmen, as did those who were married to Spanish women (or men) and had their place of abode in Spain, those who had lived in the country for at least ten years, and those who had acquired property, practised a manual trade or kept a shop. All others were considered transients. This distinction had both legal and fiscal effects, which in the latter case were far-reaching. Everybody was required to pay *alcabalas* and *cientos*, which provided an important source of revenues for the Royal Treasury, but only townsmen or *vecinos* (in the sense of taxpaying, legally entitled citizens), though not transients, were required to pay local taxes (e.g. *sisas* and *pontazgos*).[43]

The Spanish authorities sought to apply the status of *vecino* to the maximum number of French nationals. Years later in 1773, the French ambassador in Madrid informed his government that the legal classification of transients envisaged in the decree of 1716, which was not provided for in either the Treaty of the Pyrenees (1659) or the Treaty of Utrecht (1713), had been applied only to pilgrims and travellers, claiming that periodic protests against the measure had been made by successive French ambassadors. Their argument was that the conferral of citizenship, which implied naturalization, was a legal change of a kind requiring that the subject seek it as a voluntary act.[44] We shall consider the important question of naturalization and immigration policy below.

The order of 8 March 1716 also had other implications. Aside from benefitting Spain in terms of social integration and legal clarity, it also meant that all of the French nationals now deemed to be *vecinos* lost their fiscal privileges and became liable to pay taxes. Of course, nobody wants to pay taxes for the sake of it, and still less so as a foreigner, and the status of *vecino* was now the legal frontier. Accordingly, many temporary French migrants went out of their way to seek treatment as transients in order to duck possible taxes. The complex migratory circuits followed by these itinerants and mule drivers, and the range of their occupations and varied residence status allowed them to escape the fiscal clutches of the Royal Treasury, acting at all times in their own personal interest with the more or less active connivance of other French townsmen. As they occupied prominent positions in certain economic activities in many towns and cities, the alliance between French *vecinos* and temporary migrants may have been a factor in certain social conflicts.

The decree of 1716 was of course applied in a monarchy where the tax system was still far from unified, producing important secondary effects. For instance, *alcabalas* were paid in the Crown of Castile but not in the Crown of Aragon until the abolition of its local legislation in 1707–1711. The distinction between townsmen of French extraction and transients raised complex fiscal issues in a region that was not part of Castile, and was therefore not subject to either *alcabalas* or *cientos*. The first direct tax in Aragon, called the *real contribución*, was designed as an equivalent to the *alcabalas*, which meant that resident French nationals found themselves liable. Many of the most powerful among them were merchants, and as such they were able largely to avoid the *real contribución*, which taxed commercial activities very ineffectively. Logic dictates that the situation would have been similar in Valencia and Catalonia, with some local differences. French merchants were numerous in Valencia and Aragon, as we shall see, and it would seem likely that neither *vecinos* nor transients paid the tax (called the *equivalente* in Valencia) for many years. This could only have raised hackles among those who did have to pay.

The legal effects were likewise considerable. The decree of 1716 was aimed rather at French migrants, whether transient or not, than at the great merchants and traders in the ports, and its primary objective was to oblige them to pay taxes, as is evident from the testimony of French diplomats, who themselves recount that the Spanish authorities' purpose had been to prevent the majority of the French nationals resident in Spain from seeking the protection of their consuls (whose jurisdiction was confined to wholesale merchants), to oblige them to form communities and guilds in the towns where they lived, and to make them pay taxes like everyone else.

> Ils soutinrent qu'ils avoient toujours distingué les marchands en gros que leur commerce ne retient dans les différents ports d'Espagne qu'un temps passager, d'avec ceux qui prennent un domicile dans la ville de ce royaume et qui s'établissent; que ces derniers, soit qu'ils fussent artisans, vendeurs en détail ou autres, n'étoient pas dans le cas d'être protégés par les consuls nationnaux, qu'ils devoient être réputés faire corps de communautés des métiers ou professions qu'ils exerçoient, que ces étrangers ainsi domiciliés avec leur familles auraient toujours été soumis aux imposts de mesme que les sujets du Roy Catholique avec qui ils partageoient les avantages de leur résidence, et que les françois de cette espèce n'avaient commencé à s'en plaindre que depuis peu d'années autorisant par cette conduite les autres étrangers domiciliés en Espagne, à refuser de payer aussy les taxes qu'ils avaient jusqu'à lors portées conjoinctement avec les espagnols. Sur ce principe le Roy d'Espagne rendit pendant le cours du mois de mars 1712 un décret qui établissait clairement cette distinction.[45]

I have not been able to locate the decree of March 1712 referred to in this text, but it is clearly an antecedent of that issued in 1716.

Years later in 1775, the French ambassador in Madrid would himself recognize that the principal effect of the royal decree of 1716 had been to make almost all of the French residents in Spain into *vecinos* (a term equivalent to the French *habitants*) with the result that they had lost their rights under military law and their commercial privileges:

> Les cas dans lesquels les négotiants françois residents en Espagne ne doivent pas jouir du for militaire selon les dispositions d'une cédule de Philippe V de l'année 1716, sont au nombre de 13. Savoir:
>
> 1° Tout étranger qui acquiert le privilège de naturalization dans ces royaumes doit y être réputé et traité comme habitant.

2° Que celui qui est né dans ces royaumes y soit consideré comme habitant et y soit traité comme les autres sujets.
3° Que l'étranger qui se sera converti dans ces royaumes à la foi catholique soit considéré et traité comme habitant.
4° Que ceux qui demeuront dans ces royaumes et y auront établis leur domicile, y soient considérés et traités comme habitants.
5° Que celui qui démande et obtient l'habitation dans ces royaumes y soit considéré et tenu comme habitant.
6° Que l'étranger qui se mariera avec une Espagnole et qui demandera domicile sera tenu pour habitant.
7° Que la femme etrangère qui se mariera avec un natif ou sujet de ces royaumes soit tenue pour habitante et traité comme telle.
8° Que celui qui s'établira dans ces royaumes en y achetant des terres et biens inmeubles soit considéré habitant et comme espagnol.
9° Que celui qui viendra habiter dans ces royaumes et y exercer son métier, soit tenu pour habitant.
10° Que l'étranger qui aura boutique pour vendre en détail, soit réputé et tenu pour habitant.
11° Que l'étranger qui occupe des emplois dans les tribunaux et des charges qui ne peuvent être exercées que par les naturels de ces royaumes, soit traité comme habitant
12° Que celui qui jouira des pâturages et des commodités péculiaires des sujets, soit réputé comme habitant.
13° Que celui qui aura eu maison et un ménage pendants dis [=dix] ans dans ces royaumes, soit réputé comme habitant.

Il est remarqué que la cédule de 1716 n'accorde le for militaire qu'aux françois *transeúntes* [sic, author's italics], et qu'elle déclare que tous ceux qui se trouveront dans les cas prévus par les 13 articles ci-dessous ne doivent pas être réputés *transeúntes* [sic, author's italics].[46]

Despite being something of a rehash of the decree of 8 March 1716, this text is interesting for its end, which clearly demonstrates that the wholesale merchants who competed with the British by sea and in the American colonies were considered transients, which meant that they came under military jurisdiction and benefitted from the protection of their own consuls and judges conservator. The rest of the French residents in Spain, who were far more numerous, enjoyed no such privileges however. This contrast in status between a privileged minority of transients with their own consuls and judges conservator subject to the military jurisdiction, which meant that appeals went straight to the *Consejo de Guerra*, and a majority of resident townsmen consisting of shopkeepers, carriers, tradesmen and servants who paid taxes and were subject to the jurisdiction of the ordinary civil courts did not go unnoticed at the time, although the consequences have remained largely unexplored to date.

At the turn of the eighteenth century, military tribunals were much quicker than the civil courts, and depending on the issue at stake it could be an advantage to be deemed a transient under the military jurisdiction with the added benefit of exemption from taxes, than a taxpaying resident townsman subject to the civil jurisdiction. What was the status of the French migrants from the Auvergne to whom I shall refer below, who would move to Spain to work in the retail trade for three or four years only to return to France, repatriating their earnings in order to buy land and marry in their places of origin? What were the carriers, pedlars and artisans who would wander for years around Spain with no fixed abode? Or that of the transhumant French shepherds who benefitted, according to point 12 of the French ambassador's report interpreting the decree of 8 March 1716, from supracommunal rights of pasture in highland valleys according to the agreements contained in the *pactos de facería* between Spanish and French municipalities? The following pages will endeavour to throw light on these questions, if only in a small way.

The royal decree of 8 March 1716 remained in force until the end of the *Ancien Régime*. Seizures of property belonging to British merchants were regulated in 1724,[47] and the jurisdiction of the British, French and Dutch judges conservator was fixed in 1727. This office was reserved for a Spanish judge, magistrate or *oidor* of the Chancelleries and Courts assigned to hear exclusively cases arising between transient residents belonging to the same nation.[48] Finally, the requirements for the establishment of consuls and vice-consuls, who were considered agents of their nation and enjoyed military status, were regulated in 1765.[49] The legal status of foreigners did not begin to change until 1761, when the third of the Hispano-French compacts known as the *Pactos de Familia* was made. As explained below, the first register of foreigners was made in 1764.[50] Policy became more nationalistic between 1774 and 1778,[51] and intensifying anti-French sentiment after 1791 resulted in the creation of registers of foreigners which included both those who were permanent residents and transients.[52]

In any event, it seems clear that the French diplomatic service, which had proved able to look after migrants' interests during the War of Succession, gradually abandoned a broad swathe of its nationals who lived long-term in a grey area between temporary migration, organized peddling and permanent residence in Spain. This situation was encouraged by the emerging identification of the *homeland* with the state in France and other European nations, a development which excluded those who opted to seek their livelihoods beyond its bounds. By 1738 the French state was interested mainly in protecting the merchants who exported manufactured goods and returned with Spanish silver, but those who settled yet wished to remain French were largely ignored:

> [. . .] ne convient de protéger que ceux qui viennent s'établir en Espagne et qui après un certain espace de temps sont en situation de remporter en France les biens qu'ils y ont amassés; mais pour ce qui est de ceux qui s'éstablissent dans le pays, s'y méritent, achètent des biens fonds, et un mot, portent tout le caractère de gens qui ont abandonné leur patrie et qui ne longuent qu'à devenir habitants d'Espagne, je ne crois pas qu'ils méritent la protection de France puis que leur génération et leur fortune ne peuvent plus procurer aucun bien à l'Estat; et sont pour l'ordinaire ces sortes de françois renégats à leur patrie qui font de plus de bruit et qui voudroient que toute la France se sacrifiât pour eux, parce que moyennant cela, ils jouïssent du bénéfice de deux estats sans contribuir aux charges d'aucun et se servant toujours d'une jurisdiction contre l'autre, ne soyent soumis à aucune[53]

By this time, France had taken up the gauntlet of British economic nationalism, and not much later the *querelle* or debate over the merchant nobility began, in which it was argued that the aristocracy should change its attitude towards trade because it was at the heart of the balance of power and should be encouraged for the good of the nation.[54] In this way, trade became a matter of patriotism, and it was far from being a secondary issue in a country where the nobility were the depositaries of political sovereignty and guardians of the basic laws to which even the king himself was subject.[55]

This single testimony may not, of course, represent the whole of French political thinking with regard to their émigré compatriots in Spain, but it shows in any event that the broad social spectrum of the emigrants was something real and known. The diplomats were well aware of it and sometimes took it into account. Under the treaties of 1713–1714, the British merchant diasporas in Spain had been confined to two largely unconnected spheres, and only that consisting of the wholesale merchants in the ports was of real significance. However, the royal *cédula* of 8 March 1716 created two classes of French nationals in Spain who were never clearly demarcated in fact, so that the dealings of both the Spanish authorities and population with the French diasporas were often much more complex, changeable and confused than in the case of other groups of foreigners.

In any event, I believe it is clear that the political circumstances of the war had created significant differences between the British and French diasporas. The former were firmly settled in the ports and their trade spread into the interior over intermediary commercial networks. French maritime trade was accompanied by a significant presence of merchants and financiers in Madrid, however, and in addition they were able to reach into every corner of the Iberian Peninsula through their own distribution networks organized from Cadiz, Madrid and the manufacturing areas of the home country itself. French goods arrived in Spain both through the ports and overland across the long Pyrenean frontier, but above all through the Basque provinces and Navarre.

It is also clear that French commerce had by the beginning of the eighteenth century already gained a position of dominance in Spain's interior market which it never lost, combining armed force and diplomacy with the activities of wholesale merchants and the ability of migratory diasporas to penetrate the hinterland.

Comparison of the position of the British and French in Spain thus reveals two very different situations. Great Britain had a powerful merchant diaspora in Cadiz, along Spain's coasts and in the American colonies, and at Utrecht it had succeeded in driving the reorganization of customs tariffs, but its presence in the interior was maintained only through networks of intermediaries. France too had maritime commercial networks, above all in Cadiz, but it also enjoyed three additional advantages: a strong political base with the new dynasty; an extensive network of French emigrants, artisans and merchants in the interior; and a financial elite established in Madrid, which would eventually play a decisive role in the big business of lending to the Spanish Treasury, currency exchange, writing bills of exchange and providing commercial credit. These were not the only reason for the preponderance of French manufactures in Spain for most of the eighteenth century, however. There were others.

The ingredients of French predominance: costs, fashion and the state

One key factor, which we have not so far mentioned, was the capacity for social penetration displayed by the French emigrant community, many of whose members settled in Spain while maintaining close links with the homeland. In 1775, Ossun, the French ambassador in Madrid, re-examined the decree of 8 March 1716, which established the circumstances in which French residents might be reputed *vecinos* or townspeople, noting the numerous cases in which non-resident (i.e. transient) traders might be deprived of their right to the military jurisdiction. According to the marquis, the decree, summarized by himself as cited in the preceding section, had resulted in numerous French citizens who had emigrated in previous decades becoming *vecinos*. These included artisans and shopkeepers (articles 9 and 10), settled residents (article 4) and those who had purchased property (article 8), numerous people who had taken Spanish wives (article 6), and the transhumant shepherds of the Pyrenees who enjoyed communal pasture rights with associations of Spanish highland and valley livestock farmers under the *pactos de facería* (article 12).[56] However, he ignored the poor French migrants, who were not permanent residents and consisted of pedlars, chapmen, day-labourers and small traders who would stay only for a season or for just a few years. For example, the Auvergnese traders, whose case is discussed below, tended to live for a number of years in Spain but marry in France, and they could not become naturalized Spaniards because they were not resident in accordance with article 2, and their children were not born in Spain. Naturalization would have been possible if they bought property, but this they usually did in their homeland. Were they, then, treated as *négociants* or merchants and accorded military status and diplomatic protection? We do not know, but it seems unlikely.

However, there were other more visible non-resident French people in Spain, like the merchants in Madrid. One thing is clear in any event: the order of 1716 encouraged cohesion among those who escaped naturalization, because they formed part of a special class with their own judges, diplomatic protection and military status. They also enjoyed other benefits, such as exemption from taxation and a better legal forum, because Spanish military justice was considerably faster than the civil courts. This meant that contractual non-performance, bankruptcies and cases of default could be resolved more quickly than in the civil jurisdiction which was the only option open to the trade diasporas of the poor French, and of their Galician, Cantabrian, Basque, Navarrese and Catalan peers.

However, the continuous, strong French presence in the Spanish market throughout most of the eighteenth century was also a product of other factors, which deserve examination, including lower wages than those of either the Spanish or the English, superior technology (copied from the British), fashion, and a singular entrepreneurial culture in which the state played a key role. Let us consider each of these factors in turn.

Industrial wages in London were higher in the eighteenth century than in more distant parts of Great Britain like Scotland. However, the price of grain, a basic commodity, was lower, which had allowed an increase in consumption and the development of an internal market. As a consequence, the purchasing power of wages with regard to a staple like wheat was very high. This is, of course, well known and it was noted at the time among others by Adam Smith in *The Wealth of Nations*, which appeared in 1776.[57] Overall, English wages were significantly higher than in other parts of Europe.

In Spain, meanwhile, real wages had risen faster than prices in the early 1600s, and although they fell in the following decades[58] they recovered by some 50 per cent in the second half of the seventeenth century, remaining at that level until the mid-eighteenth century, when they fell in real terms in the face of sharply rising prices.[59]

In contrast, wages in France were lower than in either England or Spain in the eighteenth century, and manufacturing costs were therefore also lower. This was another factor behind the penetration of French goods in the domains of the Spanish monarchy. The English were able to offset their disadvantage in production costs by higher productivity achieved through technological innovations, but these were quickly copied by the French, whose technologies were often ahead of those employed by the Spanish.

Contemporary accounts confirm this. A French report of 1715 discussing opportunities for the penetration of French manufactures noted the scant competitiveness of Spanish stuffs and silks owing to the use of obsolete technologies. The cloth produced in Valencia, Segovia, Valdemoro and Béjar combined different grades of wool poorly in the picking, carding and spinning processes, and fine combing meant that the threads would break during weaving, which obliged masters and weavers to use thicker yarn for strength. Dyeing processes were also poorly executed, and colours were often flawed because the dyes were often badly mixed.[60]

High quality silks (damask, taffeta, satin and medium silk) were made in Madrid and Valencia, but manufacturing techniques were costly: the yarn was thicker because the know-how to make fine thread like that of Lyon did not exist, and the resulting fabrics were both expensive and long-lasting.

Silk workers' wages, another key factor, were also higher than in Lyon, which the French attributed to the 'natural indolence' of the Spanish:

> [...] différence qui vient de la seur [=de sure] de la peresse [=paresse] naturelle des ouvriers de Valence que le maitre fabriquant est obligé a payer beaucoup plus cherement que ne fait celuy de Lyon, [et] ainsi ceux y se sont payés preferés a ceux de Valence.[61]

However, the French diplomats omit a key point: strong French demand for commodities raised costs in Spain. This was recognized in a Spanish report of 1721 on the industrial crisis that had begun even before the War of Succession. The report shows how foreign demand for silk yarn affected prices and drove up costs and, ultimately, prices:

> La pérdida de las fábricas de tegidos [de seda] la ha motivado tam[ié]n en gran parte la extracción de la seda en madeja a reinos extrangeros contra lo prevenido en diferentes pragmáticas r[eale]s, con cuia saca los extranjeros además de no dejar ni los útiles del torcedor alteran y suben los precios de ella [la seda en madeja] y como al mismo t[iem]po introducen y venden con conveniencia sus tegidos, más endebles que los de la[s] fábrica[s] de España [así] se halla el M[inist]ro

> [=fabricante] español que compra la seda a precios subidos por causa del extranjero, precisado a tener atraso en la venta de su tejido [que es] de más ley por no poder costearla [la madeja], y expuesto a abandonar la fábrica.[62]

Exports of wool were also in the hands of merchants who had sufficient capital to purchase the commodity in advance, which drove up prices and put raw materials out of reach of local manufacturers. An official Spanish report of the time complains about:

> [...] el modo con que los extrangeros extrahen la lana ajustándola con los dueños 4 y 5 meses antes del [tiem]po de la esquila aunque sea a precios crezidos por tenerlas aseguradas, contraviniéndose en esto las ordenes reales que mandan que hasta después de 15 días de la esquila no se saquen las lanas al pregón y que estén otros tantos días en los pregones y se avise a las justicias de las ciudades, villas y lugares donde se vendieren para que los fabricantes puedan surtirse [...].[63]

These accounts reveal the power of French (and other nations') mercantile capital in the Madrid wool market, where the owners of the great transhumant flocks sold their produce directly, and in the silk market of Valencia.

After the war ended, the Crown partially recovered control over exports of bulk wool and silk yarn, and manufacturing expanded. The situation of wages, a key factor, did not change until the 1770s, however, when prices rose sharply, depressing real wages in Spain as Hamilton has shown. It was only then that Spanish manufactures began to become truly competitive in terms of costs.

The French consul in Cadiz, Mongelas, filed a revealing report on these structural developments in 1777 in the context of the French foreign ministry's obsession with tracking the country's trade strengths in comparison with Great Britain and with Spanish manufactures. This document describes how the differing relative cost of labour in Europe (meaning France, Great Britain, Germany and Spain) was a key factor underlying measurements of the competitiveness of French fabrics in different markets in general, and in particular in the markets of Spain and America taking Cadiz as the benchmark.

Referring to the increasing competition from toile (linen or cotton cloth) made in Silesia, Saxony and other parts of Germany, he remarks that labour was more expensive than in France and that the prices of these fabrics were rising:

> Ces toiles sont d'une qualité inférieure, cependant chères, mais beaucoup moins que nos bretagnes et autres. Les prix de ces toiles étrangères haussent continuellement. La main d'oeuvre en est chère. Cette augmentation, et leur mauvaise qualité peuvent ajouter à un prochain déscredir [= discrédit?].

In order to compete with the Spanish, it was necessary to develop the cultivation and manufacture of hemp in some of the poorer French provinces, where wages were presumably lower:

> [...] celles où les moyens sont les moins abondants, où le paysan, où l'homme vit malheureusement pour le travail et la commodité de ses semblables, doivent

être celles qui peuvent plûtot anéantir les manufactures d'Allemagne, en les contrefaisant.

Some of these were precisely the provinces whence French emigration and trade networks in Spain originated, and the new manufactures therefore had possible markets with which the producers were already well acquainted:

> La situation de quelques-unes de nos provinces, comme la Franche-Compté, le Limousin, l'Auvergne, et autres, semble frayer à leurs habitants une nouvelle ressource pour améliorer la vie dure qu'ils mènent. Il sérait facile à ces provinces de se livrer à une grande culture du chanvre, d'établir, de former des fabriques, et de les exposer en Espagne en comparaison avec celles d'Allemagne.[64]

Auvergne and Limousin were highland provinces which not only enjoyed excellent natural conditions for growing hemp but also produced demographic and labour surpluses, resulting in low wages.

The text explicitly mentions various types of woollen cloth (baize, *sempiterne* and *camelot*) in a comparison of the saleability of different French and English stuffs in Spain and the Americas, revealing that labour was still cheaper in France around 1777 and that the only reason the English were able to compete with France was that they had access to their own raw materials.

> Les Bayetes ont toujours été un objet décidé en faveur des anglais. Plusieurs de nos villes, Beauvais et Nimes, ont essayé de les contrefaire, [et] elles n'ont pu reussir. Elles n'ont en cela aucun reproche à se faire. Chaque pays a des produits, a des resources à luy seul. Nous avons dans les draps d'Elboeuf, le même avantage que les anglais à l'égard de Bayetes. Les Sempiternes ont eu à peu prés la même sort, mais elles peuvent être imitées et contrefaites dans le Quercy. L'intendant de cette province peut y porter ses regards. Cette branche est une des plus grandes richesses de l'Angleterre, et il ne faut nullement désespérer de la partager avec elle. Notre industrie est égale, et nous avons en retour l'avantage dans la main d'oeuvre. C'est un objet très essentiel auquel le gouvernement doit donner des forces et des encouragements. Nos camelots, surtout ceux de Lille ont un assez bon débit et soutiennent passablement la concurrence des anglais. Ceux de Lille sont tous goûtés aux Indes. Ils commencent à s'y faire connaître, et on doit beaucoup attendre de cette fabrique.
>
> Le plus grand avantage de l'Angleterre est de se fournir à elle même les belles laines qu'elle recolte. Sans cela il luy sérait imposible de soutenir l'etendüe de ces fabriques. La main d'œuvre en est excessivement chère.
>
> Je n'ose approfondir pourquoy nos provinces ne s'adonnent pas avec plus de soin à un entretien considérable des bêtes à laine. L'Espagne récolte les plus belles laines de l'Europe.[65]

The comment in the last paragraph is revealing: the French made enormous efforts to acquire flocks of Castilian and Aragonese merino sheep, which produced the finest wool in Europe, eventually achieving their goal in the Napoleonic Wars. The policy of introducing flocks of Spanish merinos into France was adopted to meet rising domestic demand for woollen draperies and upholstery, counter the improved quality of English cloth and, above all, save the cost of importing wool from Spain. All of this hampered the development of factories to produce fine stuffs in Spain. The *Pacto de Familia* of 1761 included the first measures to facilitate exports of merino sheep, which had been strictly prohibited until that time. The policy of importing sheep was initially developed by the *Intendant des Finances*, Daniel-Charles Trudaine, and it was continued by Turgot as *Contrôleur-Général des Finances* and the new intendant, Jean Charles Philibert Trudaine, a son of the former. Exports took off in the 1790s following the Revolution and the Consulate, and they positively soared after 1800.[66]

A point of note in the text of 1777 cited above is the absence of any reference to a technology gap between France and England. This is probably because Mongelas did not see this lag as a problem, for their tenacious espionage allowed the French to copy English innovations in machinery and manufacturing processes almost as soon they appeared.

This explanation in any event tallies with the analysis of Spanish as compared with French woollens made by García Sanz, who has shown that superfine French stuffs remained highly competitive in late eighteenth-century Castile, because of the favourable price conditions of Castilian wool exports and because French manufacturing processes created a productivity gap at this level of quality. Returns were lower, however, in the case of fine (thread count of twenty-six or less), mid-fine and coarse cloth, because transport costs and customs duties ate up a higher share of the product's total value. According to García Sanz, it was this which allowed a vigorous woollens industry to survive in Castile until after 1800.[67] I believe the same reasoning is also applicable to Aragon, although the Castilian textiles were less competitive in the region, because French stuff benefitted from lower transport costs and Catalan cloth was free of customs duties, which were abolished in the early eighteenth century, and the expanding Catalan trade networks provided distribution channels every bit as good as those of the French.

Referring to the silks (*étoffes de soie*) produced in Lyon, the Cadiz-based consul noted in 1777 that lower French labour costs compared with Spain were a decisive factor, to which he added the quality of French designs, a new but nonetheless important feature. As a result, the Lyon silk industry enjoyed a position of clear advantage in the Spanish market:

> Quoique chaque pays de l'Europe fabrique des étoffes de soye, Lyon peut se flatter d'obtenir en Espagne le débouché le plus avantageux. Les étoffes d'or et d'argent en ont un[e] décidé[e sortie] aux Indes Espagnoles. Cette faveur est düe à l'avantage qu'elles ont de ne connaître aucune concurrence, ainsy que dans plusieurs autres objets de ses fabriques dont cette ville est seule en possession, comme ses Persiennes, ses gros détours, ses rubans riches et autres en dorure. On dirait que cette ville contient une industrie qui n'appartient qu'à ce grand nombre d'ouvriers. Chaque jour, l'invention s'y reproduit. Les goûts y varient avec le renouvellement des saisons et offrent aux yeux du consommateur le désir de se satisfaire. L'imagination féconde des dessinateurs assure une faveur entière aux étoffes de

> Lyon. On ne peut se cacher que les fabriques d'Espagne leur font quelque tort et leur deviendraient plus préjudiciable encore, si le goût et l'agrément étaient joints aux facilités naturelles qui trouvent ces fabriques. La cherté de la main d'oeuvre en Espagne est supplée par les belles soyes que récolte ce Royaume, et en cela nos avantages respectifs son compensés. Il en est de même des galons fabriqués à Séville. Ils portent préjudice à ceux de nos fabriques, mais ceux y ont l'avantage de la nouveauté de l'agrément, et de fournir même aux fabriques d'Espagne, et deux ans après, les desseins et les formes qui ne sont plus de mode en France. C'est ce qui nous doit assurer la preference.[68]

The raw silk of Aragon, Valencia and Granada was of superior quality, and for this reason it was avidly sought after as an export commodity by the French and Catalan trade networks in the eighteenth century. Nevertheless, the key strength of French stuffs in Spain and the Americas, as the text itself remarks, was fashion – *être de mode.* Design was associated with the buyer's self-image and position in society and was not merely a matter of low production costs, and this made it an increasingly important factor in the textiles industry.

The development of fashion in European society was intimately linked with rising consumption of textiles and progressive changes in the use of dress as a means of differentiating social status. A market in clothing had already become established in the sixteenth century, driven by the desire of the common people to dress like their betters despite the sumptuary laws promulgated by both the state and local authorities in an effort to ensure that a person's attire would continue to mark his or her rank, as it always had done. This *consumer revolution* not only brought new garments (stockings, underclothes, the embroidered fabrics and neckerchiefs) in its wake but also a confusion of social status as fashion was progressively taken up by the middle and lower classes in towns and villages across Europe.[69] Consumption depended not only on price, but also on how wearers wished to look and the social image they sought to project. Insofar as it began to depend on design – on what a person had to wear to be somebody – English and French fashion also competed in Europe, becoming for some a badge of belonging to the upper class elites, and for others a way of giving the outward appearance of belonging even when they did not.

The spread of *les modes*, of French fashion, throughout Europe and to Spain in particular, was probably driven by factors which we cannot explore in detail here, such as appreciation of the French in other Catholic countries, the puissance of the Sun King and his successors, and the enormous influence of the Parisian intellectual vanguard in eighteenth-century Europe. Social practices were also an important part of the equation. The cafés and salons, the theatre, the opera and the new sexual conventions of the Parisian urban elites aroused intense interest in garments like silk stockings, lingerie and underclothes in general. Trappings designed for the purpose of social ostentation, like ruffs, neckerchiefs, cuffs, brocades and pinafores, also played a role. By the early eighteenth century, Paris, the showcase of France, had become the capital of sex and fashion, and the French themselves were well aware of the fact. The city not only set new trends in designs and garments, it also invented the idea that fashions must change periodically, and that what was worn in Paris was definitively the latest thing. These ideas – the use of new garments and the renewal of wardrobes *à la mode* – were enthusiastically adopted in Spain.

French fashion dominated Europe until around 1750, when an important change occurred. English fashion, which was influenced by a different political culture from French, increasingly addressed the tastes of the common people, eventually causing a social inversion of taste in Great Britain, so that people began to buy clothes not to ape the upper classes but to identify with each other as a group.[70] Hence, the political differences between a country governed according to a representative, parliamentary system (which progressively raised the prestige of the parliamentarians) and a country ruled by an absolute monarch (where the aristocracy continued to hold sway politically and to enjoy all the privileges of rank) would also have a determining influence in the field of fashion.

The dominance of French fashion in Spain, another absolute monarchy, was clear and lasting, so that English fashion made little headway in the eighteenth century. This is clear from the following testimony, dating from around 1709 in the midst of the War of Succession, in which the special envoy of the King of France in Spain, the Marquis of Bonnac, advised the King of France:

> [...] d'entretenir les Castillans dans le goût de nos modes par ce que ceux qui gouvernent l'Amerique viennent solliciter a Madrid leurs emplois; que pour cela ils ont obligés de se vêtir à la mode de la Cour et portent ensuite dans les Indes leurs habillements semblables aux nostres; de là il s'ensuit que nos draperies, nos soyries, nos dorures et tout ce qui se fait en France par rapport au vestement demeurera nécessaire dans les Indes, qu'il y sera vendu par préférence et que par là les sujets du Roy acquèreront une espèce d'exclusion en faveur de leur commerce.[71]

Mongelas' report, written decades later, reveals that *les modes* consisted of much more than cloth by 1777, but also included haberdashery, jewellery and costume jewellery, silver pins and brooches, fans and other adornments and accessories, huge quantities of which were also exported to the Americas.

> Paris et Lyon sont les seules villes de l'Europe en possession de faire tous les ouvrages que fixent le caprice des femmes, amusent leur caractere et font l'occupation d'une partie de leur vie et de leur existence. Ces bagatelles frivoles rapportent une bénéfice inmense par le prix que ce sere [?] leur attache et nos marchandes de modes ont su mettre à contribution toutes les femmes de l'Europe. Il ne manquait plus d'autre debouché à leur productions que celui des Indes Espagnoles. Le [=Il est] voilà en fin ouvert,[72] il est incroyable ce qu'a embarqué d'ouvrages de modes la dernière flotte, et il est plus etonnant encore les demandes que les femmes de Mexique font continuellement de ces ouvrages. On en est partie redevable à l'épouse du Viceroy de Mexique. Son goût pour la parure élégante de nos femmes a entraîné celui de toutes celles de Veracruz. Il fallait faciliter ce penchant naturel à la coquetterie dans les femmes de ces contrées pour faire le parallel de luxe qui y domine les hommes. Le gouvernement doit voir avec joye cette nouvelle branche de commerce [...] Les Eventails de Paris ont également un

> débouché considérable et forment un objet très important [. . .] Les bas de soye de Paris, Lyon, Nîmes, Gauge, rapportent des sommes inmenses.[73]

The texts cited clearly described the strengths of French manufactures in their competition with the English, namely low wages and a dominant position in fashionable design, which made French stuffs, accessories and adornments very attractive.

One other factor also exercised a steady influence, even if it did not actually drive the triumph of French manufactures in any specific case. This was a business culture in which the state played an active role.

In England, the revolution, which had in the long run brought representative politics and consolidated capitalism, was to an extent made against the state, and individual free enterprise lay at the heart of the country's economic development. In France, however, economic competition with England had actively involved the state since the seventeenth century, although without disdaining private initiative.[74] As a result, growth in French manufacturing was driven by a business culture in which the entrepreneur was a hybrid of pure capitalist in the English style and *state industrialist*. The contrasting roles of the trader are encapsulated in two books which had enormous influence on the commercial culture of the two countries: Jacques Savary's handbook for merchants *Le parfait négotiant* published in 1675, and the almost identically titled work *The Complete English Tradesman*, published in 1727 by the naturalized Englishman[75] Daniel Defoe.[76] The result in France was a combination of individual interest and patriotic duty: when they succeeded in making money, French manufacturers acted in the service of the state, and it was therefore only proper that the state should intervene actively to help them overcome any difficulties they might face. I shall provide two testimonies (both from diplomatic sources) in support of this argument.

The first source refers to the French merchants trading in Spain. The object of the French ministry was to protect the merchants who exported manufactured goods and returned with Spanish silver, but not those who settled yet wished to remain French. They were Frenchmen who had renounced their country, *la patrie* to use a phrase which at this time was beginning to replace 'king' or 'state':

> [. . .] ne convient de protéger que ceux qui viennent s'établir en Espagne et qui, après un certain espace de temps, sont en situation de remporter en France les biens qu'ils y ont amassés; mais pour ce qui est de ceux qui s'establissent dans le pays, s'y méritent, achètent des biens fonds, et un mot, portent tout le caractère de gens qu'ont abandonné leur patrie et qui ne longent qu'a devenir habitants d'Espagne, je ne crois pas qu'ils meritent la protection de France puisque leur génération et leur fortune ne peuvent plus procurer aucun bien à l'Estat; ce sont pour l'ordinaire ces sortes de français renégats à leur patrie qui font le plus de bruit et qui voudroient que toute la France se sacrifiât pour eux parce que, moyennant cela, ils jouïssent du bénéfice de deux estats sans contribuer aux charges d'aucun, et, se servant toujours d'une jurisdiction contre l'autre, ne soyent soumis à aucune.[77]

The French state had, then, no obligation towards these 'renégats à leur patrie' and should not bring them under its protection.

It was a different matter when emigrant traders brought back cash to France, however. Not only were they entitled to assistance from the French state (as evidenced by its diplomatic activity), but the state itself recognized its obligation to foster trade and industry in general and, specifically, to aid industries which for one reason or another might be struggling.

The second source is the report cited above, which was filed by Duplessis de Mongelas, the French consul in Cadiz, who explains that the hitherto high quality of goods produced by certain French industries had begun to decline in the 1770s. This was a problem that required the intervention of the state via its provincial intendants to correct matters.[78] In the case of a failing industry, the intendant would report and then:

> Sérait de la sage vigilance d'un Intendant de province de ne point laisser dépérir une telle fabrique, d'en informer le gouvernement qui doit la protéger, ou même en confier le soin à un homme qui, par ses travaux et son industrie, en affermît la force et la solidité. *Un fabriquant n'est que le dépositaire des biens de l'État, et il fait tort à sa Patrie lorsque son activité cesse.* Qu'on jette les yeux sur l'Angleterre, et l'on verra que la protection qu'on y accorde au commerce, est moins l'ouvrage du Gouvernement que l'exemple que les Pères transmettent à leurs enfants de leur veilles et de leur industrie. Si nos préjugés ne peuvent permettre ce goût perpétuel dans la famille d'un fabriquant, le Gouvernement doit y remédier, et en est mille moyens.[79]

The text displays a conception of trade and industry which reserves an active role for the state. A struggling business was a political problem, and it was the responsibility of the intendant in whose charge the factory lay to investigate the causes. As described by the consul in a different passage, this would be the case of a cloth factory passed on to the founder's son, who now enjoyed the income from higher quality stuffs without bothering to maintain the market for lower quality, cheaper products, where competition was fiercer and sales were more difficult. In this case, the state should protect the factory, granting it privileges to ensure recovery of the business and even appointing an administrator to save it, if necessary. Once again, the author holds up the mirror of England, which in this case reflects the model of a business culture based on individual and family endeavour.

Though its author could hardly be anything other than an advocate of free trade, industry and labour, the text nonetheless assigns a key role in industry to the state, which is to ensure quality by official inspection of manufactures and to create a legal and political architecture which would further the expansion of French trade. However, this discourse contains a number of serious contradictions. To begin with, the author asserts that industrialists in an absolute state, whose inhabitants were subjects and servants of the king, were the 'depositaries of state assets' and their failure was treason to the Crown, which, to complicate matters further, was already evolving into *la patrie* before the events of 1789.[80] In an absolutist political system like that of France, the relationship between the industrialist and the king-state-country-*patrie* could not be other than one of subordination.

As a consequence, the absolutist French state acquired a role in private enterprise which was completely absent in Great Britain.[81] As could hardly be otherwise, these matters also came very much to the fore in Spain, a country also governed under a system of enlightened absolutism, when its rulers addressed the task of restructuring the state and began to plan a mercantilist and nationalist economic policy.

Based on these premises, competition between France and England for the Spanish market led the English to develop a strong, direct trading position in the Madrid–Cadiz–America axis, while the French dominated trade with the interior, as we shall see.

The situation in 1760–1780

In terms of the total value of imports and exports, British trade with Spain enjoyed spectacular growth in the eighteenth century. In 1696–1697, the trade was worth some 324,566 pounds sterling, rising to around 750,000 pounds by 1717. By 1750, however, the trade was worth 2,169,191 pounds, most of which was accounted for by British exports to Spain (1,783,075 pounds sterling). In 1752, the volume of trade dipped to 1,392,566 pounds sterling, but overall the figures for the mid-eighteenth century are considerably higher than in its early decades. Thereafter, British exports to Spain never fell below one million pounds sterling under normal circumstances. In 1772, Great Britain exported goods worth some 1,200,000 pounds sterling to Spain, equal to 114,000,000 *reales* at an exchange rate of 95 billon *reales* to the pound, while French exports in the same year totalled 44,184,081 *livres tournois* or 176,736,324 *reales* at a rate of 4 billon *reales* to the *livre*. France was the leading exporter to Spain, followed by Great Britain. British imports from Spain in 1772 amounted to around half a million pounds sterling.[82]

It would be more than a little interesting to know how these figures break down, and above all what proportions relate to Spain's domestic market and to the Americas. Furthermore, we may note that English goods were sold in the Spanish interior via third-party retail networks, but the French mainly retailed their exports directly through their own networks. Hence, the English figures would not include retail profits. We may ask whether the French figures do. It would seem not. Nevertheless, there is evidence of major outflows of silver coins to France as a result of the illegal repatriation of earnings, and this practice did include retail profits. It is possible that the retail value of English and French goods was very similar, but logic dictates that the cash sums accruing to France from trade with Spain must have been much greater than the amounts returned to the English, as the French trade included the profits from export sales and from retailing to the end consumer.

In the second half of the eighteenth century, growth in British trade with Asia, Africa and North America had the effect of diminishing Spain's relative share of Britain's balance of trade, although it remained significant. In 1773, British exports to Spain accounted for 3.15 per cent of the total, and imports from Spain accounted for just 4 per cent. Meanwhile, the perennially bad relations between Madrid and London, which resulted in the expulsion of British merchants each time a crisis broke, hampered the formation of stable trade networks inside Spain. The British merchants operated above all at the ports as wholesalers for Spanish traders, who would market their imports. There were only a few Irish and Jacobite merchants who maintained direct commercial links with the British, the most representative being Joyes' bank in Madrid.[83] In contrast, the French maintained highly developed trade networks in the Spanish interior, competing directly with Spanish merchants.

Further detail is provided by Duplessis de Mongelas, French consul in Cadiz, in his report of 1777 examining the situation of trade in Spain and America, who noted that the English dominated the market in mid-priced cloth, which generated a smaller unit profit but sold in large amounts, while the French did best in the market for high-priced stuffs:

> [...] l'Angleterre nous a enlevé le débit de nos draps, les a tous imités, et nous éprouvons malheureusement que cette branche est presque en son pouvoir en Espagne. Yl n'ya guère que nos draps fins de Sedan et autres qui y ayent un plein funés [=succèss?]. Le luxe qui a percé aux Indes, le goût que ces nations ont pour tout ce qui est beau, doit assurer à nos fabriques de draps fins un débit certain, mais ce n'est pas là la grande consommation. Les draps de moyen prix sont ceux qui rendent aux anglais des sommes considérables. Toute la France cependant abonde en manufactures de ce genre.

By this time, however, the English and French were not the only competitors. Other European countries like Prussia and the United Provinces had begun to enter the market by imitating French fabrics, and their efforts had depressed sales of medium quality cloth.

> Tous les Princes d'Allemagne ont établi chez eux des manufactures de lainages. Le Roy de Prusse luy-même [...] la Hollande [...] le pays de Liège nous portent des coups sensibles, sont redevables de leur succès à la fraude et à la supercherie. Ces fabriquants en imitant nos draps, leur donnant un lustre qui plaît, plient les leurs comme nos fabriquants, y tracent le nom de ceux-cy, y ajoutent même le plomb de nos douanes. Toutes ces manufactures ont fait tomber nos draps de moyenne sorte.

The informant goes on to recommend care in manufacturing processes, forecasting rising demand for certain products in America and advising successful manufacturers not to let their guard down by ignoring lower quality fabrics, which generated smaller profits per unit but nonetheless commanded a large market. He then continues with a long digression on the relative advantages of the cloth produced by various British and French manufacturers, in which he also explains that the cloth produced by the Real Fábrica de Paños de San Fernando was of poor quality and was badly marketed, closing with a brief reference to the outlook for French fabrics in Spain and America:

> Nous ne devons nullement redouter leur concurrence [la de los paños de San Fernando]. Il n'y a que celle des anglais et du pays de Liège que peut nous être

> funeste. Mais des fabriques bien conduites dans toutes les provinces, dans les qualités de leurs draps, et telles que les desires l'espagnol, doivent à la longue nous assurer la moitié des richesses que nos rivaux trouvent a Cadis dans cette branche de commerce.[84]

The commercial goal of the French at this time was to sell half of all Spain's imports, equalling all of their competitors together.

However, matters did not turn out as planned. British maritime trade was dominant in Spain in the second half of the eighteenth century, especially through Cadiz, where British vessels were by a long way the main users of the port. They could not be searched, as attested by the British ambassador in Madrid in 1776:

> [. . .] we must not by any means suffer the practice of searching our vessels in the Mediterranean to grow into a right; for if it was once allowed, that they could examine into the property of the cargoes, we should lose the whole trade, which very nearly altogether consists in being the carriers; and the respect the British flag is held in makes every country prefer our bottoms to those of any other nation; we must therefore be very attentive to preserve this respect, by insisting on our right, that the flag itself exempts from all search, at least from farther inquiry than the ascertainment of it's being a British vessel.[85]

This crucial privilege meant that British ships were preferred as carriers, and third-party charters were a significant source of revenues for English trading companies. This was the case not only because of the political confidence inspired by Great Britain, but also undoubtedly because freedom from searches allowed the charterer to practise contraband with almost complete impunity.

The British had also enjoyed a dominant position in trade with the American colonies (whether or not Spanish) at least since the mid-eighteenth century:

> A Decrease in the exportation of bullion from Portugal.
>
> Having already mention'd a trade commenced between the Portugueze & Spaniards on the River Plate thro' the means of the low prices at which our commodities are transported hither from Portugal, your memorialists, Sir, beg leave to observe that this commerce grew to be considerable during the last war between England and Spain, & was carried on & encouraged by the cheapness with which the Spaniards were supplied with English goods sent from Lisbon in the Rio de Janiero fleet & from thence transported by sea to the Nova Colonia de Sacramento whither the Spaniards resorted to purchase these goods, which were mostly paid in Dollars returned to Lisbon by the Rio fleet, the greatest part of which may be said to center in England.
>
> The later years of the Spanish war the importance of this trade began to shew itself by the large sums of silver brought to Europe in the Brazil fleets; & had the war lasted a few years longer, we should by this inlet have suppli'd with English goods the greatest part or the Spanish settlements in South America.

> The consumption this market gives at present to our manufactures, is far from inconsiderable & may be estimated from the sums of Spanish silver sent from hence [Lisbon] anually to England, which are entirely in payment for the Spanish goods.[86]

The imbalance in trade between Spain and Great Britain was paid for mainly with Spanish silver arriving at Cadiz and Seville, and the remainder in dollars carried by the English Brazil fleet from Rio de Janeiro to Lisbon, and from there to Great Britain, and in Spanish silver sent from Cadiz and Seville to Lisbon.

Faced with British dominance at sea, the French sought with considerable success to defend their dominant position in trade with the Spanish interior throughout the eighteenth century. Of course, they also endeavoured to improve their trading position with the Spanish Americas, and they were a significant presence in Cadiz,[87] but this was where competition with the English was fiercest in fish, fabrics, cotton and silks, and indeed anything exportable.[88]

Let us end by turning our attention once again to the interior market, where French dominance rested on the pillars described above (low wages, design and a business culture in which the state played a major role). As a result, politics was also a crucial factor. The French monarchy intervened more or less actively to remedy the inefficiencies affecting French manufactures sold abroad, and the government also used its strong position in Spain to influence Spanish policy and assure the ascendancy of France's economic position in the country, which it was able to achieve without difficulty until the 1770s.

Both the English and the French had obtained privileged legal status in their respective treaties of peace, friendship and trade, and both defended their positions by means of political action undertaken through their embassies in Madrid, although the French enjoyed a key advantage in this respect. Their functionaries were Catholics, and as such were better regarded, and they could naturally count on the support of the networks of French people living both at the Court and elsewhere in the country. The French and British embassies were, then, important instruments in their countries' efforts to maintain trade ascendancy, as is clear from diplomatic sources. New testimonies from the 1760s and 1770s support this idea.

The first such source is an analysis of the riots of 1766, which according to the British ambassador were fanned by the French embassy to undermine the position of the king's favoured minister, the Marquis de Esquilache, because he allowed the king to spend immoderately on his pleasures and showed no interest in investing in the army or navy to protect trade, as the French wished:

> Sir,
>
> Ever since the late tumult here, I have given my whole attention to find out it's source; and though not only the Spanish ministers but even the Court have affected the greatest secrecy, yet from the observations I have made I can venture to conclude with a great deal of certainty, that the French were the first movers of it, in order to ruin Squillacci, who, they plainly saw, pursued no other thence than such as could raise money for his Catholick Majesty to disipate in his pleasures, while the army and the fleet, to which the French were continually pressing him to

> give attention, were totally neglected. Thus far the court of France succeeded in ruining M. de Squillacci; but the old Spaniards[89] seeing the pusillanimity of the Court, and his Catholick Majesty's retreat, took advantage of it; and I now plainly see, they will not be quiet without some other changes; and I should think M. de Grimaldi cannot possibly stand his ground. I have learnt from undoubted authority, that the language which is held at the meetings of the principal old Spaniards is this; that is, if M. de Squillacci had not used his influence with the king of Spain, Portugal would not have been attacked nor the family compact have subsisted; and their present sentiments are that this court should if possible avoid any demêle with us, and not think of molesting Portugal, but attend to the re-establishing good order in the State, and that then in ten years time, with prudent management, they will be again in a formidable situation. Wherever I have had a safe opportunity, I have talked on this subject with those I could trust; and if I do not err in my judgement this last affair will in the end run out advantageous to us, and the French will of course lose a great deal of their influence here.
>
> I have received the strongest assurances from Musquiz, that there shall be the greater impartiality posible in all commercial affairs; and I really believe there will, but as he has not so much authority as M. de Squillacci had, I am afraid there will be a great deal more dilatoriness.
>
> As for political affairs, if M. Grimaldi remains he will be certainly an agent for the French, but he will be so far controlled, that the venom will be dispersed before it can take effect [. . .].[90]

Múzquiz guaranteed impartiality in trade matters, but Grimaldi was in the service of the French. Esquilache, meanwhile, was not sufficiently cooperative for the French but had ordered an attack on Great Britain's Portuguese allies and supported the *Pacto de Familia* between France and Spain. The British expected the aristocratic lobby to distance the king from his alliance with France and draw him into their fold. The Earl of Rochford's testimony reveals the backstairs politicking of the British and French in Spanish domestic affairs so that, if we are to believe the ambassador, the French were in the thick of things even in a matter as serious as the 1766 riots, in which the state of the economy, the provisioning of Madrid, and the various pressure groups existing in the capital (the religious orders, the Jesuits and the aristocracy) all played a role.

A few weeks later, the British were able to confirm, apropos of the riots, the extent to which the Spanish government was beholden to the French:

> In other circumstances the late troubles would have had one good effect and detached this court from its close connection with France, and such were the wishes of the people; but the servility of the nobles, and the weakness of the government is likely I fear to increase its dependance, and little more can be done at present than to insinuate on every opportunity their unhappy situation.[91]

France's strong defence of its commercial interests not only embraced the official, diplomatic field, but also extended to other more shadowy areas. In 1777 the French ambassador in Madrid employed an agent apart from his official secretary to follow cases and proceedings in the courts and ministries of Madrid, and to use his physical presence, dialogue, coercion, bribery and any methods necessary to secure the desired outcomes:

> [...] la multiplicité d'affaires que les français qui résident en Espagne sont obligés de suivre devant les tribunaux, exige nécessairement que nous ayons à Madrid un agent qui connaisse à fonds les formes judiciaires et tout le détour de la chicane, qui conoissa aussi personellement les juges, leurs secrétaires, les employés des Contaduries, les Greffiers des Conseils suprêmes, les commis des archives; enfin, une infinité de subalternes qui influent souvent sur la décision des affaires; il n'est pas possible que l'ambassadeur du Roi ni le chargé des affaires de la navigation et du commerce de France fassent certaines démarches et traitent personnellement avec certaines personnes.[92]

The methods of the French diplomatic mission in Madrid were not in fact much different from those of other nations, but the above testimony shows how far economic affairs were bound up with wider political action.

Spain thus became one of the most interesting scenarios in which the commercial and political contest between England and France was played out. In trade treaties and diplomatic correspondence the agents of the respective states voice their opinions and state their interests, sketch the image of their rivals, and recognize the strategic interests of their respective kings and countries to reveal a confrontation which had major, long-term effects on the situation of trade with the Spanish interior.

However, if we are to arrive at a more accurate idea of the reality, it remains to consider one other key actor – the Spanish monarchy. Spain had once been the most powerful state in Europe, and its crisis in the mid-seventeenth century had been a landmark event in continental politics. The War of Succession brought major changes, eventually allowing the Spanish monarchy to regain its leading role and to address the Enlightenment goal of fostering the prosperity of its subjects. The result was that the country's new, enlightened rulers and politicians were able gradually to take measures which limited and channelled the ambitions of the English and the French in the Iberian Peninsula, to solve old problems, to modernize the state, and to facilitate the activity of both foreign and Spanish commercial networks, thereby shaping Spain's emerging interior market.

5

The Enlightenment State and Reform

The weakness of the Habsburg monarchy after the Peace of Westphalia and the trade treaties signed with Britain and France was reflected in its vacillating response to the active mercantilist policies deployed by both powers in their pursuit of political dominance and influence in Spain's interior market. There was little it could do. Yet this and other things began to change with the new century and the resolution of Spain's dynastic conflict. The change of dynasty injected new blood into the monarchy, which under the Habsburgs had been constrained by the intransigence of the Counter-Reformation, lying prostrate and exhausted by fiscal crisis, incessant warring and intermarriage.

The events of the War of Succession are well known and need not detain us here, but we may recall the long postscript to the Peace of Utrecht, which would not end until 1724. Philip V never fully accepted the treaties, and he soon launched fresh military campaigns to recover lost territories, even before making peace with the Austrian Empire. In 1717 an expedition to Sardinia recovered the island, which had been occupied by the English in 1708 and ceded to the Austrian Empire, and in 1718–1720 a Spanish army invaded and reconquered Sicily, also in the hands of the Empire, from Austrian and Savoyard troops supported by a squadron of English warships.

On 2 August 1718, the Austrian Empire, the Kingdom of Savoy, England and France signed the Quadruple Alliance against Spain. England declared war in December 1718 and France in January 1719. Between April and August 1719 the Duke of Berwick, once on the side of Philip V, seized Fuenterrabía, Pasajes, San Sebastián and eventually all of the three Basque provinces, which declared themselves willing to recognize the new French government provided it respected local laws. At the same time, the French invaded Catalonia over the Pyrenees, taking Seo de Urgel in 1720, and their fleet destroyed the Spanish shipyards in Santoña (Santander) and attacked Spanish possessions in the Americas. The British fleet, meanwhile, attacked Galicia and razed the shipyards of Vigo and Marín, although these were punitive expeditions which made no attempt at conquest. As a distraction, the Spanish struck back in Scotland in support of the Jacobites in 1719, and they also planned an assault on Normandy, although it never went ahead. Following the Peace of Cambrai signed with the Austrian Empire, France and England after negotiations lasting from 1720 until 1724, the three Basque provinces were officially returned to Spain in August 1722. It will be of interest to recall later on that France held these important territories from 1719 until 1722, when the customs barriers between France and Spain in the province of Guipuzcoa ceased to exist.

Many lines have been written about the regeneration of Spanish policy after the War of Succession and the proper historiographical interpretation of this process, and these will certainly not be the last, if only because their purpose is limited. Our aim here is merely to outline the initiatives taken, which put an end to the economic crisis, lifting the state out of its enfeeblement, and creating instruments which contributed directly to the formation of a domestic market in Spain. As an approximate point of reference, we may take the dismissal of the Marquis of Ensenada from office on 20 July 1754. The politicians who succeeded him in the government of Spain found themselves equipped with a series of new instruments and adopted a more independent, mercantilist policy, which would be tested by the Seven Years' War (1756–1763), the new *Pacto de Familia* of 1761 and the riots of 1766. In this period the state, which had fully recovered the essential tools of government in the preceding decade, began to develop a more independent, mercantilist economic policy,[1] keeping a close eye on what were already coming to be called 'national' interests, until the French Revolution finally reduced the reformist ideals of the Spanish Enlightenment to naught but broken dreams.

There is a core factor which cannot be ignored in our examination of this long process, and which is at the same time linked to the central argument of the present work. This is the close relationship between the commercial networks that helped develop the domestic market and the social and political networks which emerged within the state at this time. Hence, it could be said that the state itself contributed to the development of a domestic market in Spain in two ways: formally through its political action, and informally through the direct action of certain individuals working within and belonging to social networks, who in turn influenced other members of the same networks on the fringes of the state's power. This explains the confusion that arose between the public and private spheres, especially in economic matters, which eventually became a source of grave problems as the public sphere grew in the second half of the eighteenth century, following a trend already in progress in other parts of Europe.[2]

Administrative reorganization

Let us begin with the reform of the monarchy's political structure. The abolition of the local laws and Parliaments of Aragon, Valencia, Catalonia and Majorca extended the jurisdiction of the existing Castilian institutions, and the concomitant legislative and administrative simplification expanded the scope for the action of government. However, the centralization of political power in Castile was also accompanied by far-reaching institutional reform, beginning with the creation of the *secretarías del despacho universal*,[3] government departments which partly absorbed the powers of numerous councils, and crucially with the emergence of what in modern terms would be called a civil service.[4] This new form of government, which has been called *administrative monarchy*,[5] was also a French innovation[6] and its object was to replace the previous system of government by a series of councils with legal, official and executive powers, which though prestigious was inefficient. According to their design, the *secretarías del despacho* created in 1714 should have been vested only with executive powers, leaving judicial competences to the councils, but this separation was never clearly made, resulting a certain jurisdictional overlap and confusion. The new system of government through the *secretarías del despacho* took root when the offices of secretary of the treasury, secretary of state and secretary of war were simultaneously discharged by José Patiño in 1726–1736, followed by the ministries of José Campillo (1741–1743) and then by Zenón Somodevilla, Marquis de La Ensenada (1743–1754) who each in turn held office as secretary of the Treasury, secretary of war, secretary of the navy and secretary for the Indies. By accumulating the majority of the *secretarías del despacho*, these three ministers were able to lead the administration of the state between 1726 and 1754, side-lining the members of the different councils and successfully unifying the action of government.[7]

This transformation led to the creation of an embryonic civil service by a royal order of 28 January 1721, which provided for exclusive dedication on the part of officials, who were to be employed for life, with the important proviso that each secretary would be directly responsible for appointments in his own department.[8] This provided an incentive for the spread of patronage within the emerging central administration to the direct benefit of the ministers in charge of the *secretarías del despacho*. We do not know whether the exclusive dedication of the new functionaries reduced corruption, but it is clear at least that the scope for clientelism expanded exponentially as the new Bourbon administration took shape. In his recent analysis of the system established for the recruitment of officials by the *secretarías del despacho* following the royal order of 1721, Castellano argues that the bureaucratic career structure created was similar to that existing in the councils, allowing little room for the influence of merit or patronage in appointments, because officials were normally promoted based on seniority and they enjoyed security of tenure. In general, however, the secretaries appointed *entretenidos*,[9] who would only later become officials and rise in the service. These posts were highly desirable to people of lower social status, who could not aspire to win office in the councils directly.[10] This interpretation does not necessarily mean, however, that those who were initially appointed as *entretenidos* (at the discretion of the secretary) were not themselves the beneficiaries of patronage, or that permanent officials, not to mention other ancillary functionaries, did not place them at the service of client networks. The *secretarías del despacho* were responsible for numerous key decisions, and it was important for any lobby to place its people, whether sympathetic family members or spies, in their offices.

In all likelihood, such client structures took hold and spread in the military also. Aside from the ordinary line regiments, F. Andújar has recently shown that the troops of the Royal House formed by Philip V at the beginning of his reign (and especially the royal guard) allowed members of the nobility privileged access to commissions regardless of merit or their knowledge of military affairs:

> The power networks threading through the Court in Madrid meant that relationships based on family, patronage and friendship were a key factor in the formation of a core of officers who found in their service at the king's side a source of preferment of all kinds. One of the most important such benefits was the opportunity to ascend almost to the rank of general by using privileged access to commissions as *exemptos* to enter the military directly with the rank of colonel.[11]

The king exercised his power to grant commissions to the members of families with power and influence at court, leapfrogging the order of merit and in despite of military ordinances, a practice which had disastrous long-term consequences for the professionalism and training of both army and navy officers, as Spain would find to its cost when war broke out at the end of the eighteenth century, for example at the decisive battle of Trafalgar.

Cronyism was also widespread in other areas of the government, including the councils. For example, extensive social networks of Castilians existed in the Council of Castile, with a greater or lesser admixture of *naturals* of other parts of Spain, and advancements were almost always handed out based on family patronage to nephews, grandsons or other family members or friends, whose alleged merits would then be taken into account in successive promotions.[12]

As we shall see, the tax farms leased by the Royal Treasury declined sharply but the sale of offices and commissions continued. It is possible that clientelism also encouraged corruption in this area. Such a scenario would certainly be borne out by developments in the absolute monarchy of France between the mid-seventeenth century and the end of the eighteenth, by which time cronyism had become universal.[13]

The new dynasty also oversaw the reorganization of other bodies of functionaries, although there is no need to consider them in detail here. The courts and chancelleries were also restructured, and the Castilian office of *corregidor*, the royal official with jurisdiction for municipal affairs, was extended to the towns and cities of Aragon, Valencia, Catalonia and Majorca. Finally, in 1711 a new and decisive body of royal servants was created – the intendants, whose functions were regulated by the ordinances of 1749. Among other matters, the intendants established revenue offices in the different kingdoms, provinces and regions. For the first time, they also addressed the demands of their constituencies and they were responsible for transmitting the king's commands throughout the country, especially in matters of economic policy (agriculture, trade and industry) and taxation.

There can be no doubt that the number of state functionaries rose over the course of the eighteenth century, increasing the executive power of the monarch and his ministers accordingly, although I have no information to quantify this phenomenon. This trend occurred in the wake of similar changes in other European countries. In 1708 there were 4,780 full-time officers of the Crown in Great Britain, but by 1726 there were 6,497 (due to growth in the excise office) and by 1763 there were as many as 8,292.[14]

The Enlightenment reform movement of course fed on the opportunities presented by the politics of the day and the individuals in power, but it cannot be said that it was wholly improvised. The government encouraged the emergence of a fresh generation of political economists, and like their predecessors of the sixteenth and seventeenth centuries these new *arbitristas* were at pains to examine the problems of the monarchy and seek solutions based on Enlightenment ideas. Leaving aside authors who left only incomplete projects or who never gained much influence, like Melchor Macanaz,[15] the Marquis de Santa Cruz, Bernardo Aznar and Francisco Moya,[16] and considering only the dozen or so most distinguished thinkers, it is striking how close most of them were to the new administration.

Initially, their projects were to some extent divorced from the reality of government, which was in the hands of a king who remained determined to press ahead with military adventures abroad despite the empty coffers at the Royal Treasury. Works produced in these early decades include the writings of Gerónimo Uztáriz,[17] whose ideas were later taken up by the politician José Patiño,[18] the anonymous *Representación universal* of 1725,[19] and the essays and papers of Miguel Zabala[20] and José Campillo,[21] Patiño's political protégé.

After the bankruptcy of the state in 1739,[22] a new policy of neutrality finally put an end to unaffordable military spending, while the recovery of the customs and revenue administrations, and the policy of debt reduction provided a fresh boost for reformist economic thinking. This second wave gave rise to more elaborate and complex projects for the regeneration of Spain, including the works of Bernardo Ulloa,[23] Teodoro Argumosa,[24] Zenón Somodevilla Marquis de la Ensenada,[25] his government colleague José Carvajal[26] and Bernardo Ward.[27] It was through their work that the nascent science of political economy and modern intellectual thought entered Spain.[28]

Without going into a detailed examination, one of their most interesting features of these works, which were by this time completely orthodox, was that almost all of their authors held offices involving responsibility for economic affairs, for example in the reformed *Junta General de Comercio y Moneda*, where economic policy was hammered out, or in the *secretarías del despacho* themselves. In this light, the works of the reformist *arbitristas* of Spain in the first half of the eighteenth century can hardly be seen as an intellectual movement like that of the British political economists. Rather, the new ideas were fostered, and in some cases directly penned, by individuals who were in the service of the Bourbon state, chief among them being José Patiño, José Campillo and the Marquis of Ensenada, who would himself complete the task of defining Enlightenment reformism, preparing the ground for the emergence of the leading political figures of the second half of the eighteenth century like Rodríguez Campomanes and José Moñino, Count de Floridablanca. The need to think and govern at the same constrained the intellectual activity of Patiño, Campillo and Ensenada, who almost always focus very narrowly on the realities of government. However, it also meant that the writings and projects of these servants of the Spanish Crown, whether detailed plans or mere sketches, consisted of ideas which they actually tried to put into practice, however sound or fanciful their judgement and proposals.

As a result, the intellectual movement which emerged in the first half of the eighteenth century was put to full use by the leading figures in the resurgence of Spanish politics and government, many of whom were the authors of the canonical works. The cohesion of government action made it possible to coordinate policies designed to achieve predetermined ends and meet the demands of the king's subjects, who in light of Enlightenment principles could no longer be treated as merely passive. As the head of the body politic, the king could not increase his power alone – only by achieving the prosperity and welfare of his subjects could he decisively augment his own wealth and power. The progress of the country was therefore the basis for the advancement of the monarch, and in a way it could even be considered the same thing. Thus, the fate of the king and of the political community at whose head he stood became intertwined in a way that they never had been before.

Be this as it may, our aim is not to consider what the state was able to do, but what it actually did and what the effects of the government's policies were.

The return of politics: corruption and clientelism

After the collapse of the seventeenth-century system of *validos* or royal favourites, the new *secretarías de despacho* raised up new figures, some of whom had already won positions of influence in the preceding century, while others had risen to power, or strengthened their grip, in the shifting circumstances of the dynastic war. These were the seeds of a new ruling class which began to take shape alongside the old one dominated by the nobility. The newcomers were no longer necessarily aristocrats and they did not serve the king in the councils but in the departments of state and in the conciliar agencies, and it was only later that they were ennobled, and sometimes granted council seats as a reward. It was a reverse process. The accession of Philip V had strengthened the king's personal authority through the *secretarías de despacho*, which in turn partially undermined the dominion of the high nobility in the councils, many of which were dissolved or stripped of effective power. The hour had struck for new political groups – Basques, Navarrese, French, Galicians, Catalans, Castilians, Riojanos and Aragonese, all terms used to pigeonhole cliques, parties and national factions (according to the terminology of the eighteenth century), although in reality the membership and position of such groups varied considerably and was not necessarily a matter of territorial origin.

We know something of the groups identifiable in the Madrid of the early eighteenth century. Several, including the Basques (from Vizcaya, Guipuzcoa and Alava) and the Navarrese, coalesced around existing emigrant communities, which had grown up in the seventeenth century, occupying positions of considerable power in the century of the Enlightenment. The members of these social networks spread throughout the offices of the state, the military hierarchy and the clergy, especially senior ecclesiastics, by means of a narrow process of patronage exercised by those in office over new arrivals, as Imízcoz has shown.[29] This resulted in numerous spectacular cases of social climbing and the creation of a new enlightened aristocracy, at the same time as it displaced a part of the old nobility as the hegemonic ruling class. In my opinion the very extent of these networks and their internal cohesion and strength were key unifying factors in the political renovation of the Bourbon state.[30] The networks also helped bind together a monarchy whose American elites were more closely dependent on their patrons in the metropolis in political than in economic terms, in contrast to the situation in the French and English colonial empires.

It would seem that some migratory groups, such as the Galicians, did not create cliques or factions of this kind, or if they did they were small. A few leading individuals also succeeded in forming groups around themselves, whose members were not all of the same regional origin although they may have been called by national (i.e. regional) names, as in the case of the *riojanos* and *aragoneses*. Communities of foreigners of differing sizes and stations also existed, made up of the nationals of other European monarchies and republics. The aristocracy also acted as a political group, as did the *colegiales mayores* in some cases.

The War of Succession greatly enriched a clique of *asentistas* or government contractors from the province of Vizcaya and Navarre, who had long held positions at court, as members of their families had been in the service of the monarchy sometimes for centuries. Thus, the *Congregación de San Fermín de los Navarros* was founded in Madrid in 1684 and the *Congregación de San Ignacio de Loyola* (Basques) in 1715.[31] After the overwhelming influx of French courtiers and hangers-on in the first three years of Philip V's reign (1706–1709), a minority became established at Court, playing a key political role together with the French diplomatic service. Furthermore, the King's second marriage to Isabel de Farnesio, who was herself very active politically, ended by increasing the influence of certain groups of Italians.[32] The King's son by his first marriage, the future Ferdinand VI, was named successor in 1724 and his youthful marriage to Barbara de Braganza in 1729 increased Portuguese influence and further inflamed French and British rivalry for influence at the Spanish court. By this time, the *cuartos* (i.e. the royal household and its servants) of the Queen, the King, the Princess of Asturias and the Prince of Asturias had become the lodestones for actual or pretended lobbies in a Court where rumour was often more politically influential than actual events. Gómez Urdáñez describes the court of the Princess of Asturias, Bárbara de Braganza as consisting of the *camarera mayor* (first lady of the bedchamber), ladies-in-waiting, the princess' confessor, footmen and equerries, and that of her mother-in-law the Queen, who was supported at this time by the *vizcaínos* and the Navarrese party, who were able to place numerous agents and officials in ministerial departments until they were ousted by the new King Ferdinand VI in 1746.[33] Another of the power groups active in that year was the aristocratic lobby formed by the grandees of Spain, whose most conspicuous leaders were the Count of Maceda and the Marquis of San Juan de Piedras Albas.[34]

In a political system where the sway of the councils had been considerably diminished and the king was more than ever the sole source of power, politics came to depend both on the character of the monarch himself and on the informal mechanisms used to influence his decisions either via the staff of the royal households or the *secretarias del despacho*, and even diplomats, in particular the French and British ambassadors. In this light, the reconstruction of the Spanish state around the monarchy seems to have been influenced not only by the objective circumstances of international politics (British and French colonial expansion, wars of succession, the influence of the European Enlightenment and economic growth) but also by an accidental combination of individuals and particular political circumstances.

Gómez Urdáñez has admirably described the happy political combination, though it lasted just a few decisive years (1746–1754), between a king who eventually became a convinced neutralist and just two ministers, Zenón Somodevilla, Marquis of Ensenada, and José Carvajal Lancáster, who together forged an overarching political plan for the state. The king's reliance on only two ministers avoided the kind of inter-ministerial tussles which had all too often hampered political action in the past, and it simplified coordination with the monarchy's councils. Each respected the other (or at least they refrained from open rivalry), and the fact that the Marquis of Ensenada held four of the five departmental secretaryships then existing meant that he was able to assume the leading role, for the first time achieving coordinated and effective government action.

The talented Marquis had a political plan of his own for the monarchy, partially written down in his government programme of 1749,[35] and he immediately began to implement it. Meanwhile, the political coalition formed by Marquis himself, the influential Barbara de Braganza, wife of Ferdinand VI, and an intelligent and persuasive royal confessor, the Jesuit Francisco Rávago, succeeded in passing the king appropriately redacted summaries of political affairs to ensure that his decisions were almost always attuned with the plans of his principal minister. It could be said without fear of overstatement that the first truly coordinated government of the Bourbon monarchy with clear goals, a financial plan and a timetable for action was the administration led for these brief years by Somodevilla, culminating the work of his reformist predecessors Campillo, Patiño and the ongoing efforts of José Carvajal.

According to the logic of absolutism, this political leadership was supported by a network of faithful executors. When the Marquis of Ensenada took over the government de facto, he created his own political group, the *partido riojano*, a somewhat equivocal term given that his right hand was the Basque Agustín Pablo de Ordeñana.[36] The *hermandad riojana* or brotherhood had been founded in Madrid twenty years earlier in 1723.[37] Ensenada's administration marked the beginning of a political style that would last for decades until Floridablanca's plan for the creation of a council of ministers and collegiate government.

This political context provided fertile ground for cronyism, however. Let us make some comparisons. According to Hilton Root, corruption increased but cronyism declined in seventeenth-century England as a result of the revolution, while in France, which remained an absolute monarchy, there was little corruption but cronyism was rife. The main economic impact of corruption was to reallocate resources because favours, being public, could be priced. Cronyism, in contrast was secretive, and it was therefore economically inefficient because a favour could not be priced, since its existence was not known to all parties concerned.[38] In this regard, we may consider conditions in late seventeenth-century France, where de facto power was exercised not by Louis XIV, a king who was past the pinnacle of his power, but by just two ministerial dynasties, the descendants of Colbert (Colbert de Torcy, Nicolas Desmaretz) and the Phelypeaux family (Louis Phelypeaux, Count of Pontchantrain and Louis Phelypeaux, Marquis de La Vrillière), who each protected their own financial groups.[39] It was only in the 1770s that public concern began to mount in France over the blurring of public and private interests, as was also the case in Austria.[40]

According to this argument, corruption and cronyism had differing effects on the interior market. In this regard, the Spanish case appears much more similar to France than to England, with pernicious effects for the efficient allocation of resources to the factors of production This may have been one of the reasons why the Spanish state, like its French model, found itself obliged to adopt such an active role in the economy. In the 1750s, the government was largely in the hands of one man, the Marquis de Ensenada, who never became particularly rich, but was unusually successful and so developed a huge personal following of clients and hangers-on, as other ministers also did. Be this as it may, contrasting corruption with cronyism as Root does must eventually prove fruitless, because cronyism also spawned corruption as a system for the distribution of power based on the venality of office, though the price of favours may have remained secret. Eighteenth-century Spain provides countless examples.

Cronyism and corruption were in fact concepts which came to have obnoxious political connotations only when a new idea of the public sphere began to emerge. In this regard, the history of Spain again coincides with that of France so far as the development of a public sphere and the delimitation of public and private interests in politics is concerned. The dealings of Cabarrús in the 1780s and the 1792 trials of key figures in the economic functioning of the Spanish monarchy like Jean Baptiste Condom, François Cabarrús and the Count of Floridablanca, who were accused of blurring the lines between the public weal and their own private interests,[41] may be interpreted, I believe, in the context of a change of mentality like that which occurred around the same time in France and Austria. It was, in fact, the growing political importance of the public interest which provided the context for the reformers to undertake the measures described in the next section.

Tax reform: direct taxation

The tax reforms of the early eighteenth century were essential to the progress of the new state not only because they prepared the ground for growth in the revenues raised by the Royal Treasury in the 1740s, allowing policies that would otherwise have been unaffordable, but also because they changed the distribution of the tax burden. This had two important consequences. In the first place, it created territorial imbalances and in the second it resulted in substantial differences in the taxes actually paid by individuals, companies and industries. The two key measures that were taken were the creation of a single direct tax, the *única contribución,* and the recovery of tax management, until the reform largely in the hands of revenue farmers.

The War of Succession brought the first efforts to establish direct taxation in Spain, though this was a long process which would not be completed until well into the nineteenth century. The reform initially affected Aragon, Valencia, Catalonia and Majorca, the four countries whose political and fiscal conditions had been changed by the abolition of their *fueros* and local institutions. The *Nueva Planta*[42] abolished the existing taxes, reneged on the interest due on debt contracted by the old institutions and created a new tax equivalent to the fiscal package of *alcabala*, *cientos*, *millones* and other taxes levied in Castile, which soon came to be called the *rentas provinciales* or provincial revenues. The same methods (quotas and levies) were initially used to collect the new tax, but three politically important innovations were also made. The first was that ecclesiastics were liable, although this depended on the district and other circumstances, and the details remain hazy.[43] Second, the tax charge was to be established based on the estimated income generated by individual property and chattels, as officially recorded by the new appraisal boards in land registers and cadastres. Third, town and village census data had to be updated, an essential measure applicable to any tax collected by means of a general quota in order to ensure that the tax burden is evenly distributed. Political circumstances meant that the new tax was called by different names, and it took several years to establish it fully after the abolition of the *fueros* was begun in 1707. In Aragon, the *real contribución*, also known simply as the *contribución*, was first applied in 1714. Dubbed the *equivalente* in Valencia because it was equivalent to the *rentas provinciales* of Castile, the tax was first levied in 1715. In Catalonia, where the tax was also implemented in 1715, it was called the *real catastro* or simply *catastro* because assessments were based on the cadastral registers. Finally, a royal order of 6 October 1717 imposed the *talla general* in Majorca. In Castile, it would eventually come to be called the *única contribución*,[44] because as a package it replaced most of the former taxes.

Direct taxation was not in itself a new idea. The distribution of a tax charge not by means of a fixed charge but based on the estimated wealth of each citizen or taxpayer had already been tried in some regions (for instance the *tallas* in Majorca), and a single tax based on the individual wealth of each taxpayer had been mooted in Castile in the seventeenth century. What was new, was that the estimates were to be so detailed and were to be registered in cadastres, which would be regularly updated. Furthermore, ecclesiastics would also be liable for the tax (an innovation in Spain) and the plan was, or eventually became, universal.

The new tax policy also borrowed from measures taken in France, where the *taille royal*, a permanent tax based on rudimentary cadastres, the *compoix*, had existed since 1439. The *taille* was in some ways a form of direct tax.[45] In the matter of mandatory taxation without exemptions, meanwhile, Louis XIV had imposed the first universal tax, the *capitation*, in 1695–1698 and then again in 1701–1709 to pay for the War of the League of Augsburg, because his enemy, the Emperor, had also created such a tax in his hereditary lands of Austria. The famous Sebastien Le Prestre de Vauban advocated a general *capitation* in 1695,[46] and Boisguillebert proposed far-reaching reform of the *taille* to boost consumption in 1607.[47] Finally, Vauban once again argued for levying a *dixme (dîme) royal* on all rents in 1707,[48] and shortly afterwards a second direct tax, the *dixième*, was actually imposed (1710–1717, 1733–1737 and 1741–1749). This tax would later come to be known as the *vingtième* (1749–1790).[49]

For an extremely pro-French government, then, the notion of creating a direct general tax was grounded in the debates and policies of France since the late seventeenth century. This is not to belittle the Spanish decision, however. Making the necessary assessments, resolving appeals and organizing collection of the tax meant creating a whole new revenue service and overcoming obdurate resistance from the aristocracy and above all the Church. The government faced enormous difficulties applying the tax, and its progress goes to the very heart of Enlightenment reformism in Spain, affecting the majority of the political measures taken in one way or another.

Collection of the *única contribución* in the large cities of the former Crown of Aragon involved special difficulties. In Valencia, the *equivalente* was initially collected by means of quotas and a port charge, and after 1729 by a port charge only, so that it seems to have lost the character of a direct tax.[50] In Zaragoza, and probably in other cities, the guilds paid a fixed sum negotiated for all their members. Unfortunately, it is not possible to make very precise comparisons between Aragon, Catalonia, Valencia and Majorca based on available studies. However, the evolution and characteristics of the tax, and the collection methods applied were clearly very similar in all four regions. In Aragon, the imposition of a new tax in 1707 and of the *real contribución* in 1715 presented serious bureaucratic and economic problems, which were not resolved until the 1740s. Over the course of the century, the quota fluctuated between 5 and 8.5 million (billon) copper *reales*. Meanwhile, the Royal Treasury had assumed liability for the debt of the defunct *Diputación del Reino*, but as it had no administration to organize revenue collection, this task was assigned to the town councils, which found themselves obliged to extract the money from their own citizens and from the Church, which was very unwilling to pay and, to make matters worse, was the municipalities' own creditor as the owner of municipal perpetual debt. This resulted in numerous conflicts, and eventually in a wave of municipal bankruptcies, most notably the city of Zaragoza. Furthermore, the work of the cadastres was beset by problems and progressed only at a snail's pace.[51]

In the Kingdom of Valencia, the *equivalente* replaced the revenues of the former *Generalidad*. The 1715 quota was 800,000 pesos. Ecclesiastics were required to pay only in respect of income obtained from trade, but they resisted even this.[52] Furthermore, the development of the tax was conditioned by the debt inherited by the *Real Hacienda* after the abolition of the local institutions and administrative irregularities.[53] Minutely detailed property registers were prepared, which were required to be revised and updated every 22 years.[54] The new *talla general* was imposed on 21 October 1716 in Majorca, where direct taxes (*tallas*) based on rudimentary cadastres had existed since the second half of the fourteenth century,[55] six months after the *Decreto de Nueva Planta* affecting the island's *Audiencia* was promulgated on 16 March 1716.[56] The tax was calculated based on cash rents, and the quota of 32,000 pesos or 480,000 *reales* seems hardly to have varied over the course of the century. As in Aragon, it was collected annually based on registers of secular taxpayers, merchants and ecclesiastics.[57]

In Catalonia the cadastre was set up by José Patiño after his appointment as the region's superintendent on 21 March 1713. It was created by a decree of 9 December 1715, just one month before the *Decreto de Nueva Planta de la Real Audiencia* (16 January 1716)[58] and its general regulations were enacted on 15 October 1716. Taxable property and income were recorded in three books: the *catastro real* listing land and property, the *catastro ganancial* recording pledged property and holdings of perpetual debt, rents from capital including the profits of trading and manufacturing companies, tax farmers, government contractors and artisans, whether or not members of a guild, and the *catastro personal* detailing wages and salaries, but excluding the incomes of nobles and army officers. The data was reviewed periodically in procedures known as *recanaciones*, but the total quota remained unchanged overall throughout the eighteenth century.[59] The system employed to estimate wealth was very similar to that used in Aragon, where it was first applied.

The debate on the effects of the tax in Catalonia is far from over. Despite the somewhat hackneyed argument that the new tax was deliberately unfair and hampered the principality's growth,[60] it is today generally admitted that it in fact generated positive rather than negative economic outcomes. The *catastro real* did not in fact cover more than a small part of agrarian rents, ignoring much newly tilled land on which nothing was paid. Furthermore, growth in the region's population reduced the *per capita* tax from 30 to 16 copper *reales* over the course of the eighteenth century, a time when prices tripled, so that the actual tax burden was even less[61] given that quotas were paid in cash.[62] This explains the repeated praise of the *catastro real* by Enlightenment commentators as beneficial to growth in Catalonia, especially after 1750.

Assets acquired by ecclesiastics before 1716 were exempt from the *catastro real*, the most important category excluded from the tax. This, however, opened the door to the fraudulent practice of putting properties in the name of family members who had taken holy orders. The conflict with the Church, which began around 1730 or even earlier, was not finally resolved until the important instruction regulating payment of the tax issued by the intendant Antonio de Sartine in 1735.[63] Even so, ecclesiastical foot-dragging continued. As we shall see below, however, a papal bull of 1735 abolished numerous Church holidays (saint's days and other such festivals) in order to allow Catalan labourers to work longer in order to pay the *catastro*, a measure which would have important consequences.

Having established the *única contribución* in a part of the monarchy, the Enlightened reformers sought to implement it in the Crown of Castile also. Though it bequeathed a statistical monument to historians, the *Catastro de Ensenada*, this endeavour was a failure in fiscal terms, because the new tax never actually replaced the old *rentas provinciales*.[64] As early as 1732 Zavala Auñón had already advocated the recovery of tax management from private hands and the creation of a *real contribución* or *única contribución* along the lines of the Catalan *catastro*.[65] However, the work of establishing the new tax in Castile finally fell to José Campillo, who had managed the Aragonese *contribución* after his appointment as intendant in 1737 and who became secretary of the Treasury in 1741, and José Patiño, who had been superintendent in Catalonia and had successfully set up the *catastro* there. The royal decree of 10 October 1749 started the process. The huge task of preparing the cadastre was practically completed between 1750 and 1757, although the process began to lose impetus after the death of Ferdinand VI (1759).[66] In 1762 Bernardo Ward continued to propose the general application of a direct property tax like that applied in England, but copying the system of cadastral assessment used in parts of France.[67] Various royal decrees were issued on 11 July 1770 in an effort to get the process moving again, but in the end the tax was never applied and the project was abandoned in 1776.[68]

The new *única contribución* had important economic and social consequences in the regions where it was applied, to wit Aragon, Valencia, Catalonia and Majorca. This was partly because of the tax's own characteristics, but also because it was established when the economic growth of the eighteenth century was just beginning. In each region, the *Real Hacienda* established a quota for distribution among towns and villages based on population, and among their citizens based on the local cadastre. The contents of the cadastres, the concealment of assets, the inclusion or otherwise of the nobility, and the level of opposition from the Church all conditioned the actual tax burden, which varied from one locality to the next. Overall, assessments of rural wealth and property were fairly reasonable, but measurements of wages and industrial assets and income were poor, and the assessments of commercial incomes were even worse, making them very easy conceal, so that the new tax tended to fall more heavily on agrarian rents and hardly at all on industry and trade. Meanwhile, the quotas established in each region were barely raised at all, which mean that they fell in real terms in a general context of population growth.[69]

The new tax also had one important differential effect. Where the population and disposable income from agriculture, industry and trade were expanding, delays in updating censuses and cadastres meant that the tax burden would gradually shrink,[70] and all the more so the longer the hiatus, a phenomenon which particularly benefitted some areas like the burgeoning agricultural districts along the coast of Valencia. The advantage was even greater for the new proto-industrial districts of Catalonia and Valencia, and for commercial activities in general, many of which were linked to industry via trade networks, because these were the sectors in which income growth was fastest, and the effect was greatest where the census data used in setting the local quota was out of date. However, where the population was afflicted by poor harvests or epidemics the burden shifted from those who could no longer pay or who had died on to the rest of the population, intensifying their distress and frequently causing emigration and the abandonment of villages.[71] This may have been one reason for the anti-tax protests which occasionally erupted. Angry complaints were voiced in Aragon in the 1750s, and in Valencia there were riots over the *equivalente* and municipal debt at least in 1715 in Peñíscola, the only town that had always supported the Bourbon cause, and in the 1760s and 1770s in Traiguera, Sagunto and Vinaroz.[72]

Implementation of the *única contribución* led to renegotiation of the perpetual debt contracted by both the local institutions and the municipalities in Aragon, Catalonia and probably the other regions affected, and even to municipal bankruptcies as way for local governments to reorganize their finances. In Castile, the indebtedness of the municipalities had already brought them under the control of local magnates in the seventeenth century. All of this spurred the reformers to address the reorganization of local finances with the encouragement of the Marquis of Ensenada.[73] The *Contaduría General de Propios y Arbitrios* was created in the first chamber of government of the Council of Castile by a royal order of 1745, the terms of which were reiterated a decade and half later in a royal order of 30 June 1760 concerning the administration of municipal properties and taxes.[74] Many town councils had laboured under the burden of municipal debts since the seventeenth century, and their largest creditor in the eighteenth was the Church,[75] which would necessarily be affected by any measures taken to rationalize liabilities and reduce interest payments.

The new tax also had important repercussions for the political culture of absolutism. As Kwass argues with reference to France, though equally applicable to the Spanish case in my opinion, direct taxation radically changed the nature of fiscal obligations. In the case of taxes raised by means of quotas, the liability and payment were a collective matter and the taxes were payable to local or communal *asentistas* or tax farmers. However, in the case of direct taxes (*capitation*, *vingtième*, *contribución*, *catastro*, *equivalente*, *talla general* or *única contribución*), the individual citizen was the tax payer (via the head of the family) and the creditor was the king himself. For the first time, each subject stood in a direct relationship to the monarch without the intervention of communal institutions, and the government in turn had to develop a tax administration from scratch based on the networks of intendants which grew up in both France and Spain. The king thus ceased to be a distant, quasi-sacred idea. Taxes had previously been collected by grasping, unscrupulous tax farmers, but this function was now performed by the servants of the monarch, almost one might say by the monarch himself. Over the course of the century, this changed political relations with the monarchy's subjects, as awareness gradually spread that both parties had both rights and duties towards each other.

The other key objective of tax reform was to recover fiscal sovereignty, which was achieved when taxes in Castile ceased to be farmed and began to be managed directly. The state's revenues rose from 106 to 180 million copper *reales* in the period from 1713 to 1726, partly supported by the *única contribución* and partly on the strength of economic recovery. By the last year of this period, taxes covered 80 per cent of state expenditures. The idea of taking back management of the Royal Treasury and doing away with the pernicious system of leasing revenue collection to 'bankers' had already been mooted in 1725,[76] and in 1732 Zavala Auñón showed that the application of the direct tax would immediately affect their interests by removing the *rentas provinciales*, which were farmed, and ultimately the tax farmers themselves.[77] Both reforms were thus linked – the creation of the *única contribución* implied eliminating the network of interests concerned in tax farming.

However, the bellicose policy followed by the monarchy between 1726 and 1739 meant that expenditures far outstripped tax revenues, and in the end it was the royal decree suspending payments issued on 21 March 1739 which finally triggered the political decision to recover the administration of taxes for the government and restructure its historic debt, as Fernández Albaladejo explains.[78] These measures were gradually implemented in the 1740s.

By this time, the Basque, Navarrese and French networks in Madrid had acquired considerable size and influence. It is significant that the suspension of payments by the government was negotiated in 1741 by José Campillo with Esteban or Etienne Drouilhet, a French businessmen from Bayonne who had stayed on after the War of Succession to found the firm of Etienne Drouilhet y Cía in Madrid together with his brother, Gracian. In the same year we also find him negotiating certain expenses for the queen dowager, Maria Anna of Neuburg, at the request of a group of Bayonne merchants, providing further evidence of his financial standing at court.[79]

Until this time, the state's revenues in Castile had been in the hands of tax farmers and *asentistas*,[80] and they were not collected by royal officials or functionaries. Thompson describes how the Habsburg monarchy ceded tax collection and the administration of war, two key instruments of state sovereignty, in the late sixteenth and early seventeenth century.[81] However, a third essential area of sovereignty remained which was still not in the hands of the king, namely customs revenues, which held the key to the formulation of any kind of protectionist policy. This will be the subject of the next section. Most customs revenues were in the hands of regional Parliaments and were leased. In the 1730s there was a strong current of opinion in favour of recovering the administration of all three of these economic instruments for the state, not only in Spain but also in France and England.[82]

Around 1740, the recovery by the state of tax collection, the administration of war (i.e. provisioning of the army) and customs duties were still merely political goals of the Enlightenment reformers. However, it was precisely at this time that the state began to take back the administration of tax and customs revenues in a process which remains largely unexplored by historians, but which resulted, among other outcomes, in the metamorphosis of the *asentistas* into state functionaries. In some cases, contracts for the supply of provisions, materiel and weapons to the army were taken over by the state via the *Contaduría General de Provisiones*, but in general they remained in the hands of private contractors, who continued to enjoy substantial business opportunities, not to mention the privilege of military jurisdiction, as has recently been shown.[83] The resulting mix of public and private interests among *asentistas*, merchants and politicians, acting through client networks, would in the long run have decisive political consequences when the revolution came.

Once again, the decisive measures were taken by the Marquis of Ensenada. On 11 October 1749, one day after the decree establishing the *única contribución* was promulgated, another ordered the administration of all revenues by the state, and the position of intendant was created on 13 October, just two days later. Obviously, all three decrees were related. The state took charge of most taxes between 1748 and 1752, and the revenues it administered already represented almost 70 per cent of the total by 1751–1752. Tax farming continued to decrease over the following decades.[84]

The *única contribución* redistributed the tax burden in the monarchy as a whole, but it did not substantially increase revenues. As Uztáriz had already argued as far back as 1724, it was customs duties that could achieve this, as well as providing an instrument for a protectionist policy to support industry.[85] The customs reform discussed in the next section indeed allowed the *Real Hacienda* to raise revenues, but if this policy merits attention here, it is rather because it was essential to the development of a unified commercial space and, eventually, of an authentic internal market in Spain. A mercantilist policy was unworkable without a tariff policy, and this was in turn impossible without a unified customs system controlled directly by the state. In fact, it took the politicians of the Enlightenment just a couple of decades to come to see the customs rather as a key instrument of economic policy than as a mere source of revenues for the Royal Treasury.

The abolition of internal tolls and the exception of the Basque provinces

Customs reform began in the early eighteenth century in an economic context of rapid growth in both domestic and foreign trade, the balance of which was clearly favourable to France. The volume of trade in the Basque provinces multiplied four times between 1730 and 1789,[86] and the testimony of both the French intendants responsible for specific localities and Spanish customs reports along the border of Navarre[87] concur in their account of the cross-border traffic. The growth in trade was a fact, but it must have been influenced by the reforms.

As far as the Iberian Peninsula was concerned, the Spanish composite monarchy of the seventeenth century was formed by six different political communities, namely Portugal (though only for a time), Castile, Navarre, Aragon, Catalonia, Valencia and Majorca, each of which had its own political institutions and exchequer. Within Castile, moreover, the three Basque provinces and the *Cuatro Villas de la Costa del Mar* in what is present day Cantabria formed a series of differentiated fiscal constituencies with their own independent institutions. There were also internal customs barriers between Galicia, Asturias and the rest of Castile, and the tolls charged at all of these provided a source of revenue.

The maritime ports belonged to the four realms of Castile (including Vizcaya and Guipuzcoa, and the Cuatro Villas de la Costa del Mar), Valencia, Catalonia and Majorca. The land border with Portugal was in the hands of Castile alone, but the frontier with France passed through four territories (Castile via the province of Guipuzcoa,[88] Navarre, Aragon and Catalonia), each with its own decision-making institutions, which the king and his viceroys sought to harmonize, though not always successfully. All of these territories were also separated by internal customs barriers, and each had its own inland ports, customs offices and tolls of one sort or another (*peajes*, *pontazgos* and *derechos de puertas*), from which the cities, lay and ecclesiastical lordships, local institutions and the monarchy all obtained revenues. In short, Spain's internal space was highly fragmented, making it all but impossible to establish a tariff policy based on mercantilist criteria. The situation of the land border with France, our area of interest here, was also extraordinarily complex, as any tariff policy required measures in at least four different political jurisdictions – Castile through Guipuzoa, Navarre, Aragon and Catalonia.

Between 1700 and 1714 when implementation of the *única contribución* began, taxation in the Kingdom of Aragon was gradually aligned more closely with the Castilian fiscal system. The revenues of the *Real Hacienda* in Castile basically comprised the *rentas provinciales* made up of *alcabalas*, *cientos* and other minor taxes, and the *rentas generales*, which consisted basically of customs duties. The *rentas generales* raised by the Castilian customs were generally farmed, and as late as 1703 tariffs continued to vary depending on the region and even the tax collector. There was no overarching tariff policy, nor could there be one. The Bourbons initially undertook their reorganization of the customs system as just another reform of the exchequer. Though customs duties may initially have been regarded as simply another source of tax revenues, however, reform changed them in just a few decades into a key instrument to structure the internal market and economic policy.

The first general tariff was established in 1709,[89] shortly after the abolition of the local institutions and laws of Aragon and Valencia. A little later, a royal decree of 8 December 1714 placed the administration of customs in the hands of a *Junta y Administración General de Aduanas* beginning in 1715,[90] a decision which paved the way for control both of the duties themselves and the commercial traffic generating the revenue. Meanwhile, a royal warrant of 20 December 1714 ordered the reduction and unification of all general revenues and a return to the tariffs applied in the reign of Charles II until the new rates provided for in the Treaties of Utrecht could be agreed with the commissioners appointed by England, France and the United Provinces.[91] Tariffs held the key to any reform, as they regulated the notional prices applied to each product as the basis for the collection of duties. They could be set badly, and the prices of goods could change. Furthermore, tax farmers had the power to interpret and therefore to disregard them.[92] Nevertheless, the basic step of deciding and applying a single, general tariff would still take decades, and it was not until 1782 that the first such unified tariff was published to replace the eight existing at that time.[93]

Meanwhile, the customs network itself was undergoing decisive change. A first *real decreto* of 25 January 1714 removed the inland ports between Castile, Aragon, Catalonia and Valencia, and a few months later they were finally abolished by a *real cédula* of 7 December 1714.[94] Not long afterwards, a *real cédula* of 21 December 1717, following on various partial edicts including a royal order of 31 August 1717 abolished all internal tolls at dry ports, which were to be moved to the maritime ports and land borders with France and Portugal, resulting in the suppression of inland customs barriers between Castile and Asturias, Galicia, the Basque provinces (what was then known as the *distrito de Cantabria*) and Navarre.[95] The next year, a royal decree of 26 October 1718 abolished the *derechos antiguos* levied at a rate of 5 per cent on the wholesale clothing trade in Valencia, and the *derecho general de mercadería* charged at rates of 5–10 per cent on exports from the kingdom, depending on the goods concerned.[96]

These measures greatly simplified the situation of internal tolls, and for the first time the mainland political frontiers of the Spanish monarchy matched its customs borders. The change was permanent except in the Basque provinces and Navarre, where it lasted only five years before it was reversed by the exceptional circumstances of French occupation between 1719 and 1722.

The Marquis of Campoflorido was entrusted in 1717 with the mission of persuading the representatives of the lordship of Vizcaya, the provinces of Guipuzcoa and Alava, and the kingdom of Navarre of the benefits of shifting customs barriers to the political frontier. His overtures mixed rational arguments with occasional veiled threats.[97] According to Rafael Floranes, however, the measure met with fierce opposition that same year when tolls were moved from the inland border of Vizcaya to the city of Bilbao:

> [al] mudar las aduanas de la raya de Vizcaya a Bilbao . . . los vizcaínos de tierra llana que por costumbre inmemorial y por sus fueron generales estaban exentos de pagarle [el derecho de aduanas] y las villas que tenían la misma libertad por estar pobladas al fuero de Logroño (como Vitoria) se opusieron fuertemente a esta novedad [trasladar las aduanas a la costa]. Los diputados generales tomaron la voz y acudieron al rey.

This was because the population of the interior had formerly been exempt from the payment of *diezmos* and duties but now found that the relocation of tolls to the points of entry to the province (i.e. to the coast and land borders) meant taxes had already been paid when goods were brought inland.[98]

The king sent Floranes' memorandum to Luis de Salazar y Castro, a member of the *Consejo de Ordenes*, who issued a report[99] in favour of maintaining the exemption:

> haciendo mérito de tres principios: primero la escasez, penuria y estrechez del país, motivo, decía, de que la misma naturaleza le hubiera privilegiado para un comercio completamente libérrimo y franco, y de que aun cuando no tuviera privilegios algunos positivos para esta exención se le debiesen conceder ahora como de nuevo. Segundo: los fueros generales del señorío que con la misma atención fijaban su franquicia; y el último los particulares privilegios de cada villa, que alegó por extenso por los cuales constaba estar concedido a todas ellas desde su fundación el fuero de Logroño.[100]

Interestingly, the exemption is justified in terms of the 'poverty of the territory' and because it affected privileges. Clearly, the latter point would have carried more weight than the former with those charged with defending a prerogative in negotiations with the government. Furthermore, the idea that freedom of trade and even of industry in the Basque provinces was a logical consequence of the region's original poverty (a notion which appears to be a hangover from medieval times) contradicts the view of the region's trade and industry as sources of wealth, which was widely held among the apologists of local privileges, including Floranes. In the end, Salazar's and other reports persuaded the Royal Treasury to desist from its intention of moving the tolls. A royal order initially reinstated only the Vizcaya tolls on the border with the province of Alava. However, the other two Basque provinces (Alava and Guipuzcoa) immediately challenged the limited scope of this measure,[101] and a royal decree of 16 December 1722 eventually restored the internal tolls of the kingdom of Navarre, the provinces of Alava and Guipuzcoa and the lordship of Vizcaya to their original locations.[102]

This measure was followed by a series of negotiations on the matters of tax evasion and smuggling, and an agreement was finally made by the Marquis de Campoflorido with the province of Alava on 17 July 1723.[103] Similar agreements were later reached by José Patiño with the provinces of Vizcaya and Guipuzcoa in 1727. Finally, a royal warrant of 26 May 1748 published another *convención* with the province of Alava, which also confirmed the accords made with the other Basque provinces.[104] The result of these three accords was to maintain internal freedom of transit within the three Basque provinces and the tolls in the Ebro Valley, as well as the *aduanillas* (lit. 'little tolls') between Guipuzcoa and Navarre (at Tolosa, Segura and Ataún), and between Alava and Navarre (at Salvatierra, Bernedo and Campezo), which were used to offset duties.

This decision was a step backwards for Bourbon policy, and it was influenced by at least two main factors. The first was the French invasion of the Basque provinces in 1719, which were not returned until August 1722 in the context of the negotiations (1720–1724) held before and during the Congress of Cambrai (1721–1727). In the three years of the French occupation, the Spanish customs barrier with France did not exist in the region and it seems likely that the invaders had a considerable influence on the restoration of the former arrangements. The second factor was smuggling and the strong commercial links between French and Basque traders in the area, not to mention the fact that numerous people of Basque origin were employed in the royal administration.[105] The influential networks known to have existed in the Treasury department and the *Consejo de Hacienda* were closely connected with the municipal oligarchies of the Basque provinces,[106] and the same was true of Navarrese power networks, although I have only indirect information about these.[107] Those functionaries with first-hand knowledge of the decision-making process and the interests of the oligarchies had an advantage, because they could both pass on information and anticipate responses, earning rewards for their collaboration. The Basque provincial leaders were mainly rural magnates, the owners of iron foundries, grand houses and large estates, and they were among the first to benefit from smuggling after the reinstatement of the internal customs posts.

The Basque provinces (sometimes referred to at the time as the *Provincias Exentas*) and Navarre were not the only regions to win customs privileges. In Navarre, the chain of events was similar although the case was different, and it is discussed in the next chapter. Meanwhile, in what is modern Cantabria the ports of the *Corregimiento de las Cuatro Villas de la Costa del Mar* (Laredo, Santander, San Vicente de la Barquera and Castro Urdiales) had enjoyed their own *fueros* since medieval times, granting them exemption from the payment of tithes and customs duties on goods for local consumption, and in 1726 they demanded the continuation of this privilege, which was granted by the king in a royal order issued on 27 June of the same year.[108] The tolls remained in the ports, but all goods destined for local consumption were declared duty-free, which opened the doors to contraband by the simple expedient of swearing that any imported goods qualified for exemption and then re-exporting them to the Castilian hinterland via the networks of mule drivers operating out of the Cantabrian Mountains, chief among them the highlanders of the Pas Valley. Intense smuggling continued to be reported along the coast of Cantabria and in the Basque provinces by the directors of the *Rentas Generales* as late as 1779, and it was mentioned by Floranes in 1776.[109]

Customs reform in Catalonia and Aragon, and its territorial effects

Let us now examine how local tolls were extinguished both in Aragon and Catalonia, and between the two regions.[110] Before the abolition of its internal tolls, Aragon set significantly higher protectionist tariffs than Catalonia. In an effort to protect the feeble local market and provide an incentive for exports as a means of halting the economic crisis and the rapid spread of French manufactures, the Aragonese *Cortes* of 1684–1686 had established a general duty of 10 per cent on exports and imports of manufactured goods, and 5 per cent on commodities exports from Aragon.

In contrast, Catalonia was a much more open region before 1700. The duty known as the *derecho del general* or *dret de entrades i eixides* was calculated based on tariffs set every three years when the rights to collect the tax were leased. The tariff varied depending on the products taxed, but it was generally lower on essential goods. Wheat was untaxed, while the tariff on wool was 1.66 per cent for imports, but 11.25 per cent on exports of unwashed and 22.5 per cent on washed fleeces. Oil was taxed at a rate of 1.66 per cent on imports and 5 per cent on exports, and cloth at 1.66 per cent on imports, plus a surcharge of 3.32 per cent on French stuffs in transit to Aragon and Valencia, and 1.25 per cent on exports. The only truly protectionist tariff was applied to fleeces in order to provide an incentive for weaving, a growth industry at the turn of the eighteenth century.

As most Catalan cloth exported overland to the Spanish interior had to travel through Aragon, the abolition of the *derecho del general* and of the internal tolls between Castile, Aragon and Catalonia meant that the 1.25 per cent export duty levied in the principality itself, the 10 per cent import duty in Aragon and the 15 per cent import duty in Castile no longer applied. Hence, exports of Catalan cloth to Castile suddenly benefitted from tax savings of between 11.25 per cent and 26.25 per cent depending on the level of tariffs. The removal of internal tolls thus provided a clear incentive for the penetration of Catalan stuffs and manufactures into Aragon and the interior of the Iberian Peninsula.

Meanwhile, Aragon basically exported wheat and wool to Catalonia, and the end of the 10 per cent Aragonese export duty removed all taxes on the trade in wheat (a low value-added commodity which was only profitable when prices in Catalonia were high) and in unwashed and washed fleeces. This in turn incentivized exports of these two commodities from Aragon,[111] encouraging the growth of a budding Catalan woollens industry and the availability of Aragonese wheat in Barcelona, which in turn drove the development of the city's economic region.

Meanwhile, the abolition of internal tolls in Spain shifted the 15 per cent import duty levied in Castile to the country's external borders (except the Basque provinces and Navarre).[112] The duty was not, in fact, always 15 per cent, because of the survival of certain legacy charges and because the actual percentage charged might vary depending on the tariff applied and the method used to assess the value of goods. Be this as it may, the reform was not without consequences in Aragon and Catalonia. In the former region, it increased tariff barriers to the north and northwest, because the former Aragonese import duty on French cloth had been 10 per cent but this was increased to 15 per cent in 1717, and the tax continued to be levied at the borders with both Navarre and France. However, the kingdom was practically stripped of protection on the Catalan side, as we shall see.

In Catalonia, where the local import duty payable on French fabrics had been set at a rate of 1.66 per cent until 1717, a *Tarifa dels preus de les teles y alters sorts de robes y merceries* printed in 1718 established a general tariff of 3.33 per cent on exports and imports, rising to 7.92 per cent on imports and 7.1 per cent on exports in Barcelona.[113] However, this fiscal reorganization did not touch the *dret de bolla*, one of the few local taxes to survive the process. It was levied on local fabrics in Catalonia at a rate of 15 per cent of intrinsic retail value, and a wax seal or *bolla* was attached to each bolt of cloth as proof of payment. The *dret de bolla* was only abolished years later by a royal order of 11 December 1769 shortly before the free trade decrees were enacted, by which time industrialization had made enormous progress in Catalonia.

The continuation of *la bolla* affected customs traffic between Aragon and Catalonia. Fabrics entering Catalonia from the north, mainly originating from France and England, paid lower import duties (3.33 per cent) than they would at other customs barriers, where the tariff was 15 per cent. As a result, the cost to the merchant of importing via Catalonia for re-export to Aragon, Castile and Valencia was lower, excluding transport costs, than if the goods were imported via Aragon. To correct this anomaly, two secondary customs posts were created by way of 'reinforcement' at Fraga and Tortosa, two towns which lay on the main cartage routes to Aragon and Valencia.[114] Nevertheless, in 1742 the king's functionaries reported that:

> los comerciantes de Aragón, Valencia y Castilla hacen su comercio de los géneros extranjeros para el surtimiento de dichos reinos por las aduanas de mar y tierra del Principado de Cataluña.[115]

As the customs posts were situated on the high roads, the duty would have to be paid on any goods carried by carts, which could not travel by any other route. However, much of the traffic between Aragon and Catalonia went on mule back along tracks and byways, and it cannot have been very difficult for drivers to avoid tolls if they had a mind to do so. In fact, it would seem that the only constraint on evasion was the fear of running into the customs officers who patrolled the lowlands of Aragon, Castile and northern Valencia. Nevertheless, little is actually known about the contraband trade in French and English cloth through Catalonia to the Spanish interior, and it would be necessary to establish not only the duty actually payable to gauge the incentives, but also how goods were valued in terms of the tariffs and assessments applied. Unfortunately, this information is as yet lacking.

In light of the overall customs reorganization, however, we may conclude that the resulting geographical situation in the northeast of Spain was unique, and that the key was Aragon. No duties were paid on merchandise entering the country via the Cuatro Villas of Cantabria, the Basque provinces or Navarre as far as the long customs barrier formed by the Ebro valley and the border with Aragon, where smuggling was intense, especially in goods destined for Madrid. The protectionist tariff barrier of 10 per cent set by the *Cortes* of 1684–1686 in the former kingdom of Aragon, which was fully integrated with the interior market to the south, was further strengthened by the application of Castilian tariffs (15 per cent) on the northern border with France and the western border with Navarre (15 per cent). However, the disappearance of the customs barrier with Catalonia meant that manufactured goods, whether Catalan or passed off as such, poured in from the east both legally and illegally, some destined for sale in Aragon and others on their way to Castile. The weak Aragonese economy thus became increasingly peripheral and structured in line with the economic growth of Barcelona and Catalonia.[116] The former kingdom also experienced intense inflows of manufactured goods and immigrants from the north and west, as well as outflows of emigrants and cash to France, either directly or via Navarre, basically via Pamplona and Bayonne. Most of these imports were bound for Madrid and to a lesser extent Valencia. The ease with which French immigrants from Basse Navarre could become naturalized Castilians only encouraged these flows.

All of this made Aragon into a kind of economic way station, an internal commercial peninsula to echo the original Spanish title of this work. It was sparsely populated except for Zaragoza, but it was criss-crossed by an intense commercial traffic of migrant labourers, wandering artisans, merchants, mule drivers, pedlars and carters all seeking their own place or on their way to the neighbouring territories. This traffic shaped the trade flows from Barcelona, Valencia, Madrid and Bayonne-Pamplona described in the previous chapter, which would in turn form the economic spaces that would become the internal market of Spain in the country's north-east.

Customs reform

As we have seen, the 1720s and 1730s marked the end of the seventeenth-century system of tax management, in which revenue collection was leased to tax farmers. The reorganization of the Spanish customs system opened the way for the direct administration of taxes by the state, although no action was taken until the 1740s.

Direct administration of the *rentas generales* or customs duties was first tried in 1726, but the experiment was abandoned between 1733 and 1739, when these revenues were again farmed. The bankruptcy of 1739 was a watershed, however, and the arrival in the Treasury of José Patiño, once again the standard-bearer of reform, marked a radical change of approach. From 1740 onwards, the royal revenues would be administered directly by the state, a situation that would become permanent under the ministry of the Marquis of Ensenada.[117]

Meanwhile, a royal decree of 22 September 1740 created the office of *director de rentas* or director of revenues, a body of functionaries who gradually took over the administration of the *rentas generales*[118] and other taxes as and when they ceased to be farmed. Another decree of 1 January 1742 entrusted the collection and administration of all tax revenues belonging to the *Real Hacienda* to its superintendent general, along with the power to appoint sub-delegates and jurisdiction for disputes in the first instance, subject to appeal to the *Consejo de Hacienda*. Yet another, of 31 January 1742, granted the superintendent exclusive jurisdiction in cases of evasion of customs and excise duties.[119] Shortly beforehand, a royal decree of 6 June 1741 had abolished the *Juzgado de Contrabando de Mar y Tierra*,[120] and a few years later an ordinance of 13 October 1749 completed the task by defining the powers of provincial and military intendants in revenue matters.[121]

The reform of 1740–1742 thus placed the *rentas generales* in the hands of the state and curtailed the functions of the *Consejo de Hacienda*, which was left to act as an appellate court in matters of contraband and evasion of customs duties. The superintendent general was also usually the governor of the *Consejo de Hacienda* and as secretary of the Treasury.

The missing piece in this picture is Navarre. To fill this gap, we need to consider an important fact, which has been known for some time but is all too often ignored, namely that the customs duties or *derechos de tablas* raised in Navarre did not belong to the kingdom as such, but rather to the king and his *Real Hacienda*. These revenues were managed by the *Cámara de Comptos*, which farmed them to a merchant every three years.[122] In 1749, the *tablas* were placed under the direct administration of the *Dirección General de Rentas*[123] acting through the offices of its own functionaries who were issued with the pertinent ordinances, thus ending three centuries of tax farming. This reduced the competences of the *Cámara de Comptos* almost to nothing while swelling the powers of the regent or president of the *Consejo Real*, who became the delegate magistrate for the *renta de tablas* answerable to the directors general of revenues and the superintendent of the Royal Treasury.[124] As the revenues belonged to the king and not to the kingdom, they were managed differently from the *derecho del general* in Aragon and the equivalent duties in Catalonia and Valencia, which legally belonged to the realms concerned rather than to the king. When the abolition of the local institutions in the three territories bordering on France came under consideration at the beginning of the eighteenth century during the War of Succession, the king directly controlled the *derechos de tablas* in Navarre but not the customs duties raised in Aragon and Catalonia. Hence, the suppression of the *fueros* gave the king no extra power over the *derechos de tablas* in Navarre, because these revenues were already in his hands, but it did allow the monarchy to control the customs revenues of Aragon,

Valencia and Catalonia. In this light, the royal counsellors quite reasonably understood that there was no need to abolish the Navarrese *fueros* to control cross-border trade with France, but every need to suppress the *fueros* of Aragon.

Meanwhile, the political function of customs duties changed significantly in the first half of the eighteenth century. In his *Proyecto económico*, completed in 1762, Bernardo Ward explained the new political meaning of customs barriers in an Enlightened monarchy, showing that tariffs were destined to become the key instrument of economic policy:

> El objeto de las aduanas e imposición de tributos, en su primera institución, se dirigió únicamente a dar réditos al Príncipe, esto fue la infancia de la verdadera política: pero desde que ha hecho fuertes progresos en Europa esta ciencia, las naciones más sabias han sacado de estos establecimientos utilidades muy superiores, de suerte que hoy, en manos de un ministro hábil que las entienda, son las aduanas la clave del gobierno económico del Estado y la regla por donde se nivelan y dirigen con acierto el comercio, las fábricas y la agricultura de una Nación.[125]

These statements reflect the enormous political significance of the customs reform of 1709–1742, culminating in the recovery of administration by the state in the 1740s.

As in France, however, the process did not immediately remove the numerous internal tolls and customs barriers,[126] each with its own specific tariffs.[127] The tolls continued to be used to pay for the upkeep of bridges and roads, but they did not have the same fiscal and political importance as customs duties.

Though it made the Spanish monarchy into a legally and politically defined economic space, if not yet into a single market, the customs reform of the eighteenth century was not entirely independent of the abolition of the Aragonese *fueros* and the reform of other taxes. The *derechos del [impuesto] general [de mercaderías]*, the name given, with slight variations, to the customs duties applied in the Spanish realms belonging to the Crown of Aragon until the War of Succession, were originally created in the fourteenth century to pay the debts incurred by the regional institutions and Parliaments to make investments and, in part, to finance the king's wars. As I have shown elsewhere,[128] one of the factors that drove the customs reform in the kingdom of Aragon was the monarchy's assumption of the debts owed by the former regional institutions upon their abolition, and money was urgently needed to meet these liabilities. I believe this is equally applicable to Catalonia and Valencia, the other two mainland realms of the Crown of Aragon. The public debt of the Aragonese lands, which unexpectedly fell to the *Royal Hacienda*, spurred a customs reform which at the outset was merely a revenue raising solution but eventually became a fundamental instrument of Spanish mercantilist policy.

Reorganization of the postal service

Another major reform undertaken by the state in terms of its influence on the development of the internal market was the reorganization of the postal service. This was essential not only for official business but also for economic activities of all kinds, because it allowed the movement of cash, bills of exchange and securities, as well as the delivery of commercial dispatches containing information about prices and the situation of markets, and letters ordering the purchase or sale of goods. Crucially, the state recovered the direct administration of the postal service through the office of *Correos y Postas*, a department of the Royal Treasury. Furthermore, the progressive creation of state posts[129] gradually side-lined seignieurial and private services. Aside from these systems, trading companies commonly maintained an active correspondence using their own carriers and carters.

The Spanish road network, radial until almost the present day, evolved from the postal network organized and operated, according to Madrazo, under a monopoly held by the Tasis family from the late fifteenth century until the reign of Philip V.[130] It originated from an order issued by Charles I on 28 August 1518, which naturalized the Italians Bautista, Mateo and Simón de Tasis and appointed them joint postmasters general *'según lo gozaba y debió gozar . . . Francisco de Tasis vuestro tío'*. The office thus passed from the uncle, Francisco de Tasis, to the nephews, and from them to the family, which held it until the eighteenth century.[131]

Once again, the War of Succession changed everything. In a royal decree of 21 November 1706, the young Philip V repossessed de facto all fiscal offices which had until then been sold or leased, as well as the attached revenues.[132] This included the office of *correo mayor* or postmaster general. The seizures were handled by a *Junta de Incorporación* created by a royal warrant of 21 November 1706, which remained in force until it was superseded by a decree of 8 January 1717.[133] A year later, the postal service was leased for four years to the Alava-born *asentista* Diego Zárate Murga, Marquis of Montesacro, who was a member of the Basque *Congregación de San Ignacio* in Madrid,[134] in accordance with a royal warrant issued on 10 September 1707. Thereafter, the service was again leased for five years to a Navarrese contractor, Juan Francisco Goyeneche Irigoyen, Marquis of Ugena, a member and eventually prefect of the Navarrese *Congregación de San Fermín* in Madrid.[135] These Basque and Navarrese contractors supported Philip V in his struggle with the pretender, the Archduke Charles, and they were quick to take control of a service that was still privately organized but was used to deliver the king's orders, diplomatic dispatches and government moneys, not to mention private correspondence, bills of exchange and commercial paper, a matter of no small import to merchants like themselves.

However, the administration of the department[136] was transferred to the *Real Hacienda* by a royal warrant of 13 July 1716, and a *superintendente y administrador general de estafetas, correos and postas* was appointed for the first time. This warrant was approved by Juan Elizondo, secretary of the Council of State,[137] who was also from Navarre and a founding member of the *Congregación de San Fermín de los Navarros* in Madrid.[138] It was no accident, then, that the office of superintendent should fall to Juan Tomás de Goyeneche Irigoyen, the brother of Juan Francisco, the last tenant of the postal service.[139] Via this Navarrese clique, then, the state assumed direct administration of the postal service on 1 August 1716, which, so it declared, marked the end of:

> [...] los abusos introducidos en el manejo de las estafetas y postas por no haberse establecido una regla fija para los viajes y derechos que se debían cobrar; por haber estado segregado de la Real Corona el oficio de correo-mayor, y en arrendamiento después de su incorporación a ella.[140]

The same Navarrese family had switched from leasing the mail as external contractors to running it from within the administration itself as servants of the king.

Four years later, on 20 April 1720, Philip V enacted a regulation of the postal service[141] governing the king's correspondence with his ministers, Chapter IV of which established precautionary measures for the transportation of cash sums and letters from the Americas. Couriers and messengers provided a variety of services in the network of post offices, collecting and making payments, exchanging horses with the postmasters, delivering and receiving mail, bills and cash from the postal service administrators and the deputies of the postmaster general. The network covered regular inland routes, non-regular routes without post offices, and also European routes. There was also a judge administrator with special jurisdiction over the service.[142]

Through these measures the monarchy recovered state control of the postal service and placed it in the hands of its own functionaries, curbing corruption (though not cronyism), wrongdoing and unpredictability in the delivery of mail and trade bills. In short, the reform assured the delivery of the mail, facilitating the circulation of bills of exchange and commercial dispatches containing essential information for the expansion of trade.

The reorganization of the service was completed by two ordinances of 19 November 1743, which regulated the administration of the head post offices and the position of *correo mayor* or postmaster general in Castile and Italy. These orders were signed by Sebastián Cuadra Llerena, Marquis of Villarias, a Basque from the province of Vizcaya, at the time secretary of state, who was responsible for the postal service.[143] Villarias was a member of the group of Basques surrounding Bárbara de Braganza. The next secretary of state, José Carvajal, was made superintendent general of *Correos y Postas* by a royal warrant of 7 June 1747.[144] Some years later, Rodríguez Campomanes drew up new regulations for the postal service.[145]

The postal service of course generated revenues for the *Real Hacienda*, and it was intimately bound up with the structure and condition of the roads. It was also the starting point for a spate of radial road and canal building designed to develop and underpin the internal market, which was based on plans first drawn up by the *arbitristas* in the first half of the eighteenth century. This new policy of public works required very significant funding, far beyond what could be paid for out of the revenues of the postal service alone. The project began with the construction of the Guadarrama road through the mountains north of Madrid and the highway from Reinosa to Santander (1748–1753), followed in the ensuing decades by a series of radial road improvement schemes and the building of the Canal de Castilla and the Canal Imperial de Aragón.[146] The post of superintendent of *Correos y Postas* was normally associated with the secretary of state as the official responsible for the posts and for diplomatic communications. However, the superintendent was also in charge of the physical transport of money, another field in which the involvement of the state was almost unavoidable.

Monetary reform and the coinage

As could hardly be otherwise, monetary reformism in eighteenth-century Spain was heavily influenced by the lopsided balance of trade, especially in manufactured goods, a problem that had dogged the country since the sixteenth century. To simplify, foreign manufactures were exported to America and silver was imported in the form of ingots and coins via the south of Spain, while the north imported manufactured goods and immigrant labour and exported fine wool and silver. In the Enlightenment period, Spain continued to be the world's leading exporter of precious metals to Europe. As in most other European countries of the time, the money market in Spain worked with two different value systems. The first provided a fairly stable means of exchange using gold and silver coins (based on face value, fineness and weight) and ingots (fineness and weight alone). Gold and silver were used for large payments in domestic and foreign trade. The second was the billon or copper coinage used in small, everyday transactions. Silver was the yardstick of monetary value.[147]

The eighteenth century saw sustained economic growth. However, it is hard to gauge whether Spanish exports of agricultural commodities (wool, cochineal and oil) benefitted or not from price fluctuations in the main European markets. Nonetheless, the value of the coinage fell compared with wheat over the course of the century and so, therefore, did the purchasing power of money. As Michel Morineau has brilliantly shown, Spain thus found itself obliged to export proportionally more precious metals as the years passed to pay for the same imports of manufactured goods. As imports in fact increased, ever more silver had to be exported. Given the negative balance of trade with Europe, the Spanish monarchy was, then, essentially a victim and not a beneficiary of the inflationary processes of the eighteenth century.[148] In this light, the matter of the exchange rate and trade in silver became a political and trade issue of the first order.

The early years of the eighteenth century saw intense demand for silver in Europe,[149] a problem that continued into the 1720s. Uztáriz remarks that there was much demand for means of payment in Constantinople, Cairo and the Near East in general, and this made it necessary for Spain to offset its trade deficit with outflows of silver. Mexican and Peruvian silver pesos were rapidly exported, flowing back out of Spain almost as soon as they arrived at Cadiz:

> [...] los comerciantes de Europa, para introducirlos [los pesos] allá [en Turquía] los negocian con el premio de seis, u ocho, y diez por ciento que dan, además de su valor intrínseco, sin que para ello se les ponga reparo, mediante experimentarse que en Constantinopla, el Cayro y otros de aquellos parages, tiene esta moneda de premio hasta el cincuenta por ciento [sobre su valor real según peso y ley].[150]

At the beginning of the eighteenth-century Spanish silver, whether in the form of bars or coins, was overvalued by 50 per cent in the Near East, whence it flowed either directly or via France, Great Britain and the United Provinces, resulting in the export of a part of the domestic coinage. This trade was principally in the hands of the Cadiz and Madrid merchants, many of them French, but it was also carried on by poor temporary migrants from France returning home with their savings in the form of silver coins. It existed, as Uztáriz remarks, because the issue of bills of exchange could never offset the balance of payments deficit, so that there must always be a certain physical outflow of silver:

> [...] parece despreciable la ciencia en que se hallan algunos de que, por medio de letras de cambio, se excusa la extracción de dinero, pues la práctica de ellas viene a ser sólo como una providencia prestada e interina de que usan algunos particulares, y por medio de la cual se anticipa la entrada del dinero en la parte donde se necesite; pero es preciso que los correspondientes que lo executen se reintegren por último, ya sea en mercaderías o en dinero físico; y como los géneros y frutos que hoy salen de España no alcanzan a la permuta en el comercio que se hace con los demás países extranjeros, es consecuente que por una mano o por otra se supla de un reyno a otro en dinero efectivo lo que en lo general no alcanza ni puede satisfacerse con mercaderías.[151]

The means by which silver and other precious metals were exported to France, an important part of the total, are well known. French merchants of course used silver in the settlement of their favourable balance of trade in Spain, but the trade also had an important political dimension insofar as it affected not only the merchants as the final recipients or as intermediaries acting on behalf of Dutch, English and German traders, but also the French state, which bought silver to mint coins.

Exports to France thus comprised a range of items. One part consisted of the net profits earned by the trading houses exporting manufactured goods and by the bankers concerned in the export of precious metals. These moneys remained in private hands. The merchants would sell the metal as paste or in bars to the silversmiths of Paris and Lyon, who would use it to make gold and silver thread, or to the directors of the state mints to strike French *écus d'or* and *d'argent*. Some went to Italy and Austria, where it was transformed into Thalers. Finally, another part was purchased by the French trading companies active on the Barbary Coast (North Africa), the Levant, the East Indies and China to pay for imports of silk and other products.[152]

Other foreign traders also exported precious metals from Cadiz, both legally and illegally. The metal, whether or not minted into coins, travelled by ship and also overland via Madrid, from where *quadruples d'or* and *piastres*[153] were taken out of Spain as contraband to France and Portugal. Once in France, they would turn up in the towns closest to the border, like Perpignan, Toulouse, Oloron-Saint-Marie and above all Bayonne, where they were readily accepted as payment by local merchants acting as the brokers, correspondents and agents of their peers in Madrid.[154] Furthermore, French labourers and artisans crossing the Pyrenees on foot brought their savings with them in silver, and these small but continuous illegal exports must also have made up large quantities of metal.

This situation conditioned Spanish monetary policy to an extraordinary degree, making it necessary to address the twin, and all too often irreconcilable, challenges of creating means of payment to support domestic growth and at the same time allowing exports of silver, which were unavoidable in the circumstances. According to Muñoz de Amador, the state consistently undervalued Spanish gold and silver in the eighteenth century, while it overvalued copper.[155] Furthermore, urgent action was needed in the early years of the century to put an end to the monetary chaos left over from the years before the War of Succession.

Consequently, early monetary reforms focused on the withdrawal of debased coinage minted in the years before the War of Succession and stabilizing value in order to normalize use as a means of payment.[156] With the declared aim of equalizing Spanish *reales* and French *écus*, a royal decree of 15 August 1709 ordered that coins be minted with a fineness of 11 *dineros* (916.6 per cent) and a weight of 68 *reales* to the mark (3.38 g) in coins of 4 and 8 *reales* (*reales de a cuatro* and *reales de a ocho*), exactly equal to the fineness and weight of the French coins. This was the first milled issue, which contained an inscription on the edge of the coin to prevent clipping.

The fundamental dual system for silver *reales* was created not long afterwards. A royal decree of 31 October 1716 ordered that silver coins be minted with a lower intrinsic value than the issue of 1709, consisting of a fineness of 10 *dineros*, a weight of 75 to the mark, and smaller nominal values (2, 1 and 0.5 *reales*) for use in small transactions. The new *plata provincial* coins could only be used in domestic trade, while the *reales* minted in 1709, called *plata antigua* or *plata nacional*, became the standard in foreign trade. This system thus created an exportable *real* made of *national silver* and a *provincial silver* coin for domestic use.

Twelve years later, the values of gold, silver and copper coins were adjusted, so that the gold *escudos* appreciated with respect to national silver (from 16 to 18 *reales*, 14 January 1726); national silver in turn appreciated against provincial silver (8 double national silver *reales* to 9.5 and then to 10 provincial silver *reales* according to orders of 8 February 1726, 23 March 1726 and 8 September 1728); and silver appreciated with respect to the billon coinage (1 *peso grueso* of 18 *reales* and 28 *maravedís* to 20 copper *reales*, 6 May 1737).[157]

The dual system was also consolidated. A *real pragmática* of 9 June 1728 fixed the fineness of *national* silver coins minted in Spain and the Americas at 11 *dineros* with a weight of 68 *reales* to the silver mark, equal to the coins minted elsewhere in Europe, which facilitated exports. Two months later, another *real pragmática* of 10 and 20 August 1728 fixed the weight and value for *provincial* silver coins first at 9 *dineros* and 22 grains (10 August) and finally at 10 *dineros* (20 August) with a weight of 77 *reales* per mark of silver (slightly less than in 1716). The coins were to be minted in 1 and 0.5 *real* pieces to facilitate everyday use. The next month, an order of 18 September 1728 established a fixed rate of exchange, according to which 8 *reales* (= one *real de a ocho*) of national silver would be worth 10 *reales* of provincial silver (i.e. a rate of 1:1.25). Meanwhile, the value of the *provincial* and *national* silver *reales* was once again raised with respect to the billon coinage: until this reform 1 *national* silver *real* was worth 64 copper *maravedis*, and 1 *provincial* silver *real* was worth 51 copper *maravedis*; afterwards 1 *national* silver *real* was worth 80 copper *maravedis*, and 1 *provincial* silver *real* was worth 64 copper *maravedis*. This placed the dual silver system at the heart of the Spanish economy.

The continuous outflows of silver coins and ingots to France caused frequent shortages, affecting domestic trade. The high value of gold coins meant that they could not fill the gap, and so the creation of a low-denomination gold coin was ordered in an *auto* of 25 November 1738. This was the *medio escudo* issued with a fixed value in relation to the billon coinage as an alternative to the silver *real*. Created to compensate for the shortage of silver and to circulate with it, the value of the half *escudo* piece was initially set at 18 copper *reales* and 28 *maravedís*, although parity was later fixed at 20 copper *reales* earning the new coin the name of *veintén*.[158]

The dual system of *national* and *provincial* silver *reales* launched by the orders of 1709 and 1716 and cemented by the legislation of 1728 and 1738 was a response to the need for an easily exportable silver coin, the *national real*, that would be equal in value to its French equivalent, and for another coin, the *provincial real* (which was worth 25 per cent less) in order to discourage outflows and normalize circulation of the coinage domestically.

The silver coinage provided a means of payment for transactions above a certain value, but in the rural world most payments were made in copper coins, or even in kind. Silver coins were rare. Hence, the reformers also had to adapt the billon coinage, which was essential for use in small, everyday payments. A *real cédula* of 24 September 1718 ordered the withdrawal of the billon coins issued before the abolition of the regional *fueros* and the issue of a new copper coin with a weight of 102 *maravedís* to the mark, which was declared the only legal tender throughout the monarchy. These coins were issued in units of four (9 g), two (4.5 g) and one (2.25 g) *maravedís*.[159] The rate of exchange with silver was thus set at 64 copper *maravedís* to one double silver real.[160] The stability of this rate was essential to allow payments to be made using both silver and copper coins, and thereby to incentivize the use of coins.

Over the course of the century, however, silver appreciated against copper, although I do not have precise details of the rate of change, probably as a result of outflows of *reales* to France. This was the reason for a phenomenon that is repeatedly mentioned in contemporary accounts, namely the frequent scarcity of silver coins, which made it necessary to use copper coins in transactions that should have been made in silver, and it also obliged the authorities to mint small gold coins with a fixed parity with silver (*veintenes*) as explained above. The low value of the copper used in such transactions meant that many more coins had to be used, which drove up transaction costs because they were heavy and expensive to transport. Furthermore, the actual exchange rate for the billon coinage was variable and swindling was relatively easy, so that the services of money changers were often required, making transactions even dearer.

The Enlightenment monetary policy also involved other important measures. In the early years of the eighteenth century, the minting of coins came under state control. An ordinance of 26 January 1718 brought the mints, which until then had enjoyed considerable autonomy and were administered by a treasurer who received a percentage of production, under the control of the *Real Hacienda*. Meanwhile, the treasurer and other mint officials were to be employed as salaried functionaries. Private parties taking gold or silver to the mint were strictly prohibited from striking their own coins in return for a fee, and the institution would henceforth buy the gold, silver and copper it used. Only the king could issue coins.[161] The mints ordinance of 1730 further strengthened and refined these arrangements.[162]

In the early eighteenth century, the nominal value of the different coinage was merely a point of reference. Coins actually served as a means of payment based on their fineness and weight, a system which required the use of money changers, which complicated transactions and raised their cost. Some coins might bear a *premium* in exchanges with others, so that they had differing values, and the amount of debts and payments varied depending on the coins used. In a process that persisted over the whole course of the eighteenth century, the state gradually succeeded in imposing the nominal value of the coins in circulation, ushering in monetary modernity in Spain.

After the order of 9 June 1728 all coins were minted using improved techniques and coining presses. The coins were milled to prevent clipping and shaving, which had been common practice in the seventeenth century, and it was made compulsory to tender the coinage without demanding a premium, so that exchanges were carried out at the exact nominal value of the coins used. These measures were reiterated in a *pragmática* of 22 December 1747.[163] The much more precise relief stamped on the new coins, an apparently unimportant detail, in fact had one important economic effect: illicit filing to reduce the weight of coins became more easily visible, allowing them to be rejected on sight. Meanwhile, milling prevented clipping the edges to remove metal. The intention was to ensure that coins would circulate at their nominal value, so that it would not be necessary to assay their weight and fineness to determine their true value. This saved the cost of money changers and sped up payments.

Monetary policy was also firmly established within a stable institutional framework. A royal decree of 15 November 1730 made provision for various monetary matters, including the creation of a new institution, the *Real Junta de Moneda*,[164] a currency board formed by six councillors (at least two of them magistrates and the rest laymen), one military procurator and a secretary. The new institution was chaired by the secretary of state, at the time José Patiño, who was appointed judge conservator and superintendent of the mint, the *Reales Ingenios y Casas de Moneda*. Three weeks later, a royal decree of 9 December 1730 combined the *Junta de Comercio* with the *Junta de Moneda*, which was renamed *Junta de Comercio y Moneda*. The secretariats of the two institutions were merged[165] and the official posts existing in the former *Junta de Comercio* were terminated.

The first-hand testimony of José Carvajal in his *Testamento politico* of 1745 not only reflects the monetary problems described above but also underscores the high priority of monetary issues in the Enlightenment reform agenda:

> Moneda, es punto que se trata en una Junta, como [la de] el Comercio […] en lo que más se fatigan las gentes es en impedir su extracción, y de eso me río yo por lo que acabo de decir.[166] En cuanto a su valor intrínseco, soy de sentir que se proporcione con el de las potencias, y sobre esto diré dos cosas: una es que en pesos y en doblones dan algo más en las ciudades libres de Alemania (que corren en todas) que lo que valen aquí. Otra es que, en cuantas pragmáticas del reyno he leído, nunca he visto la desigualdad entre plata y oro que ahora veo, porque siempre una onza de oro ha valido 16 onzas de plata y ahora no, y no sé la razón. Si es porque se extrae más la plata me río por lo dicho arriba y porque la plata es necesaria para vajillas, estofas y comercio de Oriente. Por esta razón de que [los mercaderes] han de sacar más plata y oro me parece convendría hacer moneda de oro más menuda; esto es, medias monedas de lo que vale un peso grueso, que

> aunque dicen que por menudas son expuestas a perderse todos tendrán el cuidado que corresponde a su valor.
>
> Dos cosas quiero advertir utilísimas del comercio. Una es que no hay nación donde se pesa la moneda sino es en España, y esto hace al comercio gran detención y perjuicio. Hágase toda la moneda de cordoncillo y mándese que no la pesen: tomarla como la del príncipe; y aunque hay malicia, que en la lima en no saliendo lo gravado de ella muy profundo la pueden quitar [peso] sin borrarla, [hay que] dar orden pública para que la que se vea borrada en lo grabado se denuncie.
>
> Otra cosa es que a toda moneda de plata y oro quisiera que se le pusiera a los lados del sello su valor en número de maravedises como lo hacen con la de Portugal en reis, habiendo moneda de 20.000 de ellos de valor. Esto quitará muchas confusiones de cuentas.
>
> La de vellón quisiera se redujera a más manual o dándola una mezcla de plata, según un proyecto que yo tengo, o mudando la materia, aunque fuese a una de poco valor. Lo que encargo sobre todo es que con dificultad se toque en [el] valor de la moneda, que cualquiera alteración causa una alteración horrible.[167]

Value by weight, the outflow and resulting shortage of silver coins, forgery and clipping, circulation of the coinage at values other than its face value – the problems described by Carvajal were precisely those tackled by monetary reform. Despite the dual system of *national* and *provincial* silver, Spain continued to experience currency problems, which frequently posed an obstacle to the development of the market. Little by little, the Enlightenment reformists had realized that the solution was to render the export of silver superfluous, but to achieve this it would be necessary to develop Spanish industry and at the same time to control the activity of foreign, and especially French, immigrants and merchants in Spain. Monetary policy and manufacturing soon appeared as directly linked. This was precisely what Carvajal had meant in the paragraphs preceding the text cited above, which were not included for reasons of space. His testimony, however, was not that of just another reformist. In 1745 he had been the Marquis of Ensenada's right hand in trade affairs, in the following year he was appointed chairman of the Trade and Currency Board, and he then went on to hold office as secretary of state and superintendent of *Correos*. The text is not a mere speculation, then, but a thoroughgoing statement of political intentions.

The business of exporting silver fell increasingly into the hands of French merchants around the middle of the eighteenth century. Meanwhile, rising demand and appreciation of the metal (and of gold) in Europe triggered a fresh raft of reforms in 1771–1772. This package maintained the differentiation between *provincial* and *national* silver, ordered the withdrawal of all old issues of copper coins still in circulation, and apparently maintained the fineness and weight of silver coins established in the early years of the eighteenth century. However, a secret document of 18 March 1771 ordered a slight dilution in the fineness of silver coins. Thus, the exportable *national real* was reduced from 11 *dineros* to 10 *dineros* and 20 grains (903 per thousand pure), while the fineness of the provincial *real* was lowered from 10 *dineros* to 9 *dineros* and 18 *grains* (813 per thousand). The fineness of gold was also reduced slightly,[168] probably to maintain their parity with the silver coinage.

The monetary history of Spain in the eighteenth century is too important, complex and little known to deal with in just a few lines here. Suffice it to say that the legislation regulating monetary values, issues and the reform of the mints were effective, but the old, bad coinage remained in circulation for decades (the *Novísima recopilación* documents repeated orders to withdraw issues, but compliance was always only partial). Meanwhile, shortages of silver and copper coins were frequent (which encouraged the use of agricultural commodities like wheat as barter), and the crucial change from telling coins by weight to counting them at their nominal value was slow to take hold, as Carvajal's memoir of 1745 attests.

Nevertheless, these reforms succeeded in unifying and rationalizing the Spanish monetary system, stabilizing the value of the coinage, laying the foundations for the development of the market and trade, and bringing the modern monetary practices of Europe to Spain.

Having stabilized and readjusted the monetary system, the next avenue of attack for the reformists was to seek control of the trade in silver, which was far and away Spain's largest export together with merino wool. This market was in the hands of the great English and above all French merchants and financiers of Cadiz and Madrid.

To this end, Ensenada created the *Real Giro*, Spain's first public bank. The royal decree setting up the bank and its original ordinances were enacted in 1748, and it began its operations in June or July of the same year.[169] Meanwhile, its first regulations were issued on 19 August 1752.[170] The *Real Giro* was created to receive deposits from private parties and judicial bonds. It undertook deliveries of money abroad in cash, jewellery and silver, initially to Rome, and it wrote bills of exchange. The bank's initial equity of one million copper *reales* was obtained from the revenues of the Post Office,[171] which had included the transportation of money among its services since they were first regulated in 1720. The main purpose was to reduce the cost of sending money, which the state usually did in the form of bills of exchange or silver,[172] although it was hoped to capture a part of the enormous profits made from the export of American silver to Europe.

The bank was founded along the lines of the Bank of England, which the Spanish ambassador in London, the Marquis del Puerto, had described in detail in reports filed not long before. Though its equity was for a time more than 100 million copper *reales*, the Conde de Valparaíso, who succeeded Ensenada after his fall, limited these funds to 30 million under pressure from the English, whose trade had been affected.[173] The *Real Giro* continued to function until 1782, when it was absorbed by the new *Banco de San Carlos*. As a state institution, it was little liked by the merchant bankers of Madrid, whether Spanish or foreign, because it had been created to manage part of a lucrative private business. Furthermore, the regulations of 1752, which were implemented by a *real decreto* promulgated in late August 1755, granted the *Real Giro* preferential rights to collect claims in commercial bankruptcies affecting its business partners. This measure sparked protests from the English merchants of Cadiz, Seville and Sanlúcar, though these do not appear to have achieved much.[174] The bank's annual profits began to decline in the early 1760s and it made losses after 1781, according to Pulido because the gap between the official value of silver and its actual value in the foreign market redirected exports through unofficial channels.[175]

The *Real Giro* presents yet another case of cronyism. The Marquis of Ensenada used the Madrid office, the six branches abroad (Paris, Rome, Naples, Lisbon, London and Amsterdam) and the Spanish branches (Barcelona, Bilbao, Cadiz, Malaga, Seville and Valencia) to finance operations outside the network of embassies under the control of the secretary of state, Carvajal, and he filled all positions of power and responsibility with members of his Rioja 'party' or clique.[176] These included the offices of director, treasurer general and the senior functionaries at the Madrid office. For the other positions in the bank, Ensenada selected men who were already in one way or another agents of the king, basing his choice above all on their professional experience in finance and business know-how, except in the cases of Bilbao and Cadiz, where he also influenced appointments.[177] A prosopographical analysis of the 37 employees of the *Real Giro* in 1752 reveals that 12 were certainly or very probably cronies of the Marquis of Ensenada, and they in turn had family members in other posts in embassies and ministries.[178]

Restructuring of the national debt

The monetary reforms allowed the monarchy to benefit from the progressive fall in interest rates which occurred all over Western Europe in the seventeenth and eighteenth centuries as capital markets developed. In Amsterdam, the maximum rate charged on short-term loans fell from 5 per cent in the 1620s to 2.3 per cent in 1723, while in London it dropped from 10 per cent in 1571 to 8 per cent in 1624, then to 6 per cent by 1651 and to 5 per cent in 1714. The trends in Paris, Lyon, Venice, Genoa and Hamburg were similar.[179] In the Dutch capital market, which was the cheapest, this meant a fall of more than 50 per cent in the price of loans in a century. These circumstances affected long-term loans especially, interest on which also fell progressively, shifting the balance of European power politics in favour of those states that were able to issue more debt at lower interest, like England and the Netherlands. Debt issues and their terms had far-reaching economic consequences in each state, as money could be spent on war or economic development, but when interest rates were high it represented an important slice of government expenditures, which could thwart the achievement of goals. It was at this time that the modern debate over the economic role of public debt and its potentially disastrous political consequences first emerged, as Sonenscher has recently shown in his excellent study of French Enlightenment thinking on this issue.[180]

The Bourbons implemented a very different public debt policy from that of their predecessors, although this matter has as yet received little attention. As in other fields, the early Spanish reformers of the Enlightenment were faced with an additional problem in their efforts to come to grips with changing circumstances. This was the urgent need to address the debt hangover left over from the sixteenth and seventeenth centuries, which had remained untouched although the Royal Treasury was exhausted by interest payments.

The task began in 1717, when restructuring of the perpetual debt or *juros* issued during the war was ordered, resulting in reductions of 40 per cent to 60 per cent of principal on which the interest due was calculated.[181] Just ten years later, in 1727, another important edict cut the interest paid from 5 per cent to 3 per cent, and the savings obtained were applied to purchase and repay existing recognized debts.[182] Meanwhile, the debt held by the *asentistas* was fixed and interest was cut to 3 per cent in 1742, immediately after the suspension of payments of 1739 and the first measures taken to recover the public utilities leased.[183] Meanwhile, three edicts of 1747, 1748 and 1749,[184] the period of the Marquis of Ensenada's ascendancy, redeemed certain types of perpetual debt, including the so-called *juros usurarios*. The perpetual debt held by contractors to the *Real Hacienda* was also fixed and a *Junta de Juros* was formed to negotiate terms. In 1748, Ensenada obtained a specific fund from the king for the redemption of this debt.[185] Finally, a decree of 1752 recognized the debt assigned to *asentistas* in respect of capital outlays made under the terms of their contracts as valid.[186]

Torres Sánchez's analysis of the national debt only confirms and adds detail to the general outline of the process as described here. As early as 1715 a *Pagaduría de Juros* had been established with its own funds, under the control of the *Contaduría General de Distribución*, and in the 1740s the monetary authorities reduced the number of debt certificates recognized and cut the interest rate. Following José López-Juana Pinilla, Torres informs us that the capital invested in *juros* totalled some 1.9 billion *reales* in 1748 but only 1.2 billion in 1788. Though this 36.2 per cent reduction may not seem like much, it was in fact important, because total annual interest payments, which had been around 98 million copper *reales* in the early years of the eighteenth century fell to 26 million in 1748, 24.4 million in 1758 and 20.4 million in 1799, when the actual sum paid was in fact only 12.9 million *reales* taking into account certain discounts.[187] The principal on the debt may only have been reduced by around one third, but interest payments had been slashed by almost 90 per cent and no longer represented a burden for the Royal Treasury.

All of these decrees were issued in parallel with the legislation by which the state regained direct control over the administration of the revenues belonging to the *Real Hacienda*, and provisioning of the army and navy. Considered as a whole, these measures clearly reveal the political will to recover the sovereignty of the state and enter the international game of nations as a full player, and to assure the economic progress of the country and of the king's subjects.

Other forms of legacy debt also existed in addition to the *juros*. These amounts were probably smaller, but they were also reduced. In 1754 a package known as the *deuda de testamentaría de Felipe V* (referring to the unpaid balance of public expenditures incurred during his reign and recognized by the Royal Treasury) totalled 520 million copper *reales*. According to Torres Sánchez, around 40 per cent of the payments due in respect of loans made by government contractors and tax farmers were settled between 1760 and 1769, rising to almost 50 per cent by 1793.[188]

With regard to other debt, known as the *deuda de rentas y oficios enajenados*, it was decided in 1732 to recover all of the leased *alcabalas*, *tercias*, *servicios ordinarios y extraordinarios* and *cuatro medios por cientos* belonging to the *Real Patrimonio* or royal estate,[189] and in 1748 all of the offices sold in relation to the *renta de Cruzada* were likewise redeemed.[190] Some time later, a decree of 1760 provided for the redemption of the *juros*, *alcabalas* and *tercias*, and other assigned claims belonging to the *Real*

Patrimonio,[191] and another decree of the same year earmarked 10 million copper *reales* per annum for the repayment of debts incurred in wars and military provisions between the reigns of Charles V and Philip V.[192] In political terms, these measures may be interpreted in the same way as the treatment of the historical *juros*.

Aside from Torres' calculations of the debt in respect of the *juros*, the most important such item, the percentage of the total debt that was actually amortized as a result of the legislative measures taken cannot currently be established. This would require an analysis of the Royal Treasury's budgets, which is not possible here. Nevertheless, the data clearly reflect the thrust of the state's actions, which was to recover fiscal and political sovereignty and reduce the budgetary burden of the debt, whatever that may actually have been. A recent analysis shows that debt amortization peaked between 1730 and 1750.[193]

By restructuring the national debt, the Spanish state also sought to improve the rating of its debt, and thereby its credit, in the international markets, especially Amsterdam. This would in turn enhance its ability to seek fresh loans at lower interest rates. This was not an unusual policy at the time. The French state also found itself obliged to restructure and reduce the debt incurred by Louis XIV. To this end it created the *Banque General* (1716) and stabilized the *livre tournois* (1726).[194]

Financial success allowed the Spanish monarchy to launch numerous projects, which it financed using various modern forms of debt in the second half of the eighteenth century. The *Real Establecimiento del Fondo de Rentas Vitalicias* was created in 1769 in partnership with the company of the Cinco Gremios Mayores de Madrid. Torres Sánchez, who has studied this institution, describes it as a form of debt issue.[195] The Spanish state had begun to issue bonds and similar instruments in the Amsterdam capital market, the most developed in Europe, at least in 1770, and the *vales reales*,[196] a kind of warrant, were created in 1780.[197]

Debt restructuring expanded the state's room for manoeuvre and must also have had an influence on the growth in the Royal Treasury's revenues in 1740s, although the details of this process are not clear. Domestically, however, the reduction in the cost of funds in the international market also had one direct and highly positive effect on the formation of the domestic market, which was to reduce the interest on the *censos*.

Reduction of the *censos*, increase in land rents and agrarian policy

The interest or *pensiones* payable on the medieval system of property-backed perpetual loans known in the Crown of Castile as the *censos al quitar* and as *censales* in the Crown of Aragon[198] had risen in the sixteenth century to 14 per cent and more. Average interest rates began to fall again in the seventeenth century, however, especially after 1650, due to a fall in the mortgage values of estates (caused by demographic crisis and shrinking agricultural output) and the oversupply of credit available from ecclesiastical institutions, which had surplus cash from the donations they received but scant investment opportunities. The fall in interest rates in European markets must also have played a part, although I am not yet able to say exactly what. Be this as it may, the minimum interest rates on *censos* in the Crown of Castile, which were set by the king,[199] were lowered from 5 per cent to 3 per cent.[200] The same cut was applied in the Crown of Aragon, though somewhat later in 1750.[201] The reasons for this difference in timing are not known. As far as I have been able to discover, the lag in the kingdom of Aragon may have been a consequence of the need to keep interest rates high in order to encourage the clergy to continue investing in municipal debt, which was in turn required to pay war contributions, and in order to win the cooperation of the local treasuries, which were already heavily indebted before the War of Succession, in the implementation of the new *real contribución*. In any event, interest rates were generally lower than in the sixteenth century whether the *pensiones* were set at 5 per cent or 3 per cent.

In this context of falling interest rates, renewed Malthusian population growth drove up land rents. The combined action of these factors caused the interest rate and land rents curves to cross like scissors at different moments depending on the place, but in any case in the decades between 1730 and 1770. This phenomenon had extraordinary consequences. When interest rates crossed the rising land rent curves, the creditors holding the *censos*, most of them ecclesiastical institutions, progressively moved large amounts of capital into agrarian investments. This shift was accomplished by the execution of the *censales*, land purchases and other more or less lawful and morally acceptable methods. Hence, both investments in land and trade in agricultural commodities began to grow, while investment in *censos* dwindled, prey to declining returns.

The following testimony provides a clear description of the phenomenon. It refers to the moment in 1757 when the Carthusian monks of the monastery of Aula Dei near Zaragoza sought permission to buy farmland.

> El P. D. Pedro Casamayor nos dice: que por la Audiencia de Zaragoza se venden unos campos de labor en la ribera del río Jalón, vecinos de otro de este monasterio. La buena calidad de la tierra, la comodidad de traer los granos al monasterio, pues sólo distan de él una corta jornada, la necesidad que tenemos de ellos para el gasto ordinario, y considerarnos *casi obligados a establecernos sobre tierras, que a más de su permanencia dan sus frutos sin las contingencias y defectos de los censales, casi perdidos ya en este reino con notable atraso de esta santa casa*[202]; nos precisa a suplicar a S. P. Vdo. se digne concedernos grata licencia para comprarlas [...] [18 June 1756].[203]

The italicized words reveal that investments in *censales* were no longer attractive compared with land in this district.

The monarchy's officials, and in particular the intendants and *corregidores*, were aware of what was happening, and in the mid-eighteenth century they sought to benefit by diverting the capital sunk in dormant and unprofitable *censales* into new government initiatives, frequently resorting to more or less sincere patriotic arguments. I believe this is why numerous convents and ecclesiastical institutions are found buying shares in local manufacturing companies, trading concerns and banks in state-sponsored schemes in the mid- and late eighteenth century. The purchase of shares in the royal trading companies and factories in the mid-eighteenth century, considered below, is a case in point.

However, most of the capital locked up in the *censos* was moved into exploitation of the land and the trade in agricultural commodities, which remained a lucrative business for several decades. This benefitted the nobility and the Church, who owned extensive landholdings and farm surpluses, as well as their factors and the social and commercial networks with access to the market in farm products. As we shall also see, the better-off local peasants and the members of the trade networks described in the following chapters also turned the changing circumstances to their advantage. For example, the networks of French migrants who baked bread in the towns and were paid in grain found themselves able to engage in small-scale speculation based on seasonal price fluctuations in the countryside. The networks of Basque and Navarrese traders who supplied the army and the Court with provisions, operating privileged mechanisms through the Five Guilds and other companies, also did well. The Catalans also exploited the situation, penetrating deep into Aragon to lease seigneurial rents and trade in grain, wool, oil and other commodities. Many started out as factors but soon themselves became merchants, developing local credit in both cash and grain. We shall see below how the partners of one of the main such networks, the *Compañía de Aragon*, engaged in speculative and usurious lending, allowing them to gain control of entire villages under highly advantageous conditions. The phenomenon must have been widespread throughout Spain, although varying in the details from place to place. As we now know, networks of merchants and mule drivers from Valencia carried on a similar trade in grain in La Mancha, and something very much the same must have occurred in the lands of Old Castile and other regions.

In these circumstances, under pressure first from Malthusian population growth and rising land prices, and then from the riots of April and May 1766, the reformists' agrarian policy included numerous initiatives to bring unused municipal and crown land into cultivation, and to foster colonization and irrigation schemes, although they were at pains to avoid affecting seigneurial or ecclesiastical entailments.

Zavala Auñón was already proposing a raft of agrarian reforms in 1732, including cultivation of new land, reform of the communal granaries and abolition of the grain tax.[204] In my opinion, however, the first major measure enacted was the *ordendanza de Montes y Plantíos* of 1748,[205] because it transferred jurisdiction for disputes over the use of forest land belonging to seigneurial villages from the lords to the local magistrate or *corregidor*, allowing appeal to the *Consejo de Castilla*, the *Consejo de Hacienda* or indeed to the *Superintendencia de Marina*, as occurred in the marquisate of Cuéllar according to Yun.[206] The landlords thus lost their ability to manage the cultivation of seigneurial lands and, especially, they found themselves deprived of certain jurisdictional rights allowing them to appoint game wardens and foresters, for which they now had to seek royal permission. This undermined their control just at a time of increasing demographic pressure on numerous resources found on uncultivated land, including plants like dyer's madder, saffron, firewood, walnuts, acorns and game. The monarchy, meanwhile, strengthened its power in the area of farm policy, for example in the case of initiatives to till new land.

Demand for land was intense in the mid-eighteenth century. Cultivation of both communal land and *tierras novales*[207] had been on the increase for decades. A papal decree issued by Benedict XIV on 30 July 1749 confirmed the allocation of tithes on new land to the king, where cultivation had been financed by the monarchy.[208] In 1760, meanwhile, the process of drafting a farm bill began,[209] and in the following decades numerous decrees were issued authorizing the enclosure and cultivation of *tierras novales*.

Agrarian growth made the grain trade into a highly lucrative business. The regulations of 1523 and 1528 governing the purchase of *pan adelantado* (literally, 'forward bread') were still in force,[210] but on 15 July 1765 a *real pragmática* finally repealed the grain tax and freed the domestic trade.[211] Various decrees were issued in the following years in an effort to control the activities of the grain merchants,[212] including the collectors of tithes,[213] who were not permitted to form companies,[214] and an order of 1785 renewed the terms of the 1765 decree.[215] Speculation was rife in the 1770s, and huge sums were made by both individuals and companies on wheat loans payable out of the next harvest or harvests.

The trade in grain and other agricultural commodities, which were mostly low-priced but relatively expensive to transport, played a key role in the development of the emerging economic regions structured around cities like Madrid, Barcelona and Valencia. These regions expanded their boundaries driven by prices and increasing transport capacity in a process that created markets which were no longer confined to the historical political regions but were defined by the opportunity to make money out of transportation given the level of demand and prices, because the tariff barriers of the seventeenth century had been removed.

Despite these initiatives, however, the monarchy continued to rule an essentially agrarian political community. In order to complete the regeneration of the country, the Enlightenment reformers needed to address the vexed question of industrial development, a matter that was conditioned by the balance of payments and by French and English commercial interests.

Industrial and trade policy

When peace finally returned, Philip V ordered a report on industry and the trade in manufactured goods in Spain in 1721.[216] Trade with the Americas occupied 20 of its pages compared with only six for domestic manufacturing (focusing on wool and silk), attesting to the ever-present concern about the colonies at this time. The description of Spain's domestic market reveals the decline in the woollens industry:

> [. . .] no tanto por defecto de buenos operarios, que los hay y muchos, [. . .] sino de la falta del consumo de las ropas que se fabrican [. . .]. Y así parece indispensable discurrir y practicar medio de que facilite el despacho y venta de las ropas; porque en su defecto serían inútiles las providencias de restablecer las fábricas.[217]

Consumption had collapsed and the situation was compounded by the crisis of war to an extent we need not discuss here. Furthermore, Castilian merino wool was bought up and exported by foreign merchants. These two factors also played an important role in the ruin of the Castilian silk industry, whose output had plunged in the preceding decades. In this case, however, it was the production of the finished fabric that had collapsed. The raw silk harvested was still spun, but this had become a peripheral industry which was entirely dependent on foreign demand, mainly from France, the expansion of which was unaffected by the parlous situation in Spain:

> La pérdida de las fábricas de tejidos [de seda] la ha motivado tamb[ié]n en gran parte la extracción de la seda en madeja a reinos extranjeros, contra lo prevenido en diferentes pragmáticas r[eale]s; con cuia saca los extranjeros además de no dejar ni los útiles del torcedor alteran y suben los precios de ella [la seda en madeja]. Y como al mismo t[iem]po introducen y venden con conveniencia sus tejidos, más endebles que los de la[s] fábrica[s] de España, se halla el m[inistro] [=artesano] español, que compra la seda a precios subidos por causa del extranjero, precisado a tener atraso en la venta de su tejido, [que es] de más ley, por no poder costearla [la madeja de seda], y [queda] expuesto a abandonar la fábrica. A [lo] que también la [=le] ayuda la libertad y el rigor con que los arrendadores de rentas r[eale]s solicitan la cobranza de varios d[e]r[ech]os r[eale]s [...][218]

In short, war and the collapse in consumption had had grievous consequences for key industries like the production of woollen cloth and silks, deindustrializing whole regions and driving a peripheral trade in commodities to the benefit of French and British manufactures. Fiscal revenues were still in the hands of the *asentistas* and measures to reform customs policy remained unthinkable. Action was needed, but the instruments required had not yet been created in 1721.

In this situation, the reformers' first move was to address the management of the economy, starting with the *Real Junta General de Comercio, Moneda, Minas y Dependencias de Extranjeros*, which was simultaneously a deliberate, legislative, executive and judicial body, and the key instrument of Enlightenment industrial and trade policy. Tariffs and fiscal policy were mainly the province of the treasury secretary and the *Consejo de Hacienda*, while infrastructure fell within the purview of the secretary of state and the *Junta de Correos y Postas*. Historically, the *consulados*, a form of commercial courts located in the ports or otherwise associated with maritime trade, also played a role, providing a forum for the *cuerpos de comercio* or merchant communities in each town. There were eleven in the eighteenth century. The merchant communities were overseen by the *Junta General de Comercio* via the *consulados* and local boards of trade or *juntas particulares de comercio*, whose officers were proposed by the merchants. Where no such institutions existed locally, supervision was direct. The *Junta* regulated the actions and policy of all of these bodies by means of ordinances.

The functions of the *consulados* were confined exclusively to their jurisdiction as commercial courts after 1737, and the organizational model and ordinances of the *Consulado de Bilbao* were applied to them throughout Spain. Meanwhile, executive functions associated with the Crown's economic policy were vested in the *Junta General de Comercio*, which took over responsibility for the *consulados* and certain local boards of trade created in cities like Barcelona,[219] Valencia,[220] Granada, Seville, Antequera and Valladolid over the course of the eighteenth century.[221]

The *Junta General de Comercio* was the principal institution targeted for reform. Its roots went back to the *Junta de Reformación* created by Philip III in 1620 and a *Junta de Población y Comercio* set up in accordance with a royal warrant issued by Philip IV on 18 November 1625. However, it was Charles II who would finally establish it as a regulatory institution in a royal decree of 29 January 1679.[222] It was vested with jurisdictional powers by a royal decree of 25 December 1682 and it was made an appellate court by a royal decree of 4 March 1683. The activity of the *Junta* was low-key in this difficult period. Under Philip V a royal decree of 5 June 1705 again ordered the creation of a *Junta de Restablecimiento del Comercio* or *Junta General de Comercio* to include ministers of the Crown and merchants, and two years later it was officially formed by a president, a procurator, four counsellors and a secretary in accordance with a royal warrant of 15 May 1707, which confirmed the board's exclusive jurisdiction in matters of trade.[223] Some years later, a royal decree of 15 November 1730 providing for various monetary matters created the *Real Junta de Moneda*,[224] whose members comprised six councillors (at least two of them magistrates and the rest laymen), one military procurator and a secretary. The new institution was chaired by the secretary of the Treasury, José Patiño. Not many days afterwards, a royal decree of 9 December 1730 amalgamated the *Junta de Comercio* and the *Junta de Moneda* to create the *Junta General de Comercio y Moneda*. The secretariats[225] of the two institutions were merged and the official posts existing in the former *Junta de Comercio* were terminated. Another institution, the *Junta de Minas*, was absorbed by a royal decree of 3 April 1747, and just a year and a half later a decree of 21 December 1748 added the *Junta de Dependencias de Extranjeros*, a body created by José Grimaldo in 1714 as the *Junta de Dependencias y Negocios de Extranjeros*, which was dissolved after the War of Succession but restored in 1721. The resulting *Real Junta General de Comercio, Moneda, Minas y Dependencias de Extranjeros* thus acquired its longest title and all of the associated competences.[226] In a nutshell, the institution took off in the second third of the eighteenth century.[227]

The activity of the *Junta General de Comercio* was supported by the intendants, who were vested with the power to adopt measures for the improvement of industry by articles 33, 41–43 and 57–59 of the instruction for intendants of 4 July 1718. For the first time, then, oversight and the condition of local industries were assigned to provincial functionaries, even if they also had other responsibilities.

The *Junta General de Comercio* sought to develop manufacturing by implementing a range of policies with varying outcomes. On 20 October 1719, it ordered that the army was to be provisioned with Spanish products, marking the start of the institution's role in driving demand,[228] a practice which became common over the course of the eighteenth century. Meanwhile, the *Junta* created scores of new undertakings and granted numerous privileges to existing and newly created enterprises manufacturing above all woollen stuffs, linens and silk fabrics, although we have no exhaustive (or even detailed) list of these schemes.[229] Another important initiative was the abolition of the monopoly on the production of *aguardiente* or distilled spirits following a consultation of 7 March 1739.[230] In Catalonia, where controls had existed since the seventeenth century, the production of wine for distilling had been a factor in the development of the market in the principality, and the measure thus levelled the playing field for the vineyards and distillers in the rest of Spain.

However, the most interesting of the measures taken by the *Junta General de Comercio* consisted in the creation from scratch of the *companías de comercio y fábricas*. The four short years between 1746 and 1750 saw the launch of the *Compañía de Comercio y Fábricas de Extremadura* (1746), *Compañía General de Comercio y Fábricas de Zaragoza* (1746), *Compañía de Comercio y Fábricas de Toledo* (1748), and other similar initiatives in Granada (1747), Seville (*Real Compañía de San Fernando*, 1747). The *Real Fábrica de Paños de Santa Bárbara y San Carlos* in Ezcaray, La Rioja, was founded some years later.[231] Other companies were also founded in La Unión (1748), Requena (1753) and Burgos (1767).[232] All of these factories were deliberately created following the model developed in France by Louis XIV in the 1660s.[233]

The result of this industrial policy, in combination with others, was generally positive: according to a survey of industries carried out in 1746, the majority of the 204 factories belonging to the *Junta General de Comercio* were either making progress or actually growing. Only 86 of them enjoyed any kind of privilege,[234] and almost all of these had been granted for limited periods of between eight and fifteen years. Normally, they consisted of exemptions from *quintas* and *levas*, tax exemptions and reductions (*alcabalas* and *cientos*, *rentas provinciales* and municipal charges, and in some cases permits allowing exports to the Americas). The exemptions from *quintas* and *levas* spared apprentices, employees and officers from enlistment into the army, while the tax benefits awarded had no impact on the revenues raised by the Royal Treasury, as the *rentas provincials*, *contribución* and *cadastre* were all collected by way of quotas, and the exemption of privileged enterprises did not reduce the tax payable by the host district.

The *Junta* also sometimes awarded additional privileges, including its own legal forum (ensuring that litigation would be heard in the board's tribunal), priority purchase rights for commodities (particularly important in the wool trade) and the right to trade in certain protected markets like Madrid.

In short, the factories created or supported by the *Junta* did receive privileges, generally in the form of tax benefits, but these were almost always temporary and never in the form of cash transfers, even though the state frequently took political action to secure private financing given the abundance of idle capital existing in Spain. Meanwhile, the intendants succeeded, at least in some cases, in enlisting the active support of members of the nobility and church institutions, obtaining donations, loans and *censales*, and placing share purchases.[235]

A new identity: natives and foreigners

Let us consider one final state policy, which affected the legal and political identity of the individuals and groups of people present on the Spanish stage. This matter turns on two issues, namely the emergence of a single naturality (almost) throughout the monarchy's domains in the Iberian Peninsula and the application of a policy that distinguished aliens from natives, who enjoyed certain privileges (and obligations) in matters of trade which foreigners lacked.[236]

The question of naturality was no small matter. To be a *natural* meant being a subject of the Crown, an important political quality because it allowed a man to serve his king, which is to say it opened the gateway to office and other benefits. Until 1700 there were six different nationalities in the Spanish monarchy – Castilians, Navarrese, Aragonese, Valencians, Catalans and Majorcans. Meanwhile, the inhabitants of the Basque provinces, who were naturals of Castile, could not only claim nobility and a 'clean' bloodline (*limpieza de sangre*) but also enjoyed *provincial* naturality, a matter which there is no space to discuss here.[237] As a result of the political circumstances surrounding Ferdinand the Catholic's conquest of the kingdom of Navarre in 1512, Navarrese naturality was recognized as legally equivalent to Castilian for all legal purposes within Castile.

Naturality had important political ramifications in relation to the *reservation of offices*. This meant that certain offices were set aside for the naturals of each kingdom or principality and could not be held by outsiders. Where they could, the Parliaments of each kingdom intervened actively in naturalization processes, but first they had to be convened by the king, except in Navarre, where the *Cortes* convened themselves every three years. The relationship between naturality and the reservation of offices has been described in great detail for Castile and Aragon,[238] and the wholesale trafficking in offices under the Habsburgs is also well documented. Another effect of the privilege inherent in naturality derived from the sale of offices to aliens. As there could be no office without naturality, the king had an interest in securing parliamentary consent for naturalizations.

In order to sidestep occasional opposition from local Parliaments and institutions, the royal functionaries had begun in the late seventeenth century to distinguish between naturalization on grounds of the candidate's integration in the country in accordance with the laws of the realm, and naturalization by means of a *carta de naturalidad*, which is to say by royal privilege or charter. By this time, such charter naturalizations, which were sometimes granted to aliens as a reward for their services had begun to blur the privilege of naturality itself. Others earned it by meeting the legal requirements of residence, loyalty, citizenship and marriage, and they were therefore treated as naturals without further ado. The Castilian *Cortes* did not meet at any time in the seventeenth century, and this de facto dissolution facilitated the monarchy's efforts to control naturalizations, paving the way for the sale of offices.[239]

The abolition of regional laws and institutions in the realms belonging to the Crown of Aragon transformed the situation in the early eighteenth century. Between 1715 and 1723, the monarchy's plethora of naturalities were unified around Castile, and the king finally won complete control over the grant of *cartas de naturalidad*. The monarchy's policy led to a rapid increase in charter naturalizations, which undermined the reservation of offices for naturals and broadened the social base of the potential candidates.[240] A ruling of Philip V issued on 26 August 1715 in response to a query from the *Cámara de Castilla* ordered that Castilian naturality should not be granted 'without seeking the consent of the towns and cities with a vote in the *Cortes*' where it affected pensions, or ecclesiastical and municipal office.[241] As a consequence, four different types of *carta de naturalidad* for 'foreigners' were defined by the important addition made on 7 September 1716 to the order of 1588 creating the *Cámara de Castilla* and governing its functions:

> [...] se declara que las naturalezas para extranjeros corresponden despacharse por este Tribunal sin necesidad de consulta, excepto las que sean para gozar renta

> eclesiástica, en cuyo caso debe preceder [consulta]. Esta gracia es una habilitación de la persona extranjera para que pueda gozar y tener en estos reinos todos y cualesquier oficios, honores, dignidades, rentas y preeminencias que tienen los naturales, sin distinción ni diferencia alguna. Sus clases son cuatro: la primera, absoluta, para gozar de todo lo eclesiástico y secular sin limitación alguna; la segunda, para todo lo secular, con la limitación de que no comprenda cosas que toque a lo eclesiástico; la tercera para poder obtener cierta cantidad de renta eclesiástica en prebenda, dignidad o pensión, sin exceder de ella; y la cuarta es para lo secular, y sólo para gozar de honras y oficios como los naturales, exceptuando todo lo que está prohibido por las condiciones de millones. Para las tres primeras precede a su concesión el consentimiento del reino, escribiendo cartas a las ciudades y villas de voto en cortes, excepto cuando tales naturalezas son del número que ha solido conceder el reino al tiempo de disolverse las cortes generales.[242]

The final sentence holds the key. Its cryptic wording replaced the vote of the *Cortes*, which was the *sine qua non* for the grant of Castilian naturality in the sixteenth and seventeenth centuries, by the individual, bureaucratic consent of the enfranchised cities whatever the realm concerned. Furthermore, the king extended the power of his council to grant *cartas de naturalidad* to foreigners, while setting bounds depending on the privileges granted. The enfranchised cities continued to have some competences in matters of naturalization, although not necessarily through meetings of the respective regional Parliaments. However, it was the council of the *Cámara de Castilla* and the king who ultimately conferred naturality with the tacit consent of the towns and cities, the only estate convened in the Castilian *Cortes* for the last two hundred and fifty years. Meanwhile, the decrees by which the *fueros* and Parliaments of the former Crown of Aragon were abolished had assimilated the representatives of the cities into the Castilian *Cortes*. In principle, then, the same naturalization procedure applied. The kingdom of Navarre, however, remained aloof from these arrangements because its Parliament enjoyed the right to convene and debate petitions without the king's permission.

Not long afterwards, a royal decree of 7 June 1723 allowed naturals of Castile, Aragon, Catalonia and Valencia reciprocally to hold ecclesiastical office and station without being considered aliens outside their respective territories,[243] which would previously have been impossible without due validation according to the laws of each realm. Finally, in response to a query raised by the Council[244] on 1 October 1721, the applicability of the order of 1716 in the territories of the Crown of Aragon was confirmed when:

> [...] se declaró que en los reynos de Aragón, Valencia, Cataluña y Mallorca debe pedirse el consentimiento de las ciudades de voto en cortes para efectuarse en ellos la gracia de naturaleza que S. M. dispensare a fin de que extraños gocen allí de renta eclesiástica determinada; y en los casos en que por conceder S. M. naturaleza limitada o absoluta para todos los reynos de España se pidiere el consentimiento a las ciudades de voto en cortes de los reynos de León y Castilla deberá practicarse lo mismo con los de la Corona de Aragón.[245]

This clarified any remaining doubt. As the Parliaments of these realms had been abolished, consultation with the Aragonese cities following a similar procedure to that established in Castile in 1715 and 1716 would be sufficient.

In legal terms, this effectively integrated naturalization processes in the Iberian Peninsula, suppressing the role of Parliaments while retaining a place for the enfranchised cities. The subjects of the Crown of Aragon could now hold office in Castile and vice versa, as could foreigners at the discretion of the king. This power was used by government not only to reward foreign nobles with rents and office in Spain, but also to attract engineers, draughtsmen, mathematicians and architects from France, Italy, Ireland and elsewhere, who were brought in to develop and manage industries, public works and industrial machinery, and to help foster economic growth. Many had previously been involved in industrial espionage, especially in England. As an added bonus, more than a few were granted commissions in the army, which vested them with the benefits of the military jurisdiction.

Having resolved the question of naturality, the reformists addressed the matter of immigration policy with the aim of defining who was a natural and who a foreigner. In principle, the debate turned not on identity but on taxation, for the subjects of the king were fiscally liable. This led to the creation of a specific institution, the *Real Junta de Dependencias y Negocios de Extranjeros*, to handle matters which had until then been the remit of the Council of State. The new *Junta* was formed under a royal decree of 12 March 1714[246] by the secretary of state, José Grimaldo, at the request of the French ambassador in order to expedite certain affairs both of his own and of other French subjects, which had run into the sand in various different councils. However, it was abolished in 1717 by the 'new system of government established for all tribunals'[247] only to be created anew by a royal decree of 3 November 1721[248] under the authority of the secretary of state. It was finally merged with the *Real Junta General de Comercio y Moneda* in 1748, which added its name to its own lengthy title.[249] By the mid-eighteenth century, then, the authorities were less concerned to determine whether a person was a Castilian or a natural of any of the monarchy's other realms, than they were to establish whether he was a (Spanish) natural or a foreigner.

Until the 1750s, the legislative activity of the *Junta de Dependencias de Extranjeros* was concerned with regulating the activities of foreigners, especially the French, given the privileges accorded to them by the applicable peace and trade treaties,[250] and with implementing the important order of 1716, which distinguished between resident immigrants and transients. The procedure for the execution of assets owned by British merchants was fixed in 1724,[251] and in 1727 the jurisdiction of the British, French and Dutch judges conservator was established, an office reserved for a Spanish magistrate, *alcalde* or *oidor* of the Chancelleries and *Audiencias*. These magistrates were exclusively concerned with cases arising between transients of the same nation.[252]

By 1750 the restructuring of the state was well advanced, and new goals began to appear on the political agenda in relation to the matter of naturality. Thus, the authorities began to take an interest in the fraudulent use made by the French of declarations of residence or transience. This was the origin of the new aliens policy, which became more clearly based on identity and nationalist in tone after 1758 and resulted in the first register of aliens in 1765.

Changes in the naturality laws affected the legal and political situation of significant swathes of people, which in certain cases had important consequences for the development of social and commercial networks in the interior of Spain. There were no longer any legal or political distinctions drawn between the naturals of the different Spanish realms (Catalonia, Aragon, Valencia, Majorca, Navarre and Castile) as there had been before 1715. Rather, the new legislation differentiated between the king of Spain's subjects, who shared the same nationality, and foreigners. Compared with the custom of the preceding two centuries, this was a major change. It created a common identity without breaking up existing social and commercial networks based on family ties, lineage and language, and it was perfectly compatible with the fact that different social groups should identify themselves in their dealings with each other as belonging to different *nations*, a term which had for centuries connoted common kinship or geographical origin.[253] As it evolved over the course of the eighteenth century, however, the term 'nation' became ever more identified with the political community of which the king was the head and with the notion of country or *patria*. Spain was by no means unique in this. In France too, the semantic shift was sharp.[254]

In this way, a new Spanish nationality, that of the king's subjects, began to take shape over the course of the eighteenth century. This new concept discriminated increasingly between those who were nationals and those who were not, benefitting the former. The Catalan case stands out. After 1715 the people of Catalonia became merely Spanish naturals but without ceasing to form part of the social and commercial networks which for other reasons were rapidly expanding in Aragon and the interior of the Iberian Peninsula at that time. When the reformers later came to discriminate between naturals and aliens, the Catalans were insiders. It may be that this difference was initially unimportant, but as the ideals of the Enlightenment took hold it became ever more of an advantage, especially after the hour of the *patria* struck around 1766. Non-naturals, especially the French, who also formed a trade diaspora, became aliens and were more or less strictly controlled. An emerging Spanish nationalism also did its work, so that even those French residents who were naturalized as Spanish were progressively looked on as foreigners, and after 1789 all of them were seen as invaders of the Spanish *patria* and were attacked, persecuted and mostly driven out of the country.[255]

In the case of Navarre, meanwhile, the equivalence of the kingdom's and Castilian naturality had permitted its people to hold office in Castile since the seventeenth century, and the naturalization process remained under the control of the Navarrese Parliament. Moreover, it was recognized early on that French Navarrese, whether Basque speakers or *Bajonavarros* (i.e. people originating from Basse Navarre, the French part of the kingdom which was not conquered by Ferdinand the Catholic) could seek naturalization, for example on grounds of religion. Beginning in the sixteenth century the conflicts caused by the Reformation in France encouraged a migratory movement southwards, and in these circumstances the *Cortes* of Navarre came to see naturalization as a powerful legal instrument to further the kingdom's interests. Consequently, the Parliament's members allowed the French Navarrese to become naturalized, and if the candidates belonged to cross-border kinship or client networks, this process allowed them to strengthen and extend links. Furthermore, naturalization in Navarre meant that the beneficiaries would also be treated as naturals in Castile. Regardless, the French Navarrese repeatedly requested the king that they be treated equally with Castilians, and after various rulings by the Chancellery (appellate court) of Valladolid a royal warrant of 26 March 1697 provided for naturals of Basse Navarre to receive the same treatment as any other subjects of the king of Spain,[256] which greatly facilitated settlement in the Basque provinces and other territories belonging to the monarchy. In the eighteenth century, the French Navarrese could thus obtain naturalization as Navarrese or Castilian for the asking. It is not currently known how this privileged access to naturalization was actually applied to people who were in fact foreigners, especially after the order of 1716. Logic dictates that it was a further factor behind the significant presence of French merchants from the Basse Navarre region in eighteenth-century Spain.

As trade expanded in the second half of the seventeenth century and French manufactures began to enter Spain in increasing quantities, destined especially for the Court in Madrid, social and kinship groups rooted in both Basse Navarre and the (Spanish) kingdom gradually developed trade networks on both sides of the political frontier, which mingled with other Navarrese networks that had sprung up since the sixteenth century. Meanwhile, the powerful Navarrese community in Madrid became increasingly keen to preserve its links with the homeland, because it was necessary to keep a house in the kingdom in order to remain a natural of Navarre. These two factors – the requirement that Navarrese naturals resident in Madrid should maintain a house in their homeland, and the increasing importance of commercial links between the Navarrese and their French cousins – and the common strand of Navarrese or Castilian naturality played a key role in the development of overland trade between the south of France and Madrid via the kingdom of Navarre in the eighteenth century. Family and commercial links between the merchants of Bayonne and Pamplona, and with the Navarrese community in Madrid, grew ever closer.

Meanwhile, political support for the new dynasty in Navarre helped ensure the continuation of the kingdom's *fueros* and differentiated tax status, which provided exceptional opportunities for a lucrative contraband trade and helped strengthen the flow of goods southwards into Castile and along the Ebro valley to the Spanish Levant. The Navarrese were joined in their efforts by the Basques, who also enjoyed an independent tax status and their own *fueros* though they were Castilian naturals, not to mention a strong position at Court. Once again, then, the Basques and Navarrese found an incentive to maintain what was a highly advantageous alliance, as they had during the customs reform, when their influence in Madrid kept them outside the new cordon, allowing them to retain their own fiscal space and to evade the payment of duties with consummate ease. Though the Basques were naturals of Castile, many of them and the Navarrese shared the use of the Basque tongue and had common interests in the trade with France.

Meanwhile, the French players in the trade were often natives of Basse Navarre or *navarros franceses*, who could easily become naturals of Navarre or Castile, and they were well placed to move easily within the confines of the new legislation governing aliens and to benefit from kinship links with the Navarrese in Madrid. The fact that control of naturalization in Navarre remained with the *Cortes* was a further advantage for the French Navarrese, as was the equivalent of the kingdom's naturality with that of

Castile. Many of the Navarrese merchants in Madrid were from the French provinces of Basse Navarre in the eighteenth century, and in Buenos Aires at least eight of the hundred or so Navarrese settlers are positively known to have been from the French side of the Pyrenees.[257] If they had been born in France but had emigrated to America, this must be because they had obtained Navarrese or Castilian naturality. In order to establish the fact beyond doubt, however, it would be necessary to examine the records of Navarrese naturalization processes in Pamplona, which is beyond the scope of this work. Nevertheless, as Floristan revealingly remarks:

> [. . .] applications for naturalization as Navarrese seem to have been made more in pursuit of tax and trade benefits than to win offices or benefits. This at least is suggested by the almost 700 memorials filed by petitioners to the *Cortes* between 1545 and 1829.[258]

In this light, it would seem that the privilege (for such it was) of Navarrese naturality was a further instrument in the service of the Navarrese, French Navarrese and French trade networks, who used it to expand their activities throughout Spain and reach America.

* * *

To attempt a detailed evaluation of the policies implemented by the Spanish monarchy and state as described in this chapter would open up a discussion that would be unlikely to change the reader's initial impressions all that much. Moreover, it could always be argued that the picture is incomplete. For example, no space has been devoted here to the rationalization of weights and measures, and the development of commercial legislation, the currency market and the use of bills of exchange are hardly mentioned. Moreover, the restructuring of the debt carried over from the former regional institutions after their abolition is described only in passing, as is the reform of the municipal treasuries, which were awash with debts in the early eighteenth century forcing many towns and villages into bankruptcy throughout Spain.

Nevertheless, I believe that the measures considered, some of them well known and others less so, reflect a sustained reformism which shines through even today in the works penned by the Enlightenment political economists associated with the government of eighteenth-century Spain. The state's policies were in many cases remarkably successful, creating more favourable conditions for trade and the development of economic regions. This new scenario in turn offered fertile ground for the growth of trade networks. Let us now look at what they did.

6

French Migrant Networks: Navarre

Spain became one of France's principal foreign markets in the seventeenth and eighteenth centuries in large part thanks to the extensive social and commercial networks developed by French emigrants in the country. As a key point of our argument, then, let us enquire into their nature, emergence, membership, activities, and economic and social impact.

There is no need here to explain how or why these networks formed. As we have already seen, merchants and traders who belonged to a network enjoyed certain social advantages. In reality, however, all migrants seek points of reference and make use of preferably interconnected links both upon departure and upon arrival in order to increase their chances of success in the personal and all too often forced venture of emigration. In the case of trade migrations, membership of a network brought the added advantage of sharing in a supply circuit, which not only facilitated business but also made things harder for rival purveyors of the same goods. Successful commerce requires a customer base, a supply system to secure the flow of goods and information about prices, and the French networks in Spain on the whole created admirably stable circuits of this kind, which proved capable of fulfilling all three of these conditions in the seventeenth and eighteenth centuries. Let us consider two examples, the first of which refers to the maritime trade in *toiles* and linens with Cadiz, which an account of 1777 describes as always sourced from the same place:

> tous nous nationaux établis à Cadiz sont accoutumés depuis un temps immémorial à tirer leur toiles par [le port de] Saint-Malo. Leurs parents, leurs amis y demeurent, et l'intérêt les engage à rester fidèles à leurs anciens usages.[1]

The second example concerns French retailers. There were eight in Murcia around 1740, two from Provence and six from Béarn, and all of them enjoyed a competitive advantage over the 30 or so local shopkeepers because the French wholesalers would sell them alone goods on credit, which was denied to the Spanish.[2] As French stuffs were fashionable and much sought after, this was a considerable handicap for the city's Spanish mercers.

Such relationships were based on kinship, geographical origin and roots, language and the use of the same commercial instruments, all ties which generated trust and helped maintain the network. Those who could also resolved their disputes through the French consuls and the military tribunals. The French were among those who enjoyed this privilege.

French emigration to Spain had a long history. Considering only large movements of people, there were two major migratory flows in the modern period, consisting of short-range migration emanating from the northern side of the Pyrenees, and a longer-range trek undertaken by people from the highland districts of the Auvergne and Limousin in the Massif Central. The full spectrum of French migration was of course more complex, involving other smaller diasporas, which may not have been statistically relevant but were nonetheless important in economic terms, sometimes extremely so. This was the case of the merchants at the ports. Overall, it could be said that the French in eighteenth-century Spain were organized in five clearly identifiable levels:

1. The merchants of Bayonne, Basse Navarre and Béarn, and people connected with them, tended to settle in Navarre.
2. The merchants and bankers of Madrid, most of whom were from Béarn and arrived via Navarre, although some were from further afield, including Bordeaux and Brittany. Together with the Cadiz-based merchants, this was the most powerful French community in Spain.
3. The merchants and companies of Cadiz and other Spanish ports, who engaged in trade with the Americas and had links with partners in French ports like Bordeaux.
4. The extensive, diverse and complex networks of temporary migrants found in the Spanish interior, especially Aragon, Castile and Valencia, who engaged in occupations of all kinds from labouring on the land to craft manufacturing, mining and petty retailing. A number of these formed trading companies, most notably the *Espagnols Françaises* of the Auvergne and Limousin.
5. Settled French residents from earlier migrations, who had become naturalized citizens, married or otherwise, and were more or less integrated in the towns and villages of Spain.

These five groups engaged in every kind of business imaginable, and it would not be possible to consider them all here, or to make a complete study of the French presence in Spain. My aim is rather more modest, and I consider each group only insofar as they engaged in some form of commerce. In fact, all of the groups defined above did so in one way or another, so we shall concentrate on those whose principal or secondary occupation was trade. The most visible were the port merchants and the wholesalers established in the cities. However, there were many more.

French maritime trade with Spain was already fairly significant in the sixteenth century, mostly run by merchant networks from Brittany and Normandy operating out of ports like Vitré, Saint-Malo and Rouen. In the seventeenth century, the Gallic presence in Spain gradually increased despite bans on French merchants and goods, which were sidestepped using middlemen, neutral ships and other such ruses, many of them also employed by the English. By the middle of the century, the French presence in cities like Madrid and Barcelona was larger than ever. Meanwhile, French trade with Spain continued to grow, especially after the Treaty of the Pyrenees (1659), which granted numerous trade concessions to France, and as a result of the cut in tariffs at Cadiz enacted to reduce smuggling and Colbert's decisive support for French textiles.

There were numerous French jewellers in late seventeenth-century Madrid, who even had a kind of commercial representative to the king, and they controlled wholesale and retail trade in Zaragoza, a way station for much of the French commercial traffic bound for Castile and Valencia. Many were from Oloron (Béarn), and numerous French houses were torched in 1694 when a French army invaded Aragon. It was this overwhelming French presence that triggered the mercantilist and protectionist reaction of the Aragonese *Cortes* of 1677–1678 and 1684–1686[3] described in the preceding chapter.

Contemporary accounts provide fairly precise details of the number and occupations of the French migrants in Spain. The diplomatic source of 1715 mentioned above estimates that there were upwards of 60,000 of them at the end of the seventeenth century. Pierre Villars, Marquis of Villars and the French ambassador in Spain, affirmed in 1680 that:

> It might be added that more than seventy thousand Frenchmen bring money out of Spain every year. This number is needed in all provinces to cultivate the land, reap the harvest, carry water, make bricks and tiles, dig lime and coal, and do all such work as the Spanish, through idleness or lack of men, either cannot or will not do. All of these people bring or send the money they earn back to France each year.[4]

Some 70,000 people, then exported their own labour, attracted by the 'lack of men' and hence high wages in Spain.

The Marquis goes on to offer further details:

> However, there is a darker trade that is as beneficial to France as it has long since become necessary to Spain, and it is also one of the principal reasons for its enfeeblement. As the country [Spain] is very sparsely populated and the few inhabitants left spurn the fatigue of all lowly or hard occupations, either out of idleness or vanity, great numbers of poor Frenchmen were to be found in all parts, whose labour and industry attended to all matters forsaken by the Spanish. Having work they profited, and though their profit may seem very small given the tiny sums earned by each man, it amounts to a prodigious total given their large number. In recent years, there have come to be around seventy thousand. Each one of them remains in Spain without settling down only for the time necessary to make his money there. Others replace those who retire, and this wandering tribe, made up of people ceaselessly entering and leaving Spain, constantly makes up such a great number that the country cannot do without them.
>
> It is hard to reckon exactly the sums they make, but if each one of them sent home from Spain no more than ten pesetas, they would together account for seven or eight million *livres* [*tournois*]. It is certain that even the most impoverished do not take less, and that many must bring home much more. Entire provinces of France, which themselves have little commerce, are enriched by this trade, which is all the more considerable because those who ply it obtain such great benefits from Spain with no more than their own store of industry and labour.[5]

Leaving aside some misconceptions, the passage faithfully describes the constant flow of migrants in a movement, which was not one-way but circular (some going and others returning home) and seasonal (although not always so), as well as the poverty of the French migrants (manual labourers who sold their toil), and the importance of their cash remittances not only for them personally but also for France's balance of payments.

Another memorial of 1679–1680 penned by the Marquis of Villars based on the reports of the French consuls in Spain provides a more precise picture.[6] There were 65,000 'hommes' or 'françois' in the country (so that there would have been significantly more counting their families) living mainly in sparsely populated regions like Aragon (20,000 'Frenchmen'), Valencia and Murcia (16,000 'men'), Castile including Madrid (16,000) and Andalusia (16,000). In contrast, there were very few in Galicia, Asturias, Santander, the Basque provinces and Extremadura (around 1,000 in total). The same was also true in Catalonia (around 1,000), where there was considerable antipathy towards the French at the time, and in Navarre (around 1,000 'hommes'), although this was probably because many were naturalized Navarrese and were therefore not counted. At most 5–10 per cent of the total are described as merchants ('marchands', 'marchands en gros', 'negotiants' or 'vendeurs en detail'), which obviously ignores small-scale seasonal trading. The majority of the French immigrants were, then, manual labourers ('valets', 'bergers', 'laboreurs', 'porteurs', and in general 'gens servilles'). Nevertheless, all of them exported coins, often earned from labour ('argent net') but also as the proceeds from sales of French manufactured goods in Spain.[7]

French penetration increased as a result of the War of Succession and the Bourbon victory, and for a time even their political presence in Madrid was overwhelming.[8] The *Compagnie des Mers du Sud* had already been created in Cadiz in 1698 to trade in goods of all kinds, and the *Compagnie de l'Asiento* was formed in 1701 to handle the slave trade. There were 29 French wholesale merchants in the city in 1700, and by 1713 their number had risen to 80. In reality there were more. The city had some 5,000 inhabitants in 1709, of whom 445 were foreigners, one third of them (154) French. Almost all of these were merchants, which is to say wholesalers. Numerous French merchants and bankers also set up in Madrid.[9] Meanwhile, the long-standing immigration of poor French artisans, porters, seasonal labourers, pedlars and coppersmiths, continued its own course, driven less by political events and more by differences in prices and wages.

The French maintained their presence in Spain throughout the eighteenth century, despite growing commercial competition from networks of Galicians, Riojanos, Catalans, Castilians and others, and with the smaller networks formed by other foreigners with a foothold in the country, like the Portuguese and the Maltese. These were important taken as a whole, but they are not considered individually in this work. The census of aliens carried out in 1764, which has been minutely analysed by J. A. Salas, counts a total of 26,504 individuals, of whom 1,398 were German, 2,686 Portuguese (who imported English goods), 6,951 Italian and 13,873 French. Including the French immigrants counted in other surveys carried out between 1764 and 1767, then, the French made up almost two-thirds of the total foreigners officially recorded in Spain.[10] Meanwhile, commerce with Spain gradually declined in proportion to the total monetary value of French foreign trade. However, this was not because the

Peninsular trade declined in absolute terms but because of the spectacular growth in trade with the Antilles. Examination of France's balance of trade in 1777 clearly shows that Spain was the country's primary market in Europe in both absolute and relative terms, and that the Spanish trade was even larger than commerce with the Eastern Mediterranean.

To return to the census of aliens carried out in 1764 and the following years,[11] Zylberberg and Salas provide some figures but the data are incomplete because some provinces were omitted and, as we shall see, the surveys failed to include the whole foreign population. Even so, the French presence merits detailed explanation.

In total, the census of 1764–1767 included 26,054 foreigners, 13,873 (53 per cent) of whom were French. More than half of them (6,950) lived in the lands of the former Crown of Aragon, although no specific details are recorded. Another 3,978 (around 25 per cent) lived in Andalusia and there were 1,506 in Madrid.[12] The census provides some interesting data. To begin with, it bears witness to the general absence of French migrants in Catalonia, who had been numerous just a century earlier, and to the continued French presence in Andalusia (most likely the majority living in or around Cadiz), the city of Madrid, and above all Valencia and Aragon. The two regions that had suffered the greatest harm from the expulsion of the converted Moors or *Moriscos* 150 years before had, then, become the destinations for the greatest numbers of French immigrants.

Estimates of the number and distribution of merchants in the census reflect similar proportions to the total migrant headcount. According to Zylberberg, there were 1,483 *negociants* or wholesale merchants settled in Spain in June 1764, of whom 913 (61.5 per cent) were French. The next largest group were the Maltese, accounting for 14.4 per cent. Four hundred and seventy (45 per cent) of these French merchants lived in just nine large commercial cities. The most important was Cadiz, which was home to 219 merchants, followed by 53 in Valencia, 48 in Alicante, 38 in Madrid, 22 in Zaragoza and smaller numbers in Bilbao, San Sebastián, Seville and Malaga. The rest of the merchants counted were scattered throughout Castile, Aragon and above all Valencia. Symptomatically, there were only six French merchants in Barcelona. The French network in Catalonia failed to grow, and indeed it shrank over the course of the eighteenth century, according to Zylberberg because of pressure from the dynamic local bourgeoisie.[13] He seems, however, to ignore the strength of Catalan retail networks and the competitiveness of the region's textiles.

The census of 1764–1767 puts the French population at 13,000, in sharp contrast to the figure of 60,000 or more according to the country's diplomatic service in 1715 and Villars' 1680 estimate of 65,000–70,000 individuals and their families. There are various reasons to believe that the 1680 figure is closer to the truth than the census figures of 1764–1767. In the first place, if French activity in Spain increased over the century, as it in fact did, it is not logical that the number of French residents should have declined. Even excluding the possibility of concealment from the census officials, there is a second argument, which is that the majority of local and regional headcounts may refer to entire families or commercial companies, and not to individuals. However, this cannot be claimed with certainty in the absence of an exhaustive analysis. The Madrid census, the only one I have examined, takes this approach, so that a single name embraces a whole family or company. If this is also the case in the other provincial censuses, the figures would have to be multiplied by at least 5, making approximately 65,000 French residents, the Marquis of Villars' figure.

The third argument is, I believe, the clincher. This refers to the nebulous legal classification of the census' subjects. An instruction issued by the *Junta de Extranjeros* in 1716 had drawn a distinction between transient foreigners, who enjoyed the rights applicable to aliens and were subject to the jurisdiction of their own consuls and the military courts, and those who were settled residents. This reinforced the idea that to be resident was akin to being naturalized, and it also had one other important consequence, namely that foreigners were required to choose whether they wished to be considered in this or that light, which implied interpreting their intentions and caused all kinds of situations. Attitudes spanned the whole range from those who were settled but still preferred not to be considered resident in Spain to those who had arrived only recently but actively sought the condition of citizen, not to mention those who were interested in the benefits of residence (e.g. guild membership) but had no desire to pay taxes. The classification was far from simple and abuse was common. Indeed, the motivation for the census itself was precisely to begin registering the foreigners living in Spain. In response to a query of 30 July 1763 raised by the *Junta de Comercio*, the king ordered that an annual census of aliens be made beginning in 1764 'de modo que se corte el abuso experimentado de haber sujetos que pasan hoy por extranjeros para disfrutar los derechos de los tratados y mañana se declaran españoles si les acomoda'.[14]

In this light, it would appear that the merchants mentioned by Zylberberg were wholesalers, *négociants* who could be classified as transients with little trouble, but other small traders carrying on seasonal businesses like pedlars, mule drivers and chapmen were not so easy either to locate or to pigeonhole.

A fourth and final argument is how thin the line was between being French or not. The French immigrants who settled down might gradually forget their own tongue and assimilate after one or two generations so that in effect they disappeared. In times of crisis, however, there was always someone around to remind such people of their origins. If the census had included these people, the French population it reflected would have been much higher. In his studies of the border district of Barbastro in the sixteenth, seventeenth and eighteenth centuries, Salas himself refers to annual census data reflecting a multitude of French immigrants scattered throughout the territory. This distribution once again points rather to the figure of 60,000 than to 13,000 for the whole of Spain. Furthermore, when anti-French feeling boiled over in 1791 unleashing a wave of counter-revolutionary persecution, numerous people suddenly found themselves threatened, even though they had settled 20–30 years earlier and were completely assimilated.[15]

Most French immigrants engaged in trade of one sort of another, but their businesses were often very different. The *négociants* or wholesale merchants and bankers who appear in Zylberberg's figures were a small minority living in Cadiz and above all Madrid. There were many others in commerce, however. To discern them, however, we need to focus on the mass immigration of the poor French. For reasons of space we may pass over the details in the south of Spain (Cadiz, Andalusia in general and Murcia) in order to concentrate on the regions closest to the northern border, above all Navarre, Aragon, Valencia, Castile and Madrid, the capital. However, I shall begin with the cases of Catalonia and the Basque provinces, which are equally interesting but differ from the rest.

The absence of French immigrants in Catalonia and the Basque provinces

Many years ago now, Nadal and Giralt documented the large-scale French immigration into Catalonia in the sixteenth and early seventeenth centuries. They place the origin of this movement in the depopulation of Catalonia, which had been devastated by war, and the end of serfdom following the arbitration of Guadalupe of 1486, which had granted peasants the right to stable tenure of leasehold land. Wage differences were a further pull factor. The arrival of precious metals from America drove up prices and wages in lockstep in Catalonia, but in France there was a lag between inflation and earnings. This meant that wage-earners like farm hands and artisans could improve their lot by emigrating.[16]

According to a census of 1637, the French immigrants were mainly young males (11–30 years of age) engaged in unskilled occupations (83.6 per cent were ploughmen, farm labourers and shepherds). There were few artisans (12.5 per cent) and hardly any of them were engaged in 'commerce' (1.2 per cent), by which the census officials meant shopkeepers (*botiguers*) or retailers with an open establishment. There were also some wholesale merchants or *négociants*, who were found mostly in Barcelona, where they founded the *Cofradía de San Luis Rey de Francia* in 1616, which had its own chapel in the monastery of Santa María de Jesús and donated the church's main altarpiece in 1646.[17] Finally, there were the wandering pedlars, chapmen, mercers and clothes sellers, almost all of whom were unmarried men.[18]

In 1620 Narcís Peralta, an attorney of the Catalan High Court or *Real Audiencia*, referred to these wandering chapmen in the following terms:

> [...] los franceses que con sus mercaderías van por las alquerías y casas apartadas de labradores y venden lienço, lino y lo demás conveniente, recibiendo al encuentro huevos, gallinas y cualquer cosa que les den, que vale mucho más de lo que truecan [...].

He then goes on to accuse them of ruining local shopkeepers:

> [...] como los dichos extranjeros van por las alquerías y caseríos, los labradores que viven en ellas, tomando la ocasión que tienen de comprar, no envían ni van a los lugares, y así sucede que el pobre mercader [=tendero local] se queda con la mercadería en la tienda

and of returning to France each year, taking their profits with them:

> [...] con lo poco o mucho que han ganado, dexándolo allí empleado o guardado para cuando ellos saben, volviendo a su negocio, tomando fiado de quien se lo da, y sabe Dios si el día que les parece dan con todo en Francia.[19]

In a document of 1687 the French authorities themselves mention that these pedlars, who plied their trade all along the Pyrenean border, constituted one of the three principal channels for imports of silver from Spain, a fact that gives some idea of their economic importance.[20]

As for their origins, almost all of the emigrants concerned hailed from the districts of the Massif Central (Auvergne and Limousin), the long chain of the Pyrenean foothills, mainly the eastern and central dioceses (e.g. Commenges) in the case of migrants to Catalonia, while those entering Navarre and Castile were mainly from the western dioceses including the Basque provinces of France.[21]

The French practically vanished from Catalonia after the Peace of the Pyrenees, driven out by the constant warring between Spain and its northern neighbour and the hostility provoked by French sieges and attacks. They seem to have become numerous again in Barcelona after the city was taken in 1714, and in 1719 there were two merchant bankers, 25 wholesalers and 35 other merchants. This may have been only a temporary situation, however, given that there were only four French merchants left in 1740 according to Zylberberg, as well as some others whose efforts to do business in the city were thwarted by the local guilds. In 1764 they still numbered only six. However, this figure may be understated as it is taken from the census of that year, which was incomplete in Catalonia.[22] Around this time, meanwhile, the French colony in Barcelona slowly began to grow. In 1780 there were once again 31 merchants, and the defeat of the English in the American War of Independence led some British merchants to leave the city, which favoured the French. However, they never occupied a dominant position, leaving ample scope for local Catalan merchants, as well as the Maltese, Dutch and British. Available data throw no light on French immigration in the rest of Catalonia.[23] It must have existed, however, because a report of 1716 mentions that French beggars were numerous in Barcelona.[24] Nevertheless, events in the Catalan capital in the eighteenth century show that the French faced a new development in the form of stiff competition both from the city's merchants and from local networks of pedlars, porters and itinerant labourers, who gradually spread first throughout the principality itself, and then into Aragon and the rest of Spain.[25]

Zylberberg's data from the 1764 census show that this source provides an accurate account of the urban transients and wholesale merchants, but that it is much less precise in the case of rural labourers, pedlars and other such drifters. This was also the case in the Basque provinces, where the French were also scarce. The French faced a different order of difficulties in this region. To begin with, the local bourgeoisie used the *fueros* to hinder the settlement of foreigners, requiring them to lodge with a local, for whom they had to provide full board.[26] Proof of nobility and a clean bloodline was demanded for naturalization, and even the appointment of a French consul in Bilbao was fraught with difficulty.[27] The city had 10 French merchant houses around 1740 and in 1763 there were 22, eleven of them with the status of *lodgers*. This was a very small proportion for a city which only three years previously had 244 shopkeepers, 145 merchants and 22 brokers.

The legal basis for this restriction was probably the requirement for a clean bloodline rooted in the *fueros* of Vizcaya. This was certainly the case in Guipuzcoa, where an ordinance of the *Juntas Generales* issued in 1557 had established that only naturals of the kingdoms of Spain could hold municipal and provincial office, and that candidates must prove *limpieza de sangre* and *hidalguía*, thus adding further conditions to the general requirement for naturality. The king ratified this legislation on 9 April 1664.[28] It appears that the obstacles in the way of those who did not intend to practise a trade were less severe. Over time, however, the commercial interests of local merchants, especially retailers, were increasingly raised as an argument to oppose the settlement of foreigners in San Sebastián and other ports and towns of Guipuzcoa, especially on the grounds of bloodline and nobility. This occurred above all in the second half of the seventeenth century, when numerous Flemings and many more French people tried to settle than previously, and when a royal order of 26 March 1697 fully recognized the right of the French inhabitants of *Basse Navarre* to Navarrese and Castilian naturality.[29] In 1764 there were twenty-two French merchants resident in San Sebastián, almost all of them from Bayonne and Lower Navarre. Their position was bound up with the contraband trade, in which all of them were involved. There was an intense export traffic in smuggled cash from San Sebastián, both by land and sea, in which the French played an important part, although they did not control it.[30]

The Navarrese tangle: the role of the border and the *fueros*

Though Catalonia and the Basque provinces were important to the issue in question, it was Navarre and its links with Labourd, Basse Navarre and Béarn, not to mention Guipuzcoa, Vizcaya and Álava, which held the key. The Basque provinces formed part of the Crown of Castile, and their political privileges only applied to each severally. Each province was in itself a part of the Crown of Castile so it was defined as the individual possessor of its own *fueros*, and in these matters the monarchy dealt with each one alone and never with all together. Navarre, in contrast, was a separate kingdom from Castile, although it shared the same king. Furthermore, the *fueros* of the three Basque provinces meant that each had its own separate system of taxation, internal tolls and, above all, customs barriers with Castile and Navarre.[31] The fact that they maintained both *fueros* and their own tolls and tariffs throughout the eighteenth century in the circumstances described gradually took shape as an awareness of difference between the Basque provinces and Navarre, and above all with respect to the other territories of the Spanish Crown.

The French achieved a particularly strong commercial and political position in Navarre, and the kingdom was the principal route by which they entered Spain in the eighteenth century. In his analysis of the 22 censuses of French residents taken in Navarre between 1764 and 1791, J. A. Salas[32] counts between 30 and 60 French merchants in Pamplona, all of them highly stable residents. He also provides varying figures running from just a few heads to as many as a hundred resident in towns like Estella, Tudela, Corella and other localities of southern Navarre who engaged in more or less skilled occupations, including labourers, artisans, servants, shepherds and pedlars. Most of these were also to some degree smugglers. A 1778 account of French tinkers in Corella describes them in the following terms: 'estos once individuos no tienen domicilio fijo y andan de continuo por los pueblos de Navarra con sus tiendas de quincallerías y otros géneros'.[33]

In addition to confirming the census data for the period 1764–1767, Azcona discovered that there were in reality 208 French citizens resident in Pamplona, a city of around 12,000 at that time, and not a mere fifty as Salas' census figures suggest.[34] Multiplying this figure by five to take account of their households, this would make some 1,000 French inhabitants, 8.3 per cent of the city's population. Azcona's splendid and minutely detailed study of French commerce in Navarre[35] confirms over and over again the intense French immigration into the kingdom, and the presence of these migrants at every level along the Bayonne–Pamplona–Madrid trade route, from porters and smugglers operating across the border to the great French merchants of Pamplona, who acted as intermediaries and distributors for their peers in Bayonne, not to mention the numerous poor French itinerants to be found in the Navarrese towns and villages along the borders with Aragon and Castile. From there, small groups of more or less occasional porters and smugglers linked with the merchant distributors of Pamplona would carry goods across the flats of the *merindad* or district of Tudela and on into Castile, fording the Ebro at numerous points.

The census figures provide some idea of who was considered French for official purposes, but they throw little light on the numerous transients and temporary residents, and they say almost nothing about settled residents who continued to maintain their French culture and contacts, despite having arrived decades earlier and having become more or less assimilated with the local community. They are also silent on the matter of who controlled trade circuits and flows, and of course about the influence of the merchants of Bayonne in Navarre and especially in Pamplona.

To understand the French presence in Navarre, we must consider the peculiarities of what had been a trans-Pyrenean kingdom in the middle ages but was split in two when the Catholic King, Ferdinand of Aragon, conquered it in 1512. The southern part of its territory was initially annexed as the Kingdom of Navarre to the Crown of Aragon and finally to the Crown of Castile, maintaining its local laws, political institutions (*Cortes* and the *Diputación del Reino*, a kind of standing committee of the Parliament) and customs barriers.[36] Lower Navarre, the northern half of the kingdom, called *Basse Navarre* in French and *Baja Navarra* in Spanish, remained under the rule of Queen Catherine de Foix (1483–1518), who was married to King John III (Jean d'Albret). Their successors, Henry II (1518–1555) and Joan III (1555–1572), who imposed Protestantism in her realm, continued to hold themselves kings of Navarre until Henry III of Navarre (1572–1610) ascended the throne of France as the country's first Bourbon monarch under the title Henry IV (1589–1610), having abjured Calvinism. He annexed his Pyrenean kingdom to his new domains.

Except in minor details, then, the political division of Navarre into two states became permanent. However, a part of the *bajonavarros*, mostly Catholics, who now found themselves subjects of the King of France demanded to remain subjects of the King of Spain. This split took no account of linguistic diversity. Different dialects of the Basque tongue were spoken in part of the neighbouring Basque provinces and in the highland districts of Navarre, and the language was used alongside Spanish in the southern parts of both territories. Basque was also widely spoken in Lower Navarre, alongside Gascon and French.

An important point for our present topic is that the region's religious and political geography never matched. There were communities of Huguenots and Jews scattered throughout the area, but above all the Catholic parishes of Labourd and a part of Basse Navarre belonged to the diocese of Bayonne, which at the end of the sixteenth century also included part of the Basque province of Guipuzcoa (the area around Pasajes and Fuenterrabía) and in northern Navarre the district of the Cinco Villas and the valleys of Lerín and Baztán.[37] This mattered because the bishop of Bayonne, like any other, owned and leased land in these areas, received tithes and ruled on matters of canon law, generating monetary flows from Spanish to French Navarre. It was especially consequential in the Valley of Baztán, which was Spanish territory but extended further than the northern slopes of the Pyrenees, taking the political frontier beyond the highland crest and watershed down into the open land beyond and facilitating the passage of the mountains. Because of this, Baztán became in time the main route for trade and contraband traffic between Bayonne and Pamplona.

In any event, flows of migrants and goods bound from France to Castile and Madrid could travel by either of two alternative routes via the Basque provinces or Navarre from the early sixteenth century onwards. Both territories had their own local laws and representative institutions, and their customs duties represented one of their main, and most secure, sources of revenues.

Aragon and Catalonia, the other frontier realms, also had their own laws, institutions and tolls but lost them at the beginning of the eighteenth century, unlike Navarre, Vizcaya and Guipuzcoa, which succeeded in holding on to their *fueros*, perpetuating a situation of political and fiscal fragmentation at the western end of the Pyrenees with important consequences in several ways.

A first point, which is nearly always ignored, is that a customs frontier had existed between Navarre and Guipuzcoa for centuries, and it remained in place throughout the eighteenth century. As Azcona correctly argues:

> though there were no customs barriers between Guipuzcoa, Álava and Vizcaya, there were between Navarre and the [Basque] Provinces, which created two distinct customs spaces. This greatly reduced the opportunity to supply the markets of Aragon and the upper Duero from Guipuzcoa via Navarre, given the existence of a double customs barrier. The first consisted of the *aduanillas* of Tolosa, Segura and Ataún on the border between Navarre and Guipuzcoa, and the tolls at Bernedo, Santa Cruz de Campezo and Salvatierra on the confines [of Navarre] with Álava, and the second was formed by the line of the Ebro – customs districts of Logroño and Ágreda – on the south-southeast border with Castile and Aragon.[38]

There was no problem, then, if goods entering and leaving Bilbao were despatched to Castile via the southward route through Vitoria and Burgos, but the northwestern border between Navarre and Guipuzcoa and Álava discouraged traffic between Bilbao and Castile via Ágreda, and above all it obliged the mule drivers of San Sebastian to reach Ágreda via a roundabout route, preventing them from heading directly to the southeast towards Navarre, Aragon, Catalonia and Valencia. Political geography thus imposed its reality on the region's physical topography.

The *fueros* were the second differentiating factor. While the naturalization of foreigners was always difficult in the Basque provinces, this was not so in Navarre. However, it remains unclear whether this was really a decisive factor in the long run, as we shall see, or quite what its effects may have been. The thorny issue of religious differences may have made it important in the sixteenth century but less so in the seventeenth and eighteenth. In any event, the Basque provinces were home to a sizeable Jewish community in the late fifteenth century, and Jews were also prevalent in the monarchy's bureaucracy. When they were expelled from Vizcaya (1486), Guipuzcoa (1482), Álava (1492) and the rest of Castile (1492), the Basques stepped into their shoes in the Bilbao wool trade and in the service of the king. To prevent their return, the provincial *Juntas* enacted highly restrictive settlement laws applicable exclusively to converted Jews.[39] However, Navarre, which was not absorbed into the Spanish monarchy until 1512, was still a foreign realm at this time, and it stood aloof from these events. Many Jews sought refuge there, and when the kingdom was annexed to Castile some simply moved to Basse Navarre, the part of the kingdom which came under the aegis of the king of France, where a large colony of Jewish merchants were already settled in Bayonne, the region's hub. This early group continued to grow. Many of those expelled from Castile in 1492 had sought refuge in Lisbon, but when Portugal was annexed by the Hispanic monarchy at the end of the sixteenth century they were forced to migrate again. Some found their way to Bayonne, further swelling the city's Jewish colony. As mentioned above, the Navarrese *fueros* created incentives for the French to settle in Navarre, and this became much easier for them in the kingdom than it was in the Basque provinces at least until the end of the eighteenth century. It is far from certain, however, that the *fueros* of Vizcaya, Guipuzcoa and Álava actually prevented foreigners from settling in the Basque Country. After all, some fifty English and a number of Dutch merchants are recorded as being permanently established in Bilbao in the mid-seventeenth century.[40] Be this as it may, the difference in French settlement patterns was rooted in the provincial *fueros* which had developed the notions of *limpieza de sangre* and innate *hidalguía*. Many of the inhabitants of Álava, Vizcaya and Guipuzcoa spoke Basque, the tongue of Túbal, and they believed themselves to be the original inhabitants of Spain, the last pure and noble remnant of its people. Moreover, they linked these ideas to the notion that they were more Catholic than anybody else, which separated them from both Protestants and Jews. Religion thus exacerbated competition between the Catholic Spanish merchants of Bilbao and San Sebastián, the Protestant British of Bilbao and the Catholic French and French Jews of Bayonne, where they dominated trade while maintaining close links with the French and Spanish merchants of Navarre.

In the seventeenth century the wool trade centred on Burgos shifted to Bilbao, increasing the city's commercial importance, but the provincial laws throttled the activity of trade diasporas. As a result, Bilbao gradually developed an autochthonous commercial and financial bourgeoisie over the course of the seventeenth and eighteenth centuries, made up of merchant-banking families who used the city's port, the trade in wool and iron, and their links with the Castilian market to run the distribution of imported goods both in their immediate geographical region and in America. They also invested in rural manufacturing, especially iron foundries and tanneries, and in animal husbandry, raising livestock for wool and meat, managing the whole supply chain using credit and forward purchases. Other ventures included rope making and the manufacture of nets and rigging.

These merchants also formed modern commercial partnerships, which engaged in general, unspecialized trade. Around the middle of the eighteenth century, they added *compañías comanditarias*, a kind of partnership in which one partner, the *comanditario*, contributed capital, and the other, the *complimentario*, managed the business. Such partnerships made up 8 per cent of all companies formed between 1737 and 1829. However, there were few joint stock companies, which were common in Cadiz, in industry and in the maritime insurance business run from Barcelona.[41] The French, and French companies, meanwhile, were largely absent from trade in the Basque Country, as has been amply demonstrated.[42]

The difficulty of entering Vizcaya and Guipuzcoa to trade, whether by land or by sea, had consequences which even today are not given all the attention they deserve. One of these was the matter of control of the frontier towns of Irún and especially Fuenterrabía, which was constantly disputed by France and for a short time even belonged to Navarre (1521–1523). The historical bounds of the kingdom of Navarre stretched as far as Vera de Bidasoa, adjacent to the port of Fuenterrabía, which is the last town before the border of the Castilian provinces of the Basque Country with France, and is also the only point where Navarre could aspire to an outlet to the sea that was not actually in France. As Fuenterrabía belonged to Guipuzcoa, the province bordered with France, leaving Navarre bereft of a seaport for its trade or any connection with a Castilian port without crossing a customs border. Hence, the Navarrese necessarily had to trade through France, which is to say through Bayonne.[43]

Customs duties and taxation in Navarre, and their relationship with immigration

The difficulty of settling in the provinces of Vizcaya and Guipuzcoa contrasted with the ease of the process in Navarre. From some time probably in the fifteenth century, and certainly from 1628 onwards, the naturals of Navarre enjoyed among other privileges that of importing goods without paying the customs duties or *tablas* set by the *Cámara de Comptos* until 1749, which provided a large part of the revenues of the *Vínculo*, as the Navarrese Royal Treasury kingdom was known.[44] Furthermore, it had already been clearly established by 1580 that the Navarrese *Cortes* were vested with the sole authority to grant *cartas de naturaleza*, the charter by which a person could be made a natural of Navarre and enjoy the rights and freedoms of the kingdom's inhabitants. Foreigners enjoyed certain limited privileges, such as the right to hold fairs or to pay lower *alcabalas*. However, the Navarrese Parliament had also approved the grant of *cartas de naturaleza* to any foreigners who might settle at least since the *Cortes* of 1628 and 1645, in order to maintain the kingdom's commercial links with Béarn, which went back at least as far as the fourteenth century.[45] According to legislation enacted in 1645, non-naturalized foreigners were required to pay customs duties, even if they were settled and married to Navarrese women: 'los que no son naturales, o no están naturalizados por los tres Estados paguen los derechos reales en las tablas, aunque estén casados y domiciliados en él, y con mujeres naturales'.[46]

This decision was taken for reasons and in circumstances which we cannot go into here,[47] but it had important consequences in the long run. Though Pamplona was still connected to the sea via the port of San Sebastian in the sixteenth century, the incentive for French merchants to settle tightened the city's links with the traders of Bayonne, and it became increasingly integrated in the economic orbit of the French port, strengthening commercial networks based on exports of Navarrese, Castilian and Aragonese wool, and the import of colonial goods and French or Dutch manufactures. Via their partners in Pamplona or in concert with local companies, the merchants of Bayonne and Béarn were easily able to import their goods into Navarre, which offered them a low-tax trading area.

Navarre also attracted imports of French manufactured goods in the late sixteenth century, a time when the Aragonese were busy strengthening their land borders with new tariff barriers and tightening the conditions for settlement by French immigrants. Commercial ties between Pamplona and San Sebastian gradually loosened, and Basque xenophobia in Guipuzcoa and Vizcaya only strengthened the links between Bayonne and Pamplona, which became a way station for French goods on their way to the south of Navarre, whence they were imported or smuggled by the highways and byways into Castile and Aragon.

The French networks in Navarre expanded in the second half of the seventeenth century, and by the outbreak of the War of Succession, their agents, some of whom were by this time naturalized, became an interested party in the transformations brought about by the conflict, in particular the plans to reorganize the map of Spain's customs arrangements by removing internal tolls and establishing new posts at the ports and at the monarchy's land borders, an initiative that was intended as a rationalization and as a means of reorganizing the Crown's revenues. This brings us to the heart of the question – the existing customs barriers. Let us, then, describe the customs arrangements in place in Navarre, the duties established and the nature of the taxpayers.

One of the main sources of revenue for the royal treasury of Navarre, the *Vínculo*, had been the *tablas* or customs duties since the late medieval period. These revenues, the *renta de tablas*, were managed by the *Cámara de Comptos* and were usually leased every three years. This remained the case until 1749, when their administration was transferred to the *Dirección General de Rentas* as part of a broad national reform plan. Legal and official powers, meanwhile, were vested in the *Consejo Real de Navarra*, whose regent was appointed as a sub-delegate magistrate presiding over a Treasury tribunal with jurisdiction in matters of contraband. This body in turn answered to the directors general of the revenue and to the superintendent general of the *Real Hacienda*. The key to this new phase was the end of the system of farming the *renta de tablas*, which came to be administered directly by the king's functionaries. Meanwhile, new tariff ordinances were published by a royal decree of 11 November 1749.[48]

The above factors combined from the sixteenth century onwards to heighten the economic and political importance of trade with France. The merchants of Pamplona increasingly managed Spain's trade deficit with France, importing manufactured goods from over the border and exporting Castilian and Aragonese wool. The decrees of 13 August 1717 and 18 December 1718, which moved the Castilian tolls on the Ebro north to the Basque ports and the French frontier, and the subsequent decree of 16 December 1722, which restored the previous situation, bracket a four-year period of extraordinary economic importance. No tariffs were charged on either frontier in these years, allowing a simply colossal increase in smuggling,[49] racking up huge fortunes for the Navarrese merchants, who had already made succulent profits as military contractors during the War of Succession and acquired strong positions in government and in the financial affairs of the capital.

It was the opposition of these groups allied to the Basques and pressure from France that eventually led to the restoration of the Castilian tolls to their original situation, thwarting the incipient Spanish customs union. The Navarrese *tablas* remained in place throughout the eighteenth century despite the king's continual overtures to reach an accommodation to shift the customs border northward to Navarre's frontier with France, as reflected in the debates of the *Cortes* held in 1757 and 1780–1781.[50] In fact, the monarchy almost succeeded in its endeavour when the free trade decrees of 1778 authorized the port of San Sebastian to trade with the Americas. However, the question of tolls had become ever more closely associated with the *fueros*, so that they were seen as an essential right. The defence of the *fueros* thus came to be associated with keeping the tolls on Navarre's southern border while maintaining free trade with France. Thus, the interests of the merchants of Pamplona and Baztán eventually prevailed in the kingdom's institutions over those of the southern landowners, personified by figures like the Marquis of San Adrián, who wished to see the customs barrier moved north to allow the integration of their agricultural output with Spain's incipient national market. Associated as it was with the defence of the *fueros*, Navarre's so-called 'free trade' spawned an extensive literature in the eighteenth and nineteenth centuries, though we can do no more than mention it in passing here.[51]

As García-Zuñiga correctly argues, the agricultural growth of the southern part of the kingdom resulted in a fracture in Navarrese society between the commercial bourgeoisie of Pamplona, and the mule drivers and smugglers of the highland valleys in the north, all of whom were interested in keeping up the free or almost free trade with Béarn, and the large agricultural landowners of the south, who wanted to end the customs border with Castile and Aragon so as to benefit from demand for grain in the economic regions of Aragon, Catalonia and Castile,[52] and probably also in the Basque provinces.

All of these matters have a bearing on the present issue, which is to establish who actually paid duties in Navarre. For centuries, the kingdom's laws had enshrined the right of naturals and naturalized foreigners freely to import goods for their own consumption without paying taxes. The legislation in this regard is both abundant and consistent.[53] After 1632, however, both naturals and foreigners were required to pay export duties in the form of the *derechos de registro y salida*, and in 1642 they began to pay a specific export duty on wool, the most significant export good. According to the tariffs published by the *Cámara de Comptos* in 1713, foreigners were required to pay import duties of 3.33 per cent on a list of 39 products in that year.[54] In short, naturals of the kingdom paid no import duties while foreigners paid a tariff of 3.33 per cent (although the tax farmers leasing the *tablas* in fact only demanded 1 per cent), and both paid certain export taxes at rates varying between 5 per cent and 2.5 per cent on wine. In addition, foreign merchants were permitted duty-free entry into the kingdom to attend fairs, of which the Pamplona fair was the most important. Meanwhile, the city of Pamplona restricted liability for the *alcabala* to settled foreigners (i.e. those who were at least temporarily resident without necessarily seeking naturalization). As a consequence, French merchants continued to enjoy tax incentives to establish themselves in Pamplona,[55] or at least to find partners there.

After the War of Succession, the local freedom to import goods tax free was sharply curtailed. In 1716 the naturals of the kingdom began to pay the same taxes as foreigners, when a resolution of the *Cortes* concerning the payment of royal levies (discussed below) required the Navarrese temporarily to pay import duties of 1.5 per cent for a period of four years and foreigners to pay a duty of 3.33 per cent to the Royal Treasury plus a temporary surcharge of 1 per cent to the *Vínculo* (the Navarrese treasury). The *Cortes* of Navarre continued to approve the new tax, called the *impuesto* or *derecho de mercaderías*, in its next five sessions, linking periods so that, though temporary, it came to function as a permanent or quasi-permanent tax. Foreigners continued to pay import taxes of 3.33 per cent plus the temporary 1 per cent surcharge as explained above, but the tenants of the *tablas* allowed them a de facto rebate '*con el fin de facilitar el más copioso comercio*' according to the Royal Council in 1747. In total, then, the tax was less than 4.33 per cent, but as naturals paid even less (1.5 per cent), the principal foreign traders present in Navarre, the merchants of Bayonne, adopted the practice known as *encabezamiento*, which consisted of bringing goods into Navarre in the name of a local partner in order to pay less tax.[56] For a French merchant in Bayonne, the best possible partner in Pamplona was a natural of Navarre, especially if he was of French origin but had become naturalized in the kingdom.

The amount of the *derecho de mercaderías* or import duty fluctuated over the course of the eighteenth century and various exemptions were established until it was eventually equalized for all taxpayers. In 1716, it was payable only by merchants who were naturals of Navarre, but resident foreign merchants were included in 1744 and non-resident foreign merchants in 1780. The tariffs approved by the *Cortes* fluctuated over the years, so that naturals were required to pay 1.5 per cent after the Parliament of 1716 and again in 1744, which was cut to 1 per cent by the Parliament of 1766. Foreigners, meanwhile, paid 3.3 per cent after the Parliament of 1715–1716, 1.5 per cent after 1724 and 1 per cent after the Parliaments of 1744 and 1766.[57] Hence, the import tax payable by naturals came to equal the charge for foreigners in 1766.

It was against the background of this peculiar customs regime that the events of the War of Succession were played out, and the ensuing political reforms designed, among other matters, to reorganize the map of Spain's customs and tax system. As could hardly be otherwise, then, the French merchants present in Navarre and beyond found themselves caught up in these processes. In 1714 the internal dry ports between Aragon, Valencia, Catalonia and Castile were abolished and, as explained above, the *real cédula* of 21 December 1717 removed the dry ports separating Asturias and Galicia from Castile, and 'Cantabria' (i.e. the Basque provinces) and the Cuatro Villas from Castile, as well as the dry ports between Navarre and Castile and Aragon.

This affected the legal status of the customs duties in Navarre, where the *fueros* had not been abolished and local Parliaments continued to be held, unlike in Aragon and other regions.[58] At the kingdom's *Cortes*, the viceroy and the three estates (nobles, the church, and the universities or cities) negotiated the financial contribution to be made by Navarre to the Spanish monarchy, which continued to take the form of a royal levy, payable by the *Diputación del Reino de Navarra* out of its own revenues and funds, and, where necessary, quotas charged to the municipalities and so ultimately payable by their citizens.

The parliamentary records provide interesting additional information about the how and why of the changes made to the customs regime. After the War of Succession, the king convened the *Cortes* and requested the kingdom to pay a new levy, obliging the *Diputación del Reino*, which at the time was short of money, to consider the application of customs duties to goods imported by natural and naturalized citizens. This was the genesis of the *derecho de mercaderías*. In light of the king's request to the *Cortes* of 1716–1717 for a new four-year levy, the session held on 26 August 1716 debated:

> [. . .] el expediente de pagar los naturales [del reino] d[e]erechos de entrada como los extranjeros en los dichos quatro años [de recaudación] tan solamente, excepto en los géneros acordados como son granos, ganados mayores y menudos de qualquiera especie y condic[i]ón que sean y se yntrodujeren en este reyno, vivos y muertos, para comer, para el uso de la labranza u otro qualquiera, ni de los pescados franqueza y libertad de la feria de la ciudad de Pamplona que tiene para no pagar derechos de entrada y saca, y las demás franquezas y libertades que tienen las demás ciudades, villas y pueblos del reyno en sus ferias [. . .].[59]

The *Diputación del Reino* could pay a part of the levy, but to complete the sum it was necessary to impose new duties in the *tablas* for a period of four years. Negotiations between the viceroy and the *Cortes* were rarely quick or easy, however. The day before, 25 August 1716, a proposal to pay a levy of 117 *cuarteles*, 12 *tandas de alcabala* and 20,000 pesos for five years, and another to pay 15,000 ducats were both voted down. Another slightly different proposal was also rejected on 26 August.[60] The resolution approving the final conditions for the payment of the levy was approved in the following month on 22 September 1716, and the viceroy expressed his gratitude two days afterwards.[61] The merchants of Pamplona were naturally well aware of what was happening in the Parliament and speculated against the outcome. Thus, the *Cortes* complained on 21 September, one day before adopting their resolution, that even before it came into effect:

> [. . .] se sabe que los referidos mercaderes naturales no hayan ni han cesado de llenar sus lonjas de mercado en esta intermisión de tiempo, en que no puede dejar de sentirse grande menos cabo [. . .].[62]

Such stockpiling only shows that the merchants clearly foresaw that duties were about to be imposed on their imports.

The new tax charge imposed on naturalized merchants was to be applied at least between 1717 and 1720. I cannot say how the employees of the Navarrese customs office were supposed to distinguish between goods destined for the Pamplona fair, which were exempt from the duty, and other goods, on which it was payable.

In any event, this was a fiscal problem. In an important speech to the *Cortes* made a little over a month before the approval of the duty on 16 August 1716, the viceroy requested that the levy, imposed for a limited period, should be paid annually on a continuous basis.[63] Philip V was also seeking the fiscal harmonization of Navarre with the other kingdoms of Spain. This is revealed by the viceroy's argument two days later (18 August 1716) that continued payment of the levy was necessary to maintain the military garrison and the defence of the realm:

> [...] sin poderse para este fin aplicar las rentas y servicios de otros reynos, que tienen sus aplicaciones precisas, pues cobrándose en Castilla seis contribuciones además de los antiguos y crecidos tributos sin que ninguno se haya impuesto en Navarra, sus importes y el de las grandes contribuciones de todos los otros reynos no equivalen para acudir enteramente a las urgencias y necesidades presentes de la Monarchía.[64]

This text highlights the contrast between the integrating (rather than uniform) political discourse of the new dynasty, which made its proposals taking into account the goals and interests of all of the realms belonging to the Crown, and the localist positions taken by the Navarrese Parliament, deferring to the voice of its constituency. The king applied the same policies everywhere. Thus, the new intendants appointed in the realms of the former Crown of Aragon spent the years between 1715 and 1722 seeking to increase their scant fiscal contribution to the monarchy by implementing the new system of direct taxation known as the *contribution* in Aragon, the *catastro* in Catalonia, the *equivalente* in Valencia and the *talla general* in Majorca.

The Crown achieved only relative fiscal success in Navarre, however. The Navarrese Parliament did not make a sufficient contribution to cover the monarchy's costs in the kingdom at any time in the eighteenth century, and for decades the *Real Contribución* raised in Aragon was applied in large part to pay for the military garrisons in Navarre (and also in Guipuzcoa, another province with its own *fueros*). The fiscal imbalance between Navarre and the other realms of the Spanish monarchy does not appear ever to have been resolved.

Tax reform and customs reform happened at the same time but not in concert. Hardly five months after the Parliament ended its sessions on 20 February 1717, the king promulgated the key decree of 31 August 1717 abolishing the tolls between Castile, Aragon and Navarre and shifting the customs border north to the Pyrenees.[65] Meanwhile, the naturals of the kingdom also began to pay the *derecho de mercaderías* in the same year.

The combined effects of these two measures are still not clear. Azcona claims that the Royal Treasury incurred substantial losses when the Spanish customs border was moved north to the Navarrese frontier with France, citing the testimony of Pablo de Trell, a member of the *Diputación del Reino*, according to whom revenues contracted by some 20,000 doubloons.[66]

Five years later, a royal decree of 21 July 1722 restored the customs borders between Guipuzcoa, Vizcaya and Navarre, and Castile and Aragon. This was supposedly done for political reasons,[67] although I believe the decision was influenced by the interests of the Royal Treasury, which needed the revenue, and of the Navarrese merchants, who wished to maintain their privileges, and who must have had their advocates among the university members of the *Cortes* of Navarre. Shortly beforehand, the Navarrese had completed payment of the royal levy, and the king would therefore shortly need to seek fresh funds from the Parliament, a further argument for ceding to its wishes.

There may also have been other factors involved. Moving the customs border also affected the Basque provinces, where tortuous negotiations were in progress. It is unlikely that events in one case would have had no influence on the other. Furthermore, many Navarrese merchants conducted their business on behalf of French partners in Bayonne, and it seems reasonable to suppose that the French ambassador would have applied pressure to protect his compatriots' interests.

There is a third factor which is well known – the presence of Navarrese decision-makers in a matter that was very close to them. When the royal order of 7 October 1720 set up a *Junta* to examine the question of keeping the former Ebro tolls at the frontier, three of its seven members, the Marquis of Andía, Francisco de Aperregui and Sebastián de Eusa y Torreblanca, were Navarrese.[68] According to their biographical data, all three had served the king in the Privy Council of Navarre, and they were all well aware of the issues of smuggling and tolls, not to mention the interests of the monarchy's Navarrese contractors and the merchants of Pamplona.[69] As a founder member of the *Congregación de San Fermín de los Navarros*, Juan Remírez Baquedano, Marquis of Andía, was at the head of a powerful Navarrese pressure group in Madrid. Moreover, it is known that Sebastián de Eusa Torreblanca was in permanent contact with the agent of the Navarrese *Diputación* in Madrid.[70] Accordingly, it cannot be said that the interests of the Navarrese merchants were not well represented on the *Junta*, which decided for pragmatic reasons to return the customs barrier to the line of the Ebro. In my belief, it was a decision which served their interests, because it bolstered the existing commercial networks.

Not long after the customs barrier was returned to the Ebro, the viceroy read a letter from the king dated 5 April 1724 on the first day of *Cortes* held in Estella between 15 July 1724 and 23 March 1726, in which he addressed the kingdom seeking an extension of the levy of *cuarteles* and *alcabalas* established in 1721 and the imposition of a 3.5 per cent duty in respect of the *derechos de mercadería* payable by naturals of the kingdom.[71] The *Cortes* turned down successive proposals in repeated votes held on the 11th, 14th, 17th, 18th (when the rate was lowered to 3 per cent) and 19th of October 1724 until the Parliament finally agreed on the 31st day of the month in the following terms:

> [...] se cargaran veinte y cinco mil pessos para en parte del servicio que se ha de hazer a Su Magestad, que se han de sacar de las cargas de géneros que introdujeren los naturales de este reino en él, arreglándose el impuesto a los derechos del arancel presentado por los comerciantes [...].[72]

A further sum was approved on 2 November, and certain minor details on the 15th of that month. As a result, the Parliament offered to pay the king an estimated levy of

133,903 pesos, which once again included the *derecho de mercaderías*. The new tariff tables applicable to this import tax were approved on 9 November.[73] However, this proposal cannot have seemed enough to the viceroy, who turned it down. On 15 November, the deputies of the *Cortes* responded, explaining to the viceroy the difficulty of collecting a levy by imposing quotas on the few landowners in the kingdom, especially since the *apeos* or local censuses were completely out of date:

> [...] [el repartimiento] únicamente comprende a los que en propiedad tienen casa y haziendas, de suerte que los colonos o arrendadores no pagan por este medio cosa alguna, y siendo en aquel reyno [hay] muchos en número destos, y iguales los braceros, oficiales y arrieros, especialmente en las montañas, en que hay poca o ninguna labranza, a causa del [=de lo] montuoso del país, recae aquel servicio[74] sobre los labradores, que se hallan en la mayor miseria por la esterilidad continua de muchos años y por la del presente [...].[75]

Meanwhile, the viceroy proposed setting the *derecho de mercaderías* applicable to the naturals of the kingdom at 3.3 per cent:

> El impuesto de tres y tercio por ciento limita el tráfico a los comerciantes estrangeros, naturales de los reynos de Francia, de que abunda aquel reyno [Navarra], porque pagando sus naturales a el [=al] sacar los géneros de los referidos reynos, con la práctica del tres y tercio vuelven a hacerlo en la entrada de éste, quedando los estrangeros, que sólo pagan a la entrada de este reino y no a la salida del de Francia, de mejor calidad y sus mercaderías y géneros menos gravados, por cuyo motivo los venden a menores prezios que les aseguran el despacho, dificultando este a aquellos naturales, que por razón del mayor gravamen de sus géneros, no puedan darlos a igual combeniencia, faltando por ello el comercio a los naturales de aquel reino.[76]

The border between Navarre and France was indeed thick with French *fermes* or tolls.[77] This testimony clearly reveals France's mercantilist policy, which allowed local goods bound for Spain to pass the *fermes* without payment, while levying duties on Navarrese goods travelling in the other direction. To put this another way, if the naturals of the Spanish kingdom of Navarre exported goods to France, the cost would be higher than if the goods were imported by French naturals. In fiscal terms, then, it was an advantage to be French. This demonstrates how important it was for the merchant or carrier to be a French or Navarrese natural.

Four days later, the kingdom again petitioned the king, proposing a payment of 149,003 pesos over four years (from 1725 to 1728) and seeking authorization to charge the *derecho de mercaderías* on goods imported by naturals. The viceroy once again refused the offer.[78] The explanation is known from the Parliament's protests voiced a few days later at the session held on 29 December 1725. Via the viceroy:

> [...] expressó su Magestad [que] sería de su real agrado se le sirviese con el impuesto de que los naturales de aquel reyno no pagasen en tres y tercio por ciento

> de los géneros y mercancías extranjeras por el tiempo que el Reyno pareciesse, y esa es la única parte que se ha considerado impracticable y en que sin embargo insiste el virrey. Su utilidad [=beneficio] se consideró en las últimas cortes [que] sería anualmente de 12 mil pessos, pero acredita la experiencia que apenas passaba de ocho mil. [...] Pero porque no parezca quieren los Estados cumplir con esperanzas, aunque bien fundadas, sirven en dinero a más de esta suma otra mucho mayor de la que podía producir aquel impuesto en el tiempo de quatro años que se concedió en las últimas cortes [...] y así resulta claramente que el servicio concedido por los Estados es, como el nuevo aumento [propuesto del servicio], mayor en todo que el que insiste el virrey.[79]

As the text reveals, the king's goal was to establish regular customs tolls and duties, but this was precisely what the *Cortes* of Navarre wished to avoid.

The Bourbon monarchy's policy of tax and customs harmonization did not end with Navarre, or indeed in 1726. As an analysis of relations between the monarch and the *Cortes* in the turbulent years of the changes in the customs border shows, the customs measures were part of a wider fiscal policy. The Royal Treasury pursued similar reformist objectives in different political contexts, and it was because of this that internal customs barriers were abolished in other regions, but not in Navarre and the Basque provinces. In this situation, the Navarrese Parliament successfully defended the continuation of the strong commercial ties woven by the French merchant networks in Labourd and Béarn, especially in the second half of the seventeenth century.

The somewhat dry subject of the customs negotiations between the king and the Navarrese Parliament in the early part of the eighteenth century is closely related with the central theme of this chapter, which is the action of French social networks in Spain. The link was pervasive smuggling along the Navarrese frontier, from which the merchants of Pamplona profited hugely, whether Spanish or French. It was because of this that Navarre, through its connections with Bayonne, became the main overland route for Spanish imports and exports in a century which saw continuous growth in trade with France. In this region, Bayonne displaced San Sebastian. The vast contraband trade also extended to the Basque provinces, where smugglers availed themselves of the legal and territorial fragmentation of the Basque–Navarre region, control of which was one of the monarchy's key political objectives. It could be said that the old kingdom of Navarre had become a merchants' paradise, where commercial interests eventually prevailed over the agricultural concerns of what remained a fundamentally rural society. This only spurred contraband trading via the networks linking Pamplona's merchants with those of Madrid, among other places. These merchants in turn recruited Castilian, Aragonese, Navarrese and French labourers and drifters, pedlars and porters in the service of their trade. Peasant labour and farming in general were meanwhile saddled with a heavier tax burden than (contraband) trading, where taxes were low and profits immediate.

The state eventually gained direct control over the Navarrese *tablas* in the mid-eighteenth century. The tax continued to be managed by the kingdom's own treasury office, the *Cámara de Comptos*, until a royal warrant of 2 November 1748 placed it in the charge of the Crown. Beginning in 1749, contraband was prosecuted more vigorously and the penalties for smugglers were stiffened considerably. Revenues increased, although enforcement continued to generate deficits between 1749 and 1780 because of the enormous numbers of customs officers that it was necessary to maintain both within Navarre itself and along the kingdom's extended, flat borders with Castile and Aragon. [80]

Administration of the tobacco monopoly, which the king had granted to the *Vínculo* or regional treasury in 1642, was also taken over directly by the Crown in 1717 in an effort to reduce pervasive smuggling. The *Cortes* of Pamplona held in 1765–1766 reduced the royal levy to a fixed sum, with the result that a significant part of the monies raised could be applied for the first time to pay the army. Overall, Navarre's contribution in this respect increased by 100 per cent in the course of the century: between 1700 and 1793 the per capita tax burden increased from 100 to 360, and the gross tax charged increased by 4.5 times.[81] The final result was that the tax burden increased over the eighteenth century, but the kingdom's customs arrangements continued to favour the interests of the natural Navarrese and French merchant groups centered on Bayonne and Pamplona. Navarre continued, then, to act as funnel through which French goods were poured into the Spanish interior market.

The French moved skilfully to secure dominant positions in this highly complex territorial and social context, and it was almost always the redistribution centre of Bayonne that held the key to their success. The port's activity was basically to act as an entrepôt for goods bound for re-export to Spain. In 1775, over half of the value of the inbound goods handled and two thirds of outflows were destined for the Peninsula market.[82] Azcona has shown that the merchants of Bayonne continued to enjoy tax incentives to set up and conduct their business from the Navarrese capital throughout the eighteenth century, and she goes on to argue that the French firms operating in Pamplona were in reality much more numerous than the established French merchants recorded in the census. The majority of these firms conducted their business via *commission agents*, so that export goods were sold for import by a resident merchant, who was either a Navarrese natural or a foreigner settled in Pamplona and therefore paid less tax.[83] This system was the reason for the major role of re-exporting in the business of Pamplona's merchants. As control over the grant of Navarrese naturality lay with the *Cortes* and not the king, it became a key factor in driving the agency trade in French goods, which became a veritable commercial magnet in the eighteenth century.

There can be little doubt that the commercial networks centred on Bayonne made intensive use, as a pressure group, of the French government and the embassy in Madrid to lobby in their favour, for example when the Navarrese Parliament embarked upon a plan to increase the *derecho de mercaderías* in 1744.[84] We also know how they behaved on a personal and family level, where they practised a highly endogamic system of marriage. Most merchants sought and obtained noble titles, using entailments to consolidate their estates and seeking to marry a wealthy spouse who would further improve the family's position. Meanwhile, they tended to train as merchants either in the family firm, or in trading houses belonging to relatives or close associates.[85]

The efforts made by the French merchants to strengthen their ties of nationality and parentage with the home country and seal themselves off from outsiders were identical to the behaviour of their countrymen in Valencia, Madrid and Castile. The Pamplona-based commission agents of the Bayonne trading houses formed a particularly exclusive and aloof social group, although they shared many common interests with those among the local Navarrese merchants who also acted as agents. The two groups made up the city's commercial elite. However, these wealthy French traders were not the only foreigners to settle. The lower layers of French immigration made up of pedlars, porters, artisans and small retailers were far more numerous, often working as intermediaries for the rich houses. In contrast to the migrant elite, these people actively sought integration and social advancement alongside their local peers, occasionally managing to earn fortunes in the southern towns of the kingdom like Cascante, Corella, Fitero and Tudela, as Alfaro Pérez has recently shown.[86]

The penetration of French immigration from Navarre into Spain followed two routes, both starting from Pamplona. One led to Aragon and then on to Valencia via the town of Segorbe. The other pointed south towards Madrid. The numerous mule tracks which crossed the Ebro at a dozen or so fords converged on the frontier towns of Castile and the Aragonese cities of Borja and Tarazona, whence they mingled to enter Castile by way of Ágreda. This town and its neighbour, Cervera de Río Alhama, were key way stations for both lawful and contraband trade, because they lay on the highroad, the '*carrera de Madrid*' running north to south from Bayonne. Moreover, the route from Bilbao and the ports of the north coast passed through La Rioja to join up with the main route at Ágreda. From there, travellers could strike southward for Madrid or to the east, skirting Navarre in order to avoid paying duties on their goods, and make for Aragon and Valencia following the natural line of the Ebro.

The French in Aragon

Let us now turn to Aragon, the region with the highest influx of French migrants (some 20,000 individuals in 1680) and a key route for commercial traffic in north-eastern Spain, lying athwart the central portion of the Ebro Valley. It was also the region in which the Spanish customs reform of the early eighteenth century had the greatest impact.

The old medieval kingdom, which had lost its *fueros* in 1707, received short-range immigrants and trade via the Pyrenees, and as the customs border with Navarre remained in place throughout the eighteenth century but there were practically no tolls between Navarre and France, the long, flat frontier between Navarre and Aragon became a smuggling hotspot. Upon reaching Zaragoza, flows of immigrants and commercial traffic continued on their way by two routes. The first led to Valencia and Murcia via Caminreal, Teruel, Sarrión, Segorbe and Sagunto, the route of the modern motorway. The second headed south for Castile and Madrid either via Daroca, Molina de Aragón and Sigüenza or via Calatayud and once again Sigüenza. The Calatayud road became the principal highway between Madrid and Zaragoza in the eighteenth century thanks to improvements to the road and posts.[87]

Aragon was also important because it bordered on Catalonia. Most Catalan migrant and trade networks carrying goods overland to Castile and the rest of the Peninsula market (much Catalan trade also went by sea down the Mediterranean coast) necessarily passed through Aragon using Zaragoza as a way station, so that the city became a redistribution centre for the whole of north-eastern Spain.

The French had long migrated to Aragon, and the immigration of the eighteenth century was merely the continuation of a movement that had been going on for some three hundred years. Studied in detail, parish records for the period 1550–1650 bear witness to the presence in Aragon of migrants above all from the French side of the Pyrenees and Pyrenean foothills and from the area around the Garonne river, though still few from the Massif Central. They came because the land was empty, because wages were higher and they could save a part of their earnings, and to escape the depredations of bandits and the political convulsions of the Wars of Religion. These migrants were mostly young men, and at least half of them found work in relatively skilled labouring jobs, particularly in the textiles industry. Only 6.7 per cent of them declared themselves merchants by profession,[88] which does not of course mean that the others never traded any goods.

The French migrants did not make only for the towns and villages from which the Moriscos were expelled in 1609 but mainly entered other localities whose Aragonese inhabitants had in part left to repopulate former Morisco settlements, so that they only replaced the exiles indirectly. Overall, the flow was enormous. Testimonies dating from 1577, 1609 and 1635 put the kingdom's French population at between one fifth and one third of the total.[89] According to the records of the parish of San Pablo in Zaragoza, which included around half the population of the city in the first half of the seventeenth century, some 20 per cent of residents were of French origin.[90] In the census of 1642, Zaragoza's French citizens numbered 990,[91] adding up to some 5,000 people, households included, out of a total population of 22,000 (22.8 per cent). Finally, a report of the councillors of Zaragoza dated 1635 affirms that the absent Moriscos:

> [...] [les] suplieron en parte los franceses, los bearneses y gascones, que, a lo que entendemos, son la tercera o la cuarta parte del [Reino] [...] en la agricultura son los que tienen arrendadas las tierras y los campos blancos y la mayor parte de los jornaleros que cultiva las heredades son [=es] de esta nación.[92]

There was also some French immigration in Catalonia, although it seems to have been rather more skilled.[93] In any event, it is significant that the French presence in the principality had dwindled almost to nothing by the end of the seventeenth century, but it remained enormous in Aragon, sparking anti-French riots in 1694, and spurring debate on the matter of customs and tolls at the *Cortes* of 1677–1678 and 1684–1686.[94] The resulting protectionist trade policy[95] would shortly after become one of the factors leading to the abolition of the Aragonese *fueros*.

Immigration patterns in the southern Pyrenean district around Barbastro are known in detail, and it would have been similar to the rest of Aragon. Most French immigrants were from the northern foothills of the Pyrenees[96] and they often married widows, as in Catalonia:

> [...] son muchachos de cortísima edad (las chicas suelen quedarse en casa casi siempre) comprendidos entre los siete y los veinte años, que llegan para faenas

> estacionales, hacen el viaje de ida y vuelta durante unos años consecutivos y acaban estableciéndose definitivamente. Entonces procuran casarse con una mujer indígena – no pocas veces la hija o incluso la viuda del amo – arraigando para siempre más.[97]

Beginning in the early years of the seventeenth century, Aragon was progressively flooded with imports of woollen textiles, especially after 1620. The first import restrictions were enacted by the *Cortes* in 1626, and these measures were followed by an almost complete ban in 1635.[98] A report by Aragonese merchants to the Parliament of 1645–1646 bears witness to the way in which the French merchants, who had begun by importing wholesale, had little by little deployed tactics based on inter-family support to take over the retail trade, inveigling French apprentices into positions in local shops, where they would eventually assume control. The French also exported silver coins in large amounts, engaged in contraband whenever they could, and imported low quality goods which could be sold cheaply beyond the control of the guilds.[99]

The activities of the French in Aragon changed little in the eighteenth century. The penetration of French textiles was similar to the seventeenth century,[100] and if anything was new it was only the intensity but not the nature of these imports. This invasion of the weak Aragonese market caused the ruin of guild manufacturing in Zaragoza and other towns in the second half of the seventeenth century, and though these industries recovered somewhat in the mid years of the eighteenth century they collapsed once again at its end.[101]

The data provided by Salas on the French population living in the district of Barbastro are drawn from the censuses of 1791 and 1793, which were taken to keep tabs on the French population after the Revolution of 1789, and they clearly reveal the make-up and social organization of the immigrants. According to the census of 1787, there were 598 French residents in the district, of whom 145 were clerics, out of a total 55,517 inhabitants. This represents barely 1 per cent of the population, an apparently small percentage. Most of the immigrants were male, and 90 per cent of them came from the Pyrenean dioceses of Comminges and Tarbes just across the border. A quarter of them lived in the town of Barbastro and the majority (around 80 per cent) practised a trade of some sort, while only 13–15 per cent called themselves merchants.[102] Occupational association was common among them, and they were frequently organized in teams, groups and networks based on common origin or kinship. For example, the coppersmiths, of whom there were over 70 in Aragon according to a report of 1765, were spread over nine companies based in Calatayud, Tarazona, Teruel, Calamocha and Luco de Jiloca. The following account exists of two who jointly owned a shop in Fraga:

> [...] residen en esta ciudad de continuo el uno o el otro y en el entretanto, el compañero a quien toca pasa a Francia y reside en ella seis meses poco más o menos, y no tienen otro ni más negocio que la venta de los calderos que hazen [...].

Meanwhile, the company in Calamocha was formed by 28 men, of whom 20 were present when the census was taken, and according to the report 'los referidos tratantes se consideran transeúntes, mediante hallarse los más casados en su Patria y que muchas temporadas pasan a ella'.[103]

This testimony is of particular interest, because it reflects the seasonal movements of these organized groups of immigrants/citizens/transients, whose members would stay for a while (six months in the case of the pair in Fraga, but up to two or three years in other cases) and then return home, rotating between their places of origin and destination. Only 8 of the 28 members of the Calamocha group were actually in the town at the time of the census. This was probably the usual state of affairs. According to the source, these people were classed as transients ('se les considera transeúntes'), which means that a distinction continued to be drawn with settled residents. The network functioned socially along the same lines as those of the Auvergnese migrants in Castile, as we shall see below.

Other details show that many immigrants trafficked in textiles, and it is noted in numerous reports that they procured their wares from wholesalers in France. They were settled, but this did not mean that they were permanently resident in one place, travelling for short periods to other nearby localities where they would stay at inns for some time, taking their wares with them. Salas cites only one case of a merchant resident in Graus but temporarily in Barbastro,[104] though this situation must have been common. Indeed, the French migrants who travelled from Aragon to Valencia to sell fabrics from the Maestrazgo district would stay at inns, which played an important role in wholesale and retail trade, serving as entrepôts and providing a forum for the exchange of news, a function which has not received all the attention it deserves.

These characteristics can be extrapolated to the rest of the French immigrants in Aragon, who in the long run headed for the more fertile plains of the centre rather than staying in the mountain areas of the Pyrenees. Immigration was also accompanied by short-range migratory movements between towns and their surrounding districts, and by a certain trend to move down from the Pyrenean highlands into the valleys, as Salas has also shown.[105] All of this reflects a general phenomenon of highland migrations, which filled Europe with pedlars, *gagne-petits,* drifters, chapmen, porters and similar figures, who organized networks to traffic in goods, news and their own labour and made especially for the cities as may be observed in the case of the Alps.[106]

Let us end this section by considering a singular fact which we have already mentioned in passing. None of the scholars who have studied French emigration to north-eastern Spain has given a thought to the fact that the numerous migrants found all over the region in the first half of the seventeenth century all but disappeared from Catalonia in the second half, although they stayed on in Aragon. In 1680 there were around 20,000 French immigrants in Aragon, but only 1,000 in the principality, despite its considerably larger population. Nadal and Giralt deal with this matter in a brief aside, remarking that the economic situation in Catalonia was better than in the rest of Spain. This claim is unsustainable, however, because the change in the economic outlook was general, as has recently been shown,[107] occurring in Aragon too and not just in Catalonia. The disappearance of almost all the French migrants from Catalonia cannot be attributed to earnings, because both unskilled and skilled labour (e.g. building labourers and carpenters) commanded higher wages in the second half of the seventeenth century than in the first half, and the same was true in terms of bread purchasing power.[108] The reasons, then, lay elsewhere, in particular in anti-French feeling aroused by occupation during the Catalan Revolt and in the incipient industrialization of the territory.

In any event, the contrast between the practical disappearance of the French from Catalonia and their permanence in Aragon was the prelude to another singular development: the Catalans themselves became emigrants, and in the eighteenth century the abolition of internal tolls allowed their trade and social networks to spread throughout the interior of Spain. For obvious regions, both the old French and new Catalan migrant networks rubbed shoulders in Aragon, the main magnet for immigrants.

Itinerants, artisans and pedlars in Valencia

Valencia is another case in which the nature and occupations of French migrants are clearly visible. The region had suffered serious demographic decline in the seventeenth century, but population growth in the eighteenth century was spectacular, rising from around 317,000 people in 1646 to 410,000 in 1713 (annual growth rate of 0.5 per cent), and 740,000 by 1768 (annual growth of 1 per cent).[109] The French had spread rapidly in the best agricultural districts, but they were also found in smaller numbers throughout the region. There were 66 resident French merchants in the wealthy Alcira district on the banks of the Júcar river to the south of the city of Valencia, living in 15 small towns and villages like Alcira, Sueca, Algemesí, Cullera, Carcagente, Carlet, Poliñá, Alcudia de Carlet, Llombay, Real, 'Tarsis' (probably 'Turís'), Picasent and Guadasuar. By 1774 there were 80. Meanwhile, the district of San Felipe (today's Játiva) was home to 79 French immigrants settled in 14 villages, and they were found in similar numbers in other coastal towns like Denia and in more mountainous area like Morella, Los Puertos (or Els Ports) in Castellón, Alcoy and the highland districts of Alicante. There were also French migrants in the southern town Orihuela on the banks of the River Segura, almost on the boundary with Murcia. These local data show, then, that French immigrants were ubiquitous. In Valencia itself, they formed a strong merchant colony consisting of 12 wholesalers and 34 retailers. Most of the migrants came from the Dauphiné, Provence and Béarn.[110] Spain was easily reachable from the first two regions along the coast of Catalonia and Valencia, and even by sea in one of the numerous coastal vessels bringing goods from Marseille. However, the presence of Béarnese immigrants from the other side of the Aragonese Pyrenees shows that a regular line of communication also existed between the French traders in the Levant region and those coming down from Pamplona, Zaragoza, Teruel and Segorbe.

It would be very interesting to learn how these rural traders conducted their business. The only competition facing French pedlars in Valencia came from the Maltese,[111] who sold very cheap Saxon cloth, and a small number of Irish traders.[112] The French commercial network appears to have covered the whole region. In the larger towns like Alcira and San Felipe (Játiva) there were merchants who imported goods directly, using bills of exchange in their traffic with the major ports of Valencia and

Alicante. These merchants in turn supplied the secondary networks of shopkeepers and retailers who sold French fabrics to consumers among the population at large. They also provided credit for small but nonetheless important transactions, for example lending to the many peasant farmers, smallholders and farm hands who would borrow to buy mules or obtain dowries for their daughters. As a result, the French merchants and shopkeepers played a role as retail bankers, offering alternatives to the antiquated *censales* and cash or in-kind loans from municipal granaries and the *montes de piedad* (institutional pawnbrokers). In this way, they created rural credit networks, some of which became powerful but also the butt of much ill will in times of unrest. As we shall see below, Catalan merchants operated a very similar system in Aragon at around this time.

According to the available data, then, the French had penetrated deep into the social fabric and created extensive occupational, kinship and business networks, and they maintained a regular migratory traffic between their areas of settlement and France, whence they brought goods, apprentices, relatives and other people from their home villages and districts. These networks grew throughout the course of the eighteenth century, and the anti-French riots that erupted in Spain when the War of the Convention began in 1793 bear witness to their dominant position in activities like the negotiation of bills of exchange, the trade in silks produced by the artisans of Valencia (which they controlled by means of forward purchases at fixed prices), lending to peasants against their harvests,[113] forward purchases of crops (and the resale of produce at higher prices), and the lease of draught animals to peasants for terms of 4–6 years. In the city of Valencia they also monopolized the trade in linens and woollen cloth, which they imported from France almost completely, and they only employed French apprentices and assistants in their shops. Again, almost all of their wares were sourced from France.[114] Salas cites a report on the activities of the French in Valencia *Junta Particular de Comercio y Moneda* sent to Madrid in 1764:

> Ils ne se servent jamais d'autres jeunes employés que ceux de leur pays, et dans ce but s'octroient le commerce du détail et les jeunes Espagnols ne pourront jamais s'instruire dans cette branche du commerce ni dans celle du commerce de gros.[115]

The text is revealing about the instruction of apprentices in the secrets of a trading company's business: only insiders were admitted.

It is probable that French was used in bookkeeping and commercial correspondence as a means of keeping each company's business away from prying eyes. Because of this, apprentices had to be French, a requirement which is also found in the workings of Catalan, Navarrese and Basque companies, whose members were all, or almost all, of the same nation. In short, the French commercial networks in Valencia provide an illustrative example of how they were organized and operated in other areas.

It was mentioned at the beginning of this section that one of the overland trade routes entered Spain via Pamplona, passing through Aragon eventually to reach Valencia and Murcia. Let us now consider the other route, which also began in Navarre but led to Castile and thence to Madrid, the largest city of the interior and the political capital of the kingdom.

The *franceses pobres*: commercial networks from the Auvergne and Limousin in Castile and Andalusia

Aside from the case of Madrid, which we shall consider below, French immigration to Castile was not a cross-border phenomenon, and the same was true of French commercial activity. Most of the pedlars and wholesalers operating in Aragon and Navarre were from the frontier regions (Béarn, Bigorre and Labourd), where Spanish demand had helped foster proto-industrial manufacturing. However, many of the immigrants who reached Valencia via the Navarre–Aragon route were not from these border areas but from further afield in the highland districts of the Auvergne north of Toulouse and Limousin in the Massif Central. Many of the immigrants scattered throughout rural Castile also came from these areas. This eighteenth-century migratory flow did not initially involve trading companies, which developed later. The historiography has focused principally on the *Compañía de Chinchón*.

Any examination of this company cannot but begin with the evocative text written in 1783 by the Enlightenment financier Francisco Cabarrús (cited by Jaume Torras) describing the position achieved by the French immigrants in the domestic commerce of Spain:

> Hay varias compañías de franceses en Aragón, Valencia, la Mancha, Andalucía y la provincia de Madrid: quasi todas son de limosines o auverñaces; pero sin hablar de todos me ceñiré a las dos de Chinchón y Navalcarnero. Cada una de estas compañías consta de ciento o más individuos, todos activos, todos industriosos. Mediante la variedad de sus destinos abraza cada compañía todo el comercio, desde las composturas de calderas hasta las especulaciones mayores de comercio. Chinchón surte de géneros desde el Manzanares aquende y Navalcarnero del Manzanares allende.[116] En cada lugar hay un cajero[117] individuo de la Compañía que da los géneros fiados y cobra poco a poco su importe, se deja discurrir en qué ganancia. Todos los años la mitad de la compañía se va a Francia y lleva la mitad de las ganancias de dos años. Allí compran tierras, tienen sus mujeres y sus hijos, pagan las contribuciones y al fin del plazo señalado vuelven a relevar a sus compañeros que se van igualmente; será difícil evaluar con exactitud las riquezas de estas compañías, pero se puede dar una idea de ellas con dos hechos q[u]e me constan.
>
> 1°) Que estas compañías que venden al fiado compran todo de contado, lo que supone un caudal inmenso.
>
> 2°) Que hay individuo q[u]e lleva por su mitad de las ganancias de dos años hasta 10.000 r[eale]s v[elló]n; aora pues, suponiendo q[u]e haya como hay tres mil individuos que ganan unos con otros 5.000 [rs. vn. al año] sale todos los años un millón de pesos, producto de la industria de estos hombres. Qué adquisición p[ar]a la España si pudiese precisarlos a traher sus mugeres y sus hijos, y a adquirir posesiones q[u]e mejorarían anualm[en]te con el fruto de su industria. Estos tres mil hombres no son tres mil individuos. Son 3.000 vecinos.[118]

Cabarrús goes on to describe another type of short-term, seasonal migration involving labourers and artisans rather than merchants, similar to that seen in Navarre, Aragon, Valencia and Catalonia (in the latter case only until around 1650).

> [. . .] la Francia envía todos los años desde sus provincias limítrophes una porción de labradores mozos que son el sobrante de su población, gente robusta, de buenas costumbres, sana, endurecida al trabajo, y que se emplean aquí en los tejares y otras faenas penosísimas.[119]

There were, then, two different kinds of immigration – long distance long-term, but not permanent, movements, and short distance, seasonal migrations. Cabarrús stresses that immigration was not permanent and did not create new citizens, which was precisely the situation he hoped to foster in his report. He wanted to see the French naturalized and settled so that they would not export the profits from their businesses. However, this was not in the nature of their emigration. We may also ask what brought them from the Auvergne and Limousin.

The activity of these French migrants, symptomatically referred to as *espagnols* in their own country, has been broadly described in the work of Abel Poitrineau and Rose Duroux. It is known that they emigrated as pedlars or *cajeros* (colporteurs) or as tradesmen of different kinds in the seventeenth century. Little by little, they took to stable retailing out of shops and even wholesaling, creating ever larger commercial and social networks.[120] It is known that many of the immigrants were highlanders from the Haute-Auvergne (the south-eastern part of the Massif Central) in the second half of the eighteenth century, and that they formed part of a vast migratory movement, which at that time was sending out whole contingents of people related by occupation, origin and highly specific destinations. These flows did not only make for Spain, but also for different cities and districts around France. Immigrant communities coalesced around the initial migrations of men specializing in certain occupations, who formed groups based on kinship, place of origin and destination. Upon returning home or sending news, these forerunners encouraged others to follow in their footsteps until they developed into large, interlinked communities of cobblers (*sauvetiers*), coppersmiths and tinkers (*chaudronniers*), knife grinders (*gagne-petits*), ploughmen and woodcutters (*pionniers-scieurs*), pedlars (*commerce ambulante*), hemp carders (*peigneurs de chanvre*), builders (*maçons*), water carriers (*porteurs d'eau*) and other such occupations. In general, the migrants who came to Spain were thought of as *comerciantes*, meaning pedlars or members of companies like those of Navalcarnero and Chinchón, although it is clear that this was not necessarily true of those who made their circuit as artisans, as casual and skilled labourers in agriculture and the building trades, or as shepherds and goatherds.

The Haute-Auvergnese diaspora is another of the frequent cases of migration from highland regions found throughout Europe in the early modern period, which brought people down in their thousands from the mountains of Sweden, the Highlands of Scotland, and the French and Italian Alps to the lowlands in search of work, higher wages and prosperity. By offering their labour, these migrants played an important role in the development of trade, driving the progressive spatial and social division of labour, and acting as an oral conduit for the transmission of news and cultural values through their travellers' tales and the recitation of ballads, as well as the sale of printed matter.[121] In Great Britain, migration from Scotland goes back as far as the sixteenth century, a hundred years before the phenomenon appeared in France, and in my opinion it was a key factor in structuring the country's internal market, which developed earlier and with greater intensity than on the Continent. The final stage of the process in Britain was the nationwide spread of retail shops, a phenomenon studied by Hoh-cheung Mui.[122] Meanwhile, Fontaine quite rightly associates the development of these areas of permanent emigration, which constantly pushed their people out into the world, with the process of proto-industrialization, though he makes the argument only in passing.[123]

Thus, at some time in a few short decades the growth in demand outside the migrants' areas of origin allowed family workshops to raise their output and sell the surplus via related emigrant networks. Over time, in many cases not until the nineteenth century, this eventually fixed migratory commercial networks, which were no longer needed to absorb people from their highland homelands, so that the additional resources obtained stabilized the population. The case of Geneva and the Jura mountains in the seventeenth and eighteenth centuries illustrates this point.[124]

The emigration of *montagnards* from the Auvergne and Limousin districts in the south of the Massif Central, one of the great sources of emigration together with the Haute Dauphiné, dated back as far as the middle ages. The phenomenon appears with certainty in the fifteenth century along the pilgrim way to Santiago. In the modern period, the emigrants from this region basically followed three Pyrenean routes to reach Castile and Andalusia, travelling by the pass of Le Boulou-Figueres to Barcelona, Valencia and Murcia; by Oloron-Saint Marie, the valley of the river Gave d'Aspe and the pass of Somport to Jaca and on into Aragon; and by Mont-de-Marsan, Saint-Jean-Pied-de-Port and the pass of Roncesvalles to Pamplona. From the way station of Pamplona on the third route, the immigrants headed south by various mule and cart tracks (Cervera del Río Alhama, Tarazona, Ágreda, Sigüenza and Guadalajara, scattering throughout Old and New Castile, some of them making it even as far south as Cádiz), and southeastwards via Zaragoza (another important way station), Teruel and Segorbe to reach Valencia and Murcia.

Over the course of the eighteenth century, their occupational profile broadened. The migrants of the seventeenth century and before were artisans, pedlars and, above all, unskilled labourers, but as the years passed their professional status changed, and some rose so far in the social scale as to direct major commercial enterprises. Even so, the majority continued to work in agriculture and above all in service. In Seville, the census of 1773 shows that the 502 French residents counted were mainly innkeepers (almost 50 per cent), knife grinders (12 per cent), coppersmiths (6 per cent) and carpenters, as well as other tradesmen of different kinds. The census taken in Aragon in 1764 also mentions numerous coppersmiths. Almost all of these immigrants were from the Auvergne.[125] Let us recall once again, however, that these censuses did not include all of the French immigrants in the areas concerned, because numbers of transients were never counted. Many of these, whether in the towns or in rural districts, eventually became settled or semi-settled merchants and retailers with their own seasonal circuits. For example, many who had begun as coppersmiths and tinkers went on to become ironmongers. Some charcoal burners went into mining, and some labourers and artisans ended up as mule drivers or pedlars, trafficking in pack animals, woollens and other fabrics.

The numerous immigrants who found work in *cabarets* or taverns sometimes went on to trade directly in the wares needed to supply these establishments. Others who practised wandering trades, like tinkers, would often carry goods with them to sell along the way. All those who travelled far were in contact with others, providing them with information about demand and the prices of goods in other regions, and the circulation of such intelligence made networks an important instrument of business.

There were numerous active companies. Known examples in the eighteenth and early nineteenth centuries include the company of Navalcarnero (30 km to the southwest of Madrid on the road to Extremadura); the company known as Maisonobe, Ribeyrols et Compagnie in Chinchón (south of Madrid on the road to Toledo), which was broken up in 1792 only to be refounded in 1796 and again in 1807; a company in Alcázar de San Juan and one in Estremera; some affiliates of the Chinchon company, which were broken up after 1808 (Torrejón de Arcos, Pinto, Colmenar de Oreja); and the Plandiens company of Segorbe in Valencia. Some of these enterprises were refounded after 1808, as in the case of the Parla company.[126] Zylberberg mentions the same companies: Chinchón and Navalcarnero in Castile; the Compañía de Estremera founded around 1750 and another such enterprise in Torrejón de Ardoz which operated along well-documented endogamous lines; the Compañía de Maury in Aragon (probably Hispanicized as Maurín) and the Compañía de Segorbe in Valencia.[127] Until around 1760, these companies had only a handful of partners, who were generally related and engaged primarily in itinerant trading, retailing fabrics or ironmongery, and dealing in draught animals. Their heyday was between 1760 and 1808. The Chinchón company, formed by immigrants from the Aurillac district, had between 120 and 200 partners by the early nineteenth century, all of them temporary migrants and all men. They were not allowed to marry in Spain, so that the organization formed a *société perpetuelle de famille*.[128] These companies represent the final stage in an evolutionary process that had been going on since the late middle ages and had already known several moments of expansion.

The migratory stream carried people of all sorts in its flow, including some who were running away from problems, a troubled past or failure in France. Only in some cases was it related with the selective immigration of highly skilled French individuals contracted by the leading figures of the Enlightenment to provide specific services. These included civil engineers and technicians with experience in public works and canal building, like Charles Le Maur, Etienne Bellecare, Joseph ('Roque') Bieu and Gil Pin, and expert artisans with advanced industrial know-how like Jacques Reboul, who set up a silk factory in Vinalesa (Valencia).[129] Some of them caused scandals of enormous proportions, like the French *ingénieurs* contracted in Aragon in 1768–1778 to design and build the new *Canal Imperial de Aragón*, who turned out to have no relevant skills and were merely on the make, taking advantage of the Spanish authorities' inexperience of such projects.[130]

Let us consider some further testimony. In 1730, the French priest, Abbé Labat, describes the French migrants from the Auvergne and the Pyrenees present in and around Cadiz in the following terms:

> Aussi l'Espagne est remplie de toutes sortes d'étrangers qui travaillent pour les Espagnols, et qui emportent en même temps le plus clair de leurs revenus. Sans parler dels artisans qui ont boutique ouverte, et des marchands dont il y a toûjours au moins vingt étrangères contre un Espagnol. On assuroit dans le tem[p]s que j'etais à Cadis qu'il y avoit dans la seule Andalousie plus de vingt mille françois des provinces d'Auvergne, de la Marche, du Limousin et des environs de la Garonne, dont le métier étoit de porter de l'eau dans les maisons, de vendre dans les ruës du charbon, de l'huile, du vinaigre, de servir dans les Hôtelleries, de labourer les terres et faire ses moissons, et d'y travailler les vignes. Ces gens ne manquent guère de faire tous les trois ans un voyage dans leurs païs y d'y porter trois ou quatre cents piastres, et souvent davantage, quoi qu'on leur sasse payer une somme tous les mois pour avoir droit de vendre du charbon, de l'huile, du vinaigre, et même de l'eau, qu'ils sont encore obligués d'acheter avant de la pouvoir vendre. Car comme je l'ai dejà remarqué, il n'y a ni fontaine ni [d']eau courante dans toute l'Isle [Cádiz]. Ceux qui ont des cîternes les gardent pour l'usage de leur maisons, ou la vendent à ces porteurs d'eau. Les propietaires des puits qui sont hors de la ville les tiennent environnés de murailles avec un gardien qui ne laisse tirer de l'eau qu'a ceux qui la payent.
>
> Ces marchands d'eau ne dépensent jamais rien pour leur nourriture ni pour leur logement; ils se mettent dans les hôtelleries ou dans des grosses maisons, ils fournissent de l'eau necessaire, et font tout le gros service dans les heures qui n'empêchent pas leur négoce ordinaire, et on leur abandonne le reste et quelque coin pour se retirer.
>
> Ce qui leur donne plus d'embarras c'est de transporter leur argent en leur païs et se sustraire à la vigilance des fardes préposés pour empêcher le transport des espèces hors du royaume, et pour le sauver des mains des voleurs, dont toute l'Espagne est abondanment pourvuë. Pour se délivrer des voleurs ils s'assemblent, vont en troupe bien armés, et il es rare qu'on les dévalise. Ils evitent les grandes routes et les passages où sont les gardes, et prennent presque tous le chemin de Saint Jacques. La ils se métamorphosent en pèlerins, et passent les Monts Pyrénées demandant l'aumône en chantant et dans un équipage qui ne donne guere lieu de soupçonner qu'ils son chargés d'argent. On connoît grand nombre de ces marchands de charbon qui après quelques annés se sont trouvés en état de revenir en Espagne avec una balle de toillerie et autres menuës merceries, et qui sont à présent des plus gros commerçants du Royaume.[131]

Labat may be wrong about the migrants' numbers but not about their activity. However, he is not talking about the French merchants, shopkeepers, wholesalers and established artisans, whether permanent or temporary residents, who usually appear in official data, but about the bottom class of transient migrants. These people came to Spain penniless to work as manual labourers. They received cash wages and were tenaciously thrifty. A few years later, they would return home taking their savings with them in silver coins, even crossing the border via Roncesvalles on the *Camino de Santiago* disguised as pilgrims to avoid detection. Having learned the route, many would later return with goods to trade. They brought with them woollen stuffs and linens in chests or knapsacks, and after they had sold their wares they sold their labour. Many never settled, preferring to return to France to marry according to their own self-imposed rules, returning later to Spain to work at their trades or ply their wares.

The French companies financed themselves internally, and they recruited new members exclusively from their kinship groups. They never used bills of exchange and had little to do with notaries, keeping only very rudimentary books, normally without employing double-entry accounting. They were retailers and by supplying the towns and villages of Spain with fabrics and other consumer goods, they played an important, though unquantifiable role in extending and structuring the interior market.

The *modus operandi* of these traders, and their social and commercial organizations are amply documented in contemporary accounts. According to Labat, French immigrants did not reach Cadiz by sea alone but also overland, crossing the whole of Spain like the Cadiz to Paris post,[132] though they did not necessarily make a direct journey.

Girard also describes the poor French living in both Cadiz and Seville, describing them as pedlars and hawkers, labourers, water sellers, servants, shopkeepers, artisans and sailors.[133]

The following testimony of a French diplomat writing in 1768 shows that they too traded in goods alongside the large merchants of Cadiz, though conducting a very different business from that of the wholesalers:

> From time to time immemorial, men from the province of Limousin who travel round Spain have been able to peddle their wares in the streets of Cadiz and sell oil, vinegar and coal. The value of their activities has always been recognised; these commodities were good value, and beyond that, individuals had the advantage of being furnished with goods at their home by these men [...] Spain, especially Cadiz, is a real source of wealth for this province [Limousin]. None of these men who came to Spain settled here. After three or four years spent in Cadiz, the pedlar goes back to his own country, returns to Spain, undertakes four or five campaigns in Spain, then goes back to his homeland with the fruits of his labour, gets married there and settles down surrounded by his family. When they leave Spain, those such as the oil-sellers, who have their own occupation, as it were, hand it on to their children or nephews, or sell it – what they call 'passing on the pitcher' ['passer le jarròn']. Each group in the same line of trade combines forces and has a common fund to finance their expenditure.[134]

Another account from the early nineteenth century describes how self-financing allowed a strategy of capillary expansion of the business beginning with a first shop, like the veins which carry blood from the major arteries to areas of the body further away from the heart:

> [...] the main shops were established about 15–20 leagues apart, under the management of two or three shareholders. Each shop served a surrounding area

> made up of a good number of towns or large villages where other shareholders went to sell on a retail basis merchandise which they obtained from the region's shop – some operated from the fixed base of an open-air stall in the larger towns; others peddled their wares using mules in the villages assigned to them, travelling there each week on set days. Opening a new shop at a suitable distance from the others was enough to provide work for 12–15 new shareholders. Many of these businesses consisted of 100 partners or more, who traded over an area of 30–40 leagues. They had a very considerable amount of capital, with established credit arrangements with factories in France, Switzerland and Spain – and they realized profits in proportion to this. It would be no exaggeration to value them at 2,000 francs for each full shareholder, although they didn't reach this point until after a period of around 16 years of partnership, during which time the business had increased in value over a series of 4-year periods.[135]

These French traders, who were still coming in the nineteenth century,[136] were not permitted to marry in Spain, but only in the homeland with French women, returning and repatriating profits periodically, a system that fostered the system of mutual marriage ties that was common under the *Ancien Régime*. The rule was to pass on the lion's share of inheritances to a single heir.[137] Commercial practice followed similar lines, so that mutual loans, transfers of funds and guarantees, and the repatriation of shared profits all combined to strengthen ties of kinship and family solidarity.[138]

The companies developed alongside extensive, complex commercial networks, and they were often based on purely verbal agreements between family members, although deeds were sometimes used. Their activity was woven around guarantees, transfers of funds and common interests. Examination of notarial records reveals that they repatriated their earnings in the form of large amounts of Spanish coins, which were sometimes exchanged for French coins at the border. In their places of origin, they tended to be better off than their sedentary neighbours and those who emigrated only within France. They owned agricultural land, much of it bought with the profits earned from their business in Spain, which they reinvested in their home districts. The extent of these holdings cannot be accurately determined, but they provided the necessary solvency for migrants' commercial dealings. The French Revolution and the ensuing wars eventually broke these companies, although some reformed when peace returned. Before 1808 the *Compañía de Chinchón* had 80 partners, all of them from Crandelles in the Auvergne, and when French creditors claimed the restitution of expropriated assets through the French consulates in Spain in 1818 under the terms of the Treaty of Vienna of 30 May 1814, there were more than 2,000 of them.[139]

Given the presence of French traders in Castile and Valencia, we may safely assume that many of them passed through Navarre and Aragon, where they would also do business. This is dictated not only by logic, but also by some contemporary accounts, such as the testimony of the sub-delegate of Saint-Flour, who affirmed in 1784 that there were emigrants from the Haute-Auvergne region who travelled only as far as the northern and southern Pyrenees (Aragon and Navarre), where they worked as labourers because wages were higher and the cash they earned could be profitably exchanged.[140] The highland region of the Massif Central is large, but there must also have been traders from Béarn in the Pyrenees who carried on a similar activity. The border area was where traders from other districts would stock up on goods for sale in Spain, not to mention the pedlars and chapmen of the Auvergne passing through on their way south.

The networks of Cantal and the Haute Auvergne had in fact provided a steady flow of migrants for centuries, which was vastly increased by the circumstances of the eighteenth century. On the one hand, the highland economy of areas like Limousin and the Haute-Auvergne underwent a sharp decline in terms of exchanges with the lowlands, so that the barter price of wheat increased from 19.30 pounds of cheese, the main local product exchanged for lowland grain, in 1715–1730 to 24.25 pounds in 1769–1789. According to Poitrineau, demographic growth in the region and the scant elasticity of the highland economy were the key factors underlying the crisis and driving the migratory movements of the eighteenth century.[141]

In the highlands of the Auvergne, where peasant smallholders predominated, the price of land rose by 3.5 times in the period between 1729–1734 and 1780–1785, while population pressure increased inexorably in the Basse-Auvergne region, growing at an annual rate of around 0.9 per cent.[142] We may note here that some rural craft industries existed in textiles (production of camlet and passemantarie) and woodworking, but in general they were neither very developed nor the artisans' principal occupation and remained subordinate to farming,[143] leaving little alternative to emigration and trading with Spain.

In addition to trans-annual migration to Spain, there was also intense internal emigration from the region to Gascony and the Pyrenees, the seaports of France's west coast and to the cities. These movements involved people from occupations of all kinds, including sawyers (*scieurs de long*), woodcutters and charcoal burners, ploughmen, peasant smallholders, and farm labourers. All of them had working time available in winter, and they specialized by region and trade. Like the long-range emigration to Spain, these movements brought large sums of cash back to the highland regions, a matter which did not escape the notice of the French exchequer. Finally, emigration could always be supplemented by begging where necessary in straitened economic circumstances.[144]

Overview

The action of networks, whether formed by French immigrants, Castilians, Galicians, Valencians, Basques or Catalans, among others, helped shape the interior market of Spain, and they are important not only for their existence per se but also for their economic impact. In this light, it would be more than slightly interesting to attempt a quantification of their incomes. However, this would require investigation of their business in Madrid, the centre and lynchpin of their activity, which is not considered in detail in this work.

Let us begin by considering the whole. The Massif Central, and especially the historical regions of Haute-Auvergne and Limousin, was the source of much French emigration to Spain, as well as to Bordeaux and Paris. Southward migratory flows also existed from the northern side of the Pyrenees (comparable to the exodus of other French highlanders from the Briançonnais and Haute-Embrunais regions to Italy). In 1760, the Abbé Beliardi, a commercial agent in Madrid, estimated that there were around 100,000 French people in Spain, and in 1765 Savary des Bruslons' dictionary put the number of immigrants arriving in Spain each year from the Auvergne alone at between 5,000 and 6,000. A further 4,000–5,000 entered Spain annually from what is today the *Département des Pyrénées Orientales*, and Zylberberg estimates that some 20,000 French migrants may have crossed the frontier every year.[145] Movements may have been merely seasonal in the case of migrants from the neighbouring Pyrenean districts, while those from the Auvergne tended to come for a few years or even longer. Others settled permanently, however. These included some of the artisans working in the countryside or who had set up shop in the towns, as well as certain urban tradesmen and members of the merchant elites. These 20,000 French migrants would each year meet and mingle with approximately 40,000 Galicians, who also left their homes for Portugal, Castile and Andalusia in search of work,[146] and with an indeterminate number of Cantabrians, Basques and Navarrese. We have very little information about the poorer Basques and Navarrese, as their wealthier compatriots have so far stolen the limelight. I do not have the means to quantify this migration, though it must have been fairly large and it is clearly observable at least in Madrid. There were also Catalans, who from the early eighteenth century spread throughout the interior of Spain.

Other migratory flows also existed, which in their turn generated trade networks all over the Iberian Peninsula, but there is no room to describe them all here. I refer, of course, to the mule drivers and transhumant shepherds from La Rioja, who sold their own cloth; the Aragonese shepherds of the Tierra Alta district in Teruel, who migrated towards the coasts of Valencia and Murcia; and both specialized and unspecialized migrant groups from Castile, the former including the mule drivers and porters of the Bierzo and Maragatería districts in León, and the latter itinerant labourers from La Mancha and Old Castile. It also seems reasonable to suppose that there would have been emigration from Asturias, given that the phenomenon existed in Galicia to the west and Cantabria to the east. All of these people contributed in their own, not always well understood, ways to the formation of Spain's nascent interior market.

Difficult though it may be to compare the threads of this commercial traffic, it is essential to do so, because it is only in this way that we can measure the relative importance of the different networks. Leaving aside farm produce to focus only on the networks trafficking in manufactured goods, we find the Galicians selling linens produced by proto-industrial methods in their home region. The Catalans, meanwhile, sold proto-industrial woollens, although the social context differed, given that industrialization was already beginning in Catalonia, and these networks also traded in printed cotton fabrics known as *indianas*, aquavit and lingerie, which were probably imported and re-exported from the region including from France. In turn, the French sold all kinds of woollen stuffs and lingerie, fashion items and countless small manufactured articles. However, the impact of their activities was probably greater given the special features of their networks. French immigration was accompanied by their control of entire sectors of the economy in the cities, and they enjoyed the political support of their homeland, a boon for which the Galicians and Catalans would have to wait decades yet.

To end this chapter, let us look at the question of French immigration in terms of income. In general, the poor French migrants in Spain, who were vastly more numerous than the wholesalers and monopoly merchants of the cities, lived a life of scrimping and saving. However, the remittances they sent back to their homes, whether legally or more often illegally, were very considerable. Estimates of the trade imbalance between Spain and France in the eighteenth century are generally based on the trade passing through customs, but much of the cash and bills of exchange exported by French traders went as contraband, and the actual figures were therefore significantly higher. In 1765, Savary des Bruslons reported that the Auvergnese emigrants sent between 700,000 and 800,000 *livres tournois* back to France every year. Meanwhile, Cabarrús estimated in 1783 that there were as many as 3,000 family and regionally based French companies in Spain, and that the net profits they sent home amounted to around one million pesos, which is to say between 3,150,000 and 5,000,000 *livres tournois*, much of which was smuggled out. Cabarrús is quite credible, not only because we know that he was personally very well informed, but also because there are reasons to believe that he himself engaged in large-scale contraband exports of coin and was intimately acquainted with such affairs.

It is no easy matter to estimate the incomes of wage-earning temporary migrants, itinerant artisans, or the members of commercial companies engaged in peddling and the transport of goods. Let us for the moment pass over the traffic carried on by the great merchants, whose operations based in Cadiz and above all Madrid were conducted using bills of exchange and other financial instruments. The main sources of income for the rest of the French migrants in Spain consisted of wages, the proceeds from the sale of mainly manufactured goods, and as most rural sales were made in credit, in-kind or cash payments made at harvest time, as well as lending and transactions involving grain. Based on the fragmentary data offered by Zylberberg, I estimate that all of these people together may have sent home cash sums totalling over 20,000,000 copper *reales* per year in the period around 1760–1780, consisting of small remittances which were not declared at the border and on which no tax was paid. Hence, these amounts would never have been recognized for the purposes of the balance of trade. Much of this cash would have gone as contraband via Navarre and Aragon, where flows from all over the Spanish interior converged, and a sizeable amount must also have passed through Valencia and Murcia, resulting in the emergence of the French *Compañía de Segorbe*, alluding to the way station on the road to the coast. In this sense, the name is similar to that of the *Compañía de Aragón* formed by the Catalan networks operating in that region. The rest of the cash exports to France went by way of Catalonia.

These estimates of the illegal trade in coins must be added to the official figures, on the basis of which Spain's balance of trade deficit was quantified. This means, then, that the outflow of capital from Spain to France was even larger than the figures reflected in the Archives Nationales, which are probably based on the customs revenues obtained at French ports and on the land border, principally with Navarre. The evidence for the export of coin is a matter which is too broad and complex to go into here, and it has in any case been examined elsewhere.[147]

However, it is known that the French were not alone in this trade. Economic growth and the new political circumstances of the country fostered the development of other *national* Spanish commercial networks. In the next chapter, we shall look at those of the Catalans, which were among the most successful.

7

Catalan Commercial Networks

In the early eighteenth century, the Peninsula market, which had hitherto been dominated by French, Basque, Navarrese and French Navarrese networks was suddenly invaded by a dogged new force – the Catalans. Though they were the last on the scene, they arrived with a vigour that was rooted in the economic and social transformations wrought in Catalonia in the seventeenth century, and their expansion was favoured by the conditions existing in the Spanish hinterland after the War of Succession.

The region's head start in demographic growth played a key role. At the beginning of the eighteenth century, Spain had a very low population density of only around 15.4 people per square kilometre, compared with 40 in France, 43.2 in Italy, and 21.6 even in Portugal.[1] In 1718 Catalonia had a similar population density of around 12.72 people per square kilometre, but the two adjacent regions, Aragon and Valencia, were less densely populated. Aragon had just 7.43 people per square kilometre, and perhaps even less.[2] This situation had arisen from the demographic catastrophe of the seventeenth century in both Aragon and Valencia, which was driven by the expulsion of the Moriscos, plague and, in Aragon, by the war of the Catalan Revolt.

The eighteenth century, however, saw strong Malthusian growth. By 1787 the population of Spain had risen to 20.6 people per square kilometre, but in Catalonia it was 27.5, in Valencia 34.9 and in Aragon 13.1.[3] Demographic growth in the eighteenth century was strong all along the Mediterranean coast and in the Ebro valley. The populations of Catalonia and Murcia multiplied by 1.8 and 1.7 times, respectively, but the more backward neighbouring regions of Valencia and Aragon grew even faster (2.1 times), catching up with Catalonia, if only partially in the case of Aragon. In this scenario, the demographic gap between Catalonia and the adjacent regions in the eighteenth century became a push factor for emigration. This was clearly the case in Aragon, as we shall see, although we cannot say whether Catalan emigrants were drawn to the kingdom by an earnings gap like that which attracted the French, given the absence of detailed information on wages and prices. The population factor must also have had an influence on Catalan emigration to Valencia, where wages had remained stable throughout the seventeenth century, though prices rose sharply according to Hamilton.[4] In this light, it seems reasonable to suppose that the main pull factor was growth in demand. Overall, the difference between Catalan *development* and mere *growth* in the neighbouring regions and the rest of Spain was not just a matter of population growth, but was driven mainly by other internal and external factors, which are discussed in the following pages.

The emergence of an economic region around Barcelona

The case of Catalonia in the eighteenth century must be placed in the context of the emerging Spanish national market, a long and complex process about which much remains to be said. The classic interpretation of these phenomena is based on price convergence, which it is argued occurred in the central decades of the nineteenth century when the railway provided a decisive boost. In reality, the process began in the eighteenth century. Unpublished estimates of convergence in farm prices in the eighteenth century suggest that the process was already largely complete by 1808, when it was halted by the decades of revolution from 1808 to 1840, only to recommence thereafter. However, this conventional view of events suffers from a serious methodological problem inherent in the use of exclusively statistical measurements of market formation via price convergence. This is questionable, because powerful undercurrents existed in the pre-industrial economy of eighteenth-century Spain, which did not necessarily drive convergence.

This argument is based on a fact that we have already established – the considerable progress made towards the integration of Spain's interior market in the eighteenth century. As the traditional system of seasonal fairs and markets decayed in Old Castile, numerous district and regional exchange networks grew up, fostered by rising incomes and consumption, and the progressive spatial specialization of production.[5] Structured exchange flows also developed around the large cities like Cadiz, Seville, Valencia, Barcelona and Madrid, which acted to drive growth. In the case of the capital, the spatial and social division of labour was also strongly conditioned by demand in the city and from the Court.[6] In short, then, economic regions were beginning to coalesce around urban centres where high prices drove exchanges with surrounding low-price areas, which progressively increased in size. The city at the head of such a region organized demand via prices, drove the development of trade networks and exerted a huge influence over production in its area of influence. This occurred, for example, in the case of Madrid with Old and New Castile,[7] Valencia and its hinterland,[8] and Barcelona with both Catalonia and Aragon.

Over the course of the eighteenth century, Barcelona and Catalonia developed into a dynamic economic region, which also extended into Aragon. The regional historiography on this subject is particularly abundant, beginning with the seminal work *Cataluña en la España Moderna* by Pierre Vilar (first published in French in 1957, in Catalan in 1964–1968 and in Spanish in 1977) who analysed in detail the intimate relationship between agricultural growth in the Catalan interior and the growth of Barcelona, the capital, which played a key role in structuring the territory and providing contact with external markets. This has since become a canonical truth in the historiography. Numerous subsequent studies have shown how demographic and agricultural growth in rural areas beginning in the seventeenth century coupled with an intense and early spatial and social division of labour to undermine the importance of seigneurial rents, shape Catalonia's regional market, raise demand for manufactured goods, and drive the development of rural manufacturing and, in particular, of a thriving woollens industry. By the latter decades of the eighteenth century, meanwhile, the Barcelona cotton industry had taken over as the main engine of growth, outstripping even the colonial trade. The Spanish interior market was crucial to the development of this new trailblazer of Catalan industrialization.[9]

The influence of Barcelona on its economic region was very different from that of Madrid on the two Castiles. In the capital, seat of the monarchy and the wealthy aristocratic elite, luxury goods were an important factor, and the city was always a centre of consumption, and a distribution and service hub. In contrast, Barcelona shaped and developed a territorial sphere in which agriculture prospered alongside significant rural industries, including iron smelting, textiles, tanning and myriad other manufactures, while the city itself became an ever more important centre of consumption and the port provided contact with the wider world.[10] Catalonia's burgeoning industrial output was sold initially within the immediate region, but as time went on goods were increasingly sent to Aragon and then to the rest of Spain. J. M. Oliva Melgar, E. Martín, J. K. Thompson, V. Vázquez de Prada and Giménez Blanco all highlight the importance of the interior market for Catalan manufactures. Meanwhile, A. Muset Pons was the first to realize the importance of the Catalan commercial networks existing in the interior of Spain, and Rúa Fernández has recently shown that the principal market for Catalonia's expanding industrial output was not in fact America but Madrid.[11]

It is precisely the economic growth of the principality and its area of commercial influence which explains the early and growing presence of Catalan merchants, industrialists and mule drivers outside the region. Such people were found above all in Aragon but also in other regions belonging to the Spanish Crown, and their activity was noted by the politicians and thinkers of Enlightenment Spain, not always with enthusiasm.[12] The former kingdom of Aragon was progressively absorbed into the Catalan economic sphere early on, and the process was intense. Jaume Torras points to the significant penetration of Catalan woollens in Aragon, while Fradera and Peiró have amply demonstrated Aragonese dependence on the Catalan market as an outlet for the kingdom's exports of fleeces and oil, not to mention the significant quantities of Aragonese grain consumed in Barcelona.[13]

Demography coupled with various other internal factors arising from the transformation of rural Catalonia to drive this commercial expansion. Centuries before, Ferdinand the Catholic had ended strife between the feudal lords of Catalonia and the *campesinos de remensa* or serfs at the Arbitration of Guadalupe (1486), quashing the *malos usos* or 'bad rule' of the feudal lords and granting tens of thousands of peasants rights to the land they worked. The cash rents payable by these emphyteutic peasants were frozen by the king's ruling, shrinking in real terms as a result of inflation in the sixteenth and seventeenth centuries, so that the farmers themselves were able to keep a substantial portion of the incomes generated by their labour on the land – more at least than was usual in parts of the Spanish monarchy. This in turn permitted the emergence of a class of quasi-landowning peasants, who had an incentive to expand and improve their farms. This latent economic stimulus failed to operate between 1500 and 1650 because the population was too small, but demographic growth in the second half of the seventeenth century provided an ever stronger boost for farming. The family farms known as *masías, masadas* or *masos* held under emphyteutic leases by the *masadero* or *masover* began to expand at this time, and the exploitation of the land under agrarian sublets in a kind of agrarian contract called a *subestabliment* in Catalan.[14] These peasant farms were able to expand significantly in the eighteenth century by leasing additional land under *establiment* contracts and the *rabassa morta* system (a form of sharecropping) applied to vineyards. The widespread use of these instruments allowed the owners of the more prosperous *masías* (*masos benestants*) to increase their incomes through a process of colonization of the land, which did not require the commitment of capital. Meanwhile, it encouraged the peasants exploiting the new winegrowing *masías* (*masos de rabassaires*) to employ any available surplus labour in small-scale manufacturing.[15]

Under these conditions, the expansion of the market had highly beneficial effects. Meanwhile, differential trends in the prices of agricultural products like wheat, wine, oil, wool and almonds drove specialization, so that winegrowing areas appeared alongside other niche crops. This in turn drove intra-regional trade, the engine of which was always the city of Barcelona. All of this prompted continual growth in agricultural earnings,[16] raising the disposable incomes, and hence consumption, of the former emphyteutic peasants, who were able to keep most of the profit.

Population growth was a determining factor in this process. The fact that the region was sparsely populated when the process began in the latter decades of the seventeenth century made room for decades of Malthusian growth. Growth in seigneurial rents gradually shifted westwards until it eventually stopped in the last three decades of the eighteenth century.[17] Meanwhile, Malthusian growth marked by an increasing population, the colonization of new land and the creation of new irrigation systems continued in the westernmost part of Catalonia around Lerida right up to the end of the century.[18]

After 1760, the progressive decline in wine prices relative to grain depressed the disposable incomes of the small peasant winegrowers or *rabassaires*. In turn, the gap between grain prices in the Catalan countryside and in Barcelona began to close.[19] The combination of these two factors resulted in episodes of demographic stress after 1783, accompanied by declining fertility rates and a fall in seigneurial rents and rural incomes generally, creating the conditions for anti-aristocratic resistance and the definitive crisis of the *Ancien Régime*.[20]

Meanwhile, political factors related with the military situation and the increasing power of the state also favoured growth in Catalonia. While the Bourbon victory in the War of Succession resulted in the loss of the Catalan *fueros*, it also created great opportunities for the region's industry, a fact that is all too often overlooked. As we have already seen, the restructuring of the customs system consolidated the tolls on the Basque and Navarrese border, as well as creating a Catalan customs area where tariffs were low for foreign goods in transit to the Spanish interior. This was accompanied by lower taxation of goods sold inland resulting from the abolition of internal tolls between Catalonia, Aragon and Valencia, encouraging the penetration of imports via the principality while facilitating trade in Catalan goods, which could now be carried into Aragon and Castile[21] at lower cost together with foreign merchandise in transit to the Spanish interior.

Another key factor was the policy of tax rationalization, which resulted in the creation of a direct tax in each of the realms of the former Crown of Aragon – the *real contribución* in Aragon, the *equivalente* in Valencia, the *catastro* in Catalonia, and the *talla general* in Majorca. The resulting tax burden was not evenly distributed. Catalonia and Aragon paid less taxes than Castile, and the burden was comparatively smaller in Catalonia than it was in Aragon. Furthermore, the gap widened over the course of the eighteenth century because of the conditions of the tax itself and the collection methods applied.[22] Moreover, it seems likely that the new taxes which replaced the local customs revenues in the different regions had little impact on trade, so that the commercial networks existing in Catalonia, Aragon and Valencia (and for different reasons those of Castile and other regions too) would have paid little or no taxes. That, at least, is what happened in Aragon.[23] The combined effect of a bright economic outlook, and low customs duties and direct taxes was to encourage growth in Catalonia and the expansion of Catalan trade throughout the Iberian Peninsula. A further factor that may have been significant was the reduction in the number of church feast days (when no work was done) in Catalonia compared with other parts of Spain. This generated productivity gains for proto-industrial manufacturing in the region, which were in open competition with the proto-industries of Aragon and the formidable manufactures of the British and French from the beginning of the eighteenth century. To sum up, conditions were highly favourable for the expansion of Catalan trade in the interior of Spain in the years after the War of Succession.

Reasons for the expansion of Catalan trade networks in the interior of Spain

Catalan development, and that of the whole economic region which emerged as a result, is well documented today. However, the Catalan expansion in the interior of Spain is less well understood, and indeed only partial evidence existed until the work of A. Muset and others, which have revealed the importance of this phenomenon.[24] The process was led by merchants and trading companies whose activities have so far been rather described than explained, and studies have focused rather on Catalonia itself than the markets beyond the region's borders. Much recent Catalan historiography addresses the expansion of the market in eighteenth century Catalonia as if it were a purely internal and endogenous phenomenon, without taking into account the influence of the port and the consumer market of Barcelona on other areas outside the principality and above all in Aragon, the region that was affected earliest and most intensely, as Muset's data show.[25] One might add that it was also the most profoundly affected.

The contributions made at the first conference held to discuss this topic in 1996 at last addressed the phenomenon in depth, beginning with an analysis of the reasons for the expansion of Catalan manufacturing and commercial networks. The conference highlighted two factors, which I believe were crucial. One, the customs union imposed after the War of Succession, has already been considered. The other has not. While the Catalan trade diasporas operated a very similar network strategy, they enjoyed a significant legal advantage over the French – they were not foreigners.[26] The effect of the four royal orders of 1715, 1716, 1721 and 1723 had been to merge all of the different naturalities of the Spanish monarchy into one,[27] so that Catalan naturals, who had hitherto been treated differently from Castilian naturals, were not subject to the legislation governing aliens enacted in the eighteenth century, as the French were.

The data included in the conference report reflect 820 Catalan merchants in the whole of Spain except Cadiz between 1700 and 1860,[28] and 2,283 between 1760 and 1914, of whom 1,453 were active in the period 1760–1807.[29] The actual figure must have been much higher, because many left no trace in the records. They were yet another minority, which increased as the eighteenth century progressed although it is doubtful that they were ever as numerous as the French, of whom there were around 100,000.

Their expansion was general. The Catalans reached Valencia, Murcia[30] and the interior of Andalusia via Malaga by land and by sea.[31] They spread to America from Cadiz, where they first arrived in coastal vessels trading down Spain's Mediterranean seaboard. Between 1720 and 1730 they began to trade directly with Cadiz, and they finally reached America directly after the free trade decrees of 1776–1778.[32] Some also went to Galicia, once again with the aim of reaching America.[33] Meanwhile, Castile gradually filled with Catalan pedlars and shopkeepers, whose numbers increased at the end of eighteenth century, when they were particularly favoured by the temporary absence of British goods, the result of war with England and the blockade of 1797.[34] It is not clear, in my opinion, whether they found penetration of the Basque provinces and Navarre more difficult and progressed more slowly there due to the peculiarities of the region's customs regime, as Torres argues.[35]

Finally, there were at least 112 Catalan merchants running their own shops or organized in trading companies in the highly competitive and tightly controlled market of Madrid between 1730 and 1809.[36] Exports of Catalan goods throughout the interior of Castile continued to increase and they had already grown very large by the end of the eighteenth century, although they never dominated the market. According to the testimony of Larruga in 1787, the situation in Madrid, the monarchy's main consumer centre, was as follows:

> el comercio extrangero importa casi dos tantos más que el nacional. Las provincias de estos dominios que más intereses sacan de la corte por un verdadero comercio suyo activo[37] son las de Valencia y Cataluña, la primera con los varios artículos de sus manufacturas de seda, paños de Alcoy, Enguera, y Bocayrente; loza de Alcora y Manises; papel de Segorbe, Alcoy y otras fábricas; y según un cálculo prudente pasa de treinta millones de reales lo que anualmente introduce. Y la segunda [Cataluña] saca mucho más en los diferentes géneros de sus fábricas que entran continuamente, siendo los renglones más principales paños, bayetas, estameñas, indianas, lienzos pintados, papel y medias de seda, aunque este último ha decaído mucho por la mala calidad con que vienen trabajadas las más. De curtidos entra un renglón considerable; sólo de zapatos admira el gran número que se consume, y éste es un exemplar de lo industriosa que es Cataluña, pues sólo de este género vende en España más que los demás zapateros.[38]

Based on these estimates, one third of the goods purchased in Madrid by value came from Valencia and Catalonia, reflecting the success of both regions' commercial expansion, despite the increasing differences between them. The process had been going on for almost a century.

Catalan industrialization was a relentless process, continuing on into the nineteenth century, when the period of revolutionary turbulence was followed by even faster growth, though under different conditions, based on the networks that had already been formed in the eighteenth century. These developments are described by the authors cited in the preceding footnotes and in numerous other places. In the long run, the protection of the Spanish interior and colonial markets (Cuba, Puerto Rico and the Philippines) further underpinned the process of industrialization begun in Catalonia in the eighteenth century.

However, it was above all in neighbouring Aragon of all the territories belonging to the Spanish monarchy where the expansion of Catalan trade was felt soonest and most intensely. This can be explained not only by the factors described above, but also by the logical development of the commercial networks themselves, which gradually pushed outwards seeking the support of fellow countrymen who had already established shops and stores along the way in order to pare down the costs of management, warehousing and transport as far as possible. The Catalan carters and mule drivers, shopkeepers and merchants thus used basically the same methods as the French.

The overland expansion of Catalan trade into the Spanish interior basically followed three *caminos carreteros*[39] from Barcelona. The first followed the coast and must have supplemented the cabotage route from Barcelona via Tarragona, Valencia, Alicante and Murcia to Andalusia. The second was the Barcelona–Lerida–Fraga–Zaragoza route, which split at the Aragonese capital, one fork heading west into Old Castile via Tarazona, Borja, Ágreda, Almazán and Valladolid, while the other continued on to Madrid by one of two alternative routes – Zaragoza–Daroca–Guadalajara–Alcalá de Henares–Madrid or Zaragoza–Calatayud–Medinaceli–Sigüenza–Guadalajara–Alcalá de Henares–Madrid. The latter route eventually became the main road from Zaragoza to Madrid, and it remains the line of the modern motorway.

These roads were used by carters and *llogaters de mules* (mule drivers) from Barcelona, who formed their own guild, the brotherhood of San Antonio Abad de Barcelona. The guild had some fifty members, and it included both those who ran the service in Barcelona itself, and drivers who owned their own cart and could undertake long distance haulage trips. The brotherhood's records are revealing about the organization of transport services.[40] The guild members must have worked side by side with other carriers who were neither themselves members nor even necessarily Catalans, in view of the evidence described below. Outside the city of Barcelona, there were also many mule drivers and carters in towns like Calaf and Igualada on the Zaragoza route. It is no accident that the Cortadellas family, whose activities are recounted in detail below, were from Calaf and its environs.[41]

The high roads could take wagons large enough to make long-distance goods transport more profitable than trains of pack mules. However, these were not the only, or even necessarily, the principal routes. The network of highroads was fleshed out by countless tracks joining and leaving the main roads all along their routes, and these could only be used by pack animals. The two key points on the road networks used by the Catalans were Zaragoza, the way station from which they would continue their journeys in almost any direction, and Madrid. Both cities were the main centres for the overland distribution of Catalan goods, fulfilling the same role as Bayonne, Pamplona, Zaragoza (to a lesser extent) and Madrid in the case of the French.

The Catalan trade diaspora is a matter of interest not only for its own intrinsic importance in the formation of Spain's interior market, but also because comparison with the French networks and the English port colonies highlights the contrasts between the different migratory groups and the conditions under which each developed and operated.

There were notable distinctions between the long-standing French and English incumbents, and the upstart Catalan networks. In general, the Catalans who emigrated to the interior of Spain took with them their own tongue, like the French and English, which afforded certain benefits. They used Catalan to strengthen their own identity, as their language of commerce, in bookkeeping and to transmit commercial information. Like the French, they were Catholics, giving them an edge over the English. However, they lacked the key advantages of diplomatic support, favourable trade treaties and the possibility of recourse to the military jurisdiction.

However, their activities benefitted from certain other factors, some of which we have already mentioned. To begin with, they were no longer trammelled by internal customs, they paid very low taxes, and after the decrees of 1715–1723 they enjoyed the inestimable benefit of Spanish naturality, like the Basques (who had always been treated as Castilian naturals) and the Navarrese. This offered advantages for the trade diaspora: the Catalans were sufficiently different to maintain internal coherence and to be seen as separate, but at the same time they were sufficiently similar to be considered equals. It is not that they were treated as Spanish – they were Spanish. This social acceptance is, in my belief, historically compatible with the continuation of a certain pro-Habsburg tradition and the expression of grievances over the abolition of Catalonia's local laws and institutions in more restricted intellectual, legal and political circles,[42] which were in any case not confined to the Catalans but were shared by the Aragonese and in Valencia.

In this regard, we may reproduce a passage by the eighteenth-century Aragonese writer Eugenio Larruga cited by Jaume Torras, which reflects the generally good opinion of the Catalans entertained by the people of the Spanish interior (in this case the Castilian province of Soria), who saw them as hard-working and enterprising:

> Apenas hay pueblo de consideración en esta provincia [de Soria, Castilla] en que no se haya establecido algún catalán con tienda de algunos géneros, especialmente con medias, cotones, y sobre todo zapatos. Lo mismo acontece ya[43] en el día generalmente en toda la península. La actividad de la Cataluña la hace una provincia agricultora, industriosa, comerciante y traficante. La población se aumenta, los intereses entran en ella a medida de sus negociaciones y trabajos útiles para la sociedad. Todo es aplicación, todo es meditación, y todo ánimo y valor para buscar cada uno sus comodidades en donde las hallen. Los que aman la pereza, los que se avienen con la desidia y los que quieren hacerse ricos con poco trabajo a costa del descuido de sus convecinos no se avienen bien con los establecimientos que hacen los catalanes fuera de su principado; pero las gentes

> sensatas piensan de muy distinto modo, pues aprecian a estos hombres a quienes miran como hermanos y buenos españoles, que se desvelan por su conveniencia sin perjuicio del Estado, y sí con mucha gloria y utilidad de él. Cuando hablemos de este principado sacaremos pruebas evidentes de haberse equivocado muchos de los que han escrito en la causa de la decadencia de la nación,[44] y con más singularidad sobre las Castillas.[45]

The Catalans were, then, regarded as industrious and capable, and as 'hermanos y buenos españoles' according to Larruga. Once again, this does not contradict the fact that their activities were not always viewed in a positive light, as was also the case with other trade diasporas. In another passage discussing the wool industry in the province of Burgos, next door to Soria, Larruga protests that:

> acuden a comprar las lanas de esta provincia valencianos, catalanes, aragoneses y manchegos, sin saberse a dónde las destinan; y así la saca de éstas como las compras que hacen muchos almacenistas y revendedores perjudican a las fábricas de este país [Burgos] no sólo porque alteran los precios sino también porque, imposibilitando a los fabricantes hacer sus acopios y compras, se quedan por falta de géneros los telares en muchos meses del año parados, y por consiguiente los maestros y operarios sin tener que trabajar.[46]

This was an old complaint in Castile. Foreign demand caused outflows of commodities and raised the price of wool, so that the freedom of trade and formation of internal markets dear to the politicians of the Enlightenment became scarcity and unemployment for the working man. The proto-industries of Catalonia, Valencia and La Mancha needed wool and they were prepared to pay more, so the wool went to them.

The testimonies cited above show that wages in France remained below their level in Spain throughout the eighteenth century, which explains why so many French immigrants continued to seek work in Spain. However, we now know that wages in Catalonia remained as high as they were in the second half of the seventeenth century, and even rose further in the latter decades of the eighteenth century.[47] In this light, the Catalan trade diaspora cannot be attributed to wage incentives, but was driven rather by the progressive geographical expansion of demand and the evolution of prices in the principality. Successful business bred further business, and this in turn stimulated the development of an initially small entrepreneurial class. Accounts exist of *catalanes pobres* (the equivalent of the *franceses pobres* seen in the preceding chapters), who migrated to sell their labour especially at harvest time in Aragon. However, they were very few in number. In general, the Catalan migrants were not labourers in search of work who would later return home with their savings, but people of higher social status, who would usually have no problem settling down, marrying and becoming permanent residents at their chosen destinations.

Territorial and geographical links with the rest of the Iberian Peninsula were also an important factor. The Catalan trade diaspora grew out of the expansion of the Catalano-Aragonese market centred on the city of Barcelona. Its origins were not, therefore, overpopulated highland areas whose people lived by animal husbandry and cottage industries, like the emigrants from the Auvergne, the northern valleys of the Pyrenees, the Sierra de Cameros in La Rioja or the Tierra Alta of Aragon. Furthermore, the initially sparsely populated adjacent territory of Aragon to the west of Catalonia allowed the continuation of the Malthusian growth experienced in the principality's interior, expanding the influence of Barcelona's high prices and demand for commodities like wool, wheat, oil and mules for use as draught and pack animals.

A considerable amount is known today about the basic features of French migratory diasporas thanks to the study of public sources, but we still have relatively little understanding of how their businesses functioned and how they managed to make money in the Spanish interior market. This would require analysis of the private records of the companies they formed, which left very little data behind,[48] or a long trawl through the notarial archives of the time.

However, the case of Catalonia to some extent compensates for this lack, because just two archives[49] hold extensive information on numerous companies formed by Catalan migratory networks both in the Spanish interior and in the Americas. Thanks to this information, we know that the trade diaspora consisted of waves of people, who seized on the new economic and political opportunities and the advantages of a common Spanish identity to deploy highly varied commercial strategies based around three key economic factors, namely extensive Malthusian growth in the adjacent region of Aragon; demand for commodities driven by high prices in the economic powerhouse of Barcelona; and demand for manufactured goods in the Spanish interior, and particularly in Madrid.

As far as we now know, the majority of Catalan companies were originally formed to trade in the interior of the principality, or conserved a part of their business there, or built upon businesses which had been successful locally. They formed a range of increasingly specialized undertakings, which followed diverse business strategies that were more or less successful depending on the capacity of their partners to adapt to conditions in the new markets they opened up and to rising transport costs, which could only be offset by trading in higher value-added goods. Broadly, these companies' activities can be classified on three levels.

The first is that of the farm labourers who worked over a seasonal cycle in specialized and unspecialized agricultural occupations. Given the circumstances explained above, these emigrants must have been few in number, and the only mention of such people that I have been able to find appears in companies trading in farm products in western Aragon, whose partners would occasionally hire labourers from their places of origin.

The second level of activity consisted of mule drivers and carters from rural Catalonia, where a process of agricultural diversification and industrialization was under way, especially in the district around the River Anoia and in particular the villages of Capellades and Calaf[50] on the road from Barcelona to Lerida and Zaragoza. In general, these people were either peasants themselves or had peasant origins. However, this was not necessarily or completely so, because a long-standing rural woollens industry also existed, and numbers of rural artisans, most of them weavers who engaged in farming only as a secondary activity, moved from selling their wares locally to other markets further afield, as Jaume Torras has recently shown in the case of the weavers of Torelló de Igualada.[51] Meanwhile, mule drivers and carters easily recast themselves as pedlars of the fabrics they transported, or they formed partnerships with the producers and sellers of such goods. In any event, we may note that those who traded in agricultural commodities did so as a secondary business derived from the management of farms and estates, an activity which itself originated from leasing tithes and seigneurial rents. This was the business of Soler, Bosch, Figarola y Compañía, which we shall consider below, although there were other such firms.[52] The Catalan newcomers wrought profound social changes by combining their land agency and transport businesses, particularly in Aragon. Their endeavours developed and structured the interior market, at the same time influencing the growth of agriculture, transforming rural districts and changing the nature of peasant farming.

The third level of activity comprised the business of the *botiguers*, merchants and storekeepers, and the manufacturers of *indiana* cottons and other fabrics in Barcelona, who had no direct contact with agriculture. Let us consider first the case of the storekeepers belonging to the firm of Francesc Jofré and Josep Vila, in business between 1717 and 1733 or thereabouts. The firm had a '*casa de comercio*' selling Catalan agricultural products and manufactured goods, as well as imported wares which were re-exported to the interior of Spain. This activity grew up around the city and the port. The business was supported by the growth of consumption: for example, they were able to sell their wares in Zaragoza for the simple reason that there was demand in what was an undersupplied market. Such companies sometimes expanded the scope of their business to include discounting bills of exchange, and they frequently acted through agents and intermediaries (carters, mule drivers, pedlars and other merchants), although they rarely became merchant banks or moved into manufacturing.

The case of the cotton manufacturers was different. Firms like María Formentí y Cía. and Joan Baptista Sala y Cía. manufactured printed cotton fabrics, a highly specialized business. Having acquired the necessary industrial know-how, they were keen to increase sales, hence their interest in expansion to find new outlets for their products. This meant either setting up their own shops or *boticas* in target towns, forming partnerships with existing merchants, or using the services of agents. Their business strategy was industrial rather than commercial, however, and they did not engage in retailing.

Many of these companies conducted significant operations inside Catalonia itself. Some began their businesses in the principality and then expanded their territory, while others remained exclusively Catalan. However, a part of the sales made in Catalonia would always be made to individuals or other firms whose intention was to sell the goods on in the interior of Spain. We shall go no further into this matter here, or the traffic in goods imported by Catalan firms from France for consumption in the principality or for re-export to other regions of Spain, sometimes under the guise of local manufactures to avoid paying customs duties.[53] This business was in all likelihood common and lucrative, but it cannot be understood without an analysis of the traffic passing through the Catalan customs posts, which is not possible here for reasons of space.

Numerous contemporary accounts and modern studies exist of Catalan business activity in the Spanish interior and periphery, and in America (which is not considered here). These range from Muset Pons' recent, general work on Catalan trade as a whole to the numerous studies of their presence in different cities and regions, many of which cover the nineteenth century.[54] This is a broad subject, then, and to address it we shall employ a different strategy to that used to examine the activities of the French. To begin with, I have opted to concentrate on Aragon, given the nature of the Catalan trade diaspora, which was not the product of emigration by people from poor highland districts in search of work, but rather of a successive, overlapping and linked combination of three different kinds of migrants. Hence, the only way to gain an overview of the phenomenon is to examine it in a single region, and it was Aragon that received the largest number of Catalan migrants in all possible combinations. People of all kinds stopped or passed through the former kingdom, from those selling seasonal labour at harvest time to merchants trading in low value-added agricultural commodities like grain, whose reach was limited by the rising transport costs imposed by distance. Meanwhile, the carriers of manufactured goods of all kinds, whether of Catalan origin or re-exported from France, also passed through Aragon on their way to more distant markets in the Spanish interior, where the higher prices commanded by products like lace and medium to high quality fabrics were worth the additional cost of transport. These people were merchants, pedlars and traders, who would return with equally valuable commodities like wool for the textiles industry and mules, and combinations of all sorts were possible between the extremes.

Agrarian rents and the grain trade

Let us look first at the role of the Catalans who leased tithes and seigneurial rents. Many operated only in Catalonia, but some did so simultaneously in Aragon and Catalonia and others only in Aragon, creating numerous small companies. The most important was Soler, Bosch, Figarola y Compañía, which was also known, significantly, as the '*Compañía de Aragón*'.[55] Analysis of this firm will throw light on the activities of all the companies engaged in the lease of tithes and seigneurial rents, and trading in farm commodities like grain, oil, wool, wine, silk and mules. Notarial records in Zaragoza, the principal centre for the negotiation of agrarian rents in Aragon, mention as many as six Catalan groups – Cortadellas, Goser, Castaño, Cos, García Molas and Iglesias – leasing tithes and seigneurial rents. Of the 81 transactions involving feudal rents recorded in contracts made in the city, the Cortadellas group was party to 40, while the Goser group and the Castaño group each accounted for 13, the Cos group for 6, the García Molas group 6 and the Iglesias group for 2. The contracts made by the Cortadellas and Goser groups were the largest, entailing disbursements of rather more than 700,000 *libras jaquesas* in each case, though none of the transactions entered into by any of the others exceeded 100,000 *libras jaquesas*. The group with which Soler, Bosch, Figarola y Compañía maintained links was the most active and the firm contributed 766,399 *libras jaquesas*[56] out of total disbursements of 1,768,120 *libras jaquesas*, or 43.34 per cent of the total. The partners also leased agrarian rents in Barcelona, Lerida, Huesca and other places, but Zaragoza was always the most important part of their business.

Each of these six groups was formed by various companies, which might be set up and then dissolved within the space of just a few years, and it is likely that there were others of which we are unaware because they left no trace in the notarial records. A case in point is that of the two linked companies founded by Josep García and Josep

Bover, the *Compañía de Altafulla* and the *Compañía de La Pobla de Montornés*, which in the 1760s, 1770s and 1780s leased agrarian rents in Ulldecona, in Bujaraloz, from estates owned by the Aragonese monastery of Sigena, as well as the *bailías* of Miravete and Caspe, and the *encomienda* of Calatayud belonging to the *Orden de San Juan de Jerusalen*.[57] How these rents were commercialized is not known in detail. We may also mention the 'Cardona group' formed around two citizens of the eponymous town, Celedonio Garriga and Josef Martí, who conducted a considerable business (and were rivals of the Cortadellas) in Catalonia at least.[58] There must also have been others, because the majority of the lease contracts and the instruments forming companies were never witnessed by a notary[59] and have therefore left no trace in the archives.

Like its peers, the *Compañía de Aragón* was promoted by wealthy members of the Catalan peasantry. They were the beneficiaries of the emphyteutic *establiments* and *subestabliments*, some of them specializing in winegrowing under the *rabassa morta* system, who at some time switched from the operation of the family farm to the lease of agrarian, seigneurial and ecclesiastical rents, and the trade in grain and other commodities. The economic growth of the early eighteenth century drove up prices in the east of Catalonia around Barcelona, while agricultural profits shifted to the west of the principality and Aragon, driven by low demographic pressure coupled with the absence of physical barriers and the removal of tolls. It was to this area that these new Catalan entrepreneurs were attracted in search of higher returns. In some cases, they also entered urban trade, vying with the companies formed by the *botiguers* and manufacturing companies. This was the case of the Torres family from the town of Copons,[60] who probably began as carters and pedlars in the area around Daroca but settled in Zaragoza in the second half of the eighteenth century to engage in the import of cloth and export of wool to Catalonia via intermediaries.[61]

The structure and operating methods of Soler, Bosch, Figarola y Compañía, the *Compañía de Aragón*, are well known.[62] The firm was formed in Huesca on 12 June 1777 out of an earlier company of six partners, who had been operating individually and in partnership in Aragon for many years. The original partners[63] contributed most of the new company's capital.[64] Two of them, the nephew–uncle team of Josep and Francesc Cortadellas, had joined forces between 1730 and 1776 to lease tithes and seigneurial rents in various localities and engage in goods transport in Catalonia. They also set up their carriage business in the towns of Binaced, Velilla de Ebro and Sástago in eastern Aragon in the 1730s, and they succeeded in establishing commercial contacts in Zaragoza in 1733 and in Huesca in 1736.[65] By 1777 they already had factories in Manresa and Calaf.[66]

The new company was formed to bring two new partners, Josep and Francesc Cortadellas, into the business. The former contributed his business in Calaf, and the latter a factory in Barcelona, while both put up further capital. Josep Cortadellas, partner and treasurer of the firm, soon became its business brain. By the time he died on 30 November 1809, several of the company's partners had changed, making room for sons and other kin. The accounts also mention a profusion of in-laws, grandchildren and neighbours.

The inventory of the new company's assets and capital drawn up in 1777 (Table 7.1) reflects the share in the business owned by each partner, as well as the firm's structure.

Table 7.1 Capital of Soler, Bosch, Figarola y Compañía in 1777

[. . .] 'capitalidades fornidas [=capitales aportados] a la Cía., firmado por sus socios en Huesca a 12 de junio de 1777'.

(in *libras catalanas, sueldos* y *dineros*)

Partner, place of origin (share)	'Capitales'	'Apéndices capitales'
Tomás Ignasi Soler, de Manresa (1/7)	10740/10/6	4200
Josep Sagristá, de Manresa (1/7)	10740/10/6	4200
Maurici Soler, de Reus (1/14)	5370/5/3	2100
Total	26851/6/3	10500
Isidro Bosch, de Calaf (1/7)	10740/10/6	4200
Antonio Figarola y Sala, de Calaf (1/7)	10740/10/6	4200
Josep Figarola y Sala, de Calaf (1/14)	5370/5/3	2100
Total	26851/5/3	10500
Francesc Cortadellas, de Barcelona (1/7)	10740/10/3	4200
Josep Cortadellas, de Calaf (1/7)	10740/10/6	4200
Total	21481/1/-	8400

Notes:
Total capital contributed to the company: 104583/13/6 *libras catalanas*.
The column headed *apendices capitales* or additional capital shows amounts 'por los que según el propio inventario han igualmente entrado sus socios a la cía. y de que esta debería contribuirles el premio anual del 6%'.

Source: AHT, FC, book C14.

The company was, then, formed by three groups of partners with total capital of more than 100,000 *libras catalanas* already invested in a range of businesses (as we shall see below), and 29,400 *libras catalanas* in cash contributions in a kind of capital increase, which was expected by the partners to provide a return of 6 per cent per annum. The inventory of assets (Table 7.2) shows how this capital was invested.

Table 7.2 Inventory of assets owned by Soler, Bosch, Figarola y Compañía in 1777

Assets	Libras jaquesas	Libras catalanas
[A]Granos existentes en los graneros y fiados a grano por grano, valorados	8148/6/-	14379/7/-
[B]Mercaderías existentes en la botiga de Pedro Vallés de Huesca y lanas y sedas en Calaf, Manresa y Barcelona	2598/13/1	4585/17/1
[C]Dinero efectivo en Huesca de que se hace entrada el Sr. Mauricio Soler en relación de Huesca	4806/8/13	8481/18/11
[D]Dinero efectivo en poder del Sr. Isidro Bosch de Calaf y de que éste se hace entrada en cuentas de su adm(inistraci)ón	1752/10/7	3092/13/9
[E]Dinero efectivo en poder del Sr. Thomás Ignacio Soler de que este se hace entrada en cuentas de su administración de Manresa	3153/6/7	5564/13/8
[F] Desembolsos por varios arriendos	9169/-/9	16180/12/9
[G] Desembolsos por lanas y sedas	5171/1/1	9125/7/9
[H] Deudas activas en Aragón	4094/16/15	7226/4/-

[I] Deudas activas en Cataluña	23105/8/7	40774/6/1
[J] Muebles	485/7/3	856/10/3
[K] Caballerías	150/1/4	264/16/9
[L] Comestibles	379/18/6	670/8/9
Total crédito según inventario	63,014/18/9	111,202/16/4
Total arriendos y compras de lana y seda (F+G)	14,340 (22.76%)	
Total deudas activas (H+I)	27,199 (43.16%)	

Source: AHT, FC, book C14. The records reflect the current accounts of the partners in the Compañía de Aragón with each other in 1777 (ff. 1–9) and the distribution of profits between the partners from 31 December 1818 until 15 December 1879. The complete inventory drawn up when the firm was founded was included in a *Libro titulado de relaciones de los Sres. Soler, Bosch, Figarola y Compa.*, which I have not been able to locate. There is a small difference between the capital reflected in Table 7.1 and in Table 7.2.

The use made by the new company of its initial capital is eloquent: 43 per cent was invested in *deudas activas*, which is to say loans made above all in Catalonia, and a further 25 per cent was sunk into advance payments of seigneurial rents and tithes, and forward purchases of wool and silk. Current assets made up almost all of the total, and there was minimal long-term investment in fixed assets. The new company was formed with three shops selling 'lanas y sedas en Calaf, Manresa y Barcelona', Soler's shop and business in Huesca, various leases of agrarian rents, and the wool, silk and grain traded individually by the partners. Aside from joining forces in general, the company was very probably created to bring in Josep Cortadellas, a shrewd manager, and Francesc Cortadellas, whose business in Barcelona offered excellent opportunities for the investment of the profits earned in the interior markets. The main business in Catalonia was shifted into other firms, and the new company specialized in operations in Aragon. This does not mean that the partners did not already have a presence in Aragon – they had done for years, but severally.

A review of the 155 books of account conserved to the present day, which reflect the dealings of a host of small firms generally formed by only two to four partners, shows the surprisingly unified and coordinated functioning of the whole. The key to the group lies in the few surviving books of account kept in the personal archives of the Compañía de Aragon's treasurer in Calaf, Josep Cortadellas. The debits and payments entered in one of these books, which covers the period 1808–1809, allow identification of all company cash in the possession of the merchant at that time, revealing the composition of the whole group.[67] The most important fact to emerge from an examination of these books is that a very real business strategy existed, though it may not have been written down. The various factories and offices worked according to a plan.

As shown by the journals, each unit operated independently and was not even necessarily legally owned by the firm itself, but by one or more of the partners. This is the case of the Barcelona counting house, which was never actually owned by the Compañía de Aragón but always, and solely, by Francesc Cortadellas, a partner of the firm. The accounts reflect large movements of goods and capital, but the accounts appear carefully balanced at zero. This is a crucial point, because it means they were designed for management control and not to reflect profits, which the partners received directly by way of transfers in cash and in kind into their own accounts, or via the salaries paid by the firm. The books used to keep account of leased tithes and seigneurial rents do, however, include profit and loss accounts, as may be observed in the firm of García Bover, which has been studied elsewhere.[68]

One may wonder, then, what point there was in forming a company of this kind. In my view, the answer is clear – it was created to channel the agrarian earnings obtained by the Catalan partners in Aragon back to their offices in Catalonia, and principally to the counting house in Calaf. The partners, who were basically carters and the tenants of feudal rents, also conducted large-scale operations in Catalonia, which the books of the Compañía de Aragon reflect only in part.

The most surprising thing, however, is that the commercial agents were the partners themselves and not the company. Though this may appear odd, it was in reality an original and very efficient solution. The whole functioned like a spiderweb, in which most of the threads belonged to the company but others belonged to the partners, depending on the moment and the circumstances. The Catalan partners moved at will within this structure organized in small specialist groups. The Compañía de Aragón itself entered into certain transactions as a legal entity, but in other cases it merely placed the necessary infrastructure (stores, premises and management) at the service of the partners' private dealings (whether undertaken alone or in association with other partners under a variety of arrangements) or, as mentioned above, it paid them a salary as employees of the company.

In support of these claims, we may note that the contracting tenants in all 40 known cases in which the Cortadellas obtained the lease of tithes and other seigneurial and ecclesiastical rents in Zaragoza between 1774 and 17811 were partners of the group, either individually or as members of a firm of between two and four people, but never Soler, Bosch, Figarola y Compañía as such.[69] The profits from these undertakings were recognized only in the personal accounts of each partner, but never in those of the company itself. This had important consequences, insofar as the books did not allow calculation of the group's actual profits, effectively preventing taxation of its business. According to his own books, Josep Cortadellas earned money and would have paid the *catastro* in Catalonia, but the company as such had no profits, and its tax obligations, whether real or potential, remain an open question.

However, we do know fairly clearly how the business functioned. Broadly speaking, at least seven differentiated business levels can be made out based on a rough east–west territorial logic between 1777 and 1808, the pinnacle of the company's success.

1. Merchants, commercial agents and correspondents in Zaragoza and Madrid. The agents in Zaragoza leased seigneurial rents and tithes in Aragon, competing with other Catalan firms and the city's own local merchants, and they also paid the sums contracted over to the landlords either in the Aragonese capital or in Madrid, where many among the aristocracy lived and wished to collect. They also negotiated bills of exchange in Madrid and Zaragoza, and sold the goods brought by the Catalan carriers on commission. The intense relationship maintained by Josep Cortadellas with the important Catalan merchant Ramón Ferrer y Guardia is known. In Zaragoza, the partners actively engaged in leasing tithes and seigneurial rents in association with local Aragonese merchants.[70]

2. Land agents managing estates in Aragon factored for varying periods, usually between three and ten years.[71] These factors managed the leased seigneurial rents and tithes, which meant bringing in harvests, collecting rents and making numerous small local payments, for which purpose they employed associates, some Catalan labourers and local people.
3. Carters and mule drivers specializing in the trade in pack animals,[72] the wool trade and silks.
4. Agents in Catalonia who engaged above all in the sale of Aragonese grain at their own factories. The most important of these was probably the Lerida factory, although there were others in Tortosa and at other points along the River Ebro, from where grain and other products were shipped in barges, which were also sometimes chartered by associates to form river transport firms.[73]
5. Merchants engaged in the sale and transformation of farm produce in Catalonia. There was a factory in Calaf which commercialized fleeces brought from Aragon and manufactured soap using oil brought from the western part of Lerida province and eastern Aragon. The wool was sold for a time to the weavers of Sant Martí de Sasgaioles and to another factory belonging to the firm in Manresa. This business operated at least between 1777 and 1799. The Manresa factory used the wool obtained from Calaf to produce mattresses and other products. It seems reasonable to suppose that the Cortadellas-Calaf-Compañía de Aragón group may itself have moved from selling wool into manufacturing, sourcing production to cottage weavers.[74] It also operated a distillery or *oficina* producing aquavit, which transformed wine from vineyards in the Calaf district owned by the partners themselves. The distillery functioned at least between 1784 and 1793, buying up wine for distillation only when local prices fell beyond the point where exports via the ports of Reus and Barcelona were profitable.[75]
6. The central treasury in Calaf, which was controlled by Josep Cortadellas, who made his living both by managing the affairs of the Compañía de Aragón and from his own business dealings between 1777 and 1809. Much, though not all, of the income generated by the factories[76] flowed through this counting house.
7. The factory and counting house in Barcelona, which provided the connection with the city's commerce. Information on its activity exists for a number of years (1793–1801).[77] It was used by groups of partners to obtain the lease of seigneurial rents and tithes in Catalonia and sometimes Aragon in their own names rather than that of the firm. It also negotiated the partners' bills of exchange, many of which were from Madrid and Zaragoza, and managed trade with America.

The functioning of the network of firms was highly complex, but the business rested basically on the commercialization of agrarian income from the lease of tithes and other seigneurial rents in Aragon. These contracts were obtained at auction, and sometimes by the use of bribes.[78] In general terms, profits consisted of diverse flows resulting from transfers of goods and cash from the factories and farm businesses in Aragon to the partners, the manufacturers of consumer goods and the beneficiaries of agrarian rents. A first step in the realization of profits was the sale of wheat, corn and mules in local and district markets, especially in Aragon, along with rural lending. The second step consisted of bulk sales of wheat in the market of Lerida[79] and other entrepôts on the banks of the Ebro. The third stage occurred at the factories in Calaf, where wool and a part of the oil was sold, and Manresa, which both consumed wool and sold imported fleeces, and may also have operated cottage industries. The fourth stage took place at the Calaf counting house and the Barcelona factory, although the monetary nature of their relations with each other remains to be investigated. The factory paid large amounts of endorsed bills,[80] which suggests that there was a flow of debt transfers to Barcelona, where the obligations were settled using the profits obtained from trade with America. In any event, it is quite clear that the business strategy of these Catalan merchant networks began with the optimization of profits from the lease of tithes and seigneurial rents. This was the core of their business strategy throughout the 31 years of their greatest activity, from 1777 to 1808.

The agrarian origins of trade

What, we may ask, was the reason for the Cortadellas' interest in agriculture? The explanation lies in the origins of the family's business in Catalonia, which goes back at least to 1736. On 17 May 1736 a first Josep Cortadellas, who died in 1754 or 1755[81] and who may already have founded a commercial house, joined up with the firm of Josep Argullol. The partners contributed two thirds and one third of the capital, respectively. The new firm was small, with capital of just 1,215 *libras catalanas*. Between 1730 and 1775, two (or more) men by the name of Josep and Francesc Cortadellas, leased various tithes and seigneurial rents, trading in the agricultural produce received by way of in-kind payment.[82] This activity was confined to Catalonia alone. Most of the leases were managed by means of alliances with other groups of merchants.[83]

The first generation of Cortadellas also traded in cloth, wool (white and black fleeces), raw silk (*fina* and *adúcar*), silk cloth, hemp, wine, cocoa from Guayaquil, alum (for dyeing), worsted, hats, coloured thread, women's stockings and donkeys, and they even paid the *catastro* on behalf of third parties. Their commercial relations seem to have been confined to the Burgués house in Barcelona until the 1760s, when other merchants appear.[84]

Meanwhile, the Cortadellas' initial relations with Aragon (Zaragoza from 1733 and Huesca from 1736) were sporadic and indirect, being conducted, for example, through the offices of Odón Burgués of Barcelona. In May 1736, however, they established direct relations with Lucas Goicoechea, a merchant of Zaragoza, and in 1774 the books show them carrying on a two-way trade on both sides of the border with Catalonia.[85]

To sum up, the Cortadellas' business began with the lease of tithes and seigneurial rents in Catalonia and was later expanded to commercial intermediation via the provision of transport services first in Catalonia and then in Aragon. Finally, the business grew westwards in the 1770s to encompass the lease of agrarian rents in Aragon.[86] Meanwhile, other family members set up factories in the Catalan interior and in Barcelona, linking them directly with the maritime trade with Majorca and America.

After the foundation of Soler, Bosch, Figarola y Compañía, Josep Cortadellas remained as treasurer in Calaf, and Francesc Cortadellas undertook the management of the company's affairs in Barcelona. Both also continued with their own private businesses. In addition to his existing interests, Francesc Cortadellas also invested intensively in animal husbandry (sheep and goats), the lease of pasture and animal feed, and the meat trade.[87] In these years, Josep Cortadellas maintained 68 current accounts with customers in different Catalan towns,[88] as well as managing three estates in Catalonia, trading in hemp, sheep, silk (some of which was local) and wine, and he also went into industry, creating at least one soap factory. All of this brought in sufficient income to create a religious foundation for parents and grandparents, '*per los avis y pares*', in which he probably sank money into perpetual loans (*censos*) and masses for the souls of his family. Thereafter, neither Francesc nor Josep had any dealings in Aragon. They had specialized, and others continued the business for them.[89] The company they created survived for 102 years, although the business described here lasted only until 1809, the year in which Josep Cortadellas died. All of its activity was recorded in the journal,[90] allowing detailed analysis.[91]

Business organization and economic and social impact

The study of these merchants' activities in both Catalonia and Aragon reveals their extraordinary efficiency and organizational flexibility, as well as their considerable social impact wherever they set up their businesses. Meanwhile, the study of their factories and counting houses throws light on some surprising aspects of their operations.

Let us begin with the Huesca factory, a trading post situated in the central part of the firm's area of influence,[92] where two members of the Compañía de Aragón who had already been working in the region for years established a factory, which they took turns managing between 1777 and 1803. Analysis of the accounts shows[93] that it functioned as a coaching inn, a warehouse and an entrepôt for the group's carters and traders, where they could pick up or leave goods and cash on deposit. It also managed seigneurial rents and tithes in the area on behalf of the (more or less) absentee landlords. The partners were not employees but each had their own businesses, which they kept separate from the factory accounts where inflows of wheat, barley, oil, wool and wine, and cash deposits made by associates were recorded. Even the *factor* or agent had his own business dealings. The merchants, traders, carters and mule drivers using the factory came and went. For example, a series of individuals[94] dropped out in the 1780s only to reappear years later conducting their affairs in other places.

It is hard to know exactly what impact the factory had on the local market, or the social standing of the factory agents. Soler paid servants and labourers. He also deployed debt collectors in the villages, and he even contracted reapers who in turn contracted unskilled labourers at harvest time.[95] The Catalans also made cash loans, which allowed them to penetrate the key rural credit business, and they made forward purchases of raw silk, enabling them to control the peasant producers. Hence, they not only performed the functions of commercial agents (trading in grain and wool, and providing financing) but they also controlled, or were beginning to control, production through the lease of seigneurial rents and tithes, and by means of forward purchases, wages and rural credit. Profits could be substantial. Though I have not been able to determine them in the case of the Huesca factory, I have done so for the factory at Mallén on the banks of the Ebro. This establishment was engaged almost entirely in the lease and management of seigneurial rents and tithes, and its accounts reflect a considerable surplus between July 1787 and June 1788, resulting in a profit (income less expenses) of around 55–60 per cent.[96] Fontana describes another of the Cortadellas' ventures, this time with the Americas, undertaken between 1793 and 1795, in which the profit was also more than 50 per cent.[97]

Another interesting case is that of the important counting house or factory in Ballobar,[98] a village with irrigated land in the Bajo Cinca district close to the border of Aragon with Catalonia. Probably created in 1792, the factory engaged in the early 1800s in the lease of tithes under contracts which were sometimes very stable in various villages belonging to the diocese of Lerida, although they were actually situated in Aragon.[99] These contracts were probably awarded at auction in the nearby city of Lerida, where the partners of the Compañía de Aragon drove a considerable trade in the city's active wheat market. The Ballobar factory concentrated a business that had hitherto been fairly fragmented, leaving only half a dozen leased stores in the surrounding villages.[100] The factory generated significant income of between 0.25 and 5 million copper *reales* per year between 1801 and 1809, when war almost caused its disappearance.

Its main business was managing and collecting seigneurial rents, which were paid in kind, mainly in wheat and to a lesser extent in barley (these two crops made up more than 90 per cent of the total). Everything indicates that the grain collected was either sold or loaned back to the local community. Analysis of the factory's costs in a normal year (1801–1802) shows that the costs of managing rents (wages, transport and others) were small in terms of cash movements (9.3 per cent of total outflows), while in-kind loans of grain were very important (48.25 per cent) and internal transfers also accounted for large amounts of money (33.2 per cent).

The factory's treasury also served as a 'bank' which held cash deposits on behalf of the partners, whose personal purchases of wool and silk were recorded in separate accounts,[101] and could be used to transfer profits earned further west back to Catalonia. In 1801–1802 the costs incurred in collecting the leased tithes and seigneurial rents, and in making payments to the landlords accounted for only 20 per cent of outflows, but the income generated from these operations represented 50–90 per cent of inflows. The factory's net profits, meanwhile, would have been between 30 per cent and 69 per cent, a level which may be explained in terms of the highly speculative nature of the business.

The company's wheat sales and loans had a considerable social impact. The list of debtors for two years, 1801–1802 and 1807–1808, shows more than 300 scattered around some 30 villages, although they are mainly concentrated in five manors located within a radius of 20–30 km, which is to say one day's travel. Most of the inhabitants of these localities were in debt to the Catalans. Many loans were made either to buy seeds or for the payment of rents. A number were backed by mortgages but only the largest were witnessed by a notary.[102] The business was, then, based on personal credit, private contracts and good faith.

Calaf always held the keys to management of the company and its assets, but it did not control the accounts, which were decentralized, or the realization of its profits, which went directly to the partners and associates in the form of cash payments. Like the establishment in Huesca, the Ballobar factory scarcely made cash remittances to Calaf, but it did make considerable payments to the Catalans operating in the area. Meanwhile, money circulated within the organization not by means of bills of exchange but via a singular system of endorsed money orders. These transferable payment orders avoided the need to use bills of exchange (which entailed a financial cost) or ready cash within the network,[103] benefitting only creditworthy insiders.

The last case we shall consider is that of another Catalan factory in Luceni,[104] a village some 50 km to the west of Zaragoza on the banks of the Ebro. Its municipal bounds were not large but the area was very fertile, lying on both sides of the river, and almost half of the local fields were irrigated though the rest consisted of poor, unirrigated land. It was home to some fifty peasant families who lived under a harsh seigneurial regime, paying high rents to the landowner, the countess of Fuenclara and lacking any land of their own.

The little water Luceni had for irrigation was drawn from the River Jalón, though the villagers were in hope of receiving more when the Canal Imperial de Aragón was rebuilt in the 1770s. However, it was only in 1800 that their hopes were finally realized.[105] Two years earlier, on 1 June 1798 the Cortadellas family had leased certain seigneurial rents in Luceni and other places for a five-year term, and when irrigation was eventually allowed in 1800, the lease was amended, probably to include an increase in the payment and to let the villages cultivate and earn rents from the *novales*, the new irrigated fields. An agreement was then made to obtain additional water in order to raise the productivity of the leased fields and undertake improvements to a seigneurial mill.

Irrigation had amended the seigneurial rents, and it was therefore necessary also to change the terms of the agreement. The opportunity to irrigate the land and increase its productivity had existed for more than 20 years, yet the landlord had not only failed to apply for more water but had actually taken steps to prevent its arrival. The Catalan rent farmers, however, made sure to bring irrigation water to the village, and when it arrived the peasants, much to the annoyance of the countess, preferred to cultivate the new fields, where they were required to pay irrigation charges but much lower seigneurial rents, and where access to water was secure. She complained to Josep Cortadellas, protesting that the Catalan managers refused the peasants wheat to sow in the seigneurial fields, but were happy to provide seeds for the newly irrigated land. They were, she claimed, against her and in favour of the peasants.[106]

Factories like those of Huesca, Ballobar, Mallén and Luceni transferred large sums of money earned from the peasantry back to Catalonia, and they played a decisive role in driving social change wherever they operated. The polyvalent Huesca factory not only managed seigneurial rents and tithes, but also contracted numbers of local labourers and activated the silk and wool markets. Meanwhile, the Ballobar establishment, which specialized in the grain trade, ended up by reinvesting profits in rural lending operations, further strengthening the social standing of the Catalan partners and agents, which was already considerable given their position as the tenants of seigneurial rents and tithes. They collected payments in kind, allowing them to sell significant quantities of grain and lend the rest back to the peasants as seed stock and for food. As they were in contact with everybody in the local community, they became the essential intermediaries between the peasants and the clergy, the clergy and the bishop, the tithe-paying peasants and the bishop, and between everybody concerned and the market. The Catalans also purchased fleeces and silk in bulk, which they would either export to supply the industries of the principality or sell in the open market.

Finally, the case of Luceni perfectly illustrates the role of these Catalan merchants in undermining the feudal regime existing in much of Aragon, which was pervasive in the Ebro Valley and was harsher, more primitive and more paternalistic than in Catalonia. By managing the irrigation of new fields they assured and increased agrarian rents. At the same time, they stood between the peasants and the landlord, thereby limiting opportunities for seigneurial control. At the same time they turned a blind eye to the use of seed stock preferentially to sow newly irrigated land rather than the fields belonging to the landlord, allowing the peasants every opportunity to wriggle out of paying seigneurial rents.

In each area, there was a group of specialized merchants who had adapted their activities to the opportunities available locally. Many were permanent residents, and some had Aragonese wives and children. It could be said, in fact, that they were Aragonese, but they were identified in terms of their business interests and membership of migratory, commercial and social networks: they were the Catalans. All of them originated from the rural milieu. Each group consisted of dozens, sometimes up to a hundred, individuals, who would in turn mobilize both Catalan and Aragonese labourers, mule drivers, carters, artisans and servants. Their business ultimately rested on farming, and they were happy to stick to what they knew, primarily the trade in agricultural commodities, an activity which was much more limited by transport costs than the distribution of cloth and metalwork, linens, haberdashery, trinkets and small consumer articles. It was nonetheless an important business, even if it was necessarily confined to the more immediate sphere of Aragon and, perhaps, certain areas on the coast of Valencia. Much further away from the hub of Barcelona, transport costs became prohibitive for this kind of intuitive, tactical business, in which short-term moves were controlled from Calaf but which was not governed by any overarching long-run strategy, though it prospered greatly in times of economic growth. Such a trade could not, however, adapt to major changes in the social fabric, so that the crisis of the *Ancien Régime* and the outbreak of Spain's War of Independence led to the collapse of the firms involved.

The Catalan firms formed by partners like Soler, Bosch, Figarola y Compañía were not like the companies of French pedlars, artisans, merchants and financiers, or indeed the companies of Barcelona and the surrounding towns. The merchants of Calaf and Copons were of peasant origin, and their undertakings grew out of the management of agrarian rents and the trade in agricultural commodities, later moving into transport services and the sale of higher value-added products like cloth. The management of agrarian rents was an activity that deeply penetrated Aragon but could not progress farther afield. However, such firms made a crucial contribution to the development of the Catalan regional market, and to the transformation of Aragon and the creation of close links between the former kingdom and Barcelona. They provided Catalonia with capital, which was reinvested in internal commerce, in manufacturing and in maritime trade. Finally, they reached even the remotest corners of the Catalan and Aragonese countryside, demonstrating a remarkable capacity to effect social change wherever they appeared.

The companies engaged in the management of agrarian rents failed during the War of Independence as rents dried up. However, there were others ready to take their place. These were firms which had also been active in Aragon and the rest of the Spanish interior for decades, but they were not involved in agriculture. Though they did not spurn farming, their real business was the organization of proto-industrial manufacturing in the villages of the pre-coastal mountain ranges of Catalonia, close to the capital's area of influence, and the sale of their products (mainly woollen cloth), combined with the sale of French goods imported over the border or via the port of Barcelona, as well as manufactures produced in the city by the firms themselves. Their reach was longer, because transport costs were lower in proportion to the value of their goods. In the next section, we shall consider these companies in order to throw light on the expansion of trade throughout the interior of Spain.

Proto-industrial and Barcelona-based companies

The development of proto-industrial manufacturing in the Catalan pre-coastal ranges, in particular in the areas closest to Barcelona and the high road to Zaragoza and Madrid is a well-documented process, although not so much from the standpoint we are interested in here, which concerns the activity of the manufacturing companies that emerged between approximately 1690 and 1790.

Fortunately, a case study exists in the firm of Josep Torelló (in fact there was more than one person of that name) based in the town of Igualada, which has been examined in great detail by Jaume Torras through the surviving records in the family archive.[107] His analysis is illustrative of the likely course of other firms both in Igualada and in other towns. The Torelló family were traditional craft *pelaires* or carders and members of the local guild, who had progressed since the seventeenth century to become, in Torras's words '*fabricantes sin fábrica*', which is to say they were the organizers of a *fábrica*, a proto-industrial system of work which in their case comprised 19 looms and marshalled the output of 380 wool spinners from the town and the surrounding district, providing work for a total of some 500 people. Proto-industrial manufacturing, then, consisted of traditional craft industries which at some point grew beyond production for local consumption to take in other markets further afield. These *fabricantes* as they liked to be called at first sold coarse woollen cloth at local fairs like that of Verdú, but in a few decades they graduated to the production and sale of semi-fine and fine fabrics in order to add value and reach more distant markets like Zaragoza, the fair at Valdemoro near Madrid, and Madrid itself.[108] Based on the available data, the proto-industrial rural *fabricantes* of the Torelló family did not come directly from the peasantry like the networks of merchants trading in grain and other agricultural commodities, but this is not important here. This is, after all, only one case, and other such manufacturers may have had peasant origins.

The Torelló family and others like them bought fine wool in Zaragoza, which was highly prized, in the Tierra Alta of Teruel and in Albarracín, a town which formed part of the Castilian Mesta. In particular, the *fabricantes* were assiduous buyers in the town of Molina de Aragón. They used bills of exchange and they had correspondents in Zaragoza, Madrid and elsewhere. They would travel periodically following very regular circuits, but they never engaged in the business of transport themselves, preferring to hire the services of third-party mule drivers and carters. Jaume Torras stresses that the vast majority of these individuals, and the members of the networks and companies which provided support for their purchases of commodities, were Catalans.[109] This in itself shows that firms of this kind sought the assistance both of the national groups trafficking in grain and other agricultural commodities, and of the networks of carriers and merchants established in other towns and cities. They also availed themselves of contacts in Barcelona-based companies, which formed the third wave of Catalan commercial expansion into the interior of Spain, and whose pivotal role we shall now consider.

The merchant groups of Barcelona and its immediate environs obtained their capital from different sources to the rural groups described so far, spreading throughout Spain by land and by sea. They also penetrated Aragon, overlapping the activity of other networks, and they maintained a much larger presence in the former kingdom than elsewhere for reasons of proximity and because the simultaneous activity of Catalan rural firms provided an added advantage. Examination of the business conducted by some of these Barcelona-based firms in Aragon provides a general outline of how they operated in the rest of Spain. They used bills of exchange to trade in high value-added products, which reduced their transport costs relative to the value of goods. [110] Meanwhile, their only common feature was that they had their head offices in Barcelona, and it will be of interest here to consider the nature and trajectories of their different businesses. We shall look at a random sample of seven firms which, though insufficient to describe them all, will be enough to sketch an outline of the business ventures undertaken by the merchant groups that expanded throughout the interior market of Spain.

1 Jofré y Vila y Compañía (1717–1733): unspecialized storekeepers

The firm was created by Francesc Jofré and Josep Vila, and it operated in Catalonia and Aragon from early in the eighteenth century, remaining active at least between 1717 and 1733. The business was large with some 400 or 500 customers (between 1717 and 1724), achieving significant growth in the volume of its commercial transactions, and it was concentrated above all on Valencia and Zaragoza. At this stage, the partners were not yet industrialists but still only merchants.[111] Jofré and Vila exported traditional goods and manufactures, and re-exported a diverse range of merchandise imported from abroad, including fabrics. Zaragoza was the firm's second market after Valencia in terms of customer accounts (1717–1720) but the first in terms of the volume of revenues (1721–1733). Goods were taken overland to Zaragoza by Catalan and Aragonese carriers, and to Valencia by coastal trading vessels.[112] The strategic location of Zaragoza made the city an almost obligatory way station for goods on their way to the rest of

Spain by road. It is not clear which of the intermediary carriers worked as partners with the firm for a commission and which bought the goods directly. In the case of the former, the company decided what goods the carrier brought back on the return journey to Catalonia. Carriers operating on their own behalf could themselves choose when to return and what products to buy for sale on their arrival back home. In the later years of the business (1725–1733), all of the cash income earned in Aragon came from just two buyers in Zaragoza, Domingo Sabatier[113] and Ignacio Abadía. Sales in Zaragoza consisted of a wide variety of consumer goods – clothes, shoes, books, luxury articles, silks and other imported items, although not foodstuffs. These goods were despatched using Catalan and sometimes Aragonese mule drivers (but not carters). The first customer in Madrid, a merchant, appears in an entry dated 22 March 1732,[114] as the Barcelona-based firm progressively expanded its original business, which consisted of selling manufactured goods produced by third parties.

The firms of Jofré y Vila and of the Zaragoza-based merchant Domingo Sabatier collected and paid countless bills of exchange drawn on third parties in Barcelona and Zaragoza, as well as arranging purchases of goods.[115] This in itself shows that they conducted merchant banking operations, given that each was vested with reciprocal powers of management and representation, and that they granted each other credit, paying and collecting mutual debts with third parties by drawing and discounting bills of exchange. These incipient *merchant banking* transactions[116] were in fact very much of the same kind as the financial operations known to have been carried on in Madrid around this time, although the negotiation of bills of exchange was probably always a secondary business for these firms.

2 Joan Baptista Cirés y Compañía (1770–1812): manufacturers (static business)

The company's operations spanned the last quarter of the eighteenth century. It was founded by two majority silent partners, Miquel Alegre Roig and Agustí Gibert (2,105 *libras catalanas*, 8 *sueldos* and 9 *dineros*), and the firm of Joan Baptista Cirés y Cía., as the minority partner (5,528 *libras catalanas*, 14 *sueldos* and 5 *dineros*). Its activity spanned the period between 1770 and 1812. The inventory of its assets shows that it began with two factories making yarn,[117] and there is also evidence that it manufactured cloth. Above all, then, the partners were industrialists seeking to expand their market by selling in the interior of Spain. They sold to storekeepers, artisans and local customers (the records mention figures like *notari*, *fuster*, *botiguer*, *comerciant*, *sastre* and *teixidor de lli*), and to *traginers* or mule drivers, who bought their wares directly to market them on their own behalf. A certain Francisco Monistrol is mentioned as selling in Castile ('comerzian per las Castillas').[118]

3 María Formentí (or Formantí) Gusta y Compañía (1774–1796): manufacturers of *indianas*

The company was in business between 1779 and 1796, and it is the only one examined which sold its goods basically outside Catalonia, mainly in Aragon. Procurements of raw materials reveal that the factory essentially produced *indianas* (printed cotton cloth). Payments were made to a *Compañía de Filats* in which the firm held interests and investments, and it paid salaries to family members and partners working in the factory, showing that the factory operated as an urban employer, a very different situation to rural companies, in which the partners confined themselves to distributing profits (or losses) in the regular settling up known as the *passament de comptes* or *pase de cuentas*[119] at the close of each business period. The partners of the Barcelona firm changed over time, but all of them initially joined as wage-earners in what was intended as a static business.[120]

Meanwhile, dealings with merchants in Zaragoza reflect sales of a range of fabrics, including 'mocadors' and 'pessas de cutó' (i.e. cotton stuffs), 'indianes' (printed cotton fabrics), 'mucadors' and 'mucadors de sidería' (silk handkerchiefs), revealing that the company sold its own products and other textiles in the Spanish interior market, at least in some years. It seems that the sale of these goods in Aragon provided a second string in a business dedicated above all to the manufacture of *indianas*.

4 Ignasi Parera Morell y Compañía and Antón Parera y Compañía (1767–1820): from artisans to carriers

These were two different companies. The former was created on 12 August 1767 by Ignasi Parera Morell, Josep Llor and Antón Gomis, who probably started out as silk weavers,[121] in order to operate a transport business and 'per negociar nostres cab[d]als[122] junts tan[t] en Catalunya com en los Regnes de Aragó, Valencia y Castilla, com y també a colsevol altre paratje que nos aparega convenent'. Its starting capital was 15,000 *libras catalanas* split into three equal shares. The company was a scion of an earlier firm with only two partners, Ignasi Parera and Josep Llor. On 12 August 1771, the firm's starting capital was increased by 28,626 *libras catalanas* to undertake trips 'de anar fora a vendre mercaduríes' and to buy silk in Aragon and Valencia, sometimes on credit. The firm's offices were at the house of Ignasi Parera, and a part of its *cabdals* or funds were held by Antón Gomis. A *balans* or *passament de comptes* was held each year to distribute profits (or apportion losses). The settlement or *passament* for 1805 was prepared by Antón Parera 'major', Antón Parera 'menor' (perhaps the son and grandson of the original Antón Parera), Josep Parera (presumably Ignasi's son or a member of his family), Albert Llor (probably the son or kin of Josep Llor) and a new partner, Antón Omedes.[123]

The firm was, then, a family undertaking formed around the core of the Parera family, and it conducted a highly stable business (at least between 1767 and 1820). Its partners were silk artisans who had switched to trading in silks and other manufactured goods in different regions of Spain. A certain functional specialization existed within the firm so that some partners contributed capital and another managed its cash. The absence of any inventory of assets indicates that it did not engage in manufacturing. There is no evidence of any factory, and if the firm had a store in Barcelona it must have been small. The business seems rather to have been based on the purchase of small lots for sale outside Catalonia and the associated return trade. The business in Aragon seems to have been concentrated mainly in Zaragoza at the end of the eighteenth century.[124] In contrast to the firms engaging in the lease of agrarian rents, in which profits and losses were settled at the end of the 2–5 years' duration of the venture, the company closed its accounts annually, a clear indication of the partners' stable, long-term commitment to the business.

A second company also appears in the accounts. This was Antón Parera y Compañía, which was owned by one of the two people by the name of Antón Parera mentioned above. The data are intriguing: the firm had 115 customers between 1797 and 1807, only two of them outside of Aragon, and almost all of them resident in small towns in what is today the province of Teruel. The accounts were kept in *libras jaquesas* and not *libras catalanas*, while the entries made in the accounts show that the company was active both before 1797 and after 1807.[125] Clearly, it was engaged in purchasing raw silk and selling silk fabrics in Aragon.[126] It also had a store in Barcelona where it sold agricultural produce brought from Majorca.[127]

The two companies were complementary and formed part of a coordinated business strategy. The original Barcelona weavers had shifted their business to peddling via the firm of Ignasi Parera, specializing in goods destined for cities like Zaragoza. Meanwhile, another member of the group, Antón Parera, carried on a supplementary business in the rural areas of Teruel and set up a store to sell farm commodities in Barcelona. The clan had thus moved out of their original craft trade of silk weaving and into small-scale itinerant retailing of silks and other fabrics in Aragon, as well as the distribution of agricultural commodities and produce in Barcelona.

5 Francisco Ribas y Compañía: manufacturers (static business)

The principal business of Francisco Ribas y Cía.,[128] documented for a period of almost 40 years (1766–1804), consisted of a factory producing printed cottons. Almost all of its sales were made via intermediary retailers and volumes were high, generating revenues of 50,000–80,000 *libras catalanas* per year in the period 1780–1794.[129] In the 1760s, the firm's commercial activity was centred mainly on Madrid via a well-known merchant, Ramón Nadal Guardia, who acted as intermediary. By around 1800, the company was selling its wares to a dozen or so cloth merchants in Zaragoza (Pedro Lasala, José Orcet and Juan Torón), Barbastro (José Fortacín, José Chavarría and the firm of López y Navarro) and Tarazona (José Minguella), sometimes buying madder, a highly prized dye used in textiles manufacturing.[130] Outside of Barcelona they were manufacturers but not merchants. They did not travel, and they sold their wares to retailers who were never partners of the firm or family members.

6 Nicolás del Frago (1788–1794): unspecialized storekeeper of Aragonese origin

All the evidence suggests that this merchant was an Aragonese immigrant to Barcelona,[131] which would certainly explain his business. We do not know whether Frago ever formed a company.[132] However, it appears that he was an unspecialized storekeeper who at least initially engaged in the purchase of commodities in Aragon, especially raw silk but also livestock for slaughter, at the same time selling cloth and imported goods in the kingdom. His original business in Aragon consisted, then, of trading in farm products and not manufactured goods.

This surmise is supported by the network through which he operated at the time: in 1789 he was in correspondence with 36 merchants, 24 of whom were Aragonese (19 from Zaragoza) and 15 were from Catalonia. All of them, however, were based in inland ports on the River Ebro or seaports (Mequinenza, Escatrón and Caspe in Aragon, and Flix, Tortosa, Mora de Ebro and Tarragona in Catalonia). Out of a total of 223 surviving letters, no fewer than 186 were sent to merchants in Zaragoza, and Frago's correspondence with some of them reveals a special familiarity that went beyond merely commercial relations. This shows that the key to his business was his knowledge of the Zaragoza market in general, and especially the grain market. The Zaragoza merchants trading in agricultural commodities performed an essential agency function for him, as his own business actually consisted of selling Aragonese grain and meat in Barcelona. No small towns appear in his records. Rather, the usual procedure was to buy commodities in Zaragoza and 'float' them down the Ebro as soon as the river was navigable. In this case, as in almost all of the businesses described here, Frago's activity had developed over the years and must have begun in Zaragoza, whence he eventually emigrated to Barcelona in search of new opportunities.

To sum up, of the seven cases described in this section, three firms were manufacturers, three were unspecialized Barcelona storekeepers, one of them of Aragonese origin, and one was a firm of artisans who had switched activity to set up a transport business. This sample is too small to provide a basis for statistical analysis, but it does show that the commercial expansion of Barcelona was based on at least two very different types of business. The first group comprises storekeepers whose business had grown in step with the regional interior market, trading in goods arriving at the port of Barcelona and imported over the border with France. The second group was formed by textiles manufacturers seeking to expand the market for their products to the Spanish interior. This they did without creating any associated companies or moving into the transport business, preferring to operate via pedlars and urban storekeepers with whom they maintained contact via mule drivers, carters and private couriers carrying correspondence, bills of exchange and cash. Many, though not all, of the storekeepers were Catalans. Other social groups also joined in this growth fever, like the artisans of Barcelona who abandoned their traditional trades to become mule drivers or pedlars.

The development of these companies had little to do with that of their rural peers, which always expanded by bringing in new partners or associates who were linked by bonds of patronage, kinship or common origin. This divergence in business strategies may have created synergies between the two networks in those areas where both operated, basically the former kingdoms of Aragon and Valencia. However, there was a key difference between the two: an economic region was also growing up around the city of Valencia, which complicated mutual exchanges, while Aragon belonged to Barcelona's economic sphere.

Sales in the interior of the Iberian Peninsula took multiple forms, including peddling, at fairs and from fixed shops, whether directly by independent traders operating on their own behalf or on commission. Moreover, many merchants made use of hostelries, inns and taverns, an important resource which to my mind has been unjustly ignored to date, where they could operate as if they had a shop and circumvent local ordinances regulating the activities of pedlars and hawkers.[133]

While there were some similarities, the Barcelona companies conducted a diverse range of commercial activities. In this scenario, it is necessary to distinguish the principal business, normally connected with the proprietors' original trade or occupation, from secondary lines taken up to meet demand, in response to business decisions (such as the diversification of risk, or the attachment of assets and businesses originally owned by other firms in settlement of debts) or dictated by personal circumstances (marriage, the death of partners or the proprietor, or absorption by another firm).

The surviving commercial correspondence illustrates the use of bills of exchange, providing details of individual cases and the most common circumstances. This is perhaps best illustrated by an example like the case of María Formentí y Gusta between 1783 and 1785.[134] This firm was in correspondence with three merchants in Aragon, Pedro Torón and Pedro Lasala of Zaragoza, and Pablo Juncosa of Barbastro, who also had an associate, José Fortacín, in the same town. All of them bought *indianas*, preferably in blue and white patterns, which they sold either directly or to other retailers. Meanwhile, the Barcelona firm would occasionally buy dyers' madder from these merchants.[135]

Though somewhat monotonous, the correspondence is revealing of the use of bills of exchange to pay for sales where the transaction involved intermediaries. The amount of each purchase was entered in the customer's current account,[136] and when the balance payable reached a certain level, the company would draw a bill of exchange with a term of three or four months, which might or might not include a commission (depending on whether the sale was considered a cash or credit transaction), payable against the account of a third-party debtor of the bill's issuer. If the beneficiary was in a hurry to collect the sum concerned before maturity, the bill could be discounted at interest for the days remaining.

Finally, it will be of interest to consider another aspect of this trade, namely relations with the mule drivers and carters entrusted with the transport of goods and the key role of the Barcelona to Zaragoza highway. This may be observed in the entries made in 1770 in the current account of Pedro Carrica, a merchant of Zaragoza, with the Barcelona-based firm of Joan Baptista Cirés y Compañía,[137] which we have not hitherto mentioned. Table 7.3 summarizes Carrica's account, just one among several carriers mentioned in the ledger.

Table 7.3 Summary of the current account of Miguel Carrica of Zaragoza with Joan Baptista Cirés y Compañía of Barcelona, 1770

DEBIT	**libras catalanas/ sueldos/dineros**
Deu lo Sr. dn. Miquel Carrica corredor de cambis de Zaragoza per lo que li tenim rem[e]s de compte. de la fabrica lo seguent, per lo arriero Fran[ces]ch. Molins, a saver:	
P[ri]mo se li fa carrech per las indianas que li quedavan existens [. . .]	-
[Various consignments of goods described as 'colors corrents, blau y blanch de tina, encar[nat]s, fondo Groch (=yellow) tina, encar[nat]s blau fort, blau y blanch, grisetas', total '364 pessas'] [. . .]	-

(*Continued*)

Table 7.3 (continued)

DEBIT	**libras catalanas/ sueldos/dineros**
Per lo compte presentat a 18 de novbre. 1771 dona [Carrica] per venudas 300 pesses indianas en junts 6574 1/2 varas que a diferents preus valen	2255/5/12
[Other consignments to the value of]	65/10/6
Mes en deu [la] dit compa. de 3 Dezre. de 1770 [que] tenía que cobrar lo dit sr. Carrica de diferents [. . .]	619/1/14
En dit día 3 Deze. 1770 tenía en son poder dit Carrica [. . .]	96/5/7
[Total debt owed by Carrica]	3036/3/7
Mes se li fa carrech de 233/4/1 lc que son del valor dels mocadors de seda y vellut de cotó que compra al cambi del vale e indianas que nos havía pres Frenco. [=Francisco] Fuenteduch	233/4/1
[Total DEBIT	548/15/9
CREDIT	
Ha de haver el [. . .] sor. Carrica Per los ports de quatre remesas de indian[e]s que li aportaren los arrieros seguents y sels dona, a saver. A Fran[cis]co Molins de 21 arrobas a 9 s ard[dit]s	5/8/-
A Joan Bonich [Juan Sallarés, 'Bonich'][138] de 9 @ 13 ff [=*arrobas, fanegas*] a 14 s ard[dit]s [=*sueldos de ardit*]	3/6/-
A Jau(m)e Ymbert de 19 @ 13 ff a 12 s ard[it]s [=*sueldos de ardit*]	6/13/11
A Joan Lapiera de 19 @ 13 ff a 9 s ard[it]s [=*sueldos de ardit*]	5/6/8
[Total, together with an annotation stating 'no sen deu, porta res']	21/8/3
Mes a mes [= 'also'] en 15 D[e]z[embr]e 1770 ¿Casau de Craias?, de valor al 15 En[e]r 1771 post en caixa	260/14/15
En 21 Abril 1771 me remet p[e]r lo ordinary	120/-/-
En 24 Juny me remet p[e]r Ramón Jové	200/-/-
En 30 Jun. me remet p[e]r lo correu 21 vales per cobrar a son temps de diferents	1498/-/10
Per granza que compra a Antonio Gil de La Almunia [de Doña Godina], men fas entrada a 1 Julio 1771, y nos la remete, de import	77/9/4
Per 52 varas de drap de canam [=hemp] p[e]r enb. [?] a la granza [. . .] [a] 32 s 9 d [la] vara	6/9/4
Per corredorias de granza [. . .]	9/-/-
P[e]r corredorías de pel de camell que hans a venut de mon comp[añí]a [. . .]	9/2/-
P[e]r corredorías de 300 pessas indianas que a venut [. . .] y 19 p[es]sas blauetas [. . .]	15/-/14
En 18 Novbre. me remet 4 vales p[e]r solicitar son cobro	267/18/14
Mes per un vale fet a 8 Jener 1771 q[u]e es de indian[e]s, prengé Fran[cis]co Fuentes, y per temor de no perdre a la cobranza lo cambia a[m]b mocadors de seda y vellut de cotó, y dits generos son en poder de Carrica	233/4/1
[Total CREDIT]	2720/8/3

Notes:
@ = *arrobas*, ff = *fanegas*, s = *sueldos*, d = *dineros*.
I have expanded abbreviations and added accents and punctuation to make the text readable.
The references to the carriers mentioned in the text are underlined.

Source: Current accounts ledger 1770–1771, AHMB, FC, B 270. The accountant began booking entries on 6 November 1770.

The document details Pedro Carrica's relations with the partners of Joan Baptista Cirés y Compañía.[139] He charged *correduría* or a commission to sell the firm's *indianas* and camel hair, and he was also a *corredor de cambios*, which is to say a broker who charged a fee to handle the negotiation of bills of exchange. Thus, he sold goods obtained from the firm of Cirés either on commission or on his own behalf, but above all he drew and negotiated *vales*[140] or promissory notes and bills of exchange, and he changed gold coins. Carrica paid a part of his purchases in madder, a highly prized dye, and part in *vales*. However, the most interesting feature of the relationship is that the parties maintained contact via the numerous carriers of goods and information (another good) travelling the highroad between Barcelona and Madrid. The shipments listed mention no fewer than six different mule drivers or carters (with French, Catalan and Aragonese surnames), an 'ordinary', which is to say, regular transport service, and a courier who carried *vales*.

One of them, Juan Sallarés, nicknamed 'Bonich' or 'Bonny John', who reappears thirteen years later as a *carromatero* or wagoner, would transport goods carriage due, so that the buyer would pay the cost on the manufacturer's behalf, booking the resulting debt.[141] In December 1783, the firm of María Formentí wrote to its customer Pedro de Torón of Zaragoza to explain the late delivery of goods in the following terms:

> si no ha recivido vm. el todo o parte de los quatro fardos que le tenemos expedidos, no lo admire Vm. tanto porque hace dos mese que llueve, de suerte que las aguas han hecho estragos en este prin[cipa]do y no hay que poder hacer salir los carromateros, porque los caminos están intransitables, de suerte que han sucedido muchas desgracias de malbaratarse los géneros y otras peores. No obstante d[ic]ho carretero Bonich nos acaba de decir que saldrá dentro 4 ó 5 días como no vuelva a llover, que un día hace que ha cesado.[142]

These merchants were, then, able to expand their business thanks to the existence of the Barcelona to Zaragoza road. The carts and wagons plying this route reduced the relative cost of transport, allowing goods to be sold for a reasonable price at ever greater distances in the interior of Spain. This was the basis for the Catalan manufacturers' trade, as attested by numerous accounts contained in contemporary commercial correspondence.

The effects of overlap in the development of the interior market: the move into finance

Let us now turn to a common feature of all of the Barcelona-based companies – the scant relationship between their commercial activity and the processes involved in the generation and distribution of agricultural income. None of these companies was in any way concerned with the lease of seigneurial and agrarian rents or their commercialization, or even with the sale of products in the countryside. Nevertheless, they profited from such rural earnings, which raised disposable incomes in the Catalan countryside, where their partners and associates had opened up markets, established points of sale and created consumer habits. Furthermore, the products manufactured and traded by the Barcelona-based companies also reached these rural areas via other agents, like pedlars and the factors of firms like that of the Cortadellas family.

However, their principal business was the manufacture and sale of their products in relatively large markets, whether directly or through the agency of mule drivers, pedlars and local shopkeepers, which they expanded to include other wares demanded by a firm's customers as a secondary line. Developments were, then, driven more by consumer demand and less by the factors influencing the production and distribution of agrarian incomes.

Only a few Barcelona-based companies traded agricultural commodities like grain, wine, oil, wool and silk, and still fewer occupied themselves with the management of seigneurial rents and tithes. In the former case, we find the firms of Ignasi Parera and Cía and Antón Parera y Cía, small-scale silk weavers who at some time switched to buying up their raw material in the place of origin, and then moved into cartage and peddling in Aragon, eventually opening a store selling foodstuffs in Barcelona. However, it was the nature of the founders' original craft business that allowed this extension of the business into trading primarily in silk and then in other agricultural commodities rather than into manufacturing. The second case would include only Nicolás del Frago, who may have been a grain dealer or carter based in Zaragoza and trading in agricultural commodities between Aragon and Barcelona before he set up his food store in Barcelona. He is the only such entrepreneur who may have started out by leasing agrarian rents and trading in farm products, though this is mere surmise.

To sum up, this Barcelona-based commerce was directed essentially to meeting the demand for manufactured goods in Zaragoza and other towns without any concerted effect to penetrate rural markets. The main business was the factory, the shop and the development of networks of agents, who provided information about differences in prices and communications, especially along the Barcelona–Zaragoza–Madrid high road, allowing expansion throughout Spain.

The Barcelona firms also invested their capital in America and other areas, but their main interest remained the markets of the interior.[143] The extensively studied Gloria family and their associates are a case in point. Originally artisans, they developed an important textiles business involving both commerce and manufacturing, exemplifying the considerable economic success achieved by people like themselves in the second half of the eighteenth century. Between 1778 and 1782, the total volume of their business was some 1,664,766 *libras catalanas*, consisting above all of transactions carried out in the Mediterranean market (almost one million *libras*, half of it in Genoa), the Catalan regional market (almost 500,000 *libras*, half of it in Barcelona) and the Spanish interior market, worth around 130,000 *libras catalanas*. Ten years later, when the firm sank into bankruptcy in 1791–1793, its volume of business in the Mediterranean had fallen by half in absolute terms (25.14 per cent of the total) and the situation was the same in Catalonia, but the business in Spain as a whole had grown by almost 300,000 *libras catalanas*, more than 100 per cent. Though it had shrunk in some cities like Zaragoza, where the Gloria family purchased wool for its textiles manufacturing, and in Madrid, where the firm maintained contact with the Bourbon government, negotiated bills of exchange and distributed goods to the interior of Castile, their business had grown in other cities along the Mediterranean coast of Spain.[144]

The events of 1808 and the ensuing years of war disrupted commercial channels and halted Catalan commercial expansion, but the effects of the conflict differed depending on the type of firm. Firms operating in the rural world suffered a collapse in agrarian rents, the basis for their business, forcing them to abandon factories like that of Ballobar, which closed its doors in 1812.[145] The company collected a part of its debts through litigation and the attachment of mortgaged properties, but even so it incurred swingeing losses as the crisis drove down land values. The Catalan rural merchants had lost their main asset in the region, their lending business, which caused them to draw in their horns, reducing the scope of their activities and the diversification of their operations.[146] In the nineteenth century, the Compañía de Aragón, which would survive for many decades yet, confined itself merely to collecting agrarian rents obtained from the execution of mortgages securing its loans.[147] The former partners were concentrated in Catalonia, and they simplified the structure of operations to eliminate businesses like the soap factory and other manufactures, and the American trade.

In contrast, the Barcelona-based firms, whose business model was less bound up with relational and kinship networks and was based rather on more advanced commercial instruments like financial accounting, the negotiation of bills of exchange, high value-added products allowing the de-localization of sales and the use of third parties to provide transport services, were able to rebuild and restart their business in the Spanish interior as soon as market conditions, and the state of the country's infrastructure, allowed. This fits with the interpretation that the dislocation of growth in the Spanish economy at the turn of the nineteenth century was not as bad as was once believed, despite the turbulent years of revolutionary war, the collapse of the *Ancien Régime* and the loss of Spain's hold in America.[148]

To sum up, the Barcelona-based firms were better able to adapt to the conditions of the war and post-war period than the rural companies engaged in the business of agriculture. However, we cannot ignore the enterprising peasants of rural Catalonia, whose companies were perhaps the most original feature of the expansion of the region's trade into the interior of Spain in the eighteenth century. The Goser, Castaño, Cos, García, Molas, Iglesias and Cortadellas groups not only exercised a transforming social influence in the areas where they were active; they also brought with them large amounts of capital, which was invested in a process that need not concern us here to provide a fresh boost for the industrialization of Catalonia in the nineteenth century. Though we may observe a certain polarity in assessing the activity of these Catalan networks between negative outcomes, chiefly the peripheralization of Aragon, and positive outcomes like the mobilization of productive resources, this is actually a false dilemma. In reality, these were complementary effects of the same historical process, and they are by no means incompatible.[149]

Finally, the financial aspects of the process deserve consideration. Analysis of the proto-industrial businesses in significant regions of Great Britain, like the West Riding of Yorkshire, reveal that the internal credit[150] granted to artisans in their commercial transactions was sharply reduced from eight months to around four as capital began to circulate ever more quickly. Meanwhile, many of these artisans sought financing from the local banks which emerged from within the community itself.[151] We may wonder, then, whether anything like this may have occurred in Catalonia. Could a part of the capital generated have been used to finance Catalan rural industrialization?

Though it is not possible to answer this question fully at present, certain evidence suggest that this was in fact the case. In the proto-industrial area of the Tierra Alta in the province of Teruel and in the Maestrazgo, an area of Catalan influence, work contracts were made from one season to the next, indicating that there was little or no acceleration in the circulation of capital.[152] Naturally, the rural companies granted loans, but those we know about were made in kind, and they did not use bills of exchange in their internal traffic. However, their earnings, which were very considerable, must have played some role in the rural industrialization of Catalonia, and there can be no doubt that credit developed in the areas where such groups operated. Meanwhile, the Barcelona-based companies used bills of exchange to varying degrees, and it would seem logical to suppose that if they came to represent a significant portion of the total volume of a firm's business, it would de facto begin to perform the functions of a merchant bank.[153] Credit, whether direct or based on the negotiation of bills of exchange, would therefore certainly have developed wherever they operated and naturally in Barcelona, where they were based. However, little more can be said on this topic for the present.

I know of no research of this kind for the eighteenth century, but one such study does exist for the nineteenth, examining and describing the formation of the Garriga Nogués bank in Zaragoza and Barcelona, a process which began in 1831 when the firm of Garriga Hermanos was founded in Zaragoza primarily to purchase cloth from Catalonia for sale in the city as the continuation of the trading house established in the city by the brothers' father.[154] We now know that Catalan companies had been negotiating bills of exchange in Zaragoza for at least 110 years before this time. Indeed, bills of exchange played an important role in the case of Jofré y Vila y Compañía, analysed above, in the early eighteenth century. It seems reasonable to suppose, then, that the banking operations of this firm, and others like it, would have grown over the course of the century, and that in some of them such transactions may have become an important part of the business, although this could only be confirmed by a detailed analysis of their accounts. However, an intriguing point in support of this argument is the fact that the firm of Garriga Nogués' list of trade debtors and other borrowers for 1843 includes individuals and companies in Aragonese towns like Alcañiz, Almudévar, Zuera, Pedrola, Borja and Tauste, as well as Zaragoza itself.[155] These were places that had been the sphere of operations of Catalan groups like the Cortadellas family, Goser and others engaged in the management of seigneurial rents and tithes until the turn of the eighteenth century, which in turn suggests that the ruin of these companies in Aragon caused by the War of Independence left a gap in the financial market that was filled by other Catalan and local firms operating in Zaragoza. The business of credit which had begun shortly after the War of Succession, and partly because of it, was thus reborn from the ashes of the War of Independence.

Notes

Preface

1 Of course, such music cannot be reproduced by definition, as no scores have been preserved. An example can be found at www.ancestral.co.uk/romanmusic.htm (accessed 17 October 2015). Demand for such historical recreations is increasing all the time for use in the opening ceremonies of restored monuments, visits to archaeological sites, and models and pieces made for historical interpretation centres, museums and suchlike. By way of example, see www.reconstruccionhistorica.com (accessed 17 October 2015).
2 For example *Civilization III*. A demo version can be found online at www.civ3.com (accessed 20 March 2012).
3 For example at Satzvey in North Rhine Westphalia in Germany. For further details, see www.burgsatzvey.de (accessed 17 October 2015).
4 Casado (1995) and (2003).
5 Casado (2008).
6 Ringrose (1970) and (1996), Yun (1987) and Bernardos Sanz (2003).

Chapter 1

1 Sereni (1966). For the new historiographical approach, see Vicens (1968). The article referred to is Fontana (1967).
2 The quotations from Fontana (1967) are on pages 17 and 14, note 2, respectively.
3 Sánchez Albornoz (1974a, 1974b, 1975 and 1977).
4 See the innovative analysis of the eighteenth century recently published by Ocampo (2009).
5 Álvarez Junco (2001), pp. 595–597, including the reference to Jaime Balmes.
6 The term 'polarized' is derived from 'polarize', which means to 'divide into two sharply contrasting groups' (*New Shorter Oxford Dictionary*, Oxford University Press, 1993 edition, volume II, p. 2,272). In this light, I believe the terms 'specialized' and 'specialized economic region' are more appropriate.
7 Marshall (1890).
8 Hirschmann (1958), Myrdal (1959).
9 Germán (1995), pp. 19–34. The term is distinguished from *historical region*, which includes a series of political factors. A practical application of this concept is found in the analysis of Spanish industrialization in Gallego, Germán and Pinilla (1993). Torras also underlines the role of concentration in creating a broader labour market, ensuring the supply of cheaper inputs and spreading information (prices and technology), Torras (1998), pp. 85–86.
10 An excellent analysis of the role of regions in European industrialization is found in Pollard (1991), pp. 43–110.

11 Only Jaume Torras has applied the concept of increasing returns due to economies of agglomeration to eighteenth-century Catalonia; Torras (1998), pp. 79–96. I will refer below to the work of Ringrose, who also uses the concept of economic region.
12 Germán, Llopis, Maluquer and Zapata (2001).
13 The respective authors of these studies are Rafael Domínguez Martín and Patricio Pérez González (Cantabria), Emiliano Fernández de Pinedo and Fernández (Basque provinces), Alejandro Arizkun Cela (Navarra), Luis Germán Zubero (Aragón), Jordi Maluquer de Motes Bernet (Catalonia), Jordi Palafox (Valencia) and José Ramón Moreno Fernández (Rioja); all in Germán, Llopis, Maluquer and Zapata (2001).
14 García Delgado and Carrera Troyano (2001), pp. 209–237. References on pp. 210–213.
15 Llopis (2001), pp. 507–524.
16 García Sanz (1989).
17 Llopis (2002).
18 That is, the deviation of prices in each market compared with the mean for all markets grows progressively smaller.
19 Llopis and Jerez (2001), pp. 35, 53 and 57–60; and Llopis and Sotaca (2005).
20 Llopis and Jerez (2001) and (2004).
21 Llopis, Jerez, Álvaro and Fernández (2000).
22 Surprisingly, because Navarre is a region that is usually overlooked in studies. The reason is probably that Navarre had close commercial ties with France, as we shall see below, and customs frontiers/barriers with its neighbour were practically non-existent in the eighteenth century. It is my belief that a comparison of grain prices in Pamplona with those of Bayonne would show that dynamic correlation with prices in the French port was greater than with any city in Spain.
23 Reher (2001), pp. 539–572.
24 The existence of inflation is documented in Hamilton (1947), pp. 29–33, and the gap between price rises and wages on pp. 243–256, in particular in the chart on p. 248.
25 Arizcun Cela (1989).
26 Feliu (1991).
27 Hamilton (1947) and Palop (1977).
28 Peiró (1987).
29 For the eighteenth century, see J. M. Martínez Carrión, J. Moreno Lázaro (Palencia), R. Garrabou and E. Tello (Catalonia), and the statistical appendix included in Martínez Carrión (2002).
30 Domínguez Martín (2002).
31 Despite some errors. See Domínguez Martín (2002), pp. 25–32.
32 Domínguez Martín (2002), pp. 60–70 and 146–209.
33 Polanyi (1944); Granovetter (1973) and (1985). The sociology of social networks has since developed enormously, resulting in the appearance of journals like *Social Networks. An International Journal of Structural Analysis* (www.elsevier.com), which is pure sociometry and is in no way concerned with social history.
34 Christakis and Fowler (2010).
35 To whom I owe the reference: Imízcoz (2010). See the application of these categories, for example, in Imízcoz Beunza (2009).
36 These twelve categories are described in the seminal paper: Granovetter (1973).
37 Granovetter (1985).
38 Granovetter (2004).
39 As the term is used in Nell (1984), pp. 62–68.
40 Ringrose (1996), pp. 83–87.

41 See Moutoukias (1992), pp. 889–915.
42 For example, see the description of the networks formed by the Marquis de la Ensenada and Count de Aranda in Gómez Urdáñez (1996), pp. 220–236, and Olaechea (1969), respectively.
43 Curtin (1984), pp. 1–14.
44 The argument set out in the following paragraphs is based on Greif (1989), pp. 857–882.
45 A temporary alliance or union formed for the purposes of combined action and with its own identity. Such commercial coalitions or leagues gave rise to trade networks, the preferred term here, although it does not mean quite the same thing.
46 Chacón (1998), pp. 17–26.
47 Dedieu and Windler (1998), pp. 201–233.
48 Hernández Franco (1998), pp. 179–199.
49 Antón Pelayo (1998), pp. 67–101.
50 Fontaine (1996). The networks studied are described in chapters 1 and 2, pp. 8–49, and the credit system in chapter 6, pp. 120–139. See also Fontaine (1999).
51 Muldrew (1998).
52 The following paragraphs are based on Geertz (1963), pp. 30–47.
53 For a discussion of such legal factors, see the case of Savoy in Siddle (1997), pp. 1–20.
54 For further details, see Poitrineau (1985), pp. 156–163.
55 Ringrose (1996).
56 In the following paragraphs, I follow the reasoning advanced by Ringrose (1996), pp. 66–81, although not necessarily his thesis, which I have taken the liberty of adapting to the arguments I wish to present in this work.
57 The central idea of this paragraph, which I have adapted to my own analysis, is found in Ringrose (1996), pp. 74–75.
58 Ringrose (1996), p. 76 and map on p. 77.
59 Unlike in France, see Rosenthal (1992).
60 Some of these statements are based on truths which until recently were assumed to be set in stone but have since been shown to be questionable. For example, Reher (2001) has shown that the Spanish market was already well on its way to integration before the creation of the railway network.
61 For further references, see Tedde (1994).
62 The book has gone through no fewer than six editions, the last of them Fontana (2002), pp. 11–48. It has been suggested that Fontana's argument is merely a rehash of ideas propounded by Douglass C. North. As far as I am aware, however, Fontana nowhere directly cites the Nobel Prize-winning historian, although it is quite possible that North's reasoning influenced him indirectly through other authors.
63 See Fontana (1987), pp. 157–168, among others.
64 Fontana (2002), pp. 16–17.
65 For details of this process, see Tedde (1987), pp. 169–195.
66 This idea comes from Fontana (2002), pp. 11–20.
67 Root (1994), pp. 14–58. Root actually uses the term 'cronyism' to refer to the fiscal and financial favours done for family members, friends and privileged insiders.
68 Root (1994), p. 39.
69 Root (1994), p. 44.
70 Root (1994), pp. 46 and 46 note 62, respectively. A definition of economic rationality will be found on p. 20, note 12.
71 Referring to the use which the French ministerial families made of their posts in government to further their private interests, Root has no hesitation in defining the

French systems as 'bureaucratic capitalism', a phrase coined by K. Wittfogel for China, and he illustrates his point by the case of the *ferme general* or revenue service, which was a byword for efficiency and was relatively free of corruption, but was given over entirely to cronyism; Root (1994), pp. 49–50, with examples.

72 I owe both the idea and the citation to Armitage (2000), p. 5. Marc Bloch's actual words can be found in Bloch (1949), chapter I, section IV, 'L'idole des origins'.

Chapter 2

1 It is usual to distinguish between England, the term used to refer to the country in the sixteenth and seventeenth centuries, which included Wales and Ireland but not Scotland, and Great Britain, referring to the country formed after the Act of Union with Scotland in 1707. I have not found this distinction to be confirmed in contemporary documents, where the terms England and Great Britain are consistently used as synonyms in the seventeenth century.
2 See the classic work by Stone (1965).
3 See the important article published by Wrigley (1967).
4 See Brenner (1993), chapter 1, among others.
5 Mendels (1972).
6 Elliott (2002) provides an example.
7 See Wrightson's classic work (1982).
8 Wrightson (2000).
9 Weatherill (1996).
10 Muldrew (1998).
11 Mandeville (1729).
12 Hundert (1994).
13 Defoe (1727).
14 Brewer (1989) and Riley (1980), pp. 119–126.
15 Daunton (1995), pp. 518–520.
16 The following ideas are drawn from Crouzet (1996), prologue, pp. VII–XII.
17 Some also emigrated to Spain.
18 Colley (1992), pp. 5–6.
19 Kidd (1999), pp. 211–249.
20 Davenant, *A discourse upon Grants and Resumptions*, in Davenant (1771), III, pp. 59–60, in Kidd (1999), p. 215.
21 Eagles (2000).
22 The British, in turn, saw Holland as a more developed country than their own. See, for example, the interesting comparisons between Scotland, England, France and Holland in Smith (1776), pp. 88–90.
23 Crouzet (1985), pp. 127–147, data on p. 129. The original article, 'The sources of England's wealth: some French views in the Eighteenth century', was originally published in *AESC* (Paris), XXI-2 (1966), pp. 254–291.
24 Tot (1736), p. 31.
25 Crouzet (1985), p. 142.
26 A sample of these debates is found in the commentary on a book by John Nicholls published in *Journal de Trévoux*, t. III (1754), pp. 1,000–1,021.
27 Turgot (1913–1923). For a discussion of Turgot's thought, see Moilhat (1988).
28 Lopez (1996).

29 Dubois (1996).
30 Morange (1996).
31 Aymes (1996). For a discussion of France's image in Spain, see also *Les Français . . .* (1990).
32 Lénardson (1986) provides an index.
33 *Journal de Trévoux*, t. IX (1754), pp. 1655–1670.
34 *Encyclopédie . . .*, t. III (1753), pp. 690–699.
35 *Encyclopédie . . .*, t. III (1753), p. 953. For more detail, see Expilly (1762–1770), passim.
36 See Crouzet (1985), pp. 17–20 and 215 ff.
37 I have personally established this fact based on the balance of British metals trade in the early eighteenth century. Details will be found in TNA, CO, various catalogue numbers.
38 TNA, BT, 6/113, in Crouzet (1996), prologue, p. VII.
39 Crouzet (1985), pp. 12–43. The original article was published in *AESC*, XXI-2 (1966), 254–291.
40 Crouzet (1985), pp. 44–104 (chapter 2).
41 Ciriacono (1994).
42 Harris (1998), pp. 535–537. See also Harris (1992).
43 Weber (1904–1905).
44 Harris (1998), pp. 8–9 and chapter 1 in general.
45 Probably silk velvet woven onto a cotton base.
46 The machine consists of various rotating cylinders and is used to press and glaze certain kinds of fabrics and paper. In the eighteenth century they were essential to improve the finish of cotton fabrics.
47 Harris (1998), pp. 36–171.
48 Harris (1998), pp. 361–423.
49 Examples would be the adoption of French techniques for the manufacture of plate and cylindrical glass, the use of chlorine to bleach fabrics, and dyeing using the Turkey or Adrianople Red process. The British also copied the system used to make washing soda out of common salt from France, ending the need to import saltwort from Spain (Harris 1998, pp. 540–541). Saltwort is a halophyte (salt-tolerant) plant which was used to make soap. It was once economically important in some areas of Aragon and south-eastern Spain, whence it was exported via the port of Alicante (see Giménez López 1981).
50 Harris (1998), pp. 506–526.
51 Harris (1998), pp. 544–565.
52 Probably an Anglicism or calque of the English 'to its proper goal'. A more natural translation into modern Spanish would be *al fin adecuado* or *al mismo fin*.
53 A calque of the English word 'constituency'.
54 Virio (1792), t. I, pp. XVII–XX. Juan Bautista de Virio (1754–1837) was an authority on the England of his time. He was born in Vienna, and his father was probably a diplomat. He became an official in the embassy (1777) and then a member of the Counsel of State. Later, he was once again appointed secretary to the Spanish ambassador to the Court of James (1783). He was a close associate of the Count of Floridablanca, who commissioned him to make various studies of customs tariffs, craft manufacturing and smuggling, probably in relation to the publication of the first general list of Spanish customs duties in 1788. This work led him to travel widely throughout Europe with José Gardoqui Orueta, who would subsequently hold the

post of *intendente* in Valencia, Majorca and Aragon. He appears in 1791 as a royal pensioner sending boxes of books to Floridablanca from London, Lyon and Geneva, which the statesman returned to him via the Spanish consul in Bayonne (Rafael Floreusa to the Count de Floridablanca, Bayonne 23-V and 24-VI-1791, AHN, Estado, leg. 3994). In 1796 Virio penned yet another report on the development of commerce and the economy, as well as editing the famous journal *Semanario de agricultura y artes dirigido a los párrocos*. The biographical details on Virio were obtained from *Fichoz* No. 05454 (query dated 8 June 2005). For further information, see Pradells (1990).

José Gardoqui Orueta was born in Bilbao (Vizcaya) in 1772, and we know that he was an important merchant, manufacturer and financier. His father, Diego Gardoqui Arriquíbar, was secretary to the Treasury Office in that year. The two were the successive owners of the firm of José Gardoqui e Hijos. These details were obtained from *Fichoz* No. 010971 (query dated 8 June 2005). The Spanish consul in Bayonne at the time was the Frenchman Rafael Floreusa (in reality Floreuse), who assisted the Spanish government. In 1790 his sister María Teresa Florensa Bordenave (Floreuse Bordonnave) had married the Aragonese economist Ignacio de Asso y del Río, who was consul in Bordeaux. The biographical details are from Pérez Sarrión (1999), pp. 441–449, and *Fichoz* No. 000028 (query dated 16 July 2011).

55 Gómez Urdáñez (2002).
56 Pérez Sarrión (2008).
57 Treasure in the form of ingots, bars and coins.
58 Heckscher (1935), I, chapter VI, pp. 266–294.
59 Heckscher (1935), I, chapter VI, pp. 266–294. The Act of 1662 was not changed until the nineteenth century.
60 Heckscher (1935), I, pp. 294–325.
61 For a discussion of the policy followed by the Conseil de Commerce, see Smith (2002).
62 Heckscher (1935), I, pp. 37–166. My analysis of France is based on Heckscher, although my argument differs. I have, thus, used Heckscher's data but not his interpretation of them.
63 Heckscher (1935), I, pp. 167–178 ff.
64 Heckscher (1935), I, pp. 203–212.
65 Heckscher (1935), I, pp. 184–192.
66 For a discussion of industrial espionage, see Harris (1992), cited above, and Heckscher (1935), I, pp. 193–203.
67 The literature is extensive. See, for example, Cary (1695), Postlethwayt (1757) and Davenant (1771).
68 Finkelstein (2000).
69 Harvey (1628).
70 See Carney (1975), pp. 61–99.
71 Finkelstein (2000), p. 249.
72 Deyon and Guignet (1980).
73 Deyon and Guignet (1980).
74 In Deyon and Guignet (1980), translated.
75 Deyon and Guignet (1980).
76 Roland de la Platière (1784–1790), p. 4.471, s. v. 'Commerce', translated.
77 Deyon and Guignet (1980).
78 *Encyclopédie . . .* (1751–1780), t. III, 1753, pp. 690–699.

Chapter 3

1 Alloza (2006).
2 This question is discussed in great detail in Shillington and Chapman (1907), pp. 177–204 and 205–226.
3 Alloza (2006), pp. 149–179. The treaty is discussed in Abreu (1751–1752), I, 145–192. The text itself is on pp. 152–187.
4 The full text can be found in Abreu (1746–1750), VII, pp. 114–246.
5 Alloza (2006), pp. 181–199 and 201–220.
6 To understand the gestation of these treaties, it is necessary to consider the events of the preceding decades, which is not possible here. For a discussion of diplomatic and commercial relations between Spain and England in the second half of the seventeenth century, see the paper by Sanz (2002).
7 The full text can be found in Abreu (1746–1750), VII, pp. 114–246. Girard (1932), pp. 132–143, contains an initial analysis of the circumstances in which the treaty was signed and of the trade clauses it contained. In general, the international treaties made by Spain in the seventeenth and eighteenth centuries are contained in Abreu and Cantillo (see bibliography). Many of these treaties may also be found in Israel (1967).
8 The marriage was formalized in a separate document. However, it was no minor matter for trade, as it would form the basis for Louis XIV's claim to the Spanish Crown on the death of Charles II, which eventually resulted in the arrival of the Bourbons and French hegemony in Spain after the War of Succession.
9 Abreu (1746–1750), VII, pp. 139–246.
10 Abreu (1746–1750), VII, p. 122.
11 In articles 30, 10, 8, 11–12 and 14–24, respectively. See, Abreu (1746–1750), VII, pp. 123–136.
12 Abreu (1746–1750), VII, p. 122–123.
13 Abreu (1746–1750), VII, p. 124.
14 Abreu (1746–1750), VII, p. 134.
15 Pradells (1992), chapters I and II (pp. 13–43). The consuls were peculiarly unwelcome to the Spanish Crown, which did its utmost to limit their jurisdiction. See the interesting remarks ibidem, pp. 37–42. For further information about foreign consuls, see Hidalgo (1806) and Virio (1792).
16 Abreu (1746–1750), VII, pp. 133–134.
17 Abreu (1746–1750), VII, pp. 27–32.
18 Abreu (1751–1752), VII, pp. 436–487.
19 Abreu (1751–1752), VII, pp. 84–93.
20 Abreu (1751–1752), VII, pp. 291–308.
21 Abreu (1751–1752), VII, pp. 436–462.
22 The treaty provided for the recommencement of traffic and trade (article 15), the end of war levies (article 17), the reinstatement of all civil and ecclesiastical officers (article 18) and the revocation of debts arising from military confiscations (article 19). In Abreu (1751–1752), III, pp. 449–452.
23 Royal *cédulas* of 26 August 1667 and 27 August 1667, and royal *cédula* of 1 September 1667. In Abreu (1751–1752), I, pp. 2136–2154.
24 Declarations of war between Spain and France of 19 December 1673 and 31 December 1673, in Abreu (1751–1752), I, pp. 636–637 and 650–669; royal *pragmática* of 26 January 1674; royal *cédula* expanding the scope of the trade ban of 11 April 1664,

and royal order of 11 February 1675 extending the term of the ban; in Abreu (1751–1752), II, pp. 38–42 and 162–172.

25 Royal *cédula* of 19 February 1684 prohibiting trade with France, in Abreu (1751–1752), III, pp. 50–64.

26 Royal *cédulas* of 7 June 1689 and 15 September 1689 prohibiting trade with France, in Abreu (1751–1752), III, pp. 214–228 and 242–243.

27 At least the royal *cédulas* of 31 October 1689, 13 April 1689, 9 January 1691 and 1 February 1697, in Abreu (1751–1752), III, pp. 254–258, 280–281 and 429–430, respectively.

28 This was not an international treaty, although it was treated as one. Abreu (1746–1750), VI, p. 198. There were probably other such agreements. Such local cross-border accords were common in the Pyrenees at the time, another instance being the *pactos de fazería* made by highland communities in Spain and France to regulate common use of mountain pastures, exchanges of seasonal labour and other matters of mutual interest.

29 Abreu (1751–1752), I, pp. 145–192. The text itself is on pp. 152–187.

30 Abreu (1751–1752), I, pp. 1–26.

31 Abreu (1746–1750), VII, pp. 261–287.

32 The treaty enshrined the freedom to trade and to contract (article 2), and to buy and export products for their value (article 5), as well as freedom of residence (article 30), respecting the laws of the host nation and paying the applicable duties (article 4). All customs posts were required publicly to display the tariffs, duties and taxes payable, which could be applied only to the goods listed (article 6). The free circulation of goods was provided for in minute detail. Exports of English cloth to Flanders were permitted (article 20), as well as mutual trade with third nations (articles 21 and 22) and in all goods and commodities including corn and other agricultural produce (article 25), except for contraband goods, arms, people, horses and military material (article 24). However, all traffic in gold- or silverware from one country to the other was forbidden (article 15), and any cargo shipped on vessels belonging to enemy nations of the other party could be confiscated (article 26). Finally, the treaty removed the requirement to guarantee residual charges (article 11), and it allowed free entry and departure from ports without unloading cargo (article 13), unrestricted sale of any goods on which port charges had already been paid at any other port (article 12), and visits by up to eight warships provided they did not hinder the movement of other shipping (article 16). All in Abreu (1751–1752), I, pp. 152–187.

33 Abreu incorrectly gives the date of the first *cédula* as 10 March 1645. Each of these three statutes was included word for word in the text of the treaty in 1713, Capmany (1796–1801), I, pp. 297–313, together with various petitions concerning their actual application or revocation made until 1695, idem, pp. 313–324.

34 A century later, Abreu noted that the term 'solely' did not appear either in the Latin text of the treaty dated 1667 or in the first text of the treaty dated 17 December 1665, which demonstrates the jurisdictional significance of this article and the concerns arising from its interpretation; Abreu (1751–1752), I, p. 174.

35 For a discussion of the consuls and their multiple functions, see Pradells (1992), pp. 35–89.

36 Abreu (1751–1752), I, pp. 159–160.

37 As Abreu himself recognizes in a note; Abreu (1751–1752), I, p. 165, notes a and b.

38 'con tal que conste por testimonio de los diputados de la compañía de la dicha India Oriental, residentes en Londres, que los referidos frutos y mercaderías han sido

trahidos o proceden de las conquistas, colonias o factorías de ingleses, en la misma forma . . . y efectos que las ordenanzas y concesiones que se despacharon a favor de los vasallos de las Provincias Unidas de los Países Bajos en las reales cédulas expedidas acerca de las mercaderías prohibidas o de contrabando en 27 de Junio y 3 de Julio del año de 1663 y publicadas en 30 de Junio y 4 de Julio de dicho año. Y por lo que mira a ambas Indias, y a otras qualesquiera partes, quiere la Corona de España que todo lo que se concedió a los Estados Generales de las Provincias Unidas de los Países Bajos por el Tratado de Münster celebrado en el año de 1648 se entienda concedido y otorgado al rey de la Gran Bretaña, y a sus vasallos', Abreu (1751–1752), I, p. 161.

39 Abreu (1755–1752), I, pp. 181–182.

40 See the summary of the treaty in Rubio (s.a.), pp. 70–71.

41 The English envoy extraordinary was a diplomat sent by the English king in addition to the ambassador in Madrid to perform a specific mission in the role of a plenipotentiary. The envoys cited here were charged with resolving trade and related issues. This was, or became, a standard diplomatic office, and as we shall see the French also had their own *envoyé extraordinaire.*

42 Lord Lansdowne to the Secretary of State, TNA, SP 94/72, ff. 1–24v.

43 Copy of the memorandum sent by the French ambassador in Madrid to the Marquis de los Balbases, circa 25 April 1686, perhaps 31 December 1685; TNA, SP 94/72, ff. 25–26.

44 Pablo Spínola y Doria, Marquis de los Balbases, to the French ambassador, 10 June 1686, TNA, SP 94/72 ff. 59–60.

45 Lansdowne to the Secretary of State, Madrid 7 November 1686, TNA, SP 94/72, ff. 116–117.

46 Lansdowne to the Secretary of State, Madrid 21 November 1686, TNA, SP 94/72, ff. 118r–118v.

47 In the context of the economic crises which beset Spain in the reign of Charles II, the major monetary stabilization of 1680–1686 and its impact on English trade is a less straightforward matter than would initially appear if the billon currency is taken into account. Some years before Lansdowne wrote his letter in November 1686, a *pragmática* of 10 February 1680 had cut the nominal value of billon coins by 75 per cent, and various other decrees had ordered the withdrawal of older copper coins from circulation. This caused a sharp deflation in prices set in billon. Meanwhile, the *pragmática* of 14 October 1686 mentioned above revalued the silver *real de a ocho* by 25 per cent, producing a de facto devaluation of the silver coinage and sparking equivalent price inflation in silver. Lansdowne writes just one month after this measure was adopted.

Creditors whose debts were denominated in billon had benefitted, but the effects of these policies on those owed sums in silver were highly detrimental. Most of the contracts, debts and bills of exchange held by the English merchants were in silver, which explains the English ambassador's complaint that his countrymen were being ruined – they had stood aloof from the deflation affecting the billon currency but price inflation in silver hit them where it hurt.

For a more detailed account of the monetary reform of 1680–1686 and its political context, see Santiago Fernández (2000), pp. 195–248 and Font de Villanueva (2005 and 2008). Supplementary information will also be found in García de Paso (2000 and 2002).

48 Lansdowne to King Charles II of Spain, Madrid 23 November 1686, TNA, SP 94/72, ff. 120v–121r.

49 Lansdowne to King Charles II of Spain, Madrid 23 November 1686, TNA, SP 94/72, ff. 120v.
50 Lansdowne to King Charles II of Spain, Madrid 23 November 1686, TNA, SP 94/72, ff. 119–121v. He also requested that certain English traders who had been imprisoned in Bilbao be freed, reflecting the English interest in the wool trade carried on at this port.
51 Marquis de Mancera to Lansdowne, Madrid 13 January 1687, TNA, SP 94/72, ff. 137–138v.
52 Meaning the 'increase in the value of gold and silver'. If the bill of exchange set a price in a currency which had been devalued, a higher nominal price would be required to settle the debt. Meanwhile, the value of the debt was reduced for the debtor by the same amount as it increased for the creditor. As the English basically sold goods to the Spanish, they found themselves in the position of the latter.
53 Letter from twenty-two merchants to the King of England, February 1687, TNA, SP 94/72, ff. 159–162. The language of this document differs from that of the letters cited above. The English used in late seventeenth-century manuscripts was very similar to modern English, but when nobles, or in the present case merchants, wrote to the king, they would use a much more archaic and grave style, as in this case.
54 In 1686–1688, TNA, SP 94/72 passim.
55 Memorandum from a group of English merchants to the King, 1687, TNA, SP 94/72, ff. 210–212.
56 Alexander Stanhope to the Secretary of State, Madrid 5 December 1691, TNA, SP 94/73, ff. 49–49v.
57 Alexander Stanhope to King Charles II of Spain, Madrid 24 January 1693, TNA, SP 94/73, ff. 86–92v.
58 Alexander Stanhope to King Charles II of Spain, Madrid 24 January 1693, TNA, SP 94/73, ff. 86–92v.
59 Meaning the peace treaty of 1667. Alexander Stanhope to the Secretary of State, Madrid 25 February 1693, TNA, SP 94/73, ff. 103–104v.
60 Two memorandums submitted by Alexander Stanhope to the Marquis de Mancera, both dated 8 February 1693, TNA, SP 94/73, ff. 107–112v.
61 Alexander Stanhope to the Marquis de los Balbases, Madrid 15 August 1695, TNA, SP 94/74, ff. 1–3.
62 Alexander Stanhope to the Marquis de los Balbases, Madrid 15 August 1695, TNA, SP 94/74, ff. 1–3.
63 Pablo Spínola to Alexander Stanhope, Madrid 26 December 1695, TNA, SP 94/74, ff. 66–66v.
64 Pedlars, hawkers.
65 Carriers.
66 Salt cod.
67 Négociations entre la France et l'Espagne, au sujet de leur commerce réciproque. Depuis l'année 1659 jusq'en 1716. [Paris] 1716, AMAEP, MD, Esp. livre 153, ff. 8v–9r. The fascinating complete document can be found in ff. 4r–35v.
68 Most likely double entry bookkeeping, which was already practised by Spanish merchants trading with the Americas in the sixteenth century.
69 Négociations entre la France et l'Espagne, au sujet de leur commerce réciproque. Depuis l'année 1659 jusq'en 1716. [Paris] 1716, AMAEP, MD, Esp. livre 153, f. 10v.
70 Négociations entre la France et l'Espagne, au sujet de leur commerce réciproque. Depuis l'année 1659 jusq'en 1716. [Paris] 1716, AMAEP, MD, Esp. livre 153, ff. 9v–10r.

71 Act of the *Cortes* of 20 January 1678 and *fuero* (local law) of 11 January 1686, in Savall and Penén (1866), I, pp. 526–537 (*fuero*) and II, pp. 400–411 (Act of the *Cortes*).
72 Mules were always in demand for farm work. However, mules are also pack animals, and anybody bringing them into Spain was therefore at least potentially a carrier.
73 The proposal to delay enactment until after the next meeting of the Aragonese Parliament in fact meant that it would only enter into force at the discretion of the King, in whose power it lay to convene the *Cortes*.
74 Literally, 'forestall the privileges of the Aragonese', which is to say infringe local laws.
75 The local and customary laws, and acts of the *Cortes* of Aragon.
76 The Zaragoza magistrates and councilors.
77 Négociations entre la France et l'Espagne, au sujet de leur commerce réciproque. Depuis l'année 1659 jusq'en 1716. [Paris] 1716, AMAEP, MD, Esp. livre 153, ff. 9r–10r.
78 For the meaning of the term *aggregate* or *composite monarchy*, see Fernández Albaladejo (1992) passim, especially chapters II-1 and III-1.
79 Négociations entre la France et l'Espagne, au sujet de leur commerce réciproque. Depuis l'année 1659 jusq'en 1716. AMAEP, MD, Esp. livre 153, ff. 9v–10v.
80 Profit, gain.
81 Verbatim text from a letter discussing the trade deficit with Aragon sent by the Count de Rubenac to the Marquis de Croissy, Minister and Secretary of State for Foreign Affairs, on 21 August 1688. Negotiations entre la France et l'Espagne, au sujet de leur commerce reciproque. Depuis l'année 1659 jusq'en 1716, [Paris] 1716, AMAEP, MD, Esp. livre 153, f. 10r.
82 Idem, [Paris] 1716, AMAEP, MD, Esp. livre 153, f. 10v.
83 Local laws.
84 William Aglionby to the Secretary of State, Madrid 19 March 1692, TNA, SP 94/75.
85 William Aglionby to the Secretary of State, Madrid 19 March 1692, TNA, SP 94/75.
86 Negotiations entre la France et l'Espagne, au sujet de leur commerce reciproque. Depuis l'année 1659 jusq'en 1716, [Paris] 1716, AMAEP, MD, Esp. livre 153, f. 12r.
87 Negotiations entre la France et l'Espagne, au sujet de leur commerce reciproque. Depuis l'année 1659 jusq'en 1716, [Paris] 1716, AMAEP, MD, Esp. livre 153, f. 16r.
88 Larruga (1789), III, f. 19v.
89 Aglionby to the Count de Oñate, 4 June 1691, from the copy sent to England, TNA, SP 94/75.
90 Pablo Spínola to Alexander Stanhope, Madrid 26 December 1695, TNA, SP 94/74, ff. 66–66v; Stanhope to the King of England, Madrid 25 June 1698, TNA, SP 94/74, ff. 311–312.
91 Alexander Stanhope to the King of England, Madrid 26 November and 10 December 1698, TNA, SP 94/73, ff. 132–134.
92 Here and previous quote, Alexander Stanhope to the King of England, Madrid 10 December 1698, TNA, SP 94/104, ff, 133–134v.
93 The extraordinary envoy, Francis Schonenberg, to the Secretary of State, Vernon, s.l., 15 June 1701, TNA, SP 94/75.
94 The extraordinary envoy, Francis Schonenberg, to the Secretary of State, Vernon, s.l., 24 August 1701, TNA, SP 94/75.
95 Capmany (1796–1801), I, pp. 83–97.

96 In Capmany (1796–1801), I, pp. 83–97, and also Cantillo (1843), pp. 75–86. On the matter of trade, all of the previous treaties and agreements (including the treaty of 1667) were renewed in so far as they did not conflict with the new terms (article 15); navigation and mutual trade were re-established subject to a new trade agreement to be drawn up in the future (article 8); Menorca (article 11) and Gibraltar were ceded to the British Crown subject to the absolute prohibition of smuggling (article 10); a slave factory with a monopoly similar to that enjoyed by the French was permitted in the Americas (article 12); and at the request of the English Queen Anne, the King of Spain granted a full pardon and amnesty to the people of Catalonia, allowing them full possession of their goods and privileges (article 13). This latter point was a somewhat cynical attempt by the British to appear as the protectors of the Catalan losers. The 20-year contract for the slave factory was made on 26 March 1713.

97 However, the key articles 3, 5 and 8 were amended in the treaty ratified by Phillip V in Madrid on 21 January 1714 and by Queen Anne at Windsor on 7 February 1714. All in Capmany (1796–1801), I, pp. 267–356. Furthermore, a separate article of 'minor' import signed in Utrecht on 9 December 1713 was added to the treaty together with another 'Treaty of Declaration and Explanation' made in Madrid on 14 December 1715 and ratified on 24 January 1716. In Capmany (1796–1801), I, pp. 357–362.

98 Capmany (1796–1801), I, pp. 269–325. The treaty made between Great Britain and Spain in America in 1670 was also confirmed, provided it did not conflict with the 1712 treaty and the contract of 26 March 1713 regulating the slave monopoly. In addition to the matters mentioned above, the treaty included the usual clauses governing debt recognition, procedures in the event of war and matters of personal liability (articles 6, 7, 13 and 16).

99 Capmany (1796–1801), I, p. 326.

100 Capmany (1796–1801), I, pp. 328–329.

101 *Arancel* . . . (1709).

102 Capmany (1796–1801), I, pp. 336–339.

103 The Catalan tax known as the *derecho de bolla* is not mentioned.

104 Capmany (1796–1801), I, pp. 336–339. Furthermore, the same duties would be paid on products brought from Africa as on other goods (article 10), and no extra duties were to be applied in the Canary Islands (article 12); Capmany (1796–1801), I, pp. 332 and 334.

105 Capmany (1796–1801), I, pp. 329–330.

106 Capmany (1796–1801), I, pp. 336–340. Terms were also fixed for the payment of *millones* on fish at the point of sale, allowing settlement within two months (article 8 and amended article 8); Capmany (1796–1801), I, pp. 331 and 340.

107 Capmany (1796–1801), I, p. 332.

108 Capmany (1796–1801), I, pp. 334–335.

109 Separate article signed at Utrecht on 9 December 1713; Capmany (1796–1801), I, p. 350.

Chapter 4

1 In Cantillo (1843), pp. 48–52.

2 The Envoy Extraordinary, Paul Methuen, to the Secretary of State, Stanhope, Madrid 10 May 1715, TNA, SP 94/83, p. 8.

3 Kamen (1969), pp. 161–174.

4 Translated; Amelot to Louis XIV, 31-III-1708, AMAEP, CP, Esp., livre 179, f. 187; in Kamen (1969), pp. 173–174.
5 Created by Colbert, it was established by an *arrêt* of 29 June 1700.
6 Paul Methuen to the Secretary of State, Stanhope, Madrid 10 May 1715, TNA, SP 94/83.
7 NR, lib. X, tít. XV, ley VII–V, p. 79–.
8 Paul Methuen to the Secretary of State, Stanhope, Madrid 10 May 1715, TNA, SP 94/83.
9 There are several more in TNA, SP 94/87.
10 Lists for 31 August 1715 are in TNA, SP 94/84.
11 The consul, Crow, to Geoffrey Bubb Doddington (1691–1762), first Baron Melcombe, Barcelona around September 1715, TNA, SP 94/98.
12 'now we are in danger of loosing a very considerable branch of our trade in these parts by a late order restraining ye sale of our tobacco', to Burch, Bilbao, 18–I–1715, TNA, SP 94/83.
13 'the trade in this place [Bilbao] is beyond expression dull and besides got into ye hands of the townes men who sell at very low prices', to Burch, Bilbao 11–I–1715, TNA, SP, 94/83.
14 Paul Methuen to Cardinal del Giudice, Madrid 22 April 1715, TNA, SP 94/83.
15 Paul Methuen to Cardinal del Giudice, Madrid 22 April 1715, TNA, SP 94/83. The treaty is in Capmany (1796–1801), I, pp. 363–399. French was commonly used as the language of diplomacy at this time, including by the English.
16 This was the case between 1714 and 1717, and again in 1722, although the customs posts were ultimately restored in both cases.
17 Geoffrey Bubb to the Secretary of State, Madrid 23 December 1715, TNA, SP 94/98.
18 'as the commerce here [=Spain] can never be of much utility to us, while the Indies are overrun by the French in the manner that you will see by the enclosed copies of letters from one Spaniard to another', Geofrey Bubb to the Secretary of State, Madrid 23 December 1715, TNA, SP 94/84. 'Utility' here means 'profit' rather than 'use'. Hence, what the diplomat is saying is that trade with the Spanish interior was less profitable than the transatlantic trade, although that does not mean it was of no interest to English merchants. The letters written by the two Spanish functionaries are dated in Cartagena de Indias, 8 February 1715, and Buenos Aires, 8 June 1715.
19 Geoffrey Bubb to the Secretary of State, Madrid 23 December 1715, TNA, SP 94/98.
20 NR, lib. X, tít. XV, ley VII–V, pp. 309—.
21 NR, lib. VI, tít. X ley I -III, p. 165–.
22 NR, lib. VI, tít. X ley II–III, pp. 165–166–.
23 Paul Methuen to the Secretary of State, Stanhope, Madrid 10 May 1715, TNA, SP 94/83.
24 This is thanks mainly to the efforts of three scholars, O'Scea (2010 a, 2010 b, 2015 a and 2015 b), Pérez Tostado (2005, 2008 and 2010), and Recio Morales (2004, 2007 a, 2007 b, 2011 and 2012).
25 These figures are based on Recio (2004). There were also Irish soldiers in Flanders, see Gráinne (1992).
26 References in Pérez Sarrión (2007).
27 See Téllez (2006) and (2009) on Wall.
28 Recio (2004) suggests that some Irish émigrés traded in English goods through the port of La Corunna around the end of the sixteenth century, which is certainly possible.

29 These lines are from the *bando* of 16 June 1703 cited below.
30 NR, lib. VI, tít. X ley II —III, pp. 165–166–. 'Correspondence' here means 'commercial relations'.
31 Mémoire touchant le commerce de France en Espagne pour le marquis de Bon[n]ac, envoyé extraordinaire du Roy au Roy d'Espagne, s.l., some days after 16 September 1709, AMEAP, MD, Esp., livre 32.
32 Mémoire touchant le commerce de France en Espagne pour le marquis de Bon[n]ac, envoyé extraordinaire du Roy au Roy d'Espagne, s.l., some days after 16 September 1709, AMEAP, MD, Esp., livre 32.
33 Mémoire touchant le commerce de France en Espagne pour le marquis de Bon[n]ac, envoyé extraordinaire du Roy au Roy d'Espagne, s.l., some days after 16 September 1709, AMEAP, MD, Esp., livre 32.
34 Kamen (1969), p. 161.
35 Member of the Council of Castile since 20 September 1706 and judge conservator of the French nation since 5 September 1706 (Fichoz, no. 005903, consulted 7 September 2010). The deed was witnessed by the judge conservator's *escribano* (scrivener), Lorenzo Martínez.
36 *Representación y recopilación general*... (1710). This document lists all of the privileges enjoyed by foreign merchants in Spain at this time.
37 Kamen (1969), p. 162.
38 Kamen (1969), pp. 177–181.
39 The verb 'contribuir' means 'pay taxes' in this context.
40 Manuel de Vadillo y Velasco to Blécourt, 12 May 1712, ANF, Aff. étr., BIII 360, in Kamen (1969), pp. 180–181.
41 Melchor de Macanaz was a member. See Kamen (1969), pp. 180–184.
42 NR, lib. VI, tít. XI, ley III —III, pp. 166–167—.
43 In fact, where *alcabalas* were farmed and were collected by means of a levy, as was commonly the case, they too were payable only by citizens.
44 Ossun to the French government, 31 March 1773, AMAEP, livre 132, f. 99v.
45 Négociations entre la France et l'Espagne, au sujet de leur commerce réciproque. Depuis l'année 1659 jusq'en 1716. AMAEP, MD, Esp. livre 1716, ff. 153. 4–35v.
46 Interpretation of the *real cédula* of 8 March 1716 attached to a letter of 30 June 1775 sent by the French ambassador in Madrid, Ossun, to Paris; AMEAP, CP, livre 576, ff. 354–355.
47 NR, lib. VI, tít. XI, ley IV —III, p. 167—.
48 Royal *cédula* of 7 July 1727, NR, lib. VI, tít XI, ley V —III, pp. 168–169—.
49 Royal *cédula* of 1 February 1765, NR, lib. VI, tít XI, ley VI —III, pp. 169–170—.
50 By a royal *cédula* of 28 June 1764. A copy will be found in AHN, Estado, leg. 629-1/2.
51 Royal order of 20 November 1778, NR, lib. VI, tít XI, ley VII —III, p. 170—.
52 NR, lib. VI, tít XI, leyes VIII a X —III, pp. 170–174—.
53 Anonymous memorandum written around 1738, AMAEP, MD, Esp., livre 153, ff. 78–83v.
54 This position was defended for example by the Abbé Coyer in his *Noblesse commerçante* (1756), in Greenfield (2001), pp. 132–139. This work and the debate in general also reached Spain, though with some delay: Coyer (1781).
55 See the interesting observations in this regard in Greenfeld (1992), pp. 230–233.
56 Document cited above. As interpreted in the annex to the letter sent by Ossun, French ambassador in Madrid, to Paris on 30 July 1775; AMAEP, CP, livre 576, ff. 354r–355v.

57 Smith (1776), pp. 72–77.
58 Hamilton (1933), p. 295 and in general pp. 277–298.
59 Hamilton (1947), pp. 254–255 and in general pp. 243–256. Real wages also appear to have risen in terms of wheat purchasing power in Catalonia in the second half of the eighteenth century; see Feliu (1991), II, pp. 100–101 at least, and passim.
60 Report of 17 May 1715, AMAEP, MD, Esp., livre 32, ff. 69r–105v, data in ff. 74r–74v.
61 Report of 17 May 1715, AMAEP, MD, Esp., livre 32, ff. 69r–105v, data in ff. 85v–86r.
62 Consulta de una Junta q[u]e el año de 1721 mandó el Rey formar sobre la pres[en]te decadencia de el comercio de España [con Indias] y su forma de restablecimiento en todos los ramos, 30 September 1721, AMAEP, MD, livre 252, ff. 94r–126r, text in ff. 124r–124v.
63 Consulta de una Junta q[u]e el año de 1721 mandó el Rey formar sobre la pres[en]te decadencia de el comercio de España [con Indias] y su forma de restablecimiento en todos los ramos, 30 September 1721, AMAEP, MD, livre 252, ff. 94r–126r, text in ff. 121r–121v.
64 Here and previous two quotes, report filed by the French consul in Cadiz, Mongelas, 20 January 1777, AMAEP, MD, livre 132, ff. 145v–146r.
65 Report filed by the French consul in Cadiz, Mongelas, 20 January 1777, AMAEP, MD, livre 132, ff. 149v–150r.
66 Teissier (1997), pp. 11–43.
67 García Sanz (1994), pp. 397–434. See also García Sanz (1977), (1987) and (1996).
68 Report filed by the French consul in Cadiz, Mongelas, 20 January 1777, AMAEP, MD, livre 132, ff. 151–152v.
69 Belfanti and Giusberti (2000), pp. 359–365. For a discussion of dress in England, see Lemire (1997) and (2000); for France, see Reddy (1984); and for both, see Ribeiro (1995). The question of the *consumer revolution* in Europe as a phenomenon which preceded and then accompanied the industrial revolution was first raised by Neil McKendrick (McKendrick, Brewer and Plumb, 1982). Important recent references to these issues include Berg and Clifford (1999) (in particular, Berg on England, and Colin Jones and Rebecca Spang on France, in both cases referring to the eighteenth century), Wrightson (2000), *Continuity and Change* (2000), and with reference to Spain, Torras and Yun (1999 and 2001).
70 Ribeiro (1995).
71 Report of the Marquis of Bonnac, c. 1709, AMAEP, MD, livre 132, f. 63v.
72 This remark must refer to the liberalization of trade with the Americas in 1776.
73 Report filed by the French consul in Cadiz, Mongelas, 20 January 1777, AMAEP, MD, livre 132, ff. 156v.
74 As Greenfield has recently shown (2001), pp. 107–135.
75 In reality Defoe was of Dutch origin but settled in Great Britain.
76 See Defoe (1727) and Savary (1675 and 1688). The author Jacques Savary (1622–1690) should not be confused with his son, Jacques Savary des Bruslons (1675–1716), himself the author of a famous posthumous dictionary; Savary des Bruslons (1723–1730).
77 Anonymous report, 1738, AMAEP, MD, livre 153, ff. 78r–83r, text in ff. 80v–81r.
78 For a discussion of the key role played by the intendants in France, see Gruder (1968).
79 Report of the French consul in Cadiz, Etienne-Louis Duplessis de Mongelas, Cadiz 20 January 1777, AMAEP, MD, livre 132, ff. 140r–161v, text in f. 148v. Author's italics.
80 In other passages, the term is replaced by *pays* or country, and even the word *citoyens* or 'citizens' occasionally turns up in other texts.

81 English commercial handbooks like Defoe's *Complete English Tradesman* (1727) concentrate on the development of the merchant's individual abilities, and they make no mention of the state.
82 Zylberberg (1993), pp. 51–52, drawing on Whitworth (1776), I, p. 38 and McLachlan (1940), p. 6.
83 Zylberberg (1983), p. 272.
84 Here and previous two quotes, report of the French consul in Cadiz, Etienne-Louis Duplessis de Mongelas, Cadiz 20 January 1777, AMEAP, MD, livre 132, ff. 140r–161r, texts cited in ff. 140r, 147v and 151v.
85 H. S. Conway to the ambassador Earl of Rochford, St. James, 31 January 1766, TNA, SP 94/173.
86 Memorial submitted by British merchants in Lisbon to the Earl of Kinnoul, British ambassador in the Portuguese capital, and forwarded by him to William Pitt, Libon, 6 June 1760, TNA, CO 388/53. The British merchants stressed the low prices of their goods in America as an argument in favour of free trade and against the creation in Portugal of privileged companies to trade with Brazil, as seems to have been planned.
87 In 1773 a merchant (*négotiant*) from Bayonne, Dufourquez, proposed to the King of France that a Spanish company should be created to trade with Louisiana (a colony which had been ceded to France under the recent peace treaty) because, 'Yl est de l'intérêt de la France de chercher les moyens de donner la plus grande extension à son commerce, et de préférence avec les Espagnols, qui tirent inmensément de marchandises de nos fabriques, lors qu'au contraire elles sont prohibées en Angleterre, comme celles d'Angleterre en France,' although he then adds, 'Il est certain que les Anglois sortent de France annuellement en effectif plus de sept ou huit millions de livres [tournois] en remboursament du tabac qu'ils fournisserent aux Fermiers generaux'. AMAEP, CP, livre 572, ff. 401r–402r.
88 'De toutes les places de l'Europe, Cadiz est sans contredire la plus importante pour la France. Toutes nos fabriques, toutes nos manufactures y envoyent le fruit de leurs soins et de leur industrie. La consommation qui s'y en fait pour les expéditions des flottes pour la nouvelle Espagne et par les vaisseaux particuliers pour la mer du sud est inmense', Report of the consul in Cadiz, Mongelas, 20 January 1777, AMAEP, MD, livre 132, f. 143r.
89 This seems to refer to an aristocratic lobby.
90 The Earl of Rochford to the Secretary of State, Aranjuez 5 May 1766, TNA, SP 94/174, ff. 20–21v.
91 L. Devisne to the Secretary of State, Conway, Aranjuez 18 June 1766, TNA, SP 94/174, ff. 65–70, cited from ff. 68–69v.
92 Letter from the Marquis of Ossun to the minister, Count of Vergennes, Aranjuez, 15 May 1777, AMAEP, CP, livre 576, ff. 61r–62v.

Chapter 5

1 The relationship between this policy and internal trade is discussed in Franch (2004), pp. 103–132.
2 See the excellent study by Melton (2001).
3 Dedieu (2000 a).
4 Numerous papers have recently been published in this field, in particular by the PAPE group. See, for example López-Cordón (1995 a) and (1995 b), Jean Pierre Dedieu

(1996), (1997), (2000 a) and (2000 b), Teresa Nava (2003) (2005), and Castellano (1996) and (2006).

5 Because it was organized in ministerial departments, compared with the earlier form of government, sometimes called *judicial monarchy* or simply composite monarchy, which was based on the exercise of royal power through various councils (Castellano (2006), p. 124).

6 For a discussion of the influence of the French political model on administrative reform in Spain, see Dubet (2007).

7 Following Castellano (2006), pp. 104–112, 124–129 and 132–155. For a discussion of the political circumstances surrounding the *secretarías de despacho*, ibid, pp. 17–71.

8 NR, lib. III, tít. VI, ley VI —II, p. 35—.

9 An *entretenido* was an interim appointee, who would take a position, often without pay, to earn merits until a vacant post became available. Castellano (1996), p. 41.

10 Castellano (2006), pp. 87–91.

11 Andújar (2008). The text is a translation from the abstract found at: www.moderna2008.org/comunicacionesaceptadas/index.html (consulted 26 February 2008).

12 This was the case of the *escribanos reales*, or royal notaries. One of these, Juan de Peñuelas Zamora, was the uncle of another, Pedro Escolano de Arrieta, an *hidalgo* whose great grandfather was Diego Escolano de Arrieta, a native of Guipuzcoa who had emigrated to Sigüenza. The service also included other families with roots in Aragon and Navarre (Vallejo 2007, pp. 80–104 and 130–154). Another notary, Antonio Martínez Salazar (1705–1794), never petitioned for a letter patent raising him to the status of *hidalgo*. He must have ascended through service in the king's household, as we know that he was treasurer to the Infante Don Luis in 1735 (*Fichoz* No. 0019002, consulted on 16 December 2009). He went on to lease a notarial office in Madrid and held several other positions until he was eventually appointed notary to the Council of Castile in 1740 (Vallejo 2007, pp. 188–190, 202 and 210).

13 Root (1994), pp. 14–58.

14 There would also have been between 100 and 300 clerks of one sort or another in administrative departments between 1692 and 1755. All according to Kozub (2003), chart 1, p. 366. The figures are taken from contemporary printed sources.

15 Macanaz (1714), (1722) and (1889). Further biographical details and a selection of papers can be found in Macanaz (1972).

16 Santa Cruz (1732), Aznar (1728) and Moya (1730).

17 Uztáriz (1724). See Fernández Durán (1999) on the author and his work.

18 Biographical details in Bethencourt (1954), Pulido (1998) and Pérez Fernández-Turégano (2006).

19 *Representación universal*... (1725). I have taken the initial reference from Fernández Albaladejo (1977).

20 Zavala Auñón (1732). Two further editions were published by Herederos de Martínez, Pamplona 1747 and a 'third edition, corrected and augmented' (in reality the fourth edition) by Antonio Espinosa, Madrid 1787. Zavala's work thus went through four editions in total.

21 Campillo (1739). For further biographical detail and references to other government writings by the author, see the 'Estudio preliminar' (pp. IX–LXXXIX) of the 1993 edition by M.D. Mateos. His other work is Campillo (1743). I have not been able to locate a third work attributed to this author, the *Tratado de los intereses de la Europa*, which was not published until 1819.

22 See Fernández Albaladejo (1977) for further details of the relationship between the crisis and some of these works of political economy.
23 Ulloa (1740).
24 Argumosa (1743).
25 Surviving works by the Marquis of Ensenada comprise two *Representaciones* addressed to Fernando VI dated 18 June 1747 and 27 May 1748, which were published only in the nineteenth century in Rodríguez Villa (1878), and the better known *Representación* . . . (1751), which was only printed and published in part in 1788, years after Somodevilla's death. It was published in Ozanam (1980).
26 Carvajal (1745). In the prologue to *Mis pensamientos* (ff. 145–180), dated 5 July 1745, the author tells how he wrote the work while convalescing from a serious illness, and that he later decided to write his *Testamento politico* (ff. 3–144v), which is dated 12 September 1745. Carvajal never intended it for publication, and he wrote it all straight off from memory beginning on 5 July 1745 and finishing on 12 September 1745 (ff. 1–2). The citation is from the BNE manuscript, Mss/10687. For a discussion of Carvajal and his writings, see also Delgado Barrado (1999) and (2001), Delgado Barrado and Gómez Urdáñez (2002), and Molina (1999).
27 Ward (1750) and (1779).
28 A matter which is not discussed here. See Astigarraga (2003) and (2010), and Astigarraga and Usoz (2008) on the important matter of orthodox political and economic thought in Spain.
29 See Imízcoz and Guerrero (2004) and especially Imízcoz Beunza (2008) and (2009).
30 Imízcoz (2008), pp. 105–111.
31 At least 29 *national cofradías* or brotherhoods have been identified in Madrid. Details in Pérez Sarrión (2007).
32 Based on the data provided by Gómez Urdáñez (2001), pp. 21–95.
33 Gómez Urdáñez (2001), pp. 30, 34 and 49.
34 Gómez Urdáñez (2001), p. 50.
35 Ensenada (1751) and Gómez Urdáñez (2001), pp. 78–79.
36 Gómez Urdáñez (2001), p. 54.
37 See González Caizán (2004 a) and (2004 b).
38 Root (1994), pp. 14–58.
39 Details in Lévy (1969–1980), II, pp. 10–12 ff. I owe the initial reference to Root (1994), p. 40 note 47.
40 Root (1994), pp. 50 ff., with examples. For the development of the public sphere as an essential forum for the opposition of public and private interests in France, England and Austria, see Melton (2001), pp. 15–32 and passim.
41 See Pérez Sarrión (1996 b).
42 Meaning 'new design', because it entailed a reorganization of the institutions of government, and in particular of the high court known as the *Real Audiencia*.
43 Restrictions on the payment of taxes by ecclesiastics changed drastically after the concordat of 1737. In fact, the Castilian cadastre also included church properties, as we shall see, although ecclesiastics everywhere resisted paying taxes.
44 With some minor differences, this general interpretation is that presented in Juan (2004), the most recent general study I know. The legislation governing the *única contribución* in Aragon, Valencia, Catalonia and Majorca can be found in Ripia and Gallard (1796), pp. 33–161.
45 The *taille réelle* taxed real properties in the *pays d'état*, while the *taille personnelle* levied in the *pays d'elections* was based on the estimated ability of each individual to pay. In

both cases, the tax was collected by means of a quota or levy (*impôt de repartition*), like in Spain. The individual wealth attributable to each individual was estimated on a more proportional basis after 1716.

46 Vauban (1695), pp. 193–208.
47 Boisguillebert (1697), in his analysis of the economic situation of France in the matter of taxation.
48 Vauban (1707).
49 The information contained in this paragraph is based on Touzery (1994), passim. In time, these taxes came to be applied to pay interest on the debt contracted to pay for the wars. On this matter, see Kwass (2000), pp. 21–116.
50 See García Trobat (1999), pp. 160–165.
51 For details see Pérez Sarrión (2000) and (2004).
52 See García Trobat (1999), pp. 77–85.
53 See Franch (2003), pp. 523–542, and (2005), pp. 269–297. Ecclesiastical resistance is described in detail in Franch (2009), pp. 215–261, and the Church's involvement in regional manufacturing in Franch (2002), pp. 421–447.
54 Juan (2004), pp. 77–82.
55 See Barceló (1984), (1991) and (2001), and Cateura (1992), (2001) and (2008).
56 *Nueva Planta de la Real Audiencia del Reino de Mallorca . . .* (1716).
57 Riera Vayreda (1988). The process of preparing and updating the cadastres is described in Coll (2005), pp. 620–621; further local testimony is contained in Barceló and Servera (1993), p. 16.
58 *Nueva planta de la Real Audiencia del Principado de Cataluña . . .* (1716).
59 Data in Segura Mas (1988), pp. 31–44, and Ferrer Alós (2002), pp. 27–35. See also Nadal Farreras (1971).
60 For example, Delgado Ribas (1987b).
61 Ferrer Alós (2002), p. 34, who nevertheless very sagely points out that there must have been some increase in the tax burden in Catalonia taking indirect taxes into account, as revenues from this source increased. Idem, p. 34–35.
62 Certain testimonies regarding the tax in Aragon suggest that it was also paid in kind in that region. It is not known whether this practice was widespread in other regions. However, it is an important point, because the payment was less in real terms if made in cash, but equal or even greater if made in kind.
63 Sartine (1735).
64 For a discussion of the organization and functioning of these taxes, see Artola (1982) and, especially, Angulo Teja (2002).
65 Zavala Auñón (1732), pp. 24–28 and 53–83 respectively.
66 The process is described in Matilla Tascón (1947) and Camarero Bullón (1993), (2001) and (2002).
67 Ward (1982) [1779], pp. 200–201.
68 The tax reform also affected areas which are not discussed here, such as the matter of monopolies. For the case of Catalonia, see Torres Sánchez (2005 a).
69 As Jordá Fernández (2006), p. 305, correctly remarks.
70 Observed in the case of Catalonia by Delgado Ribas (1987).
71 As I have observed in Aragon, see Pérez Sarrión (2000).
72 Giménez López (1999), pp. 13–50, 107–108 and 111–124. For a discussion of tax issues and complaints in Aragon, see Pérez Sarrión (2000) and (2004).
73 See García García (1996).

74 See the references in NR, VI, pp. 21–22. This royal order reiterated the application of the ordinance of 3 February 1745; both in NR, lib. VII, tít. XVI, leyes XI, XII and XIII —III, pp. 385–395—.
75 This was the case in Zaragoza, as already mentioned. Madrid had the highest debt; see Hoz García (2007), pp. 98–112. These two cases suggest that it was the state which encouraged the end of revenue farming by the municipal treasuries in the eighteenth century and the switch to direct management, as was also done with the revenues of the *Real Hacienda*.
76 *Representación Universal* . . . (1725).
77 Zavala Auñón (1732), pp. 102–103.
78 Fernández Albaladejo (1977).
79 *Fichoz* nos. 010260 (José Campillo) and 033125 (Etienne Drouilhet), consulted 22 November 2007.
80 The *asientos* or contracts to provision the army were a highly lucrative business for the agents to whom they were awarded. Many of these contracts were obtained by Basque and Navarrese merchants, who had earned positions of privilege by supporting Philip V during the War of Succession. The company of the Cinco Gremios Mayores de Madrid, of which these merchants were members, was also involved.
81 Thompson (1976).
82 Torres Sánchez (2002), pp. 491–492.
83 Torres Sánchez (2002), pp. 487–511.
84 Fernández Albaladejo (1977), pp. 76–77, drawing on Matilla (1947) pp. 61–63 and 87–90 and González Alonso (1970), pp. 324–359.
85 Uztáriz (1724), pp. 241–244.
86 Zabala (1983 b), II, pp. 124–126. See also Zabala (1983 a).
87 Pérez Sarrión (2004).
88 Fuenterrabía, the coastal town where the province of Guipuzcoa borders with France, belonged to Navarre in certain periods (e.g. 1521–1524). This provided the kingdom with a seaport, but it also meant that Guipuzcoa had no land border with France.
89 A copy will be found in AGS, DGR, leg. II-471. See also Ibarra and Cuéllar (1759), all in García-Cuenca (1983), p. 237. The 1709 tariff unified duties at around 15 per cent of the value of goods.
90 Zabala (1983 a), I, p. 39.
91 LL (1996), I, pp. 45–46.
92 The following testimony of 1749 refers to the Navarrese *tables* for leased duties based on the 1723 tariff prevailing in the kingdom. According to the tribunal of the *Cámara de Comptos* 'la baja en los derechos rigurosos de los aranceles era facultativa de los arrendadores para facilitar mayor comercio y librarse de las pérdidas en el arriendo; y que la introducción de géneros prohibidos y su extracción a otros reinos no era tan fácil de tolerar ni disimularse por los arrendadores por estar dispuestos al castigo del tribunal del contrabando, establecido en este reino únicamente para celar semejantes introducciones y extraciones de géneros prohibidos. Sobre lo que lograrían mayor utilidad los arrendadores delatando este comercio que con la paga del derecho real pues como a denunciantes les tocaría la tercera parte del género prohibido si se diese por decomisado, según las reglas del contrabando'; AGN, Cámara de Comptos, Archivo Secreto, Tesorería y Tablas, fajo 6°, título 29, núms. 11 y 15; in Azcona (1996 a), p. 98, note 23.

93 The tariff is found in Ripia and Gallard (1796), IV, pp. 195–357. The methods applied to collect customs revenues and the legislation governing direct administration will be found ibid., IV, pp. 1780–1795.

94 LL (1996), I, p. 43.

95 Text in Uztáriz (1724), pp. 137–138. See also *Cuaderno de las leyes . . .* (1986), leyes 21 and 22; the reference is in Azcona (1996), p. 95, n. 7.

96 Uztáriz (1724), pp. 140–141.

97 Campoflorido was at this time the general administrator for *Rentas Generales*, which were the responsibility of the *Consejo de Hacienda*; Muñoz (1995), p. 774.

98 Floranes (1776), pp. 50v–51. See also Floranes (1771?), which may be another version.

99 'Este insigne informe se halla manuscrito en el archivo de los monjes de Monserrate en Madrid, a quienes dejó aquel hombre sabio todo su gran caudal de libros y papeles. Y para lo referido se ha tenido a la vista una copia certificada por el P. M. fray Diego Mecolaeta, archivero que fue de aquel monasterio', Floranes (1776), p. 49v.

100 Floranes (1776), pp. 51–51v. The argument of the region's poverty is again repeated in pp. 69–71. I owe the initial Floranes reference to the study by Muñoz (1955), p. 775. Floranes rests his arguments on the fundamental report by Salazar, local legislation and the treatises penned by writers like Mariana and Garibay. A defender of local laws, Rafael Floranes (1743–1801) appears to have spent much of his life in the regions where the old *fueros* still prevailed. He was originally from Tanarrio, Liébana, in what is today Cantabria (but was then a part of Castile), where the territory of the Cuatro Villas de la Costa del Mar had its own *fueros*. As a young man he lived in the Basque provinces, where he married Ignacia Goicoechea Sagarmínaga. In 1768 he was appointed to the post of procurator in the jurisdiction of Vizcaya, an office he was finally prevented from taking up because he was not a native of the province. He lived in Vitoria between 1770 and 1775, and then in Valladolid from the early 1780s. Biographical details in García López (1991), pp. 74–82.

101 Floranes (1776), p. 84v.

102 This decree is contained in another document in *Cuaderno de leyes de la provincia de Alava* (1761), pp. 154–156. It is also copied in Floranes (1776), pp. 85–87v. It can also be found in COGR t. 4, ref. 416, f. 25; in Muñoz (1955), p. 776 n. 74. Also in RORG.

103 At this time, Campoflorido was governor of the *Consejo de Hacienda*, secretary of the treasury and superintendent of the *Rentas Generales*. The accord is in *Cuaderno de leyes de la provincia de Alava* (1761), pp. 153–165.

104 According to Floranes (1776), pp. 87v–88, who makes no reference to the 1723 accord with Alava. The text is in *Cuaderno de leyes de la provincia de Alava* (1761), pp. 110–148. I owe the reference to Muñoz (1955), p. 776.

105 Angulo Morales (1995), p. 222. Mediation by leading members of a network in favour of their home communities was nothing new. Between 1550 and 1640 leading figures from Guipuzcoa in Madrid had interceded in defence of its laws and freedoms, some of them in the capacity of secretaries to the king (Idiáquez, Peñarrieta, Ibarra and Aróstegui), promoting natives of the province and consolidating its political statutes and the nobility or *hidalguía universal* of its citizens in the seventeenth century. For a discussion of these matters, see Truchuelo (2004).

106 Angulo Morales (1995), pp. 38–40. For example, the 1723 accord with Alava was negotiated on behalf of the king by Andrés Ignacio de Ansotegui, judge conservator of the *Rentas Generales*, and on behalf of the province by José Ignacio de Landázuri, its procurator general, José Során, procurator general of the *hermandad*, and the citizens, Pedro Gregorio de Albiz and Juan Bautista Sanz Navarrete; in *Cuaderno de*

leyes de la provincia de Alava (1761), pp. 153–165. I have no biographical details about Andrés Ignacio Ansotegui, but a person of that name appears redeveloping an iron foundry in Echevarría, Guipuzcoa, in 1729 (www.bizkaia.net/Kultura/Ondarea_Bizkaia/pdf/ondare/147%20c.pdf, consulted 3 September 2010), and it is probable that he was from the town. The negotiations thus involved Basques on both sides of the table.

107 Pérez Sarrión (2007).

108 The matter is mentioned in Muñoz (1955), pp. 778–779. The text of the royal order is in COGR t. 4, ref.ª 456, ff. 208–258, supplement 1; in Muñoz (1955), p. 779, note 84.

109 In a report of 17 February 1779 and a royal order of 12 April 1779 in COGR t. 32 ref.ª 2857, ff. 141–142, in Muñoz (1955), p. 779. Floranes' testimony is given in Floranes (1776), pp. 92–94v, and the whole of the last part of the manuscript, pp. 122–132, which originated precisely in response to the problem of smuggling.

110 In general, I have followed the sequence of events established in Torras Elías (1990), pp. 17–32.

111 Exports of Castilian wool to Catalonia continued to be taxed until 1746; Torras Elías (1990), p. 21.

112 But not export duties, because silk and wool, the main export products were strictly regulated; see the legislation in Muñoz (1955), pp. 760–761.

113 I have not seen this document. The references are in Torras Elías (1990), p. 25, and Uztáriz (1724), p. 358.

114 I have no further information about these secondary customs posts, although we may assume that they levied the difference between the 3.33 per cent duty applicable in Catalonia and the 15 per cent applied in the rest of Spain.

115 Royal order of 8 August 1742, in COGR t. 6, ref. 744, ff. 460–462, all in Muñoz (1955), p. 780.

116 See Pérez Sarrión (1999), pp. 246–251 and ff.

117 Fernández Albaladejo (1977), pp. 51–85, especially pp. 63–69.

118 Details in García-Cuenca (1982), pp. 473–475, together with a summary text of the first decree. Based on Gallardo (1805), and Ripia and Gallard (1796).

119 García-Cuenca (1982), pp. 473–475.

120 The reference is in Angulo (1995), p. 36.

121 A part of the text will be found in NR, lib. VI, tít. X, ley VII — pp. 140–141—.

122 The legislation is in NRN, libro I, título XVII, leyes I a XLVI —III, pp. 15–55. See Ostolaza (2007) for a discussion of the king's exchequer in Navarre.

123 Azcona (1995), pp. 96–101.

124 Azcona (1996 a), p. 97.

125 Ward (1779), p. 193 (quoted from the 1982 edition).

126 Studied in Madrazo (1984), II, pp. 673–774, based on an earlier work, Madrazo (1982).

127 See Conchon (2002).

128 Details in Pérez Sarrión (2005 a).

129 The term 'mail' means the letters and parcels sent by post, the bag or sack used to carry deliveries, or the vehicle (mail coach) used in the service. A 'post', meanwhile, was the stage or station established at regular intervals where both couriers and private parties could obtain fresh horses and supplies for a price. Posts were commonly associated with *posadas* or inns offering private accommodation and other services, including in particular those of a *post office* or *estafeta*, which would handle local deliveries of official and private mail, and pass mail on to secondary routes.

130 This section is based largely on Madrazo (1984) II, pp. 503–532 and Rodríguez Campomanes (1761) pp. XII–XIII, providing a complete overview of the development of the postal service in Spain, especially in the eighteenth century.
131 The order granting title is contained in *Anales de las ordenanzas de correos de España* (1879–1881), I, pp. 3–5. The *correo mayor* in turn leased or sold the offices of local and territorial postmaster, though always by royal appointment. See for example, *Anales de las ordenanzas de correos de España* (1879–1881), I, pp. 57–65 for the cases of the *correos mayores* of Galicia, Salamanca and other localities in 1646.
132 The new king thus declared his intention to 'valerme por ahora de las alcabalas, tercias reales, cientos, millones, servicio real, portazgo, puertas y peazgos, fiel medidor, hornos, servicio y montazgo, y todos los demás oficios y derechos que por cualquiera título, motivo o razón se hayan enajenado y segregado de mi Corona'. The order (in the king's own hand) is in AHN, Fondos Contemporáneos, Ministerio de Hacienda, lib. 8010 ff. 189–190.
133 See Morán Martín (2007).
134 From 1707 until the end of 1711. His business partner was the Dutchman, Umberto Hubrechtz from Zeeland, who was naturalized as a Spaniard in 1700. Both held contracts to farm royal revenues in Asturias and Galicia, among other places. Details in *Fichoz*, nos. 013362 and 020713 respectively (consulted 8 June 2005).
135 From late 1711 to the end of 1716. Details of Goyeneche will be found in *Fichoz* No. 010971 (consulted 8 February 2005).
136 At this time, the mail was viewed more as a department or revenue division of the *Real Hacienda* than a service.
137 See Rodríguez Campomanes (1761), p. xiii.
138 *Fichoz* no. 005834 (consulted 8 June 2005).
139 *Fichoz* no. 039910 (consulted 8 June 2005).
140 Rodríguez Campomanes (1761), p. xiii.
141 *Reglamento general*... (1761). Rodríguez Campomanes made certain additions to the document of 1720 in his edition: Rodríguez Campomanes (1761), pp. lii–liv.
142 Details in *Reglamento general*... (1761), pp. xviii–li.
143 Rodríguez Campomanes (1761), p. xvi and *Fichoz* no. 010545 (consulted 8 June 2005).
144 Rodríguez Campomanes (1761).
145 Manuel Jesús González and John Reeder, 'Introducción', in Rodríguez Campomanes (1761), p. 25.
146 See Palacio Atard (1960) for a discussion of the Reinosa to Santander highway, the most politically significant road-building scheme. Recent papers by Arenas de Pablo (2005) and Pérez Sarrión (2005 c) address the question in general.
147 See Bordázar de Artazu (1736) for further information about the Spanish monetary system.
148 Morineau (1985), p. 597, in Zylberberg (1993), p. 68.
149 See, for example, the interesting proposals to increase the circulation and re-export of silver in England made in 1702 by Isaac Newton, at the time Master of the Mint in London; J. Stanley, I. Newton and J. Ellis, *Report of the Officers of the Mint about the Preservation of the Coyne*, 17 July 1702, with attached documents, in Shaw (1896). The originals are in TNA, Treasury Board Papers, vol. XXX, no. 105 and in Newton's private papers; see Shaw (1896), pp. 132–134.
150 Uztáriz (1724), pp. 7–8.
151 Uztáriz (1724), p. 8.
152 Data provided by Zylberberg (1993), p. 313.

153 The French names for the gold *escudos*, and the silver *pesos, pesos fuertes, pesos duros* and *reales de a ocho.*
154 Zylberberg (1993), p. 313.
155 Muñoz de Amador (1755), pp. 7–8.
156 In general, the legislative information contained in this section is taken from Santiago (2000), pp. 249–261 and the NR. The interpretation of events is my own.
157 Legislative references in Muñoz de Amador (1755), pp. 9–11.
158 NR, lib. IX, tít. XVII, ley IX —IV, p. 358—.
159 We may assume that 1 billon *real*, which was worth 34 *maravedís* (as the accounting unit) was in reality made up of various copper coins; for example eight copper 4 *maravedí* bits and one 2 *maravedí* bit.
160 NR, lib. IX tít. XVII ley VI —IV, p. 355—. The fineness of the metal is not specified because the coins were copper. We may assume that the *real de plata doble* or double silver *real* mentioned is the *real de a dos*, which is to say the *provincial* silver two-*real* coin.
161 *Autos acordados* . . . (1777), libro V, tít. XXI, auto XLV —III, pp. 291–304. Also cited in Santiago (2000), p. 259.
162 *Ordenanza de S. M. de 16 de julio de 1730* . . . (1745). Also in *Autos acordados* . . . (1777), libro V, tít. XXI, auto LXV —III, pp. 384–435. Part of the text is in NR lib. IX. Tít. XVII ley VII —IV, pp. 355–356—.
163 Santiago (2000), p. 259 and NR lib. IX, tít. XVII, ley XII —IV, p. 360—.
164 NR, lib. IX, tít. I, ley III —IV, pp. 210–212—. Another copy of the Royal Decree of 15 November 1730 will be found in AHN, Estado, leg. 3216.
165 NR, lib. IX, tít. I, ley IV —IV, pp. 212–213—.
166 In the preceding lines, Caravajal explains that a satisfactory fiscal policy would foster Spanish industry, and as outflows of silver were unavoidable due to the trade deficit (*comercio pasivo* as he calls it), preventing the entry of foreign manufactures would end the export of silver.
167 Carvajal (1745) ff. 57–58v. In the prologue dated 5 July 1745, the author explains that he wrote the work while convalescing from a serious illness, He wrote it all straight off from memory, as he never intended it for publication, beginning on 5 July 1745 and finishing on 12 September 1745 (from the manuscript in the BNE, Mss/10687, ff. 1–2). He then decided to write *Mis pensamientos* (ff. 145–180), which he began on 7 June 1753 (BNE, Mss/10687, f. 146).
168 Santiago (2000), p. 260, in Céspedes del Castillo (1988), p. 79. The *pragmaticas* of 5 and 29 May 1772 will be found, together with other minor documents, in NR lib. IX, tít. XVII, leyes XIII a XIX —IV, pp. 360–366.
169 The ordinances were drawn up in the second quarter of the year but neither they nor the decree starting up the bank's operations, nor indeed its first ordinances have been located; Pulido (1994), pp. 44–46.
170 The regulations were amended on 19 August 1754, clearly an outcome of Ensenada's fall. All in AGS, Estado, leg. 5067 and AGS Dirección General del Tesoro, Inventario 23, leg. 8–3; in Pulido (1994), pp. 46–47, 152 and passim.
171 AGS, Estado, leg. 5067; according to Pulido (1994), p. 125.
172 See Pulido (1994), pp. 30–37.
173 The dispatches of the English ambassador, Keene, are in AHN Estado, leg. 4294, in Gómez Urdáñez (1996), pp. 190–192.
174 According to letters dated 1 September and 18 September 1755 in AGS, Estado, leg 6938; in Pulido (1994), pp. 155–161.

175 All according to Pulido (1994), pp. 165–166. The gap between the official and market prices of silver does not seem a sufficient explanation for the decline in profits. It is my belief that other factors, which the same author mentions without considering them causes, may also have been to blame. Chief among these was increasing contraband exports of silver coins.

176 Gómez Urdáñez (1996), pp. 193–194.

177 González Caizán (2004 b), p. 112.

178 Information obtained by cross-checking the data provided by González Caizán (2004 b), pp. 111–120 and *Fichoz*.

179 Pulido (1994), pp. 24–25, based on the work of H. van der Wee, Ch. Wilson, G. Parker, H. Luthy and F. C. Spooner.

180 Sonenscher (2007).

181 These details are taken from an instruction of 16 January 1717, CLDPE, I, pp. 16–22, note 3.

182 Royal decree of 18 August 1727 containing a *real pragmática* of 12 August 1727, CLDPE, I, pp. 28–31. Also of interest in this context is a *real cédula* of 5 November 1727, in CLDPE, I, pp. 31–33, and also in NR, lib. X, tít XIV, ley V —V, pp. 77–78—.

183 'Habiendo entendido que á diferentes herederos de casas de negocios del siglo pasado se han declarado y pagado en éste, sin la debida reflexión y justificación, créditos en que se han duplicado, triplicado y cuadruplicado los capitales por el exceso de los intereses y poco examen de las cuentas: he resuelto suspender la paga de estos créditos y que de nuevo se reconozcan en una Junta particular [en] que mandaré formar los documentos que los han producido, declarando que en adelante por ninguna especie de créditos atrasados de esta naturaleza se haya de abonar más intereses que el 3 por 100, y éste señaladamente solamente de aquellos créditos que constare que sin ninguna intermisión se han solicitado y no pagado, pues sobre los que hayan dormido por largo tiempo [. . .] está contra ellos la presumpción de que se hayan satisfecho. Y suplantándose los instrumentos de que debiera resultar la noticia, no se debe admitir instancia, aun [=a menos] que [medie] especial orden mía, si no fuese con derogación de esta providencia' *real decreto* of 7 June 1742, in CLDPE, IX, pp. 244–247; text in pp. 244–245. Furthermore, certain *asientos de provisiones* dating from the period 1684–1686, which bore interest of 8 per cent, were also cut to the 3 per cent rate established in 1742; *real orden* of 20 November 1743, in CLDPE, IX, pp. 245–246. Ten years later, a *real orden* of 12 January 1752 stipulated that payment would only be made subject to recognition of the debt; in CLDPE, IX, pp. 246–247. The decree of 1742 was signed by the Basque, Nicolás de Aristizábal Olloqui, then secretary to the governing board of the *Consejo de Hacienda; Fichoz* no. 005644 (consulted 3 September 2010).

184 They were preceded by a royal order of 10 April 1731; *reales decretos* of 14 July 1747, 16 December 1748 and 1 July 1749, in CLDPE, I, pp. 33–42. The decree of 1747 is also in NR, lib. X, tít. XIV, ley VII —IV, pp. 67–68—; and that of 1748 is in NR, lib. X, tít. XIV, ley XI —IV, pp. 73–74—.

185 By means of two decrees dated 16 and 20 December 1748 for Castile and 9 August 1750 for Aragon, which reduced the interest on the *juros* to 2 per cent; Gómez Urdáñez (1996), pp. 195–196.

186 'todos los Juros compuestos de capitales consistentes en efectivos desembolsos hechos por los asentistas en las diferentes partes adonde con sus caudales se obligaban a proveer con sus contratos, bien se les diesen juros para su resguardo o por cuenta de lo que proveyesen o en pago de alcances por tanteo, sin formal

liquidación de cuentas, siempre que por la que se ajuste en el día resulte caudal para ello', *real decreto* of 1 January 1752, CLDPE, I, pp. 42–45, text on p. 43.

187 Torres Sánchez (2008), pp. 263–282. See also the general remarks made by the same author in Torres Sánchez (2007), pp. 13–45, and more specifically pp. 40–44.

188 Torres Sánchez (2008), pp. 271–274. The *deuda de testamentaría* or 'legacy debt' was left by each king to his successor when he died. In 1754, all other legacy debts carried over from the reigns of kings before Philip V amounted to no more than 4.3 million *reales* (Torres Sánchez (2008), p. 271), which is to say they were irrelevant compared with the debts left by the last king.

189 Royal decree of 18 November 1732, CLDPE, appendix 1, pp. 18–20.

190 *Real resolución* issued by Fernando VI on 10 December 1748; CLDPE, I, pp. 128–129. Also in NR, lib. VII, tít. VII, ley XXI —III, pp. 313–314—. This measure was related with the recovery of offices, which began with the royal decree of 21 November 1707 issued by Philip V, as discussed above. The process was again a long one, and it remains to be examined in detail.

191 Decree of 31 January 1760, by now in the reign of Charles III; CLPDE, I, pp. 46–48. Other edicts of 1765, 1787 and 1799 only confirmed and fleshed out the terms; CLPDE, I, pp. 49–54.

192 Royal decree of 22 February 1760. Another decree of 1788 recognized the debt of Charles III; both in CLPDE, I, pp. 100–115.

193 Debts referred to in treasury terms as *atrasos* or 'arrears'; Jurado (2007), p. 94. The analysis refers only to expenditures and not to revenues, so it is not possible to establish the actual share of debt amortization in the budgets.

194 Hoffman, Postel-Vinay and Rosenthal (2001), pp. 97–127. See also Hoffman (1996).

195 Torres Sánchez (2006), pp. 139–172.

196 See Riley (1980), pp. 165–174.

197 See the legislation in *Recopilación* . . . (1802).

198 The *censo al quitar* or *censal* consisted of a loan (*dar dinero a censo*) made by a *censualista* to a borrower or *censatario* in consideration of interest payable in the form of a pension or annuity secured against property (in an arrangement akin to a mortgage). The system developed as a legal ruse to sidestep the progressive prohibition of usury (i.e. lending at interest) by the Church in the eleventh and twelfth centuries. It was derived from the feudal system of emphyteusis (in which the *censualista*, who held direct title to a property, assigned its use to a *censatario* in consideration of a fixed annuity, making it somewhat similar to the English leasehold). These *censos* or *censales* were already in widespread use in Spain and Portugal in the fourteenth century, and they survived until the 1830s when full freedom to lend was eventually allowed. For a discussion, see the illuminating paper by Clavero (1977), pp. 107–131.

199 See the abundant legislation in NR, lib. X, tít. XIV. The king also fixed the interest or *denier légal* payable on public debt and *cens* in France, and the trend followed by the rate was similar to the Spanish case; see Grenier (1996), pp. 196–197.

200 *Real pragmática* of 10 February 1705, NR, lib. X, tít. XIV, ley VIII —V, p. 79—.

201 *Real pragmática* of 6 July 1750, NR, lib. X, tít. XIV, ley IX —V, pp. 79–80—.

202 Author's italics.

203 AHN, Clero, leg. 8432, in Atienza (1993) p. 72. The land was probably sold by the *Audiencia* following the enforcement of an order for distraint against a smallholder. The informant may have been a French merchant settled in Zaragoza, Pedro Casamayor, Pierre Casamayor or Pierre Casamajeur, whose business dealings

involved farm rents. This gentleman appears again some years later, when he became involved in a major agricultural investment, the construction of the Canal Imperial de Aragón irrigation scheme.

204 Zavala (1732), pp. 110–184.

205 Royal decree of 7 December 1748, NR lib. VII, tít. XXIV, ley XIV —III, pp. 516–523—.

206 Yun (2002 a), p. 242 and passim.

207 Wasteland tilled and cultivated for the first time.

208 In the decision issued in response to a query of 13 November 1765 and *real cédula* of 21 June 1766, NR lib. I, tít. VI, ley XIII —I, pp. 59–61.

209 See Anes (1970), pp. 95–138, and Ortega López (1986).

210 NR, lib. VII, tít. XIX, leyes I y II —III, p. 445—

211 *Real pragmática* of 15 July 1765 and *real provisión* of 30 October 1765, NR, lib. VII, tít. XIX, leyes XI y XII —III, pp. 452–454—.

212 *Real provisión* of 20 August 1768, NR, lib. VII, tít. XIX, ley XIII —III, p. 454—

213 *Real cédula* of 1 February 1785, NR, lib. VII, tít. XIX, ley XIV —III, p. 454—.

214 *Real pragmática* of 15 July 1765, NR, lib. VII, tít. XIX, ley XI, artículo 6 —III, pp. 452–453—.

215 *Real provisión* of 22 July 1789 and *real cédula* of 16 July 1790, NR, lib. VII, tít. XIX, leyes XVIII y XIX —III, pp. 456–457—.

216 A copy ended up in the French archives: *Consulta de una Junta q[u]e el año de 1721 mandó el Rey formar sobre la pres[en]te decadencia del comercio en España [y con Indias] y forma de su restablecimiento en todos los ramos*, 3 September 1721, AMAEP, MD, livre 252, ff. 94–126. In general, this section is a summary of another broader study, see Pérez Sarrión (2011 a).

217 It was proposed to form a 'tribunal [...] que vele continuamente de [=por] la conservación y augmento de las fábricas, maniobras y comercios de lo interior del Reino [...]', and a privileged 'Compañía de Españas' to boost trade with America; idem, ff. 120–120v.

218 Idem, ff. 124–124v.

219 A *Junta Particular de Comercio* was created in 1692, and another was formed in 1735, although it did not actually commence its activity until 1758. Details in Molas (1977), pp. 241–264. The legislation governing the *Junta Particular de Comercio de Barcelona* is in Larruga (1789) VI, ff. 29–429. See also Ruiz i Pablo (1919) and Iglèsies (1969) on this institution.

220 The Valencia board of trade was not approved until 1762; Molas (1977), pp. 308–328, whose information about the *Junta Particular de Valencia* also draws heavily on Larruga (1789), I, ff. 795–1390. The legislation is in Larruga (1789), VI, ff. 410–577 and 707–728.

221 The activities of these local boards are described in Larruga (1789), I, ff. 539–794 (Barcelona and its *consulado*) and 795–1,390 (Valencia and its *consulado*), and II, ff. 2,273–2,615 (Granada, Seville, Antequera and Valladolid).

222 Text in Larruga (1789), V, ff. 29–41.

223 Text in Larruga (1789), V, ff. 14–15.

224 NR, lib. IX, tít. I, ley III —IV, pp. 210–212—. There is another copy of the royal decree of 15 November 1730 in AHN, Estado, leg. 3216.

225 NR, lib. IX, tít. I, ley IV —IV, pp. 212–213—.

226 Both decrees in NR, lib. IX, tít. I, leyes V y VIII —IV, pp. 213–214—.

227 In 1727 its permanent staff consisted of four officials, rising to six in 1730 when the *Junta de Moneda* was absorbed. By 1737 the board had seven officials and in 1754 it

had nine officials, two *entretenidos*, one archivist and two attendants, making a total of fourteen, according to Larruga (1789), I, ff. 412–458. In 1727 the familiar figure of Gerónimo de Uztáriz, at the time a member of the *Consejo de Indias*, was appointed secretary and a member of the *Junta*. In 1730 he was replaced as secretary by his son Casimiro de Uztáriz (1727–1735) while remaining a member of the board (Larruga 1789, I, ff. 412–458). Gerónimo Uztáriz greatly influenced the Board's economic tenets. Both he and his son belonged to the Navarrese clique at Court, which filled a number of posts in the institution. Details and lists of *Junta's* members will be found in Larruga (1789), I, ff. 307–458.

228 Larruga (1789), III, ff. 81–81v.

229 Larruga (1789), III, passim. Initiatives were launched to create factories or grant privileges to successful enterprises, especially in the wool, linen and silk industries (ff. 56v–57v, 68–68v and 74–74v), though care was taken to balance the privileges accorded in each case (consultation of August 1731, ff. 75–75v). It was also proposed to create factories for baize and Turkish-style carpets in Madrid and other cities (consultations of 15 and 20 April 1741, f. 94–94v), as well as strings for musical instruments, iron looms for the manufacture of stockings (consultations of 16 June 1742, ff. 93v–94) and other important goods (f. 94–96). Larruga examines each of these initiatives and their outcomes in detail in his magnificent *Memorias políticas y económicas* (Larruga, 1787, passim).

230 Larruga (1789), III, ff. 93–93v.

231 Larruga (1789), III, ff. 197–200.

232 Matilla (1982), pp. 323–390.

233 Memorial in defence of the *compañías de comercio y fábricas*, s. a., late 1752, AHN Estado leg. 3188-2 exp. 402.

234 According to the institution's secretary, Juan Fernández de Jamieles: *Estado general de las fábricas que hay en España sugetas a la Real Junta General de Comercio y de Moneda, con distinción de las provincias y pueblos donde se hallan extablecidas, géneros de su construcción, privilegios que se les han concedido, por qué tiempo, consistencia de ynstrumentos, oficinas y personas de que se componen, y estado en que hoy subsisten, según lo que consta en la Secretaría de la citada Junta General.* Madrid, 7 August 1746, AHN, Estado, leg. 3515.

235 Details can be found in Pérez Sarrión (2011 a).

236 In general, this section is a summary of another broader study, see Pérez Sarrión (2011 b).

237 The *real cédula* of 13 November 1710 contained in *Cuaderno de leyes de la provincia de Alava* (1761), pp. 104–109, provides incontestable evidence of these matters. Everything appears to indicate that the privileges of *hidalguía* or nobility and *limpieza de sangre* had been broadened until they created a provincial *naturality*, which was beginning to take shape just as Spain's other naturalities began to coalesce around Castile. However, it is also possible that something else was happening in the Basque provinces. As a new fiscal *naturality* developed, distinguishing the Basques from other Spanish naturals, it may have begun to overlap Castilian naturality, which conferred the right to serve the king and hold office. Basque identity in fact became increasingly defined in fiscal terms in the eighteenth century. For the moment, I am unable to clarify this ambiguous semantic change in a term which in any case underwent a shift in meaning over the course of the century.

238 Pérez Collados (1993), pp. 171–230.

239 For a discussion of the absence of any meetings of the Castilian *Cortes* in the seventeenth century, see Fortea (2003), republished in Fortea (2008).
240 Herzog (2003), pp. 76–93.
241 NR, lib. I, tít XIV, ley VI —I, pp. 109–110—.
242 NR, lib. I, tít. XIV, ley VI, nota 5 —I, p. 110—.
243 NR, lib. I, tít. XIV, ley V —I, pp. 108–109—.
244 The text does not actually say whether it is the *Consejo de Castilla* or the *Consejo de la Cámara de Castilla.*
245 NR, lib. I, tít. XIV, ley VI, nota 4 —I, p. 110—.
246 Text in Larruga (1789), V, ff. 72v–73.
247 Larruga (1789), I, f. 201.
248 Larruga (1789), V, ff. 73v–74v.
249 Royal order of 21 December 1748, in AHN, Estado, leg. 647-14 and Larruga (1789), I, ff. 204–205 and V, ff. 76–76v.
250 The peace treaty of 1648 for the 'hanseaticos' (i.e. Germans); the peace treaty of 1651 for the Dutch; the trade treaty of 1667 for the English; and the Treaty of the Pyrenees of 1659 for the French, who made up the most important community of foreigners. The privileges are examined in detail, from a French standpoint, in *Representación . . .* (1710). The original is in AHN, Consejos, libro 5207. The treaties can be consulted in Andrés-Gallego (1999).
251 NR, lib. VI, tít. XI, ley IV —III, p. 167—.
252 *Real cédula* of 7 July 1727, NR, lib. VI, tít XI, ley V —III, p. 168–169—.
253 See the use of the term in Madrid, in Pérez Sarrión (2007), pp. 216–222.
254 For an excellent analysis of this matter, see Greenfeld (1992), pp. 213–244 who provides a detailed analysis of the semantic shift affecting the terms *peuple*, *nation*, *patrie* and *état* or *estat* (the latter term refers to the estates of the realm - church, lords and commons - as opposed to the state *qua* political institution).
255 See Pérez Sarrión (2005 b) and (2011 b).
256 See Vizcay (1621) and Aragón Ruano (2009), p. 193 and passim. Vizcay's book and the nature of the *bajonavarros* are examined in more detail in Aragón Ruano (2010).
257 These settlers are named in Frías and García Belsunce (1996), p. 45, as Pedro de Alvarado (Otardazuri, Basse Navarre); Juan Anchordoqui (Basse Navarre); Fernando de Arizaga (valley of Uriarte, Basse Navarre); Bernardo Artayeta (Basse Navarre, or perhaps Hasparren, Lapurdi [Labourd]); Juan Bidondo (Saint-Etienne de Baigorri, Basse Navarre); Juan Salvador de Echepare (Basse Navarre); Martín Iribarren (Saint-Etienne de Baigorry, Echepare); and Pedro Sabores or Saforet (Echepare).
258 Floristán (1999), p. 483 note 90 (author's translation). The naturalization processes consist of eight bundles in AGN, Naturalizaciones.

Chapter 6

1 Report of the French consul in Cadiz, Mongelas, 21 January 1777, AMAEP. MD, Esp., livre 132, f. 146v.
2 Zylberberg (1993), pp. 113–114.
3 Zylberberg (1993), pp. 42–44.

4 Pierre Villars (1733). Pierre Villars was Marquis of Villars, Seigneur of La Chapelle, Baron of Masclas, Sarras, Rèvirant and Oriol and ambassador in Spain in 1680. He was in the country in 1668–1669, 1671–1673 and 1679–1681. His biographical details and the Spanish translation of the passage cited above (in García Mercadal (1959), 1999 edition, volume III, p. 703) are taken from Sanz (2005), p. 284. Translation by Daniel Duffield.
5 García Mercadal (1959), 1999 edition, volume III, p. 734. The passage is also cited in Sanz (2005), p. 284. Translation by Daniel Duffield.
6 Marqués de Villars, *Memorie des françois qui sont en toute l'ettendue de l'Espagne*, c. 1679–1680, manuscript, AMAEP, CP, Espagne, 64, pp. 273–274v, document 111. This document was originally brought to light by Nadal and Giralt (1960), pp. 223–235, who attribute it to the Marquis of Villars.
7 Nadal and Giralt (1960), pp. 223–235, including the table on p. 232. These scholars read the document rather differently, however. They count some 45,000 individuals, not including Catalonia, and only around 5,000 merchants. However, the document clearly says 'environ 65 mil' though the partial figures given actually total 67,000.
8 See the recent, important paper by Desos (2009).
9 Zylberberg (1993), pp. 33–47
10 Salas (1990), pp. 158–159 and passim.
11 The census is in AHN, Estado, legs. 629–1, 629–2 and 629–3. Reference in Zylberberg (1993), p. 80 and Salas (1990), p. 170, note 2.
12 Data in Salas (1990), pp. 155–171.
13 Zylberberg (1993), pp. 80–84. The author says nothing about the French in Aragon, where they were most numerous, or those of Navarre.
14 22 December 1763, AHN, Estado, leg. 647–15.
15 See Salas (1977) and (1992–1993).
16 Nadal and Giralt (1960), pp. 171–186. The authors appear to overlook the fact that these migratory movements also occurred in other areas of the monarchy like Aragon, where the wage factor, which was not specific to Catalonia, would have worked in the same way.
17 Nadal and Giralt (1960), pp. 210–211.
18 Nadal and Giralt (1960), pp. 187–213. The immense majority of French immigrants worked on the land, especially sowing and reaping. Nadal and Giralt (1960), pp. 215–221.
19 BCB, Bonsoms, fullet 253, pp. 142–144, in Nadal and Giralt (1960), pp. 211–212.
20 Instructions issued to the new French ambassador in Spain, the Count de Vauguyon, Fontainebleau 29-IX-1687; ANF, Afers Estrangers, BI 766, in Nadal and Giralt (1960), p. 212.
21 Nadal and Giralt (1960), pp. 142–145.
22 Salas (1990), p. 157.
23 Data in Zylberberg (1993), pp. 109–111.
24 The reference is in Zylberberg (1993), pp. 109–111.
25 French trading activity in and via Catalonia in the eighteenth century is not well documented, and it is possible that some supposedly Catalan merchants were in reality French, or of French origin, given that the historically Catalan county of Rousillon had belonged to the Spanish Crown until it was ceded to France in the Treaty of the Pyrenees (1659). Hence, there may have been a conflict over the Catalan naturality of the area's inhabitants (and their Castilian naturality after 1714) of a similar nature to that between *navarros franceses* and *navarros españoles* at the western end of the

Pyrenean border. Trade in Catalonia in the eighteenth century may therefore have involved not only merchants of French origin who had already settled in the seventeenth century, but also specifically French traders who were in reality Catalan (and then Castilian), allowing them to trade freely in Spain. Such would have been any *catalanes franceses* who had stayed on after 1659. In any event, the trade and client networks knitting together Rousillon and the rest of Catalonia until 1659 must have lingered on for long afterwards, at least in part. A detailed examination of the 1764 census taken in Catalonia might perhaps throw light on this matter, which is here raised merely as a conjecture. References to French trade in Catalonia will be found in Torra (1997), (2001) and (2005).

26 This custom appears to have fallen gradually into disuse around 1740, Zylbergerg (1993), p. 108.

27 'tout nouveau venu non espagnol, était tenu de se loger en tant qu'hôte [huésped] chez l'habitant. Cela représentait une charge plus lourde qu'il paraît puisque l'huesped devait nourrir la famille qui l'hébergeait. Pour échapper à ce statut, il fallait accepter de perdre sa qualité de Français et se faire naturaliser, mais cela occasionnait de grans frais puisq'il fallait présenter des preuves de noblesse et réunir des preuves de sa filiation, donc établir une généalogie', Zylberberg (1993), pp. 106–107. The author bases his account on a *Mémoire des négotiants français de Bilbao*, 1773, ANF, AE III 334, which I have not seen. He regards these arrangements as a discrimination against the French, although they applied in fact to all strangers coming from outside the provinces of Vizcaya and Guipuzcoa, including the Navarrese and any other Spaniards. As explained above, the restriction was based on the local laws prevailing in Vizcaya and Guipuzcoa.

28 Título XLI capítulos III and IV of the *fueros*: *Nueva recopilación de los fueros . . .* (1696), in Aragón Ruano (2009), pp. 162–164.

29 This is the author's interpretation. Details and data will be found in Aragón Ruano (2009). The *cédula* is in AGG, Juntas y Diputaciones, IM 4/10/68, in Aragón Ruano (2009), p. 173.

30 Zylberberg (1993), pp. 108–109.

31 The question of customs and contraband in the Basque Country, including the seaports, is not discussed here given its complexity, and because it does not bear directly on the present argument. For further information, see the interesting work published by Angulo (1995), (1997), (2001) and (2003).

32 Salas (1986).

33 In Salas (1986), p. 70.

34 Azcona (1996), pp. 439–440.

35 Azcona (1996), pp. 439–488. This work contains a detailed study of the eight principal French merchant families in Pamplona, seven of which were from the nearby Basque-speaking areas of Basse Navarre (*Baja Navarra* in Spanish, *Behenafarroa* in Basque), Labourd (*Laborrt, Lapurdi*) and Soule (*Sola, Zuberoa*). Most of the other French immigrants were also from this area. See Azcona (1995) and (1996 b).

36 I follow the interpretation of Floristán Imízcoz (1991), pp. 55–62, in this matter. The arguments presented by Esarte (2001), pp. 251–257, from a Basque nationalist perspective do not seem to me acceptable. This author decontextualizes the documents of Ferdinand the Catholic and the Burgos *Cortes* of 1515 cited by Floristán, and he adds a pan-Basque map of Navarre, which is again decontextualized and is constructed based on the testimony of the secretary to the deposed Henry II of Navarre and a map contained in the *Gran Enciclopedia Vasca*. See Ostolaza (2007), pp. 313–336, for a discussion of the legal formalities involved in the issue of

documents by King Ferdinand the Catholic in the years immediately after the occupation of Navarre in August–September 1512 until its annexation to Castile in 1515 and Charles I's coronation as Holy Roman Emperor at Aix-la-Chapelle in 1520, and in the rest of the sixteenth century (under Charles V and Philip II).

37 The rest of the parishes in the region belonged to the French dioceses of Dax (western part of Basse Navarre) and Oloron (Soule).

38 Azcona (1996 a), p. 43.

39 Juaristi (1992), pp. 13–17.

40 For further details, see Zabala Uriarte (1994) and Grafe (2005).

41 Azcona Gutiérrez Muñoz (1994), pp. 74–76, 287–295 and passim.

42 See the citations of J. J. Laborda Martín, T. Guiard Larrauri, L. M. Bilbao, J. J. Laborda and A. Zabala in Azcona (1996), p. 51 note 50.

43 See Pontet (1991) for a discussion of Bayonne's role.

44 Azcona (1996), pp. 93–99. See also Bartolomé Herranz (1991 and 1993) on the customs revenues and Treasury of Navarre.

45 NRN, 1.17.12, in Azcona (1996), p. 51.

46 *Cuadernos de las leyes* (1896), ley 20 (1645), corresponding to NRN 1.10.17 (1737), all in Azcona (1996), p. 43.

47 See the considerations on this matter in Pérez Sarrión (2007).

48 Azcona (1996), pp. 93–98.

49 Based on Rodríguez Garraza (2003), pp. 139–147.

50 Azcona (1996), p. 45.

51 See the paper published by Rodríguez Garraza (2003), pp. 129–190, as well as the abundant bibliography cited, and the papers by Alberto Angulo Morales, Jesús Astigarraga and Juan-Cruz Alli Aranguren in the same issue of the journal. For a discussion of the nineteenth century, see in particular Alli Aranguren (2004), pp. 511–544. Certain documents concerning this issue will also be found in Floristán Imizcoz (1991), pp. 251–261.

52 García-Zúñiga (1993 b), pp. 320–324.

53 Azcona (1996), p. 109, especially the numerous legislative references contained in note 51.

54 Azcona (1996), pp. 109–110.

55 Azcona (1996), pp.110–111.

56 Azcona (1996), pp. 110–112.

57 Azcona (1996), pp. 112–113.

58 Parliaments were held at the beginning of the eighteenth century in 1701–1702 (Pamplona), 1705 (Sangüesa), 1709 (Olite), 1716–1717 (Pamplona), and 1724–1726 (Estella). The texts are in ACN, libros 5 a 7.

59 ACN, libro 6, pp. 145–146. I have modernized the spelling in the citations.

60 ACN, libro 6, pp. 143–145.

61 ACN, libro 6, pp. 171–175 and 180–181.

62 ACN, libro 6, p. 179.

63 ACN, libro 6, pp. 99–102.

64 ACN, libro 6, p. 100.

65 Part of the text is in Uztáriz (1724), 1737–1738. See also *Cuaderno de las leyes* . . . (1896), leyes 21 and 22; the reference is in Azcona (1996), p. 95, note 7.

66 Azcona (1996), p. 44, note 23.

67 Azcona (1996), pp. 44–45. The text of the royal decree is in Floristán Imízcoz (1991), pp. 206–211.

68 The data is from García-Zúñiga (1993 b).

69 Juan Remírez Baquedano, Marquis of Andía (1645–1743) was born in Amescoa in the north of Navarre. He was an *alcalde* and *oidor* of the Council of Navarre (1681–1685), a founder member of the *Congregación de San Fermín de los Navarros* in Madrid (1688) and interim governor of the Council of Castile (1715–1723). He also held other offices, including membership of the *Junta de Guerra y Hacienda* formed to supervise the appointment of the provincial superintendents general in 1711. *Fichoz* no. 004608 (consulted 28 June 2005).

Francisco Aperregui Asiaín (1663–1731) was born in Tudela. He had been an *oidor* of the Council of Navarre's *Cámara de Comptos* (from 1691), the body responsible for the customs administration, a counselor to the viceroy (1706), a contraband magistrate in Navarre (1711), a magistrate of the *Audiencia* of Aragon, and successively a member of the *Consejo de Hacienda* (1718), the *Consejo de Órdenes Militares* (1720) and the Council of Castile (1723). *Fichoz* no. 005755 (28 June 2005).

Sebastián Eusa Torreblanca (1660–1722) was born in Tafalla and had also been an *oidor* of the Council of Navarre (1705), as well as a magistrate of the *Real Audiencia* of Aragon (1707), a member of the *Consejo de Hacienda* (1707), and a member of the Council's *Junta del Arancel* or tariffs committee (1715). *Fichoz* no. 006063 (consulted 28 June 2005).

70 AGN, Traslación de aduanas, leg. 1, c. 11, in García Zúñiga (1993 b), p. 320 note 37.

71 'haviendo cumplido en año de 1720 la última prorrogación que hizo ese Reino del servicio de quarteles y alcavalas, y así mismo el impuesto de tres y medio por ciento de derechos de los géneros extrangeros que introducen en él sus naturales, y han estado siempre aplicados a la subsistencia de las tropas que en este dicho reino han servido'. ACN, libro 7, pp. 148–150. We may remember that the *derechos de mercaderías* imposed on the naturals of Navarre were temporary and were collected to allow payment of the royal levy.

72 ACN, libro 7, pp. 148–150, 152–153, 157, 159 and 161.

73 ACN, libro 7, pp. 177, 180, 189 and 195.

74 Meaning the part of the *servicio* or levy collected by the *Diputación del Reino* via the imposition of quotas.

75 ACN, libro 7, p. 196.

76 ACN, libro 7, p. 197.

77 See the map in Azcona (1996), p. 94. For a discussion of the complex question of French tolls, see Foursans-Bourdette (1963), and Conchon (2005) and especially (2002).

78 ACN, libro 7, pp. 402–413.

79 ACN, libro 7, p. 422.

80 García-Zúñiga (1993 b).

81 García-Zúñiga (1993 a and 1993 b).

82 Zylberberg (1993), pp. 193–244, provides a quantity of information about Bayonne. The figure cited is on p. 217.

83 Azcona (1996 a), p. 460.

84 According to a query raised with the viceroy, in AGN, cited by Azcona (1999), p. 97.

85 Azcona (1997) passim. The businesses created by these families can be studied via the records of bankruptcies affecting firms throughout Navarre, and even in Zaragoza and Ágreda, kept in APNP, and charter nobility processes in AGN. The references can be found in Azcona (1997), p. 356 and (1999), p. 356 and passim, respectively.

86 Alfaro Pérez (2006 and 2007).

87 An excellent description of these routes will be found in Rodríguez Campomanes (1761), pp. 52–53, 82, together with a detailed map of the area in idem between pp. XCVI and XCVII.
88 Langé (1993), pp. 62, 88, 90 and passim. Based on a sample of marriage certificates from around 25 parishes, as well as other marriage records (spinster and bachelor certificates, diocesan archives) and Inquisition records for the period indicated.
89 Data in Nadal and Giralt (1960), pp. 224–225.
90 Ansón (1977).
91 Salas (1977), p. 47.
92 Data in Nadal and Giralt (1960), pp. 226–227, and in Salas (1977), p. 46.
93 See Nadal and Giralt (1960), pp. 87–221 on French immigration in Catalonia.
94 Details in Nadal and Giralt (1960), pp. 226–227.
95 The measures concerned are well documented; see Sanz (2005), pp. 294–303.
96 Salas (1977).
97 Nadal (1960), in Salas (1977), p. 70 (translation).
98 Langé (1993), p. 95.
99 Langé (1993), pp. 95–96.
100 Based on the Aragonese customs revenues for 1675, fabrics accounted for 51.7 per cent of the total value of the kingdom's imports; in ADPZ, manuscript 451, ff. 194–194v, in Peiró (1990), p. 45. This figure does not take account of contraband goods.
101 See the table in Peiró (1990), p. 49.
102 Salas (1992–1993), pp. 41–51.
103 Salas (1992–1993), p. 52.
104 Salas (1992–1993), p. 54.
105 Salas (1994), pp. 260–261, 264–265 and passim.
106 Fontaine (1996).
107 Yun (2002 b), pp. 106–128.
108 Feliu (1991), vol, II, pp. 88–129.
109 Ardit (1993), I, pp. 49–53 and (1996). The territory of the Kingdom of Valencia was smaller than that of today's *Comunidad Autónoma*, because the districts of Requena and Utiel, which had been part of New Castile since the late medieval period, were not attached to Valencia until the nineteenth century.
110 All of the data in this section are taken from Zylberberg (1993), pp. 114–118.
111 See Vasallo (1997) for a discussion of the activities of Maltese merchants in the Mediterranean.
112 An interesting point. These may have been discharged soldiers who had served in the regiments formed by the noble Irish Catholics employed by the king of Spain, as explained above.
113 The amounts loaned were repaid in kind (grain) when the harvest was brought in. The lender would buy at low cost and could then sell at a higher price in times of scarcity. The difference was the lender's profit, and at the same time the system allowed the merchants involved to speculate in grain.
114 All based on Zylberberg (1993), pp. 432–433.
115 In Salas (1990), p. 169.
116 The rural districts to the west and east of Madrid, respectively.
117 *Cajero* here means the company's treasurer. The term *cajero* or *cajonero* is also used to refer to pedlars or chapmen, who sold manufactured goods out of boxes or portable chests.

118 Francisco Cabarrús, *Memoria sobre la protección que necesita el comercio y el establecimiento de los extranjeros en España*, Madrid 22 March 1783, manuscript, AHN, Estado, leg. 2944 exp. 434, ff. 6r–6v. I attribute this title to the text because the author himself uses it in his letter of submission to Floridablanca.
119 Francisco Cabarrús, *Memoria* ... cited in the preceding note, AHN, Estado, leg. 2944 exp. 434 f. 24v.
120 Duroux (2000 a).
121 Fontaine (1996), pp. 35–49.
122 Mui (1987).
123 Fontaine (1996), p. 39.
124 Landes (1983), pp. 283–329.
125 Zylberberg (1993), p. 95. The census of 1773 is in AHN, Consejos, leg. 1592; the 1764 census is in AHN, Estado, leg. 629–1.
126 Poitrineau (1985), pp. 157–158.
127 Zylberberg (1993), p. 98.
128 Poitrineau (1985), pp. 159–160.
129 Zylberberg (1993), p. 100.
130 I have investigated events involving these individuals in a number of papers, and unfortunately I must admit that I was slow to realize that many whom I had believed to be Spanish (because of the Hispanicization of their surnames) were in fact French. Overall, their activity makes sense if it is placed in the context of the powerful merchant and social networks formed by the French centred on Madrid. References to these people will be found in Pérez Sarrión (1975), (1984 a, b) and (1996 a, b).
131 Labat (1730), t. I, p. 285–288. The Abbé Jean Baptiste Labat (1666–1738) was a Dominican friar who travelled widely in Spain, Italy and America. A somewhat abridged version of this passage is cited in Girard (1932), pp. 279–480 of the Spanish edition, and also in Fontaine (1996), pp. 44–45, to whom I initially owe the reference.
132 Contrary to the assertions made by Girard (1932), pp. 415 and 455–460 of the Spanish edition.
133 Girard (1932), pp. 469–482 of the Spanish edition.
134 Mongelas to Castriès, 1 August 1786, ANF, Affaires étrangeres, B1 294, translated. The origin of the text and the passage cited in Fontaine (1996), pp. 233–234.
135 Once again in this case, I lack the original in French; ANF, F20/434, cited by Duroux (1985), pp. 284–285; in Fontaine (1996), p. 47.
136 Duroux (1992).
137 Duroux (2000 b). Whether or not a legal requirement, inheritance of the family farmhouse and land by a single heir was the norm in originally poor highland areas. It was found both in the Basque Country and Navarre (*casa* or *etxea*), in the Aragonese Pyrenees (*casa*) and Tierra Alta, in the Maestrazgo of Aragon and Valencia (*casa, masía, masada*), and in the Catalan Pyrenees (*casa, masía, masada* or *mas*).
138 Poitrineau (1985), pp. 47, 55–60; also Duroux (1985) (2000 a) and (2000 c).
139 Poitrineau (1985), pp. 158–178.
140 Poitrineau (1962), p. 21.
141 Poitrineau (1983), pp. 18–20.
142 Poitrineau (1965), I, pp. 71, 154–155.
143 Poitrineau (1965), I, pp. 572–579.
144 Poitrineau (1965), I, pp. 560–572 and II, p. 134.

145 Zylberberg (1993), p. 95.
146 Morineau (1960), p. 99, in Zylberberg (1993), p. 96.
147 See Pérez Sarrión (2005 a), (2005 b) and (2005 c).

Chapter 7

1 Llopis (2002), p. 123.
2 Pérez Sarrión (1999), pp. 41–42. I now believe that the population figure I gave for Aragon in this work is understated.
3 Figures in Llopis (2001), pp. 512–513.
4 Hamilton (1947), pp. 217–223 and 254–256.
5 Yun (1987), chap. X.
6 This is suggested by the work of Ringrose (1970), (1983 b) and (1987), Castro (1987) for Madrid, and Franch (1986) and (1989) and Catalá (1995) for Valencia.
7 See Ringrose (1970, 1983 b and 1987) and Yun (1987).
8 The phenomenon is clearly, if indirectly, observable in the data provided by Franch (1986).
9 Delgado Ribas (1995).
10 Ringrose (1996), chaps. 8 and 10.
11 Muset Pons (1997) and Rúa Fernández (2006). The reference to Rúa is taken from the abstract of a research paper presented at the Instituto Universitario de Historia Jaume Vicens Vives belonging to the Universitat Pompeu Fabra under the title *El homes de negoci Catalans a Madrid desprès del 1714*. The author presented her doctoral thesis *La xarxa catalana a Madrid en el segle XVIII. Un estudi sobre els homes de negocis catalans i el comerç* on 27 January 2010, although I have not had the opportunity to read it.
12 The Enlightenment commentators complained that the activity of Catalan carters and mule drivers caused regional inequalities. Ocampo (2009) provides a groundbreaking analysis of the effects of Catalan trade networks in Spain. It is striking how often Enlightenment testimonies account for the Catalan expansion throughout Spain in terms of the region's extreme poverty, an argument that was also used in the case of the Basques. I believe that this idea emerged in both cases as the product of Basque spin about conditions in their home provinces. In any event, the association between Basque and Catalan emigration and poverty was quite wrong.
13 Torras Elías (1990, 1991 and 1992), Fradera (1984), and Peiró (1987), (1995) and (2000).
14 Serra (1988), pp. 376 ff.
15 Ferrer (1987).
16 This process was explained by Vilar (1962 a).
17 Torras Elías (1978); Caminal, Canales and Torras (1983).
18 Vicedo (1991), pp. 56–71, 179–194 and 268–275.
19 Grain prices in markets like Lerida and Cervera were 30–40 per cent lower than in Barcelona in 1745, but the gap narrowed to only 20 per cent in the second half of the eighteenth century, and by 1800–1812 it had closed completely. The end of the process was accelerated by the post-war depression in international prices.
20 Explained in Tello (1995), pp. 109–157.
21 Torras Elías (1990).

22 The effects of inter- and intra-regional income redistribution must have been considerable, although they remain to be quantified. However, there is no space here to address this fundamental point. See Delgado Ribas (1987) and Peiró (1988) for a reference. The state also played an important role in other ways, for example as an investor. References in Pérez Sarrión (1989), pp. 253–254 and (2000), pp. 277–280.
23 For the case of Aragon, see Pérez Sarrión (2000) and (2002). The *equivalente* was not payable on goods in transit in Valencia, unless they entered a gated city where *alcabalas* were collected. See García Trobat (1999), pp. 71–72 and the legislation in pp. 231 ff.
24 Muset (1993).
25 Muset (1993), I, pp. 237–266 and II, pp. 507–532.
26 Torras Elías (1996).
27 Rulings of Philip V issued on 26 August 1715 and 1 October 1721 in response to queries from the Council of the Cámara de Castilla; addition of 7 September 1716 to the ordinance of the Cámara de Castilla of 1588 and a royal decree of 7 July 1723. All in NR, lib. I, tít. XIV, ley VI; ley VI nota 4; ley VI nota 5 and ley V, respectively —I, pp. 108–110—.
28 Muset (1996), p. 421.
29 Foraster (1996), p. 486.
30 Pérez Picazo (1996).
31 Martínez Shaw (1978), (1980), (1981) and (1983), Alfonso Mola and Martínez Shaw (1996), and Parejo Barranco and Sánchez Picón (1996).
32 Delgado and Fradera (1996). See also Oliva Melgar (1987) for a discussion of trade with America.
33 Alonso (1996).
34 Yun (1996).
35 Torres (1996).
36 Muset (1996 c). Rúa Fernández's research, which I have not had the opportunity to see, could significantly change these figures.
37 The expression 'comercio activo' means a trade surplus or favourable balance of trade.
38 Larruga (1787), I, pp. 82–83.
39 Roads suitable for carts and wagons.
40 The surviving records run from 23 August 1753 to 23 January 1815. AHMB, Gremis, libros 3-101, 3-104 and 3-105. The ordinances of the Barcelona mule drivers' guild were approved in 1765; AHN, Consejos (Consejo de Castilla), libro 5462. Carriers' guilds appear to have been common in the larger cities. There was also a carters' guild in Valencia whose ordinances date from 1778; AHN, Consejos (Consejo de Castilla), libro 5167. A *Hermandad del Camino de San Antonio Abad* existed in Madrid from the end of the seventeenth century. It was formed in the parish church of San Ginés, probably in 1697, and its members engaged in the hire of mules and litters. AHN, Consejos (Consejo de Castilla), libros 5023 and 5024, libros y papeles de 1698–1726. It was linked to the guild of *esparteros,* artisans who manufactured articles out of esparto grass (AHN, Consejos (Consejo de Castilla), libro 5105, de 1716). Its ordinances date from 1724 and its privileges were confirmed in 1765; respectively in AHN, Consejos (Consejo de Castilla), libros 5025 and 5026.
41 See also Muset (1995), pp. 85–86.
42 There is a very extensive literature on *foralismo* and the question of the abolition of the *fueros*. Among other recent references, see Simón Tarrés (1999), Lluch (1999), the

compilation of papers edited by Albareda Salvadó (2001), the papers published in *Revista de Historia Moderna* no. 25, and Albareda Salvadó (2010).

43 The author is referring to a process of commercial expansion. Catalan shops existed by this time, but not much earlier.

44 The author means the Spanish nation, to which the Catalans, the principality of Catalonia, the Castilians and the two Castiles all belonged.

45 Larruga (1787), vol. VII, t. XXI, pp. 168–169. The author intended to extend his *Memorias* to the realms of the Crown of Aragon, but he was unable to bring this idea to fruition, and his monumental work was only published for the Crown of Castile.

46 Larruga (1787), XI, volume XXXII, p. 240.

47 See the table in Feliu (1991), II, pp. 88–93.

48 Though they left some. Certain archives have been examined, but not in detail to my knowledge. The only such archive I know of left by the companies of emigrants from the Auvergne and Limousin is that of the *Compañía de Parla*, for which we have books of accounts dating from the end of the eighteenth and early nineteenth century; reference in Poitrineau (1985), p. 157. Documents also exist concerning the bankruptcies of French and Navarrese companies in Pamplona; Azcona (1997), p. 356 and (1999), p. 975 and passim. Logic suggests that other private archives must exist, probably in Bayonne and other places in France, which will appear over time.

49 These are the Arxiu de l'Institut Municipal d'Història, Barcelona, sección Fons Comercial (AHMB, FC), and the Arxiu Històric de Tarragona, Tarragona, sección Fons Comercial (AHT, FC).

50 These towns form the core of Muset's research (1996 a, 1996 b and 1997).

51 Torras Elias (2007).

52 For example the firm of Josep García and Josep Bover, and the companies of Altafulla and La Pobla de Montornés, respectively, which also leased agricultural rents in Aragon in 1760s, 1770s and 1780s. See below. Their accounts are in AHMB, FC, B191.

53 I refer to the ancillary customs office at Fraga just over the border with Aragon on the high road from Barcelona to Zaragoza.

54 See the titles of Muset's works in the bibliography, and the numerous other references included in the miscellany published by Pérez Picazo, Segura and Ferrer Alós (1996).

55 A detailed analysis will be found in Pérez Sarrión (1984 b).

56 Gómez Zorraquino (1988), figures in pp. 412–413, and (1990).

57 Book of accounts covering various years, AHMB, FC, B 191.

58 Caminal, Canales and Torras (1983), pp. 277–278. Some members of this group must also have had business dealings in Aragon, as they sometimes appear acting in concert with the other groups mentioned. I have not been able to establish this with certainty, however.

59 The *botiga* (i.e. shop) contracts were usually verbal: 'They were mostly "de fe i paraula"', Vilar (1962 a), IV, p. 166.

60 A Catalan town which was a centre for mule drivers and carters in the eighteenth century, as Muset has shown.

61 Gómez Zorraquino (1989).

62 Given the survival of a significant part of its archives. See Navarro (1977), Herrera (1979), Sales (1983), Muñoz (1984 and 1985), Pijuan (1984 and 1985), Gómez Zorraquino (1988, 1989 and 1990), Muset (1993) and Pérez Sarrión (1984 b, 1995 and 1996 a).

63 Antón Figarola y Sala, of Calaf; Josep Figarola y Sala, of Calaf; Isidro Bosch, of Calaf; Tomás Ignaci Soler, of Manresa; Josep Sagristá, of Manresa; and Maurici Soler, of Reus.

They were joined by Josep Cortadellas of Calaf and Francesc Cortadellas of Barcelona, nephew and uncle. Readers will observe an apparent unconcern as to the use of Catalan and Castilian forms for names. This is deliberate. The documents constantly switch from one language to the other depending on circumstances, such as the place where they were made or to whom they might have been addressed, so that the form of names frequently switches between Castilian and Catalan. In this light, it seems we do not need to make an issue out of what was clearly not one for the principals themselves. To respect this ambivalence and indifference, as well as its social significance, is the best homage we can pay to these cross-border entrepreneurs, who made a virtue out of necessity, living and integrating in two different communities, and who played a key role in the economic and cultural exchange between Aragon and Catalonia.

64 They contributed 44,675/5/10 *libras jaquesas* or 78,838/4/10 *libras catalanas* out of a total of 63,014/18/9 *libras jaquesas* or 111,202/16/4 *libras catalanas*; AHT, FC, C14, f. 2r.

65 As shown by the company's journal (1750–1775), AHT, FC, C72. Book C1 shows Francesc Cortadellas performing multiple transactions involving the purchase of agricultural commodities between 1733 and 1795. In C2 we find him leasing seigneurial rents and trading in silks between 1750 and 1775, both in partnership and individually. C4 reflects identical activities between 1771 and 1788.

66 The Manresa factory's books of account begin precisely on 12 May 1777, while those of the principal factory in Calaf managed by Isidre Bosch y Bosch and Isidre Bosch y Ribalta start on 12 June 1777, the very day on which the company was founded. These facilities already existed, then, and their owners integrated them with the new company's network. The Manresa accounts run from 12 May 1777 to 31 May 1797; AHT, FC, C11. The Calaf book spans the period 12 June 1777 to 31 May 1801. Isidre Bosch y Bosch was replaced on 5 May 1799 by another partner, Josep Figarola y Sala; AHT, FC, C12.

67 AHT, FC, book C95. Another current accounts ledger, C36, covering the period 1788–1797 refers to yet another beginning in 1775, before Soler, Bosch, Figarola y Compañía came into existence, which shows that these books had nothing to do with the firm itself. The archive of Josep Cortadellas comprises dozens of books of account belonging both to his own house and to other manufacturing and mercantile undertakings, including the Barcelona factory and a soap factory, as well as the commercial archive of the Satorras of Reus, where all of the documents ended up in the nineteenth century. The Cortadellas collection contained in the Arxiu Històric de Tarragona contains books of account and commercial correspondence, including orders dispatched by the firm to its partners and associates, and information revealing the functioning of the networks overall. These documents show that there was always something happening: a partner might die or another might marry; a son suddenly appears as an employee or a partner; a new business emerges at a greater distance; a little later an office is closed but another appears holding the same leases as its forerunner; and not long afterwards new partners turn up selling mules, silk or some other new product.

68 Feliu (1985). It is in a different archive, AHMB, FC, libro B191.

69 Based on data in Gómez Zorraquino (1988), pp. 416–418.

70 See Gómez Zorraquino (1988) and (2002), pp. 131–164 for a discussion of family strategies.

71 The absence of a factory does not necessarily mean there was no business. The books of account recorded income from localities where there was no factory, as shown by

the central journal kept in Calaf, in AHT, FC, C13. Figures in Pérez Sarrión (1984 b), table II, pp. 227–229.

72 See Sales (1983).

73 Described in detail in Navarro (1977).

74 Based on the information provided in the excellent studies by Muñoz (1984 and 1985).

75 Segarra (1994), pp. 223–258.

76 Examined in Pérez Sarrión (1984 b).

77 Thanks to the excellent studies by Pijuan (1984 and 1985).

78 It was sometimes necessary to pay sweeteners to secure the lease of seigneurial rents at the auctions attended by the Cortadellas group. Such amounts, known as the *aumento callado* in Spanish or *augment callat* in Catalan, would be handed out among other bidders to ensure their acquiescence. The evidence for this comes from two notarial instruments formalizing leases in Barcelona; Pijuan (1984), p. 773.

79 The Lerida market was tightly regulated. Public granary tariffs exist from 28 July 1750, as well as ordinances of the *almudí* (granary) dated 1 April 1761 and weights and measures from 13 March 1761; APL, Administració/Proveiments i Consums, box 1540. The books of wheat and barley prices at the city granary have been conserved, APL, llibres 305 (29 November 1727 to 1 December 1755), 306 (28 July 1757 to 31 December 1781) ff., together with the maximum and minimum prices for wheat ('xexa' and 'mescladis') and barley for each day. Some books of account kept by the city's flour mills have also survived for the years 1711–1752 ff. in APL, Administración/Proveiments i Consums, books 293 to 301 ff. The Catalan merchants acquired properties in the city, either by investing directly or in settlement of loans. These transactions can be traced through the almost 250 books of the Catastro: APL, Hisenda/Cadastre, 1716–1837.

80 Pijuan (1985), pp. 263–286.

81 He was therefore a forbear of the Josep Cortadellas who lived at the end of the century.

82 They leased tithes and rents from the Marquis de Santa Cruz in Balaguer, in the villages of Puigvert and Tarrós, from the priory of the Order of Malta in Urgel (several times), rents in Santa Fe, Sant Grim de la Plana, Ceró and in Agramunt, in Termes, in the barony of Alguaire, half tithes belonging to the Carthusian monastery and to the lord of Albesa, in Ardévol and rents in other villages belonging to the Duchy of Cardona.

83 For example, the tithes and other seigneurial rents of Balaguer were leased by Teresa Cortadellas between 1755 and 1759 'como usufructuaria dels bens que foren del q.° Josep Cortadellas y Josep Argullol', who formed a company with Odón Burgués of Barcelona, while the rents of the county of Prades in the duchy of Cardona were leased between 1768 and 1771 by the partners, who held the following interests in the transaction: Teresa (1/4) and Francesc Cortadellas (1/4), associates of Josep Freixas y Mallada y Cía. of Lérida (remaining 2/4). Many of these activities appear in AHT, FC, book C2.

84 Antón Valldejuli (broker), Ramón Pujol Cantarell y Cía., Agustí Roig, Salvador Molet Valer, Joaquim Roca i Batlle, all of Barcelona; Jaume Roig, of Valencia; Bartolomeu Cerdá, of Sitges; Josep Freixas i Mallada y Cía., of Lerida; AHT, FC, book C2, ff. 88v and 99v. Others who later become their partners also appear, including Josep Argullol i Comes (who became a partner in the lease of rents in the duchy of Cardona), Miquel and Andreu Puiggrós, Josep Argullol i Vidal, Josep Iglésies, and other merchants of Mataró, Barcelona (the main distribution centre) and from the towns of the interior like Calaf, Sabadell and Vich; AHT, FC, book C1.

85 They sold *indianas* to F. Laventana ('en Verdú') and raw silk ('fina' and 'adúcar') to Francisco Piñol, both of Sástago; silk and cotton cloth (*indianas*) to Pelegrín Muñoz of Velilla de Ebro; and salt cod and rice from the Ampurdán district to Francisco Espuñes of Binaced; AHT, FC, book C2.

86 The last general ledger and journal kept together by Josep and Francesc Cortadellas before the formation of Soler, Bosch, Figarola y Compañía runs from 30 May 1775 to 26 August 1777, and it provides clear evidence that they already had dealings in Aragon at this time. It also includes backdated accounts of Teresa Puiggrós y Soler (widow of the merchant Andreu Puiggrós and probably kin to the future partners of Soler, Bosch, Figarola y Compañía) with Miquel Puiggrós of Calaf; the leases of rents from the baronies of Bellpuig and Llinyola (as of 7 September 1768), the *noveno* of Vilanova de la Aguda and the manor of Falcons, and the rents of the Marquis de Rubí; AHT, FC, book C0. Further testimony is provided by the map in Navarro (1977), pp. 160–161.

87 AHT, FC, book C1.

88 As well as one customer in Adahuesca, Aragon, and the chapter of Lerida cathedral.

89 According to the journal covering the period 30 May 1788 to 15 May 1807; AHT, FC, book C36. Other books reflect the business of Josep Cortadellas, conducted either alone or with other partners, which was not included in the accounts of Soler, Bosch, Figarola y Compañía; see C35, C48, C58, C72, C80, C95, C96 and C97. As a whole, these accounts run to 1809. The last two, which end in 1802, refer to Josep Cortadellas y Cía. A new company was created to continue the founder's business on his death.

90 *Libro de caja de la Sociedad de los señores 'Soler, Bosch, Figarola y Cía.' de Calaf, vulgarmente conocida por la Compañía de Aragón, a cargo de Josep Cortadellas de dicha villa, que empieza en 14 de mayo de 1777 en que se formó la contrata de la sociedad y concluye en 11 diciembre de 1809 en que falleció dicho señor Cortadellas*. This journal is followed by the liquidation accounts kept after 1 December 1809 by Manuel Lasala as the liquidator of the business of Josep Cortadellas; AHT, FC, book C13. The Compañía de Aragón continued its business, however, although it was much changed.

91 Pérez Sarrión (1984 b).

92 Huesca was the Aragonese city with the largest community of Catalans in relative terms in the eighteenth century, because the closure of the Catalan universities as a result of the *Decretos de Nueva Planta* brought large numbers of students from the principality to the University of Huesca. Catalans figured prominently among the students enrolled in almost all faculties between 1700 and 1845: Medicine (65.17 per cent of the total), Civil Law (48.15 per cent), Arts (25.07 per cent), Canon Law (29.34 per cent) and Theology (5.58 per cent). There were regularly around 200 Catalan students in the city for a period of around 140 years. Excluding the period 1809 to 1845, when their numbers dropped sharply, there would have been even more. In 1720–1769 there were 1,711 Catalan out of a total 3,750 students, and in 1770–1809 there were 1,714 Catalans out of 4,060 students, because at this time bachelors from the University of Cervera began to arrive to complete their degrees and study for doctorates, which they could only do in Huesca according to prevailing regulations. If each student remained at the university for five years, there would have been 171.1 Catalan scholars in Huesca permanently between 1720 and 1769, and 214.2 in the period 1770–1809 when the Cortadellas expanded their business to the city. The primary data are taken from Gracia (1994), pp. 277–327.

93 All, or almost all, of the books of account survive: AHT, FC, at least books C7 (12 June 1777 to 25 June 1785), C26 (1 June 1785 to 29 June 1790), C40 (1 July 1790 to

30 September 1792), C54 (1 April 1794 to 31 May 1801) and C19 (loose papers and accounts of the Huesca office with third parties for the period 1801–1803).

The books contain a wealth of information. One alone may provide sufficient material for a monograph like the splendid study published by Pierre Vilar (1962 b) on the *Companya Nova* of Gibraltar, or provide the basis for complex analyses of the office's affairs and management like Feliu (1985). Several together, whether referring to one or more companies, provide the elements for such illuminating work as the recent papers by Rodríguez González (1995) (on the Castilian merchants of the sixteenth century, including the famous Simón Ruiz), Maixé (1994) and Lobato (1995), both of whom examine Catalan firms.

94 For example, those cited by Salas (1983), p. 65, note 1.

95 See, for example, the reference in AHT, FC, book C7, f. 18.

96 AHT, FC, book C29.

97 Fontana (2002), p. 28.

98 Information comes from the surviving general ledger and journal (1801–1812), which bears the title *Ballobar. A cargo de Francisco Soler y Solanes. Relaciones dadas a los señores Soler, Bosch, Figarola y Cía. de Calaf* and runs from 7 August 1801 to 28 February 1812; AHT, FC, book C69. The accounts are annual from 1801 until 1809, except the last, which spans a little less than three years from June 1809 to February 1812 because of the war. This case is studied in detail in Pérez Sarrión (1996 a), pp. 271–284. The company's activity in this area was also the subject of another interesting study in Berenguer Galindo (1966).

99 At least five different, mostly ecclesiastical, rents were managed between 1794 and 1834. Details in AHT, FC, book C49.

100 See inventories, for example in AHT, FC, book C69, ff. 7r–8r and 27v–28r.

101 At this time, the partners were buying up considerable quantities of silk and wool in the area, but these purchases were not recorded in the factory's books, as it confined itself to receiving cash and financing transactions.

102 The loans were made *con comanda* (i.e. witnessed by a notary), *con vale* (ordinary written contracts) and *de palabra* (verbal contracts). An early sixteenth-century notarial record from Aragon contains a *comanda*, at that time called a *carta de encomienda*, in which the declarant represents as follows: 'manifiesto tener *en comienda* puro y fiel depósito de vos N. . . . "un préstamo de dinero, y como prenda" . . . en general y especial obligación pongo un campo tal' (the italics are my own). In principle, this was a cash loan backed by an *obligación* or mortgage charge on real property; *Formulario* . . . (1523) pp. 76–81. The record also includes deeds formalizing 'comanda concellal' transactions and *cancellations* of *comanda* and *deudo* charges; *Formulario* . . . (1523), pp. 81–83. In their treatise on Castilian and Aragonese civil law, Asso and Manuel mention different types of loan arrangements in Aragon, including the 'escritura de encomienda, o depósito', which is a 'crédito manifiesto' formalized in a public deed in contrast to other forms of private ('no manifiesto') loans; Asso and Manuel (1771), pp. 197–198. The latter formula would be a loan made *con vale*. See also Sala (1783).

103 For example, the following entry was made in the accounts by the Ballobar agent on 10 February 1802: 'Me hago cargo de 2.000 l[ibras] Jaq[uesa]s. q[u]e. he recibido de d[o]n Juan Escuer de La Almolda en virtud de carta orden q[ue] contra d[ic]ho dio en 31 Diz[iembr]e 1801 d[o]n Mig[ue]l Miguel a favor de d[o]n Josef Cortadellas, y por su dorso de 6 de febrero 1802 a d[o]n Man[ue]l Sarasa quien en 8 corriente dorsó [sic] a mi favor'; AHT, FC, C69, f. 21r. Including the intermediary and the two

endorsements, the money order had passed through five different hands and was in circulation for 40 days, avoiding the need for three movements of cash, which was transferred directly from an account in La Almolda to the account in Ballobar.

104 Based on the case of Luceni, near Zaragoza, a manor owned by the countess of Fuenclara; see Pérez Sarrión (1984 a), pp. 198–206. The case outlined here is described in detail in Pérez Sarrión (1984 b).

105 They had attempted to irrigate and cultivate three new lots of common land, but the countess demanded the same seigneurial rents as were paid on her own land. The peasants went to court, winning their suit in 1800.

106 As may be observed in Josep Cortadellas' letter of reply to the dowager countess of Fuenclara dated 25 June 1803; AHT, FC, Ca27, f. 624, reproduced in Pérez Sarrión (1984 b), p. 230.

107 Torras Elías (2007). See Benaul (1992) for a discussion of the important Sabadell and Terrassa companies.

108 All of the information is taken from Torras Elías (2007), passim.

109 Torras Elías (2010), summary in Spanish of Torras Elías (2007), pp. 102–111 and 159–191. The correspondence of Josep Torelló for 1771 reflects connections with some 66 different individuals, of whom 51 were Catalan. They included carters, family members, correspondents, other manufacturers, suppliers of wool and merchants. Reference in Torras Elías (2007), p. 180.

110 The sources for the study are in the *fons de fallides* or bankruptcy archive of the Consulado de Comercio in Barcelona, which was briefly examined by Vilar and more exhaustively by Muset (1993). It holds a wealth of documents, especially books of account and letters of bankrupt companies which placed their archives at the disposal of the courts. They form the *Fons Patrimonial* or *Fons Comercial* section of the Archivo Histórico Municipal belonging to the Institut Municipal d'Historia, Barcelona.

111 Books in AHMB, FC, B 85, B 86 and B 87.

112 As shown in Muset (1993), I, pp. 222–225.

113 Given his surname, of French or Catalano-Valencian origin.

114 Current accounts ledger (1725–1733, in reality debtors), AHMB, FC, B 87. An entry dated 11 September 1728 mentions goods which 'li avem remes per Joseph Labado, arriero aragonés'. The reference to the Madrid-based merchant is in f. 204.

115 Current accounts ledger (1725–1733), AHMB, FC, B 87. See, for example, fol. 139, which lists all of the mutual transactions entered into from 25 June to 1 October 1729. Further details cannot be obtained from commercial correspondence as the letters have been lost.

116 *Comerciantes banqueros* was the term coined by the Treasury Ministry in 1870 to describe these credit agents; García López (1989), p. 115.

117 Stocks were inventoried, together with balances due to creditors and the total debt assumed by the new company.

118 According to current account ledgers. The book for the period 1770–1771 lists 139 customers, and the 1775 ledger 189; AHMB, FC, B 270 and B 271.

119 A meeting at which the profit and loss of the company was settled.

120 The partners in the period 1792–1796 were different, comprising Miquel Formantí, Antón Gasset and María Formantí Gusta; journal (1784–1802), AHMB, FC, B 143.

121 They are actually listed as *velers*. Silk weavers were called *veleros* or sometimes *velluteros* in Aragon. However, this term was sometimes applied to the makers and purveyors of ship's sails in both Spanish and Catalan.

122 *Cabals, cabdals* or *caudales*, meaning the capital or funds put up by each of the partners.
123 General ledger (1766–1806), AHMB, FC, B47. This book contains two private contracts, draft customer accounts and the *pasamientos de cuentas* or balances, which were closed annually in the case of this firm.
124 The majority of the company's Aragonese customers were resident in Zaragoza between 1789 and 1795 according to the data in Muset (1993, III, pp. 867–870) drawn from the current account ledgers in AHMB, FC, B 51 (1784–1790) and B 50 (1791–1807).
125 Current accounts ledger (1797–1807), AHMB, FC, B 339.
126 Muset (1993), I, pp. 271–272.
127 Store sales ledger (1782–1783), AHMB, FC, B 338.
128 Partially studied in Muset (1988).
129 Journal (1780–1794), AHMB, FC, B 124.
130 As shown by the commercial correspondence; correspondence books (1767–1770 and 1795–1803), AHMB, FC, B 127 and B 132.
131 All of the company's correspondence was written in Spanish, including letters sent to the firm's people in Catalonia, and it is noticeable that the distinctively Aragonese diminutive suffix *–ico* is frequently used.
132 Only a few commercial letters survive in the correspondence books (1788–1791 and 1791–1794), AHMB, FC, B 40 and B 41.
133 See the useful references in Muset (1996 c), in particular the mention of inns, pp. 55–56.
134 Correspondence book (1783–1785), AHMB, FC, B 142.
135 The dye was provided by Pedro Lasala. Letter of 2 August 1783 and 9 August 1783, correspondence book (1783–1785), AHMB, FC, B 142.
136 Showing credits, debits and the balance in cash and in kind.
137 Current accounts ledger (1770–1771), AHMB, FC, B 270.
138 His actual name was Juan Sallarés, while 'Bonich' is a nickname meaning 'handsome', which we might render in English as 'Bonny John'. See below.
139 When the new firm of Cirés was formed on 3 December 1770. The inventory of assets begins of 1 October 1770, listing tools and equipment at the Cirés factory and at the factory 'dels Sors. Alegres y Gibert'. It appears that the new company included both. Cirés provided capital of 5,528 *libras catalanas*, and Alegrés and Gibert contributed 21,015 *libras catalanas*. The book is in AHMB, FC, B 227.
140 According to a contemporary dictionary, the term *vale* denotes 'papel o seguro que se hace a favor de otro, obligándose a pagarle alguna cantidad de dinero' (*Diccionario de Autoridades*, edition of 1739, s. v. 'vale').
141 He had his own cart, which he used together with his brother-in-law, Pablo Filieu (possibly French), another partner called Félix Soler and 'su criado el Negret'. María Formentí y Gusta y Compañía of Barcelona to Pedro de Torón of Zaragoza, 31 October 1783, correspondence book of María Formentí y Gusta y Compañía of Barcelona, AHMB, FC, B 142.
142 María Formentí y Gusta y Compañía of Barcelona to Pedro de Torón of Zaragoza, 24 December 1783, correspondence book of María Formentí y Gusta y Compañía of Barcelona, AHMB, FC, B 142.
143 For a discussion of the Barcelona bourgeoisie, see Molas (1978), (1980) and (1985).
144 Fernández Díaz (1982), pp. 36–37 and 39–40.

145 In that year, the Ballobar factory complained that 'la adm[inistraci]o de mon carrech se extinguit per ella mateixa per faltar los arrendaments'. The loans made in the village by the Compañía de Aragón totalled around 15,000 *libras jaquesas* in 1801 and the same in 1809, when numerous new loans were made. The business dried up almost completely after 1809, however. In 1812, the factory's total revenues were in the region of 123,000 *libras jaquesas* but lending had practically stopped. What was left was uncollectable debt, which the borrowers could not repay.
146 Precisely the two factors which formed the basis for the success of these companies in the nineteenth century according to Chandler (1990).
147 See Pérez Sarrión (1984 b).
148 See Ringrose (1996), chap. 3, pp. 90–123, for a discussion of this interesting interpretation of Spanish economic growth in the eighteenth and nineteenth centuries.
149 The meaning of this peripheralization is addressed in Fernández Clemente and Pérez Sarrión (1985), and the mobilization of productive resource is discussed in Feliu (1985) and Gómez Zorraquino (1988).
150 The period in which an operation was deemed a cash transaction so that no interest was charged on the debt.
151 Hudson (1986), pp. 211–270.
152 See Tomás (1965), pp. 18–21, in Pérez Sarrión (1999), pp. 478–480.
153 Until they became what the Treasury Ministry began to call *comerciantes-banqueros* in 1870, a term that would survive until well into the twentieth century; García López (1985) and (1989), p. 115.
154 García López (1990).
155 García López (1990), pp. 129–135 and tables 4 and 5. The average balance of debt in the period 1843–1852 represented only around one third of assets, but the trend was for growth in such financial assets. The institution was at once a merchant bank and a trading house, as it had been in the eighteenth century.

Manuscripts and Printed Sources up to 1900

Abreu y Bertodano, Joseph Antonio (1740–1745), *Colección de los tratados de paz, alianza, neutralidad, garantía, tregua, mediación, accesión, reglamento de límites, comercio, navegación, &c. Hechos por los pueblos, reyes y principes de España con los pueblos, reyes, príncipes y demás potencias de Europa, y otras partes del mundo; y entre sí mismos, y con sus respectivos adversarios: y juntamente de los hechos directa o indirectamente contra ella, desde antes del establecimiento de la Monarquía Góthica . . . Reynado del Sr. Rey D. Phelipe III* partes I [años 1598–1621] (1740–1744, 3 tomos), y II [años 1609–1621] (1745, 1 tomo). Juan de Zúñiga, Antonio Marín, Diego Peralta, Madrid. Facsimile edition in José Andrés-Gallego (ed.), *Tratados internacionales de España 1598–1700*, Fundación Histórica Tavera (Clásicos Tavera núm. 37, CD-ROM), Madrid 2000.

Abreu y Bertodano, Joseph Antonio (1746–1750), *Colección de los tratados de paz, alianza, neutralidad, garantía, tregua, mediación, accesión, reglamento de límites, comercio, navegación, &c. Hechos por los pueblos, reyes y principes de España con los pueblos, reyes, príncipes y demás potencias de Europa, y otras partes del mundo; y entre sí mismos, y con sus respectivos adversarios: y juntamente de los hechos directa o indirectamente contra ella, desde antes del establecimiento de la Monarquía Góthica. . . Reynado del Sr. Rey D. Phelipe IV*, partes I [años 1621–1626], II [años 1627–1634], III [años 1635–1641], IV [años 1642–1646], V [años 1647–1648], VI [años 1649–VII/1659] y VII [años 1659–1665] (1746–1750, 7 tomos). Juan de Zúñiga, Antonio Marín, Viuda de Peralta, Madrid. Facsimile edition in José Andrés-Gallego (ed.), *Tratados internacionales de España 1598–1700*, Fundación Histórica Tavera (Clásicos Tavera núm. 37, CD-ROM), Madrid 2000.

Abreu y Bertodano, Joseph Antonio (1751–1752), *Colección de los tratados de paz, alianza, neutralidad, garantía, tregua, mediación, accesión, reglamento de límites, comercio, navegación, &c. Hechos por los pueblos, reyes y principes de España con los pueblos, reyes, príncipes y demás potencias de Europa, y otras partes del mundo; y entre sí mismos, y con sus respectivos adversarios: y juntamente de los hechos directa o indirectamente contra ella, desde antes del establecimiento de la Monarquía Góthica. . . Reynado del Sr. Rey D. Carlos II*, partes I [años 1665–1674], II [años 1674–1682] y III [años 1683–1/XI/1700] (1751–1752, 3 tomos). Juan de Zúñiga, Antonio Marín, Viuda de Peralta, Madrid. Facsimile edition in José Andrés-Gallego (ed.), *Tratados internacionales de España 1700–1902*, Fundación Histórica Tavera (Clásicos Tavera núm. 38, CD-ROM), Madrid 2000.

Actas de las Cortes de Navarra (1530–1829) (1991–1996), edited by Luis Javier Fortún Pérez de Ciriza, Parlamento de Navarra, Pamplona, 19 vols.

Aguirre, Joaquín de (1759), 'Abusos que se cometen en el manejo y dirección de todas las Rentas reales. Universales remedios para que logre el Erario los beneficios que hoy le faltan y a la monarquía española toda gloria y esplendor de que carece', in *Semanario Erudito* de Valladares, t. XI (20 September 1759) pp. 36–80. Cited from Muñoz (1955).

Anales de las ordenanzas de correos de España (1879–1881), Imprenta Central, Madrid, 5 vols. Volume 1 contains the legislation for the period 1283–1819.

Arancel . . . (1709) *. . . para la renta de diezmos y puertos. dado en Madrid en diez y seis días del mes de Septiembre, año de mil setecientos y nueve*, Imprenta Real, Zaragoza 1709. A copy will be found in AGS, DGR, leg. II-471.

Argumosa Gándara, Theodoro Ventura (1743), *Erudicción [=erudición] política, despertador sobre el comercio, agricultura y manufacturas, con avisos de buena policía y aumento del Real Erario, su autor don Theodoro Ventura de Argumossa Gandara, señor de Campén, Caballerizo de Campo del rey Nuestro Señor y veedor de Guerra en la costa de Granada etc. quien le dedica a la Real Junta [General] de Comercio y Moneda*, s. e., Madrid 1743.

Autos acordados . . . (1777) *. . . por el orden de título de las leyes de la Recopilación*, J. Ibarra, Madrid 1777, 4 vols. A copy can be found in BNE sig. 2/10429 to 2/10432.

Asso y del Río, Ignacio Jordán de and Manuel Rodríguez, Miguel de (1771), *Instituciones de derecho civil de Castilla, por los doctores don . . . y don . . . Van añadidas al fin de cada título las diferencias qeu de este Derecho se observan en Aragón por disposición de sus fueros*, Imprenta de Francisco Xavier García, Madrid; *. . . edicion quinta corregida notablemente y aumentada la parte histórica que comprehende la introducción*, Imprenta de Ramón Ruiz, Madrid 1792, facsimile edition Lex Nova, Valladolid 1984.

Aznar, Bernardo Francisco (1728), *Discurso que formó tocante a la Real Hacienda y administración de ella don . . ., del Consejo de su Magestad y su Contador General de Millones. En el se incluyen entre otros tratados, todas las Rentas que su Magestad goza en las dos Castilla, Galicia y Asturias; y se declara también cuáles Rentas se pueden suprimir o moderar por ser muy perjudicial su práctica y continuación; y cuáles pueden quedar en su ser sin novedad alguna*, s. l., s. e. [1728]. This work would have been printed at the earliest in 1728, although perhaps somewhat later.

Barberi, Mateo Antonio (1768), *Cartas político instructivas sobre las ventajas que facilita el comercio y proporciones del reino de Aragón para practicarlo. Primera. Escribióla D. . . .*, José Fort, Zaragoza.

Boisguillebert, Pierre Le Pesant, seigneur de (1697), *Le detail de la France. Cause de la diminution de ses biens et de la facilité de son reméde en fournissant en un mois tout l'argent dons le roy a besoin, et enrichissant tout le monde*, in *Collection des principaux economistes. Tome 1. Economistes financiers du 18e siécle . . . precedés de notices historiques sur chaque auteur et accompagnés de notes explicatives par M. Eugène Daire*, Otto Zeller, Osnabruck 1966 (reprinted from the 1843 edition), pp. 171–266.

Bordázar de Artazu, Antonio (1736), *Proporción de monedas, pesos y medidas, con principios prácticos de arithmética y geometría, para su uso*, Imprenta de Antonio Bordázar de Artazu, Valencia.

Cabarrús, Francisco (1783), *Memoria sobre la protección que necesita el comercio y el establecimiento de los extranjeros en España*, Madrid 22 March 1783, manuscript; AHN, Estado, leg. 2944 exp. 434. I attribute this title to the text because the author himself uses it in his letter of submission to Floridablanca.

Campillo Cossío, José (1739), *Lo que hay en España demás y de menos, para que sea lo que debe ser y no lo que es*, manuscript, and *España despierta: obra que sirve de segunda parte a su papel intitulado Lo que hay en España demás y de menos*, manuscript, Madrid 1739. The date of writing attributed varies between 1739 and 1742 depending on the copy. The original has been lost. The texts were published for the first time by Antonio Elorza under the same title with an introductory study, Madrid 1979. Another edition has since been published under the title *Dos escritos políticos. Lo que hay de más y menos en España. España despierta*, edited with an introductdory study by María Dolores Mateos, Junta General del Principado de Asturias, Oviedo 1993 (the unpublished manuscripts date from 1739).

Campillo y Cossío, José (1743), *Nuevo sistema de gobierno económico para la América: con los males y daños que le causa el que hoy tiene, de los que le participa copiosamente España y remedios universales para que la primera tenga considerables ventaxas y la segunda mayores intereses, escrito por el señor don. . . . Primera y segunda parte. Año de 1743*. Imprenta de Benito Cano, Madrid. There are two recent editions, one published by Universidad de los Andes, Facultad de Humanidades y Educación, Mérida (Venezuela) 1971, and other with an introduction and notes by Manuel Ballesteros Gaibrois, Grupo Editorial Asturiano, Oviedo 1993.

Cantillo, Alejandro del (1843), *Tratados, convenios y declaraciones de paz y de comercio que han hecho con las potencias estranjeras los monarcas españoles de la Casa de Borbón. Desde el año de 1700 hasta el día. Puestos en orden e ilustrados muchos de ellos con la historia de sus respectivas negociaciones. Por don . . . oficial que ha sido en la primera Secretaría de Estado y del Despacho*. Imprenta Alegría y Charlain, Madrid 1843. Facsimile edition in José Andrés-Gallego (ed.), *Tratados internacionales de España 1700–1902*, Fundación Histórica Tavera (Clásicos Tavera núm. 38, CD-ROM), Madrid 2000.

Capmany y Montpalau, Antonio de (1796–1801), *Colección de los tratados de paz, alianza, comercio etc. ajustados por la Corona de España con las potencias extranjeras desde el reynado del señor don Felipe Quinto hasta el presente. Publícase por disposición del Exmo. Señor Príncipe de la Paz, consejero y Primer Secretario de Estado, grande de España de primera clase, etc. etc.*, tomes I [1701–1716], 1796; II [1717–1748], 1800; and III [1749–1801], 1801, Imprenta Real, Madrid. Facsimile edition in José Andrés-Gallego (ed.), *Tratados internacionales de España 1700–1902*, Fundación Histórica Tavera (Clásicos Tavera núm. 38, CD-ROM), Madrid 2000. The work was published anonymously, although its author was in fact Antonio de Capmany y Montpalau according to J. Andrés-Gallego.

Carvajal Lancáster, José de (1745), *Testamento político, reducido a una idea de un gobierno cathólico, político, militar y económico como conviene para la resurección y conservación de España* (ff. 3–136v) and *Mis pensamientos* (ff. 137–168), manuscripts, Madrid 12 September 1745, bound copy, 180 ff., in BNE, Mss/10687. There are also two identical manuscripts in BNE Mss/10446 and Mss 11065. Another copy of *Mis pensamientos*, Madrid 12 September 1745, will be found in BNE, Mss/10676. The first of these works was published under the same title in Delgado (1999).

Cary, John (1695), *An Essay on the State of England In Relation to its Trade, its Poor, and its Taxes, For Carrying on the Present War against France*, W. Bonny, London.

Colección de órdenes generales de Rentas, eighteenth century, manuscript, AHN, FC, books 8009 to 8109.

Colección legislativa de la deuda pública de España, Imprenta Nacional, Madrid 1859–1870, 10 volumes and 2 volumes of appendices.

Concordia, hecha entre la c. y r. Magestad del rey don Phelipe . . . y el tribunal del Santo Oficio de la Inquisición del reyno de Aragon, que se hizo a 17 de julio de 1568, s. l., s. a., BCAZ L-632.

Copia del auto acordado de la Real Audiencia de Zaragoza para el mejor y más exacto cumplimiento de la Cédula Real acerca del extrañamiento de franceses (1793), Imprenta Real, Zaragoza.

Correo Mercantil de España y sus Indias, El, Madrid 1792–1808.

Coyer, abbé, Gabriel-François (1756), *La noblesse commerçante*, chez Duchesne, Paris.

Coyer, abbé, Gabriel-François (1781), *La nobleza comerciante: traducción del tratado que escribió en francés el abaye Coyer, hecha para utilidad de la Real Sociedad Económica de*

Amigos del País de Mallorca, con un discurso preliminar, y varias notas. Por Don Jacobo Maria de Spinosa y Cantabrana . . ., Joaquín Ibarra, Madrid.

Cuaderno de leyes de la provincia de Alava (1761) (handwritten title), s. l., s. a. (the year comes from Floranes (1776), p. 88). Earlier editions were also published. This copy is in BNE sig. 3/40546.

Cuadernos de las leyes y agravios reparados por los tres estados del Reino de Navarra (1896), Diputación Foral de Navarra, Institución Príncipe de Viana, Pamplona 1964, 2 vols (1st edition, Imprenta de Miguel de Cosculluela, Pamplona 1797–1798, complete first edition Imprenta Provincial, Pamplona 1896, 2 vols). The 1964 edition comprises the books containing parliamentary records for the period 1724 to 1829.

Davenant, Charles (1771), *Political and Commercial Works*, Whitworth, London, 5 vols.

Defoe, Daniel (1727), *The Complete English Tradesman*, Alan Sutton Publishing, Gloucester 1987 (original edition *The Compleat English Tradesman. Vol. II. In two parts. Part I. Directed chiefly to the more experienc'd tradesmen; with cautions and advices to them after they are thriven . . . Part II. Being useful generals in trade, describing the principles and foundation of the home trade of Great Britain, with large tables of our manufactures, etc.*, Charles Rivington, London.

Encyclopédie ou dictionaire raisonné des sciences des arts et des métiers, pars une société des gens de lettres. Mis en ordre et publiée par M. Diderot, de l'Academie Royale des Sciences et des Belles-Lettres de Prusse; et quant à la Partie Mathématique, par M. D'Alembert, de l'Académie Royale des Sciences de Paris et celle de la Prusse, et de la Société Royale de Londres (1751–1780). Various publishers (Briasson, David, Le Breton and Durand), Paris, 35 vols. Facsimile edition published by Friedrich Fromann Verlag, Stuttgart-Bad Cannstatt 1966.

Ensenada, Marquis of (1751), see Somodevilla.

Expilly [J. J.] (1762–1770), *Dictionaire géographique, historique et politique des Gaules et de la France. Par l'Abbé . . .*, ed. Desaint & Saillant, Bauché, Durand, París, 6 vols. Floranes, Rafael de (1771?), *Discurso sobre el origen del derecho de diezmo, la antigüedad de las aduanas de Cantabria y libertad del comercio de las tres Provincias Vascongadas*, written after 1771, BRAH, ms., 12-24-1-B-10. Cited from Muñoz (1955).

Floranes, Rafael (1776), *Discurso histórico y legal sobre la esención y libertad de las tres nobles provincias vascongadas. Origen del derecho de diezmos y el de las aduanas de Cantabria. Escribíale por su encargo D. . . . hoy señor de Tavaneros, socio y académico de mérito de las reales sociedad y academias de Jurisprudencia y Cirugía de Valladolid. Hallándose en la ciudad de Vitoria el año. . .*, manuscript, BNE, Manuscritos, MSS/10601.

Floridablanca, José Moñino Redondo, Count of (1788), 'Memorial presentado al rey Carlos III y repetido a Carlos IV, por el conde de Floridablanca, renunciando a su ministerio', in Conde de Floridablanca, *Escritos políticos. La Instrucción y el Memorial*, Edited with a study and biographical notes by Joaquín Ruiz Alemán, Academia Alfonso X el Sabio, Murcia 1982, pp. 287–416.

Formulario de actos extrajudiciales de la sublime arte de la notaría [1523], Junta de Decanos de los Colegios Notariales de España, Editorial Reus, Madrid 1968.

Gallardo Fernández, F. (1805), *Origen, progresos y estado de las rentas de la corona de España, su gobierno y administración*, Imprenta Real, Madrid, 2 vols.

Garriga, Juan Bautista (n.d.), *Recopilación de órdenes de Rentas Generales. Por D. . . ., administrador general de las de Galicia*, manuscript, 6 tomes, AMH sig. 961 to 966. Retrieved on 10 November 2015 from http://biblioteca.meh.es.

Hidalgo González, Joaquín (1806), *Historia de las Dependencias de Extranjeros*, ms., 3 vols, AMAEP Mss, 141–143 and 203.

Ibarra y Larrea, Luis de, and Cuéllar, Francisco de (1759), *Memoria sobre el establecimiento y origen de todas las rentas que componen el Real Herario*, Madrid 1759, AHN, Estado, leg. 3211-1. The authors were Directores Generales de Rentas in 1766 (AGS, SSH, leg. 1062). Cited from García-Cuenca (1983).
Journal de Trévoux, o Memoires pour l'histoire des sciences et Beaux-arts, commencés d'etre imprimés l'an 1701 à Trévoux, et dédiés à son Altesse Serenissime Monseigneur le Prince Souverain de Dombes (1701–1767), Paris, republished in facsimile, Slatkine, Geneva 1969.
Jovellanos, Gaspar M. (1984–1999), *Obras completas*, critical edition, introduction and notes by José Miguel Caso González, Centro de Estudios del siglo XVIII and Ayuntamiento de Gijón, 4 vols, Oviedo.
Junta de Comerç de Barcelona (1780), *Discurso sobre la agricultura, comercio e industria del principado de Cataluña* (1780), edited by Ernest Lluch, Alta Fulla, Barcelona 1997.
Labat, Jean Baptiste (1730), *Voyages du P. Labat, de l'ordre des FF. Prescheurs, en Espagne et en Italie*, 8 vols, Jean Baptiste Delespine, Paris.
Larruga y Boneta, Eugenio (1789), *Historia de la Real y General Junta de Comercio, Moneda, Minas y Dependencias de Extranjeros. Colección íntegra de los Reales Decretos, Pragmáticas, Resoluciones, Órdenes y Reglamentos que por puntos generales se han expedido para el gobierno de los Comercios y manufacturas del Reyno. Compuesta en virtud de Reales Resoluciones a consulta de la misma Junta. Por Don . . .*, Madrid 1789, 10 tomes in 13 volumes, manuscript, BMH 479A, 479B and 479C. Only six copies were made 'como [=porque] no ha de tener otro uso que el de personas instruidas' (Larruga 1789, I, f. XXIII).
Larruga y Boneta, Eugenio (1787), *Memorias políticas y económicas sobre los frutos, comercio, fábricas y minas de España, con inclusión de los reales decretos, órdenes, cédulas, aranceles y ordenanzas expedidas para su gobierno y fomento*, Madrid, Benito Cano (tomes I and II, 1787–1788) and Antonio Espinosa (tomes III to XLIII, 1788–1798). Facsimile edition with prefatory remarks by Ernest Lluch, Eloy Fernández Clemente and Alfonso Sánchez Hormigo and an introduction by Josep Fontana, Institución 'Fernando el Católico', Gobierno de Aragón and Instituto Aragonés de Fomento, Zaragoza 1995, 43 tomes in 12 volumes.
Legislación histórica de España, database of documents pertaining to Spanish legislation from the twelfth to the nineteenth centuries, sponsored by Real Academia de la Historia and Ministerio de Cultura, retrieved on 10 November 2015 from www.mcu.es/archivos/lhe/.
Libro de las leyes del siglo XVIII, El. Colección de impresos legales y otros papeles del Consejo de Castilla (1708–1781) (1996), edited by Santos Coronas González, Boletín Oficial del Estado and Centro de Estudios Constitucionales, Madrid, 5 vols. (previously unpublished manuscript; the index was completed in 1782).
Macanaz Fernández, Melchor (1714), *Memorial con las proposiciones que dió al Rey Felipe Quinto, Don Melchor de Macanaz, Fiscal General del Reyno*, ms., 1714, in BN Mss/12946/141.
Macanaz Fernández, Melchor (1889), *Discursos políticos y testamento de España, en principios del reinado de Felipe V* Imprenta de Primo Andrés, Madrid, s. a., nineteenth century, perhaps 1889.
Macanaz Fernández, Melchor (1972), *Testamento político [Texto impreso]: Pedimento fiscal/ Noticia biográfica*, by Joaquín Maldonado Macanaz. Edited with notes by F. Maldonado de Guevara, Instituto de Estudios Políticos, Madrid.
Macanaz Fernández, Melchor Rafael (1722), *Auxilios eficaces para bien gobernar una monarquía católica, o documentos que dicta la experiencia y aprueba la razón para que el*

monarca merezca justamente el nombre de grande. Obra que escribió y remitió desde París en 29 de agosto de 1722, al Rey Nuestro Señor don Felipe Quinto, don. . . . La da a luz don Antonio Valladares Sotomayor, Imprenta de don Antonio Espinosa, Madrid 1789.

Mandeville, Bernard (1714), *La fábula de las abejas, o los vicios privados hacen la prosperidad pública*, Fondo de Cultura Económica, Mexico 1997 (Spanish original 1982 based on the English edition of 1729; the first edition dates from 1714).

Moral y economía en el siglo XVIII. Antología de textos sobre la usura: Zubiaur, Calatayud, los Cinco Gremios Mayores y Uría Nafarrondo (1995). Edited with a preliminary study and notes by José M. Barrenechea, Gobierno Vasco, Vitoria.

Moya Torres y Velasco, Francisco Máximo de [1730], *Manifiesto universal de los males envejecidos que España padece, y de las causas de que nacen, y remedios que a cada uno en su clase corresponde, sin que tenga nota de arbitrio; antes sí para que se conozca el daño de los que se establecieron*, Librería de Francisco Laso, s. e., s. a. An original copy though with a different title can be found in BNE 2/41467. Quotations are taken from the new edition and preliminary study by Antonio Domínguez Ortiz, Instituto de Estudios Fiscales, Madrid 1992.

Muñoz de Amador, Bernardo (1755), *Arte de ensayar oro y plata, con breves reglas para la theórica y la práctica. En el qual se explica también el oficio de ensayador y marcador de los reinos; el de los fieles contrastes de oro y plata; el de los marcadores de plata y tocadores de oro; y el de los contrastes a[l]motacenes, según las leyes de estos reinos*, Imprenta de Antonio Marín, Madrid.

Novísima recopilación de las leyes de España. Dividida en XII libros. En que se reforma la Recopilación publicada por el Señor Don Felipe II en el año de 1567, reimpresa últimamente en el de 1755: Y se incorporan las pragmáticas, cédulas, decretos, órdenes y resoluciones Reales, y otras providencias no recopiladas, y expedidas hasta el de 1804. Mandada formar por el señor don Carlos IV, s. i., Madrid 1805, 6 vols. The collection includes the *Suplemento de la novísima recopilación de leyes de España, publicada en 1805. contiene las Reales disposiciones, y otras providencias expedidas en los dos años de 1805 y 1806, y algunas de las anteriores no incorporadas en este Código: y se distribuyen por leyes y notas de los libros y títulos a que corresponden*, s. e., Madrid 1807. Second facsimile edition, Boletín Oficial del Estado, Madrid 1992 (the first edition was published in 1976).

Novissima recopilación de las leyes de el reino de Navarra, hechas en sus cortes generales desde el año 1512 hasta el de 1716 inclusive. Que con especial orden de los tres estados ha coordinado el licenciado don Joachín de Elizondo, síndico, y diputado que fue del mismo reino, oidor togado de la Cámara de Comptos, y ahora oidor del Real Consejo, Infiriendo en la recopilación de los síndicos y a los títulos a que pretenecen todas las promulgadas en el referido tiempo. Y dedica al mismo ilustrísimo reino y a sus tres estados. Office of Joseph Joachín Martínez, Pamplona 1735, 2 vols (a new edition exists, *Novísima recopilación de las leyes de Navarra* (1735), Diputación Foral de Navarra and editorial Aranzadi, Pamplona 1964).

Nueva planta de la Real Audiencia del Principado de Cataluña . . . (1716) . . . *establecida por su Magestad con decreto de 16 de enero de mil setecientos y diez y seis*, Joseph Te[i]xidó, Barcelona.

Nueva planta de la Real Audiencia del Reyno de Mallorca . . . (1716) . . . *establecida por su Magestad con Real Cédula de diez y seys de março de mil setecientos diez y seis*, Miguel Capó, Palma de Mallorca.

Nueva recopilación de los fueros . . . (1696) . . . *privilegios, buenos usos y costumbres, leyes y órdenes de la M. N. y M. L. provincia de Guipúzcoa*, Andrés de Gorosabel, Tolosa 1696. Facsimile editions, Lex Nova, Valladolid 1976 and 2006.

Ordenanza de S. M. de 16 de julio de 1730 de la labor de monedas de oro, plata, y cobre, que se fabricaren en las reales casas de moneda de España: Ministros, oficiales, y operarios y operarios que se ha de ocupar en ellas, sueldos que han de gozar, encargos y obligaciones de cada uno, derechos que se señalan para costear las labores de las monedas, ensayos que se han de hacer de ellas y de las barras y demas pastas y lo demas que se ha de observar, Viuda de Peralta, Madrid 1745.

Postlethwayt, Malachy (1757), *Great Britain's True System*, A. Millar, London 1757, republished by August M. Kelley Publishers, New York 1967.

Reales Cédulas de erección y ordenanzas de los tres cuerpos de comercio de el principado de Cathaluña, que residen en la ciudad de Barcelona (1763), Francisco Suriá Impresor, Barcelona. In Larruga (1789), VI, ff. 77–138.

Recopilación . . . (1802) . . . *de todas las providencias relativas a vales reales expedidas desde 1780*, Imprenta de la Viuda e Hijo de Marín, 2 vols, Madrid 1802.

Reglamento general . . . (1761) . . . *expedido por su majestad en 23 de Abril de 1720 para la dirección y gobierno de los oficios de correo mayor y postas de españa en los viajes que se hicieren; y exenciones que han de gozar y les están concedidas a todos los dependientes de ellos*, in Rodríguez Campomanes (1761), pp. XVIII–LI.

Representación . . . (1710) . . . *y recopilación general que el Cuerpo del Comercio de la nación francesa en esta Corte de Madrid pone en manos del Ilustmo. Señor Marqués de Blecour[t], enviado extraordinario de su Magtad. Cristianísima, para que los privilegios concedidos a la nación subsistan, y que se revaliden para la permanente unión y buena correspondencia entre los súbditos de ambas majestades, Cathólica y Cristianíssima*, s. l. [Madrid], s. e. Copy in AHN, Consejos, libro 5207.

Representación universal . . . (1725) . . . *de el estado de la Real Azienda, Gobierno Económico, Comercio, Marina y de las Indias; de los desórdenes, daños e inconbenientes que al presente hay con sus remedios; y con la forma fácil de su mayor y respectivo adelantamiento para la mayor gloria de su Magestad, alibio de sus vasallos y exaltación de la Monarquía de España*, ms., Madrid 28–VII–1725, XIV+270 folios, BNE Mss/1448.

Ripia, Juan de la, and Gallard, Diego María (1796), *Práctica de la administración y cobranza de las rentas reales y visita de los ministros que se ocupan de ellas. Por* . . . . *Corregida con las nuevas cédulas, decretos y órdenes que no se habían publicado hasta aquí sobre las rentas de que se trata* . . . *por el licenciado don* . . ., Oficina de don Antonio Ulloa, Madrid, 5 vols. The first edition dates from 1676. My citations are from the 1795 edition. A new edition was published by the Instituto de Estudios Fiscales, Madrid 1968, 4 vols.

Rodríguez Campomanes, Pedro (1761), *Itinerario de las carreras de posta de dentro y fuera del Reyno, que contiene también, I. Las leyes y privilegios con que se gobiernan en España las postas desde su establecimiento, II. Y una noticia de las especies corrientes de moneda estrangera reducidas a la de España, con los precios a que se pagan las postas en los varios payses*. Imprenta de Antonio Pérez de Soto, Madrid. Facsimile edition with an introduction by Manuel-Jesús González and John Reeder, Ministerio de Fomento, Madrid 2002.

Rodríguez Villa, Antonio (1878), *Don Cenón de Somodevilla, Marqués de la Ensenada: ensayo biográfico formado con documentos en su mayor parte originales, inéditos y desconocidos*, Librería de M. Murillo, Madrid.

Roland de la Platière, Jean-Marie (1784–1790), *Manufactures, arts et métiers par M*. . . . . *Encyclopédie méthodique*., 6 vols, Panckucke, París.

Rubio, fray Isidoro (s. a.), *Resumen de tratados internacionales de España en los siglos XVII y XVIII*, monastery of San Pedro de Arlanza, Burgos? s. d., early eighteenth century.

BL, Eg., 1817, ff. 67v–88. Title I have used to refer to the manuscript written by a friar at the monastery summarizing various treaties. It forms part of a collection of manuscript essays and treatises, mainly on religious subjects, written in the early eighteenth century but in any case after 1714. They were probably intended for personal use. The book contains a mark of ownership belonging to the Count of Tepa, and the inside cover bears the note 'purchased at Puttide's 15 June 1859'. I have no way of establishing whether this was the bookshop and date at which Lord Eggerton bought the manuscript for his collection, or whether it formed part of the Iriarte library which he had acquired previously.

Sala, Juan (1783), *Ilustración del derecho real de España. Ordenada por don* . . ., Imprenta de Joseph de Orga, Valencia, 2 vols. Cited from Matilla (1950) and Muñoz (1955).

Santa Cruz de Marcenado, Álvaro Navia Ossorio, Marquis of (1732), *Comercio suelto y en compañías, general y particular, en México, Perú, Philipinas y Moscovia; población, fábricas, pesquerías, plantíos, colonias en África; empleo de pobres y de vagabundos, y otras ventajas que son fáciles a la España con los medios aquí propuestos, extractados o commentados*, Antonio Marín, Madrid.

Sartine, Antonio de, Count of Albi (1735), *Dn. . . ., conde de Albi, caballero del Orden de San Miguel . . . entre los principales encargos de mi ingresso à este Ministerio, se me hizo con especial atencion el que se aplicasse todo mi mayor cuydado, y desvelo, para que el Real Tributo, establecido en este Principado con nombre de Catastro, se repartiesse, y exigiesse con la justificacion, y equidad que saviamente previenen las reglas primitivas de su imposicion* . . ., s.l., s.a., Barcelona 20 December 1735. Copies in AHN, ancillary library, sig. A-E2, F4, and in BNE. The work was reprinted again as *Práctica de los repartimientos y apremios sobre contribuciones, mandadas en la provincia de Cataluña por . . . en el año de 1735*, Viuda e Hijos de Don Antonio Brusí, Barcelona 1825, and by José López Juana Pinilla, *Biblioteca de Hacienda de España*, IV, *Contribuciones de la Corona de Aragón equivalentes a las provinciales de Castilla*, Madrid, Imprenta y fundición de Eusebio Ayguadó, 1847; and by Antonio Sanmartí, *Colección de órdenes relativas a la Nueva Planta de la Real Audiencia de Cataluña* . . ., Lérida 1806. The original is in AGS, Consejo Supremo de Hacienda, leg. 60 (Delgado Ribas 1987b, p. 39, note 27).

Savall y Dronda, Pascual, y Santiago Penén y Debesa (1866), *Fueros, observancias y actos de corte del reino de Aragón*, Establecimiento tipográfico de Francisco Castro y Bosque, 3 vols, facsimile edition, El Justicia de Aragón and Ibercaja, 1991.

Savary des Bruslons, Jacques (1723–1730), *Dictionnaire universel de commerce: d'histoire naturelle, & des arts & metiers, contenant tout ce qui concerne le commerce qui se fait dans les quatre parties du monde . . . ouvrage posthume du sieur . . . continué sur les mémoires de l'auteur . . . par Philemon-Louis Savary. Nouvelle édition, exactement revûe, corrigée, et considérablement augmentée*, J. Estienne, Paris, 3 v. The citations are taken from an expanded edition by the author's brother M. Philémon-Louis Savary des Bruslons, Chez les frères Cl. & Ant. Philibert, Copenhague 1759–1765, 5 v. Contents: v. 1, A-Ch; v. 2, Ci-F; v. 3; G-O; v. 4, P-Z; v. 5, *Tout ce qui concerne I. Le commerce qui se fait dans les quatre parties du monde . . . II. Les compagnies de commerce . . . III. Les chambres d'assurances.*

Savary, Jacques (1675), *Le parfait négociant, ou instruction générale pour ce qui regarde le commerce de toute sorte de marchandises, tant de France que des pays estrangers . . . par le sieur* . . ., L. Billaine, Paris. Among others, subsequent editions included Savary (1688), *Le parfait négociant, ou, instruction générale pour ce qui regarde le commerce des marchandises de France, & des pays étrangers: pour la banque, le change & rechange* . . .

comme aussi plusieurs pareres ou avis & conseils sur diverses matières de commerce très-importantes; enrichi d'augmentations par le feu sieur .... Huitiéme edition: revûë & corrigée sur leurs memoires & nouvellement augmentée des edits, declarations, arrêts, & reglemens intervenus depuis la précedente edition, sur le fait du Commerce & des manufactures; ensemble de la vie de l'auteur par M. Philemon-Louis Savary ... son fils. Paris, chez Claude Robustel, 1721–1724 2 vols. Volume 1 of the 1753–1757 edition includes Jacques Dupuis de la Serra, *Suite du parfait negociant, ou, l'art des lettres de change* and C[laude] Naulot, *Nouveau traité des changes étrangers.*

Savary, Jacques (1688), *Parères, ou avis et conseils sur les plus importantes matières du commerce ... par le sieur ...*, J. Guignard, Paris.

Shaw, William A. (1896), *Select Tracts and Documents Illustrative of English Monetary History 1626–1730*, Wilsons & Milne, London 1896. I have used the documents from the edition by Olaf Simons 2004, in http://pierre-marteau.com, who in turn took them from a re-edition of Shaw's work, August Kelley Publishers, New York 1967.

Smith, Adam (1776), *Investigación sobre la naturaleza y causas de la riqueza de las naciones*, Fondo de Cultura Económica, México 1984 (original edition of 1776).

Somodevilla Bengoechea, Zenón, Marquis of La Ensenada (1751), *Representación hecha al Señor don Fernando VI por su ministro el marqués de La Ensenada proponiendo remedios para el adelantamiento de la monarquía y buen gobierno de ella*, Madrid between 8 September and 8 October 1751, ms., AMAEP. The first (partial) edition was published in *Semanario erudito* (Madrid). It is cited from the edition by Ozanam (1980).

Tot (Nicolas o Pierre) Du (1736), *Histoire du systême de John Law (1716–1720)*, Edited and introduced by Antoine E. Murphy, Institut National d'Etudes Démographiques, Paris 2000. Untitled, unpublished manuscript, completed around 1736.

Turgot, Anne Robert Jacques (1913–1923), *Oeuvres de ... et documents le concernant.* Avec biographie et notes par Gustave Schelle, 5 vols, Librairie Felix Alcan, París (orig. ed. *Oeuvres*, Dupont de Nemours, Paris 1808–1811, 9 vols).

Ulloa, Bernardo de (1740), *Restablecimiento de las fábricas y comercio español; errores que se padecen en las causales de su [de]cadencia, cuáles son los legítimos obstáculos que le destruyen y los medios eficaces de que florezca. Parte primera, que trata qué sea comercio, cuáles sus partes y diferencias; cuál el que goza España y el que necesita mantener con las naciones para el restablecimiento de las fábricas y tráfico terrestre, con un extracto del libro de D. Gerónimo Uztáriz 'Theorica y práctica de comercio y marina'. Restablecimiento de las fabricas, tráfico y comercio marítimo de España. Segunda parte, que trata del comercio y tráfico marítimo que tiene España con las naciones y en la América; causales de su decadencia y medios con que se debe aumentar y extender para beneficio de estos reynos y aumento de las fuerzas marítimas de ellos y su población*, Antonio Marín, Madrid 1740, 2 vols.

Uztáriz, Gerónimo de (1724), *Theorica y practica de comercio, y de marina, para la Monarquia Española*, s. e., Madrid. There are two editions dated 1737 and 1742, and a recent edition (republication of the 1742 edition) with an introduction by Gabriel Franco, Aguilar, Madrid 1968. The citations are from the 1968 edition.

Vauban, Sebastien Le Prestre de (1695), *Projet de capitation* (1695) in idem, *Écrits divers sur l'économie*, with an introduction by Jean-François Pernot, Les Amis de la Maison Vauban, Saint-Léger-Vauban 1996 (writings and documents from 1667 to 1706).

Vauban, Sebastien Le Prestre de (1707), *Projet d'une dixme royale qui suprimant la taille, les aydes, les doüanes d'une province á l'autre, les décimes du clergé, les affaires extraordinaires et tous autres impôts onereux et non voluntaires, et diminuant le prix du sel de moitié et plus, produiroit au Roy un revenu certain et suffisant, sans frais; et sans être à charge à l'un de ses sujets plus qu'à l'autre, qui s'augmenteroit considerablement par la meilleure culture des terres*, s. l., s. e. Facsimile edition with an introduction by Jean-François Pernot, Association des Amis de la Maison Vauban, Saint-Léger Vauban 1988.

Villars, Pierre (1733), *Memoires de la Cour d'Espagne, depuis l'année 1679 jusqu'en 1681*, Chez Jean Fr. Josse, Paris. Reprinted by M. A. Morel Fatio as *Memoires de la cour d'Espagne de 1679 á 1681*, G. Plon, Murrit et Cie., Paris 1893, and translated in García Mercadal (1959).

Virio, Juan Bautista de (1792), *Colección alfabética de los aranceles de la Gran Bretaña y extractos de las leyes, reglamentos, ordenes y providencias expedidas en aquel Reyno para el régimen de sus aduanas y fomento de su comercio. Obra dispuesta por Don . . ., secretario que fue del ministerio de S. M. en Londres*, Imprenta de la viuda de Joaquín Ibarra, Madrid, 4 vols.

Vizcay, Martín de (1621), *Derecho de naturaleza que los naturales de la merindad de San Juan de Pie de Puerto tienen en los reinos de la Corona de Castilla. Sacado de dos sentencias ganadas en juicio contencioso y de otras escrituras auténticas*, Juan Lanaja Quartanet, Zaragoza. Facsimile edition, Órbigo, A Coruña, 2008.

Ward, Bernardo (1750), *Obra pía y eficaz modo para remediar la miseria de la gente pobre de España*, Vda. de Gerónimo Conejos, Valencia [1750]. The work was republished in 1767 and again 1787, and together with other texts in Ward (1779).

Ward, Bernardo (1779), *Proyecto económico, en que se proponen varias providencias, dirigidas á promover los intereses de España con los medios y fondos necesarios para su plantificación: escrito en el año de . . . por D. . . . y su Ministro de la Real Junta de Comercio y Moneda. Obra póstuma*, Joaquín Ibarra, Madrid. This work was completed in 1762. It was reprinted in 1779, 1782 and 1787, and a modern edition was published with a preliminary study by Juan Luis Castellano Castellano, Instituto de Estudios Fiscales, Madrid 1982. Citations are from the 1982 edition.

Whitworth, Sir Charles (1776), *State of trade of Great Britain in its Imports and Exports. From the years 1697 to 1773*, G. Robinson, London, 2 v.

Zavala Auñón, Miguel (1732), *Representación al Rey Nuestro Señor Don Phelipe V (que Dios guarde), dirigida al más seguro aumento del real Erario y conseguir la felicidad, mayor alivio, riqueza y abundancia de su Monarquía . . . . Hecha por don . . .*, s. i., Madrid 1732. It was later reprinted as Zabala Auñón, Miguel; Martín de Loinaz y 'un señor ministro práctico en la sugeta materia', *Miscelánea económico-política, ó Discursos varios sobre el modo de aliviar los vasallos con aumento del Real Erario*, Antonio Ulloa, Madrid 1747.

Bibliography since 1900

Albareda Salvadó, Joaquim (ed.) (2001), *Del patriotisme al catalanisme. Societat i politica (segles XVI–XIX)*, Eumo, Vic.

Albareda Salvadó, Joaquim (2010), *La Guerra de Sucesión de España (1700–1714)*, Crítica, Barcelona.

Alfaro Pérez, Francisco (2006), *La merindad de Tudela en la Edad Moderna. Demografía y sociedad*, Institución Fernando el Católico, Zaragoza.

Alfaro Pérez, Francisco (2007), *Historia de la villa de Cintruénigo*, Ayuntamiento de Cintruénigo, Cintruénigo.

Alfonso Mola, Marina and Carlos Martínez Shaw (1996), 'La expansión catalana en la Andalucía Occidental (1740–1840)', in M. T. Pérez Picazo, A. Segura and Ll. Ferrer (eds.), *Els catalans a Espanya, 1760–1914*, Afers, Barcelona, pp. 213–222.

Alli Aranguren, Juan Cruz (2004), 'Pedro Sáinz de Andino y el traslado de las aduanas del Ebro al Pirineo', *Príncipe de Viana* (Pamplona), 65 (232), pp. 511–544.

Alloza Aparicio, Ángel (2006), *Europa en el mercado español. Mercaderes, represalias y contrabando en el siglo XVII*, Junta de Castilla y León, Valladolid.

Alonso Alvarez, Luis (1996), 'Emigrantes catalanes en Galicia, 1760–1832', in M. T. Pérez Picazo, A. Segura and Ll. Ferrer (eds), *Els catalans a Espanya, 1760–1914*, Afers, Barcelona, pp. 97–108.

Álvarez Junco, José (2001), *Mater dolorosa. La idea de España en el siglo XIX*, Taurus, Madrid.

Andrés-Gallego, José (ed.) (1999), *Textos clásicos para la historia del Reino de Navarra*, Fundación Histórica Tavera, Madrid, published on CD-ROM.

Andújar, Francisco (2008), 'Nobleza cortesana: la vía privilegiada de acceso al generalato en el siglo XVIII', paper given at the X Reunión Científica de la FEHM Santiago de Compostela y Ferrol, 2008. An abstract can be found online at: www.moderna2008.org/comunicacionesaceptadas/index.html (consulted 26 February 2008).

Anes Álvarez, G. (1970), *Las crisis agrarias en la España moderna*, Alianza, Madrid.

Angulo Morales, Alberto (1995), *Las puertas de la vida y la muerte: la administración aduanera en las provincias vascas (1690–1780)*, Universidad del País Vasco, Bilbao.

Angulo Morales, Alberto (1997), 'El mundo al revés. La visión del contrabando por los representantes de la Hacienda Real y Pública en el País Vasco (siglos XVIII y XIX)', *Sancho el Sabio* (Vitoria), 7, pp. 79–96.

Angulo Morales, Alberto (2001), 'Comercialización y contrabando de tabaco en el País Vasco durante el antiguo régimen', *Vasconia*, pp. 21–43.

Angulo Morales, Alberto (2003), 'El sistema aduanero y el contrabando en el País Vasco', *Notitia Vasconiae* (San Sebastian), 2, pp. 97–127.

Angulo Teja, María del Carmen (2002), *La Hacienda española en el siglo XVIII. Las rentas provinciales*, Centro de Estudios Políticos y Constitucionales, Madrid.

Ansón Calvo, Carmen (1977), *Demografía y sociedad urbana en la Zaragoza del siglo XVII*, Caja de Ahorros de Zaragoza, Aragón y Rioja, Zaragoza.

Antón Pelayo, J. (1998), 'Comportamientos familiares y actitudes culturales durante la Época Moderna', *Studia histórica. Historia Moderna* (Salamanca), 18, pp. 67–101.

Aragón Ruano, Álvaro (2009), '"Con casa, familia y domicilio". Mercaderes extranjeros en Guipúzcoa durante la Edad Moderna', *Studia Historica. Historia Moderna* (Salamanca), 31, pp. 155–200.

Aragón Ruano, Álvaro (2010), '"Que los naturales della sienpre fueron, y han sido auidos y reputados por nauarros y naturales del dicho reyno" Bajonavarros y derecho de naturaleza en Guipúzcoa durante la "hora navarra"', in Rafael Torres Sánchez (ed.), *Volver a la 'hora navarra'. La contribución navarra a la construcción de la monarquía española en el siglo XVIII*, Eunsa, Pamplona, pp. 73–115.

Ardit Lucas, Manuel (1993), *Els homes i la terra del País Valencià (segles XVI–XVIII)*, Curial, Barcelona, 2 vols.

Ardit Lucas, Manuel (1996), 'Agricultura e industrial rural en el siglo XVIII', in Joaquín Azagra, E. Mateu and J. Vidal (eds), *De la sociedad tradicional a la economía moderna. Estudios de historia valenciana contemporánea*, Instituto de Cultura Juan Gil-Albert, Alicante, pp. 62–76.

Arenas de Pablo, Joan José (2005), 'Ingeniería y obra civil en el Siglo de las Luces', en Manuel Silva Suárez (ed.), *Técnica e ingeniería en España, II. El siglo de las Luces. De la ingeniería a la nueva navegación*, Real Academia de Ingeniería, Institución Fernando el Católico y Prensas Universitarias de Zaragoza, Zaragoza, pp. 383–427.

Arizcun Cela, Alejandro (1989), *Series navarras de precios de cereales 1589–1841*, Servicio de Estudios del Banco de España, Madrid.

Armitage, David (2000), *The ideological origins of the British Empire*, Cambridge University Press, Cambridge.

Artola, Miguel (1982), *La Hacienda del Antiguo Régimen*, Alianza, Madrid.

Astigarraga Goenaga, Jesús (2003), *Los ilustrados vascos: ideas, instituciones y reformas económicas en España*, Crítica, Barcelona.

Astigarraga Goenaga, Jesús (2010), 'La dérangeante découverte de l'autre: les (més) aventures de l'Essai politique sur le commerce' (1734) de Jean-François Melon dans l'Espagne du XVIIIe siècle', *Revue d'Histoire Moderne et Contemporaine* (París), 57(1), pp. 91–118.

Astigarraga Goenaga, Jesús y Javier Usoz (2008), 'Del A. Genovesi napolitano de Carlo di Borbone al A. Genovesi español de Carlos III: la traducción española de las "Lezioni di commercio" de V. de Villava', *Cuadernos de Historia del Derecho* (Madrid), 15, pp. 293–326.

Atienza López, Ángela (1993), *Propiedad y señorío en Aragón. El clero regular entre la expansión y la crisis (1700–1835)*, Institución Fernando el Católico, Zaragoza.

Aymes, Jean René (1996), 'L'interpretation du "caractère français" en Espagne pendant la decade revolutionaire (1789–1799)', in J. R. Aymes (ed.), *L'image de la France en Espagne pendant la seconde moitié du XVIIIe siècle*, Instituto de Cultura Juan Gil-Albert – Presses de Sorbonne Nouvelle, Alicante, pp. 283–306.

Azcona Guerra, Ana (1995), 'Contribution à l'etude des reseaux commerciaux dans une espace interregional: Navarre-Aquitaine au XVIIIe siècle', *Bulletin du Centre des Espaces Atlantiques* (Bourdeaux), 7, pp. 59–84.

Azcona Guerra, Ana (1996 a), *Comercio y comerciantes en la Navarra del siglo XVIII*, Gobierno de Navarra, Pamplona.

Azcona Guerra, Ana (1996 b), 'Une enterprise navarraise dans la réseau commercial de la France meridionale: les Vidarte (1754–1823)', *Annales du Midi*, 108 (216), pp. 479–503.

Azcona Guerra, Ana (1997), 'Pautas de análisis de la estructura familiar del negocio comercial navarro en el siglo XVIII', in F. Chacón and Ll. Ferrer (eds), *Familia, casa y trabajo*, Universidad de Murcia, Murcia, pp. 345–369.

Azcona Guerra, Ana (1999), 'La presencia de la minoría bayonesa en la dinámica del comercio franco-español del siglo XVIII', *Hispania* (Madrid), LIX-3(203), pp. 955–987.

Barceló Crespí, María (1984), 'El "Capbreu": font per a l'analisi d'una comunitat urbana', *Mayurqa* (Palma), 20(1980–1984), pp. 233–242.

Barceló Crespí, María (1991), 'Més sobre l'impost del tall (1450–1521)', *Randa*, 29, pp. 185–217.

Barceló Crespí, María (2001) *La talla de la ciutat de Mallorca, 1512*, Universitat de les Illes Balears, Palma de Mallorca 2002.

Barceló Crespí, María, and Bartolomeu Servera Sitjar (1993), *Vida municipal i Nova Planta: Porreres, 1718–1728*, Ajuntament, Llucmajor 1993.

Bartolomé Herranz, Carlos (1991), 'Las tablas de Navarra (1513–1700)', *Príncipe de Viana* (Pamplona), 193, pp. 139–161.

Bartolomé Herranz, Carlos (1993), 'Aproximación al estudio de Navarra a través de las cuentas 1513–1700', *Príncipe de Viana* (Pamplona), 199, pp. 417–430.

Belfanti, Carlo Marco and Fabio Giusberti (2000), 'Clothing and social inequality in early modern Europe: Introductory remarks', *Continuity and Change*, 15(3), pp. 359–365.

Benaul, José María (1992), 'Los orígenes de la empresa textil lanera en Sabadell y Terrassa en el siglo XVIII', *Revista de Historia Industrial* (Barcelona), 1, pp. 39–62.

Berenguer Galindo, Antonio (1966), 'La Compañía de Calaf en la Ribera del Cinca, 1784–1812', in M. T. Pérez Picazo, A. Segura and Ll. Ferrer (eds.), *Els catalans a Espanya, 1760–1914*, Afers, Barcelona, pp. 329–340.

Berg, Maxine and Helen Clifford (eds.) (1999), *Consumers and luxury. Consumer culture in Europe 1650–1850*, Manchester University Press, Manchester.

Bernardos Sanz, José Ubaldo (2003), *Trigo castellano y abasto madrileño. Los arrieros y comerciantes segovianos en la Edad Moderna*, Junta de Castilla y León, Valladolid.

Bethencourt Massieu, Antonio (1954), *Patiño en la política internacional de Felipe V*, Universidad de Valladolid, Valladolid 1954.

Bloch, Marc (1949), *Apologie pour l'histoire ou métier d'historien*, Librairie Armand Colin, Paris.

Brenner, Robert (1993), *Merchants and Revolution. Commercial Change, Political Conflict and London's Overseas Traders, 1550–1653*, Cambridge University Press, Cambridge.

Brewer, John (1989), *The Sinews of Power. War, Money and the English State 1688–1783*, Routledge, London 1994 (first published by Albert Knopf, New York 1989).

Camarero Bullón, Concepción (1993), *El debate de la Única Contribución: catastrar las Castillas*, Centro de Gestión Catastral y Cooperación Tributaria y Tabapress, Madrid.

Camarero Bullón, Concepción (2001), *Madrid y su provincia en el catastro de Ensenada. I. La Villa y Corte, 1750–1759*, Ediciones del Umbral, Madrid.

Camarero Bullón, Concepción (2002), 'Vasallos y pueblos castellanos ante una averiguación más allá de lo fiscal: el catastro de Ensenada 1749–1756', in *El catastro de Ensenada: magna averiguación fiscal para alivio de los vasallos y mejor conocimiento de los reinos, 1749–1756*, Ministerio de Economía y Hacienda, Madrid 2002 (2nd edn. 2006), pp. 113–388.

Caminal Abadía, Montserrat; Esteban Canales Gil and Jaume Torras Elias (1983), 'Sobre la renta señorial en Cataluña en el último tercio del siglo XVIII', in *II Simposio sobre el padre Feijoo y su siglo (ponencias y comunicaciones)*, Centro de Estudios del siglo XVIII, Oviedo, 2 vols., II, pp. 259–280.

Carney, Thomas F. (1975), *The Shape of the Past: Models and Antiquity*, Coronado Press, Lawrence, KS.

Casado Alonso, Hilario (1995), *Castilla y Europa: comercio y mercaderes en los siglos XIV, XV y XVI*, Diputación Provincial de Burgos, Burgos.

Casado Alonso, Hilario (2003), *El triunfo de Mercurio. La presencia castellana en Europa (siglos XV y XVI)*, Cajacírculo [Caja de Ahorros y Monte de Piedad del Círculo Católico de Obreros de Burgos], Burgos.

Casado, Hilario (2008), 'Los flujos de información en las redes comerciales castellanas de los siglos XV y XVI', *Investigaciones de Historia Económica* (Madrid), 10, pp. 35–68.

Castellano Castellano, Juan Luis (1996), 'La carrera burocrática en la España del siglo XVIII', in Juan Luis Castellano Castellano (ed.), *Administración y poder en la España del Antiguo Régimen*, Universidad de Granada, Granada, pp. 25–45.

Castellano Castellano, Juan Luis (2006), *Gobierno y poder en la España del siglo XVIII*, Universidad de Granada, Granada.

Castro, Concepción de (1987), *El pan de Madrid. El abasto de las ciudades españolas del Antiguo Régimen*, Alianza, Madrid.

Catalá Sanz, Jorge (1995), *Rentas y patrimonios de la nobleza valenciana en el siglo XVIII*, Siglo XXI, Madrid.

Cateura Bennasser, Pablo (1992), 'Fiscalidad real y municipal en la Mallorca del siglo XV', *Anuario de estudios medievales* (Madrid), 22, pp. 443–462.

Cateura Bennasser, Pablo (2001), 'El sistema fiscal del reino de Mallorca en los inicios de la crisis', *Mayurqa* (Palma de Mallorca), 27, pp. 47–61.

Cateura Bennasser, Pau (2008), 'El rey burlado: deuda pública y fiscalidad en el reino de Mallorca (siglo XV)', *Anuario de estudios medievales* (Madrid), 38(1), pp. 185–211.

Céspedes del Castillo, Gonzalo (1988), 'Economía y moneda en los reinos de Indias bajo Carlos III', in *Carlos III y la Casa de la Moneda*, Ministerio de Economía y Hacienda, Madrid, pp. 65–84.

Chacón, Francisco (1998), 'Propuestas teóricas y organización social desde la historia de la familia en la España moderna', *Studia histórica. Historia Moderna* (Salamanca), 18, pp. 17–26.

Chandler Jr., Alfred D. (1990), *Escala y diversificación. La dinámica del capitalismo industrial*, Prensas Universitarias de Zaragoza, 2 vols, Zaragoza 1996 (first published by Harvard University Press, Cambridge MA. 1990).

Christakis, Nicholas A. and James H. Fowler (2010), *Conectados. El sorprendente poder de las redes sociales y cómo nos afectan*, Taurus, Madrid 2010 (first published by Harper Press, London 2010).

Ciriacono, Salvatore (1994), *Acque e agricoltura. Venezia, l'Olanda e la bonifica europea in età moderna*, Franco Angeli, Milan.

Clavero, Bartolomé (1977), 'Prohibición de usura y constitución de rentas', *Moneda y Crédito* (Madrid), 13(1977), pp. 107–131.

Coll, Anna M. (2005), 'De Guerra de Successió i intèndencia al Regne de Mallorca', *Afers* (Catarroja, Valencia), XX(52), pp. 607–622.

Colley, Linda (1992), *Britons: forging the nation 1707–1837*, Vintage, London.

Comín, Francisco, Mauro Hernández and Enrique Llopis (eds) (2002), *Historia económica de España, siglos X-XX*, Crítica, Barcelona.

Conchon, Anne Marie (2002), *Le péage en France au XVIIIe siécle: les privileges a l'epreuve de la reforme*, Comité pour l'histoire economique et financière de la France, Ministère d'Economie, des Finances et de l'Industrie, París.

Conchon, Anne Marie (2005), 'Les péages dans les Pyrénés français (XVIIe–XVIIIE siècles)', in Jean-Michel Minovez and Patrice Poujade (eds), *Circulation des marchandises et réseaux commerciaux dans les Pyrénées (XIII–XIX siècle/Circulació de mercaderies i xarxes comercials als Pirineus (segles XIII–XIX)*, CNRS-Université de Toulouse II-Le-Mirail, Toulouse, pp. 71–96.

Continuity and Change (2000), 15(3), 'Special Issue on clothing and social inequality in Early Modern Europe'.

Crouzet, François (1985), *Britain ascendant: comparative studies in Franco-British Economic History*, Cambridge University Press-Maison des Sciences de l'Homme, Cambridge 1990 (first published in French as *De la supériorité de l'Angleterre sur la France. L'economique et l'imaginaire XVIIe–XXe siècles*, Perrin, Paris 1985).

Crouzet, François (1996), *Britain, France and International Commerce. From Luis XIV to Victoria*, Ashgate, Aldershot, Hants.

Curtin, Philip (1984), *Cross-cultural trade in world history*, Cambridge University Press, Cambridge.

Daunton, Martin J. (1995), *Progress and Poverty. An Economic and Social History of Britain 1700–1850*, Oxford University Press, Oxford.

Dedieu, Jean-Pierre (1996), 'Familia y alianza. La alta administración española del siglo XVIII', in Juan Luis Castellano (ed.), *Administración y poder en la España del Antiguo Régimen*, Universidad de Granada y Diputación Provincial de Granada, Granada, pp. 47–76.

Dedieu, Jean-Pierre (1997), 'La haute administration espagnole au XVIIIe siècle', in Robert Descimon, Jean-Frédéric Schaub and Bernard Vincent (eds), *Les figures de l'administrateur. Institutions, réseaux, pouvoirs en Españgne, en France et au Portugal, 16e–19e siècles*, EHESS, Paris.

Dedieu, Jean-Pierre (2000 a), 'La Nueva Planta en su contexto. Las reformas del aparato del Estado en el reinado de Felipe V', *Manuscrits*, 18, pp. 113–139.

Dedieu, Jean-Pierre (2000 b), 'Procesos y redes. La historia de las instituciones administrativas de la época moderna, hoy', in Juan Luis Castellano Castellano, Jean-Pierrre Dedieu and María Victoria López-Cordón (eds), *La pluma, la mitra y la espada. Estudios de historia institucional en la edad moderna*, Universidad de Burdeos and Marcial Pons, Madrid, pp. 13–31.

Dedieu, Jean-Pierre and Christian Windler (1998), 'La familia: ¿una clave para entender la historia política? El ejemplo de la España moderna', *Studia histórica. Historia Moderna* (Salamanca), 18, pp. 201–233.

Delgado Barrado, José Miguel (1999), *José de Carvajal y Lancáster: testamento político o idea de un gobierno católico (1745)*, Universidad de Córdoba, Córdoba.

Delgado Barrado, José Miguel (2001), *El proyecto político de Carvajal: pensamiento y reforma en tiempos de Fernando VI*, CSIC, Madrid.

Delgado Barrado, José Miguel, and José Luis Gómez Urdáñez (eds) (2002), *Ministros de Fernando VI*, Universidad de Córdoba, Córdoba.

Delgado Ribas, José María (1987), 'Presión fiscal y asignación de recursos en la monarquía borbónica', *Manuscrits* (Barcelona), 4(5), pp. 25–40.

Delgado Ribas, Josep María (1995), 'Mercado interno versus mercado colonial en la primera industrialización española', *Revista de Historia Económica* (Madrid), XIII(1), pp. 11–31.

Delgado Ribas, Josep M. and Josep M. Fradera Barceló (1996), 'La diáspora atlàntica. De Cadis a les Antilles, 1750–1860', in M. T. Pérez Picazo, A. Segura and Ll. Ferrer (eds.), *Els catalans a Espanya, 1760–1914*, Afers, Barcelona, pp. 31–34. The study was published incomplete by an oversight and was added in a supplement.

Desos, Catherine (2009), *Les Français de Philippe V. Un modèle nouveau pour gouverner l'Espagne (1700–1724)*, Presses Universitaires de Strasbourg, Strasbourg.
Deyon, Pierre and Philippe Guignet (1980), 'The royal manufactures and Economic and Technological Progress in France before the Industrial Revolution', *The Journal of European Economic History* (Rome), 9(3), pp. 611–631.
Domínguez Martín, Rafael (2002), *La riqueza de las regiones. Las desigualdades económicas regionales en España, 1700–2000*, Alianza, Madrid.
Dubet, Anne (2007), '¿La importación de un modelo francés? Acerca de algunas reformas de la administración española a principios del siglo XVIII', *Revista de Historia Moderna* (Alicante), 25, pp. 207–233.
Dubois, M. (1996), 'L'image de Paris dans les memorias literarias de París, de Luzán (1751)', in J. R. Aymes (ed.), *L'image de la France en Espagne pendant la seconde moitié du XVIIIe siècle*, Instituto de Cultura Juan Gil-Albert and Presses de Sorbonne Nouvelle, Alicante, pp. 201–214.
Duroux, Rose (1985), 'Les boutiquiers cantaliens de Nouvelle-Castille au XIX siècle', *Melanges de la Casa de Velázquez* (Madrid), XXI, pp. 281–307.
Duroux, Rose (1992), *Les Auvergnats de Castille. Renaissance et mort d'une inmigration au XIXe siècle*, Association des Publications de la Faculté des Lettres, Clermont-Ferrand.
Duroux, Rose (2000 a), 'Entre archaïsme et modernité – les migrations du Massif central au XIX siècle', in René Leboutte (ed.), *Migrations et migrants dans une perspective historique. Permanences et innovations/Migrations and Migrants in Historical Perspective. Permanencies and Innovations* [International conference proceedings, European Forum 1997–1998, European University Institute, Florence, October 1997], P.I.E.-Peter Lang, Bruxelles.
Duroux, Rose (2000 b), 'Estrategias patrimoniales excluyentes. Un caso francés', *Hispania* (Madrid), LX/1 (204), pp. 315–330.
Duroux, Rose (2000 c), 'Migrants et Corporations. Corporations "molles", corporations "dures" (XVIII et XIX siècles, Auvergne/Espagne)', paper presented at the International Commission on Historical Demography, 19th International Congress of Historical Sciences, Oslo (Norway), 6/13 August 2000, unpublished.
Eagles, Robin (2000). *Francophilia in English Society, 1748–1815*, Macmillan, London.
Elliott, John H. (2002), 'Una relación agitada: España y Gran Bretaña, 1604–1655', in Jonathan Brown and John Elliott (eds), *La almoneda del siglo. Relaciones artísticas entre España y Gran Bretaña, 1604–1655*, Museo Nacional del Prado, Madrid, pp. 17–39.
Esarte Muniain, Pedro (2001), *Navarra, 1512–1530. Conquista, ocupación y sometimiento militar, civil y eclesiástico*, Pamiela, Pamplona.
Feliu, Gaspar (1985), 'El negocio de los arrendamientos de rentas señoriales: examen de un libro de cuentas', *Revista de Historia Económica* (Madrid), III(1), pp. 31–54.
Feliu, Gaspar (1991), *Precios y salarios en la Cataluña moderna*, 2 vols, Servicio de Estudios del Banco de España, Madrid.
Fernández Albaladejo, Pablo (1977), 'El decreto de suspensión de pagos de 1739: análisis e implicaciones', *Moneda y Crédito* (Madrid), 142, pp. 51–85.
Fernández Albaladejo, Pablo (1992), *Fragmentos de monarquía. Trabajos de historia política*, Alianza, Madrid.
Fernández Clemente, Eloy (1986), 'La crisis de la ganadería aragonesa a fines del Antiguo Régimen: el caso de Cantavieja', *Teruel* (Teruel), 75, pp. 95–140.
Fernández Clemente, Eloy and Guillermo Pérez Sarrión (1985), 'El siglo XVIII en Aragón: una economía dependiente', in Roberto Fernández (ed.), *España en el siglo XVIII. Homenaje a Pierre Vilar*, Crítica, Barcelona, pp. 565–629.

Fernández Díaz, Roberto (1982), 'La burguesía barcelonesa en el siglo XVIII: la familia Gloria', in *La economia española al final del Antiguo Régimen. II. Manufacturas*, edited and with an introduction by Pedro Tedde, Alianza, Madrid, pp. 1–131.

Fernández Durán, Reyes (1999), *Gerónimo de Uztáriz, 1670–1732: una política económica para Felipe V*, Minerva, Madrid.

Ferrer Alós, Llorenç (1987), *Pagesos, rabassaires i industrials a la Catalunya central (segles XVIII–XIX)*, Publicacions de l'abadía de Montserrat, Barcelona.

Ferrer Alós, Llorenç (2002), '¿Modernización fiscal? La implantación del catastro en Cataluña', *CT/Catastro* (Madrid), 46, pp. 27–35.

Fichoz (Fichier Ozanam), prosopographic relational database on the ancient regime in Spain administered by Jean-Pierre Dedieu, Laboratoire de Recherches Historiques Rhône-Alpes (LARHRA) del Institut des Sciences de l'Homme, Lyon. Available for consultation online since 2008, fmnet:/fm.tge-adonis.fr/ (consulted 29 April 2015).

Finkelstein, Andrea (2000), *Harmony and the Balance. An Intellectual History of Seventeenth-Century Thought*, University of Michigan Press, Ann Arbor, Michigan.

Floristán Imízcoz, Alfredo (1991), *La monarquía española y el gobierno del reino de Navarra, 1512–1808. Comentario de textos históricos*, Gobierno de Navarra, Pamplona.

Floristán Imízcoz, Alfredo (1999), '¿Conquista o restauración? La incorporación de Navarra a la Monarquía española', *Hispania*, LIX/2(202), pp. 457–491.

Font de Villanueva, Cecilia (2005), 'Política monetaria y política fiscal en Castilla en el siglo XVIII: un siglo de inestabilidades', *Revista de Historia Económica* (Madrid), XXIII número extraordinario, pp. 329–348.

Font de Villanueva, Cecilia (2008), *La estabilización monetaria de 1680–1686: pensamiento y política económica*, Banco de España, Madrid.

Fontaine, Laurence (1996), *History of Pedlars in Europe*, Polity Press, Cambridge.

Fontaine, Laurence (1999), 'Redes de buhoneros (vendedores ambulantes) y desarrollo del consumo en Europa durante los siglos XVII y XVIII', in J. Torras and B. Yun (eds.), *Consumo, condiciones de vida y comercialización. Cataluña y Castilla, siglos XVII–XIX*, Junta de Castilla y León, Valladolid 1999, pp. 311–321.

Fontana, Josep (1987), 'El alimento del Estado. Política y hacienda en el "despotismo ilustrado"', *Hacienda Pública Española* (Madrid), 108–109, pp. 157–168.

Fontana, Josep (2002), *Obra, I. La quiebra de la monarquía absoluta 1814–1820*, Crítica Barcelona (new, expanded edition, first published in 1971, Ariel; 2nd to 5th editions in 1974, 1978, 1983 and 1987).

Fontana Lázaro, José (1967), 'Formación del mercado nacional y toma de conciencia de la burguesía', in idem, *Cambio económico y actitudes políticas en la España del siglo XIX*, Ariel, Barcelona 1980 (3rd edition, 1st in 1973; paper originally published in 1967, although it was sent to print in 1962), pp. 11–53.

Foraster, Lourdes (1996), 'Catalans a Espanya, 1760–1914. Base de dades', in M. T. Pérez Picazo, A. Segura and Ll. Ferrer (eds), *Els catalans a Espanya, 1760–1914*, Afers, Barcelona, pp. 487–499.

Fortea Pérez, José Ignacio (2003), 'Las Cortes de Castilla y su Diputación en el reinado de Carlos II: historia de un largo sueño', in A. Eiras Roel (ed.), *Estudio preliminar* to *Actas de las Juntas del Reino de Galicia, volume XII: 1701–1704*, Xunta de Galicia, Dirección Xeral do Patrimonio Histórico e Documental, Santiago de Compostela, pp. 63–98.

Fortea Pérez, José Ignacio (2008), *Las Cortes de Castilla y León bajo los Austrias. Una interpretación*, Junta de Castilla y León, Valladolid.

Foursans-Bourdette, Marie-Pierrette (1963), *Economie et finances en Béarn au XVIII siècle*, Brière, Bordeaux.

Fradera, Josep María (1984), 'El comercio de cereales y la prohibición de 1820 (el caso del mercado catalán)', *Agricultura y Sociedad* (Madrid), 30, pp. 137–177.
Franch Benavent, Ricardo (1986), *Crecimiento comercial y enriquecimiento burgués en la Valencia del siglo XVIII*, Institució Alfons el Magnànim and Institucio Valenciana d'Estudis i Investigació, Valencia.
Franch Benavent, Ricardo (1989), *El capital comercial valenciano en el siglo XVIII*, Universidad de Valencia, Departamento de Historia Moderna, Valencia.
Franch Benavent, Ricardo (2002), 'Fiscalidad y manufacturas en la Valencia de Felipe V', *Revista de Historia Moderna* (Alicante), 20, pp. 421–447.
Franch Benavent, Ricardo (2003), 'La nueva fiscalidad implantada en los territorios de la Corona de Aragón tras la abolición del régimen foral: una aproximación desde la perspectiva valenciana', *Norba* (Cáceres), 16(2), pp. 523–542.
Franch Benavent, Ricardo (2004), 'Política mercantilista y comercio interior en la España de Felipe V', in Eliseo Serrano (ed.), *Felipe V y su tiempo Congreso Internacional celebrado en Zaragoza, 15 al 19 de enero de 2001*, Institución Fernando el Católico, Zaragoza, 2 vols, vol. 1, pp. 103–132.
Franch Benavent, Ricardo (2005), 'El cambio de naturaleza de las rentas de la Generalitat Valenciana tras la abolición de los fueros: la reacción del clero en defensa de su inmunidad y los conflictos provocados por la gestión de los intendentes', *Estudis* (Valencia), 31, pp. 269–297.
Franch Benavent, Ricardo (2009), 'Los conflictos generados por la implantación del nuevo sistema fiscal en la Valencia del siglo XVIII: la resistencia del clero en defensa de su inmunidad', in Ricardo Franch (ed.), *La sociedad valenciana tras la abolición de los fueros*, Institució Alfons el Magnànim, Valencia, pp. 215–261.
Frías, Susana R. and César A. García Belsunce (1996), *De Navarra a Buenos Aires, 1580–1810*, Instituto Americano de Estudios Vascos, Buenos Aires.
Gallego, Domingo, Luis Germán Zubero and Vicente Pinilla Navarro (1993), 'Crecimiento económico, especialización productiva y disparidades internas en el valle medio del Ebro', *Cuadernos Aragoneses de Economía* (Zaragoza), 3(2), pp. 277–320.
García Delgado, José Luis and Miguel Carrera Troyano (2001), 'Madrid, capital económica', in Luis Germán Zubero, Enrique Llopis, Jordi Maluquer de Motes and Santiago Zapata (eds), *Historia económica regional de España, siglos XIX y XX*, Crítica, Barcelona, pp. 209–237.
García García, Carmen (1996), *La crisis de las haciendas locales. De la reforma administrativa a la reforma fiscal (1743–1845)*, Junta de Castilla y León, Valladolid.
García López, Jorge (1991), 'Las glosas de don Rafael de Floranes', in Alfonso de la Torre, *Visión deleytable*, critical edition and study by Jorge García López, Universidad de Salamanca, Salamanca, 2 vols, vol. 2, pp. 71–108.
García López, José Ramón (1989), 'El sistema bancario español del siglo XIX, ¿una economía dual?', *Revista de Historia Económica* (Madrid), pp. 11–132.
García López, José Ramón (1990), 'Mercado aragonés e industria catalana: el caso de la banca Garriga-Nogués', in *Actas del I Simposio sobre las relaciones económicas entre Aragón y Cataluña (ss. XVIII–XIX)*, Instituto de Estudios Altoaragoneses, Huesca, pp. 117–136.
García Mercadal, José (1959), *Viajes de extranjeros por España y Portugal. Desde los tiempos más remotos hasta comienzos del siglo XX*, Junta de Castilla y León, Valladolid 1999, 6 vols (1st edition: Aguilar, Madrid, 3 vols).
García de Paso, José Isidoro (2002), 'The 1628 Castilian crydown: a test of competing theories of the price level', *Hacienda Pública Española* (Madrid), 163(4), pp. 71–91.

García de Paso, José Isidoro (2000), La estabilización monetaria en Castilla bajo Carlos II', *Revista de Historia Económica* (Madrid), XVIII(1), pp. 49–77.

García Sanz, Angel (1977), *Desarrollo y crisis del Antiguo Régimen en Castilla la Vieja. Economía y sociedad en tierras de Segovia 1500–1814*, Akal, Madrid (a 2nd edition published in 1987 also exists).

García Sanz, Angel (1987), 'Mercaderes hacedores de paños en Segovia en la época de Carlos V: organización del trabajo productivo y estructura del capital industrial', *Hacienda Pública Española* (Madrid), 108–109, pp. 65–80.

García Sanz, Angel (1989), 'El sector agrario durante el siglo XVII: depresión y reajustes', in Miguel Artola (ed.), *Historia de España Menendez Pidal. Tomo XXIII. La crisis del siglo XVII. La población. La economía. La sociedad*, Espasa-Calpe, Madrid, pp. 161–235.

García Sanz, Angel (1994), 'Competitivos en lanas pero no en paños: lana para la exportación y lana para los telares nacionales en la España del Antiguo Régimen', *Revista de Historia Económica* (Madrid), XII(2), pp. 397–434.

García Sanz, Angel (1996), 'Verlagssystem y concentración productiva en la industria pañera de Segovia durante el siglo XVIII', *Revista de Historia Industrial* (Barcelona), 10, pp. 11–35.

García Trobat, María Pilar (1999), *El equivalente de alcabalas, un nuevo impuesto en el Reino de Valencia durante el XVIII*, Generalitat Valenciana, Valencia.

García-Cuenca Ariati, Tomás (1982), 'El Consejo de Hacienda (1476–1803)', in *La economía española al final del Antiguo Régimen. IV. Instituciones*, Alianza and Banco de España, Madrid, pp. 403–500.

García-Cuenca Ariati, Tomás (1983), 'Las rentas generales o de aduanas de 1740 a 1774', in Gonzalo Anes, Luis Ángel Rojo and Pedro Tedde (eds and intro.), *Historia económica y pensamiento social. Estudios en homenaje a Diego Mateo del Peral*, Alianza and Banco de España, Madrid, pp. 237–262.

García-Zúñiga, Mario (1993 a), 'Gasto y deuda pública en Navarra durante el feudalismo desarrollado', in J. I. Fortea and C. Cremades (eds), *Política y Hacienda en el Antiguo Régimen*, Universidad de Murcia, Murcia, 2 vols, vol. 1, pp. 271–284.

García-Zúñiga, Mario (1993 b), 'Haciendas forales y reformas borbónicas. Navarra, 1700–1808', *Revista de Historia Económica* (Madrid), XI(2), pp. 307–336.

Geertz, Clifford (1963), *Peddlers and Princes. Social Changes and Economic Modernization in Two Indonesian Towns*, University of Chicago Press, Chicago.

Germán Zubero, Luis (1995), 'Crecimiento económico y disparidades espaciales. Notas para su estudio y aplicación a la industrialización española', in J. L. Acín Fanlo and V. Pinilla Navarro (eds), *Pueblos abandonados ¿un mundo perdido?*, Rolde d'Estudios Aragoneses, Zaragoza, pp. 19–34.

Germán Zubero, Luis, Enrique Llopis, Jordi Maluquer de Motes and Santiago Zapata (eds) (2001), *Historia económica regional de España, siglos XIX y XX*, Crítica, Barcelona.

Giménez López, Enrique (1981), *Alicante en el siglo XVIII. Economía de una ciudad portuaria en el Antiguo Régimen*, Institución 'Alfonso el Magnánimo', Valencia.

Giménez López, Enrique (1999), *Gobernar con una misma ley. Sobre la Nueva Planta borbónica en Valencia*, Universidad de Alicante, Alicante.

Girard, Albert (1932), *El comercio francés en Sevilla y Cádiz en tiempo de los Habsburgo. Contribución al estudio del comercio extranjero en la España de los siglos XVI y XVII*, Renacimiento, Sevilla 2006 (first published as *Le commerce français à Seville et Cadiz au temps des Habsbourg. Contribution à l'etude du commerce étranger en Espagne aux XVIe et XVIIe siècles*, Paris 1932, English edition, Burt Franklin, New York 1967).

Gómez Urdáñez, José Luis (1996), *El proyecto reformista de Ensenada*, Milenio, Lérida.

Gómez Urdáñez, José Luis (2001), *Fernando VI*, Arlanza, Madrid.
Gómez Urdáñez, José Luis (2002), 'El absolutismo regio en España durante la Ilustración', *Brocar* (Logroño), 26, pp. 151–176.
Gómez Zorraquino, José I. (1988), 'La burguesía mercantil catalana y su presencia en Aragón (1770–1808)', *Pedralbes* (Barcelona), 8(1), pp. 405–423.
Gómez Zorraquino, José I. (1989), 'La burguesía mercantil catalana en Aragón. La familia Torres (1750–1816)', *Estudis d'Història Econòmica* (Palma de Mallorca), 2, pp. 115–132.
Gómez Zorraquino, José I. (1990), 'Las relaciones mercantiles entre Aragón y Cataluña en el siglo XVIII', *Actas del I Simposio sobre las relaciones económicas entre Aragón y Cataluña (ss. XVIII–XX)*, Instituto de Estudios Altoaragoneses, Huesca, pp. 65–76.
Gómez Zorraquino, José Ignacio (2002), 'Los lazos familiares como estrategia para la formación y gestión de los patrimonios de la burguesía mercantil. El ejemplo de la familia Romeo de Estromed (1703–1848)', in Hilario Casado Alonso and Ricardo Robledo Hernández (eds), *Fortuna y negocio: formación y gestión de los grandes patrimonios (siglos XVI–XX)*, Universidad de Valladolid, Valladolid.
González Alonso, Benjamín (1970), *El corregidor castellano (1348–1808)*, Instituto de Estudios Administrativos, Madrid.
González Caizán, Cristina (2004 a), 'La cofradía de Nuestra Señora de Valvanera: riojanos en Madrid (1723–1782)', *Mágina* (Jaén), 12 (monograph issue titled *Reformas y acción de Estado en tiempos de Felipe V y Fernando VI, 1700–1759)*, pp. 25–39.
González Caizán, Cristina (2004 b), *La red política del marqués de la Ensenada*, Fundación Jorge Juan, Madrid.
Gracia Guillén, José Antonio (1994), *El marco de actuación de la Universidad de Huesca*, Diputación General de Aragón, Zaragoza.
Grafe, Regina (2005), *Entre el mundo ibérico y el atlántico: comercio y especialización regional, 1550–1650*, Diputación Foral de Vizcaya, Bilbao 2005 (doctoral thesis, University of London 2001).
Grafe, Regina (2012), *Distant Tiranny. Markets, Power and Backwardness in Spain, 1650–1800*, Princeton University Press, Princeton NJ. (This interesting book was published in English after the Spanish version of my own work had already gone to press, and I therefore merely mention it here as an important new contribution to the literature.)
Gráinne, Henry (1992), *The Irish community in Spanish Flanders, 1586–1622*, Irish Academic Press, Dublin.
Granovetter, Mark D. (1973), 'The strength of weak ties', *American Journal of Sociology*, 78(6), pp. 1,360–1,380.
Granovetter, Mark D. (1983), 'The strength of weak ties: a network theory revisited', *Sociological Theory*, 1, pp. 201–233.
Granovetter, Mark D. (1985), 'Economic action and social structure: the problem of embeddedness', *American Journal of Sociology*, 91(3), pp. 481–510.
Granovetter, Mark D. (2004), 'The impact of economic structures on economic development', *Journal of Economic Perspectives*, 19(1), pp. 33–50.
Greenfeld, Liah (1992), *Nacionalismo. Cinco vías hacia la modernidad*, Centro de Estudios Políticos y Constitucionales, Madrid 2005 (first published in English as *Nationalism. Five Roads to Modernity*, Harvard University Press, Cambridge, MA, 1992).
Greenfeld, Liah (2001), *The Spirit of Capitalism. Nationalism and Economic Growth*, Harvard University Press, Cambridge, MA, 2003 (first published 2001).
Greif, Avner (1989), 'Reputations and coalitions in Medieval trade: Evidence on the Maghribi traders', *The Journal of Economic History*, XLIX(4), pp. 857–882.

Grenier, Jean-Yves (1996), *L'économie d'Ancien Régime*, Albin Michel, Paris.
Gruder, Vivian G. (1968), *The Royal Provincial Intendants. A Governing Elite in Eighteenth-Century France*, Cornell University Press, Ithaca NY.
Gutiérrez Muñoz, María Catalina (1994), *Comercio y banca. (Expansión y crisis del capitalismo comercial en Bilbao al final del Antiguo Régimen)*, Universidad del País Vasco, Bilbao.
Hamilton, Earl J. (1933), *El tesoro americano y la revolución de los precios en España, 1501–1650*, Ariel, Barcelona 1975 (first published by Harvard University Press, Cambridge, MA, 1933).
Hamilton, Earl J. (1947), *Guerra y precios en España, 1651–1800*, Alianza, Madrid 1988 (first published by Harvard University Press, Cambridge, MA, 1947).
Harris, John R. (1992), *Essays in Industry and Technology in the Eighteenth Century*, Variorum, London.
Harris, John R. (1998), *Industrial Espionage and Technology Transfer. Britain and France in the Eighteenth Century*, Ashgate, Aldershot, Hants.
Harvey, William (1628), *Exercitatio Anatomica de Motu Cordis et Sanguinis in Animalibus*, Sumptibus Guilielmi Fitzeri, Frankfurt. A Spanish translation exists titled *De motu cordis: estudio anatómico del movimiento del corazón y de la sangre en los animales*, Advise, Barcelona 2000.
Heckscher, Eli F. (1935), *Mercantilism* (1st edition in Swedish 1931, 1st edition in English revised by the author, 1935). Reprint of the 1st edition in English with a biographical introduction by Lars Magnusson, Routledge, London 1994, 2 vols (a Spanish edition also exists titled *La época mercantilista: historia de la organización y las ideas económicas desde el final de la Edad Media hasta la revolución liberal*, FCE, México 1943, reprinted 1983).
Hernández Franco, J. (1998), 'El reencuentro entre historia social e historia política en torno a las familias de poder. Notas y seguimiento a través de la historiografía sobre la Castilla moderna', *Studia histórica. Historia Moderna* (Salamanca), 18, pp. 179–199.
Herrera Navarro, Javier (1979), 'Los orígenes de la Compañía de Calaf: el Señorío de Sú', *Primeres Jornades d'investigació del arxius del Camp de Tarragona. Ponencies i comunicacions*, Arxiu Històric Provincial, Tarragona, pp. 216–236.
Herzog, Tamar (2003), *Defining Nations. Inmigrants and Citizens in Early Modern Spain and Spanish America*, Yale University Press, New Haven, CN.
Hirschmann, Alfred O. (1958), *La estrategia del desarrollo económico*, Fondo de Cultura Económica, México 1961 (first published by Yale University Press, New Haven, CN. 1958).
Hoffman, Philip T. (1996), *Growth in a Traditional Society. The French Countryside, 1450–1815*, Princeton University Press, Princeton, NJ.
Hoffman, Philip T., Gilles Postel-Vinay and Jean-Laurent Rosenthal (2001), *Des marches sans prix. Une economie politique du crédit a Paris, 1660–1870*, Editions de l'École des Hautes Études en Sciences sociales, Paris.
Hoz García, Carlos de la (2007), *Hacienda y fiscalidad en Madrid durante el Antiguo Régimen (1561–1833)*, Instituto de Estudios Fiscales, Madrid.
Hudson, Pat (1986), *The Genesis of Industrial Capital. A study of the West Riding wool textile industry c. 1750–1850*, Cambridge University Press, Cambridge.
Hundert, E. G. (1994), *The Enlightenment's Fable. Bernard Mandeville and the Discovery of Society*, Cambridge University Press, Cambridge 1996 (first published 1994).
Iglèsies i Fort, Josep (1969), *Sintesi de la Junta de Comerç de Barcelona: 1760–1847*, Rafael Dalmau, Barcelona.

Imízcoz Beunza, José María (2008), 'Las élites vasco-navarras y la monarquía hispánica: construcciones sociales, políticas y culturales en la Edad Moderna', *Cuadernos de Historia Moderna* (Madrid), 33, pp. 89–119.

Imízcoz Beunza, José María (2009), 'Familia y redes sociales en la España moderna', in Francisco Javier Lorenzo Pinar (ed.), *La familia en la historia*, Universidad de Salamanca, Salamanca, pp. 135–186.

Imízcoz Beúnza, José María (2010), 'El capital relacional. Relaciones privilegiadas y redes de influencia en el Estado español del siglo XVIII', in José María Imízcoz Beúnza and Ohiane Oliveri Korta (eds), *Economía doméstica y redes sociales en la España moderna*, Sílex, Madrid, pp. 227–282.

Imízcoz Beunza, José María and Rafael Guerrero (2004), 'Familias en la Monarquía. La política familiar de las élites vascas y navarras en el Imperio de los Borbones', in José María Imízcoz Beunza (ed.), *Casa, familia y sociedad (País Vasco, España y América, siglos XV–XIX)*, Universidad del País Vasco, Bilbao, pp. 177–238.

Israel, Fred L. (ed.) (1967), *Major Peace Treaties of Modern History 1648–1967*, with an introductory essay by Arnold Toynbee, Chelsea House Publishers, New York, 4 vols.

Jordá Fernández, Antoni (2006), 'Reflexions sobre el cadastre i la seva aplicació a la Corona d'Aragó', *Ius Fugit* (Zaragoza), 13–14 (2004–2006), pp. 297–308.

Juan Vidal, José (2004), 'Las nuevas estructuras de la hacienda borbónica', in Alfredo Alvar Ezquerra, Jaime Contreras Contreras and José Ignacio Ruiz Rodríguez (eds), *Política y cultura en la época moderna (cambios dinásticos, milenarismos, mesianismos y utopías)*, Universidad de Alcalá, Alcalá de Henares, pp. 65–92.

Juaristi, Jon (1992), *Vestigios de Babel. Para una arqueología de los nacionalismos españoles*, Siglo XXI, Madrid.

Jurado Sánchez, José (2007), *El gasto de la Hacienda española durante el siglo XVIII. Cuantía y estructura de los pagos del Estado (1703–1800)*, Instituto de Estudios Fiscales, Madrid.

Kamen, Henry (1969), *La Guerra de Sucesión en España, 1700–1715*, Grijalbo, Madrid 1974 (first published in English in 1969).

Kidd, Colin (1999), *British Identities before Nationalism. Ethnicity and Nationhood in the Atlantic World, 1600–1800*, Cambridge University Press, Cambridge.

Kozub, Robert M. (2003), 'Evolution of taxation in England, 1700–1850: a period of war and industrialization', *Journal of European Economic History* (Rome), 32(2), pp. 363–388.

Kwass, Michael (2000), *Privilege and the Politics of Taxation in Eighteenth-Century France. Liberté, egalité, fiscalité*, Cambridge University Press, Cambridge.

Landes, David S. (1983), *Revolución en el tiempo. El reloj y la formación del mundo moderno*, Crítica, Barcelona 2007 (first published in English by Belknap Press of Harvard University Press, Cambridge, MA and London 1983, translation of the second edition, Viking, London 2000).

Langé, Christine (1993), *La inmigración francesa en Aragón (siglo XVI y primera mitad del XVII)*, Institución Fernando el Católico, Zaragoza.

Lemire, Beverly (1997), *Dress, Culture and Commerce: The English Clothing Trade before the Factory, 1660–1800*, Macmillan Press, London.

Lemire, Beverly (2000), 'Second-hand beaux and "red-armed Belles": conflict and the creation of fashions in England, c. 1660–1800', *Continuity and Change*, 15(3), pp. 391–417.

Lénardson, Dante (1986), *Index du Journal de Trévoux 1701–1767*, Slatkine, Genève.

Les Français en Espagne à l'èpoque moderne. Ouvrage collectif (1990), CNRS, Paris.

Lévy, Claude-Fréderic (1969–1980), *Capitalistes et pouvoir au Siècle des Lumières*, Mouton, Paris, 3 vols, I. *Les fondateurs des origines à 1715*, 1969; II. *La revolution libérale, 1715–1717*, 1979; III. *La monarchie buissonière, 1718–1723*, 1980, Mouton, Paris.

Llopis Agelán, Enrique (2001), 'El legado económico del Antiguo Régimen desde la óptica regional', in Germán Zubero, Luis; Enrique Llopis, Jordi Maluquer de Motes and Santiago Zapata (eds), *Historia económica regional de España, siglos XIX y XX*, Crítica, Barcelona, pp. 507–524.

Llopis Agelán, Enrique (2002), 'Expansión, reformismo y obstáculos al crecimiento, 1715–1789' and 'La crisis del Antiguo Régimen y la revolución liberal (1790–1840)', in Francisco Comín, Mauro Hernández and Enrique Llopis (eds), *Historia económica de España*, Crítica, Barcelona, pp. 121–202.

Llopis Agelán, Enrique and Sonia Sotaca López (2005), 'Antes, bastante antes: la primera fase de la integración del mercado español de trigo, 1725–1808', *Historia Agraria* (Murcia), 36, pp. 225–262.

Llopis Agelán, Enrique, Miguel Jerez Méndez, Adoración Álvaro and Eva Fernández (2000), 'Índices de precios de la zona nortoccidental de Castilla-León, 1518–1560', *Revista de Historia Económica* (Madrid), XVIII(3), pp. 665–684.

Llopis Agelán, Enrique and Miguel Jerez Méndez (2001), 'El mercado de trigo en Castilla y León, 1691–1788: arbitraje espacial e intervención', *Historia Agraria* (Madrid), 25, pp. 13–68.

Llopis Agelán, Enrique and Miguel Jerez Méndez (2004), 'Arbitraje espacial e intervención en el mercado castellanoleonés de cebada, 1691–1788', in Josep Fontana (ed.), *Història i projecte social. Reconeixement a una trajectòria*, Crítica, Barcelona, pp. 195–211.

Lluch, Ernest (1999), *Las Españas vencidas del siglo XVII. Claroscuros de la Ilustración*, Crítica, Barcelona.

Lobato Franco, Isabel (1995), *Compañías y negocios en la Cataluña preindustrial (Barcelona 1650–1720)*, Universidad de Sevilla, Sevilla.

Lopez, François (1996), 'Ce qu'une Espagne a attendu de la France de la fin du XVIe siècle a l'époque des lumières', in J. R. Aymes (ed.), *L'image de la France en Espagne pendant la seconde moitié du XVIIIe siècle*, Instituto de Cultura Juan Gil-Albert and Presses de Sorbonne Nouvelle, Alicante, pp. 17–28.

López-Cordón Cortezo, María Victoria (1995 a), 'Administración y política en el siglo XVIII: las secretarías del despacho', *Chronica Nova* (Granada), 22, pp. 185–209.

López-Cordón Cortezo, María Victoria (1995 b), 'Oficiales y caballeros: la carrera administrativa en la España del siglo XVIII', in *El mundo hispánico en el Siglo de las Luces*, 2 vols, Editorial Complutense, Madrid, vol. 2, pp. 843–854.

Madrazo, Santos (1982), 'Portazgos y tráfico en la España de finales del Antiguo Régimen', *Moneda y Crédito* (Madrid), 160 (1982), pp. 39–84.

Madrazo, Santos (1984), *El sistema de transportes en España, 1750–1850*, Turner and Colegio de Ingenieros de Caminos, Canales y Puertos, Madrid, 2 vols.

Maixé Altés, Joan Carles (1994), *Comercio y banca en la Cataluña del siglo XVIII. La Compañía Bensi & Merizano de Barcelona (1724–1750)*, Departamento de Historia e Instituciones Económicas, Universidade da Coruña, La Coruña.

Manera, Carles (1988), *Comerç i capital mercantil a Mallorca 1720–1800*, Consell Insular de Mallorca, Palma de Mallorca.

Marshall, Alfred (1890), *Principios de economía: un tratado de introducción*, Aguilar, Madrid 1963 (first published in English, Cambridge 1890).

Martinez Carrión, José Miguel (ed.) (2002), *El nivel de vida en la España rural, siglos XVIII–XX*, Universidad de Alicante, Alicante.

Martínez Shaw, Carlos (1978), 'Las relaciones económicas entre Cataluña y la Baja Andalucía en el siglo XVIII. Un intento de interpretación', in *Actas del I congreso de Historia de Andalucía. Andalucía Moderna*, 3 vols, vol. II, Publicaciones del Monte de Piedad y Caja de Ahorros de Córdoba, Córdoba, pp. 347–356.
Martínez Shaw, Carlos (1980), 'El comercio catalán en el siglo XVIII: mercado peninsular, mercado europeo y mercado colonial', *Quaderns d'Història Econòmica de Catalunya* (Barcelona), 21, pp. 103–112.
Martínez Shaw, Carlos (1981), *Cataluña en la Carrera de Indias, 1680–1756*, Crítica, Barcelona.
Martínez Shaw, Carlos (1983), 'Andalucía y el abastecimiento agrario de Cataluña, la coyuntura de 1721–1722', *Actas del II Congreso de Historia de Andalucía*, 2 vols, Consejería de Cultura y Medio Ambiente y Obra Social y Cultural de Cajasur, Seville, pp. 639–650.
Mateos, María Dolores (1993), 'Estudio preliminar', in Campillo (1993), pp. IX–LXXXIX.
Matilla Quizá, María Jesús (1982), 'Las compañías privilegiadas en la España del Antiguo Régimen', in M. Artola (ed. and intro.), *La economía española del Antiguo Régimen. IV. Instituciones*, Alianza and Banco de España, Madrid, pp. 269–402.
Matilla Tascón, Antonio (1950), *Catálogo de la colección de órdenes generales de Rentas: aportación para la historia de los tributos y del comercio españoles*, Servicio de Estudios de la Inspección General del Ministerio de Hacienda, Madrid.
Matilla Tascón, Antonio (1947), *La Unica Contribución y el Catastro [del marqués] de la Ensenada*, Servicio de Estudios de la Inspección General del Ministerio de Hacienda, Madrid.
McKendrick, Neil, John Brewer and J. H. Plumb (1982), *The birth of a consumer society: the commercialization of eighteenth-century England*, Europa, London.
McLachlan, Jean Olivia (1940), *Trade and peace with old Spain, 1667–1750: a study of the influence of commerce on Anglo-Spanish diplomacy in the first half of the eighteenth century*, Cambridge University Press, Cambridge.
Meijide Pardo, Antonio (1960), *La emigración gallega intrapeninsular en el siglo XVIII*, CSIC Instituto Balmes de Sociología, Madrid.
Melton, James Van Horn (2001) *La aparición del público durante la Ilustración europea*, PUV, Valencia 2009 (original 2001).
Mendels, Franklin (1972), 'Protoindustrialization. The first phase of the industrialization process', *Journal of Economic History*, XXXII (1972), pp. 241–261.
Moilhat, Claude (1988), *La prise de conscience du capitalisme. Economie et philosophie chez Turgot*, Klinksiech, París.
Molas Ribalta, Pere (1977), *Comerç i estructura social a Catalunya i València als segles XVII i XVIII*, Curial, Barcelona.
Molas Ribalta, Pere (1978), 'Los cuerpos generales de comercio: la pequeña burguesía mercantil a fines del Antiguo Régimen', *Cuadernos de Historia Económica de Cataluña* (Barcelona), XIX (1978), pp. 213–246. Reprinted in Molas (1985), pp. 81–110.
Molas Ribalta, Pere (1980), *Historia social de la administración española. Estudios sobre los siglos XVII y XVIII*, Institución Milá y Fontanals, Departamento de Historia Moderna, Barcelona.
Molas Ribalta, Pere (1985), *La burguesía mercantil en la España del Antiguo Régimen*, Cátedra, Madrid.
Molas Ribalta, Pere (1997), 'The industrial policy of the Board of Trade in Spain', *Journal of European Economic History* (Roma), 26(2), pp. 269–293.
Molina Cortón, Juan (1999), *José de Carvajal: un ministro para el reformismo borbónico*, Institución Cultural 'El Brocense', Cáceres.

Morán Martín, Remedios (2007), 'La Junta de Incorporación. Instrumento de la Nueva Planta', *e-Legal History Review*, 3 (www.iustel.com).
Morange, Claude (1996), 'Le voyage en France d'Antonio Ponz ou l'Espagne au coeur', in J. R. Aymes (ed.), *L'image de la France en Espagne pendant la seconde moitié du XVIIIe siècle*, Instituto de Cultura Juan Gil-Albert - Presses de Sorbonne Nouvelle, Alicante, pp. 241–260.
Morineau, Michel (1985), *Incroyables gazettes et fabuleux métaux. Les retours des trésors américains d'après les gazettes hollandaises (XVIe–XVIIIe siècles)*, Cambridge University Press and Maison des Sciencies de l'Homme, London and Paris.
Moutoukias, Zacharias (1992), 'Réseaux personnels et autorité coloniale: les négotiants de Buenos Aires au XVIII siècle', *AESC* (Paris), 47(4/5), pp. 889–915.
Mui, Hoh-Cheung Lorna (1987), *Shops and Shopkeeping in Eighteenth Century England*, Methuen, London.
Muldrew, Craig (1998), *The Economy of Obligation. The Culture of Credit and Social Relations in Early Modern England*, Macmillan, London.
Muñoz Melgar, Rafael (1985), *La Compañía de Aragón en Calaf (1777–1799)*, unpublished degree thesis, Universitat Rovira i Virgili [formerly Facultad de Filosofía y Letras de la Universidad de Barcelona], Tarragona.
Muñoz Melgar, Rafael (1984), 'Una aportación al estudio del comercio catalán a finales del siglo XVIII: la 'Fábrica de Sabó dels Senyors Cortadellas y Satorras' de Calaf', in *Primer congrés d'Història Moderna de Catalunya*, Universitat de Barcelona, Barcelona, 2 vols, vol. II, pp. 321–331.
Muñoz Pérez, José (1955), 'Mapa aduanero del XVIII español', *Estudios Geográficos* (Madrid), XVI (61), pp. 747–799.
Muset Pons, Assumpta (1988), 'La conquesta del mercat peninsular durant la segona meitat del segle XVIII: l'exemple de la casa Francesc Ribas i Cia. (1766–1783)', *Pedralbes* (Barcelona), 8(1), pp. 395–404.
Muset Pons, Assumpta (1993), *Catalunya i el mercat espanyol al segle XVIII*, tesis doctoral, Universidad de Barcelona, Departamento de Historia Económica, Barcelona.
Muset Pons, Assumpta (1995), 'Els transports per terra entre Catalunya i la resta de regions espanyoles al segle XVIII', *Recerques* (Barcelona), 31, pp. 73–92.
Muset Pons, Assumpta (1996 a), 'Catalunya y el mercado español en el siglo XVIII', in M. T. Pérez Picazo, A. Segura and Ll. Ferrer (eds), *Els catalans a Espanya, 1760–1914*, Afers, Barcelona, pp. 419–428.
Muset Pons, Assumpta (1996 b), 'La diáspora de Copons y su integración en la sociedad española del siglo XVIII', in M. T. Pérez Picazo, A. Segura and Ll. Ferrer (eds), *Els catalans a Espanya, 1760–1914*, Afers, Barcelona, pp. 429–436.
Muset Pons, Assumpta (1996 c), 'Penetració i expansió del comerç catalá en el mercat espanyol al segle XVIII', *Estudis d'Historia Econòmica* (Palma de Mallorca), 14, pp. 45–65.
Muset Pons, Assumpta (1997), *Catalunya i el mercat espanyol al segle XVIII: Els traginers i els negociants de Calaf i Copons*, Abadía de Montserrat, Barcelona.
Myrdal, Gunnar (1959), *Teoría económica y regiones subdesarrolladas*, Fondo de Cultura Económica, Mexico 1962 (1st edition 1961, first published in English in 1959).
Nadal Farreras, Joaquim (1971), 'Una font important per a la història economica de Catalunya: el Reial Cadastre (1715–1845)', in *Homenaje al Dr. Juan Reglá Campistol*, Universidad de Valencia, Valencia, 2 vols, vol. II, pp. 209–222.
Nadal Oller, Jordi and Emili Giralt (1960), *Inmigració y redreç demogràfic. El francesos a la Catalunya dels segles XVI i XVII*, Eumo, Vic 2000 (reprint, first published in France as

La population catalane de 1553 à 1717: l'inmigration française et les autres facteurs de son dévelopement, SEVPEN, Paris 1960).
Nava Rodríguez, Teresa (2003), 'Las redes del poder: Campomanes y la administración borbónica, 1745–1762', in M. D. Mateos Dorado (ed.), *Campomanes: doscientos años después*, Universidad de Oviedo-Instituto Feijoo de Estudios del siglo XVIII, Oviedo, pp. 435–454.
Nava Rodríguez, Teresa (2005), ' "Nervios de bóveda": Las tesorerías centrales de la Hacienda borbónica (1716–1743)', in Enrique Martínez Ruiz (ed.), *Vínculos y sociabilidades en España e Iberoamérica: siglos XVI–XX*, Ediciones Puertollano, Puertollano (Ciudad Real), pp. 111–132.
Navarro Miralles, Luis (1977), 'La Compañía de Aragón (1777), *Miscelánea en honor a J. M. Madurell Marimón* (Estudios Históricos y Documentos de los Archivos de Protocolos, t. V), Barcelona, pp. 216–236.
Nell, Edward J. (1984), *Historia y teoría económica*, Crítica, Barcelona (first published in English in 1984).
Ocampo Suárez-Valdés, Joaquín (2009), in Jesús Astigarraga Goenaga, María Victoria López-Cordón Cortezo and José María Urkía Etxabe (eds), *Ilustración, ilustraciones*, Sociedad Estatal de Conmemoraciones Culturales y Real Sociedad Económica de Amigos del País, Madrid, 2 vols, vol. 2, pp. 561–594.
Olaechea Albistur, Rafael (1969), *El conde de Aranda y el 'partido aragonés'*, Universidad de Zaragoza, Zaragoza.
Oliva Melgar, José María (1987), *Cataluña y el comercio privilegiado con América en el siglo XVIII. La Real Compañía de Comercio de Barcelona a Indias*, Universitat de Barcelona, Barcelona.
Ortega López, Margarita (1986), *La lucha por la tierra en la Corona de Castilla al final del Antiguo Régimen. El expediente de Ley Agraria*, Ministerio de Agricultura, Madrid.
O'Scea, Ciaran (2010 a), 'From Munster to La Coruña across the Celtic Sea: emigration, assimilation and acculturation in the Kingdom of Galicia (1601–1640)', *Obradoiro de Historia Moderna* (Santiago de Compostela), 19, pp. 9–38.
O'Scea, Ciaran (2010 b) 'The search for inmigrant rights and naturalization papers among Irish emigrants in early modern Spain (1598–1665)', in *Emigrants and exiles from the Three Kingdoms in Europe, 1603–1688*, Brill, Leiden, pp. 107–124.
O'Scea, Ciaran (2015 a), 'Los exiliados de las Islas Británicas', in J. J. Ruiz Ibáñez and Igor Pérez Tostado (eds), *Los exiliados del Rey de España*, Fondo de Cultura Económica, Madrid, pp. 107–130.
O'Scea, Ciaran (2015 b), *Surviving Kinsale: Irish emigration and identity formation in early modern Spain, 1601–1640*, Manchester University Press, Manchester.
Ostolaza Elizondo, María Isabel (2007), 'La hacienda real en Navarra durante la etapa de los Austrias', *Príncipe de Viana* (Pamplona), 240, pp. 225–262.
Ozanam, Didier (1980), 'Representación del marqués de La Ensenada a Fernando VI (1751)', *Cuadernos de Investigación* Histórica (Madrid), 4 (1980), pp. 67–124.
Palacio Atard, Vicente (1960), *El comercio de Castilla y el puerto de Santander en el siglo XVIII: notas para su estudio*, Escuela de Historia Moderna del CSIC, Madrid.
Palau Claveras, Agustín (1943), *El archivo del Consulado de Mar y el de la Real Junta de Comercio de Barcelona. Sus restos*, Imprenta de la Caridad, Barcelona.
Palop Ramos, José Miguel (1977), *Fluctuaciones de precios y abastecimiento en la Valencia del siglo XVIII*, Institución 'Alfonso el Magnánimo', Valencia.
Parejo Barranco, Antonio and Andrés Sánchez Picón (1996), 'La colonia catalana en Andalucía Oriental (1780–1860). Estado de la cuestión', in M. T. Pérez Picazo,

A. Segura and Ll. Ferrer (eds), *Els catalans a Espanya, 1760–1914*, Afers, Barcelona, pp. 223–232.

Peiró Arroyo, Antonio (1985), *Las Cortes aragonesas de 1808. Pervivencias forales y revolución popular*, Cortes de Aragón, Zaragoza.

Peiró Arroyo, Antonio (1987), 'El mercado de cereales y aceite aragoneses (siglos XVII–XIX)', *Agricultura y Sociedad* (Madrid), 43, pp. 213–279.

Peiró Arroyo, Antonio (1988), 'La única contribución', in Antoni Segura Mas (ed.), *El catastro en España 1714–1906. De los catastros del siglo XVIII a los amilllaramientos de la segunda mitad del siglo XIX*, vol. I, Lunwerg Editores, Madrid, pp. 75–87.

Peiró Arroyo, Antonio (1990), 'Comercio de trigo y desindustrialización: las relaciones económicas entre Aragón y Cataluña', in *Actas del I Simposio sobre las relaciones económicas entre Aragón y Cataluña (ss. XVIII–XX)*, Instituto de Estudios Altoaragoneses, Huesca, pp. 35–64.

Peiró Arroyo, Antonio (1995), 'Especialización productiva y crisis social: la Tierra Baja en la crisis del Antiguo Régimen', in Pedro Rújula (ed.), *Aceite, carlismo y conservadurismo político. El Bajo Aragón durante el siglo XIX*, special issue of the journal *Al-qannis. Taller de arqueología de Alcañiz* (Alcañiz) 5, pp. 17–30.

Peiró Arroyo, Antonio (2000), *Especialización olivarera y crecimiento económico in Caspe*, Centro de Estudios Comarcales del Bajo Aragón-Caspe, and Institución 'Fernando el Católico', Caspe.

Pérez Collados, José María (1993), *Una aproximación histórica al concepto jurídico de nacionalidad. (La integración del Reino de Aragón en la monarquía hispánica)*, Institución 'Fernando el Católico', Zaragoza.

Pérez Fernández-Turégano, Carlos (2006), *Patiño y las reformas en la administración en el reinado de Felipe V*, Ministerio de Defensa, Madrid.

Pérez Picazo, María Teresa (1996), 'Los catalanes en Murcia, 1750–1850. Del pequeño comercio al mundo del negocio', in M. T. Pérez Picazo, A. Segura and Ll. Ferrer (eds), *Els catalans a Espanya, 1760–1914*, Afers, Barcelona, pp. 243–254.

Pérez Picazo, María Teresa, Antoni Segura i Mas and Llorenç Ferrer i Alós (eds.) (1996), *Els catalans a Espanya, 1760–1914*, Afers, Barcelona.

Pérez Sarrión, Guillermo (1975), *El Canal Imperial y la navegación hasta 1812*, Institución Fernando el Católico, Zaragoza.

Pérez Sarrión, Guillermo (1984 a), *Agua, agricultura y sociedad en el siglo XVIII. El Canal Imperial de Aragón, 1766–1808*, Institución Fernando el Católico, Zaragoza.

Pérez Sarrión, Guillermo (1984 b), 'Capital comercial catalán y periferización aragonesa en el siglo XVIII. Los Cortadellas y la "Compañía de Aragón"', *Pedralbes* (Barcelona), 4, pp. 187–232.

Pérez Sarrión, Guillermo (1989), 'Crecimiento sin desarrollo e integración de mercados. El sector agrario aragonés en el siglo XVIII', in *Estructuras agrarias y reformismo ilustrado en la España del siglo XVIII*, Ministerio de Agricultura, Pesca y Alimentación, Madrid 1989, pp. 235–265.

Pérez Sarrión, Guillermo (1995), 'Compañías mercantiles rurales y urbanas de Cataluña en el interior peninsular durante el siglo XVIII', in M. Lobo and V. Suárez (eds), *El comercio en el Antiguo Régimen*. III *Reunión Científica Asociación Española de Historia Moderna 1994*, Universidad de Las Palmas de Gran Canaria, Las Palmas de Gran Canaria, pp. 233–244.

Pérez Sarrión, Guillermo (1996 a), 'Compañías y redes mercantiles rurales en Aragón a fines del Antiguo Régimen', in M. T. Pérez Picazo, A. Segura i Mas and Ll. Ferrer i Alòs (eds), *Els catalans a Espanya, 1760–1914*, Afers, Barcelona, pp. 271–284.

Pérez Sarrión, Guillermo (1996 b), 'Política hidráulica y capital financiero en la España ilustrada, 1766–1792', in Guillermo Pérez Sarrión and Guillermo Redondo Veintemillas, *Los tiempos dorados. Estudios sobre Ramón Pignatelli y la Ilustración*, Diputación General de Aragón, Zaragoza, pp. 225–299.
Pérez Sarrión, Guillermo (1999), *Aragón en el Setecientos. Crecimiento económico, cambio social y cultura, 1700–1808*, Milenio, Lérida.
Pérez Sarrión, Guillermo (2000), 'Los efectos de la Real Contribución de Aragón en el siglo XVIII. Una aproximación', in J. A. Ferrer Benimeli, E. Sarasa and E. Serrano (eds), *El conde de Aranda y su tiempo*, Institución Fernando el Católico, Zaragoza, 2 vols, vol. I, pp. 251–286.
Pérez Sarrión, Guillermo (2003), 'Sobre la crisis de la Ilustración en España', in Manuel Retuerce, Manuel Motilva and Ascensión Bayona (eds), *La Guerra de Independencia en el Valle Medio del Ebro*, Universidad SEK and Ayuntamiento de Tudela, Tudela, pp. 55–78.
Pérez Sarrión, Guillermo (2004), 'El nacimiento de la contribución directa en España. La política de la puesta en marcha de la Real Contribución de Aragón', in Eliseo Serrano (ed.), *Felipe V y su tiempo Congreso Internacional celebrado en Zaragoza, 15 al 19 de Enero de 2001*, Institución Fernando el Católico, Zaragoza, 2 vols, vol. II, pp. 405–447.
Pérez Sarrión, Guillermo (2005 a), 'Emigrantes y traficantes entre Francia, Navarra y Aragón en el siglo XVIII. La práctica social del contrabando', in Jean-Michel Minovez and Patrice Poujade (eds), *Circulation des marchandises et réseaux commerciaux dans les Pyrénées (XIII–XIX siècle/Circulació de mercaderies i xarxes comercials als Pirineus (segles XIII–XIX)*, CNRS-Université de Toulouse II-Le-Mirail, Toulouse, pp. 97–117.
Pérez Sarrión, Guillermo (2005 b), 'Los franceses y la crisis financiera de la Ilustración en España', *Spagna Contemporanea* (Torino), 27, pp. 3–26.
Pérez Sarrión, Guillermo (2005 c), 'La política de construcción de canales. Una aproximación', in Manuel Silva Suárez (ed.), *Técnica e ingeniería en España, II. El siglo de las Luces. De la ingeniería a la nueva navegación*, Real Academia de Ingeniería, Institución Fernando el Católico y Prensas Universitarias de Zaragoza, Zaragoza, pp. 429–467.
Pérez Sarrión, Guillermo (2007), 'Las redes sociales en Madrid y la Congregación de San Fermín de los Navarros, siglos XVII y XVII', *Hispania. Revista Española de Historia* (Madrid), LXVII(225), pp. 209–254.
Pérez Sarrión, Guillermo (2008), 'Intereses financieros y nacionalismo. La pugna entre mercaderes banqueros españoles y franceses en Madrid, 1766–1796', *Cuadernos de Historia Moderna. Anejos* (Madrid), VII, pp. 31–72.
Pérez Sarrión, Guillermo (2011 a), 'La formación de la política manufacturera de la Ilustración española en la primera mitad del siglo XVIII. Una aproximación', in Guillermo Pérez Sarrión (ed.), *Más Estado y más mercado. Absolutismo y economía en la España del siglo XVIII*, Sílex, Madrid, pp. 181–234.
Pérez Sarrión, Guillermo (2011 b), 'The idea of "naturality" in Hispanic Monarchy and the formation of Spanish identity between the sixteenth and the eighteenth centuries: an approach', in Guido Abbattista (ed.), *Encountering Otherness. Diversities and Transcultural Experiences in Early Modern European Culture*, Edizioni Università di Trieste, Trieste pp. 67–96. Also available in *CROMOHS, Cyber Review of Modern Historiography* (Firenze), 16 (2011), retrieved on 10 November 2015 from www.cromohs.unifi.it/.
Pérez Tostado, Igor (2005), 'Una política de 'conveniencia y piedad': el despliegue diplomático de la monarquía hispánica en la confederación de Kilkenny y la

transformación de las relaciones hiberno-hispanas' in F. J. Guillamón, D. Centenero and J. D. Muñoz Rodríguez (eds), *Entre Clío y Casandra: poder y sociedad en la monarquía hispánica durante la Edad Moderna*, Universidad de Murcia, Murcia, pp. 163–186. Also in *Tiempos Modernos*, 7 (2002).

Pérez Tostado, Igor (2008), *Irish Influence at the Court of Spain in the Seventeenth Century*, Four Courts Press, Dublin.

Pérez Tostado, Igor (2010), 'Os Irlandeses e a Inquisição Portuguesa: Processados e Reduzidos', in Igor Pérez Tostado and Enrique García Hernán (eds), *Irlanda y el Atlántico ibérico. Movilidad, participación e intercambio cultural (1580–1823). Ireland and the Iberian Atlantic: mobility, involvement and cross-cultural exchange (1580–1823)*, Albatros Ediciones, Valencia, pp. 111–126.

Pijuan Domènech, M.ª Rosa (1984), 'La factoría barcelonesa de la Companyia d'Aragó: dades sobre els arrendaments de drets senyorials (1793–1801)', in *Primer Congrès d'Història Moderna de Catalunya*, Universitat de Barcelona, Barcelona, 2 vols, vol. II, pp. 771–777.

Pijuan Domènech, M.ª Rosa (1985), *La factoria barcelonesa de la Companyia d'Aragó (1792–1801)*, degree thesis, Universitat Rovira i Virgili [formerly Facultad de Filosofía y Letras de la Universidad de Barcelona], Tarragona.

Pocock, John G. A. (2002), *Historia e Ilustración. Doce estudios*, Marcial Pons, Madrid.

Poitrineau, Abel (1962), 'Aspects de l'emigration temporaire et saisonière en Auvergne a la fin du XVIIIe et au debut du XIXe siècle', *Revue d'histoire moderne et contemporaine*, IX(1962), pp. 5–50.

Poitrineau, Abel (1965), *La vie rurale en Basse-Auvergne au XVIIIe siècle (1726–1789)*, Presses Universitaires de France, 2 vols, Paris.

Poitrineau, Abel (1983), *Remues d'hommes. Les migrations montagnards en France au XVIIe et XVIIIe siècles*, Aubier Montaigne, París.

Poitrineau, Abel (1985), *Les Espagnols de L'Auvergne et du Limousin du XVIIème au XIXème siècles*, Malroux and Mazel Librairie Editeur, Aurillac.

Polanyi, Karl (1944), *La gran transformación: crítica del liberalismo económico*, La Piqueta, Madrid 1989 (first published in English as *The Great Transformation: the political and economic origins of our time*, New York, Farrar & Rinehart, 1944).

Pollard, Sidney (1981), *La conquista pacífica. La industrialización de Europa, 1760–1970*, Prensas Universitarias de Zaragoza, Zaragoza 1991 (first published 1981).

Pollard, Sidney (1991), 'Mercados regionales y desarrollo nacional', in Maxine Berg (ed.), *Mercados y manufacturas en Europa*, Crítica, pp. 43–110.

Pontet, Josette (1991), 'La cheville ouvrière du commerce avec l'Espagne', in Josette Pontet (ed.), *Histoire de Bayonne*, Privat, Paris, pp. 127–150.

Pradells Nadal, Jesús (1990), 'Juan Bautista Virio (1753–1837): experiencia europea y reformismo económico en la España ilustrada', *Revista de Historia Moderna* (Alicante), 8–9, pp. 233–271.

Pradells Nadal, Jesús (1992), *Diplomacia y comercio. La expansión consular española en el siglo XVIII*, Universidad de Alicante and Instituto de Cultura Juan Gil-Albert, Alicante.

Pulido Bueno, Ildefonso (1994), *El Real Giro de España. Primer proyecto de banco nacional*, Artes Gráficas Andaluzas, Huelva.

Pulido Bueno, Ildefonso (1998), *José Patiño: el inicio del gobierno político-económico ilustrado en España*, self-published, Huelva.

Recio Morales, Oscar (2004), ' "Una nación inclinada al ruido de las armas". La presencia irlandesa en los ejércitos españoles, 1580–1818: ¿la historia de un éxito?' [online], *Tiempos Modernos. Revista electrónica de Historia Moderna*, 10, retrieved on 10 November 2015 from www.tiemposmodernos.org.

Recio Morales, Óscar (2007 a), 'Identity and loyalty: Irish traders in seventeenth century Iberia', in David Dickson, Jan Parmentier and Jane Ohlmeyer (eds), *Irish and Scottish mercantile networks in Europe and overseas in the seventeenth and eighteenth centuries*, Academia Press, Gent, pp. 197–210.

Recio Morales, Óscar (2007 b), *La presencia irlandesa en los ejércitos de la monarquía hispánica 1580–1808. The Irish military presence in the Spanish Armies, 1580–1818*, Ministerio de Defensa, Madrid.

Recio Morales, Óscar (2011), 'Los extranjeros y la historiografía modernista', *Cuadernos de Historia Moderna. Anejos*, X, pp. 33–51.

Recio Morales, Óscar (2012), 'Redes de nación y espacios de poder en la monarquía hispánica: un estado de la cuestión', en Óscar Recio Morales (ed.), *Redes de nación y espacios de poder: la comunidad irlandesa en España y la América española, 1600–1825. Power strategies: Spain and Ireland 1600–1825*, Albatros Ediciones y Ministerio de Defensa, Madrid, pp. 37–54.

Reddy, William (1984), *The rise of market culture. The textile trade and French society, 1750–1900*, Cambridge University Press, Cambridge.

Reher, David S. (2001), 'Producción, precios e integración de los mercados regionales de grano en España', *Revista de Historia Económica* (Madrid), XIX(3), pp. 539–572.

Ribeiro, Aileen (1995), *The art of dress: fashion in England and France 1750 to 1820*, Yale University Press, New Haven Conn.

Riera Vayreda, Francesc (1988), 'La talla general', in Antoni Segura Mas (ed.), *El catastro en España 1714-1906. De los catastros del siglo XVIII a los amilllaramientos de la segunda mitad del siglo XIX*, vol. I, Lunwerg Editores, Madrid, pp. 61–72.

Riley, James C. (1980), *International Government Finance and the Amsterdam Capital Market 1740–1815*, Cambridge University Press, Cambridge.

Ringrose, David (1970), *Los transportes y el estancamiento económico de España (1750–1850)*, Tecnos, Madrid 1972 (first published in English in 1970).

Ringrose, David (1983), 'El desarrollo urbano y la decadencia española', *Revista de Historia Económica* (Madrid), I(1), pp. 37–57.

Ringrose, David (1987), *Ensayos sobre historia económica de España (siglos XVI–XIX)*, Siglo XXI, Madrid.

Ringrose, David (1996), *España, 1700–1900: el mito del fracaso*, Alianza, Madrid (first published by Cambridge University Press 1996).

Rodríguez Garraza, Rodrigo (2003), 'El tratamiento de la libertad de comercio y las aduanas en Navarra (1717–1841)', *Notitia Vasconiae* (San Sebastián), 2, pp. 129–190.

Rodríguez González, Ricardo (1995), *Mercaderes castellanos del Siglo de Oro*, Universidad de Valladolid, Valladolid.

Root, Hilton L. (1987), *Peasants and Kings in Burgundy: Agrarian Foundations or French Absolutism*, University of California Press, Berkeley, CA.

Root, Hilton L. (1994), *The Fountain of Privilege. Political Foundations of Markets in Old Regime France and England*, University of California Press, Berkeley, CA.

Rosenthal, Jean-Laurent (1992), *The fruits of revolution. Property rights, litigation, and French agriculture, 1700–1860*, Cambridge University Press, Cambridge.

Rúa Fernández, Carolina (2006), 'Els catalans y el mercat madrileny al segle XVIII', *Boletín del Institut Universitari d'Historia Jaume Vicens Vives*, 6(May), pp. 18–21. The paper is an advance of the author's doctoral thesis, *La xarxa catalana a Madrid en el segle XVIII. Un estudi sobre els homes de negocis catalans i el comerç*, directed by Josep M. Delgado Ribas, read at the Institut Universitari d'Historia Jaume Vicens Vives de la Universitat Pompeu Fabra, Barcelona, on 27 January 2010.

Ruiz i Pablo, Angel (1919), *Historia de la Real Junta Particular de Comercio (1758–1847)*, Henrich y Cía., Barcelona. Reprint with notes of the edition by Josep María Fradera, Alta Fulla, Barcelona 1994.

Salas Auséns, José Antonio (1977), 'La inmigración francesa a Barbastro en los siglos XVI y XVII', *Estudios*, Departamento de Historia Moderna de la Universidad de Zaragoza, Zaragoza, pp. 41–84.

Salas Auséns, José Antonio (1986), 'Extranjeros en Navarra en la segunda mitad del siglo XVIII', *Actas del I congreso de historia de Navarra en los siglos XVIII, XIX y XX*, Pamplona, Anejo 5 of the journal *Príncipe de Viana*, 2 vols, vol. I, pp. 67–78.

Salas Auséns, José Antonio (1990), 'Les Français en Espagne dans la seconde moitié du XVIIIe siècle', in *Les Français en Espagne à l'époque moderne (XVIe–XVIIIe siècles)*, Centre National de la Recherche Scientifique, pp. 155–171.

Salas Auséns, José Antonio (1992–1993), 'Extranjeros en el corregimiento de Barbastro en el siglo XVIII', in *Somontano. Revista del Centro de Estudios del Somontano de Barbastro* (Barbastro), 3 (1992–1993), pp. 41–64.

Salas Auséns, José Antonio (1994), 'Migraciones internas y medium-distance en Aragón (1500–1900)', in *Migraciones internas y medium-distance en la Península Ibérica, 1500–1900*, Xunta de Galicia, Santiago de Compostela, pp. 247–273.

Salas Auséns, José Antonio (2003), 'Buscando vivir en la ciudad: trayectorias de inmigrantes franceses en los siglos XVII y XVIII', *Revista de Demografía Histórica* (Zaragoza), 21(1), pp. 141–165.

Salas Auséns, José Antonio (2001), 'Las otras leyes de extranjería: migraciones francoespañolas a través de la frontera pirenaica en la Edad Moderna', paper given at VI Congreso de la ADHE, Castelo Branco 2001.

Salas Auséns, José Antonio (2009), *En busca de El Dorado. Inmigración francesa en la España de la Edad moderna*, Universidad del País Vasco, Bilbao.

Salas Auséns, José Antonio and Encarnación Jarque Martínez (1990), 'Extranjeros en España en la segunda mitad del siglo XVIII', *Actas del Coloquio Internacional Carlos III y su siglo*, Universidad Complutense, Madrid, 2 vols, vol. II, pp. 985–997.

Sales, Nuria (1983), 'Ramblers, traginers i mules (s. XVIII–XIX)', *Recerques* (Barcelona), 13, pp. 65–81.

Sánchez Albornoz, Nicolás (1974 a), 'La integración del mercado nacional, España e Italia', in J. Nadal and G. Tortella (eds), *Agricultura, comercio colonial y crecimiento económico en la España contemporánea*, Ariel, Barcelona, pp. 158–187.

Sánchez Albornoz, Nicolás (1974 b), 'Las regiones económicas de España en el s. XIX. Su determinación mediante análisis factorial de los precios del trigo', *Revista de Occidente* (Madrid) 134, pp. 212–227.

Sánchez Albornoz, Nicolás (1975), *Los precios agrícolas durante la segunda mitad del siglo XIX. vol. I: trigo y cebada*, Banco de España, Madrid.

Sánchez Albornoz, Nicolás (1977), 'Congruencia económica entre regiones económicas', in idem, *España hace un siglo. Una economía dual*, Alianza, Madrid, pp. 101–121.

Santiago Fernández, Javier de (2000), *Política monetaria en Castilla durante el siglo XVII*, Junta de Castilla y León, Valladolid.

Sanz Camañes, Porfirio (2002), *Diplomacia hispano-inglesa en el siglo XVII. Razón de Estado y relaciones de poder durante la guerra de los Treinta Años, 1618–1648*, Universidad de Castilla-La Mancha, Cuenca.

Sanz Camañes, Porfirio (2005), 'La colonia francesa en Aragón a finales del reinado de Carlos II', in José Manuel de Bernardo Ares (ed.), *La sucesión de la monarquía*

hispánica, 1665–1725 (I). Lucha política en las Cortes y fragilidad económica-fiscal en los Reinos, Servicio de Publicaciones de la Universidad de Córdoba, Córdoba, pp. 279–304.
Segarra Blasco, Agustí (1994), *Aiguardent i mercat a la Catalunya del segle XVIII*, Eumo, Vich.
Sereni, Emilio (1966), *Capitalismo y mercado nacional*, Ariel, Barcelona (first published by Italiano Editori Riuniti, Rome 1966).
Serra, Eva (1988), *Pagesos i senyors a la Catalunya del segle XVII: baronía de Sentmenat, 1590–1729*, Crítica, Barcelona.
Shillington, Violet Mary, and Annie Beatrice Wallis Chapman (1907), *The Commercial Relations of England and Portugal*, Burt Franklin, New York 1970, reprint (first published 1907).
Siddle, D. J. (1997), 'Migration as a strategy of accumulation: social and economic change in eighteenth-century Savoy', *The Economic History Review* (London), 1, pp. 1–20.
Simón Tarrés, Antoni (1999), *Els orígens ideològics de la revolució catalana de 1640*, Publicacions de l'Abadia de Montserrat, Barcelona.
Smith, David Kammerling (2002), 'Structuring politics in early eighteenth-century France: the political innovations of the French Council of Commerce', *The Journal of Modern History* (Chicago), 74(3), pp. 490–537.
Sonenscher, Michael (2007), *Before the Deluge. Public Debt, Inequality and the Intellectual Origins of the French Revolution*, Princeton University Press, Princeton NJ.
Stone, Lawrence (1965), *La crisis de la aristocracia 1558–1641*, Revista de Occidente, Madrid 1976 (first published by Clarendon University Press, Oxford 1965).
Tedde de Lorca, Pedro (1987), 'Crisis del Estado y deuda pública a comienzos del siglo XIX', *Hacienda Pública Española* (Madrid), 108–109, pp. 169–195.
Tedde de Lorca, Pedro (1994), 'Cambio institucional y cambio económico en la España del siglo XIX', *Revista de Historia Económica* (Madrid), XII(3), pp. 525–537.
Teissier, Eric, 'La introducción de los merinos en Francia a fines del siglo XVIII y principios del siglo XIX. La pérdida del monopolio español de una materia prima', *Revista de Historia Industrial* (Barcelona), 11(1997), pp. 11–43.
Téllez Alarcia, Diego (2006), 'D. Ricardo Wall. Un ministro olvidado', *Tiempos Modernos. Revista electrónica de Historia Moderna*, 10, retrieved on 10 November 2015 from www.tiemposmodernos.org.
Téllez Alarcia, Diego (2009), *D. Ricardo Wall. Aut Caesar aut nullus*, Ministerio de Defensa, Madrid.
Tello i Aragay, Enric (1995), 'El fin de la expansión agraria en la Cataluña del siglo XVIII: factores económicos y crisis social', *Agricultura y Sociedad* (Madrid), 74, pp. 109–157.
Thompson, I. A. A. (1976), *Guerra y decadencia: gobierno y administración en la España de los Austrias, 1560–1620*, Crítica, Barcelona 1981 (first published in English, London 1976).
Tomás, C. (1965), 'La Casa de Misericordia de la ciudad de Teruel', *Teruel* (Teruel), 32(1965), pp. 5–122.
Torra Fernández, Lídia (1997), 'Comercialización y consumo de tejidos en Cataluña (1650–1800)', *Revista de Historia Industrial* (Barcelona), 11, pp. 177–196.
Torra Fernández, Lídia (2001), 'Botigues de teixits, crèdit comercial i crèdit al consum. Xarxes comercials a la Cataluya del segle XVIII', *Recerques* (Barcelona), 41, pp. 5–30.
Torra Fernández, Lídia (2005), 'Distribució, difusio i venda de teixits procedents de França a les botigues catalanes (1650–1800)', in Jean-Michel Minovez and Patrice Poujade (eds.), *Circulation de marchandises et réseaux commerciaux dans les Pyrénées (XIII–XIX siècle)*, 2 vols., CNRS and Université de Toulouse-Le Mirail, Toulouse, vol. 1, pp. 39–56.

Torras Elías, Jaume (1978), 'Moviment de l'ingrès senyorial a Catalunya (1770–1835). Els arrendaments de la casa de Medinaceli', *Recerques* (Barcelona), 8, pp. 51–72.
Torras Elías, Jaume (1982), 'La economía aragonesa en la transición al capitalismo. Un ensayo', in *Tres estudios de historia económica de Aragón*, Departamento de Historia Económica de la Facultad de Ciencias Económicas, Universidad de Zaragoza, Zaragoza, pp. 9–32.
Torras Elías, Jaume (1984), 'Especialización agrícola e industria rural en Cataluña en el siglo XVIII', *Revista de Historia Económica* (Madrid), II(3), pp. 113–128.
Torras Elías, Jaume (1990), 'Relaciones económicas entre Aragón y Cataluña antes del ferrocarril', *Actas del I Simposio sobre las relaciones económicas entre Aragón y Cataluña (ss. XVIII–XX)*, Instituto de Estudios Altoaragoneses, Huesca, pp. 17–32.
Torras Elías, Jaume (1991), 'Redes comerciales y auge textil en la España del siglo XVIII', in Maxine Berg (ed.), *Mercados y manufacturas en Europa*, Crítica, Barcelona 1995 (first published by Routledge, London 1991), pp. 111–132.
Torras Elías, Jaume (1992), 'Gremio, familia y cambio económico. Pelaires y tejedores en Igualada, 1695–1765', *Revista de Historia Industrial* (Barcelona) 2, pp. 11–30.
Torras Elías, Jaume (1993), 'From craft to class: the changing organization of cloth manufacturing in a Catalan town', in T. M. Saftley and L. N. Rosenband (eds), *The Workplace before the Factory. Artisans and Proletarians 1500–1800*, Cornell University, Ithaca NY, pp. 165–179.
Torras Elías, Jaume (1994), 'Corporations et liberté de fabrication en Espagne au XVIIIe siècle', *Revue du Nord* (Lille), 307(1994), pp. 745–751.
Torras Elías, Jaume (1996), 'La penetració comercial catalana à l'Espanya interior en el segle XVIII. Una proposta d'explicació', in M. T. Pérez Picazo, A. Segura and Ll. Ferrer (eds), *Els catalans a Espanya, 1760–1914*, Afers, Barcelona, pp. 27–30.
Torras Elías, Jaume (1997), 'Productes vitícoles i integració mercantil a Europa, ss. XVI–XVIII. Una panorámica', *Estudis d'Història Econòmica* (Palma), 14, pp. 23–33.
Torras Elías, Jaume (1998), 'Small towns, craft guilds and proto-industry in Spain', *Jahrbuch für Wirtschaftsgeschichte*, 1998-2, Akademie Verlag, München, pp. 79–96.
Torras Elías, Jaume (1999), 'Gremis i indústria rural a la Catalunya moderna', in A. Carreras, P. Pascual, D. Reher and C. Sudriá (eds), *Doctor Jordi Nadal. La industrialització i el desenvolupament econòmic d'Èspanya*, Universidad de Barcelona, 2 vols, Barcelona, vol. II, pp. 925–935.
Torras Elías, Jaume (2007), *Fabricants sense fàbrica. Els Torelló, d'Igualada (1691–1794)*, Eumo, Vic.
Torras Elías, Jaume (2010), 'De Verdú a Valdemoro. Sobre la comercialización de tejidos catalanes en la España interior (siglo XVIII)', *Estudis* (Valencia), 36, pp. 9–20.
Torras Elías, Jaume and Bartolomé Yun Casalilla (eds) (1999), *Consumo, condiciones de vida y comercialización, Cataluña y Castilla, siglos XVII–XIX*, Junta de Castilla y León, Avila.
Torras Elías, Jaume and Bartolomé Yun Casalilla (2001), 'Presentación' a la sesión 'Pautas de consumo 1550–1800', in *Asociación de Historia Económica. VII Congreso 19/20/21 septiembre 2001, Zaragoza. Addresses and papers*. Published on CD-ROM, Asociación de Historia Económica and Universidad de Zaragoza.
Torras Elías, Jaume, Montserrat Durán and Llidia Torra (1999), 'El ajuar de la novia. El consumo de tejidos en los contratos matrimoniales de una localidad catalana, 1600–1800', in J. Torras and B. Yun (eds), *Consumo, condiciones de vida y comercialización. Cataluña y Castilla, siglos XVIII–XIX*, Junta de Castilla y León, Valladolid, pp. 61–70.

Torre, Joseba de la (1996), 'Obstáculos a la concurrencia de comerciantes y géneros de Cataluña en Navarra (c. 1780–1880)', in M. T. Pérez Picazo, A. Segura and Ll. Ferrer (eds), *Els catalans a Espanya, 1760–1914*, Afers, Barcelona, pp. 149–158.
Torres Sánchez, Rafael (2002), 'Cuando las reglas del juego cambian. Mercados y privilegio en el abastecimiento del ejército español en el siglo XVIII', *Revista de Historia Moderna*, 20, pp. 487–512.
Torres Sánchez, Rafael (2005 a), 'The failure of the Spanish crown's tobacco tax monopoly in Catalonia during the XVIIIth century', *The Journal of European Economic History* (Rome), 34(3), pp. 721–760.
Torres Sánchez, Rafael (2006), 'Seguro de hombres y auxilio de reyes. El Fondo Vitalicio y la Real Hacienda Española de Carlos III', *Obradoiro de Historia Moderna* (Santiago de Compostela), 15, pp. 139–172.
Torres Sánchez, Rafael (2007), 'The triumph of the fiscal-military state in the eighteenth century. War and mercantilism', in idem (ed.), *War, State and Development. Fiscal-Military States in the Eighteenth Century*, Ediciones Universidad de Navarra, Pamplona, pp. 13–45.
Torres Sánchez, Rafael (2008), 'Incertidumbre y arbitrariedad. La política de deuda pública de los Borbones en el siglo XVIII', *Estudis* (Valencia), 34, pp. 263–282.
Touzery, Mireille (1994), *L'invention de l'impôt sur le revenu: la taille tarifée, 1715–1789*, Comité pour l'Histoire Economique et Financière de la France, Ministère de l'Economie et du Budget, Paris.
Truchuelo García, Susana (2004), *Gipuzkoa y el poder real en la Edad Moderna*, Diputación Foral de Guipúzcoa, San Sebastián.
Usoz Otal, Javier (1998), 'Mateo Antonio Barberi: el ideario de la Junta General de Comercio en Aragón', *Cuadernos Aragoneses de Economía*, 8(2), pp. 501–523.
Vallejo García-Hevia (2007), *El Consejo Real de Castilla y sus escribanos en el siglo XVIII*, Junta de Castilla y León, Valladolid.
Vasallo, Carmel (1997), *Corsairing to commerce. Maltese merchants in XVIIIth Century Spain*, Malta University Publishers, Malta.
Vicedo Rius, Enric (1991), *Les terres de Lleida i el desenvolupament català del Set-cents. Producció, propietat i renda*, Crítica, Barcelona.
Vicens Vives, Jaime (1968), *Coyuntura económica y reformismo burgués y otros estudios de historia de España*, Ariel, Barcelona. Preliminary note and selection of texts by José Fontana Lázaro.
Vilar, Pierre (1964), *Catalunya dins l'Espanya moderna. Recerques sobre els fonaments econòmics de les estructures nacionals*, Edicions 62, Barcelona 1986, 4 vols (first published in French, 1957).
Vilar, Pierre (1962), *Manual de la Compañya Nova de Gib[r]altar*, Centre de Lectura, Reus 1990 (first published as *Le 'Manual de la Compañya Nova' de Gibraltar 1709–1723*, SEVPEN, Paris).
Weatherill, Lorna (1986), *Consumer Behaviour and Material Culture in Britain 1660–1760*, Routledge, London 1996 (first published 1986).
Weber, Max (1904–1905), *La ética protestante y el espíritu del capitalismo*, Istmo, Madrid 1998 (first published in 1904–1905, translation of the 2nd German edition, revised by the author, 1919–1920).
Wrightson, Keith (1982), *English Society 1580–1680*, Routledge, London 1995 (first published 1982).
Wrightson, Keith (2000), *Earthly necessities. Economic lives in Early Modern Britain*, Yale University Press, New Haven Conn.

Wrigley, E. A. (1967), 'Un modelo sencillo de la importancia de Londres en la sociedad y la economía inglesas de la transición, 1650–1750', in E.A. Wrigley (ed.), *Gentes, ciudades y riqueza. la transformación de la sociedad tradicional*, Crítica, Barcelona, pp. 189–220. The article was originally published in English in *Past and Present*, XXXVII, pp. 44–70.

Yun Casalilla, Bartolomé (1987), *Sobre la transición al capitalismo en Castilla. Economía y sociedad en Tierra de Campos (1500–1830)*, Junta de Castilla y León, Valladolid.

Yun Casalilla, Bartolomé (1996), 'Los catalanes en Castilla. Apuntes para un estado de la cuestión (1750–1868)', in M. T. Pérez Picazo, A. Segura and Ll. Ferrer (eds), *Els catalans a Espanya, 1760–1914*, Afers, Barcelona, pp. 169–178.

Yun Casalilla, Bartolomé (2002 a), *La gestión del poder. Corona y economías aristocráticas en Castilla (siglos XVI-XVIII)*, Akal, Madrid.

Yun Casalilla, Bartolomé (2002 b), 'Las raíces del atraso económico español: crisis y decadencia (1590–1714)', in Francisco Comín, Mauro Hernández and Enrique Llopis (eds), *Historia económica de España siglos X–XX*, Crítica, Barcelona, pp. 85–120.

Zabala Uriarte, Aingeru (1983 a), *El comercio y tráfico marítimo del norte de España en el siglo XVIII*, Haranburu, San Sebastián.

Zabala Uriarte, Aingeru (1983 b), *La función comercial del País Vasco en el siglo XVIII*, 2 vols, Haranburu, San Sebastián.

Zabala Uriarte, Aingeru (1994), *Mundo urbano y actividad mercantil, Bilbao 1700–1810*, Bilbao Bizkaia Kutxa, Bilbao.

Zylberberg, Michel (1983), 'Un centre financier péripherique: Madrid dans la seconde moitié du XVIIIe siècle', *Revue Historique* (Paris), CCXXIX, pp. 265–309.

Zylberberg, Michel (1993), *Une si douce domination. Les milieux d'affaires français et l'Espagne vers 1780–1808*, Comité pour l'Histoire Economique et financière de la France, Ministère des Finances, Paris.

Index

Lightning Source UK Ltd.
Milton Keynes UK
UKHW02f0032201217
314793UK00003B/212/P